THE COMPLETE ROMANCES OF

CHRÉTIEN DE TROYES

The

COMPLETE ROMANCES OF

Chrétien de Troyes

TRANSLATED WITH AN INTRODUCTION BY

DAVID STAINES

INDIANA UNIVERSITY PRESS

BLOOMINGTON & INDIANAPOLIS

The paper used in this publication meets the minimum requirements of American
National Standard for Information Sciences—Permanence of Paper for Printed
Library Materials, ANSI Z39.48-1984.

Manufactured in the United States of America

Library of Congress Cataloging-in-Publication Data
Chrétien, de Troyes, 12th cent.
[Selections. English. 1990]
The complete romances of Chrétien de Troyes / translated with an
introduction by David Staines.
p.   cm.
Includes bibliographical references.
ISBN 0-253-35440-4 (alk. paper)
1. Chrétien, de Troyes, 12th cent.—Translations, English.
2. Romances, English—Translations from French.   3. Romances—
Translations into English.   4. Arthurian romances.   I. Staines,
David.   II. Title.
PQ1447.E5S73   1990
841'.1—dc20   90-4060
CIP
1 2 3 4 5 94 93 92 91 90

This book has been supported by a grant from the National
Endowment for the Humanities, an independent federal agency.

CONTENTS

FOR BRIAN

ACKNOWLEDGMENTS

Like many teachers, I have introduced my students to the romances of Chrétien de Troyes through the translations by W. Wistar Comfort, which were first published in 1914 in the Everyman Library. More than a decade ago, I began my own translations. My dissatisfaction with Comfort's *Arthurian Romances* does not diminish my respect for his unique achievement: at a time when comparatively little editorial and critical study of Chrétien had taken place, Comfort was indeed a pioneer.

Whereas Comfort based his translations on Wendelin Foerster's nineteenth-century edition of the four romances, I have turned to MS B.N. 794, the manuscript that served as the base text for the more recent edition of the five romances in the Classiques Français du Moyen Age series. I have profited from the clarifying manuscript studies of Tony Hunt, Alexandre Micha, and Brian Woledge; their writings, cited in the bibliography, are central to the knowledge of Chrétien's text. The staff of the manuscript room of the Bibliothèque Nationale showed much courtesy as I examined B.N. 794 and other manuscripts of the romances. And Serge Lusignan, Director of the Institut d'études médiévales, Université de Montréal, allowed me to consult its computerized concordance to MS B.N. 794, since published as *Lexique et concordance de Chrétien de Troyes*, ed. Marie-Louise Ollier (Montréal: Institut d'études médiévales, 1986).

It is a pleasure and a privilege to acknowledge the many scholars who supported this translation project through much of the last decade. Alexandre Micha twice showed me both gracious hospitality and scholarly generosity: as we discussed various manuscript problems, he examined, clarified, and corrected many of the variant readings I was proposing, and our visits became lessons in editing, in which I was a privileged student. From the summer of 1979, when I was in residence at the Huntington Library, until his untimely death in 1988, John F. Benton shared with me his immense knowledge of Chrétien de Troyes and the literature of Champagne and responded with enthusiasm and interest to my questions and suggestions.

As I began these translations, Elizabeth T. Kennan and John Leyerle were the first to offer invaluable encouragement. My teachers and former colleagues at Harvard University, William Alfred, Larry D. Benson, the late Morton W. Bloomfield, and B. J. Whiting, read the translations with attentive care. My colleagues at the University of Ottawa, David Lyle Jeffrey, Pierre Kunstmann, Yvon Lepage, and Nicholas von Maltzahn, were appreciated consultants. And during the long period of revising, Nancy Bradley-Cromey, Joan Ferrante, Douglas Kelly, and especially Donald L. Maddox and Sara Sturm-Maddox responded to many queries with thoughtful advice and guidance. Sally Fitzgerald and Jonathan Griffin have been valued friends and guides in the art of translation.

In an undergraduate course at the University of Toronto, F. T. Flahiff introduced me to the world of Arthurian poetry. I have never ceased to learn from him and his scholarly example.

Finally, I should like to express my sincere gratitude to Indiana University Press, which has shown me only commitment, consideration, and patience through the many years of these translations.

INTRODUCTION

Chrétien de Troyes. Born circa 1140?—died before 1200? Perhaps born in Troyes and/or lived in the city. Medieval romancer. His extant poetry includes three finished romances, *Erec et Enide* [*Erec and Enide*], *Cliges*, and *Le Chevalier au Lion* [*The Knight with the Lion*], as well as two unfinished romances, *Le Chevalier de la Charrete* [*The Knight of the Cart*] and *Le Conte du Graal* [*The Story of the Grail*]. He also wrote two short lyric poems. He may be the author of another romance, *Guillaume d'Angleterre* [*William of England*].

Thus reads the biography of Chrétien de Troyes, the foremost poet of twelfth-century France. Even so spare a sketch is filled with hypotheses, however. Of almost no other major writer of the Middle Ages do we know so little. No records of the day offer any details about the man. All we have are his own brief comments in his romances, and with these we have to create a portrait of the writer who is accurately called the father of Arthurian romance and who is, indeed, the creator of medieval romance.

At the beginning of *Erec and Enide*, Chrétien refers to himself as Chrétien de Troyes; in his later writings, he refers to himself only as Chrétien. The designation "de Troyes" refers to the city of Troyes, site of the court and center of the province of Champagne. Although the designation might well have referred to a time when Chrétien was absent from Troyes, the reference probably indicates that he was born at Troyes or else spent a considerable amount of time there during his early years.

From the opening of *The Knight of the Cart*, we know that Chrétien was associated with the court of Champagne. The romance opens with extended praise of Marie, the wife of Henry the Liberal, Count of Champagne, and the eldest daughter of Eleanor of Aquitaine and her first husband, Louis VII of France:

> Puis que ma dame de Champagne
> vialt que romans a feire anpraigne,
> je l'anprendrai molt volentiers
> come cil qui est suens antiers
> de quan qu'il puet el monde feire
> sanz rien de losange avant treire.
> Mes tex s'an poist antremetre
> qui li volsist losenge metre,
> si deist, et jel tesmoignasse,
> que ce est la dame qui passe
> totes celes qui sont vivanz,
> si con li funs passe les vanz
> qui vante en mai ou en avril.
> Dirai je: "Tant com une jame
> vaut de pailes et de sardines,
> vaut la contesse de reines?"
> Naie voir, je n'en dirai rien,
> s'est il voirs maleoit gre mien.
> Mes tant dirai ge que mialz oevre
> ses comandemanz an ceste oevre
> que sans ne painne que g'i mete.
> Del Chevalier de la Charrete
> comance Crestiens son livre.
> Matiere et san li done et livre
> la contesse, et il s'antremet
> de panser, que gueres n'i met
> fors sa painne et s'antancion.

[Since my lady of Champagne wills me to undertake the making of a romance, I shall undertake it with great goodwill, as one so wholly devoted that he will do anything in the world for her without any intention of flattery. But another man might begin this in order to flatter her; he would say, and I could only agree, that she surpasses all living ladies as the south wind blowing in April or May surpasses all winds. On my word, I am not one who would flatter his lady. Shall I say, "The Countess is worth as much in queens as a precious gem is worth in brocades and semiprecious stones"? No indeed, I shall say nothing of this, though it is true despite my silence. I shall say only that her command is more important in this undertaking than any thought or effort I may expend.

Christian is beginning his book of the Knight of the Cart. The Countess presents him with the matter and the meaning, and he undertakes to shape the work, adding little to it except his effort and his careful attention.]

The court of Champagne was a center of literary activity. Among the many writers associated with the court were, aside from Chrétien, Andreas

Capellanus, the lyric poet Gace Brulé, and the romancer Gautier d'Arras. The remarkable literary flowering of twelfth-century France grew, as John Benton observed,

> from the fruitful meeting of representatives of different intellectual traditions, the collaboration of the laymen of the feudal courts and of those trained in monastic and cathedral schools. This mixing occurred most often at the courts of great lords, either because authors met personally in that varied and changing society or because they wrote for an audience which they knew had sophisticated and eclectic tastes. Among these centers the court of Henry the Liberal and Marie of Champagne was one of the most important, notable for the education and patronage of its count and countess, for the prominence of the many scholars and authors associated with it in one way or another, and for the quality of its literary remains.

Chrétien's praise of Marie of Champagne not only establishes his familiarity with the court but also provides a *terminus a quo* for the dating of *The Knight of the Cart*. Since Marie's marriage occurred in 1159, *The Knight of the Cart* could not have been written before that year. The only other certain date in Chrétien's skeletal biography is based on the dedication of *The Story of the Grail* to Philip, Count of Flanders. Sometime after the death of Henry the Liberal in 1181, Chrétien may well have turned to Philip as his new patron; Philip himself was a close friend and cousin of Marie of Champagne. Since Philip, who became Count of Flanders in 1168, left on the Third Crusade in 1190 and died in the Holy Land in 1191, Chrétien must have begun his final work before 1191. Because *The Story of the Grail* remains unfinished, we might assume that Chrétien abandoned his longest work upon the news of the Count's death or, more likely, that he himself died before he could complete the poem. If so, Chrétien probably died before the end of the twelfth century, perhaps not long after 1191. Eleven fifty-nine and 1191, then, are the only dates on which we can with certainty base any chronology of Chrétien's life.

At the beginning of his second romance, *Cliges,* Chrétien presents a list of his works:

> Cil qui fist d'Erec et d'Enide,
> Et les comandemanz d'Ovide
> Et l'art d'amors an romans mist,
> Et le mors de l'espaule fist,
> Del roi Marc et d'Ysalt la blonde,
> Et de la hupe et de l'aronde
> Et del rossignol la muance,
> Un novel conte rancomance

D'un vaslet qui an Grece fu
Del linage le roi Artu.

[The man who wrote of Erec and Enide,
translated Ovid's *Commandments* and his
Art of Love, composed *The Shoulder Bite*,
and wrote of King Mark and the blonde Iseult,
and about the metamorphoses of the hoopoe,
the swallow, and the nightingale,
takes up a new tale about a Greek youth of the
line of King Arthur.]

Erec and Enide, then, is Chrétien's earliest extant romance. All the other works he lists are lost, though their names suggest Chrétien's literary inheritance. Most of these lost writings are translations or, perhaps more accurately, adaptations of Ovid: *The Commandments* is probably Ovid's *Remedia Amoris*, and *The Art of Love* his *Ars Amatoria*; *The Shoulder Bite* is possibly the legend of Pelops from the sixth book of Ovid's *Metamorphoses*. The metamorphoses of the hoopoe, the swallow, and the nightingale is an adaptation of the Philomela story from the same book of the *Metamorphoses*; this same story survives in a version that may be by Chrétien.

The year 1159, the date of the marriage of Marie of Champagne and Henry the Liberal, and the year 1191, the date of the death of Philip of Flanders, together with Chrétien's list of his works in the opening of *Cliges*, do offer some guidance in dating the Arthurian romances, and references to contemporary historical events and personages in the romances have led to the possibility of even more exact dating. Scholars now ascribe the composition of *Erec and Enide* to about 1170, *Cliges* to the middle of the same decade, *The Knight of the Cart* and *The Knight with the Lion* to the later seventies and early eighties, and *The Story of the Grail* to the eighties and early nineties.

Like many of his contemporaries, Chrétien began his literary career with a series of apprentice pieces that were translations or adaptations from Latin into the vernacular. Chrétien himself was probably a *clerc*, that is, a scholar with a university education, perhaps even in minor religious orders. If this were the case, he would have been trained in theology and scripture, the liberal arts, and Latin literature. The cathedral schools emphasized classical learning, and so studies included the translation and imitation of such masters as Ovid and Virgil.

From Ovid, Chrétien and his contemporaries inherited a conception of love as an ennobling experience that transforms lovers; such, at least, was the reading given to Ovid by Chrétien's contemporaries, including Andreas

Capellanus, who, in his *De Amore*, analyzes effects of love such as those Chrétien depicts in *The Knight of the Cart*. Twelfth-century poets also found in Ovid a treasury of mythological subjects and stories for poetry.

Chrétien may have known Virgil's *Aeneid* either directly or in its mid-twelfth-century vernacular poetic adaptation, the *Roman d'Eneas*. One of the so-called romances of antiquity, the *Roman d'Eneas* is less an imitation of the Latin epic than a loose adaptation and expansion that transforms Aeneas from a classical epic hero into a twelfth-century knight torn between the power of love and his social and familial duties.

Chrétien's service to another literary tradition is evident in his reference to a version of the Mark and Iseult story, which is also lost. He alludes to the legend of Tristan and Iseult throughout his first two romances, *Erec and Enide* and *Cliges*, and echoes of the legend occur in his later romances. The reference to Mark suggests that Chrétien's treatment might well have been a depiction of a major episode from the already famous Breton story. Such a poem would have been among the first treatments of the story in French.

In addition to the classical authors he studied and the Tristan and Iseult tradition, Chrétien was familiar with the growing body of literature, both written and oral, about King Arthur. In the 1130s, Geoffrey of Monmouth completed his *Historia regum Britanniae* [*History of the Kings of Britain*], a pseudohistorical medley in Latin prose of earlier histories and chronicles, and even of Celtic genealogical material and folktales. He makes Arthur's reign the climax of his account of the British kings; Arthur receives the most attention of the many kings who people Geoffrey's panorama of British history. Amid banquets, military exploits, and martial glories, Arthur is a monarch of unparalleled prowess, a powerful and valiant warrior whose life is ultimately doomed, like the lives of other great kings in British history, to end in tragedy. Through its detailed portrait of Arthur, Geoffrey's history became a major source for Arthurian lore.

This Arthurian world was introduced into French with Wace's *Roman de Brut*, a French verse translation and expansion—and the earliest extant adaptation—of Geoffrey's book. In the *Roman de Brut*, which was completed in 1155, Arthur is still Geoffrey's warrior-king. Wace, an Anglo-Norman poet, pays less attention than Geoffrey, however, to Arthur's military successes and more to his social behavior. It remains for Chrétien, with his emphasis on Arthur's knights as the representatives or embodiment of the king's chivalric order, to complete the transformation of Arthur into a courtly monarch. And so the introduction of Arthur in *Erec and Enide* emphasizes the splendor of his court: "One springtime Easter Day, King Arthur held court in his castle at Cardigan. None so sumptuous was ever seen, for many fine knights were there, bold and proud warriors, as well as elegant ladies and beautiful and charming maidens who were the daughters of kings."

Although Geoffrey of Monmouth refers to King Arthur's founding an order of knighthood, he makes no mention of the Round Table. Wace's *Roman de Brut* contains the first extant reference: "For his noble barons— each of them strove to be the best, and each considered himself the best, and none would admit to being less—Arthur made the Round Table." There may be, as Wace suggests, a Breton source for the Round Table. Or the circular design may be a literary invention, an allegorical representation of the desire for equality, for, Wace continues, the design ensured that all barons would be treated equally. And at the time of Arthur's final battle, Wace again refers to the Round Table and the many deaths of "those of the Round Table, of whom there was such renown throughout the world." By Wace's time, then, there was already an established tradition of the renown of Arthur and also of the knights who sat at his Round Table.

Wace refers to storytellers familiar with Arthurian tales: "In that great time of peace I am speaking about—I do not know if you have heard of it— the marvels were demonstrated and the adventures found that are related about Arthur so often that they have become idle tales. They are neither all lies, nor all truth, neither total folly nor total wisdom. To embellish their tales, the storytellers have recounted so much and the fablemakers have contrived so much chatter that they have given everything the appearance of idle words." By Wace's time, there already existed an extensive oral tradition about King Arthur independent of Geoffrey's literate and comparatively erudite history, and the storytellers were usually Celtic minstrels with a large repertory of Arthurian tales. The literate and oral traditions about King Arthur were not mutually exclusive, for Geoffrey himself was not ignorant of the oral tradition.

Chrétien, then, had access to the world of King Arthur through two distinct traditions, the learned tradition as represented in Geoffrey's *Historia* and, even more, in its expanded adaptation by Wace, and the oral tradition of Celtic storytellers with their many Arthurian tales. How he knew these Celtic tales remains a matter of conjecture, but there is no doubt that he was deeply influenced by them. His romances reveal a familiarity with English geography so detailed and so exact it seems to derive from firsthand experience of the terrain. Yet even had he never crossed the English Channel, he would have heard these tales, for they were being recounted at the time in France, both by courtiers returning from official trips to England, and by jongleurs or minstrels, fluent in French and in

Celtic. He may be referring to just such minstrels at the beginning of *Erec and Enide* when he speaks disparagingly of his professional predecessors who told the same tale, "which those who wish to make their living by storytelling in the presence of counts and kings usually mutilate and spoil."

Chrétien's five Arthurian romances are set in the world of King Arthur and his knights of the Round Table. Whereas Arthur is a heroic figure in earlier histories and chronicles, which contain very few knightly adventures, the knights are the heroes of these romances, and their adventures are the romances' center. Reflecting the late-twelfth-century world with its slowly eroding monarchical power and the increasing importance of the barons, the romances make Arthur more of a figurehead, and the knights or barons the central and developing characters.

Erec and Enide, not only Chrétien's first but *the* first Arthurian romance, focuses on Erec and his beloved Enide. Their story falls into three sections: first, two simultaneous hunts, Arthur's for the white stag and Erec's for the sparrowhawk, culminate in the marriage of Erec and Enide; then a series of tests and ordeals leads them to a new understanding of their love; and finally the adventure of the Joy of the Court leads to a reaffirmation of their love in its full social significance.

In the second section, the poem moves from the realization of the couple's love, through a time of trial and doubt, to an eventual reassertion and redefinition of their love. On his return to his father's kingdom of Outer Wales, Erec's absorption in married love is opposed to the call of chivalry. Marital and martial, married love and chivalry, seem natural enemies, for though Erec continues to equip his men properly and generously, he himself abstains from all chivalric exploits. When he overhears his wife lamenting his behavior, her words, ironically her first words in the poem, sting his pride, and also reflect her own immaturity. The couple set out on a long series of adventures in which Erec tests Enide as well as himself. Their encounters with robbers and thieves, amorous counts and envious nobility provide the realm of social experience their love needs. Enide begins to understand the value of silence and of speech, Erec the meaning of married love.

Before the resolution of their story, Erec and Enide must undergo one last adventure, the Joy of the Court. In Maboagrain and his lady, they confront a couple who have cut themselves off from their relatives, their friends, and their society. The restrictive and confining love-service of Maboagrain contrasts with the love Erec now shares with Enide. On Christmas Day, at Nantes, both Erec and Enide are crowned. Through their adventures they have become worthy of their regal roles in Outer Wales, and Erec, at the beginning a great knight of the Round Table, is now an Arthur in his own land.

Although it is not difficult to trace the influence of *Erec and Enide* on later literature, it is difficult to ascertain the romance's antecedents. Chrétien himself declares that his story is not original; he elicits, he tells his audience, "a most pleasing pattern from a tale of adventure." This "tale of adventure" probably refers to one of the many Celtic tales circulating about Arthur and his knights.

Erec and Enide had an almost immediate literary impact. Within a decade or two of its composition, Hartmann von Aue wrote a Middle High German verse adaptation. And in the early to mid-thirteenth century there was *Erex Saga*, an Old Norse prose adaptation. "Gereint Son of Erbin," a tale from the Welsh *Mabinogi* dating from the thirteenth century, reveals sufficient parallels to *Erec and Enide* to suggest Chrétien's influence, or at least some common Celtic source, however remote. The Welsh tale became the source of the Erec and Enide story for later generations, including Alfred Lord Tennyson, who retold the couple's love and subsequent trials in the third and fourth of his *Idylls of the King*.

Although *Cliges*, Chrétien's next romance, begins and ends in Constantinople, it is not a romance of Byzantium, but an Arthurian romance in which Greece plays a secondary role to Arthur's realm. The tripartite structure of *Erec and Enide* gives way here to a double plot where the adventures of Alexander are the subject of the first third of the poem, the adventures of his son Cliges the subject of the remainder.

In the first section, Alexander travels from Greece to England to become a knight of the Round Table. After proving himself a valiant knight, he marries Soredamor, Gawain's sister, then returns to regain his rightful kingdom from his treacherous brother. On his deathbed, Alexander advises his son Cliges to travel to Arthur's court to measure himself against the knights and, in particular, if occasion arises, his uncle Sir Gawain. The first section, a prelude and anticipatory parallel to the second and major section, ends with Alexander's death.

The parallel between father and son, while not always exact, provides the romance's structure. In England, Cliges too proves his valor. He falls in love with Fenice just as Alexander fell in love with Soredamor, and both lovers are forced to hide their feelings, Alexander out of naivete, Cliges out of need because his beloved is engaged to his uncle. And for Alexander and for Cliges alike, Arthur's kingdom is the world where they must win honor and renown.

Much of the second part of the poem focuses on Cliges' seemingly hopeless love for Fenice and their efforts to hide their passion, first from each other, and then, after they have admitted their love, from Alis, Cliges' uncle and Fenice's husband. Fenice's feigned death is a successful ruse, and Fenice and her lover inhabit an earthly paradise as private and as remote from society as the garden of Maboagrain and his lady. When the couple's isolated pleasure is discovered, the two flee for safety to Arthur's courts, where they receive news of Alis' death. Like Erec and Enide, they return to their homeland. At the end of *Erec and Enide*, Erec becomes the King of Outer Wales, and Arthur's kingdom extends its influence. At the end of *Cliges*, Cliges becomes Emperor of Greece, and his bride Fenice is the daughter of the Emperor of Germany. Arthur's kingdom now has even wider influence.

Cliges also shares with *Erec and Enide* some significant references to the story of Tristan and Iseult. The love triangle of King Mark, his wife Iseult, and Mark's nephew and Iseult's lover Tristan parallels to some degree the relationship of Alis, his wife Fenice, and his nephew and his wife's lover Cliges. The love potion that unites Tristan and Iseult becomes, in *Cliges*, a magic potion that makes Alis believe he is making love to his wife when he is, in reality, asleep. And Fenice's repeated protestations that she does not wish to imitate Iseult's behavior suggest that *Cliges* is a critique of the Tristan legend.

Whereas *Erec and Enide* examines knightly prowess and its relationship to love, *Cliges* focuses, at least initially, on the pursuit of honor and renown. Alexander's statement to his father, "Rest and renown, in my opinion, are not compatible, for a powerful man who is all the time at rest adds nothing to his renown," echoes the plight of the uxorious Erec. In the opening lines, the narrator announces that Alexander traveled to England "to win honor and renown." There is no elaboration here of the meaning of the two virtues, yet their pairing recurs more often in this romance than in any other poem by Chrétien. Honor and renown, excellence and esteem: *Cliges* explores the true merit of the knight. Alexander goes to England to win honor and renown, he proves himself worthy of his lady, and his life ends in peace. Cliges follows his father's path and pattern, attempting to measure himself against the finest knights in Arthur's realm. In the course of his testing, he too falls in love, and in time proves himself worthy of his lady. And the woman he loves, Fenice, is constantly concerned not with honor but with dishonor, not with fame but with infamy occasioned by improper behavior.

Honor and renown are constantly presented alongside human love, that emotional state that renders its inhabitants blessed and foolish at the same time. "Love indeed made a wise man a fool," the narrator observes as he describes Alexander gazing on a strand of his lady's hair. *Cliges* explores much more fully than did *Erec and Enide* the psychology of love, most often through long interior monologues in which the major characters examine their emotional frustrations and their passionate longings.

The folly of love, Chrétien seems to say so often in *Cliges*, is simultaneously beautiful and ridiculous, and the course of true love never does run smooth. The narrator of *Cliges* sympathizes and laughs with his lovers, developing a richer, more bemused personality than did the narrator of *Erec and Enide*.

At the beginning of *Cliges*, Chrétien informs his audience of his romance's written source "in one of the books in the library of Saint Peter's Cathedral in Beauvais." Such a statement, common in the Middle Ages, lends authority to the story but does not necessarily mean that the source existed. If this manuscript did exist, it was probably a Latin text which Chrétien was translating and adapting into the vernacular. The text may have been some copy of the tale of Solomon and Marcolfus, the oldest known version of the feigned death ruse, in which one of Solomon's wives plays the trick on her husband. Chrétien certainly knew this story: in the poem, the three elderly physicians from Salerno refer to it. The feigned death plot, however, is only one dimension of the romance. The treacherous activities of Count Angres seem to be adapted from the account of Mordred's betrayal of Arthur in Wace's *Roman de Brut*. And there are some significant parallels between contemporary political figures and characters in the romance. The remarkably precise details of geography, complemented by historical parallels, make *Cliges* the romance by Chrétien rooted most closely in events of its time.

Both *Erec and Enide* and *Cliges* were adapted into prose at the Burgundian court in the fifteenth century. But *Cliges* did not enjoy the popularity of *Erec and Enide* or, indeed, of any of Chrétien's other romances. Apart from this single adaptation, *Cliges* made no other appearance in later literature.

Like *Erec and Enide*, *The Knight of the Cart*, Chrétien's third Arthurian romance, has a tripartite structure: Lancelot's quest for the abducted queen, his rescue of her and subsequent anxiety before their night of love, and his imprisonment at the hands of Meleagant, the personification of evil. This structure also reflects Celtic folktales of abduction with their three stages of abduction, rescue, and return. Chrétien complicates this pattern, however, by making his tripartite structure far less straightforwardly linear than the structure of *Erec and Enide*. Episodes do not follow one after another as much as they interrupt each other in an interlacing or alternating pattern; Lancelot's quest to rescue the queen is constantly interrupted by subsidiary quests that need to be resolved before the major quest can be successfully completed.

Guinevere and Lancelot, the protagonists of *The Knight of the Cart*, appear in Chrétien's earlier romances, but their appearances do not foreshadow their roles in this third romance. In *Erec and Enide* and *Cliges*, Guinevere is Arthur's queen, his wise counselor (next only to his nephew Gawain), and his devoted wife. In *Cliges*, Guinevere perceives the love tormenting Alexander and Soredamor: "I advise you never to resort to force or yield to the willfulness of loving. Join yourselves together in marriage and honor." In *The Knight of the Cart*, Guinevere, no longer the wise observer, is the beloved of Lancelot, who appears in *Erec and Enide* as third among Arthur's great knights (next only to Erec and Gawain) and in *Cliges* as one of Cliges' more worthy challengers in the tournament.

In *The Knight of the Cart*, Lancelot and Gawain are contrasted as the preeminent knights of the Round Table. Both ride off to rescue the abducted queen, yet in all the time that they share the road, Lancelot always takes the initiative, first in the incident of the Perilous Bed, and later when he offers Gawain the choice of the two dangerous bridges. In the earlier romances, Gawain was the greatest knight of the Round Table. Now his excellence is diminished in contrast to Lancelot's bravery, which originates in his love for the queen.

Lancelot's only failing in his adventures is his hesitation, for just two steps, before entering the shameful cart. His hesitation reflects his momentary unwillingness to humiliate himself in the service of love; he shows himself only the slightest degree forgetful of love's dictates. Later, he does not hesitate to humiliate himself in following the queen's will at the tournament of Noauz. And his early failing is not in the area of knightly excellence, where Lancelot is always the epitome of perfection, but in his status as a lover, and it is Lancelot as a lover that is the ultimate center of the romance.

The critical term *amour courtois* or courtly love was introduced in the late nineteenth century by Gaston Paris to describe the adulterous relationship of Lancelot and Guinevere in this romance.[1] For Paris, their love was the first romance expression of a code of love that developed as an artistic convention in and around the courts of southern France in the late eleventh and early twelfth centuries. The writings of the courtly poets who developed this convention survive in northern French translations, and Chrétien shows a marked familiarity with the lyric poetry of these troubadours. Indeed, he himself wrote two short lyric love poems, "Amors, tençon et bataille" and "D'Amors, qui m'a tolu a moi," which not only confirm the influence of the troubadour poets but also place him among the first poets of the north to write in the courtly lyric style.[2]

Governing behavior of both the lover and his lady, such love describes an all-encompassing passion that ennobles the lover through his ceaseless striving to make himself worthy of his lady. The lover rejoices in the idealized beauty of his beloved and submits himself in all humility to her service. And, perhaps most important for Chrétien, such love is irrational, indeed usually in direct opposition to reason's urgings. *The Knight of the Cart* uses the conventions of this codified system to depict the ordeals and triumphs of Guinevere's peerless lover. Guided by love and not by reason, indeed illustrating the constant battle between emotions and reason in the dedicated lover, Lancelot is an ideal courtly lover, viewed by the narrator with affectionate irony.

In her adultery, Guinevere does not seem the least troubled by the anxieties that plagued Fenice. The loving wife who is willing to lay herself at Kay's feet to please her husband is also the beloved of her husband's greatest knight. Lancelot is Tristan to Guinevere's Iseult, yet Chrétien carefully presents social consequences of their love: Lancelot rescues the queen and thereby frees the captives imprisoned in the land of Gorre.

Chrétien did not finish *The Knight of the Cart*, but left Godefroi de Leigni, perhaps his assistant, to follow his plans and complete the romance from the time of Lancelot's imprisonment in the tower. Godefroi de Leigni brought the romance to what he tells the reader was Chrétien's designated ending, and Chrétien himself seems to have turned his talents to another romance.

At the beginning of *The Knight of the Cart*, Chrétien announces that Marie de Champagne presented him "with the matter and the meaning" of the romance. Marie may well have given him a Celtic abduction tale, in which a mysterious stranger frequently carries off a married woman to his otherworldly home, and the woman is ultimately rescued by her husband, who has overcome many ordeals to free his beloved. Guinevere herself is the center of such a tale in the mid-eleventh-century Latin *Vita sancti Gildae* [*Life of Saint Gildas*] attributed to Caradoc of Llancarfan. But no extant

Celtic tale employs the character of Lancelot, and it is a tribute to Chrétien's invention that he uses such a traditional tale to develop yet another knight of the Round Table, in this instance a knight who is now Arthur's greatest knight and worthy of being the queen's lover.

The first surviving portrait of Lancelot, *The Knight of the Cart*, developed the central love affair of Lancelot and Guinevere that was destined to be a seminal and central component of future retellings of the Arthurian legends. The next presentation of Lancelot, Ulrich von Zatzikhoven's Middle High German poem *Lanzelet*, offers a long personal history of the knight and does present him as the champion of Arthur's queen, but does not even suggest their adulterous relationship. Composed at the end of the twelfth or the beginning of the thirteenth century and probably based on a lost Anglo-Norman source, *Lanzelet* shows no knowledge of Chrétien's romance. Like Ulrich's Anglo-Norman source, *The Knight of the Cart* is reflected in the great prose *Lancelot* of the thirteenth-century French Vulgate Cycle. And in the *Queste del Saint Graal*, a sequel to the prose *Lancelot*, the knight recognizes his guilt, and his penance allows him partial participation in the mysteries of the grail. The Vulgate Cycle furnished Malory with much of the material for his late-fifteenth-century *Le Morte D'Arthur*. And through Malory's work, Lancelot remained Arthur's greatest knight and Guinevere's devoted lover for all future generations.

The plot of *The Knight with the Lion*, Chrétien's fourth Arthurian romance, falls into two parts: Yvain's successful quest for fame and a lady, and his failure to keep his promise and his subsequent regeneration, which culminates in his reunion with his lady. While sharing the linear structure of a knight's quest with *Erec and Enide*, the romance also employs the interlacing pattern that is evident in *The Knight of the Cart*. Twice during Yvain's adventures in the service of others, the knight finds his immediate quest interrupted by demanding smaller adventures. Such interlacing serves to develop and complicate the seemingly simple romance plot of an individual knight's quest for a specific goal.

In *The Knight with the Lion*, Chrétien explores more fully than he has before the tension between chivalry and love. Yvain eagerly pursues the adventure of the spring in order to avenge his cousin's disgrace and enhance his own renown. Brave but rash, courageous but impetuous, he is a youthful, even innocent knight who pursues adventures for his own glory. When he defeats the lord of the spring, he makes every effort to obtain proof of his avenging achievement so that his success will be known at court.

Love enters the world of Yvain's immature chivalry when he first sees Laudine. Succumbing less to love than to her need to defend the spring, Laudine marries her husband's murderer. Immediately after the marriage, Gawain succeeds in urging Yvain to forsake his wife and engage in a year of tournaments to increase his fame. By overstaying the allotted year, Yvain forfeits his wife's love. From the despair of his madness, he begins the slow journey to self-understanding, a series of adventures that teach him to place his chivalry at the service of others rather than himself. In each of his adventures he comes to the service of people in need, and their need, not his fame, is his motivating principle. By the end of the romance, he has learned the meaning of knighthood, which is not a quest for personal glory but a quest for selfless service.

More than any of Chrétien's earlier romances, *The Knight with the Lion* presents a variety of loves, the selfless devotion of a grateful lion to his master, the equally selfless devotion of Lunete to her lady Laudine, the abiding friendship of Yvain and Gawain, the romantic avowal of devotion by Gawain to Lunete, and finally the married love of Yvain and Laudine. Yet many of these loves are presented in their complexity and, like the romance itself, do not necessarily present a final and fixed perspective.

The denouement of *The Knight with the Lion* lacks the harmonious closure of *Erec and Enide* or *Cliges*. Laudine accepts her penitent husband, not out of love or even pity, but because she cannot break her oath; she will love him rather than perjure herself. Chrétien's first two romances, like Shakespeare's early comedies, have a symmetrical and all-embracing resolution. *The Knight with the Lion*, like a later Shakespearean comedy such as *Twelfth Night*, has a symmetrical resolution that can no longer be all-embracing.

Like *The Knight of the Cart*, *The Knight with the Lion* owes part of its origin to Celtic tales. And like *Erec and Enide*, it has as an analogue one of the stories from the Welsh *Mabinogi*, "Owein, or the Lady of the Fountain," which follows the plot of Chrétien's story with enough fidelity until Yvain's rescue of Lunete to suggest Chrétien's influence, or perhaps some common Celtic source for both works. And other details of the romance, such as the magic spring and the equally magical Castle of Most Ill Adventure, find close parallels in stories of the Celtic otherworld.

Although Yvain himself never came to occupy the central position that Lancelot holds in Arthurian literature, *The Knight with the Lion* was translated and adapted into many languages. Before the end of the twelfth century, Hartmann von Aue adapted the romance into Middle High German; the thirteenth century saw versions of the romance in Old Norse and in

Swedish; and the fourteenth century produced the Middle English poem *Ywain and Gawain*, the only version of one of Chrétien's romances to survive in English.

It is difficult to assess Chrétien's final romance, *The Story of the Grail*, for it remains incomplete, with little indication of a final direction or conclusion. Its nearly nine thousand lines make even the unfinished poem longer than any of Chrétien's earlier works. It is a poem on a grand scale, in which the boyish Perceval, wholly innocent and ignorant of the chivalric life, goes through a series of adventures to achieve the selfless dedication of a true knight.

The structure of the extant portion of the romance recalls the double structure of *Cliges*, with two seemingly independent narratives, Perceval's transformation from innocent child to devoted knight beloved by man and by God, and the story of Gawain's more secular adventures. Gawain already served as a counterpart to Lancelot in *The Knight of the Cart* and to Yvain in *The Knight with the Lion*. The gulf between Gawain and Perceval is much greater than in either of these earlier contrasts, for Perceval is instructed into a knighthood that centers on divine love, a realm that would seem to be closed to the purely chivalric and earthly Gawain.

Perceval's story is interrupted by Gawain's adventures, which are in turn interrupted by the brief episode of Perceval and his uncle the hermit. Such interlocking suggests that Chrétien is here employing an interlacing pattern on a much larger scale. And just as Gawain's adventures are interrupted by Perceval's meeting with the hermit, so are the adventures of both knights constantly interrupted by secondary adventures. Perceval is on his way to find his mother when he comes upon the Fisher King, and later through the Fisher King's cousin he learns of his mother's death. Gawain's adventures begin with the charge of treason that is leveled against him, and his journey to defend himself before the King of Escavalon is constantly interrupted by other adventures.

Although some critics have claimed that the Perceval and Gawain sections are separate adventures connected by a later editor, such a theory disregards the fact that *The Story of the Grail* survives in fifteen manuscripts, many more than for any other romance by Chrétien, and in all these manuscripts the romance has the same bipartite structure. Gawain is a surrogate for Perceval, his set of adventures paralleling in meaning Perceval's offstage adventures. But while Gawain's unreflecting chivalry finds him undertaking challenges in the service of women, Perceval's adventures, higher in accomplishment than Gawain's, are qualifying him for spiritual achievement.

Just as the length of *The Story of the Grail* distinguishes it from Chrétien's earlier romances, so too does its theme. In the long eulogy to Philip of Flanders that begins the poem, Chrétien sets up an opposition between the great Alexander of pre-Christian times and the worthier Philip of the present. The contrast focuses on the opposition between vanity and charity. Alexander's good deeds originate in vanity, the selfish quest for fame, Philip's in charity, which is rooted in divine love. Just as Philip is worthier than Alexander, so too will Perceval be worthier than the heroes of the earlier romances, for Perceval, the romance implies, will return to the Fisher King's castle and finally ask the proper questions.

Perceval passes through distinct stages of education. As the only child of the lonely widow of the Desolate Forest, he receives careful instructions from his mother, which include the proper behavior of a knight in public, the proper conduct of a knight to a lady, and the proper practice of religion. From Gornemant of Gohort he learns the practical requirements of knighthood, and Gornemant's instructions too end with an exhortation to prayer. The mysterious grail procession in the home of the Fisher King and Perceval's silence reveal the essential inadequacy of his secular training, and only in his later meeting with the hermit do he and the audience learn of the higher calling of knights, indeed of mankind.

In the course of his adventures Perceval becomes the epitome of chivalry, the equal of Erec, Cliges, Lancelot, and Yvain; like them too, he falls in love with a beautiful woman worthy of his devotion. But chivalry and love, the sources of tension for the earlier heroes, now give way and are subsumed within the practice of religion and the meaning of divine love. And this theme, the relationship between knighthood and God, accounts for the massive scale of *The Story of the Grail*, Chrétien's first romance to follow its protagonist's career from childhood through knighthood to the knight's relationship with God.

At the beginning of the romance, Chrétien informs his audience that he took his story, "the finest tale that may be told at a royal court," from "the book the count gave him." If the book existed, it may have been a Latin treatise Chrétien was adapting into the vernacular, or some Celtic tale of adventure dealing with the grail. The word *grail* was a common term to designate a serving bowl usually used for fish. So far as surviving texts are concerned, it was Chrétien who first attached some special significance to this bowl. And because he did not finish the romance, it is impossible to determine the extent of the grail's religious significance.

The original grail story may not have included Perceval. The knight's earlier appearances—in *Erec and Enide* he is among the knights of Arthur's court, and in *Cliges* he is "a vassal of great renown"—give no suggestion of his association with the grail. In *The Knight of the Cart*, Chrétien introduced Lancelot into a traditional Celtic abduction story. It may be a further mark of his inventiveness that he has here brought together a Celtic tale of the grail with the undeveloped figure of Perceval.

The unfinished state of Chrétien's romance, complemented by its innately mysterious subject matter, led to a series of continuations. About the year 1200, an anonymous poet continued the romance for another nine thousand five hundred lines without reaching a conclusion. A second continuator added thirteen thousand more lines, and he did not reach a conclusion either. About thirty years later, Gerbert de Montreuil added another seventeen thousand lines to the Second Continuation; his ending for the poem is lost. And probably about the same time, in a third continuation written by Manessier, ten thousand new lines brought the poem to a conclusion with Perceval crowned Grail King.

While these four poets were completing *The Story of the Grail*, others were adapting it. By the end of the twelfth century, Robert de Boron, a Burgundian poet, composed the first cycle of grail romances, a trilogy that included *Joseph d'Arimathie, Merlin,* and *Perceval,* of which only the first and the beginning of the second survive. He was the first writer to connect explicitly the grail of Chrétien's romance with the vessel of the Last Supper; he also describes how Joseph of Arimathea used the same vessel to collect the blood of Christ on the cross. Early in the thirteenth century, Wolfram von Eschenbach translated, adapted, and completed *The Story of the Grail* in his twenty-five thousand-line German epic *Parzival*. And "Peredur," the third Arthurian tale from the Welsh *Mabinogi*, has many similarities to Chrétien's poem that suggest his influence, or perhaps, again, some remote Celtic source for both romances.

The Didot-*Perceval*, written about 1200, is a French prose adaptation of Robert de Boron's poem, of the Second Continuation, and probably of Chrétien's romance itself. At the same time there was another French prose adaptation, *Perlesvaus*, which reveals familiarity with *The Story of the Grail*, the First and Second Continuations, and Robert de Boron. Then, shortly thereafter, the Vulgate Cycle's *Queste del Saint Graal* drew upon Chrétien's romance, the First and Second Continuations, Robert de Boron, and the Didot-*Perceval*. The Continuations and adaptations, all written within fifty years of Chrétien's romance, testify to its popularity and to the pervasiveness of its influence.

For more than a century, *William of England* has been the subject of scholarly debate and controversy. In the opening line, and then again seventeen lines later, the author identifies himself as Chrétien. Although this name was not uncommon in the twelfth century, many scholars believe that this Chrétien is Chrétien de Troyes. Arguments both for and against the identification are frequent and often convincing. The Appendix contains a translation of *William of England* and a bibliography so that the reader can compare the poem with the Arthurian romances.

William of England shares no Arthurian connection to Chrétien's other romances; it contains no Arthurian references. Absent too are the long interior monologues of character revelation as well as the narrator's irony. Present, however, are the lavish court setting, though not Arthurian, which opens the poem, an interest in and knowledge of aristocratic life, and a rudimentary interlacing structure.

A story of spiritual rather than chivalric adventure, *William of England* is a romance with hagiographic overtones in which the goal is not knightly success but endurance and survival in the face of trials and tortures. The romance begins with a portrait of the pious king William and his equally pious wife Gratienne in their childless marriage. Only after Gratienne becomes pregnant does the king hear a voice admonishing him to go into exile. William, who considers himself guilty of covetousness, sets out with his wife on twenty-four years of secular rather than spiritual adventures. The episodic, linear narrative follows their wanderings, first William's, then Gratienne's, and finally those of their twin sons, before the three tales come together in a happy familial reunion.

If Chrétien de Troyes is the author of the poem, he probably wrote it after he finished *Cliges*—he does not list the poem among his works at the beginning of *Cliges*—and before he turned to the complexities of *The Knight of the Cart* and *The Knight with the Lion*. If he is not the author, then the author, perhaps even a disciple or student, was familiar with the twelfth-century romance world and, in particular, some of the romances of Chrétien de Troyes.

At the beginning of *William of England*, the author informs his audience that his tale has its source in a book at Saint Edmund's monastery in England; at the end, he explains that he himself heard the tale from his friend Roger le Cointe, a name that remains unknown. Although there is no known source for the story, the plot shares some similarities with the legends of Saint Eustachius and Apollonius of Tyre. More important is the poem's affinity with the folk motif of the Man Sorely Tried by Fate, itself evident in the Saint Eustachius legend.

William of England, which survives in only two manuscripts, had little influence, apart from a fourteenth-century Spanish translation.

The fame and even the name of Chrétien de Troyes—both in his time and since his time—rest on his five Arthurian romances. He reshaped his Arthurian inheritance, and created a design that would serve as the standard and an essential source for all subsequent Arthurian literature.

By shifting the center of the Arthurian world from King Arthur to his knights, by making the knights the embodiment of the order represented by the Round Table, Chrétien based his romances on Wace's reference to the Round Table and on the many Arthurian tales already in circulation. His Round Table is no longer an allegorical representation of Arthur's order but its living embodiment, a group of individuals, each one capable of sustaining his own adventure.

In *Erec and Enide*, Chrétien describes the Round Table: "I can certainly tell you the names of some of the finest barons who belonged to the Round Table, which comprised the best in the world." He then names the ten finest and twenty-one others. Here is Gawain, the best; Erec, next to Gawain; and Lancelot of the Lake, who is third. Here too are Yvain, who will be the hero of his own romance, and Gornemant of Gohort and Meliant of Lis, who will have important roles in *The Story of the Grail*. And Chrétien has already mentioned Perceval of Wales as one of the knights at Arthur's court. *Erec and Enide*, however, offers no hint of the roles to be played by Lancelot, Yvain, Perceval, Gornemant, Meliant, or even Gawain. In adapting or perhaps inventing tales of adventure and assigning them to individual and, therefore, individualized knights, Chrétien creates a fictional universe that is no longer the world of King Arthur but an Arthurian world.

The individual knight rather than Arthur is the center of Chrétien's fiction. Traditionally, the epic and the chronicle depict a nation; their characters are the embodiment of a national destiny; their ultimate concern is the nation itself. By contrast, the romance depicts the individual. Thus, in the twelfth century, Virgil's epic of national identity becomes the *Roman d'Eneas*, with the national concerns subordinated to a tale of an individual, his heroism, his loves, his adventures. The distance between the Arthur of the chronicles and Chrétien's Arthur is the distance between Arthur in a national context and Arthur as secondary to individual knights whose heroism and loves are portrayed through their adventures.

The romances of Chrétien distance the individuals from their society, allow them their own identities, and examine their understanding of both themselves and their world. In his focus on the individual, Chrétien creates the knights who will be central figures of the Arthurian world for all future generations.

At the beginning of *Erec and Enide,* Chrétien sets himself up in confident opposition to storytellers, who earn their living by reciting their tales. He "elicits a most pleasing pattern [une molt bele conjointure] from a tale of adventure [un conte d'avanture]," and so creates an important distinction between the *conte* and his own art. The word *conte,* meaning tale or story, occurs twenty-seven times in Chrétien's five Arthurian romances, usually signifying a simple story, either the tale Chrétien received from his source or a story such as Calogrenant's tale in *The Knight with the Lion.*

Chrétien's art is the romance. In the twelfth century, *romanz* designated the vernacular as opposed to the Latin language and, by extension, any composition in the vernacular. The word *romanz* occurs only seven times in Chrétien's five Arthurian romances. In *Cliges, romanz* opens the narrative, and appears again when the section on Cliges begins; in both cases, the word has the standard meaning of a composition adapted from Latin. In his five other uses of the term, however, Chrétien gives *romanz* a new meaning as he applies it specifically to his own creations. In the opening lines of *The Knight with the Lion* and *The Story of the Grail* and in the closing lines of *The Knight of the Cart,* he has *romanz* designate his own completed artistic creation. In *The Knight with the Lion,* the maiden at the Castle of Most Ill Adventure is reading "from a romance—I do not know about whom. A lady had come to recline there and hear the romance." A word rarely used by Chrétien is repeated within three lines. Here may be Chrétien referring to his own literary genre, a moment of self-reflection by a poet who boasted at the beginning of *Erec and Enide* that his poem would "be remembered as long as Christianity endures."

NOTES

1. Gaston Paris, "Etudes sur les romans de la Table Ronde. Lancelot du Lac, I. Le *Lanzelet* d'Ulrich de Zatzikhoven; Lancelot du Lac, II. Le *Conte de la charrette*," *Romania* 10 (1881):465–96; 12 (1883):459–534. For an analysis of Paris, see Henry Ansgar Kelly, "Gaston Paris's Courteous and Horsely Love," in *The Spirit of the Court*, ed. Glyn S. Burgess and Robert A. Taylor (Cambridge, England: D. S. Brewer, 1985), pp. 217–23, and "The Varieties of Love in Medieval Literature According to Gaston Paris," *RPh* 40 (1986):301–327. For courtly love in a historical perspective, see John F. Benton, "Clio and Venus: An Historical View of Medieval Love," in *The Meaning of Courtly Love*, ed. F. X. Newman (Albany, N.Y.: SUNY Press, 1972), pp. 19–42. An overview of courtly love is available in the variety of essays in *The Meaning of Courtly Love* and in *In Pursuit of Perfection*, ed. Joan M. Ferrante and George D. Economou (Port Washington, N.Y.: Kennikat Press, 1975).

2. *Les Chansons courtoises de Chrétien de Troyes*, ed. Marie-Claire Zai (Berne: Herbert Lang, 1974). The two lyric poems may be among Chrétien's early works, or they may have been written concurrently with *Cliges* or *The Knight of the Cart*, which employ extensively the language of the troubadour poets.

A Note on the Translation

"A true poet is strictly untranslatable," wrote Paul Valéry, poet and critic. And yet such an assertion of the impossibility of translating poetry—a humbling warning indeed—has been no deterrent, even to Valéry himself.

In these translations of the romances of Chrétien de Troyes, I have tried to capture in modern English prose the meaning and the emphases of the original French poems. I have deliberately avoided archaic words and phrases, for Chrétien's language did not employ archaisms, and I have also avoided contemporary colloquialisms, which seem inappropriate to his style. Although my prose cannot reproduce the rhyme or the rhythm of Chrétien's octosyllabic couplets, I hope these translations suggest something of the beauty and the wit of the original poetry.

The base text for the translations of Chrétien's five Arthurian romances is Bibliothèque Nationale manuscript 794, copied in the early thirteenth century—not long after the composition of the romances themselves—by the Champenois scribe Guiot. Since this manuscript served as the base text for the edition of Chrétien's romances in the Classiques Français du Moyen Age series, I have retained the line numbers from this edition for convenience in reading.

THE COMPLETE ROMANCES OF

CHRÉTIEN DE TROYES

EREC AND ENIDE

HE PEASANT HAS A proverb: "What you scorn may be worth much more than you think." For the man does well who turns to good use whatever talents he has, while the man who neglects his talents could well be being silent about something which otherwise might bring much delight. That is why Christian of Troyes maintains it is right that all always aspire and endeavor to speak eloquently and to teach well. And he elicits a most pleasing pattern from a tale of adventure, in order to demonstrate and to prove that the man does not act wisely who fails to make full use of his knowledge so long as God grants him the grace to do so.

This is the tale of Erec, the son of Lac, which those who wish to make their living by storytelling in the presence of counts and kings usually mutilate and spoil. Now I am going to begin the story that henceforth will be remembered as long as Christianity endures. This is Christian's boast.

One springtime Easter Day, King Arthur held court in his castle at Cardigan. None so sumptuous was ever seen, for many fine knights were there, bold and proud warriors, as well as elegant ladies and beautiful and charming maidens who were the daughters of kings. Before the court dissolved, however, the king told his knights that he wished to revive the custom of the hunt for the white stag. Sir Gawain was not pleased by what he heard. "Lord," he said, "this hunt will never bring you pleasure or thanks. We have all known for some time the meaning of the custom of the white stag:

whoever can kill the white stag has the right to kiss the most beautiful maiden of your court regardless of the consequences. Great peril could come from this, for there are five hundred young ladies of noble birth here, wise and charming, the daughters of kings. There is none who does not have a bold and valiant knight for her lover, and each lover would gladly affirm, whether right or wrong, that his beloved is the most charming and the most beautiful."

"I know this," the king replied. "Nevertheless I shall not renounce my plan on that account. The word of the king should not be contradicted. Tomorrow morning amid great festivity, we shall all go and hunt the white stag in the forest of adventures. This hunt will be an occasion of great wonders." And so the hunt was arranged for dawn the next day.

At daybreak the following morning, the king rose and dressed, putting on a short tunic for his ride in the forest. He had his knights awakened and the hunting horses harnessed. Armed with their bows and arrows, the men set out to hunt in the forest. After them the queen mounted. Accompanying her was her maid-in-waiting, the daughter of a king, who sat on a fine palfrey. Behind them spurring quickly was a knight named Erec, a member of the Round Table, who enjoyed great renown at the court. Since he had been there, no other knight had received so much praise. Such beauty was his that nowhere on earth could be found a knight so handsome. Though not yet twenty-five, he was most noble, brave, and becoming. Never had any man his age displayed such valor. What more can I say of his good qualities?

He had mounted a charger, dressed in an ermine-trimmed cloak, a tunic of splendid flowered silk from Constantinople, and leggings of silk brocade that were finely designed and cut. His gold spurs were fastened and he was firmly fixed in the stirrups as he came galloping along the road. He carried no other weapon but his sword. Racing along, he overtook the queen at the turning in the road. "Lady," he said, "if you please, I would like to join you along this route. The only reason I came here is to keep you company."

"Dear friend," the queen answered by way of thanks, "I delight in your company, you may be certain of that. I could have no finer companion."

They then galloped along until they reached the edge of the forest. Those who had gone ahead had already flushed out the stag. Some were blowing horns, others shouting. With a great din, the hounds dashed after the stag, running, darting, and barking. The archers sent up a shower of arrows. Leading all the hunters was the king riding a Spanish hunting horse.

Queen Guinevere was in the forest listening for the hounds, and alongside her were Erec and her courteous and beautiful maid-in-waiting. But because those who had flushed out the stag were so far away, the three could hear nothing, not horn, hunting horse, or hound. In order to listen carefully, all three had stopped in a roadside clearing, hoping to hear a man's voice or a hound's cry somewhere. They were in this place but a short time when they sighted an armed knight approaching on a charger, his shield hanging from his neck, his lance in his hand. From a distance the queen saw him: riding beside him on his right was a maiden of elegant bearing, and coming along the road ahead of them on a large packhorse was a dwarf, who carried a knotted whip in his hand. Watching this handsome and proper knight, Queen Guinevere wished to know his identity and that of his maiden. She commanded her maid to go at once and speak with him. "Young lady," the queen said, "that knight who rides there, go and tell him to come to me and to bring his maiden with him."

Her maid rode at an amble straight to the knight. His whip in his hand, the dwarf came to meet her. "Stop, young lady!" shouted the dwarf, who was full of wickedness. "What are you after? Nothing past here concerns you."

"Dwarf, let me pass on, for the queen sends me there. I wish to talk with that knight," she replied.

The evil, base-born dwarf stood in the center of the road. "Nothing here concerns you," he said. "Go back. It is improper for you to address so fine a knight."

The maid rode forward and tried to force her way past, having great contempt for the dwarf because she saw how small he was. When the dwarf saw her riding toward him, he raised his whip, intending to lash her across the face. But she raised her arm to protect herself. He struck her again, this time hitting her on her bare, unprotected hand. He brought down such a blow on the back of her hand that the entire hand turned blue. Unable to do more, the maid was forced to return whether she wished to or not. She wept as she made her way back, the tears from her eyes streaming down her face.

At the sight of her injured maid, the queen was angry and distraught; she did not know what to do. "Alas, Erec, dear friend," she said, "I am deeply pained that this dwarf has done my maid such an injury. The knight is certainly a churl to let a monster like that strike such a lovely creature. Dear friend Erec, go to the knight there and tell him to come to me at once. I wish to be acquainted with him and his lady."

Spurring his horse, Erec galloped straight to the knight. The despicable dwarf saw him approaching and went to meet him. "Vassal, stand back!" he exclaimed. "I don't know what business you have here. I advise you to draw back."

"Move away, you disagreeable dwarf," Erec replied. "You are wicked and provoking. Let me by."

"You shall not go by."

"Yes, I will."

"No, you will not."

Erec forced the dwarf aside. Of all people the dwarf was the most wicked, and he dealt him a terrible blow across the neck with his whip. The whip's stroke slashed Erec's neck and face. From one end to the other, lines appeared from the lashes. Seeing the armed knight's arrogance and ferocity, Erec realized that he could not have the satisfaction of hitting the dwarf, for fear the knight would kill him at once were he to strike his dwarf before his eyes. Folly is not valor, and so Erec, having no alternative, acted prudently by returning to the queen.

"Lady, the situation is worse now," he said. "The despicable dwarf has badly hurt me, for he slashed my face. I dared not touch or hit him. But no one should blame me for this, since I was all unarmed, and I feared the rude and arrogant knight who was armed. He would not have regarded the matter as a jest. In his conceit he would have killed me at once. Yet I make you a promise: if I can, I will avenge my disgrace or else increase it. But my weapons are too far from here when now I need them, for I left them at Cardigan when I set out this morning. If I were to go and fetch them, I might never chance upon the knight again, for he is galloping away. I must follow him at once, far or near, until I can find equipment to borrow or hire. If I find someone to lend me arms, the knight will discover me ready for immediate combat. You can be absolutely certain both of us will fight until he defeats me, or I him. And if I can, I shall be on my return within three days. You will then see me back home again either happy or sad, I don't know which. Lady, I can delay no longer. I must follow the knight. Off I go. To God I commend you." And more than five hundred times the queen similarly commended him to God to protect him from harm. Erec left the queen to pursue the knight without pause, while the queen stayed in the forest where the king had overtaken the stag.

The king had arrived before the other men at the stag's capture. They killed the white stag and carried it away. They all turned back toward home, bearing the stag, and they rode along until they reached Cardigan.

After supper, when the high spirits of all the barons pervaded the household, the king declared that in accordance with the practice, since he had captured the stag, he would go and bestow the kiss to observe the custom of the stag. Throughout the court a great din arose. Everyone was asserting and swearing that this would never happen without the dispute of swords or ash lances. Every knight wished to prove in armed combat that his beloved was the greatest beauty in the hall. That kind of talk was most alarming.

You can be certain Sir Gawain was not pleased by what he heard. He addressed the king on the subject. "Lord, these knights of yours are deeply upset. They all talk about this kiss and say it will never happen without dissension or battle," he said.

"Dear nephew Gawain," the king replied sensibly, "advise me, with due respect to my honor and my prerogative, how to avoid the dissension."

Several of the finest barons of the court hastened to council. King Yder had come there; he had been the first summoned. After him came the wise and worthy King Cadiolant. Kay and Girflet had come there, King Amauguin as well, and many other barons had joined them.

The discussion continued until the queen arrived. She recounted the adventure that had happened in the forest, telling them about the armed knight she had seen and the wicked little dwarf who had hit her maid's bare hand with his whip and foully struck Erec in the same way on the face. She continued by noting that Erec had followed the knight to avenge his disgrace or else increase it, and that he was to return, if he could, within three days. "Lord," the queen addressed the king, "listen to me a minute. If these barons agree, postpone this kiss until Erec returns in three days." Everyone there agreed with her, and the king himself approved her suggestion.

Erec continued his pursuit of the armed knight and the dwarf who had struck him until they reached a well-situated town, which was both beautiful and fortified, where they immediately entered through the gateway. In the town there was jubilation among the knights and among the maidens, for many beautiful maidens were there. Along the streets, some people were feeding molting falcons and sparrowhawks; others were bringing tercels outside, along with sorrel-hooded goshawks. Elsewhere, other people were playing games, some at dice or another game of chance, others intent on chess and backgammon. In front of the stables the grooms were rubbing down and currying the horses. In their chambers the ladies were preparing themselves in their finery. From the distance the people caught sight of the knight approaching with his dwarf and his maiden; they recognized him and went in threes to meet him. Although they all joyfully welcomed him, they paid no attention to Erec, for they did not recognize him.

Erec followed the knight closely through the town until he saw him take lodging, and was extremely pleased and happy to see that he was lodged. Proceeding a little farther, he noticed a rather elderly vavasor resting at the top of some steps. The vavasor was a handsome man, elderly and white-haired, noble and well born, though his dwelling was poor. He was seated there all alone, apparently absorbed in his thoughts. Erec assumed that he was a man of worth who would not hesitate to offer him lodging, and as he entered the yard through the gate, the vavasor hurried to meet him. Before Erec had uttered a word, the vavasor greeted him. "Welcome, dear sir," he said. "If you care to accept my hospitality, behold, my lodging awaits you."

"Thank you," Erec replied. "That is the reason I came here: I need shelter for the night."

When Erec dismounted, the host himself took his horse and led it away by the reins, rejoicing over his guest. The vavasor called to his wife and his beautiful daughter, who were busily engaged in a workroom. I do not know what work they were doing. The lady came outside at his call, as did his daughter, who was attired in a white shift of fine material with wide pleats. She wore this under a long-sleeved white linen smock, which was so old that it was worn through at the elbows; she wore no other clothing. The outside attire was meager, but the person within was attractive.

The maiden was most beautiful. In creating her, Nature had expended all her effort. More than five hundred times even Nature herself had marveled at having fashioned on this one occasion such a beautiful creature. Since that time, despite all her possible efforts, there was no way in which she could reproduce her own model. Nature bears witness that never before had such a lovely creature been seen on the face of the earth. I tell you honestly, the shining golden hair of the blonde Iseult was nothing in comparison with this maiden's hair. Her forehead and face were whiter and brighter than the lily-in-bloom. In a most wondrous fashion, Nature had given her complexion a fresh rosy hue that illuminated her face. So brilliantly glowing were her eyes that they seemed a pair of stars. God never knew how to make a finer nose, mouth, or eyes. What more can I say of her beauty? To be honest, she was made to be gazed upon, for a man could see himself reflected in her as in a mirror.

When the maiden came out of the workroom and noticed the knight whom she had never seen, she stepped back a little. Because she did not know him, she was embarrassed and began to blush. For his part, Erec was dazzled to behold such great beauty in her.

"Sweet gentle daughter," the vavasor said to her, "take this horse and lead it to the stable with mine. Make certain it has everything. Remove the saddle and bridle. Give it hay and oats. Brush and groom it that it may be well cared for."

The maiden took the horse, unlaced the breaststrap, and removed the saddle and bridle. Now, under her proper attention, the horse received excellent care. She put a halter around its neck, then rubbed it well, brushed it, and groomed it. She tied it to the feeding-trough and heaped in front fresh sweet hay and oats. Then she returned to her father.

"My dear daughter," he said to her, "take this lord by the hand and show him the highest honor."

The maiden did not know discourtesy. She did not hesitate to take him by the hand and lead him upstairs. The lady of the house had gone ahead to prepare her home. She had decked the beds with quilts and spreads where all three of them would sit, Erec beside the maiden and his host across from them. In front of them the fire blazed brightly. The vavasor had no household staff, not even a chambermaid or a serving girl, but only one serving man, who was cooking meat and fowl for supper in the kitchen. He was fast in arranging the meal, for he knew well how to prepare and cook meat quickly by boiling it in water and roasting it on a spit. When the meal had been prepared according to the instructions he had received, he offered them water in two basins, then set everything in place, portable tables with cloths and bowls. All of them sat down to eat and found they had everything they wanted.

When they had dined to their satisfaction and left the tables, Erec addressed his host, the lord of the house. "Dear host, tell me," he said, "why is your daughter, who is so beautiful and careful of herself, turned out in dress so poor and beneath her station?"

"Dear friend," the vavasor replied, "poverty harms many men, and I am no exception. Although it hurts me deeply to see her dressed so poorly, I cannot amend the situation. I have been at war so long that I have lost all my land, which I was forced to mortgage and sell. Yet she would have been well dressed had I let her accept what people wished to give her. Even the lord of this town would have clothed her in splendid style and complied with all her wishes, for she is his niece and he is a count. In all this land there is no baron, however renowned, who would not have married her gladly had I consented. But I am still waiting for a better occasion when God may show her greater honor and chance may bring a count or a king here who will lead her away.

"My daughter is so wondrously beautiful that her equal cannot be found. Is there, then, under heaven a count or a king who would be ashamed of her? Lovely she is, yet her wisdom far surpasses her beauty. God never made any creature so wise or so noble hearted. When I have my daughter beside me, the whole world is not worth one bead. She is my pleasure and my happiness, my comfort and my joy, my fortune and my treasure. There is nothing I love so much as her."

When Erec heard everything his host said, he asked him to tell him whence had come such a company of knights as was in this town. There was no street so poor or lodging so small and meager that it was not filled with knights, ladies, and squires.

"Dear friend," the vavasor answered him, "these men are barons from around this land. Young and old, they have all come to a festival, which will take place in this town tomorrow. That is the reason the lodgings are so full. There will be a huge commotion tomorrow when everyone has gathered. Before all the people, a beautiful sparrowhawk of five or six moltings, the finest known, will be set on a silver perch. The man who would own the sparrowhawk must have a wise and beautiful lady who has no trace of baseness. If there is a knight bold enough to claim the honor and title of the most beautiful on behalf of his beloved, then he will bid her take the sparrowhawk from the perch in front of everyone so long as no one else dares interfere. Such is the custom the barons now observe, and that is the reason they come here every year."

"Dear host," Erec answered him imploringly, "tell me, if you don't mind, do you know the knight with gold and azure arms who passed by here just a while ago? He was accompanied by an elegant maiden who stayed close to his side and a hunchbacked dwarf who rode ahead of them."

"That is the man who will have the sparrowhawk without opposition from any knight," the host replied to him. "There will be no blows or wounds. I don't expect anyone to stand up to him. For the last two years he has won without challenge. But if he wins it again this year, he will have claimed its possession forever. From now on he will have it always, uncontested and undisputed."

Erec's response was immediate. "I do not like that knight. You can be certain I would challenge him for the sparrowhawk if I had arms. Dear host, I call upon your noble nature. As a reward and service, advise me, I beg you, how I can procure some arms, be they old or new, ugly or beautiful."

[8]

Noble was the vavasor's response. "Do not worry about that. I have fine good arms I shall be glad to lend you. Inside I have a triple-woven hauberk, which was selected from among five hundred; handsome and expensive greaves, which are new, lightweight, and excellent, as well as a good, splendid helmet and a fresh, new shield. Shield, lance, and horse, I shall not hesitate to lend you all these. So there is nothing left to ask."

"Thank you, dear sir, but I seek no better sword than the one I have been carrying and no other horse but my own, for they will be of good aid to me. I think you are very kind if you lend me the rest. But there is one further favor I would ask of you, and I shall repay you for it, if God grants me all the honor of the combat."

"Do not be afraid to ask whatever you wish" was the vavasor's response. "I should deny you nothing of mine."

Erec then said that he wished to claim the sparrowhawk on behalf of his daughter, for there would be, in truth, no maiden with a hundredth of her beauty. And if he took her along with him, he would have just and proper cause to claim and prove that she should carry away the sparrowhawk. "Sir," he continued, "you do not know the guest you have lodged, his race or his rank. I am the son of a rich and powerful king. My father's name is King Lac; the Bretons call me Erec. I belong to King Arthur's court, where I have been for the last three years. I do not know if news of my father's renown or my own has ever reached this country. But I pledge to you, I swear, if you will provide me with arms and entrust me with your daughter that I may win the sparrowhawk tomorrow, I will take her to my own land if God grants me victory. There I will have her crowned, and she shall be queen of ten cities."

"Ah, dear sir, is this true? Are you Erec, the son of Lac?"

"Yes I am," he said.

His host rejoiced. "We have certainly heard of you in this land," he said. "Now my affection and esteem for you are even greater, for you are very bold and brave. You will be denied nothing of mine. Just as you asked, I entrust you with my beautiful daughter." The host then took her by the hand. "Here she is," he said. "I present her to you."

Erec received her happily; now he had all he wanted. Everyone there rejoiced: her father was joyous, her mother wept for joy, and as for the maiden herself, though she kept totally silent, she was overjoyed and pleased to be presented to him, for he was courteous and brave, and she realized that he would be king and she herself would be honored and crowned a powerful queen.

That night they stayed up very late. White sheets and soft pillows had been placed on the beds, and when the words were spent, they went happily to rest.

Erec slept little that night. At daybreak the next morning he rose promptly, and his host rose at the same time. They both went to church to pray; they asked a solitary monk to sing a mass in honor of the Holy Spirit and did not neglect to leave an offering. When the mass ended, they both knelt at the altar, then returned home.

Erec was eager for the combat. At his command his arms were brought to him, and the maiden herself armed him. Without pronouncing any charm or spell, she laced up his iron greaves with a deerskin strap, dressed him in a hauberk of strong meshes, attached his chinguard, placed the gleaming helmet on his head, and girded his sword at his side. She made fine work of arming him from head to toe.

Then at his command his horse was led out. Directly from the ground he mounted in a single leap. The maiden brought the shield and the unbending lance. He took the shield from her hand and hung it from his neck by its strap. She placed the lance in his hand, and he laid hold of it near the end.

"Dear sir," Erec then addressed the noble vavasor, "please have your daughter prepare herself. As we agreed, I wish to take her to the sparrowhawk."

At once, without wasting a moment, the vavasor had a bay palfrey saddled. There was nothing remarkable about the harness, for the vavasor's severe poverty did not permit any splendor. Once the bridle and saddle were in place, the maiden mounted the palfrey without prompting. She did not even wear a belt or cloak. Wishing no further delay, Erec set off with the daughter of his host beside him.

His lance upright, Erec rode on with the maiden at his side sitting her horse becomingly, followed by the lord of the house and his lady. Along the streets all the people, highborn and low, gazed up at Erec in awe. Among themselves they were wondering quietly: "Who is that knight? Who is he? He must be very proud and bold to be escorting the beautiful maiden. This man will not waste his efforts. By right this man should certainly claim that she is the most beautiful."

Then one said to another: "Surely the sparrowhawk ought to be hers."

Some praised the maiden, and there were many who asked: "God! Who can that knight be with the beautiful maiden at his side?"

"I don't know," "I don't know either," that was what all were saying, "but the gleaming helmet suits him well, as do that hauberk, that shield, and that sharp steel blade. How becomingly he sits his horse. He looks like a valiant vassal. He is so well built and well proportioned in his arms, legs, and feet."

Erec and the maiden were the focus of everyone's attention. They continued along without stopping until they were before the sparrowhawk, where they took their place and waited for the other knight.

Then behold they saw him approaching, accompanied by his maiden and his dwarf. He had already heard news of the arrival of a knight who wished to have the sparrowhawk, though he did not believe there was a knight on earth bold enough to dare fight him. He was certainly expecting to defeat and kill him. Recognized by everyone, he was greeted and escorted along his way. Racing behind him was a large crowd, knights and men-at-arms, ladies and maidens. The knight rode ahead of everyone with his maiden and his mongrel of a dwarf beside him. Quickly and insolently he rode to the sparrowhawk, but such a rush of commoners had gathered round about that you could come no closer than a crossbow's shot.

The count of the town arrived on the scene. He moved toward the commoners and threatened them, holding a staff in his hand. The people drew back. Riding forward, the knight whispered to his maiden: "My lady, this bird, which is so beautiful and finely molted, is to be yours by right because you are so beautiful and charming. As long as I live, the bird will be yours. Go ahead, my sweetheart, and take the sparrowhawk from the perch."

The maiden was about to extend her hand, but Erec rushed up to challenge the other knight, for he took no notice of that knight's willfulness. "Maiden, stand back!" he exclaimed. "Take pleasure in some other bird, for you have no right to this one here. No matter who should meddle here, this sparrowhawk will never be yours, for a finer lady than you claims it, and she is more courteous and more beautiful."

The other knight was angry, but Erec took no notice. He made his own maiden step forward. "Fair one, come up and take the bird from the perch, for it is right indeed that you have it," he said. "Step forward, maiden. I make the sure boast of claiming it, should someone else dare approach. No maiden compares with you in beauty and merit, nobility and honor, any more than the moon does with the sun."

When the other knight heard him present himself for combat with such daring, he could endure the situation no longer. "Vassal, who are you? Who are you to challenge me for the sparrowhawk?" he exclaimed.

"I am a knight from another land, and I have come to seek the sparrowhawk," Erec boldly answered. "No matter who may be displeased, it is right indeed that this maiden have it."

"Go away! That will never be!" the other shouted. "Folly has brought you here. If you would have the sparrowhawk, you will have to pay dearly."

"Pay, vassal, and how?"

"If you will not give it to me, you must fight me."

"To my mind you have now spoken like a fool," Erec said. "These threats amount to nothing. I do not fear you."

"In that case I challenge you now, for combat must take place."

"So help me God, I have never wanted anything so much as that," Erec answered.

Now you are going to hear of the blows of combat. The people gathered round on all sides of the large cleared area. The two combatants separated a distance of more than an acre. They spurred their horses to the attack. Charging at each other with the heads of their lances, they delivered such forceful blows that their shields were pierced and cracked, their lances split and shattered, and their cantles broken into pieces. Both men had to abandon their stirrups. They fell to the ground and their horses galloped off across the field. The lances had done their work.

At once the men jumped again to their feet. They now unsheathed their swords. Horrid were the attacks of their blades, and dreadful the blows they exchanged. The helmets clanged as they collided. Terrible was the clash of swords, and savage were the many blows they dealt each other on the neck, for they spared no effort in their assaults. Whatever they touched they smashed, cutting shields and breaking hauberks. Their swords were turning red with crimson blood. The combat was lasting a long time, and because the men did not stop their blows, they were becoming weak and exhausted.

Both maidens were in tears. Each knight saw his own maiden weeping, holding up her hands to God, and praying that He grant the honor of combat to the knight who was striving on her behalf.

"Vassal," the knight said to Erec, "let us withdraw a bit and pause a little for rest. Our exchanges are too weak. We should be dealing better blows since it is almost evening. What deep shame and dishonor that this combat lasts so long! For our ladies' sake we should be struggling harder with our steel blades."

"Well said," Erec replied.

Then they rested a little. The moment Erec saw his lady praying tenderly for him, his strength increased. Because of her love and her beauty, he felt his great pride reborn. He remembered his words to the queen in the forest that he would avenge his disgrace or else increase it still. "Ah, wretch that I am," he exclaimed, "what am I waiting for? I have not yet avenged the insult I suffered from this vassal when his dwarf struck me in the forest." His resentment returned, and he shouted furiously to the knight. "Vassal, I call you back to combat. We have rested too long. Let us resume our battle," he said.

"That does not displease me," the other answered.

Then they came at each other again. Both men were skilled swordsmen, and at the first clash, had Erec not covered himself well, the knight would have wounded him. The knight had struck him in an exposed area above the shield and cut a piece of the helmet close to the white padding. The sword went down farther, splitting the shield right to the buckle and cutting away more than a span from the side of his hauberk. Erec must have been stunned: the cold steel plunged right into his thigh.

This time God saved him. Had the steel not swerved toward the outside, it would have cut through the center of his body. But Erec was not dismayed. If he owed his opponent anything, he paid him back well. In a bold attack he hit him across the shoulder. The blow was so violent that the shield gave way and the hauberk could not prevent the sword from penetrating to the very bone. He made the crimson blood spurt down all the way to his waistband.

Both vassals were proud men. So evenly did they fight that neither one could gain a foot of ground from the other. Their hauberks were broken to pieces, their shields hacked to bits so that, to tell the truth, they had nothing left to provide protection. And so they fought on fully exposed. Both men were losing a large amount of blood and becoming very weak. The knight hit Erec, and Erec hit him, dealing such a blow to his helmet that he made him dizzy. Then he hit him again and again, giving him three heavy blows in succession. He split his helmet completely and cut the padding underneath. His sword did not stop until it reached his head, where it sliced bone from the skull, though it did not touch the brain. The knight was fumbling and faltering. As he staggered about, Erec pursued him, and the knight fell down on his right side. Seizing him by the helmet, Erec ripped it off his head and unlaced his chinguard. His head and his face were unprotected.

Mindful of the dwarf's disgraceful act in the forest, Erec would have decapitated the knight had he not begged mercy. "Alas, vassal, you have overcome me," he cried. "Grant me mercy. Don't kill me. Now that you have defeated and captured me, honor and renown would never be yours were your next act my murder. That would be too hideous a crime. Take my sword. I surrender it to you."

Erec did not take it, but said: "Very well, I shall not kill you."

"Ah, noble knight, thank you. What crime, what wrong has caused your mortal hatred of me? I have never seen you before as far as I know, and I have never done you any shame or disgrace."

"Yes, you have," Erec replied.

"Ah, sir, tell me when. To the best of my knowledge I have never looked on you. If I have done you any wrong, I shall be at your mercy."

Erec then spoke. "Vassal, I am the man who was in the forest yesterday with Queen Guinevere when you let your wicked dwarf hit my lady's maid. It is disgraceful to strike a woman. And after that he hit me. On that occasion you took me for a peasant, and that was a dreadful insult on your part, for when you looked on at such an outrage, you took delight in allowing such a dwarf and toad to strike the maid and me. I have a right to hate you for that offense; you showed too much contempt. You must pledge to be my prisoner. Immediately, without a moment's delay, you shall go directly to my lady. If you travel to Cardigan, you will be sure to find her there. You can arrive there tonight; I don't think it is seven leagues from here. To her you shall yield yourself, your maiden, and your dwarf to do her will. And tell her for me that I shall come tomorrow in happy spirits, bringing a maiden with me who is nowhere equaled in wisdom, virtue, and beauty. You can say this with all honesty. And now I would know your name."

"Sir," he said, whether he wished to or not, "I am Yder, the son of Nut. This morning I did not believe a single man could defeat me in knightly combat. Now I have found a man better than I and tested myself against him. You are a valiant knight. Accept my pledge. I swear to you, I will go now without further ado and surrender to the queen. But tell me your name. Do not hide it from me. Who shall I say sent me there? I am ready to go my way."

"I shall tell you. I shall never hide my name from you," he replied. "I am Erec. Go and tell her I have sent you to her.

"I am going now, I promise you. I shall place my maiden and my dwarf together with myself at her mercy, have no fear of that. And I shall tell her the news of you and your maiden."

When Erec had accepted his pledge, everyone came for the parting, the count and the people from round about, the barons and the maidens. There was happiness as well as sadness: some were upset, others were pleased. Many of them rejoiced for the sake of the maiden in the white smock whose heart was noble and true, the daughter of the vavasor. And those who were fond of Yder's maiden were sad for her and for him.

Yder did not wish to stay there longer; he had to keep his promise. At once he mounted. Why should I make the tale long for you? He rode off, taking his maiden and his dwarf with him, and they traveled through the forest and across the plain, then followed the highway until they reached Cardigan.

Sir Gawain and Kay the seneschal were together in the galleries outside the great hall. A large number of barons, I believe, had also accompanied them there. When they sighted those approaching, the seneschal, the first to notice, addressed Sir Gawain. "Sir," he said, "my instinct tells me that vassal on the road is the one the queen mentioned as being so troublesome to her yesterday. I think there are three. I see the maiden and the dwarf."

"True indeed. There are a maiden and a dwarf coming with the knight straight toward us along the highway," Sir Gawain said. "The knight is fully armed, but his shield is battered to pieces. I think the queen would recognize him if she saw him. So go, seneschal, and summon her."

Kay went off immediately and found her in a chamber. "Lady, do you recall the dwarf who insulted you yesterday and injured your maid?" he asked.

"Yes, I remember him well, seneschal. Do you know something of him? Why have you mentioned him?"

"Lady, because I have seen a knight errant in full armor approaching on an iron-grey charger. If my eyes do not deceive me, a maiden accompanies him, and coming with them, I think, is the dwarf, holding the whip that lashed Erec on the neck."

The queen then rose. "Seneschal," she said, "let us go and see if this is the vassal. If it is, you may be certain I shall tell you the truth the moment I see him."

"I shall escort you there," Kay said. "Come up to the galleries where our companions are. It was from there that we saw him coming, and Sir Gawain himself is waiting there for you. Lady, let us go. We have tarried here too long."

The queen then left and came to the windows, where she stood beside Sir Gawain. She recognized the knight clearly. "Oh, it is he!" she exclaimed. "He has fought and been in great peril. I don't know if Erec avenged his injury or if this knight defeated Erec. But his shield has received many blows and his hauberk is covered in blood. More red is visible than polished metal."

"True indeed, lady," Sir Gawain said. "I am certain you are in no way mistaken: his hauberk has been heavily pounded and hammered; it is covered in blood. He has been in a fight, that is evident. We can certainly see how severe the combat was. Soon we shall hear news from him that will bring us joy or anger; we shall know if Erec sends him here to you as a prisoner at your mercy or if he comes boldly to make the foolish boast among us that he has defeated or killed Erec. I don't think he bears other news."

"Nor do I," the queen replied.

"That may well be," all the others said.

At that moment Yder, who was bringing them the news, passed through the gateway. They all went down from the galleries to meet him. Yder reached the horseblock where he dismounted, and Gawain took the maiden's arm and helped her down from her horse. The dwarf dismounted on the other side. More than a hundred knights were present.

When all three had dismounted, they were led before the king. Yder saw the queen there and did not stop until he stood at her feet. After first greeting the king and all his knights, he said: "Lady, a noble man, a valiant and brave knight, sends me here as your prisoner. Yesterday my dwarf made him feel the knots of his whip across his face. He has overcome me in armed combat and defeated me. Lady, I lead my maiden and the dwarf here at your mercy that we may do your will."

Keeping silent no longer, the queen asked him news of Erec. "Tell me now, sir," she asked, "do you know when Erec will be coming?"

"Tomorrow, lady, and he will bring with him a maiden. I have never known one so beautiful."

When he had related his message, the queen was prudent and wise, making a courteous response to him. "Friend, since you have placed yourself as my prisoner, your imprisonment will not be at all severe. I have no desire to harm you. But now, so help me God, tell me your name."

"Lady, I am Yder, the son of Nut," he answered her. And it was evident that he was telling the truth.

The queen then rose and went before the king. "Lord, now you have seen, now you have heard about Erec, the valiant knight," she said. "I gave you good counsel yesterday when I advised you to wait for him. That is why it is good to take advice."

"That remark is true; it is no idle tale," the king replied. "A man who does not take advice is a fool. We were fortunate to follow your advice yesterday. But by your love for me, give this knight his liberty on condition that he stay here and join my court and my household. If he refuses, so much the worse for him."

As soon as the king finished speaking, the queen granted the knight his liberty in the proper manner, though on condition that he stay at the court. Yder needed little urging to agree to remain there. From that moment he belonged to the court and the household. He had scarcely agreed when waiting attendants ran up to relieve him of his arms.

Now we are to speak again of Erec, who was still at the scene of the combat. When Tristan defeated and killed Morholt on the Isle of Saint Samson, I doubt there was joy equal to the celebration here for Erec. Everyone shouted his praises, highborn and low, thin and stout, all paying homage to his knighthood. There was not a knight who did not exclaim: "God, what a vassal! He has no equal under heaven."

Afterwards, Erec went to his lodging. Lavish were the words of praise for him. The count himself, who was happier than anyone else, embraced him. "Sir," he said, "if you please, you ought, by right, to lodge in my home since you are the son of King Lac. Should you accept my offer, you will do me much honor, for I regard you as my lord. By your grace, dear sir, I beg you, stay with me."

"Take no offense," Erec replied, "but I shall not leave my host tonight. He honored me most highly when he presented his daughter to me. What do you say about this gift, sir? Is it not beautiful and precious?"

"Yes, sir, that gift is fine and beautiful," the count replied. "The maiden is most wise and beautiful, and she comes from a noble family. You may know that her mother is my sister. And so I am delighted that you are minded to take my niece. Still I beg you, come and lodge in my home tonight."

"Let me be on this subject," Erec said. "I would not do that."

The count realized further urging was useless. "As you please, sir," he said. "Now let us talk of this no more. But all my knights and I shall be with you this night for pleasure and for company."

When Erec heard this, he thanked him, and then proceeded to his host's home with the count at his side, accompanied by knights and ladies. The vavasor was delighted.

The moment Erec arrived, more than twenty squires raced out to remove his arms promptly. Anyone who was in that house could behold great rejoicing. Erec went and sat down first, then all the others took their seats in order along the couches, benches, and stools. The count took his seat near Erec, and between them was the beautiful maiden, who showed more joy than any maiden ever had for her lord.

Erec called to the vavasor and addressed him in a fine and fitting manner. "Dear friend, dear host, dear sir," he began speaking, "you have honored me most highly, and well shall you be repaid. Tomorrow your daughter will accompany me to the court of the king, where I intend to marry her.

And if it pleases you to wait a little, I shall send someone soon to conduct you to my country. Now it belongs to my father; afterwards it will be mine. It is not nearby, but far from here. I shall present to you two very fine castles there, most splendid and powerful. You will be lord of Roadan, which was built as early as the time of Adam, and of another nearby castle just as valuable, which people call Montrevel. My father does not have a more splendid castle. Within three days I shall send you a large quantity of gold and silver, spotted and grey furs, and precious silks to dress you and your wife, who is my dear sweet lady. Tomorrow, at first dawn, I shall take your daughter to court dressed as she now is. I wish my lady the queen to clothe her in her own dress of dyed red silk."

Nearby was a young lady of great wisdom, prudence, and virtue. She was seated on a bench beside the maiden in the white smock; she was her cousin and the niece of the same count. She began to address the count. "Sir," she said, "what a dreadful disgrace it would be—and for you more than anyone else—if this lord took your niece with him dressed in such poor garments."

"I beg you, my sweet niece," the count answered, "give her the dress of yours you consider the finest."

Erec heard what they were saying. "Sir, don't speak that way," he exclaimed. "Of one thing you can be certain: under no circumstance would I like her to have any other dress until the queen gives it to her."

When the young lady heard this, she answered him. "Alas, dear sir," she said, "since you wish to lead my cousin away dressed as she is in her shift and her white smock, I would like to give her a different present. Because you have decided that she should have none of my dresses, I have three good palfreys, one sorrel, one dappled, and the other white-footed. No count or king has a finer horse. Among a hundred palfreys there is truly none better than the dappled one. Birds flying through the air don't travel faster than the palfrey. No one has ever seen it take a false step. Even a child could ride it. Such a horse befits a maiden because it is not skittish or disobedient, and does not bite, kick, or become violent. Seek a better horse, and you don't know what you want. You ride this without any cause for alarm, for you move with greater ease and comfort than if you were on a boat."

"My dear friend," Erec said, "I don't object to her acceptance of this gift. Indeed I am pleased. I don't wish her to refuse it."

At that instant the young lady summoned one of her personal servants. "Dear friend," she told him, "go and saddle my dappled palfrey and lead it out here quickly." And he followed her order, bridling and saddling the horse and making every effort to caparison it well. He then mounted the long-maned palfrey.

Behold the palfrey came. When Erec looked at the palfrey, he was unstinting in its praise, for he saw how fine and handsome it was. He then ordered a servant to go and hitch the palfrey in the stable beside his own charger.

Everyone departed after the abundant joy of that evening. The count left Erec at the vavasor's home and went off to his own lodging, promising to escort him when he set out in the morning.

All that night they slept, and in the morning at daybreak Erec prepared to leave. He ordered his horses saddled and he wakened his fair beloved. She dressed and readied herself. The vavasor and his wife rose too. Every knight and lady present prepared to escort the knight and the maiden. All were mounted, including the count.

Erec rode between the count and his fair beloved, who had not forgotten the sparrowhawk. She entertained herself with her sparrowhawk, having brought no other possessions.

Everyone was delighted to escort them. When the time to separate arrived, the noble count wished to send some of his company along with Erec to honor him by their escort. Erec announced, however, that no one was to stay with him; the only companionship he sought was his beloved's. "To God I commend you," he told them.

After the couple had been escorted quite a distance, the count kissed his niece and Erec, and commended them to God the Merciful. Kissing their daughter again and again, her father and her mother could not hold back their tears. At the moment of their separation, all three were weeping, the father, the mother, and the maiden. Such is love; such is human nature; such is familial affection. The tears came from deep tenderness and the gentleness of the parents' love for their child. Nevertheless they knew their daughter would be going to a place where she would receive great homage. Only love and devotion, nothing else, made them weep at their daughter's departure; they knew she would surely be honored. At her parting their tears flowed constantly. They wept as they commended one another to God; then, without further delay, they went their separate ways.

Erec took leave of his host, for he was most eager to reach the court of the king. He rejoiced in his adventure; he found great happiness in his good fortune, for his beloved was extraordinarily wise and beautiful, courteous and nobly born. He could not gaze on her enough, and the more he gazed, the more pleasing she was. He could not keep himself from giving her a kiss. Riding beside her brought him gladness, and gazing on her brought him comfort. Long did he stare at her fair head, her laughing eyes, her clear brow, the nose, the face, the mouth. All this touched his heart with deep tenderness. He stared at her down to her hips, gazing on her chin and her white neck, her breasts and her sides, her arms and her hands. But with no less interest did the maiden stare with goodwill and a loyal heart at the vassal, as if the two of them were competing with each other. Neither would have accepted ransom not to look on the other. In courtesy, beauty, and nobility they were perfect equals. So alike were they in their manner of being, their customs, and their character that no one wishing to tell the truth could have distinguished the finer, or the wiser, or the more beautiful. Having exactly the same disposition, they suited each other perfectly. Each stole the other's heart. The natural law or marriage never united two figures of such beauty.

And so they rode on together. Then, precisely at noon, they neared the town of Cardigan, where both were expected. The finest barons of the court had gone up to the windows in the hope of catching sight of them. Queen Guinevere hurried there, and the king himself came, as did Kay and Perceval of Wales, followed by Sir Gawain and Cort, the son of King Ares. Lucan the cupbearer was present as well as many fine knights. They had spotted Erec as he approached with his beloved, whom he was leading. From the distance they could see him, and they all recognized him. The queen and the entire court were delighted by his arrival, for all without exception loved him.

As soon as Erec arrived in front of the great hall, the king and the queen went down to meet him. Everyone commended him to God. They welcomed him and his maiden, whose great beauty was the object of their praise and esteem. The king himself took her hand and helped her down from her palfrey, for the king had been well educated in the forms of proper behavior. At that moment his mood was very happy. He treated the maiden with great honor leading her by the hand up the stairs into the great stone hall. Following them hand in hand together were Erec and the queen.

"Lady," Erec said to her, "I bring you my maiden and my beloved dressed in poor garments. Just as she was presented to me, I have brought her here to you. She is the daughter of a poor vavasor. Poverty humbles many men. Although her father has extremely meager possessions, he is noble and courteous. Her mother is a noble lady whose brother is a noble count. Lack of beauty or parentage cannot be a reason for rejecting the maiden in marriage. Poverty has forced her to wear this white smock until both its sleeves are ripped away at the elbows. Nevertheless she would have had many fine dresses had that pleased me, for one young lady, her cousin, wished to give her an ermine-trimmed dress of speckled or grey silk. Yet I would not have her wear any other dress until you had seen her. My dear lady, consider this now, for she needs, as you clearly see, a beautiful dress that becomes her."

The queen answered at once. "Well said. It is right that she have one of my dresses. I shall give her immediately a fine and beautiful one, fresh and new."

The queen took her at once into her own private chamber and had her new court dress brought out and the deep-green silk cloak embroidered with little crosses that had been made especially for her. The servant carried out her instructions and brought the cloak and the dress which was trimmed with white ermine even along the sleeves; around the cuffs and the collar there was, to be precise, more than two hundred marks' worth of beaten gold enshrining exceptionally precious stones of indigo and green, of deep blue and dark brown. The dress was very costly, although, as far as I know, the cloak was certainly of no less value. The straps had not yet been placed on the cloak, for everything, both the dress and the cloak, was fresh and new. The cloak was beautiful and of fine quality. Around the neck were two sable furs with clamps that contained more than an ounce of gold: on one side there was a hyacinth, on the other a ruby brighter than a flaming carbuncle. The white ermine lining was the finest and most beautiful ever seen or found. All manner of little crosses, indigo and vermilion and dark blue, white and green, blue and yellow, had been finely embroidered on the silk cloth. The queen asked for some ribbons five ells long made of gold and silk thread. Beautiful and finely prepared, they were given to her. At once she had a skilled man, a fine master of his trade, fasten them promptly to the cloak.

When nothing remained to be done to the cloak, the noble and well-born lady put her arms around the neck of the maiden in the white smock. "My young lady, I command you to change that smock for this dress. The fabric is worth more than a hundred silver marks. There is so much I wish to give you now for your honor. Put this cloak on over the dress. I shall give you more on another occasion."

The maiden did not refuse the ensemble, but accepted it gratefully. Two maids-in-waiting took her to a private chamber. Once in the room she removed her smock and put on the dress, tightening it with a costly gold-embroidered belt. Out of love for God she asked that her smock be given away. And after this she put on the cloak. She did not then appear a drab figure, for the outfit suited her so well that she became even more beautiful. Although the two maids braided her deep-brown hair with fine gold thread, her own hair was still more radiant. The maids placed a gold diadem on her head decorated with many different colored flowers. As best they could they devoted all their efforts to perfecting her appearance so that there might be nothing wanting improvement. One maid placed around her neck two small clasps of enameled gold fixed upon a topaz. Now the maiden was so attractive and beautiful that I do not believe her equal could be found anywhere, no matter where you sought or looked—so well had Nature formed her.

She then left the chamber and came to the queen. Delight filled the queen because she loved the maiden and took such satisfaction in her beauty and fine manners. Taking each other by the hand, they came before the king. At their sight, the king rose to meet them. When they entered the great hall, there were so many knights who stood up that I cannot name a tenth, thirteenth, or fifteenth of them. But I can certainly tell you the names of some of the finest barons who belonged to the Round Table, which comprised the best in the world.

Gawain has to be first, at the head of all the excellent knights; then Erec, the son of Lac; and third, Lancelot of the Lake. Gornemant of Gohort was fourth, and the Handsome Coward was fifth. Sixth was the Ugly Hero, seventh Meliant of Lis, eighth Maudit the Wise, ninth Dodinel the Savage. Let Ganedlu, because of his many good qualities, be named tenth. The others I shall name in no particular order because the ranking embarrasses me. Yvain the Brave was seated a little farther away. On the other side was Yvain the Bastard, and Tristan who never laughed sat beside Blioberis. Farther on were Karadues the Short-armed, a knight of good cheer; Caveron of Roberdic; the son of King Quenedic; the page of Quintareus; Yder of the Dolorous Mount; Gahereit and Kay of Estral; Amauguin and Galet the Bald; Girflet, the son of Do; Taulas, who never tired of bearing arms; Loholt, the son of King Arthur, a vassal of great strength; Sagremor the Unruly should not be forgotten, nor Bedoier, the Master of the Horse, who was an expert at chess and backgammon, nor Bravain, nor King Lot, nor Galegantin of Wales.

When the beautiful maiden from the distant land saw all the knights in order with their eyes fixed on her, she bowed her head. That her embarrassment made her blush was not remarkable. Yet her bashfulness was so becoming that it made her only the more beautiful. Noticing her embarrassment the king did not wish to leave her. He took her gently by the hand and seated her beside him on his right. The queen, who was seated at the king's left, addressed him. "Lord, I think and believe that a man who can win such a beautiful lady in armed combat in another land should be welcomed at the court of a king. We did well to wait for Erec. Now you can bestow the kiss on the greatest beauty in the court. I do not think anyone will disagree with you. No one will ever say I lie in declaring that this maiden is the most beautiful of those here and those throughout the world."

"That is no lie," the king answered. "If no one challenges me, I shall bestow on her the honor of the white stag." Then he addressed his knights. "Sirs, what do you say? What do you think? In regard to her form, her face, all the personal excellences belonging to a maiden, is she not, as I believe, the most charming and the most beautiful from here to the very place where the earth meets the sky? I declare that it is right beyond any doubt that she have the honor of the white stag. And you, sirs, what would you say? Have you any objections? If someone would object, let him state his opinion right now.

"I am a king. And so I must not lie or condone any base, dishonest, or unreasonable act. I must uphold truth and right. The function of a true king is to observe the law, truth, faith, and justice. In no way would I wish to do wrong or to be disloyal to the weak any more than the strong. It is wrong for anyone to have reason to find fault with me.

"And I do not wish to let the custom and tradition observed by my family become obsolete. If I wished to establish laws and customs other than those my father the king observed, you would have cause for alarm. No matter what should befall me, I intend to uphold and to maintain the tradition of my father Pendragon, who was king and emperor. Now tell me all your thoughts. Let no one hesitate to speak the truth. Although this maiden is not of my household, she should certainly have the kiss of the white stag by right. I would know the truth."

Everyone shouted out together in agreement. "In the name of God and His cross, lord, you can definitely determine by right that she is the most beautiful. Her beauty far outshines the radiance of the sun. You may kiss her without hesitation, for we are all in complete agreement."

When the king saw that everyone was pleased with his opinion, he would not delay bestowing the kiss. With courtesy the king kissed her before all his barons. "My dear friend," he said to her, "I give you my love without base intention, dishonesty, or ulterior motive. I shall love you with a fine heart."

By this adventure the king restored the custom and the privilege that the white stag should have at his court. Here ends the first stage.

The kiss of the white stag had been taken according to the custom of the country. Then Erec, like the courteous and noble man he was, concerned himself with his poor host. Not intending to break his promise, he adhered firmly to his agreement by immediately dispatching to him five fat and well-rested packhorses loaded with gold marks and silver plate, clothes and cloths, spotted and grey furs, sables, buckrams and rich wools, velvets and silks. When the packhorses were laden with everything a man of worth needs, Erec dispatched along with the packhorses ten knights and ten men-at-arms from the men of his own company. He instructed them to greet the host on his behalf and to treat him and his wife too with the same high honor they would pay to himself. After they had presented the packhorses that they led, along with the gold, the silver, the money, and all the rich garments in the bags, they were to escort with great honor the lord and lady into his kingdom of Outer Wales. He had promised them two castles, the most beautiful, the best located, and the least threatened by war in the whole land. One was called Montrevel, the other Roadan. When they had arrived in his kingdom, they were to hand over to them these two castles along with their rents and their judicial rights just as he had promised them.

Not caring to delay, the messengers that very day presented to Erec's host the gold and silver, packhorses, clothes, and abundance of coin. With every possible honor they escorted the vavasor and his wife into Erec's kingdom, which they reached in three days. King Lac had not the slightest objection when the messengers handed over to the couple the towers of the castles. He gave them a joyous welcome, honored them highly, and held them in affection on account of Erec, his son. He ceded to them full rights to the castles and confirmed their dominion by having knights and townsmen swear to esteem them as their rightful lords.

As soon as the messengers accomplished their mission, they returned to their lord Erec. Joyful was their welcome. He asked them news of the vavasor and his wife, and of his father and the kingdom. They offered him a fine and fitting report.

Not long afterwards, the time of Erec's wedding was drawing near. The wait was a burden; he did not wish to put up with further delay. He went and asked permission of the king to celebrate his wedding at the court, provided the king had no objection. The king granted his request and sent throughout his kingdom a summons for kings, dukes, and counts, all those holding land from him, that not one of them should be so bold as not to be present there at Pentecost. Not one dared stay home; by the king's order everyone came to the court.

Now listen to me. I am going to tell you who the kings and counts were. With a powerful retinue, Count Branles of Colchester came there, leading on his right a hundred horses. After him came Menagormon, who was the

Lord of Eglimon. He of the High Mountain arrived with a powerful company. The Count of Traverain came with a hundred of his knights, and following was Count Godegrains with a group no smaller. In addition to these you have heard me name came Moloas, a wealthy baron, who was Lord of the Black Isle: thunder is not heard there, nor are there storms or lightning; toads and snakes do not inhabit the island, and the temperature is never too hot or too cold. Greslemuef of Finisterre brought twenty companions. And his brother Guinguemar came too, who was Lord of the Isle of Avalon. We have heard it said of him that he was a lover of Morgan le Fay, and that had been proven true. David of Tintagel came, who was never angry or upset.

There were many counts and dukes, but even more kings. Garras, the proud King of Cork, came with five hundred knights clad in cloaks, tunics, and leggings of silk and brocade. Aguiflet, King of Scotland, came riding a Cappadocian horse and brought with him both his sons, Cadret and Cuoi, two fearsome knights. Along with these I have named to you came King Ban of Gomeret; those accompanying him were young men without mustaches or beards; his company of two hundred was very happy: each of them, no matter who, had a falcon or another bird, a merlin or sparrowhawk, a splendid sorrel goshawk or one trained to chase cranes. Quirion, the elderly King of Orcel, did not have any young men in his company of two hundred; the youngest was a hundred years old. Because of their great age, their heads were white and bald, and their beards fell to their waists. King Arthur held these men in high esteem.

Next came the lord of the dwarfs, Bilis, King of the Antipodes. This man I tell you of was himself a dwarf and the brother of Bliant. Bilis was the shortest of all the dwarfs, and Bliant, his brother, the tallest, for he was a half-foot or full palm taller than any other knight in his kingdom. To display his lordship and his wealth Bilis brought along in his retinue two kings, who were dwarfs and held their land from him, Gribalo and Glodoalan; everyone regarded him with awe. The trio were treated with great respect when they reached the court. They all were honored and served at the court in a manner befitting kings, for they were most noble men.

At last, when King Arthur saw all his barons assembled, he was delighted. To augment the joy of the gathering, he then ordered a hundred squires bathed, wishing to knight all of them. Each one had a robe of different colors made from costly Alexandrian silk according to his own choice and fancy. They all had the same pattern of equipment as well as swift and spirited horses, the poorest horse being worth at least a hundred pounds.

When Erec took his wife, he had to call her by her proper name; a requisite for marriage is that a woman be called by her proper name. Although no one yet knew her name, everyone now learned it. Enide was her baptismal name. The Archbishop of Canterbury, who had come to the court, blessed her in performance of his duty.

In the full court assembly, all the minstrels of the area skilled in pleasant pastimes were at the court. What festive joy there was in the great hall with each one contributing to it by performing what he knew! Some were jumping, some tumbling, others making magic. One man whistled, another sang. Some were playing the flute, others the pipe, some the violin, others the fiddle. Maidens formed circles and danced. All the people threw themselves into the merrymaking. Anything that might contribute to the joy and put happiness in men's hearts occurred that day at the wedding. There was the music of drums and tambourines, bagpipes, fifes, and flutes, trumpets and pipes.

What more can I say? No gateway or wicket was closed; entrances and exits were left open all day long. Rich or poor, no one was turned away. Not at all niggardly, King Arthur gave instructions to the bakers, cooks, and butlers to be most generous in offering the people all the bread, wine, and venison they desired. Anyone making a request received his entire wish. Extensive were the joyous festivities in the palace.

I am going to leave aside all the rest, however. Now you will hear of the joy and pleasure in the chamber and the bed that night. Bishops and archbishops were in attendance when the couple retired. At this first meeting, Enide was not stolen away and Brangein was not substituted in her place. The queen, caring so much for the couple, attended to the preparations for their night.

Before the couple were in each other's arms, they came to their bedroom with more eagerness than the hunted stag, panting from thirst, seeks the spring, or the hungry sparrowhawk, when called home, makes his return. That night they recovered the time they had lost in waiting. When they found themselves alone in their chamber, they surrendered themselves to each part of their bodies. The eyes, the birthplace of love's joy, took pleasure from gazing and sent the message to the heart, for everything they saw delighted them. After the message from the eyes came the more precious sweetness from their love-arousing kisses. The couple tested this sweetness, and their hearts became so intoxicated that they could scarcely separate their bodies. Kissing was their first sport. Their love gave new courage to the maiden so that all her fears disappeared; she endured everything, however painful. Before she rose again, she had lost the name of maiden. In the morning she was newly a woman.

All the minstrels were pleased with their excellent wages that day. Whatever had been due them was paid, and many beautiful gifts were presented to them: clothes of spotted fur and ermine, of rabbit and of purple cloth, and of rich grey wool or silk. Each man received his desire, whether a horse or money, according to his skill. Thus, with such joyful magnificence, the wedding feast and the court lasted more than fifteen days. To honor Erec further, King Arthur, befitting his majesty and for his pleasure, had all his barons stay a fortnight.

At the beginning of the third week, everyone agreed to hold a tournament between York and Tenebroc. Sir Gawain advanced and presented himself for one camp, and Melis and Meliadoc presented themselves for the other camp. Then the court dissolved.

A month after Pentecost, all the people assembled on the plain below Tenebroc in preparation for the tournament. There were so many scarlet banners, kerchiefs, and sleeves, many blue ones and many white, bestowed as tokens of love. So many lances were carried, many painted azure and red, many gold and silver. And there were also many lances with other patterns such as stripes and dots. That day many laced helmets of iron and of steel were seen glistening in the sun, some green, some yellow, others scarlet. Many emblazoned shields, gleaming hauberks, swords girded on the left side, fine shields new and untested, some handsome in azure and red, others of silver with gold buckles. And there were many fine horses, white-footed and sorrel, tawny and white, black and bay, all galloping along together.

The entire field was covered with equipment. All the ranks from both camps were stirred up, and the attack produced a crash. Great was the uproar from the shock of the lances. Shields were pierced, lances split, hauberks broken and torn apart; saddles went empty as knights fell from their sweating and foaming horses. Everyone drew swords against those who tumbled with a loud crash; some raced up to exact ransom for them, others to hand over their own equipment.

Riding a white horse, Erec, all alone, came at the head of the line to joust with any opponent he could find. From the other side the Proud Knight of the Heath advanced to meet him, riding an Irish horse that carried him at top speed. Erec dealt him such a strong blow on his shield in front of his chest that he knocked him from his charger; he then left this combat and rode on ahead.

Dressed in blue silk, Randuraz, a knight of great valor and the son of the dowager of Tergalo, came to meet Erec. They charged at each other, delivering severe blows to the shields hanging from their necks. With the full extent of his lance's shaft, Erec knocked his opponent to the hard ground.

As Erec returned to the combat, he encountered the valiant and brave King of the Red City. Both of them had excellent arms and fine swift horses. Holding their reins by the knots and their shields by the straps, they struck each other so forcefully on their fresh, new shields that both lances were splintered. Never have such blows been seen. They hurled themselves at each other with their shields, arms, horses. Saddlegirths, reins, breaststraps, nothing could stop the king from falling to the ground, clutching the reins and bridle in his hand. All the spectators at the jousting were astounded and exclaimed that high indeed was the cost of jousting with so fine a knight. Erec would not wait and capture the knight and the horse, but preferred to joust and perform well in a display of his valor. Around him the combat took on new force. His valor encouraged those on his side, and he captured horses and knights only to exact further defeat from the other side.

I wish to speak about Sir Gawain and his excellent conduct. In the combat he knocked down Guincel and took prisoner Gaudin of the Mountain. He captured knights and won horses. Sir Gawain excelled.

Girflet, the son of Do, and Yvain and Sagremor the Unruly took such care of their opponents that they drove them back to the gates, where they knocked down and captured many of them.

Before the town gate, the assault erupted again between the men inside and those outside. Sagremor, a most renowned knight, was knocked down. He had already been captured and taken prisoner when Erec raced to his rescue. Erec broke his lance into splinters against one man and struck him so hard in the chest that he forced him from his saddle. Then he drew his sword, overtook them, and crushed and shattered their helmets. Some took to flight, others let him pass, for even the boldest stood in fear of him. Finally he dealt such thrusts and blows that he rescued Sagremor from them and drove them in confusion back into the town.

Meanwhile the evening bell was tolling. Erec conducted himself so well that day that he was the finest in the combat. Yet the next day he excelled even more, for he took prisoner so many knights and emptied so many saddles that no one could believe this except those who had witnessed it. All the men from both camps declared that he was victorious in the tournament with his lance and his shield.

Such was Erec's renown that everyone talked of none but him. There was no man of such noble excellence. In beauty he resembled Absalom, and in eloquence, Solomon. He had the pride of a lion. And in generosity he was the equal of Alexander.

After returning from the tournament, Erec went to speak to the king and ask his permission to leave, for he wished to set out for his own land. But first, like a noble, courteous, and wise man, he thanked the king for the honor he had accorded him; his gratitude was very deep. Afterwards, he took his leave of the king, eager to travel with his wife to his own country. Although the king wished Erec to stay, he could not deny his request. He gave him permission to leave and urged him to come back as soon as he could, for he had no baron in his court more valiant, more bold, or more brave, except his dear nephew Gawain, who had no equal. After Gawain, it was Erec whom the king regarded with the highest esteem and held dearest of all his knights.

Erec wished no further delay. As soon as he received leave from the king, he instructed his wife to make the preparations. For his escort he accepted sixty knights of renown with horses and with spotted and grey furs. The moment his baggage was ready, he prepared to set out from the court. He commended the knights to God and asked leave of the queen. The queen gave him leave to depart.

At six in the morning, Erec left the royal palace. In sight of all, he mounted his horse. After him his wife mounted her horse, which he had brought from her country. Then all his retinue mounted: at least one hundred and forty knights and men-at-arms were in his company.

For four whole days they traveled over so many hills and slopes, through forests and across plains and mountains, until one day they reached Carnant, where King Lac was staying at a most pleasant castle; one more finely situated has never been seen. Forests and meadows, vineyards and farms, rivers and orchards surrounded the town, and within were knights and ladies, stalwart and brave squires, noble and well-trained clerks who spent their income well, beautiful and charming ladies, and prosperous townsmen.

Before reaching the town, Erec dispatched two messengers to announce his arrival to the king. As soon as the king heard the news, he had knights, clerks, and maidens mount their horses; he ordered the bells rung and the streets draped with hanging tapestries and silks to offer a most joyous welcome to his son. He himself then mounted. Eighty clerks were present, noble men of honor dressed in sable-bordered grey cloaks. At least five hundred knights were there on bay, sorrel, and white-footed horses. There were so many ladies and townspeople that it was impossible to estimate their number. The king and his son raced at a gallop until they sighted and recognized each other. The two of them dismounted, then greeted and embraced. For a long while, they did not move from the spot where they met, but continued to exchange greetings. The king rejoiced over Erec, then left him and turned to Enide. With one as well as the other he was enraptured; he embraced and kissed them both, not knowing which of the two delighted him more.

Then they entered the town. All the bells rang out merrily for his arrival. All the streets were strewn with rushes, wild mint, and iris; draped above were curtains and tapestries of embroidered silk and samite. Great was the happiness in that place. All the people had assembled to see their young lord. No one has ever beheld young and old rejoicing to this degree.

The couple first came to the church, where they were devoutly received in procession. Erec prayed before the altar of the Crucifix, where he donated sixty silver marks, which he could not have put to better use, and a cross of fine gold, which had once belonged to King Constantine. It contained a piece of the true cross on which the Lord God was tortured and crucified for us: He delivered us from prison where we all were captive because of the sin Adam long ago committed on the devil's counsel. The cross had considerable value, for it contained precious stones of immense power. Gold carbuncles of unseen equal had been wondrously mounted in the center and on each side. Just like the morning sunlight, each carbuncle gave off so much radiance during the night that their glow made it unnecessary to burn lamp, candle, or candlestick in the church.

Two barons led Erec's wife before the altar of Our Lady. She prayed devoutly to Jesus and the Virgin Mary that they might give the couple, in their lifetime, an heir to receive their inheritance. Then, on the altar, she offered green silk, such as had never been seen, and a large decorated chasuble all embroidered with fine gold. It was a proven fact that Morgan le Fay had devoted all her skills to designing it at her home in the Perilous Vale. Made of gold and Almerian silk, it was not designed by le Fay to serve as a chasuble for singing the mass; not at all, for she wished to give it to her lover to make a splendid garment, since it was marvelously becoming. With great cleverness, Guinevere, the wife of Arthur the powerful king, had obtained it through the mediation of Emperor Gassa. She made it into a chasuble and, because of its exquisite beauty, kept it a long time in her chapel. When Enide was leaving, she made her a present of the chasuble, which, in truth, was worth more than a hundred silver marks. After Enide made her offering, she stepped back a little and, in the manner of a well-educated woman, made the sign of the cross with her right hand. They then left the church and returned directly to their residence, where the great festivities began.

That day Erec received many presents from knights and townsmen: from one a Norwegian palfrey, from another a gold cup; one presented to him a sorrel goshawk, another a hunting dog, still another a greyhound; one man gave him a sparrowhawk, another a Spanish charger; one presented a shield, one an ensign, one a sword, and one a helmet. No realm ever rejoiced more over its king or welcomed him more joyously. All the people devoted themselves to serving him, and still more joy did they display for Enide than for him because of the great beauty they beheld in her, and even more because of her noble nature.

In a chamber, Enide was seated on a Thessalian silk bedcovering. Many ladies surrounded her, but just as the lustrous gem surpasses the brown pebble in splendor and the rose surpasses the poppy, so was Enide more beautiful than any lady or maiden to be found anywhere on earth, look where you may. She was so noble and honorable, so wise and gracious in her speech, so well born and knowledgeable. No observer, however skilled, might detect in her any trace of folly, mischief, or baseness. So perfect was her upbringing that she excelled every woman in all the fine qualities a lady should possess, in generosity as well as wisdom. Everyone loved her because of her noble nature. Whoever might serve her esteemed himself the more worthy and honored. No one spoke badly of her, for no one could find anything ill to say. In the kingdom, indeed in the empire, there was no lady of such fine manners.

But Erec loved Enide with such love that he cared no more for feats of arms, nor did he attend tournaments. He had no desire to joust. His only wish was to lie beside his wife, whom he made his sweetheart and his mistress. Embracing her and kissing her occupied all his attention, and he longed for no other pleasure.

This situation saddened his companions. Often among themselves they regretted his excessive love for her. Often it was past noon before he rose from her side. His behavior may have displeased others, but it did please him. Rarely did he leave his wife. Yet he was no less generous to his knights with equipment, clothes, and money. He sent them to every tournament splendidly attired and equipped. No matter what the cost, he presented to them fresh chargers for jousts and tournaments. The whole company of knights remarked on the great pity and shame that such a baron as he had been was not interested in bearing arms.

He was so censured by everyone, knights and men-at-arms, that Enide heard them saying that her lord had changed his way of living and become lost to honor in arms and in knighthood. Their talk distressed her, but she dared not show it for fear that were she to speak out, her lord might immediately take it amiss. So the matter was kept hidden until one morning when they lay in a bed where they had been taking great pleasure—mouth to mouth they lay, arms around each other, as people do who are very much in love. He was asleep, and she lay awake, remembering what many men throughout the country were saying of her lord. When she recalled their words, she could not restrain her tears. She felt such grief and sorrow that she happened by ill fortune to make an utterance she later regretted, for she had meant no harm. She began to gaze on her lord from head to toe, noticing his handsome body and his radiant face. Her eyes kept flooding with tears until the tears fell on his chest. "Alas, what a pity for me!" she said. "What did I come to find here, far from my own country? Certainly the earth should swallow me up since the knight, the best, the boldest, and the bravest of all, the most loyal and the most courteous who ever was count or king, has utterly abandoned all deeds of chivalry for my sake. Therefore I have indeed brought shame on him. Not for anything would I have wished that."

She then spoke to him. "Beloved, what a pity for you!" With these words she became silent again and said nothing more.

Erec was not in a deep sleep. Though dozing, he heard her voice, and at her utterance he woke up. He was astonished to see her weeping so much. "Tell me, dear sweetheart," he asked her, "why do you weep like this? What is causing your sorrow and anger? I certainly intend to know the reason. Tell it to me, my sweetheart. Be careful not to hide anything from me. Why did you say what a pity for me? It was said for me, and for no other. I heard your words clearly."

Enide was then distraught. Feeling deep fear and dismay, she spoke. "Sir, I don't know what you are talking about."

"Lady, why do you deny this? It is useless to hide it from me. I see that you have been weeping. There was some reason for your tears. And I did hear the words you spoke as you wept."

"Alas, dear sir, you heard nothing. I imagine it was a dream."

"Now you are telling me lies. I hear you openly lie! But you will repent later if you fail to tell me the truth."

"Sir, since you press me so, I shall tell you the truth. I shall not keep the matter hidden longer. But I fear you will be upset. Throughout this land, everyone—the fair, the dark, and the ruddy—is saying it is a great pity that you have set aside your arms. Your reputation has suffered from it. Last year all were accustomed to say that no finer or braver knight was known in the entire world. Nowhere was there anyone to equal you. Now all, young and old, highborn and low, make fun of you. They all call you lost to honor. Do you think it doesn't bother me to hear of their contempt for you? Everything said distresses me. And what pains me even more is the fact that they blame me for this. They accuse me, and that does hurt me. They all say the reason is that I have entranced and captivated you so that you lose your honor and desire nothing but me. Now you must take counsel to end this reproach and regain your reputation, for I have heard you censured too many times. I never dared tell you this. Many times when this came to mind, I had to weep in anguish. Just now my distress was so great I could not keep myself from saying it was a pity for you."

"Lady," he responded, "you were right, and those who reproach me for it are right. Prepare yourself immediately and be ready to ride. Rise, attire yourself in your most beautiful dress, and have your best palfrey saddled."

Now Enide was alarmed. She rose sad and reflective. She rebuked and reproached herself for her foolish words. A goat that fouls its stall gets no rest at all.

"Oh, what a wretched fool I am!" she said. "Until now I was too happy. I had everything. Alas, alas, why was I so bold as to dare utter such madness? God! Was it because my lord loved me too much? I swear, alas, he did love me too much. And now I must go into exile. But what makes my grief deeper is that I shall not see my lord anymore. He loved me so much that nothing else was as important to him. The finest man ever born was so smitten that he cared about nothing else. And I had everything. I was at the peak of happiness. But I was too exalted by my pride when I uttered those outrageous words. I shall suffer for my pride, and it is right that I do. The person who has not tasted misfortune doesn't know what happiness is."

While lamenting, the lady attired herself beautifully in her finest dress. Nothing, however, pleased her. Everything had become a source of grief. She had a maid summon one of her squires, and she ordered him to saddle her splendid Norwegian palfrey. No count or king ever had a better horse. The moment she gave the squire the command, he followed it without delay and saddled the dappled palfrey.

Erec summoned another squire and ordered him to fetch his arms and equip him. He then went up into a gallery and had a Limoges carpet stretched out on the ground before him. According to his instructions, the squire hurried off to fetch the arms and placed them on the carpet. Erec sat opposite, on a leopard design in the rug. He prepared to put on his equipment. He first had his polished steel greaves laced up, then he put on a hauberk of such value that not one bit of the mesh could be cut away. The hauberk was so costly that on the inside as well as the outside there was not enough iron for a needle. The hauberk could never rust, for it was all made of triple-woven fine silver mesh. This work was, I can assure you, so skillfully designed that anyone who had worn it would have been no more weary or pained than if he had worn a silk jacket over his shirt.

All the knights and men-at-arms began to wonder why he was having himself armed, but none dared ask. When his hauberk had been set in place, an attendant laced over his head a helmet with a bejeweled gold band that sparkled more brilliantly than ice. He then took the sword and girded it on. Erec ordered his Gascon bay steed saddled and led out to him, then summoned an attendant. "Page, go quickly. Hurry to the chamber beside the tower where my wife is," he said. "Go and tell her she keeps me waiting here too long. She has spent too much time getting ready. Tell her to come and mount her horse immediately, for I await her."

The attendant went away and found her ready. Her tears revealed her grief. "Lady," he at once addressed her, "why do you delay so long? My lord is waiting for you outside with all his equipment on. Had you been ready, he would have mounted quite a while ago."

Although Enide wondered to herself about her lord's intentions, she behaved wisely. When she came before him, she seemed as happy as could be. She came before him in the center of the courtyard. King Lac was hurrying behind her. Knights were running as fast as they could. No one there, young or old, failed to go to inquire and learn if Erec would take any of them along with him. Although all the people presented themselves and their service, he swore and made a solemn oath that no one was to stay in his company, were it not his wife and she alone. That was the way he put it, that he would go alone.

The king was filled with anxiety. "Dear son," he said, "what do you wish to do? You should tell me your business and keep nothing secret from me. Tell me, where are you planning to go? No matter what I say to you, you don't want a knight or a squire in your company. Should you undertake single-handed combat against a knight, that is no reason to leave behind your company. Take some of your knights with you for pleasure and for companionship. The son of a king should not travel alone. Dear son, have your packhorses loaded and take thirty of your knights, or forty, or even more. Have silver and gold carried with you, and anything else befitting a man of worth."

In a final reply, Erec related all his plans for the journey. "Sire, it cannot be any other way," he answered. "I shall not take along a horse on my right, and I have no need of gold or silver, squire or man-at-arms. I seek no companionship other than that of my wife. But I do make one request of you. Whatever happens, if I die and she returns, love and cherish her out of love for me and respect for my request, and bestow on her for all her life, without dispute or strife, half of your land."

The king heard his son's request. "Dear son, I promise that," he replied. "But I am so distressed to see you setting out alone. If I had my way, you would never do this."

"Sire, it cannot be any other way. I am going. I commend you to God. But be considerate of my companions, and give them horses, equipment, and all that knights need."

The king could not hold back his tears at his son's departure, and for their part the people too were weeping. Knights and ladies did not hide their tears in their deep grief for him. There was not a single person who did not grieve, and many fainted in the courtyard. Amid all their tears and almost mad with grief, they embraced and kissed Erec. I do not believe they could have shown greater sorrow had they seen him fatally wounded.

To comfort them, Erec spoke. "Sirs, why do you weep so much? I am not crippled or captured. This grief does not help you. If I leave, I shall return at God's pleasure and when I can. To God I commend each and every one of you. Grant me leave now, for you detain me too long. To see you weeping makes me most unhappy and upset." To God he commended them, and they him. The separation took place amid great anxiety.

Erec set out on his way, taking his wife with him. He did not know his direction, but rode on according to chance. "Gallop along," he said, "and be careful not to be so presumptuous as to address me if you see something. Don't speak to me unless I address you first. Gallop along in front and ride fearlessly."

"Yes, sir, at once," she replied.

She rode silently in front, and they did not exchange a word. Enide was very sad, however, and lamented to herself in a soft low voice lest he hear her. "Alas, wretch that I am," she said, "God had exalted me to such great joy. Now, in no time at all, He has brought me down. Fortune, who had drawn me to her, has quickly withdrawn her hand. This, alas, would be of no concern to me were I to dare address my lord. But I am abandoned and dead because my lord has taken an aversion to me. He has come to hate me, I see this clearly, since he doesn't wish to talk to me. And I am not so bold as to dare look at him."

During her lament, a knight, who made his living by robberies, was emerging from the forest with two companions. All three were armed. He coveted the palfrey Enide was riding. "Do you know, sirs, what is in store for you?" he asked his two companions. "If we are not the winners here, we are shameless and lost to honor and incredibly unlucky. Here comes a very beautiful lady. I don't know if she is single or married, but she is dressed magnificently. Her palfrey and her saddle along with her bridle and her breaststraps are worth at least twenty silver marks. I want the palfrey for myself. Everything else is yours; I want nothing more for my share. So help me God, the knight shall not get away with anything belonging to the lady. I tell you this with every confidence: I intend to deal him a blow that will cost him dearly. Therefore it is right that I go and be the first to engage in combat."

The others agreed with him. He spurred on, covered up well behind his shield, while the other two stayed back. In those days it was not the custom or practice for two knights to assault one. Had they also attacked, their behavior would have been considered a treacherous offense.

Enide was terrified at the sight of the robbers. "God!" she exclaimed to herself. "What may I say? Now my lord will be captured or killed, for there are three of them and he is alone. This is not a fair contest, one knight against three. That man will strike my lord at once, for he is off his guard. God! Shall I then be so cowardly as not to dare speak to him? I shall not be such a coward. I shall speak to him. I will not fail."

At once she turned to him. "Dear sir, where are your thoughts?" she said. "There are three knights spurring after you in full pursuit. I fear they will harm you."

"What! What have you said?" Erec exclaimed. "You have too little respect for me now. I gave you a command, forbidding you to speak. How very bold of you to disobey! This time you shall be pardoned, but should this happen again, you will not be forgiven."

Then, turning his shield and his lance, Erec rushed toward the knight. Seeing him coming, the robber shouted out to him. Erec heard him and answered with a challenge. Holding their lances at their full extent, they came spurring at each other. But the robber missed Erec, who knew the right method of attack, and was placed in a bad position. Erec's blow had such force that it cracked his opponent's shield from top to bottom. His hauberk gave no protection, for Erec punctured and smashed it in the middle of his chest, thrusting his lance a foot and a half into the body. As he drew it back out, he turned his shaft, and his opponent fell. He had to die, for the lance had reached the heart.

Leaving his companion behind, one of the other two rushed forward, spurring toward Erec and threatening him. Erec took hold of the shield hanging from his neck. He made a bold attack while the other man protected his chest with his shield; each struck the other on the emblazoned shields. The knight's lance flew into pieces, and Erec thrust a quarter of his lance into his opponent's body. That man would be no further trouble that day. Erec knocked him from his charger in a swoon, then from an angle spurred at the other man.

Seeing Erec coming toward him, the other man began to flee; he was afraid and dared not wait for him. He raced to take refuge in the forest. But his flight availed him not. Erec was pursuing him closely. "Vassal, vassal," he shouted, "turn around and prepare to defend yourself, or else I shall kill you as you flee. Your flight is totally useless."

With no desire to turn about, the man continued to flee at full gallop. Erec chased him, overtook him, struck him squarely on his painted shield, and threw him down on the opposite side. He paid no more attention to these three: one was dead, one wounded, and he was free of the third since he had knocked him from his charger to the ground. He took the horses of all three and tied them together by the reins. All were of different color: the first was milk-white, the second black but not ugly, the third all dappled.

Erec returned to the road where Enide was waiting for him. Ordering her to lead and drive the three horses in front of her, he made it his particular concern to threaten her that she was not to be so bold as to utter a single word unless he gave her permission. "I shall never do that, dear sir, if this is your wish," she answered him. And as they went their way, she kept silent.

They had not traveled a league when ahead in a valley were five other knights coming toward them, their lances in their rests, their gleaming helmets laced up tight, and their arms clutching the shields hanging from their necks. They were riding along seeking plunder. At that moment they saw the lady riding up, leading the three horses, and Erec following after. On sighting them, they talked of how they would divide up all the equipment among themselves as if it were already theirs. Covetousness is a bad thing. But it was not to their liking to encounter an unexpected obstacle. Expectations are largely unfulfilled, and some people expect to win but fail. And that was what happened to them when they attacked.

One of the men announced that he would have the lady for himself or else die. Another said that the dappled charger would be his; from all the spoils he would seek nothing more. The third declared that the black horse would be his. "And I shall have the white one," the fourth announced. No coward, the fifth said that he would have the knight's charger and arms; desiring to win them by himself, he would be the first to go and attack him provided they granted him leave. They willingly agreed, and he left them and rode ahead on a fine, swift horse. Erec saw him but pretended he had not yet noticed him. When Enide caught sight of them, all her blood stirred, and deep fear and terror took hold of her. "Wretch that I am," she said, "what shall I do? My lord's threats are so severe I don't know what to say or do. He says he will punish me if I speak to him. But if my lord met his death, I would have no consolation. I would be tortured and killed. God! My lord doesn't see him. What a wretched fool I am. Then why am I waiting? Now I am too cautious in my speech since I have said nothing to him in some time. I am certain the men coming there intend harm. Alas, God, how shall I talk to him? He will kill me. Very well, let him kill me. I will not fail to speak to him."

"Sir," she then called out softly to him.

"What! What would you say?" he asked.

"Pardon me, sir. I would tell you that five knights have emerged from that thicket. They terrify me. Having seen them, I am convinced they intend to attack you. Four of them remain behind in wait, and the fifth rides toward you as fast as his horse can carry him. I am afraid now that he will strike you. The other four remain behind, though not far away. If the fifth is in need, they will all come to his aid."

"You thought wrong when you violated what I told you," Erec answered. "I expressly forbade you to do that. And yet I realized how little respect you have for me. This zeal of yours has been put to bad use, for I feel no gratitude to you. Know well that I abhor you. I have told you this before, and I tell you again. On this occasion I shall pardon you once more. But be on your guard in the future. Never turn your eyes toward me. That would be folly on your part, for your words do not please me."

Then Erec spurred toward the knight, and both of them clashed. Each sought the other and attacked him. Erec struck his opponent so hard that his opponent's shield flew from his neck and his collarbone was broken; his stirrups snapped, and he fell. There was no fear that he would get up again, for he was badly battered and wounded.

One of the others made his way toward Erec, and they struck each other violently. Without any effort, Erec plunged his sharp, well-forged lancehead into his opponent's neck underneath the chin. The lance cut through all the bones and nerves so that its head stuck out on the other side. The crimson blood spurted out hot on both ends of the wound. His spirit departed. His heart stopped.

The third robber leapt from his lookout on the other side of a ford and rode straight across the ford. Erec spurred forward and met him before he even made his way out of the ford, dealing him such a forceful blow that he laid flat both him and his charger. The charger was stretched over its rider long enough to drown him in the water. The horse struggled until it finally managed to stand. And so the three had been defeated.

The other two decided to abandon the spot and not to engage him in combat, making their escape through the stream. Erec followed them in pursuit. He gave one such a blow in the back that he pushed him forward over the pommel. Mustering all his strength in the attack, he broke his lance on the man's back and sent him falling neck first. Erec exacted a heavy price from the knight for his lance, which he had broken on him, for he soon unsheathed his sword. Acting like a fool, his opponent stood again. Erec dealt him three blows so terrible that he made his sword drink his opponent's blood. He severed his shoulder from his body and knocked him to the ground.

With his sword Erec attacked the other robber, who was fleeing rapidly without companion or escort. The man dared not wait, yet he could not get out of the way. He had to abandon his horse, for he had no more hope. Throwing down his shield and his lance, he let himself fall to the ground. Erec did not intend any further attack now that his opponent had thrown himself to the ground; he did bend down, however, to pick up the lance, not leaving it there but replacing his own which he had broken. He picked up the lance and set off. He did not abandon the horses but took all five and led them away.

Erec handed over the five horses to Enide to add to the other three. Leading them was arduous work for her. He ordered her to travel along quickly and to refrain from addressing him lest some harm or misfortune befall her. But she answered him not a word, and kept silent. Away they rode, leading all eight horses.

They had ridden along until evening without sighting any town or place of shelter. At nightfall they took refuge beneath a tree in an open field. Erec ordered his lady to sleep while he stood guard. She replied that she would not do that, for it was not proper and she did not wish to do it. He would sleep, for he was the more exhausted. Since the proposal pleased Erec, he agreed. He placed his shield under his head, and the lady took her cloak and stretched it over him. And so he slept, and she kept watch without dozing at all during the night. All through the night until morning she continued to hold on to all the horses.

Severe were her self-rebuke and self-reproach for the words she had spoken. She had behaved, she said, very badly. "Certainly I don't have half the misfortune I have deserved. Wretch that I am," she went on, "at what an evil time do I see my pride and my presumption. I could have known beyond doubt that no such knight or finer was known than my lord. I knew that. Now I know it better still, for I watched with my own eyes as he displayed no fear of three or five armed men. Damn my tongue forever for speaking from the disgraceful pride that has reduced my body to this shame." Thus she lamented all night long until dawn the next morning.

In the morning Erec rose and set out again along the road with Enide in front and himself following. At noon, in a valley, they came upon a squire, accompanied by two attendants carrying bread, wine, and five rich cheeses. The squire was a discerning fellow. When he noticed Erec and his beloved coming from the forest, he realized that they had slept in the forest that night without any food or drink, for there was no castle, town, tower, fortified dwelling, abbey, almshouse, or shelter within a whole day's journey. He then formed a most noble plan. He directed his path toward them and greeted them nobly. "Sir," he said, "I think and believe that you and this lady had a most uncomfortable time last night and lay awake in these woods. I present to you a gift of this white bread if you care to eat a little. I say this not to flatter you, for I ask nothing from you. The bread is made from fine wheat. I have some good wine and rich cheese, a white cloth and beautiful goblets. You may disarm yourself and rest a little under the shade of these hornbeam trees. Dismount, for this is my advice to you."

Erec dismounted. "Dear friend, I shall eat, thank you. I have no wish to ride farther," he answered him.

The squire performed his service well: he helped the lady down from her horse, while the attendants accompanying the squire held the horses. The three then went and sat in the shade. The squire removed Erec's helmet and unlaced the chinguard in front of his face. Then he spread out the cloth before them on the thick grass. He gave them bread and wine, and prepared and cut a cheese for them. With their sharp appetites, they were glad to eat the food and drink the wine. The squire did not overlook anything in serving them.

After the food and drink, Erec was courteous and generous. "Friend," he said, "as a gesture of thanks I offer you one of my horses. Take the one you like the best. Ride back to your town and prepare a splendid lodging there for me. I pray that may not be too much trouble for you."

The squire answered that he would gladly perform any pleasure for him. He then came to the horses, untied them, selected the black one, which seemed to him the best, and thanked him. He mounted by the left stirrup. Leaving the couple there, he went galloping into the town, where he took a suitably comfortable lodging.

Behold he has returned again. "Now, sir, mount quickly," he said, "for a fine and fitting lodging is yours."

Erec mounted, and his lady mounted after him. Since the town was quite near, they soon arrived at their lodging. Joyous was their reception. Their host welcomed them, happy and delighted to have them generously supplied with all their needs.

When the squire had done them all possible honor, he came to his horse and mounted again. On his way to the stable, he led it past the count's galleries, the count and three other vassals having come there to lean out. When the count saw his squire on the black charger, he asked him who owned it; the squire replied that he did. The count was astonished. "What! Where did you get it?" he asked.

"Sir, a knight I esteem very much gave it to me," he answered. "I brought him into this town, and he is lodging in the house of a townsman. Very courteous is the knight, and the most handsome man I have ever seen. Had I sworn and pledged my oath, I still could not have described his beauty to you, no, not completely or even by half."

"I think and believe he is not as handsome as I am," answered the count.

"On my word, sir, you are most fine and handsome," the squire said. "There is no knight born in this country as handsome as he. I dare maintain this man is much more handsome than you, were he not exhausted from carrying his hauberk and bruised by the blows he has received. In the forest he fought all alone against eight knights, and led away all their chargers. And with him he brings a lady so beautiful that no woman ever had half her beauty."

The count was seized by the desire to go and see if this news he heard was true or false. "I have never heard anything like this," he said. "So take me to his lodging, for I would know with certainty if you lie or tell the truth."

"Gladly, sir," he replied. "Here is the route and the road. The lodging is not far from here."

"I am anxious to see them," the count said, and then came down.

The squire dismounted and made the count get up on his horse. He hurried ahead to tell Erec that the count was on his way to see him. Erec had his customary splendid accommodation; tapers and other candles burned everywhere.

The count came with only three companions; he brought no more. Erec knew proper manners and rose to meet him. "Welcome, sir," he said to him, and the count returned his greeting. They sat down next to each other on a soft white couch and, as they talked, became acquainted. The count offered and proposed to him, indeed begged him, to agree to take reimbursement for his expenses. But Erec was not inclined to accept, noting that he had ample funds and did not need to accept anything from him.

Many subjects filled their long conversation. The count, however, did not stop glancing in the other direction where he had caught sight of the lady. Her beauty consumed all his thoughts. He looked at her as much as he could. He coveted her and found her so desirable that her beauty ignited him with love. Covering up his true purpose, he asked Erec's permission to speak to her. "Sir," he said, "I have a request to make of you provided you don't object. As a gesture of courtesy and as a pleasure, I would like to sit beside this lady. With good intent have I come to see both of you, and you should not take my request amiss. I would offer the lady my service in all respects. You may be assured I would do all her pleasure out of affection for you."

Erec was not jealous; he suspected no deception. "Sir," he said, "it doesn't trouble me at all. You may sit there and talk. Don't think I have any objection. I am pleased to give you permission."

The lady was seated two lance-lengths from the count, who had taken a seat beside her on a low stool. Wise and courteous as the lady was, she turned toward him. "Alas, how it troubles me that you travel in such a disgraceful fashion. This brings me dreadful displeasure and pain," the count said. "But if you would believe me, honor and profit will be yours, and great wealth will come to you. Great honor and great nobility befit your beauty. I would make you my lady if this suited your pleasure. You would be my dear beloved and lady over all my domain. Since I deign to seek your love, you should not refuse me. I see clearly and know that your lord does not love or esteem you. If you stay with me, you will be married to a fine lord."

"Sir, you are distressing me in vain; this cannot be," Enide replied. "Alas, I would rather be still unborn or else die in flaming thorns and my ashes be scattered than be untrue in any manner to my lord or wickedly plot some treachery or evil. You were very mistaken to make such a proposal to me. I could never behave in that manner."

The count became incensed. "Lady, you would not deign to love me?" he asked. "You are too proud. My flattery and begging will not make you do my will? How true it is that a woman's pride grows the more you flatter and beg her. But the man who insults and humiliates her finds her often in a better disposition. I give you my solemn promise: if you don't do my will, there will be swords drawn here. Right or wrong, I shall have your lord slain before your eyes."

"Sir, there is a better way to accomplish this than you say," Enide said. "If you killed him like that, you would be guilty of despicable treachery. But calm yourself now, dear sir, for I shall do your pleasure. You may take me as your possession. I am yours and I would be yours. I have not spoken out of pride, but rather to learn and prove if I could find in you the love of a true heart. But on no condition would I like you to commit such treachery. My lord is not on his guard against you. If you killed him that way, you would be guilty of a dreadful evil, and the blame would be mine. Throughout the country everyone would say my counsel made you do it. Take your rest until morning when my lord is about to rise. Then you could do him greater harm without incurring blame or reproach."

What the heart thinks, the mouth does not utter. "Sir," she continued, "believe me now. Don't be so impatient. But send your knights and your men-at-arms here tomorrow and have me abducted by force. My lord is brave and courageous, and he will wish to defend me. Whether the combat is real or just a game, have him captured and tortured or decapitated. Too long have I led this sort of life. I have no desire for my lord's companionship. I cannot lie about this, I would like to feel you in bed, yes, your naked body beside my naked body. We have reached a point where you may be certain of my love."

"Yes indeed!" the count replied. "Lady," he continued, "blessed was the hour of your birth. You will be treated with high honor."

"Sir, I believe this, but I would have your promise that you will cherish me. Otherwise I shall not believe you," she said.

Delighted and happy was the count as he replied. "Take my pledge. I promise you, lady, on a count's loyal word to do all your will. Never be worried about this. You will have everything you wish."

Then she accepted his promise, although it was worth little and she regarded it as valueless, except as a way of rescuing her lord. Well she knew, when she set her mind to it, how to intoxicate a fool with words. It was better that she lie to him than that her lord be slaughtered.

The count rose from her side, commending her to God a hundred times. Yet his pledge to her would be of very little value.

Erec knew nothing of the death they were plotting for him. Yet God will have the power to come to his aid, and I believe He will.

Now Erec was in grave danger, and did not think to be on his guard. The count was most wicked in plotting to steal Erec's wife and kill Erec when he was defenseless. Like a traitor he took his leave. "I commend you to God," he said.

"And you too, sir," Erec answered. Thus they separated.

It was already late in the evening. In a private chamber, two beds had been made on the floor. Erec went to sleep in one, and Enide was lying down in the other. Most unhappy and upset, she did not sleep all night. For the sake of her lord she had been on watch, for she had realized, from what she had seen, how thoroughly evil the count was. Were he to get hold of her lord, she was sure he would not fail to ill-treat him. His death would be a certainty.

Fear for her lord prevented her from knowing any comfort. All night she had to keep watch. But if she could manage, and if her lord would believe her, they would be back traveling their route before dawn so that the count would come in vain and she would never be his, nor he hers.

Erec slept soundly all night long until day drew near. Then Enide realized in her fear that she might wait too long. Like a good and loyal lady, she was tenderhearted toward her lord, for duplicity and falsehood had no place in her heart. She dressed and readied herself, then came to her lord and woke him.

"Ah, pardon me, sir," she said. "Rise at once, for you are betrayed at this very moment without cause or crime on your part. The count is a proven traitor. If you can be found here, you will never escape without being cut to pieces. He would have me. That is the reason he hates you. But All-knowing God willing, you will not be captured or killed. Last night he would have slain you had I not promised to be his beloved and his wife. Soon you would see him coming here. He would take and keep me and kill you if he finds you."

Now Erec was hearing this display of his wife's loyalty toward him. "Lady, have our horses saddled quickly and our host awakened. Tell him to come here. Treachery is already at work," he said.

The horses were soon saddled, and the lady had summoned the host. Erec dressed promptly. "Sir," his host asked when he came to him, "why are you rushing to get up before the appearance of day and the sun?"

Erec answered that a long road and a full day lay ahead of him. As a consequence he had prepared for his journey, which had been weighing heavily on his mind. "Sir," he continued, "you still have not rendered an account of my expenses. You have treated me with kindness and honor, and for this you deserve a large payment. Consider my account settled with seven chargers. I am not in a position to offer you anything more, not even to the value of a halter."

Delighted with the gift, the townsman bowed down and thanked him profusely. Then Erec mounted and took his leave. They set out again along the road. Always as he rode, he warned Enide not to be so bold as to address him should she see something.

Meanwhile, a hundred armed knights entered the house. They were all outraged not to find Erec there. The count then realized the lady had tricked him. When he discovered the horses' tracks, they all set out on the trail. The count made severe threats that if he could catch Erec, nothing would stop him from immediately taking his head. "Damn the man who makes no effort to spur quickly!" he exclaimed. "The man who can present me with the head of the knight I despise will render me the most agreeable service." They all then charged after him in full pursuit, burning with anger over a man they had never seen.

They sighted Erec riding along before he had entered the forest. One of them separated from all the others, who let him go by common accord. Enide heard the clang of their armor and the noise of their horses and noticed that the valley was filled. As soon as she saw them approaching, she could not refrain from speaking.

"Alas, sir, alas!" she exclaimed. "What an assault this count has mounted against you! Such an army he brings against you! Sir, ride faster until we are in the forest. I hope we shall escape quickly; they are still far back. If we ride at this speed, you cannot escape, for you are no match for them."

"You have little respect for me when you scorn my words," Erec answered. "In spite of my words to you, I cannot correct you. But if God takes mercy on me and I can escape from here, you will pay dearly for this unless I have a change of heart."

At once he turned about and saw the seneschal approaching on a strong and swift horse four crossbow shots ahead of the others. He had not borrowed his arms, for he was very well equipped. Making an estimate of the army, Erec saw that there were at least a hundred men. He thought he had to stop the man who was rushing ahead, pursuing him. They rode at each other, striking their shields with the two sharp, pointed heads of their lances. Erec drove his strong steel lance into the body of his opponent, whose shield and hauberk offered him no more protection than a piece of dark-blue silk.

Then behold the count came spurring on. According to the story, although the count was a good, strong knight, he behaved like a fool by coming with only his shield and his lance. So confident was he of his own strength that he wanted no other equipment. And he displayed such great daring by racing ahead of all his men by more than nine acres. When Erec noticed him separated from his troop, he rushed at him; the count was not afraid, and they attacked fiercely. The count delivered the first blow, striking him so hard in the chest that Erec would have fallen from his stirrups had he not been securely fastened. He cracked the wood of his shield so that the lancehead protruded out the other side. But Erec's costly hauberk saved him from death, and not a single mesh was torn.

The count was strong; he broke his lance. Erec dealt such a forceful blow to the yellow-painted shield that more than a yard of his own lance he thrust into the count's side, knocking him senseless from his charger.

Then Erec turned and rushed off, not staying there longer but spurring straight into the forest at top speed.

Behold Erec was in the forest, and the others had paused over those lying in the field. They declared their intentions and swore at the top of their voices to spur in pursuit of him for two days or three rather than fail to capture and kill him. The count heard their words. Seriously wounded in the side, he raised himself a little and opened his eyes slightly. He realized what an evil deed he had begun to execute. He had his knights draw back.

"Sirs, I tell all of you, there is not one of you, strong or weak, highborn or low, bold enough to dare proceed another step," the count said. "All of you, turn back at once. My behavior has been disgraceful. I am distraught at my villainous deed. The lady who tricked me is courteous, wise, and honorable. Her beauty ignited me. Because of my desire for her, I planned to murder her lord and keep her by force. How deserving indeed that misfortune came upon me. Since I acted like a fool, like a shameful and wicked traitor, evil has befallen me. That man is better than any mortal knight. I shall never let him come to harm as long as I can prevent it. I command you now to turn back."

They all rode away disconsolate. They were carrying the seneschal, and they had laid the count out on his shield. Though seriously wounded, the count lived a long time. And that was the manner of Erec's delivery.

Galloping along a road between two woods, Erec came upon a drawbridge in front of a high tower at the end of one wooded area. The tower was surrounded by a wall and a wide, deep moat. They crossed the bridge quickly but had not traveled far when the lord of the tower sighted them from high up in the turret. I can well be truthful about this man: he was small in stature, but courageous and brave. When he saw Erec riding across, he came down from his tower. He had his saddle with its gold lions placed on a large sorrel charger. He then ordered his equipment fetched, his shield and his strong unbending lance, his sharp, polished sword and his bright, gleaming helmet, his shining hauberk and his triple-woven greaves. Because he had seen an armed knight pass in front of his lists, he wished to engage him in combat to the point of exhaustion, or else the knight would exhaust him until he admitted defeat. His men carried out his order. Behold his horse was already led out. One squire brought it out saddled and bridled. Another carried his equipment. All alone without a companion, the knight galloped through the gateway as quickly as he could.

Erec was riding along a slope. Behold the knight charging down the small hill, seated on a proud horse that made such a commotion that it cracked the small stones under its hooves more easily than a millstone crushes corn. Brightly blazing sparks flew in all directions, for its four hooves seemed on fire.

When Enide heard the noise and the commotion, she almost fell from her palfrey, senseless and in a faint. The blood stirred in every vein of her body; her face turned pale and white as though she were dead. She was extremely distressed and distraught because she dared not address her lord lest he threaten and accuse her, and order her to keep quiet. She was completely torn in two, not knowing which path to follow, whether to speak or to remain silent. Giving careful consideration to the matter, she found herself ready to speak so often that her tongue moved but the voice could not come forth, her teeth being clenched in fear, keeping her words within. She was thus debating and tormenting herself. She closed her mouth and clenched her teeth, and not a word came forth.

With this war raging within, she spoke to herself. "My loss would be too terrible, I know that for certain, were I to lose my lord here. Then shall I tell him everything openly? Absolutely not. Why? I would not dare, for my lord would be furious. And if my lord is angered, he will abandon me in this thicket and leave me alone and wretched. Then I shall be even worse off. Worse off? What does it matter to me? Grief and sorrow are to be mine for the rest of my life unless my lord somehow frees himself immediately and escapes from here without fatal injury. But if I don't warn him at once, that knight who is spurring on will have killed him before he realizes, for the knight seems bent on harm. Wretch that I am, I have waited too long already. Even though he forbade me severely, I shall not stop because of his warning. My lord is so absorbed in his thoughts, I clearly see, that he forgets about himself. And so it is right that I address him."

She spoke to him. He threatened her, although he had no desire to hurt her, for he perceived and recognized that she loved him above all else and he loved her as much as it was possible to love.

He rushed against the knight who was daring him to combat. Meeting at the end of the bridge, they challenged each other and attacked, both striking with their lanceheads as hard as they could. The shields that hung from their necks were not worth two pieces of bark to them. They split the leather covering and cracked the wood, and they cut the meshes of the hauberks so that both men were stabbed and pierced to the guts, and their chargers fell to the ground. Because their shields were heavy, the men were not fatally wounded. Throwing their lances to the ground, they unsheathed their swords and attacked furiously. They did not spare each other in inflicting wounds and injuries. They delivered heavy blows to their helmets so that blazing sparks flew. They split and smashed their shields. In many places their swords plunged into the naked flesh so that both men were weakened and weary. Had their two swords remained whole a long while, they would not have drawn back, and the struggle would have ended only with the death of one.

As Enide watched them, she was almost mad with grief. Seeing her display her deep sorrow, wringing her hands, tearing her hair, and shedding tears, one could have beheld a loyal lady. And anyone seeing her who did not feel great pity for her would be a wretch indeed.

They exchanged heavy blows. From nine in the morning until almost three that afternoon, the combat raged with such intensity that one could not discern with certainty who had the advantage. Erec exerted increased efforts in the struggle, plunging his sword into his opponent's helmet all the way to the mail lining so that he made him totter. But his opponent held himself upright and did not fall. He then launched an attack on Erec and struck him so hard on the cover of his shield that his fine and valuable blade broke as he pulled it back. When he saw his sword was broken, in his rage he threw the piece that remained in his hand as far as he could. He was afraid; he had to retreat, for in combat or assault a knight without a sword cannot make a vigorous effort. As Erec pursued him, the knight begged in God's name that he not slay him.

"Mercy, noble knight," he exclaimed. "Don't be cruel or savage to me. Since my sword has failed me, you have the strength and might to kill me or to take me alive. I have no way of defending myself."

"Since you beg me, I want you to acknowledge yourself beaten and defeated," Erec answered. "I shall then spare you if you place yourself in my power."

The knight was slow to respond. When Erec noticed his hesitation, he attacked him again to make him more afraid. His sword drawn, he rushed at him. The knight was terrified. "Mercy, sir," he exclaimed. "You have defeated me, for it cannot be otherwise."

"That is not enough," he answered. "You will not go free for so little. Tell me your name and your position, and I shall tell you mine."

"Sir, you speak rightly," he said. "I am king of this land. My liegemen are Irish, and there is no man who fails to pay me tribute. My name is Guivret the Small. I am very wealthy and powerful. Throughout this land there is no baron with land adjoining mine who breaks my command or fails to perform my every wish. Every neighbor of mine, however proud or courageous, stands in fear of me. I would certainly like to be your friend and your ally from now on."

"For my part I too boast of being a man of high nobility," Erec answered. "I am Erec, son of King Lac. My father, the King of Outer Wales, has more beautiful halls, strong castles, and splendid cities than any king or emperor except King Arthur. I make an exception of him, of course, for he has no equal."

Guivret was startled by what he heard. "Sir, this is amazing news I hear," he said. "To make your acquaintance gives me more joy than anything else could. You may have at your command my land and my wealth. As long as you wish to dwell here, I shall honor you highly. As long as you wish to stay here, you will be lord over me. We both need a physician, and one of my castles is nearby, not six or seven leagues away. I would like to take you there, where we shall have our wounds treated."

"I am grateful to you for what I have heard you say," Erec answered. "I shall not go there, thank you nevertheless. I beg of you only this: if I find myself in trouble and news reaches you of my need for help, then do not forget me."

"Sir, I promise you: as long as I live, any time you need my help I will come to your aid at once with all the men I can summon," he declared.

"I have nothing more to ask of you," Erec said. "You have promised a great deal. If your actions reflect your words, you are my lord and my friend."

They embraced and kissed. Never did so strenuous a combat end with such a fond separation, for their noble natures and their deep affection for each other caused them to tear long, wide strips from the bottom of their shirts and bandage each other's wounds. After they finished the bandaging, they commended each other to God. This was the manner of their departure: Guivret rode back alone, and Erec returned to his route.

Although Erec was in dire need of ointment to heal his wounds, he did not cease from travel until they came to a plain beside a lofty forest full of stags, hinds, bucks, roe-deer, and other wild animals, as well as all sorts of game. That day King Arthur, the queen, and the finest of his barons had come to the forest. The king wished to spend three or four days there in sport and play, and had ordered various sizes of tents and pavilions to be brought. Sir Gawain, exhausted from his long ride, entered the king's tent. Before his tent was a hornbeam tree. There Gawain had hung an ash lance and a shield from his equipment. With the reins he tied Gringalet, saddled and bridled, to a branch. The horse had been standing there quite a while when Kay the seneschal came by. With speed he made his way to that spot, and in jest, took the horse and mounted it without anyone preventing him. He then took the lance and the shield from the nearby tree. Galloping away on Gringalet, Kay rode along all through a valley until, by chance, he met Erec, who recognized the seneschal as well as the arms and the horse. Kay, however, did not recognize him because Erec's arms offered no sure means of identification. Erec's shield had taken so many blows from lance and sword that all the paint had come off. And because the lady did not wish the seneschal to see or recognize her, she tricked him by putting her veil in front of her face as if protecting herself from heat or dust.

Kay rushed forward and, without greeting Erec, immediately seized his horse by the reins. Before letting him budge, he was arrogant enough to question him. "Knight, I would know who you are and from where you come," he said.

"You are a fool to take hold of me," Erec answered. "You will not know this tonight."

"Do not be annoyed," he replied. "I ask this for your own good. I see and realize that you are maimed and wounded. Pass the night at my lodging. Should you wish to come with me, I shall have you treated with great honor and respect, and put at ease, for you are in need of rest. King Arthur and the queen are nearby in a forest where they have lodged in some tents and pavilions. I advise you, in good faith, to come with me and visit the king and the queen. They will be happy to see you, and will honor you highly."

"You speak well," Erec replied, "but nothing could make me go there. You do not know my needs. Still must I travel farther. Let me go, for I stay too long. A large part of the day yet remains."

"You speak foolishly in refusing to come," Kay answered. "Perhaps you will have a change of mind, for whether you wish to or not, both you and your lady, I think, will come there, just as the priest goes to the synod. If you follow my opinion, you would be ill-treated tonight if you go as strangers. Come quickly then, for I lay hold of you."

These words angered Erec. "Vassal," he said, "you are foolish to drag me after you by force. Without challenge you took hold of me. You acted badly, I tell you, for I thought I was without threat and so made no attempt to defend myself against you." He then placed his hand on his sword. "Vassal, let go of my reins! Get away from there!" he exclaimed. "I find you most arrogant and insolent. If you hold me longer, I shall strike you, be certain of that. Let me go."

And Kay left him, and raced more than an acre across the field; then returning, like a man filled with evil, he challenged him. They rushed at each other, but because Kay was unarmed, Erec behaved courteously and turned the head of his lance around, putting the butt-end in front. Nevertheless he dealt such a blow to the largest area of Kay's shield that it was made to hit him in the temple, pinning his arm to his chest. He stretched him out on the ground, then rode to his charger, took it, and handed over the reins to Enide. He wished to lead it away, but the other man was expert in flattery and appealed to Erec's noble nature to return it. Very fine indeed were his words of flattery and praise. "Vassal," he said, "so help me God, this charger is not mine. It belongs to the most valiant knight in the world, the bold Sir Gawain. I tell you this much that you may return his charger to him and thereby win honor. That would be the act of a wise and noble man. And I shall be your messenger."

"Vassal, take the horse and lead it away," Erec answered. "Since it belongs to Sir Gawain, I have no right to take it."

Kay took the horse, mounted again, and coming to the king's tent, recounted the facts without omitting a detail. The king summoned Gawain. "Dear nephew Gawain," the king said, "if ever you were courteous and noble, follow this knight at once. Politely inquire of him his position and his business, and persuade him, if you can, to come along with you. Take care not to fail."

Gawain mounted Gringalet, and two attendants followed him. They soon overtook Erec, although they did not recognize him. Gawain greeted him, and he returned the greeting; after this exchange Sir Gawain, the soul of nobility, spoke to him. "Sir, King Arthur has sent me along this road to you," he said. "The king and the queen send you their greetings. They ask and urge you to come and relax in their company. They wish to help you, not harm you, and they are not far from here."

"I am most grateful to both the king and the queen," Erec answered, "and to you, who, I believe, are well born and of fine education. Because my body is covered with wounds, I feel poorly. Yet I will not leave my route to take lodging. You should not wait here longer. I do thank you. Now go your way again."

Gawain was a man of great prudence. He drew back and whispered to one of his attendants to ride quickly and tell the king to take immediate measures and pull down and fold up his pavilions, then come and pitch the linen tents three or four leagues ahead of them in the center of the road. "That is where he must take up quarters tonight if he would know and lodge the finest knight, to be honest, ever seen. That is my hope, for the knight has no intention of abandoning his route for the sake of shelter."

The attendant rode away and delivered his message. Without a moment's delay, the king had his tents struck. After they were taken down, the men loaded the packhorses and set off. The king mounted Aubagu, then the queen mounted her white Norwegian palfrey.

During this time, Sir Gawain continued to delay Erec. "I traveled farther yesterday than I have today," Erec said to him. "You make me anxious, sir. Let me proceed. You have caused me to lose a good part of my day's journey."

"I would still accompany you a little way," Sir Gawain said to him. "Don't be annoyed, for night is far off."

They had conversed so long that, ahead of them, all the tents were pitched. Erec noticed them and recognized the lodging arranged for him. "Aha, Gawain, aha!" he said. "Your intelligence has tricked me. Through your cleverness you have detained me. Since this has happened, I shall now tell you my name. Keeping it from you does not help me. I am Erec, who was your companion and your friend of old."

When Gawain heard this, he went to embrace him. He lifted up his helmet and unlaced his chinguard, then hugged and embraced him joyously; Erec did the same. Then Gawain stepped back from him. "Sir," he said, "this news will delight my lord. Both my lady and my lord will be pleased. I shall ride ahead to tell them. But first I must embrace my lady Enide, your wife; I must welcome her and celebrate her arrival. My lady the queen is most anxious to see her; only yesterday I heard her speak of her."

Gawain went over to her at once and asked her how she was, if she was healthy and well. Her reply was that of a lady well educated. "Sir, no pain or suffering would be mine were I not so uneasy about my lord. But this distresses me, that scarcely a limb of his body is without wound."

"I find that most upsetting," Gawain answered. "His condition is evident in his pale, discolored face. I could have wept when I saw how wan and colorless he was. But joy stifled sadness, for my joy at seeing him made me forget all sadness. Now ride along at a slow pace. I shall gallop ahead to tell the king and the queen that you follow me. I am certain both will be delighted to learn this."

He then departed. And upon reaching the royal tent, he exclaimed: "Lord, now you should rejoice, you and my lady, for Erec and his wife are on their way here."

The king jumped to his feet in joy. "I am truly delighted. I could hear no news that would make me so happy," he exclaimed.

At once the king set out from his tent. It was not long before they met Erec. The moment Erec saw the king approaching, he dismounted, and Enide dismounted too. The king welcomed and embraced them, and the queen too embraced and kissed them tenderly. All present took part in the rejoicing. In that very place they relieved Erec of his arms. When they saw his wounds, joy turned to anger for the king and all his people. The king then had an ointment brought out that had been made by Morgan, his sister. The ointment, which Morgan had given to Arthur, was so strong that within a week it would completely cure and heal the wound being treated, whether in the ligaments or the joints, provided the ointment was applied daily. The ointment, which was delivered to the king, brought Erec great relief. After the wounds had been washed, the ointment applied, and the wounds bandaged again, the king led Erec and Enide into his private chamber. He declared that out of love for Erec, he would stay in the forest a fortnight until Erec, completely healed, was restored to health.

Erec thanked the king for his kindness and said to him: "Lord, my wounds are not so painful that I wish to abandon my journey. No one could detain me. Early in the morning, I would like to depart without further delay when I see daybreak."

The king raised his head at this. "It is a great misfortune that you do not wish to stay," he said. "I clearly see that you are in severe pain. Behave wisely and stay. Too dreadful will be the loss should you meet your death in the forest. Dear friend, remain here until you have recovered."

"That is enough," Erec answered. "I have undertaken this business, and I shall not stay under any circumstance. Say no more on this now. Order the supper prepared and the tables set. The attendants are going off to see to this."

It was a Saturday night, and their meal consisted of fish and fruit: pike and perch, salmon and trout, then raw and cooked pears. After supper the tablecloths were promptly removed.

The king cared about Erec very much. He had him sleep in a bed alone since he did not wish anyone sleeping with him who might disturb his wounds. That night Erec was finely lodged. In an adjacent chamber, Enide and the queen slept soundly on a large ermine blanket until the first light of morning.

At daybreak the next morning, Erec rose and dressed. He ordered his horses saddled and his equipment fetched. The attendants ran and brought them to him. The king and all the knights continued pressing him to stay, although there was no use entreating him since he was determined not to remain.

At that moment you would have seen everyone weeping and grieving as heavily as if they beheld him already dead. Erec armed himself, and Enide rose. The separation was most painful for all the people, for they expected never to see them again. All left their tents to follow the couple, sending for their horses that they might guide and escort them. "Do not trouble yourselves," Erec told them. "You will not accompany me one step. Stay here and you have my thanks."

The moment his horse was led out to him, Erec mounted and took his shield and his lance. He then commended them all to God, and they in turn commended him. Enide mounted, and they set out.

They entered a forest and did not cease from travel until nearly six that morning. They were making their way through the forest when from afar they heard the cries of a maiden in distress. Erec listened to the screams and, from what he heard, recognized a voice in pain and in need of help. He at once called out to Enide. "Lady," he said, "a maiden is traveling through these woods crying out. As far as I can tell, she is in need of help and assistance. I wish to hurry in that direction and determine her need. Dismount here, and I shall ride there. While I am away, wait for me here."

"Gladly, sir," she replied.

Leaving her on her own, he rode away alone until he came upon the maiden. She was walking through the woods, crying for her lover, whom two giants had captured, and were cruelly torturing as they led him away. As she went along, the maiden wrung her hands and pulled at her hair and her delicate rosy face. Erec was astonished by the sight of her. He begged her to tell him the reason for her heavy sobs and tears. Continuing to sigh and to cry, the maiden answered him amid her weeping. "Sir, it is no wonder I grieve. I wish I were dead. I don't love or value my life, for my lover has been captured by two cruel and evil giants, who are his mortal enemies. God! What shall I, miserable wretch that I am, do, deprived of the finest knight alive, the most noble and most well born? Now is he in grave danger of death. Today, without cause, they will make him die a most horrible death. If ever you can aid him, noble knight, I beg you, in God's name, help my lover. You will not need to race far, for they are still very nearby."

"Young lady, since you beg me, I shall ride after them," Erec answered. "Be fully assured I shall do all I can. Either I shall be taken prisoner along with him, or I shall return him, freed, to you. If the giants let him live until I can find them, I intend to test myself against them."

"Noble knight," the maiden said, "if you restore my lover to me, I will be your servant always. God be with you. Hurry, please."

"What direction did they follow?"

"This way, sir. Here is the path and the tracks from their horses."

Erec told her to wait there for him, then galloped off. The maiden commended him to God and prayed softly to the Lord to grant him, through His command, the strength to defeat those who hated her lover.

Keeping to their tracks, Erec spurred off in pursuit of the giants. He followed them closely until he sighted them about to leave the forest. He saw the knight wearing only undergarments, barefoot and naked on a nag, hands and feet bound as if he had been arrested for robbery. The giants had no spears, shields, sharp swords, or lances, but only clubs, and both were holding whips. They had struck and beaten the knight so badly that they had already cut the flesh on his back to the very bone. The blood ran down his sides and hips so that the nag was covered in blood even under its belly. Coming after them all alone, Erec was deeply pained and saddened to see the knight treated so shamefully.

In an open field between two forests, he overtook and questioned them. "Sirs," he asked, "what crime has this man committed that you treat him so badly and lead him along as if he were a thief? You treat him too cruelly. You lead him along as if he had been captured in thievery. It is a dreadful insult to strip a knight naked, then tie him and savagely whip him. Hand him over to me, I order you, as an act of noble courtesy. I do not make this demand by force."

"Vassal," they said, "what concern is this of yours? You are quite mad to make such a demand of us. If you don't like this business, change it!"

"To be honest, I do not like it," Erec replied. "You will not lead him away today without a fight. Since you will not hand him over to me, whoever can have him, let him keep him! Take your stand here, I challenge you. You will not take him farther until we have exchanged blows."

"Vassal, you are mad to want to fight us," they exclaimed. "If there were four of you now, you would have no more strength against us than one lamb against two wolves."

"I have no idea what will be," Erec answered. "If the heavens fall and the earth crumbles, many larks will be captured. There is little worth in the man who boasts much. On guard now. I attack you."

The giants were strong and fierce, holding large square clubs in their clenched fists. Erec rode at them, his lance in its rest. For all their arrogant threats he did not fear either of them, but struck the first in the eye. The blow went through the brain so that brains and blood spurted out at the back of his neck. He fell dead. His heart stopped.

When the other giant saw him dead, he was distraught, and not without reason. He advanced to wreak furious vengeance. He lifted up his club in both his hands, intending to strike Erec's head before he could protect himself. But Erec saw the blow coming and received it on his shield. Nevertheless, the force of the giant's stroke completely stunned him, almost knocking him from his charger to the ground. With his shield Erec covered himself. Regaining his stance, the giant expected no interference in delivering another blow to his head. But Erec had drawn his sword and made such an assault that the giant was badly served. He struck him through his skull and split him down as far as the saddlebows. His guts spilled out along the ground, and his body, split into two halves, fell its full length.

The knight wept with joy. He invoked and adored God, who had sent him aid. Then Erec unbound him, had him dress and arm himself, and mount one of the horses, leading the other with his right hand. He then asked him who he was.

"Noble knight," he answered him, "you are my rightful lord. I would make you my lord, as by right I should, since you have saved my life. My soul would have been separated from my body in cruel pain and torment. In God's name, dear sir, what chance sent you here to deliver me, through your valor, from the hands of my enemies? Sir, I would do you homage. I shall accompany you always and serve you as my lord."

Erec saw the knight's eager willingness to do him every possible service. "Friend," he replied, "I have no wish for your service. You should know, however, that I came to aid you here at the entreaty of your beloved, whom I came upon in these woods in a state of misery. With a heart in deep sorrow she was grieving and lamenting for you. I would present you to her, and once I have brought you together again, I would then, all alone, return to my journey. And you will not accompany me, for I have no need of your company. But I would know your name."

"Sir, as you wish," he answered. "Since you would know my name, I ought not to hide it. My name, be assured, is Cadoc of Carlisle, for that is how people call me. But seeing I must leave you, I would like to know, if possible, who you are and where you are from, or where I could seek or find you when I leave here."

"Friend, I shall never tell you that," Erec said. "Say no more of this. But if you would know it, and honor me, then go at once to my lord King Arthur. He is hunting now with a very large retinue in this forest and, I believe, not even five short leagues from here. Ride there quickly, and tell him you are sent by me, whom he welcomed with joy last night and lodged in his own tent. Take care not to keep from him the torment from which I delivered you, both you and your beloved. I am much loved at the court. If you present yourself on my behalf, you will do me honor and service. Inquire about my identity there. Otherwise you cannot know."

"Sir," said Cadoc, "I am at your full command. Never doubt my willingness to go there. I shall tell the king the truth about your combat on my behalf."

Thus conversing, they rode along until they reached the spot where Erec had left the maiden. Seeing her lover return, the maiden was overwhelmed with joy, for she had never expected to see him again. Erec took the knight's hand and presented him to her. "Don't be sad, young lady," he said. "Here is your lover, all joyous and happy."

Most wise was her response. "Sir, both of us, he and I, should certainly be in your power. We should both be yours to honor and serve you. But who could repay this debt even by half?"

"My dear friend," Erec answered, "I ask no recompense from you. I commend you both to God, for I think I have delayed too long." Then he turned his horse about and rode away as fast as he could. Cadoc of Carlisle rode off with his young lady in another direction to report the news to King Arthur and the queen.

Erec did not cease from galloping until he reached the spot where Enide was waiting for him. At that moment she was sick with worry, for she was firmly convinced that he had abandoned her completely. And he was much afraid that she had been led off by some felon who had bent her to his will. That is why he returned to her with all possible speed. But that day's heat, as well as his equipment, was so oppressive that his wounds broke open and all his bandages burst. His wounds were still bleeding when finally he reached the place where Enide awaited him.

Enide felt great joy at seeing him, although she did not perceive or know the pain that made him groan. His whole body was soaked in blood and his heart was scarcely beating. Riding down a small hill, he suddenly fell forward onto his horse's neck. As he tried to straighten up, he left the saddle and the saddlebows and fell unconscious, as though dead. When Enide saw that he had fallen, her heavy sorrow began. Deeply despondent at the sight of him, she rushed toward him, not concealing her pain. She cried out at the top of her voice, wringing her hands and tearing away every thread of the dress at her breast. She began to pull her hair and claw her delicate face.

"My dear, dear lord," she exclaimed. "Oh God, why do you let me live thus? Death, kill me! I surrender myself to you!" With these words she fainted over his body. When she had regained consciousness, she reproached herself bitterly. "Alas, sorrowful Enide, I am my lord's murderer," she said. "My folly has killed him. My lord would still be alive now had I not acted like a presumptuous fool and uttered those words that made my lord set out. Good silence never hurts anyone, but speech is often harmful. I have put this matter to the test and proven this to be completely true."

She seated herself in front of her lord and placed his head in her lap. Then she began to lament again. "Alas, sir, what a pity for you! No one has been your equal, for you were the mirror of beauty and the paragon of prowess. Wisdom had given you her heart; generosity crowned you. Without the latter, a man is not held in esteem. But what did I say? I made a terrible mistake in uttering the words that have killed my lord, the fatally poisoned words that must be my reproach. I recognize and confess that I alone am the guilty party. I alone must bear the blame."

Then once more she fell to the ground in a faint. When she straightened up again, her cries increased in anguish. "God, what shall I do? Why do I still live? Why does Death delay? Why does she wait? Why does she not take me without delay? Death holds me in such deep contempt that she does not bother to kill me. I must take my own vengeance for my crime. And so I shall die, despite Death's refusal to help me. Mere desire cannot make me die, and laments are worth nothing to me. The sword that my lord has girded on should by right avenge his death. From now on I shall resort to no other desire, no longer to wishes and prayers."

She unsheathed the sword and began to stare at it. All-merciful God made her hesitate a moment. While she was recalling her grief and misfortune, behold a count came galloping along with a large troop of knights. From afar he had heard the lady's loud screams. God had not intended to abandon her, for by now she would have killed herself had she not been taken by surprise: the knights snatched the sword from her and put it back in the scabbard. The count then dismounted and began by asking her about the knight, and whether she was his sweetheart or his wife. "Both the one and the other, sir," she replied. "Such grief is mine I don't know what to tell you. I am in agony not to be dead."

The count did his best to comfort her. "Lady," he said, "in God's name, take pity on yourself. It is proper indeed for you to have it. But you torment yourself for nothing, for you might yet know a better fate. Do not become indifferent to everything. You will be wise to comfort yourself. God will make you happy soon. Your exquisite beauty will be your good fortune. I shall take you as my wife and make you my countess and my lady. That should bring you much comfort. And I shall have the body transported and buried with great honor. Abandon this grief of yours. It is foolish behavior."

"Go away, sir," she answered. "For the love of God, leave me be. You have nothing to gain here. Nothing you could say or do would bring me happiness."

At her words the count stepped back. "Let us quickly prepare a bier where we shall bear the body," he said. "We shall take it and the lady directly to the town of Limors, where the body will be buried. Afterwards I would like to marry the lady despite her displeasure. I have never beheld such beauty, nor have I so coveted a woman. I am delighted to have found her. Now quickly and without delay let us prepare a bier furnished with stretchers for the horses. Everybody to the task! Let no one shirk!"

Some of them drew their swords and promptly cut two poles and tied sticks across. There they laid Erec on his back. They then attached two horses. As Enide rode alongside, she did not cease her lament, often swooning and falling backwards. The knights who were escorting her kept holding her up with their arms. And thus they supported and consoled her.

They bore the body to Limors and took it to the count's palace. All the people came up after them, ladies, knights, and townsmen. They placed the body on a large table in the center of the great hall and laid it out with his lance and his shield on either side. Crowds of people filled the hall, everyone eager to ask the meaning of the remarkable mourning.

During this time, the count was taking private counsel with his barons. "Sirs," he said, "I wish to take this lady as my wife immediately. We may easily recognize from her wisdom and beauty that she comes from a most noble family. Her nobility and her beauty show that she would deserve the honor of being at the head of a realm or an empire. If I marry her, I shall not be worse off. On the contrary, I believe I shall have much to gain. Have my chaplain summoned, and go and bring the lady. If she intends to do my will, I would like to give her half of all my land as dowry."

They then summoned the chaplain as the count had instructed, and they brought the lady. By force they presented her to him in marriage, for she steadfastly refused his will. Nevertheless the count married her, as he pleased. And the moment he had wed her, the constable had the tables set up in the palace and the food prepared, for it was already time for the meal.

After dusk on that May day, Enide was deeply troubled. Her grief had not abated at all, and the count continued pressing her with pleas and threats to calm herself and be happy. Against her will she was forced to sit in a chair; she was made to sit there, whether she wished to or not, and a table was placed in front of her. Across from her sat the count, almost mad with anger at his inability to comfort her. "Lady," he exclaimed, "you must give over and forget this grief. You can trust in me that wealth and honor will be yours. You can be certain that grief for a dead man does not bring him back to life. No one has ever seen that happen. Remember the poverty that was yours and the great wealth that is yours now. Poor you were; now you are rich. Fortune has not been ungenerous to you: she has now honored you with the title of countess. Your lord is dead, it is true. If you feel sorrow and anger at this, do you think me surprised? Not at all. But I give you the best advice I can offer. You should be delighted that I have married you. Be careful not to anger me. Have something to eat since that is my order."

"Sir, I have no desire for food," she answered. "As long as I live, sir, I will not eat or drink unless I see my lord, who lies on that table, take food first."

"Lady, that cannot be. You will be considered mad for speaking such nonsense. If you upset me today, you will be severely punished."

She did not care to reply to him, for she placed no value on his threat. The count then struck her on the face. She shrieked, and the barons round the count reproached him for his act. "Stop, sir!" they told the count. "You should be ashamed of hitting this lady for not eating. Too hideous is your base offense. None should say this lady wrong for grieving at the sight of her dead lord."

"Silence, all of you," the count exclaimed. "The lady is mine, and I am hers. I shall do with her what I wish."

Then she could not keep quiet, but swore she would never be his. And the count raised his hand and struck her again. At the top of her voice, she screamed. "Ah, I care not what you say or do to me! I don't fear your blows or your threats," she shouted. "Assault me more. Strike me more. Even if you were to pluck out my eyes with your own hands at this instant, or flay me alive, I shall never think you so savage that I shall do more or less for you."

In the midst of this angry exchange of words, Erec, like a man awakening, recovered from his faint. No wonder that he was amazed to see the people round him. But he was deeply distressed and distraught to hear his wife's voice. He got down from the table to the floor and drew his sword quickly. Anger and his love for his wife emboldened him. He ran to where he saw her. Without challenging or addressing a word to him, he struck the count in the middle of the head, smashing the forehead and skull. His blood and his brains spilled forth. The knights jumped up from the tables. Everyone thought it was the devil come among them. Not a man, young or old, remained there, for they were terrified. All jostled one another, making their way out as quickly as they could. They had soon emptied the palace. Everyone, strong as well as weak, exclaimed: "Flee! Flee! Look at the dead man!"

The press of people was very dense at the exit, for each man rushed to escape quickly. They pushed and shoved one another, for the man last in the crowd wished to be first. They all fled, no man daring to wait for another.

Erec ran to pick up his shield, and he hung it from his neck by the strap. Enide took his lance. They came out into the center of the courtyard. No one was bold enough to restrain them, for all thought they were being pursued, not by a man but by a devil or a demon who had entered the dead body. All the people were in flight, and Erec was chasing them.

There was a page outside in the courtyard, planning to take Erec's horse, equipped with bridle and saddle, to the watering place for a drink. Erec was delighted by this chance happening, and he darted toward the horse. Terrified, the page handed it over at once. Erec mounted between the saddlebows. Enide then placed her foot in the stirrup and jumped over the neck of the charger, just as Erec, who made her mount, had ordered her. The horse carried them off, and finding the gate open, the two rode out without being stopped.

There was heavy desolation in the town over the slain count. But there was no one, however esteemed, who followed after for revenge. The count had been slain at mealtime.

As Erec bore his wife away, he comforted her with embraces and kisses. He held her tightly in his arms next to his heart. "My sweet sister," he said, "I have tested you in all ways. Now you have nothing more to fear, for now I love you more than ever. And I am again sure and certain of your perfect love for me. From now on I wish to be, as I was before, entirely at your command. And if you have offended me in anything you said, I pardon you completely and consider you free of the offense and the words."

Then he embraced and kissed her again. Now Enide was not discomfited when her lord, assuring her again of his love, embraced and kissed her.

They galloped through the night, relieved that the moon shone brightly that evening.

The news spread quickly, for nothing else travels so fast. The news that a knight, wounded in combat, had been found dead in the forest had already reached Guivret. With the knight was a beautiful lady whose eyes seemed like sparks and whose grief was remarkable. The proud count of Limors had found them both and had had the body carried from there; he had wished to marry the lady, but she had rejected him. When Guivret heard the news, he knew no happiness, for Erec came into his mind immediately. His heart and mind told him to go and search for the lady and have the body buried with great honor if it was indeed Erec. He had a thousand knights and men-at-arms assembled to capture the town. If the count was unwilling to hand over the lady and the body, he would burn the town to the ground. In the bright moonlight he led his men toward Limors, their helmets laced, their hauberks in place, their shields hanging from their necks. Thus they all rode along armed.

It was nearly midnight when Erec caught sight of them. He now expected to be tricked, or killed, or taken prisoner without ransom. He made Enide dismount beside a hedge. His anxiety was not surprising. "Lady, stay a while here to the side of this path until these men have passed by," he said. "I don't care for them to see us, for I don't know what men they are or what they seek. It may be that we have nothing to fear from them. Yet I see no place where we could hide should they be bent on our harm. I don't know if harm will befall me, but fear will never prevent me from riding to meet them. If one attacks me, I shall not fail to joust with him. Yet I am exhausted and in pain; it is no wonder I grieve. I intend to ride directly ahead to meet them, and as for you, remain here and keep silent. Be careful none of them sees you until they are far from you."

Behold at that moment Guivret, his lance lowered, who had seen Erec from afar. They did not recognize each other because the moon was hidden by the shadow of a dark cloud. Erec was weary and weak, whereas Guivret had recovered somewhat from the blows and the wounds he had received. Erec would now act too much like a fool were he not to make himself known at once. He advanced from the hedge, and Guivret spurred toward him without word of address. Nor did Erec utter a word, expecting to accomplish more than he was able. A man wishing to do more than he can is forced to cease combat or surrender.

They clashed in an unequal joust, for one man was weak, the other strong. The force of Guivret's blow knocked Erec over the back of his horse to the ground. When Enide, who was on foot, saw her lord on the ground, she expected to be mistreated and killed. She jumped out from behind the hedge and rushed to help her lord. If she had known grief before, it was never so great as now. When she came near Guivret, she seized the reins of his horse. "Knight!" she shouted at him. "Damn you for attacking a man alone and powerless, a man in pain and almost dead from his wounds. What an unjust assault! You cannot say why you did this. Had you been alone, without companion or aid, and my lord had been in good health, this attack would have gone badly for you. Now show your nobility and fine upbringing. Because of your noble nature, renounce this combat you have undertaken. Your reputation will not increase for capturing or killing a knight who, as you can see, has not the strength to stand again. He has suffered so many blows in armed combat that his entire body is covered with wounds."

"Do not worry, lady," he answered. "I clearly see your steadfast love for your lord, and I praise you for it. Have no fear of me or my company. But do tell me your lord's name. Do not hide it. From this you can only profit. Whoever he is, tell me, and he will then go safe and free. You have nothing to fear, you or he, for both of you are safe."

When Enide heard this assurance, her response was immediate and brief. "His name is Erec. I am not to lie, for I see you are noble and well born."

Guivret, delighted, dismounted and went to throw himself at Erec's feet where he lay on the ground. "Sir," he said, "I was taking the highway to Limors in search of you, expecting to find you dead. They gave me information, held to be true, that Count Oringle had carried a knight killed in armed combat to Limors; in his evil, the court's intention was to marry a lady he had found with the knight, although she held no such desire. And I was coming to aid and deliver her in her deep distress. If he had been unwilling to hand over to me, without resistance, the lady and you, my self-regard would have been very small had I left him a foot of earth. Be certain, had I not loved you, I would never have undertaken this. I am Guivret, your friend. If I have injured you, it is only because I did not recognize you. You must pardon me."

At these words Erec sat up a little, to the extent of his ability. "Rise, friend," he said. "You are pardoned for this error since you did not recognize me."

Guivret rose, and Erec explained to him how, while the count was eating, he had slain him, how he had recovered his charger in front of a stable, how knights and men-at-arms had fled the place screaming: "Flee! Flee!

The dead man is chasing us!", how he should have been trapped there, and how he escaped.

Guivret then spoke to him. "Sir, there is a castle of mine near here which is beautifully situated. For your comfort and your honor I would like to take you there tomorrow, and we shall have your wounds treated. Two charming and cheerful sisters of mine, skilled in healing wounds, will soon restore you to health. Tonight we shall have our army set up quarters in these fields till the morning, for I think a little rest tonight will do you good. My advice is to lodge here."

"I agree with this advice," Erec replied.

There they spent the evening. It was no easy matter for them to set up quarters with only a few accommodations for their large company. They went and took shelter among the hedges. Guivret had his pavilion set up and ordered tinder burned to give light. He had the candles taken from the chests and lit inside the tent. Now Enide's sadness was gone, for all had turned out well for her. She relieved her lord of his arms and undressed him, then washed his wounds, and dried and bandaged them again, permitting no one else to touch him. Erec now had no reason to reproach her; he had tested her well and discovered her deep love for him.

Guivret made a great fuss over Erec. With quilts of his own, he had a long, high bed made on a spot with thick grass and rushes. Erec was laid there and covered. A chest was then opened, and Guivret had three pies taken out. "Friend," he said, "now taste a little of these cold pies. You will drink some wine mixed with water. I have seven barrels filled with fine wine; yet because of your wounds and injuries, the pure wine is not good for you. Dear friend, try now to eat something. It will do you good. And my lady your wife will also eat, for she has been in great distress today on your account. Yet you have taken fine revenge for that. You are out of danger. Now eat something, dear friend, and I too shall eat.

Guivret sat down beside Erec, as did Enide, who was delighted by all Guivret did. Both urged Erec to have something to eat. They gave him watered wine to drink, the pure wine being too strong for him. Erec ate as much as a sick man might and drank a little; he dared do no more. Nevertheless, he rested most comfortably and slept all night long since no one around him made any noise.

Early in the morning, everyone rose and prepared to mount and ride off. Erec had such fondness for his own horse that he did not wish to ride another. Enide was presented with a mule because she had lost her palfrey. To judge from the look on her face, however, she was not at all frightened. She had a fine mule whose steady amble carried her most comfortably.

Her great relief was this, that Erec was not worried about anything, but told her he was making a fine recovery.

Before nine that morning they reached the strong castle of Pointurie, which was very handsome and extremely well situated. Because of its beautiful location, Guivret's two sisters lived a tranquil life there. Guivret led Erec to an enchanting, airy room, away from all noise. Following their brother's request the two sisters did their best to heal Erec, and because they inspired his confidence, he trusted them completely. They went to great lengths to heal his wounds, first removing the dead skin, then applying ointment and a dressing. Much experienced in these matters, they often washed his wounds and reapplied the ointment over them. Every day they made him eat and drink four times or more, permitting, however, no garlic or pepper. People came and went, yet Enide was always at his side, for she was the most concerned about him. Guivret came in often to see him and to learn if he lacked anything. Erec was well served and well treated, for he was given everything he needed, not reluctantly but willingly and happily.

Because the maidens devoted themselves so much to his recovery, within a fortnight he felt no pain or suffering. Then they began to bathe him so that his color might return. They had nothing to learn in this regard, for they knew all about healing. When Erec was able to come and go, Guivret had two robes made of two different kinds of silk, one trimmed with ermine, the other with spotted fur. One was a deep-blue cloth from the Orient, the other a striped silk, which a cousin of his, a lady in Scotland, had sent him as a gift. Enide received the precious silk robe trimmed with ermine, Erec the fur-trimmed silk, which was of no less value.

Now Erec was completely healthy and strong; now he was recovered and healed. Now Enide was very happy; now she had her joy and her delight. They lay in one bed together embracing and kissing; there was nothing that gave them so much pleasure. They had gone through so much pain and agony, he for her and she for him, that they had now done their penance. Each made every effort to give as much pleasure to the other as possible. Concerning the rest of this I should keep silent.

Now they had reaffirmed their deep love. They had forgotten their sorrow so completely that they had scarcely a memory of it.

But now it was time for them to set out again. They asked leave of Guivret, in whom they had found a great friend; he had honored and served them in every way he could. In taking his leave, Erec said to him: "Sir, I can wait no longer to return to my own land. Have everything I need collected and made ready. I would like to depart tomorrow morning at daybreak. I have stayed with you long enough to regain my health and strength. May God be pleased to let me live to see you again where I can honor and serve you. Unless I am taken prisoner or detained, I expect no delay in reaching King Arthur's court. I intend to see him at Quarrois or Carlisle."

Guivret replied immediately. "Sir, you shall not travel alone, for I will accompany you, and, be it your pleasure, we shall take companions with us."

Erec accepted this suggestion, saying he wished to undertake the journey as Guivret proposed. That night he had everything prepared for the journey, for they did not wish to remain there longer.

In the early morning when they woke up, they all dressed and armed, and their horses were saddled. Erec went to the chamber where the maidens were to take leave of them before departing, and Enide hurried after him, delighted and happy that the preparations for the journey were complete. They both took leave of the maidens. Erec, who had been brought up well, took his leave by thanking them for his health and his life and by pledging to be at their service. He then took the hand of the maiden nearer him, and Enide followed, taking the other's. Hand in hand, they all left the room and came up into the palace.

Guivret immediately invited them to mount without delay. Enide never expected to see the time when they would be mounted. For her a soft-stepping, noble, and elegant palfrey of great value was led out in front of the horseblock. Fine and fitting as it was, the palfrey was worth no more than her own palfrey, which she had left behind in Limors. The other was black, whereas this one was sorrel, and its head was different: the colors there were divided so that one cheek was all white, the other black as a crow, and in the middle was a line greener than a vine-leaf, separating the black from the white. I can truly state that the workmanship of the bridle, the breaststrap, and the saddle was exquisitely fine: the bridle and the breaststrap were all studded with emeralds, and the saddle, designed in another style, was covered with a precious cloth. On the ivory saddlebows was carved the story of Aeneas: how he came from Troy, how Dido welcomed him with great joy to her home in Carthage, how Aeneas deceived her, how she killed herself for him, how Aeneas then conquered Laurentum and all of Lombardy, where he was king the rest of his life. The craftsmanship here was subtle and skilled, and the entire work was set off by fine gold. The Breton sculptor who had designed it labored more than seven years, and during that time he worked on nothing else. I do not know whether he sold it, though he ought to have received a high price for it.

Enide was well recompensed for the loss of her own palfrey since they honored her with the presentation of this palfrey, resplendently harnessed, and she was pleased to mount. The lords and the squires then mounted quickly. For their pleasure and sport, Guivret had taken along with them many falcons and sparrowhawks, reddish-brown goshawks and those trained to hunt cranes, and hunting dogs and greyhounds.

From morning until dusk they rode along the highway more than thirty Welsh leagues, until they arrived before the palisades of a beautiful and strongly fortified town that was totally enclosed by a new wall. Down below in a circle ran deep water, rushing and roaring like a tempest. Erec stopped to look at it, and asked to know if anyone could tell him who indeed was the lord of this town. "Friend," he addressed his good companion, "can you tell me the name of this town and whose it is? Tell me whether it belongs to a count or a king. Since you have brought me here, tell me if you know."

"Sir, I know that well, and I shall tell you the truth about it," he answered. "The town is called Brandigan, and it is so splendid and beautiful that it fears neither king nor emperor. If France, together with the whole kingdom and all who live from here to Liège, set up a siege around it, they would never in their lives capture it, for the island where the town is situated stretches away more than fifteen leagues. Within the enclosure grows everything a strong fortress needs: crops for fruit, wheat, and wine are there, and plenty of woods and rivers too. On no side does the town fear assault, and it is impossible to reduce it to starvation. The town was fortified by King Evrain, who has held it free of duty all the days of his life and will hold it as long as he lives. He had it fortified, not because he feared anyone, but because the town is more beautiful that way. If it had no wall or tower, but only the stream that surrounds it, the town would still be so strong and secure that it would have no fear of anyone."

"God! What magnificence!" Erec exclaimed. "Let us go and see the fortress and take our lodging in the town, for that is where I would dismount."

"Sir, if you don't mind, we should not dismount here. There is a most dangerous ritual in the town," he said, deeply distressed.

"Dangerous? Do you know it?" Erec asked. "Whatever it is, tell us, for I am eager to know."

"Sir," he answered, "I would be afraid you would come to harm there. Your heart has so much boldness and valor, I know, that were I to tell you what I know of the adventure, which is most difficult and dangerous, you would want to proceed there. I have often heard tell that it has been seven years or more since anyone went to the town in quest of the adventure and returned. Proud and courageous knights have come from many lands. Sir, don't regard this matter as a jest. You will not learn this from me unless you swear to me, by the loyalty you have promised me, never to undertake the adventure that no one escapes without disgrace and death."

What Erec now heard satisfied him. He begged Guivret not to be distressed. "Ah, dear friend, let us lodge in the town," he said. "Don't worry. It is time to take shelter for the night. I don't want you to be alarmed, for if some honor should come my way there, you should be very pleased. As for the adventure, I call on you to tell me only the name. You need not worry about the rest."

"Sir, I cannot keep quiet and refuse your desire," he answered. "The name is beautiful to pronounce but difficult to accomplish, for no one may escape from there alive. The name of the adventure, I swear to you, is the Joy of the Court."

"God, there is nothing but good in joy," Erec said. "That is what I seek. Don't despair on my account over this or anything else, dear friend. But let us take our lodging, for great good may befall us as a result. Nothing could prevent me from going to seek the Joy."

"God hear you, sir, that you may find joy there and return without misfortune," he answered. "You have to go there, I see that clearly. Since it cannot be otherwise, let us proceed. Our lodgings are there, for—from what I have heard told and related—no highly esteemed knight can enter this town intending to lodge without being welcomed by King Evrain. So noble and well born is the king that he has had proclaimed to his townsmen, appealing to their love for his person, that their homes not lodge any man of worth from afar so that he himself may do the honor to all worthy men who would stay there."

Then they rode toward the town, passing the wooden barriers and the bridge. As soon as they had gone past the barriers, the inhabitants, who had gathered in great numbers along the road, caught sight of Erec. He was so handsome that they thought and believed, judging by appearances, that all the others were his men. Everyone gazed at him in awe. The whole town was bustling and buzzing with their talk and conversation. Even the maidens who were dancing in rounds stopped singing and waited; all together they looked at Erec and crossed themselves at the sight of his great beauty. Astounding was their heavy lament for him. "Alas! God! Alas!" one said to another. "This knight, passing by here, comes to the Joy of the Court. He will be sorry before his return. No foreigner has ever come to seek the Joy of the Court without meeting shame and disgrace and leaving his head there as forfeit."

Afterwards they shouted out that he might hear their words. "God protect you from misfortune, knight, for you are handsome beyond measure. The reason for our lament is your beauty, for tomorrow we shall see it erased. Tomorrow is set for your death. Tomorrow you shall die, unless God protects and saves you."

Erec heard their words clearly and understood what was being said about him through the town. More than seven thousand were lamenting for him, but nothing could dismay him. Without delay he rode on, greeting in a noble manner all the men and women together, and all the men and women greeted him. Several were sweating anxiously, for they feared, more than he, for his disgrace or his death. Just the sight of his bearing, his great beauty, and his appearance won him all their hearts so that everyone, knights, ladies, and maidens, feared that he would be harmed.

King Evrain heard news that a great company was making its way to his court, preceded by a lord who, judging from his equipment, was at least a count or a king. King Evrain came to meet and welcome them in the street. "Welcome to this company," he said, "to its lord and all his people. Be welcome," he continued, "and dismount."

As they dismounted, there were many to hold their horses and lead them away. King Evrain was not backward when he saw Enide approaching. He at once greeted her and hurried to help her dismount. Taking her soft and beautiful hand, he led her up to his palace, as his noble nature dictated. He treated her with all the honor he could, for he was well versed in the forms of proper behavior and had no foolish or ill intentions. He had a chamber perfumed with incense, myrrh, and aloe. As they entered, all the people complimented King Evrain on its beautiful appearance. Hand in hand they came into the chamber, and as he led them, the king rejoiced in his guests.

But why should I describe in detail for you the silk embroideries that adorned the room? I would waste the time in such folly, and I do not wish to lose the time. Rather, I would hurry along a little, for the man who adheres strictly to the straight road passes the man following the indirect. For this reason I do not wish to stop here.

Since it was time for supper, the king ordered the meal prepared. I do not wish to delay here if I can find a more direct route. That night there was an abundance of everything their hearts and palates desired: fowl, venison, fruit, and several wines. But the fine welcome surpassed everything, for of all dishes, the most agreeable is the fair face and the fine welcome. They were being served amid abundant joy until the moment Erec suddenly stopped eating and drinking and began to recall what was dearest to his heart. He remembered the Joy, and turned the conversation to that subject. King Evrain followed.

"Sir," Erec said, "it is time now that I tell you my thoughts and why I have come here. I have held back too long from speaking. Now I can hide it no longer. I call for the Joy of the Court. There is nothing else I desire so much. Grant it to me whatever it is, if you have the power."

"Dear friend, I clearly hear your foolish words," the king answered. "This is a painful business; it has brought suffering to many a worthy man. If you are not willing to take my advice, you too will meet your end in defeat and death. But if you care to heed me, I would advise you to forgo asking about such a distressing subject wherein you shall never come to success. Talk no more of this. Keep silent about it. You will not show good sense if you fail to follow my advice. That you seek honor and esteem surprises me not at all, but if I were to see you captured, or your body injured, my heart would be deeply distressed. Be certain of this: I have beheld and welcomed many men of worth who sought this Joy. They were never the better for it. Rather, they all perished and died. Before nightfall tomorrow, you may expect the same fate for yourself if you intend to undertake the Joy. It will be yours, but dearly will you pay. This is something you may renounce and forgo if you would act in your own interest. I speak to you in this manner because it would be treachery and evil on my part not to tell you the whole truth."

When Erec heard this, he agreed that the king had counseled him with good reason. But the greater the wonder and the more difficult the adventure, the more he desired it and the greater his concern. "Sir," he said, "I tell you that I find you a man of loyalty and valor. Whatever befalls me later, I cannot blame you for the business I would undertake. Now the question is decided, for I shall never be so cowardly as to renounce anything I have undertaken unless I have done all I can before fleeing the field."

"I knew that well," the king replied. "Against my will you are going to have the Joy you seek. But I deeply fear and despair that you will fare badly. Yet rest assured now, you will have what you desire. If you succeed with joy, you will have won greater honor than any man has ever won. God grant my desire and give you a joyous outcome."

They talked of this all evening long, and when the beds had been prepared, they went to take their sleep.

In the morning at daybreak, Erec awoke and saw the sun and the bright dawn. He rose immediately and dressed. Enide was deeply distraught, much saddened and vexed. During the night she had been sick at heart with concern and fear for her lord, who was intent on placing himself in such peril. Yet since no one could dissuade him from his purpose, he readied himself.

As soon as the king rose, he sent Erec arms to wear, which he himself had put to excellent use. Erec did not refuse them, since his own were worn out, damaged, and in bad condition. Glad to accept the equipment, he had himself armed in the hall. When he was armed, he went all the way down the stairs and found his horse saddled and the king already mounted. Everyone, those in the courtyard and those in the lodgings, prepared to mount. In the entire town, not a person remained who was able to travel. As they started on their way, there was a huge uproar and commotion through all the streets, for everyone, highborn and low, was talking. "Alas! Alas! Knight, this Joy you expect to win has tricked you. It is your grief and your death you go to seek. God's curse on this Joy that has brought so many worthy men to their deaths," everyone said. "On this very day, it will certainly do the worst that ever it has done."

Erec was listening, and heard the people constantly commenting, for everyone was saying, "What a pity for you, dear knight, handsome and proper! It would surely be wrong for your life to end so soon and for you to come to harm, suffering wounds and injuries." Erec heard their words and comments clearly, but still continued on, holding his head high and showing no sign of cowardice. No matter who was talking, he was anxious to see, know, and understand what caused all these people to be frightened, bringing them such pain and anguish.

The king led him outside the town to a nearby garden, and all the people followed, praying God to give his task a joyous outcome. But at the risk of overworking and exhausting my tongue, I must not fail to tell you from the story a fact about the garden.

The garden was surrounded, not by wall or fence but only by air. Through black magic, the garden was enclosed by air on all sides as if it were enclosed by iron, so that nothing could enter there except at one particular entrance. All summer and winter, flowers and ripe fruit were plentiful there. Such a spell was on the fruit that it could be eaten inside but not taken outside. Whoever wanted to carry some outside would never know the way out, for he would not find the exit until he returned the fruit to its place. Among the birds that fly under heaven, charming and delighting men with their joyous song, every single one could be heard there, and there were several of every species. As far as the land stretched, it bore every spice and medicinal herb effective in any kind of treatment, for everything had been planted there and was found in abundance.

Through a narrow entrance, crowds of people came in, the king first and then all the others. His lance in its rest, Erec came riding into the center of the garden, taking great delight in the songs of the birds warbling there. And their songs offered him an advance taste of the Joy, the object of his greatest yearning.

But Erec beheld an astounding spectacle, which could have terrified the most powerful warrior, Thiebaut the Slav as it was then, or of those we now know, Ospinel or Fernagu. Ahead of them on sharpened stakes were bright gleaming helmets, and Erec saw heads visible under each of the metal rims. At the end of the row of stakes, however, he noticed one where there was yet nothing, except a horn. Although he did not know the meaning of this, he was not frightened. On the contrary, he asked the king, who was near him on his right, what this could be. The king explained.

"Friend," the king said to him, "do you know the meaning of what you see here? If you cared for your own life, you would be frightened by this. That one stake that is set apart, where you see that horn hanging, has been waiting for a knight a long time. We do not know for whom, whether it is reserved for you or someone else. Be careful your head is not placed there, for that is the purpose of the stake. I gave you clear warning before you came here. I do not believe you will ever depart unless you are killed and cut to pieces. Now you know this much, that the stake awaits your head. Should your head happen to be placed there, then the moment the stake is raised and set in position, as is provided, another will be planted after that one, which will wait until someone else, I know not who, comes in his turn. I shall tell you nothing more about the horn, except that no one has so far had the ability to sound it. The man who can blow it will surpass all my countrymen in honor and renown. And such honor will be his that everyone will come to pay him homage and hold him to be the best. Now there is nothing more to this business. Have your people draw back, for the Joy will come soon and, I believe, cause you sorrow."

Then King Evrain left him, and Erec leaned over to Enide, who was by his side, deeply grieving. Yet she kept silent, for spoken grief is worthless unless it touches the heart. Erec knew her heart well. "Dear gentle sister," he said to her, "noble lady loyal and wise, well I know all you feel. Your fear is great, I see this well, and still you know not why. You have no cause for dismay until you see my shield battered to pieces, my body wounded, the meshes of my gleaming hauberk covered with my blood, my helmet smashed and broken, and myself defeated and exhausted so that I cannot protect myself any longer but must, against my will, beg and await mercy. It is then that you may express your grief, but now you have begun too soon. Gentle lady, you still do not know what is going to happen any more than I do. You worry about nothing, for you can be absolutely certain that if my bravery were only what your love gives me, I would not fear bodily combat with any man alive. I am a fool to make that boast. Yet I say this not from pride, but only from my desire to comfort you. Take courage and let this be. I cannot stop here any longer. And you will not accompany me farther since, following the king's command, I am not to take you past here."

Then he kissed her, and in turn commended her to God, and she commended him. But it troubled her most painfully not to follow or accompany him until she saw and learned what the adventure would be and how he would acquit himself. She had to stay behind, however, for she could not follow him farther. Filled with sadness and grief, she remained there.

All alone without any company, he rode along a path until he came upon a silver bed, covered with a gold-embroidered quilt, beneath the shade of a sycamore tree. Seated all alone on the bed was a maiden, attractive in face and form, displaying every aspect of beauty. I do not wish to describe her more, but anyone considering her beauty and her attire carefully could truly declare that Lavinia of Laurentum, who was so beautiful and charming, never had a quarter of her beauty. Erec drew near the spot, wishing to look at her more closely, and went to sit beside her.

Then behold an incredibly tall knight, equipped in vermilion arms, came riding under the trees through the garden. Had he not been so disturbingly tall, there would have been under heaven no man more handsome than he. As all the people testified, he was a foot taller than the tallest knights they knew. Before Erec had seen him, the knight shouted out: "Vassal! Vassal! So help me God, you are a fool to approach my young lady. To my mind you are not worthy to draw near her. Today, on my life, you will pay dearly for your folly. Draw back!" Then he stopped and looked at Erec, and the latter stood still.

Neither man moved toward the other until Erec had responded with all he cared to say. "Friend," he said, "a man may speak folly as easily as wisdom. Threaten as much as you please. I am a man who will keep silent, for there is no wisdom in threats. Do you know why? A man thinks he has won the game who later loses it. And so the man who expects too much and threatens too much is obviously a fool. If there is someone who flees, there is always someone to give chase. But I am not so frightened of you that I would flee first. Now if there is someone who wants to engage me in combat so that I would be forced to fight or else be unable to escape, I am ready to defend myself."

"No, so help me God!" he replied. "Know that combat is yours, for I challenge and defy you."

From that moment on, you can be completely certain, they did not restrain their reins. Their lances were not slender, but thick and smooth, and since they were made from very dry wood, they were the stiffer and stronger. The men struck each other's shields so forcefully with the sharp lanceheads that each plunged a fathom deep into the bright shields. But neither reached the other's flesh, and no lance had been broken. As quickly as he could, each man withdrew his lance. They then rode at each other and returned to the match according to the rules. They jousted, and so severe was their attack that both lances broke and their horses fell beneath them. Seated in their saddles, the men sustained no injuries. They got up quickly, for they were valiant and agile. On foot, in the center of the garden, they came at each other immediately with their fine blades of Viennese steel, and dealt such heavy and harmful blows to the bright and shining shields that they smashed them all to pieces and their eyes flashed with fire. They could not exert themselves more in their struggles to harm and injure each other. Fierce were their assaults with the flat sides and the sharp edges of their blades. So much did they hammer away at each other's teeth, cheeks, noses, hands, arms, and, still more, temples, necks, and throats, that all their bones ached. Severe were their sufferings and severe their exhaustion. Yet they did not give up, but struggled more and more. The sweat and the blood flowing down with it hurt their eyes so that they saw hardly anything. Very often they wasted their blows, like men who cannot see to direct their swords. One was scarcely capable of injuring the other, yet never doubt that they failed to employ all their strength. Because their eyes blurred, they lost all sight and let their shields fall, grappling with terrible rage. They pulled and tore at each other so that they fell to their knees. In this position they fought long past three in the afternoon until the tall knight, so exhausted, lost all his wind. Erec led him at will, pulling and dragging him so that he tore all the lacings of his helmet and brought him down at his feet. His opponent fell on his chest, his face toward the ground; he did not have the strength to get up again. Although it must have pained him, he had to speak and concede. "You have defeated me, I cannot deny that, although I am deeply distraught. And yet perhaps you are of such rank and such renown that only honor will come to me from this. If possible, I would beg to know your proper name that I might take some consolation from it. If a man better than I has defeated me, I shall be happy, I swear to you. But I should be deeply distressed to have been defeated by a man less worthy than I."

"Friend, you would know my name," Erec replied, "and I shall tell you before I leave here, though only on condition that you now tell me why you are in this garden. I would know the last word on this. What is your name? And what is the Joy? I am eager to hear this."

"Sir, as you please, I shall not hesitate to tell you the whole truth," he said.

Erec no longer withheld his name. "Did you ever hear of King Lac and his son Erec?" he asked.

"Yes, sir, I knew him well, for I was at King Lac's court for many a day before I was knighted, and if he had had his wish, I would never have had reason to leave him."

"Then you should know me well if you were ever with me at the court of my father the king."

"I swear then, it has turned out well. Now hear who has detained me so long in this garden. However painful it may be for me, I intend to tell everything, as you commanded. That young lady sitting there has loved me since her childhood, and I her. We both were very happy, and the love grew and deepened to the point where she asked me for a favor without naming it. Who would deny his beloved anything? Without the slightest pretense or neglect, a lover does all the will of his beloved if he possibly can. I promised to do her will, and when I had made the agreement with her, she still wanted my oath. If she had wanted more, I would have done more, but she accepted me at my word. I made a promise to her, and I did not know what it was until I was knighted.

"I am King Evrain's nephew. He knighted me, in the presence of many worthy men, here in this garden where we are. My young lady, who is sitting there, immediately called me to my word and declared that I had promised never to leave this place until a knight came and defeated me in armed combat. It was right for me to stay rather than break my promise, which I should never have given.

"From the moment I knew and understood the will of the person I held dearest of all, I had to give the appearance and expression that nothing displeased me, for had she noticed, she would have taken back her heart. I would not have desired that, not for anything that might happen. Thus my young lady expected to detain me a long time, believing the day would never come when a vassal capable of defeating me should enter this garden.

This is why she anticipated no trouble in keeping me imprisoned with her all the days of my life.

"And I would have acted disloyally had I not done everything in my power to defeat all those I could. What a base deed it would have been to make such an escape! I can certainly tell and assure you that I have no friend so dear that I would have overlooked anything in order to defeat him. I was never weary of bearing arms or tired of combat. Surely you noticed the helmets of the men I have defeated and killed. But mine is not the blame for this, if you would consider rightly. I could not avoid doing this unless I wished to be a false and disloyal perjurer.

"I have told you the truth about this matter, and be assured, the honor you have won is not inconsiderable. You have given great joy to the court of my uncle and my friends, for now I shall be released from here. And because those who will come to the court will also rejoice, those who here awaited the joy called it the Joy of the Court. They waited a long time for it to be restored to them, for the first time, by you who did so through your victory. You have bewitched and subdued my valor and my chivalry. And it is surely right that I tell you my name since you would know it. My name is Maboagrain. But I am not known by this name in places where I have been seen, but only in this country, for while I was a page, I never spoke or knew my name.

"Sir, you know the truth about your question, but I still have something to tell you. There is a horn in this garden, which, I believe, you have noticed. I am not to leave here until you sound the horn. Only then will you have released me, and then the Joy will begin. All those who hear the sound will encounter no obstacle in coming to the court the moment they hear the blast of the horn. Rise from here, sir. Go at once and quickly take the horn. You have no reason to wait. Do what you should."

Erec stood up immediately, as did the other at the same time. They both came to the horn. Erec took and sounded it, blowing with all his might so that the sound traveled far and wide. Enide was overjoyed, and the king was happy, and happy were his people. Everyone took great pleasure and satisfaction from Erec's feat. No one rested or left off singing and merry-making. That day Erec could boast that there had never been such rejoicing. That joy could not be described or related by tongue of man; yet I shall briefly tell you the essential details without too many words.

The news flew through the country that the affair had taken place as I have related. Everyone then hastened to the court without delay. People raced there from every direction, some on foot, some on horseback, one not waiting for another. Those who had been in the garden prepared to relieve Erec of his arms, and all of them, vying with one another, sang a song about the Joy. And the ladies composed a lay, which they called the Lay of Joy, although the Lay is hardly known now.

With joy Erec was well feasted and well served to his heart's content. But the lady sitting on the silver bed was not pleased; the joy she witnessed brought her no pleasure. Yet many people are forced to watch and endure what brings them pain.

Enide behaved with the utmost courtesy. Because she saw the young lady sitting alone and deep in thought on the bed, she was minded to go and tell her who she was and what she did, and to inquire if she in turn could tell Enide something about herself, provided the subject did not distress her too much. Intending to go there alone, Enide expected to have no one accompany her. But some of the ladies and maidens, among the most esteemed and beautiful, followed her to show their affection and to offer her company; they also wished to comfort the young lady, for she found the Joy strongly distasteful. Seeing her lover about to leave the garden, she assumed that he would not be with her now as much as he had been. However much she resented his departure, she could not prevent it, for the time and the hour had arrived. This was the reason tears streamed from her eyes down her face. She was sobbing and grieving much more than I am describing to you. Nevertheless she rose, though none of those trying to bring comfort meant enough to her to make her stop lamenting.

Enide, in the manner of a well-educated lady, greeted her. For a long time the young lady was unable to answer a word, prevented, as she was, by the sighs and sobs that shook her and took her breath away. Some time afterwards she returned her greeting. And when she had looked at her and studied her a while, the young lady thought she recognized and knew her from some other occasion, though she was not very certain of this. She was not hesitant to ask Enide where she was from, of what country, and where her lord had been born, asking who they both were.

Enide's reply was immediate and truthful. "I am the niece of the count who holds Laluth in his domain," she said. "I am the daughter of his own sister, and I was born and raised in Laluth."

At that moment the young lady could not stop herself from laughing; she rejoiced so much, even before hearing further words, that she felt no more concern about her grief. Her heart gave in to happiness, and she could not hide her joy. She went to embrace and kiss Enide. "I am your cousin!" she exclaimed. "Know that this is the honest truth. And you are the niece of my father, for he and yours were brothers. But I imagine that you have not heard and do not know how I came into this land. The count, your uncle, was at war. Then knights from many countries came to him to enlist as mercenaries. And so, dear cousin, it happened that with a mercenary came the nephew of the King of Brandigan. For nearly a year he stayed with my father, and that was, I believe, a good twelve years ago. I was still very young, and he was handsome and attractive. It was at this time that we made an accord between us that suited us. Because I never had any wish but his, he began to love me, and so promised and swore to me to bring me here and be forever my lover. This pleased me and him also. He prolonged his stay, and I longed to come here with him. We both came without anyone knowing our plan. At that time you and I were young girls. I have told you the truth. Now tell me, as I have told you, the truth about your lover and by what chance you are his."

"Dear cousin, he married me with the full knowledge of my father and my mother, who were delighted. All our relatives knew and were happy, as they should have been. Even the count himself was happy, for so fine a knight is Erec that no finer could be found. No longer has he need to prove his valor or excellence. No one among those his age has his renown, and I do not believe he has an equal. He loves me very much, and I love him even more, so that our love cannot be greater. Never yet has the force of my love diminished, nor should it. In truth, my lord is a king's son, and yet he took me when I was naked and poor. Through him I am arrayed in greater honor than has ever come to any helpless girl. If it is your pleasure, I shall tell you, without word of lie, how I came to such elevation. I shall never be reluctant to tell the story."

Then she talked to her, telling her how Erec had come to Laluth, for she did not care about keeping anything from her. Omitting no details, she carefully recounted the adventure to her word for word. But I am not going to tell it to you again because the man who recounts the same thing twice lengthens his tale in a tiresome way.

While they conversed together, a lady slipped away by herself and went to tell the story to the barons to increase and heighten the Joy. All her listeners felt happiness together at this Joy. And when Maboagrain knew it, his happiness was greater than that of all the others. His beloved was comforted, and the lady who hastened to him with the news suddenly made him very happy. The king himself was delighted, and if he had shown great joy earlier, his joy now was greater still.

Enide came to her lord, bringing along her cousin, who was more beautiful, more charming, and more graceful than Helen. Immediately Erec and Maboagrain, Guivret and King Evrain hurried to meet them, as did all the others. They welcomed and honored them without reluctance or reserve. Maboagrain rejoiced over Enide, as she too did over him, and both Erec and Guivret rejoiced over the young lady. They displayed their happiness, the men and women, embracing and kissing one another.

They spoke of returning to the town, for they had been in the garden too long. Everyone was ready to leave, and they went out along the way, kissing one another and rejoicing. They all left after the king.

Before the people arrived in the town, the barons from all the surrounding countryside had assembled, and all those who had learned the news of the Joy came there, those who were able to come. Huge was the assembling crowd; everyone, highborn and low, rich and poor, rushed to catch sight of Erec. They took positions one ahead of the other, greeting him and bowing to him. All without cease exclaimed: "God save the man who has caused joy and happiness to return to our court! God save the most blessed man God made the effort to create!"

Thus they escorted him to the court, making every attempt to display their joy as they followed the promptings of their hearts. Harps and viols were playing there, as well as fiddles, psalteries, symphonia, and all the stringed instruments that could be named or mentioned. But I intend to finish this for you briefly without too long a delay.

To the extent of his power the king honored Erec, as did all the others, unreservedly. There was not a person who did not place himself at his service with great goodwill. The Joy lasted three full days before Erec was able to depart. On the fourth day, he had no desire to stay longer despite their entreaties. The people took great delight in escorting him, and the crowd taking leave of him was immense. Had he wished to respond to their individual greetings, he could not have returned them in half a day. He greeted and embraced the barons. In one speech he greeted all the others and commended them to God. And Enide did not remain silent when she took her leave of the barons. She greeted them all by their names, and together they returned her greeting. At the moment of parting, she embraced and kissed her cousin most tenderly. With their departure, the Joy came to its close.

They rode on their way, and the others returned. Erec and Guivret did not delay, but joyfully pursued their route until they came directly to the town where they had been told King Arthur was staying. On the preceding day he had been bled. He had with him in his chambers only five hundred barons of his household. Never before in any season was the king to be found in such solitude, and he was distressed at not having more people at his court.

At that moment a messenger came racing up, whom Erec and Guivret had sent ahead, to announce their coming to the king. Quickly he took the lead before the company, found the king with all his people, and greeted him wisely. "Lord," he said, "I am the messenger from Erec and Guivret the Small." Then he told and related to him that they were coming to see him at his court.

"May they be welcome as brave and valiant barons," the king replied. "Nowhere do I know of men finer than these two. Their presence will enhance my court very much." Then he sent for the queen and told her of the news.

The other men had their horses saddled to go and meet the barons. They were in such haste to mount that they failed to fasten their spurs. I wish to tell you briefly about the crowd of commoners: servant boys, cooks, and butlers had already arrived in the town to prepare the lodgings. The main company arrived later; they had drawn so near that they had already entered the town. Now they had met one another and were exchanging greetings and kisses. They came to their lodgings and made themselves comfortable. After they had undressed, they prepared themselves by putting on their beautiful robes, and when attired, they returned to the court.

The king saw them as they entered the court, as did the queen, who was mad with longing to embrace Erec and Enide. So filled with joy was she that you could almost see her lift off like a bird in flight. Each of them did his utmost to welcome them. After the king asked for silence, he questioned Erec about his adventures. When the din subsided, Erec began his tale, recounting his adventures without forgetting a single one. But do you think I shall tell you what occasioned his departure? Not at all, for you know the truth of that and the rest, as I have placed these matters before you. To recount this again would be difficult for me, for the tale is not so short that anyone would wish me to begin it again and retell the words in their order just as he related the story to them. He told them of the three knights he defeated, then of the five, then of the count who wanted to bring him to such deep disgrace, and then of the giants. He related his adventures to them in their exact order, one after the other, until the point at which he broke the neck of the count, who was seated at dinner, and he told how he recovered his charger.

"Erec, dear friend," said the king, "remain now in this country at my court as you once did."

"Lord, since this is your will, I shall be delighted to stay two or three full years. But do ask Guivret to stay too. And I shall make the same request of him." The king asked Guivret to remain, and he accepted the invitation.

And so both stayed. The king kept them in his company and held them in great honor and affection.

Erec stayed at the court along with Enide and Guivret, all three together, until the death of his father the king, who was an elderly man of many years. Messengers set out at once, barons who were the most highborn men of Erec's land, and went to locate Erec. They searched and made inquiries after him until they found him at Tintagel a week before the Nativity. They related to him the details of his elderly, white-haired father's death and passing. Erec felt much deeper pain than he showed to his people. But sorrow is not proper for a king, nor does it befit a king to display his grief. There at Tintagel where he was staying, Erec had vigils and masses chanted; he made pledges to religious houses and churches, and fulfilled the pledges as he had promised. He properly executed every act required of him. He chose more than one hundred and sixty-nine poor suffering souls and presented them with a complete set of new clothes. To the poor clerics and priests he gave, as was proper, black-hooded cloaks lined with warm fur. Because of his love of God, he performed many good deeds for all. To those in need, he gave more than a barrel of coin.

After he had distributed his wealth, he acted very wisely in taking back his land in fealty from the king. He then asked and entreated the king to crown him at his own court. The king told him to make immediate preparations, for both he and his lady would be crowned on the Nativity, which was fast approaching. "We must go from here to Nantes in Brittany," he said. "The royal insignia will be carried there, the gold crown and the scepter. This is the honor and the gift I present to you." Erec thanked the king and said that he had made him a great gift.

On the Nativity the king assembled all his barons. To each and every one of them he sent the command, and he ordered the ladies to come. He summoned them all, and not one stayed behind. And Erec sent word to a large number of his men, commanding many to come there; more than he expected came to honor and serve him.

I cannot tell or relate to you the identity and name of each. Yet no matter who came or not, Erec did not forget the father of my lady Enide or her mother. Her father was the first to be summoned, and he came to the court in splendid style like a wealthy baron and castellan. His company was composed, not of chaplains or people dumbfounded or stupid, but of fine knights and well-equipped men. Each day they made a very long day's journey. Day after day they rode until, amid great joy and honor, they reached the city of Nantes on the eve of the Nativity. They made no stop anywhere until they entered the great hall. Erec and Enide saw them and at once came to meet them. In welcome they embraced them, addressing them tenderly and rejoicing as they should. After their joyous reunion, all four took one another by the hand and came before the king. At once they greeted him and the queen too, who was seated beside him. Taking his host by the hand, Erec said: "Lord, behold here my fine host and my good friend, who paid me such great honor by making me lord in his household. Before he knew anything of me, he gave me fine and attractive lodgings. He entrusted everything he had to me. Even his own daughter he presented to me without anyone's advice or counsel."

"And, friend, this lady who accompanies him, who is she?" the king asked.

Erec hid nothing from him. "Lord, this lady, I tell you, is the mother of my lady," he answered.

"She is her mother?"

"Yes indeed, lord."

"Then I can certainly attest that beautiful and charming should be the flower issuing from such a beautiful stem and better the fruit picked there, for what comes from a good source has a sweet fragrance. Beautiful is Enide, and beautiful should she be by reason and by right, for a beautiful woman is her mother, and a fine knight has she for her father. She does them no shame, for she is obviously descended from both and inherits a wealth of their traits."

The king finished speaking and remained silent; he asked them to sit down, and not refusing his command, they at once took seats. At that moment Enide was delighted, for she looked on her father and her mother, whom she had not seen in a long while. Great was the increase in her joy. Great indeed was her delight, great indeed her pleasure, and she showed her happiness as much as she could. Yet no matter how much joy she might have displayed, still greater was the joy she felt.

I do not wish to say more about this now, for my heart draws me toward the people who had all assembled there from many different countries. There were many counts and kings, Normans, Bretons, Scots and English. From England and from Cornwall came many powerful barons. From Wales all the way to Anjou, in Germany and in Poitou, no knight of high rank or noble lady of high birth stayed behind. The finest and the most noble were at the court in Nantes where the king had summoned all of them.

Listen now if you will. Before nine that morning, at the full court assembly, King Arthur had four hundred knights and more dubbed, all sons of counts and kings. To each he presented three horses and three sets of robes so that his court would be the more brilliant. Wealthy and generous was the king: he presented cloaks made not of serge or rabbit fur or light wool, but of ermine and samite, of whole fur and dappled silk, bordered with heavy gold embroidery. Alexander, who made so many conquests that the entire world stood at his feet, was very rich and very generous, yet compared to Arthur he was poor and niggardly. Caesar, the Emperor of Rome, and all the kings whose names you hear mentioned in stories and *chansons de geste* did not offer at one celebration as many gifts as King Arthur distributed on the day of Erec's coronation. Neither Caesar nor Alexander together would have dared make such large expenditures as were made at the court.

All the cloaks had been taken from the trunks and scattered everywhere throughout the halls for anyone to take what he desired. On a carpet in the center of the court were thirty large barrels of blanched sterlings, for at that time, and since the time of Merlin, sterlings were current throughout the whole of Brittany. From the barrels everyone took a supply that night, carrying away to his lodging all he wanted.

On Christmas Day, at nine in the morning, the court assembled there. The great joy approaching Erec had ravished his heart. At that moment the mouth or tongue of any man, no matter how versed he might be in the arts, could not capture in detail a third, fourth, or fifth of the ceremony that surrounded Erec's coronation. And so in my wish to attempt its description, I would be embarking on an enterprise of sheer folly. But since I must do it, and this is something feasible, I shall try to relate some of it as best I can.

In the great hall were two new and beautiful white ivory thrones of the same shape and style. There is no question about the great skill and subtlety of their designer, for he made both of them exactly alike in height, width, and decoration. Had you studied the pair from all angles to distinguish between them, you could never have discerned a detail in one lacking in the other. Not a section was made of wood, but everything was gold and pure ivory. With great art they had been sculpted: the two feet on one side represented leopards, the other two crocodiles. A knight named Bruiant of the Isles had presented them as a gift to King Arthur and the queen.

King Arthur was seated on one throne, and he had Erec, wearing a robe of watered silk, sit on the other. In reading the story, we find the description of the robe. To show that I do not lie, I draw upon Macrobius, who understood the story and put all his efforts into it, as my authority. Macrobius teaches me how to describe, just as I have found in the book, the workmanship and the pattern of the cloth.

Four fairies had designed the robe with great skill and mastery. One embroidered the figure of Geometry there: examining and measuring the dimensions of the heavens and the earth, first the depth, then the height, then the width, then the length, so that nothing is missed, and afterwards examining the entire width and depth of the sea, thereby measuring the entire world. This was the design of the first fairy.

The second fairy devoted her efforts to depicting Arithmetic, and worked hard to show clearly how Arithmetic wisely numbers days and hours of time, drops of water in the sea, and then all the grains of sand and the stars one by one. Arithmetic well knows how to tell the truth about this, and how many leaves there are in the forest; she has never been deceived in her numbers, and will never be mistaken in her calculation since she wished to put all her efforts into this. This was the design of Arithmetic.

The third design was that of Music where all pleasures find themselves in harmony: songs and counterpoints, and sounds of string, harp, violin, and viol. This was a beautiful and exquisite design, for in front of Music were depicted all the instruments and all the pleasures.

The fourth fairy, who toiled next, applied herself to a very fine design, for she depicted there the best of the arts. She set her mind to the presentation of Astronomy, who accomplishes so many wonders under the inspiration of the stars, the moon, and the sun. From no other source does Astronomy take advice about anything she may have to do, for on whatever inquiry she makes, their counsel is good and proper, and free of lies and deceptions, about all that was and all that will be.

This was the design figured and woven with gold thread on the cloth of Erec's robe. The fur lining sewn inside came from some strange beasts, which have heads completely blond and necks as black as mulberries, with scarlet backs below, black stomachs, and dark-blue tails. Born in India, such beasts are called berbiolettes and find their only nourishment in fish, cinnamon, and fresh cloves. What more can I tell you of the robe? It was costly, elegant, and beautiful. In the tassels were four stones: two chrysolites on one side and two amethysts on the other, all set in gold.

At that moment Enide had still not entered the palace. When the king noticed her delay, he ordered Gawain to go and escort Enide into the palace. In haste Gawain rushed there along with King Caroduant and the generous King of Galloway. Guivret the Small accompanied him, and Yder, the son of Nut, followed. So many barons hurried there to provide an escort for the ladies that, numbering more than a thousand, they could have destroyed an army.

The queen had put her finest efforts into the adornment of Enide. Into the palace they escorted her, Gawain the courteous on one side and the generous King of Galloway on the other, who cherished her because Erec was his nephew. On their arrival in the palace King Arthur hastened to meet them. He acted nobly in having Enide seated beside Erec, wishing to pay her high honor. He immediately commanded that two large crowns of pure gold be brought from his treasure. After he had given his command, the crowns were brought before him without delay. The crowns glittered with carbuncles, for there were four in each. The light of the moon was nothing compared to the light that the least of the carbuncles could yield. Because of the reflected light, all the people in the palace were so severely dazzled that for a moment they saw nothing. Even the king was astounded. Nevertheless he rejoiced to see the crowns so bright and beautiful. He had one taken by two maidens and the other held by two barons. He then commanded the bishops, the priors, and the abbots of monastic communities to come forward for the anointing of the new king in accordance with Christian law. All the prelates, young and old, stepped forward immediately, for there were many clerics, bishops, and abbots at the court. The Bishop of Nantes himself, who was a distinguished man of great saintliness, carried out the anointing of the new king in a holy and exact and beautiful fashion, and placed the crown on his head.

King Arthur had a most celebrated scepter brought in. Hear how the scepter was made. As large as a fist and adorned with one solid emerald, it was clearer than glass. I dare tell you the truth that in all the world there is no kind of fish, wild beast, man, or flying bird that was not designed and carved on it, each properly represented. The scepter was handed over to the king, who gazed on it with awe. Without further delay, he placed it in the right hand of King Erec, who was, at that moment, king as he ought to be. They then crowned Enide.

The bells now rang for mass. And the people proceeded to the cathedral to hear mass and the service; they went to pray in the cathedral. You would have seen Enide's father and her mother, who was named Tarsenesyde, weeping for joy. That was, in truth, her mother's name, and her father was called Licorant. Both were very happy.

When the people reached the cathedral, all the monks from the church came out to meet them, bearing relics and treasures. Crosses, holy books, censers, and reliquaries containing all the holy relics, of which there were many in the church, were all brought out to welcome them. And there was no scarcity of chants. No one has ever seen together at one mass so many kings, so many counts, so many dukes, and so many barons. The crowds were so huge and dense that the church was completely filled. No commoner could enter, but only knights and ladies. Outside the church door were still more people; so many gathered there that they could not gain entrance to the cathedral.

When the people had heard all the mass, they returned to the castle. Everything was already prepared and set out, the tables in position with tablecloths on top. There were five hundred tables and more. I do not wish to make you believe—the lie would be too obvious—that the tables were placed in rows in one palace hall. My intention is not to say that. No, there were five halls filled with them so that only with great difficulty could a passage be found among the tables. Each table had, in truth, a king, or a duke, or a count, and at each table sat a good hundred knights.

Dressed in fresh ermine tunics, a thousand knights served the bread, a thousand the wine, and a thousand the food. As for the various dishes served, even if I do not enumerate them, I can certainly give you an account. But rather than report the fare, I must attend to something else. The food was so plentiful that the people needed no restraint. With great joy and in great abundance they were served according to their desires.

When the feast ended, the king dismissed the assembly of kings, dukes, and counts, a very large numbering, as well as the commoners and others WHO HAD ATTENDED THE FEAST. BECAUSE OF HIS GREAT NOBILITY AND BECAUSE OF HIS DEEP AFFECTION FOR EREC, HE WAS MOST GENEROUS IN THE GIFTS HE BESTOWED ON HIS PEOPLE: HORSES, ARMS, SILVER, AND MANY VARIETIES OF CLOTHS AND BROCADES. ¶HERE THE TALE ENDS AT LAST.

CLIGES

HE MAN WHO WROTE of Erec and Enide, translated Ovid's *Commandments* and his *Art of Love*, composed *The Shoulder Bite*, and wrote of King Mark and the blonde Iseult, and about the metamorphoses of the hoopoe, the swallow, and the nightingale, takes up a new tale about a Greek youth of the line of King Arthur. But before I tell you about him, you will hear of his father's life, of his family and where he was from. He was so brave and stouthearted that, to win honor and renown, he traveled from Greece to England, which in those days was called Britain. The story I wish to recount to you, we find written down in one of the books in the library of Saint Peter's Cathedral in Beauvais. The fact that the tale was taken from there is evidence of the truth of the account. Hence its greater credibility.

From the books in our possession we know of the deeds of the ancients and of the world as it was in olden days. These books of ours have taught us that Greece once stood preeminent in both chivalry and learning. Then chivalry proceeded to Rome in company with the highest learning. Now they have come into France. God grant that they be sustained here and their stay be so pleasing that the honor that has stopped here in France never depart. God had lent them to the others, for no one ever speaks now of the Greeks or the Romans. Talk of them is over; their burning coals are spent.

Christian begins his tale, as the book recounts to us, with an emperor of great wealth and honor, who governed Greece and Constantinople. His empress was noble and elegant, and by her the emperor had two children. The first son had grown to such an extent before the birth of the second that the elder, had he wished, could have become a knight and held the entire empire under his sway. The first son was called Alexander, the younger Alis. Alexander was their father's name, Tantalis their mother's. For the moment we shall say nothing of the empress Tantalis, the emperor, or Alis. We shall tell you of Alexander, who was so proud and courageous that he did not care to become a knight in his own country. He had heard talk of King Arthur, who reigned at that time, and of the barons who always composed his company; as a consequence, his court was feared and renowned throughout the world. Whatever might occur, whatever the outcome, nothing in the world would stop Alexander from traveling to Britain. But it was proper that he take leave of his father before setting off for Britain and Cornwall. To ask and obtain leave, Alexander, the handsome and the brave, went to speak with the emperor. Now he would tell him of his intentions and plans.

"Dear father," he said, "in order to learn honor and to win fame and renown, I take the liberty of asking a favor of you. I beg you to do it for me. Make no delay if you are to grant me it."

The emperor thought no harm would come from the request. Above all else, he should wish and desire his son's honor. That, he thought, would be a fine achievement. Would it be? Yes, it would be a fine achievement for him to increase his son's honor.

"Dear son," he answered, "I grant you your pleasure. Tell me what you wish me to give you."

Now the young man was delighted with the success of his task, since the favor he desired so much was granted him. "Sire," he said, "do you wish to know what you have promised me? I would like a large share of your gold and your silver and such companions as I choose from your men. The reason for this is my desire to leave your empire. I shall go and present my service to the king who governs Britain that he may knight me. Never in all my life, I promise you, will I wear armor on my face or helmet on my head until King Arthur, if he so deigns, girds me with my sword. I wish to receive arms from no one else."

The emperor responded immediately. "In God's name, dear son, do not speak so. This country and wealthy Constantinople are yours entirely. Since I would present to you so fine a gift, you should not think me niggardly. Tomorrow I shall crown you, and tomorrow you will be a knight. All Greece will be yours, and from our barons you will receive, as you should, homage and oaths. Unwise is the man who refuses this."

Although he heard his father's promise to dub him knight after mass the next morning, the young man asserted that he would show cowardice or bravery in a country other than his own. "If you would act upon my wishes as I requested of you, give me now spotted and grey furs, silks, and fine horses. Before being knighted, I would like to serve King Arthur. I am not yet strong enough to bear arms. Neither entreaty nor flattery could divert me from traveling to the distant land to see the king and his barons, who have such great repute for their courtesy and bravery. Through their laziness, many highborn men lose the great renown that could be theirs were they to travel the world. Rest and renown, in my opinion, are not compatible, for a powerful man who is all the time at rest adds nothing to his renown. Thus the two are divergent and contrary. The man who always hoards and increases his possessions is slave to them. Dear father, provided I have the strength, I intend to devote my work and efforts to winning renown so long as I may."

The emperor undoubtedly felt joy and pain at this request: joy because he realized his son's interest in valor, and pain, on the other hand, because he would be separated from him. But whatever anxiety he felt, he was forced, because of his promise, to grant his son's request, for an emperor must not lie. "Dear son," he said, "since I see you strive for honor, I should not fail to do your pleasure. From my treasures you may take two barges filled with gold and silver. But take care that you be generous."

The young man was now courteous, well behaved, and happy, since his father promised to place his treasures at his disposal. And so his father honored him, and ordered him to give and to spend generously, explaining to him his reason for this. "Dear son," he said, "believe me, generosity is the lady and queen who enhances all virtues. This is not difficult to prove. Where might you find a man, however strong or powerful, who is not shamed to be niggardly? Who has so many other good qualities, with the exception of grace, that generosity will not win him further praise? By herself generosity makes a man worthy, and this cannot be accomplished through high rank, courtesy, knowledge, nobility, possessions, strength, chivalry, valor, lordship, beauty, or anything else. But as the budding rose, fresh and new, is more beautiful than any other flower, so generosity, where she comes, takes her place above all virtues, and multiplies a thousand times the good qualities she finds in a man of valor who proves his worth. There is so much to relate concerning generosity that I cannot tell the half."

The young man had achieved all he sought and requested, since his father had urged him to tell all he desired to have. The empress was saddened to hear talk of the journey her son was to make. But whoever was pained or dispirited by this, or considered it childish behavior, or reproached or praised him, the young man, as quickly as he was able, ordered his ships prepared, for he did not wish to stay longer in his own country. At his command, the ships were loaded that night with meat, bread, and wine.

The ships were loaded in the harbor. When Alexander reached the sandy shore the next morning, he was in high spirits, and his companions were delighted about the journey. The emperor escorted them, as did the empress, who was very sad. In the harbor beside the cliff they found the sailors in the ships. The breeze was calm and peaceful, the wind gentle, the air serene. When Alexander had parted from his father and taken leave of the empress, whose very soul was in grief, he was the first to go from the boat to the ship. His companions were in groups of twos, threes, and fours, vying with him to board immediately. The sail was spread at once, and the boat weighed anchor. Anxious about the young man they saw departing, those on land followed him with their eyes as far as they could see. In order to look longer and better, all went together to climb to the summit of the high ground by the water's edge. From there they watched the cause of their anxiety. For as long as they were still able to see him, they strained, out of their deep concern for the young man, to watch their friend. God bring him to good port, safe from peril and disaster!

They were at sea all of April and part of May. Without serious trouble or peril, they reached the port below Southampton, where they dropped anchor and moored between three and dusk. The young men, unaccustomed to enduring sickness or pain, had stayed so long at sea, which was not healthy for them, that all had turned pale. Even the strongest and the healthiest were weak and exhausted. Nevertheless they were jubilant that they had escaped the sea and reached their destination.

Because of the great suffering they had endured, the men spent the night below Southampton joyously happy. From their inquiries as to whether the king was in England, they learned that he was at Winchester, where they could soon be should they rise early in the morning and take the highway. The young men awakened early and prepared and equipped themselves. When they were ready, they left Southampton and followed the highway until they came to Winchester, where the king was staying.

Before six that morning, the Greeks had reached the court. They dismounted at the foot of the outside staircase. The squires remained below in the courtyard with the horses, and the young men went up the steps to present themselves to the king, the finest who ever was or ever would be in the world.

King Arthur was pleased and happy to see them. But before coming into his presence, they unfastened the cloaks from their necks lest they be considered foolish. Thus without cloaks, they all went before the king. The nobility and beauty of the handsome youths made all the barons stare at them and take them all for sons of counts or kings, as indeed they were. And most handsome were they for their age, noble men both comely and tall in stature. Their clothes were of the same cloth and cut, the same color and appearance. Without counting their lord, there were twelve. I shall tell you nothing of him except that there was none better than he, no one less prideful or more moderate in his behavior. He was most handsome and well shaped as he stood cloakless before the king, and when he knelt before him, all the other men, out of love for him, knelt beside their lord.

Alexander, who had sharpened his tongue to speak wisely and well, greeted the king. "Your Majesty, unless your reputation be false," he said, "since the time God made the first man, no king who placed belief in God has ever been born equal to you in power. Your Majesty, news of your renown spreads quickly, and it has brought me to your court to honor and serve you. If my service is acceptable to you, I would like to stay until I am knighted by no one's hand but your own. Unless knighted by your hand, I will never be named knight. If you like my service enough to wish to knight me, nobly born king, retain me as well as my companions who are present."

The king responded immediately. "Friend," he said, "I do not refuse you or your company. Be welcome, all of you, for you do appear to be, as I think, sons of great men. Where are you from?"

"We are from Greece."

"From Greece?"

"Yes."

"Who is your father?"

"On my word, sir, the emperor."

"And what is your name, dear friend?"

"Alexander was the name given me when I received the salt and chrism of Christian baptism."

"Alexander, dear friend, I am delighted to retain you. That gives me much happiness and pleasure. You did me great honor in coming to my court. I am most anxious to honor you here as the noble, wise, and gentle young men you are. Stand, I command you. You have been on your knees too long. Henceforth be of my court and my trusted men, for you have reached a good port."

The Greeks then rose, happy to be so graciously received by the king. It was good that Alexander had come, for he was in want of nothing he wished, and at the court was no baron of exalted position who did not greet him with a gracious welcome. And Alexander, though not lacking in nobility or valor, was not prideful on this account. He introduced himself to Sir Gawain and the others individually, and endeared himself to each of them. Even Sir Gawain loved him so much that he called him his friend and companion.

At the home of a townsman, the Greeks had taken the finest lodgings available to them in the town. Alexander had brought great possessions from Constantinople. He wished to heed, above all else, the counsel and command of the emperor that his heart be disposed to giving and spending well. To this end he devoted much effort and care. He lived well in his lodgings, giving and spending generously, according to the promptings of his heart and befitting his wealth. The entire court wondered where he had acquired what he spent, for to all he presented valuable horses, which he had brought from his own land. Alexander's fine services won him the love and high esteem of the king, the queen, and the barons.

It was the will of King Arthur at that time to cross over to Brittany. He had all his barons assemble in order to ask and seek their counsel as to whom he might trust to keep England safe and peaceful until his return. On unanimous advice, as I believe, it was entrusted to Count Angres of Windsor, for they still believed that in all the king's land, there was no baron more loyal. The morning after this man assumed governance of the land, King Arthur set out with the queen and her maids-in-waiting. News of the coming of the king and his barons reached Brittany, and there was jubilation among the Bretons.

The only young man to board the ship on which the king was making the crossing was Alexander, and, to be precise, the only maiden was Soredamor, who attended the queen. Scornful of love, Soredamor had never heard tell of a man, whatever the degree of his beauty or valor, his lordship or high position, whom she would care to love. Yet so beautiful and attractive was this man that she should have known about love had she been pleased to pay heed. But she desired never to give it thought.

Now Love would make her suffer. Love was planning to avenge himself well for the haughty pride and imperious disregard she had shown him always. Love had aimed well: with his arrow he pierced her to the heart. Often she grew pale; often she was bathed in sweat. And despite herself she was compelled to fall in love. She could scarcely hold herself from looking at Alexander. She was forced to guard herself against Sir Gawain, her brother. For her haughty pride and her scorn, she bought and paid dearly. Love had heated her a bath that tormented and scalded her painfully. He was kind to her one moment, harmful the next. She desired him one moment, rejected him the next. She accused her eyes of treason. "Eyes, you have betrayed me," she exclaimed. "My heart was once loyal to me. You made it hate me. Now what I see pains me. Pains? No truly, but suits me. And if I see something that pains me, still do I not focus my own eyes? I would have lost all my power, and should esteem myself but little, were I unable to govern them and make them look elsewhere. Thus I shall be able to guard myself against Love's intent to govern me, for the heart does not lament what the eye does not see. If I don't see him, I shall know no pain. Never does he entreat or implore me. Shall I love him if he loves me not? If his beauty entices my eyes, and my eyes heed the call, shall I say that I love him because of this? Not at all, for that would be false. Therefore he has no claim on me, and can make no accusation. One cannot love with the eyes.

"Then what crime have my eyes committed if they look at what I desire? What is their fault? their error? Should I reproach them? No. Then whom? Myself, who holds them under my control. My eyes look at only what brings the heart pleasure and delight. My heart should not desire something that would cause me misery. My own desire causes me pain. Pain? Then I am a fool, since my heart desires that which hurts me. If I can, I should rid myself of desires that torture me. If I can? Fool that I am, what have I said? If I had no power over myself, I might do very little. Does Love expect to guide me along the road that is accustomed to leading others astray? Others he had to place on his path. But I am not his; I have never been, and never will be. I will never accept his friendship."

Thus she argued with herself, one moment full of love, the next full of hate. She hesitated so much that she did not know which course was better to follow. Although she believed she defended herself against Love, defense helped her not. God, if only she knew that Alexander, for his part, was thinking of her! To them equally, Love dispensed the gifts that were their due. His treatment of them was right and just, because each loved and desired the other. Had they known each other's desires, this love would have been unhampered and true, but Alexander did not know her desire, and she did not know the cause of his pain.

The queen, often seeing each of them changing color and turning pale, took notice. Ignorant of the cause, she attributed it only to seasickness

[93]

from the crossing. Had the sea not misled her, she might have seen the true cause. But the sea did trick and deceive her, and so the sea prevented her from seeing their love. They were at sea, and this came from loving: the sickness that gripped them came from love. And of these three [their love, their sickness, and the sea], the queen knew enough only to blame the sea, for the other two made accusations to her against the third, and thanks to that third, the pair guilty of the crime escaped unscathed. One not guilty of fault or error often pays dearly for another's sin. And so the queen reproached the sea with bitter recriminations, though she was wrong to blame the sea, for it had done nothing wrong.

Until the ship reached port, Soredamor was heavily burdened. As for the king, it was well known to him that the Bretons were jubilant about his arrival, and delighted to serve him as their rightful lord. At this moment I wish to speak no further of King Arthur. No, you will now hear me speak of Love, how he had waged battle against the two lovers and now tormented them.

Although Alexander loved and desired the one sighing from love for him, he did not and would not know of this until he had suffered much pain and anxiety on her account. Out of love for the maiden, he served the queen and her maids-in-waiting, yet dared not address or speak to her who came to his mind most often. Had she dared claim the right over him that she believed hers, she would gladly have made it known to him; yet she dared not, nor would it have been proper to do so. The fact that each saw the other and could not speak or act distressed them very much. And the burning intensity of their love grew. But it is the custom of all lovers, if they can do no better, to nourish their eyes gladly with gazing, and, because the origin and source of their love delights them, they assume that gazing should aid them, though in truth it injures them. In like manner the man who draws near the fire burns himself more than he who stands back from it.

Their love increased and grew. But, embarrassed in each other's presence, they couched and concealed their love so that neither flame nor smoke appeared from the coals beneath the ashes. There was no less heat because of this; rather, the heat sustained itself longer beneath the ashes than above them. The two, deeply distressed, were forced to deceive all the people with false appearances lest anyone recognize them or notice their laments. But heavy were the laments each made at night in solitude.

I shall tell you first of Alexander, how he lamented and complained. Love brought to his mind the young lady for whom he felt such severe pain, for she had stolen his heart and robbed him of sleep. Alexander took such delight in remembering her beauty and her bearing, yet had no hope that some kindness from her should ever come his way.

"I may consider myself a fool," he said. "A fool? Truly I am a fool, for I dare not speak my mind, aware that matters would soon worsen for me. I have fixed my mind on folly, and so must take wiser thought lest I be called a fool. Will my desire never be known? Shall I conceal the cause of my pain completely and not know how to seek help or aid for my sorrow? He is a fool who, feeling sick, does not seek help or health if somewhere he can find them. But such a man expects to profit, procuring his desire by pursuing the source of his suffering. And since he does not expect to find it, why should he go and seek advice? He would labor in vain.

"I feel my sickness too severe ever to be healed by medicine or potion, herb or root. Not every sickness has a remedy. Mine is rooted so deeply that it cannot be cured. Cannot? I think I have lied. The first moment I felt this sickness, had I dared disclose it, I might have spoken to the physician empowered to restore me completely. But it is most painful for me to speak out. Perhaps she would not deign to hear me, or be loath to accept any fee. Therefore it is no wonder that I am worried, for I am very ill. And yet I don't know what sickness overpowers me, nor whence my pain has come. Do I not know? Yes indeed, I believe I know. Love has brought this sickness on me. Then can Love do harm? Is he not kind and nobly born? I once thought there was nothing but good in Love, yet I have discovered him to be very wicked. The man with no experience of Love does not know what jests command Love's attention. He who enlists in Love's company is a fool, for Love always desires to harm his followers. I swear, his jests are not good. Playing with him is dangerous. I believe he will harm me. What then shall I do? Shall I draw back? I think that wise, though I don't know how to do it. If Love chastises and threatens me in order to teach and instruct me, am I to scorn my master? He who scorns his master is a fool. I ought to keep and retain the teachings and instructions love gives me. They might bring me great happiness.

"But Love batters me too much, and I am frightened. No blow or wound is ever visible, yet I complain. Am I not mistaken? Not at all, for he has dealt me so fierce a wound, thrusting his arrow into my very heart, but not withdrawing it.

"Then how has Love penetrated your body when no wound is visible on the surface? Tell me this. I wish to know. How did he strike you? Through the eye. Through the eye? Then did he not put out your eye? My eye received no injury, but the severe pain is in my heart. Then tell me now how the arrow passed through the eye without wound or tear. If the arrow entered through the eye, why does the heart inside the breast complain when the eye, first struck, suffered no pain?

"I can suggest a reason. The eye does not concern itself with understanding, nor is it able to do anything of the like. But it is the mirror of the heart, and through this mirror passes, without wound or tear, the feeling that inflames the heart. And so the heart is placed in the breast like a lighted candle within a lantern. If you remove the candle, light will never shine forth. But so long as the candle endures, the lantern is not dark, and the light shining within does it no harm or injury. The same is true of a glass pane: however thick or solid it might be, the sun's ray passing through it would never shatter it, and the glass would never have such clarity that another light striking there would not enhance the vision of its own brightness. The eyes are the same, be certain, as the glass and the lantern, for the light strikes the eyes where the heart watches and gazes on whatever outside form. And the heart sees many different forms, some green, others purple, one vermilion, another blue. It blames one and praises another, considering one worthless, another dear. But when seen in a mirror, a certain object presents to the heart a beautiful appearance, and, unless on guard, the heart is deceived.

"These objects have deceived me, my eyes, and myself, for in the mirror my heart saw a ray that struck me and lodged within. Through it my heart tricked me. I am poorly treated by my friend, who deserted me for my enemy. Because of its dire crimes against me, I may charge it with treason. I once believed that I had three friends, my heart and my two eyes, but it seems to me that they despise me. Alas, God, where are my friends henceforth, since these three are my enemies? They belong to me, yet they murder me. My servants mock me, acting according to their own will and paying no attention to mine. By those who have wronged me, I now realize that a noble lord's love perishes because of wicked servants in his employ. The man who has a wicked servant in his company, whatever may come, cannot help but lament sooner or later.

"Now I shall tell you about the shape and cut of the arrow that has been entrusted to my safekeeping. The shape of the arrow is so magnificent that I fear failing in this endeavor, and should I fail, it is no wonder. Still I shall devote all my efforts to stating what I believe. The shaft and the feathers are so close together that careful examination reveals only a slight line of separation, like a narrow part in the hair. The shaft is so smooth and straight that, without question, the arrangement needs no improvement. The feathers are colored as if completely gilded, but the color was not made by gilding, for the feathers, be certain, were by nature brighter than any gilded object. The feathers are the golden tresses I beheld at sea the other day. This is the arrow that causes me to love. God, what a precious possession! Why would the man who could have such a treasure covet any other wealth in his lifetime? As for me, I could swear I would desire nothing more. Not even for Antioch would I exchange the shaft and the feathers. And since I place such high value on these two objects—who could estimate their value?—what is the rest worth? It is so beautiful and so becoming, so fine and so precious that I am eager and anxious to gaze on myself again in that countenance. God made it so clear that no mirror, emerald, or topaz would enhance it.

"But all this still remains as nothing to those who gaze on the brightness of the eyes, for, to all who look on them, they seem a pair of burning candles. Whose tongue is alert enough to describe the face, the well-shaped nose, and the bright cheeks, where the rose eclipses the lily, outshining the lily in order to light up the face? And can it describe the small smiling mouth so knowingly fashioned by God that none would see it without thinking she was smiling? And what of the teeth inside the mouth? So close together are they that they seem to be all of a piece, and that they might better achieve this effect, Nature exercised a little further care there: anyone seeing the small mouth open would never declare that the teeth were not fashioned of silver or ivory. So much is there to recount in depicting each part of the ears and the chin that it would be no great wonder were I to overlook some detail. Of the mouth I say only that beside it crystal is clouded. The neck beneath the tresses is eight times whiter than ivory. And what I saw of her bare bosom, from the base of her neck to the brooch fastening her chemise, was more white than new-fallen snow. I would certainly have found relief for my pain had I seen the whole of the arrow.

"Were I able, I would be delighted to describe the shaft, but I did not see it. I am not to blame if I cannot describe the form of something I have not seen. At that time Love showed me only the notch and the feathers. The remainder of the shaft was placed in the quiver, that is, inside the dress and chemise the maiden wore.

"On my word, this is the sickness that kills me: this is the arrow, this the ray. I would be too base were I enraged over it. In rising to anger, I behave like a churl. Never will provocation or war break any engagement I should seek with Love. Now let him do all his will with me, as he should do with one who is his, for this is my desire and my pleasure. I request only that this sickness not leave me. I would rather be in its grip always than receive health from anyone, unless health comes from the source of my sickness."

Although Alexander's lament was long, the maiden's was not more brief. Deep anxiety prevented her sleep or rest all the night. Love had locked a furious debate inside her heart that disturbed her mind and beset her with such torment that she lamented and wept the whole night long. After so much sobbing and suffering, moaning and sighing and starting up, she gazed into her heart to see the true nature of the man for whom Love tortured her. And after taking comfort in thoughts pleasing to her, she stretched out, turning and tossing again. In her mind she ridiculed all thoughts she had come to, beginning once more another discussion with herself.

"Fool that I am," she said, "what does it matter to me if this youth is nobly born, and generous, and courteous, and brave? All this is to his honor and credit. And as for his beauty, what do I care? Let his beauty go off with him, and so it will, for all I may do. I have no intention of depriving him of any. Depriving? No indeed, that is not my wish. Had he Solomon's wisdom, and had Nature presented to him all the beauty it could bestow on a human body, I, had God given me the power to destroy it completely, would not set out to anger the young man. But were I able, I would be glad to make him wiser and more handsome.

"On my word, I hate him not one whit. And because of this, am I his beloved? No, no more than I am someone else's. Then why do I think on him if he does not please me more than another? I don't know. I am confused completely. For I have never given so much thought to any man alive. Had I my wish, I would gaze on him always. Seeing him delights me so much that I would never wish to take my eyes from him. Is this love? Yes, I so believe. I would never recall him so often unless I loved him more than another. Now I am in love with him. Now let that be granted.

"And so I shall indeed acquiesce in my desire, provided he not be displeased. This is an ill desire, but Love persists in such hatred toward me that I am confounded and foolish; resistance aids me not; I must submit to his assault. For a long while I protected myself from him so prudently that never did I wish to do anything for him. But now I am too gracious toward him. And what thanks should he know from me since he cannot have my service or kindness through affection? By force he has subdued my pride, and I must be at his mercy.

"Now I wish to love. Now I have a master. Now Love will be my teacher. And what will be his teaching? How I must serve him. Here I am well instructed: I am well informed, for none could find fault with me. There is nothing more I need to learn. Love would like—and this is my wish too— that I be wise and humble, gracious and welcoming in speech, kind to all on account of one alone. Shall I love all because of one? I must show a fair expression to all, though Love does not teach me to be a true friend to all. Love teaches me nothing but good.

"Not for nothing am I called by this name Soredamor. I must love, I must be loved, and I intend to find proof of this in my name, for in my name I should find love. It is not without meaning that the first part of my name contains the color gold, and the most golden are the finest objects. I therefore value my name the more because my name contains the color that accords with the finest gold. And the end of my name reminds me of love, for whoever calls me by my proper name always makes me think of love. One half gilds the other with a bright golden radiance. Soredamor thus means the same as gilded with love. Gilding with gold is not so pure as that which enhances me. Thus Love has honored me highly by gilding me with himself. And I shall lay my cares in him that I may be his gilding, and never shall I complain.

"I love now and will love always. Whom? Truly that is a fine question. Him whom Love commands me to, for another will never have my love. What does it matter, since he will not know of it unless I tell him myself? What should I do unless I entreat him? One who wants something ought indeed to ask and beg for it. What? Then shall I beg him? No. Why not? No woman, unless she was uncommonly senseless, has ever made such a mistake as to ask a man's love. I would be found guilty of madness were I to make an utterance that would bring me reproach. When the man learned of my words, I believe he would consider me the cheaper for them and reproach me for first asking him. May Love never be so debased that I become the first to ask. For this he should cherish me the more.

"God, how could he know of it since I shall never tell him? Thus far I have not suffered enough to be desolate. I shall wait until he becomes aware, for I shall never make him know. He will certainly be able to notice for himself, if ever he experienced love or learned it from people's talk. Learned? Now I have spoken nonsense. Love is not so openly gracious that talk instructs a man, unless good experience accompanies it. I realize this from my own experience, for I could never learn of love through people's talk or flattering words. Although I have attended Love's school and often been the subject of his attentions, I stood always aloof. He makes me pay so dearly for my behavior that I now know more of loving than does an ox of plowing.

"But there is one thing that makes me despair—perhaps he never loved. And if he is not in love and has not been in love, then I have been sowing on the sea where a seed can take no more root than it would in ashes. Now there is but suffering until I see if I can lead him on with appearances and veiled references. I shall do this until he knows of my love, if he dares ask for it. Therefore all that matters is that I love him and am his. If he does not love me, I will love him."

Thus the two lamented, concealing their feelings from each other. Their days were ill, their nights worse. For a long time, as I believe, such was their anguish in Brittany until the coming of summer's end.

At the very beginning of October, a message came from London and from Canterbury, by way of Dover, with disturbing news for the king. The messengers informed him that he perhaps stayed too long in Brittany; the man he had entrusted with his land was planning to challenge him; he had already summoned a large army of his friends and men of his land and stationed himself inside London in order to defend the city when the king should come.

When the king heard the news, he was angry and resentful. He summoned all his barons, and then, that they might better execute his will to destroy the traitor, declared that theirs was the blame for his hardship and war; it was on their advice that he had entrusted his land to a scoundrel worse than Ganelon. Not a single one failed to recognize that the king's statement was right and proper, for such had been their counsel. But the scoundrel would be destroyed, they asserted, and the king could be certain that no castle or city would have the power to prevent his body from being dragged out by force. These were the assurances all offered the king, pledging solemn oaths to hand over the traitor to him or never again to hold land from him.

The king had it proclaimed throughout Brittany that no man in the host capable of bearing arms was to remain there, or fail to follow him at once. All Brittany stirred. Such an army as King Arthur assembled had never been seen. When the ships moved out, the entire world appeared to be at sea; not even the waves were visible, the ships having blanketed them. War would be a certainty. From the commotion at sea, all Brittany appeared to set out.

By now the ships had all made the crossing, and the men who had assembled took their quarters along the shore. Alexander was minded to go and ask the king to make him knight, for if ever he should win renown, he would win it in this land. Anxious that his wish be realized, he took his companions with him and went off to the king's tent.

The king was standing in front of his tent. When he saw the Greeks approaching, he called them before him. "Gentle sirs," he said, "keep not from me the business that brought you here."

Speaking for all of them, Alexander told him his wish. "On behalf of my companions and myself," he said, "I have come to ask you, as I should ask my lord, to make us knights."

"Most gladly and without delay, since this is your request of me," answered the king.

The king then ordered equipment fetched for thirteen knights. The king's command was carried out: each man asked for his own equipment, and the king presented this to each, a fine horse and excellent arms. And each took his equipment. The arms, apparel, and horses for all twelve were valuable, yet the equipment for Alexander's person was worth, if any wished to evaluate or to sell it, exactly as much as the other twelve together.

The men took off their clothing at the seashore, and washed and bathed. Not wishing or even caring that a bath be heated for them, they made the sea their bath and tub.

Far from hating Alexander, the queen loved him very much and esteemed and praised him. When she learned his request, she wished to do him a fine service. (Much greater was it than she imagined.) Searching and emptying all her chests, she pulled out a finely made white silk shirt that was most delicate and soft. In the seams there was not a thread that was not of gold, or at least of silver. On several occasions Soredamor had put her hands to the stitching, slipping alongside the gold a strand of her own hair in the two sleeves and in the collar, in order to ascertain and know if a man could ever be found who was able, on close examination, to distinguish one from the other, for the hair was as bright and golden as the gold itself—or more so.

The queen took the shirt and sent it to Alexander. God, how ecstatic Alexander might have been had he known what the queen sent him! And she who had placed her hair there would have been ecstatic too had she known that her beloved was to own and wear the shirt. She should have been delighted, for she loved the strands of hair in Alexander's possession more than all the rest of her hair. But about this each was ignorant, and for them their ignorance was a heavy hardship.

The messenger from the queen came to the harbor where the young men were washing. Finding Alexander on the beach, he presented to him the shirt. The youth was most pleased, cherishing it the more because it came from the queen. Yet had he known the rest, he would have loved it still more; not for the entire world, had it been offered him, would he have exchanged the shirt.

Delaying no longer, Alexander dressed at once. When armed and outfitted, he returned to the king's tent, along with all his companions. Interested in seeing the arrival of the new knights, the queen, as I believe, had come to the tent to be seated. Although they all might be called handsome, with his comely body Alexander was the most handsome.

Now they are knights, and I say nothing more about them. Henceforth I shall speak of the king and the army that came to London. Most of the people remained loyal to him, and a large number gathered to meet him. With gifts and promises, Count Angres assembled all the people he could win to his side. After gathering his men, he fled away secretly by night, for, hated by several, he feared betrayal. But before fleeing, he took from London as much gold, silver, and provisions as he could and distributed them to all his men.

The news was reported to the king that the traitor had fled with all his forces, taking so much food and supplies from the city that the poor towns-people were destitute and distraught. In response the king declared that he would never take ransom for the traitor, but would hang him, could he but capture and hold him.

The entire army moved immediately, journeying until the men reached Windsor. However the castle stands now, it was in those days not easily taken, were any intent on its defense. The traitor had plotted his treachery, having the walls buttressed from behind with pointed stakes so that cata-pults would not topple them, and surrounding the castle with double walls and moats. The enclosure had put him to great expense. He spent all June, July, and August building the palisades, moats, and drawbridges, the trenches, obstructions, and barriers, iron portcullises, and a tall tower keep made from quarried stones. Never, from fear of assault, had the gateway been closed.

The castle stood on a high hill overlooking the Thames. Stationed along the river, the army had time remaining that day only to find a suitable place and pitch their tents. The army set up their quarters along the Thames, the entire meadow becoming a campsite of green tents and crimson. The sun struck the colors, and the river glittered for more than an entire league.

Those from the castle had come out to disport themselves along the gravel bank, bearing no other arms but the lances in their hands and the shields clutched close against their chests. Because they had come un-armed, they appeared to show those outside that they stood in no fear of them.

From the other bank Alexander noticed, across from his men, knights engaging in feats of arms. Eager to join them in combat, he summoned his companions by name, one after the other: first Cornix, whom he loved very much; after him Acorde the Insolent; then Nebunal of Mycene; Acoriondes of Athens; Ferolin of Salonica; Charquedon from the African regions; Parmenides; Franchegel; Tor the Strong; Pinabel; Nerius; and Neriolis.

"Sirs," he said, "I long to go and meet with shield and lance those who come to joust before me. I clearly see that they consider me a coward, and I believe they esteem us but little since they have come here all unarmed to joust before our very faces. We have just now been dubbed knights. We have as yet dealt no blow to knight or quintain. Too long have we kept our fresh lances intact. Why were our shields made? They have yet to be punctured or broken. They have no value but in assault or combat. Let us cross the ford. Let us attack them."

"We will not fail you," they exclaimed.

And each proclaimed: "So help me God, the man not at your side is no friend of yours."

At once they fastened their swords, saddled and bridled their horses, mounted and took their shields. When they had hung their shields from their necks and taken the lances that were painted in quarters, all galloped immediately to the ford. The men on the opposite bank lowered their lances and raced to strike them. The others knew how to requite them, not avoiding or sparing them, nor yielding them a single foot of ground, but each dealing his foe such a powerful blow that every knight, however fine, was forced to vacate his saddle. Not regarding their opponents as boys, cowards, or fools, the Greeks did not waste their initial blows, for they unhorsed thirteen.

From their blows and the strokes of their swords the cry went up in the host. There would soon have been an excellent fray had the others dared await them. Throughout the camp, the Greeks ran to take up arms. Then, with a great din, they hurled themselves at the enemy. The latter all took to flight, seeing no point in remaining there. The Greeks followed them, striking with lances and swords and beheading many. To Alexander belonged the honor: he led away four knights bound to his person as prisoners. And the dead lay abandoned, for many were maimed, wounded, or beheaded.

As an act of courtesy, Alexander presented to the queen his prisoners, the first glory of his knighthood. He did not wish anyone else to have possession of them, for the king would soon have had them hanged. The queen had them taken and imprisoned, befitting those charged with treason. But the queen's action did not please the king, who immediately commanded her to come and speak with him, and not to detain the traitors herself. She would be compelled to surrender them or else keep them against his will. The queen came to the king, and, as they should, they held their discussion about the traitors.

All the Greeks stayed behind with the young ladies in the queen's tent. Although the twelve had much to say to them, Alexander did not utter a word. Seated close to him, Soredamor focused her attention on him; she had placed her hand by her side and appeared deep in thought. For long they sat in this manner until Soredamor noticed the hair she had stitched into the seams of his sleeves and collar. She drew a little nearer, now having a pretext for speaking to him. But not knowing how to begin, she took thought with herself.

"What shall I say first?" she asked. "Shall I call him by his name or shall I call him beloved? Beloved? Not I. Then how? Call him by his name! God, the word *beloved* is ever so beautiful and sweet to say. If I dared call him beloved . . . dared? What stops me from doing this? The fact that I might lie. Lie? I don't know what will be, but I shall be sorry if I lie. Therefore it is best that my words accord with my thoughts, for I have no desire to lie. God, he would not lie if he called me his sweetheart. And would I lie if I said this of him? We both should speak the truth, and if I lie, his will be the wrong.

"But why is his name so difficult for me that I want to give him his true title? It seems to me his name has too many letters, and I would stop in the very middle. But if I called him beloved, I would pronounce this entire name with ease. For fear of stumbling on the other name, I would shed my own blood to have his name be 'my sweetheart.' "

She pondered still these thoughts until the queen returned from the king, who had summoned her. Seeing her approaching, Alexander went to meet her and asked her what the king commanded done with the prisoners, and what would happen to them. "Friend," she said, "he asks me to yield them to his will that he may exercise his justice over them. He is most angered that I have not already handed them over to him. I must send them to him. His will is to have them close by him." Thus they spent that day.

The next morning the good knights, the loyal ones, assembled before the royal tent to render just judgment on the form of punishment and torture by which the four traitors would die. Some proposed that they be flayed, others that they be hanged or burned. The king himself judged that the traitors should be drawn. He then commanded them brought in. After they were led in, he had them bound and declared that they would be drawn all around the castle in sight of those within.

When the words ended, the king, whose will it was that they be killed, went to the royal pavilion and had Alexander summoned. Calling him his dear friend, he said: "Friend, what a splendid assault and defense I observed you execute yesterday. For this I should reward you. To your forces I add five hundred Welsh knights and one thousand men-at-arms. When I have ended my war, in addition to what I have presented you, I shall have you crowned king of the finest kingdom in Wales. In the meantime, I shall present to you cities and towns, castles and halls that will be yours until the land belonging to your father is handed over to you. Of that territory you are to be emperor."

Alexander expressed his sincere gratitude to the king for his gift, and his companions offered their thanks. All the barons of the court declared well deserved the honor the king designed for Alexander. When Alexander beheld his men, his companions and his men-at-arms, such as the king wished to present to him, he ordered horns and trumpets sounded throughout the camp. Good and bad alike, all took up their arms, men from Wales and Brittany, from Scotland and Cornwall, for strong army reinforcements had come from all directions.

Because there had been no rain all summer, the Thames was at a low level. The drought was so extensive that the fish in the river had died and the ships in the harbor were drydocked. It was possible, therefore, to ford the river at its shallowest point.

The army had crossed the Thames. Some troops occupied the low-lying ground, others climbed the slope. Those inside the castle, seeing the army's wondrous approach with forces prepared to capture and destroy the castle, placed themselves in readiness for defense.

Before any assault was made, the king ordered the traitors drawn by four horses around the castle, through valleys, over small hills, and across fallow fields. Count Angres was deeply pained to see those dear to him drawn before his eyes, and his other men were most dismayed at the sight. But despite their dismay, they had no intention of surrender. Because the king had openly displayed to all his resentment and his anger, they were forced to defend themselves, realizing that if he captured them, he would make them suffer a shameful death.

After the prisoners had been drawn and their limbs lay across the countryside, the assault began. But all efforts were wasted: no matter how strenuously the troops threw and hurled their missiles, it was impossible for the men to accomplish anything. Still they tried arduously, throwing and hurling a shower of bolts, javelins, and arrows. Crossbows and slings made a huge commotion everywhere. Arrows and round stones flew in thick profusion like rain mixed with hail. In this manner they struggled all day long, one side defending, the other attacking, until night separated them.

On his side, the king had proclaimed and made known in the camp the gift he would offer the man who captured the castle. "I will present to him a most valuable gold cup weighing fifteen marks, the most magnificent one in my treasure. The cup will be most beautiful and precious, and anyone who admires cups ought to prize it still more for the workmanship than for the material, for the workmanship on the cup is superb. To tell the truth, the jewels on the outside are more valuable than the workmanship or the gold. If a man-at-arms captures the castle, the cup will be his. And if a knight does the capturing, he will be given the cup as well as any reward he asks, provided it be found on earth."

After the proclamation, Alexander had not neglected his nightly practice of going to see the queen, and had gone there again that night. Alexander and the queen were seated beside each other. Soredamor, sitting by herself quite close in front of them, was so glad to gaze on him that she would not have wished to be in paradise. The queen took hold of Alexander's right hand and examined the gold thread, which had lost its luster. (The strand of hair became more radiant while the gold thread grew dull.) She laughed when she happened to recall that Soredamor had done this piece of stitching. Noticing her laughter, Alexander asked her to tell him the reason, if it might be told. Hesitant to answer, the queen looked toward Soredamor and summoned her. Soredamor was glad to go, and knelt down before her. Alexander was delighted to see her approaching so near that he might have touched her. He was not so bold, however, to dare even to look on her; rather, he was so disconcerted that he almost became dumb. And for her part, she was so taken aback that she did not know what to do with her eyes, but fixed her gaze on the ground, not focusing on anything.

The queen was astonished to see the young lady at one moment pale, the next blushing, and in her mind carefully pondered the bearing and the manner of each, and of the pair together. Judging by the changes in color, she perceived clearly and, as she believed, accurately that these were symptoms of love. But not wishing to cause the couple anguish, she pretended to know nothing of what she saw. She, as she should, acted well, giving no look or suggestion, except that she did speak with the maiden. "Young lady, look at this, and tell where this knight's shirt was sewn. Hold nothing back."

The maiden, though burning with anger and embarrassment, willingly told them, for she wanted him to hear the truth. When she described for the queen how the shirt was made, the hearing of her words filled him with such joy that he scarcely held himself from bowing and adoring the small strand of hair he beheld. The queen and his own companions there caused him much annoyance and discomfort, their presence preventing him from touching the shirt to his eyes and his mouth, where he would have most eagerly placed it had he thought he would be unnoticed. He was pleased to possess this much of his beloved, never expecting or believing to have any other possession of hers. His desire filled him with fear, yet when by himself in his happiness, he kissed the strand of hair more than a hundred thousand times. All night he took great joy from it, making certain, however, that no one saw him. When he lay in his bed, he took comfort, pleasure, and delight in an object incapable of offering delight. All night he held the shirt in his arms, and when he gazed on the strand of hair, he thought himself lord of the entire world. Love indeed made a wise man a fool, for the knight rejoiced over a strand of hair. Yet love would trade this pleasure for another. At that time, such was Alexander's joy and delight.

Before the bright dawn and sunlight, the traitors held council to decide what could be done and what would happen. They had the strength to defend the castle a long time (that was a certainty), were they to expend great efforts in the defense. But they knew that the king had such fierce determination that, as long as he lived, he would not turn back until the castle was captured, and there they would be forced to their deaths. Even if they surrendered the castle, they could expect no mercy for their act. So their two alternatives were equally bleak. They finally reached the decision to steal from the castle the next morning before dawn and come upon the unarmed host by surprise while the knights were still asleep in their beds. Before these men awakened, readied themselves, and armed, they would have caused such a massacre that this night's slaughter would be recounted forever. With no hope for their lives, all the traitors clung defiantly to this plan. Despair over the outcome emboldened them for the battle, which they regarded as their only resort other than imprisonment or death. Such a resort was not favorable, and no effort could provide them with a solution. Moreover, they saw no place where they might find safety in flight: the river and their enemies were all around them, and they themselves in the middle.

Spending no more time in deliberation, they made ready at once and armed themselves. They then came out through an old postern gate toward the northwest, issuing forth in close ranks. Their men split into detachments, each with a thousand knights and at least two thousand men-at-arms well equipped for battle.

That night neither the stars nor the moon had shone in the sky. But before the men reached the tents, the moon began to rise. And I believe that it rose earlier than usual to vex them, and that God, wishing to do them harm, lit up the dark night. God had no care for their host, hating them for the sin they had committed, for He hates traitors and treason more than any other wrong. He commanded the moon to shine that it should do them harm. The moon proved most injurious to them by reflecting on their glittering shields, and their helmets too were a major handicap in their reflection of the moonlight. As a consequence, the sentries charged with keeping watch over the camp sighted them and shouted throughout the host: "Up, knights, up! Rise quickly! Take up your arms! Arm yourselves! The traitors come upon us!" Through the camp men sprang to arms, struggling hard to equip themselves as men must in such a crisis. Not a single one moved forward until all had time to be armed; then all mounted their horses.

While the host armed, the other side, eager for battle, hurried ahead to take them by surprise, coming upon them before they had equipped themselves. They saw their own men, whom they had divided into detachments, advancing in five directions. The first company held its way beside the woods, the second came along the riverbank, the third entered the forest, the fourth was in a valley, and the fifth battalion spurred down alongside the rockhewn entrance ramp, expecting to fall upon the tents impetuously and easily. But they had not found the road and passageway unimpeded, for the royal forces opposed them, defiantly challenging them and charging them with treason.

Both sides attacked with their lanceheads, falling upon one another as savagely—or indeed more so—as lions falling upon their prey and devouring whatever they take. In this first attack, to be honest, the number of dead on both sides was very large. But help arrived for the traitors, who were defending themselves fiercely, selling their lives at a dear price. When they could hold out no longer, they saw their battalions coming to their rescue on four sides. And the royal forces rushed at them as fast as they could spur, delivering such blows to their shields that they overthrew more than five hundred, not to mention the wounded.

The Greeks did not spare their opponents, nor was Alexander idle, for he put all his strength into his attacks. He rode into the thickest of the fray to strike a good-for-nothing whose resistance was worth not a button; his victim's shield and hauberk were worth not a piece of dark-blue silk. When he finished with this man, he offered his service to another without wasting or losing it: he dealt him such a fast and cruel blow that he drove the soul from his body and the house remained behind without tenant. After these two, he made the acquaintance of a third, a knight of nobility and valor, striking him through his sides with such force that blood ran out the other side of the wound and the soul, breathing its last, took leave of his body.

Alexander killed many, many others he maimed, for he attacked, like a flying thunderbolt, everyone he sought out. So fast were his attacks that coat of mail or shield offered no protection. As for his companions, they were most generous in spilling blood and brains, knowing well how to deliver their blows. And the royal forces wreaked such havoc that, like base and senseless people, they smashed and scattered the bodies.

The onslaught continued, so many dead lying strewn across the fallow fields, until, well before daybreak, the battle array was routed and the line of dead extended five leagues down the river.

Abandoning his banner in the battle, Count Angres fled, taking with him seven of his companions. He returned to the castle along a hidden path where he thought no one might see them. But Alexander, who had sighted him fleeing from the host, resolved to go and engage with them, could he but steal away without any noticing where he had gone. But before he was in the valley, he saw as many as thirty knights, six Greeks and twenty-four Welsh, coming after him along a path; they planned to follow him at a distance and come to his aid if he needed them. When Alexander noticed them, he stopped to wait for them, noting the route those returning to the castle followed until he saw them enter. He then began to plot a dangerous deed of daring, a marvelous trick. And after he had devised all his plans, he turned to address his companions. "Sirs," he said, "if you wish my love, do not object, but grant my will whether it be wisdom or folly."

They pledged never, in any matter, to oppose his will.

"Let us change our insignia," he exclaimed. "Let us take the shields and lances of the traitors we see here, and with them proceed toward the castle. The traitors will believe that we are from their side. Whatever the outcome, the gates will be opened for us. And do you know how we shall repay them? Provided the Lord God permits, we shall take them all, either dead or alive. If any of you regrets his pledge, be assured that as long as I live, he will never know my heartfelt love." All acceded to his will, going and taking the shields of the dead and outfitting themselves in their equipment.

The men in the castle, who had gone up to the battlements of the keep, recognized the shields and believed that the men approaching were from their side. They did not suspect the trap concealed behind the shields. The porter opened the gates and received them within. A victim of their deceit, he did not address a word to them, nor did any of them speak to him. Mute and silent they passed on, displaying such grief that they dragged their lances behind them and leaned on the shields. Giving the appearance of pain, they continued on where they wished until they had passed the three walls.

Up ahead they found many knights and men-at-arms with the count—I am not able to give you the exact number. But all were unarmed, except for the eight who had returned from the foray, and even they were preparing to remove their equipment. Yet they might well be too hasty, for the Greeks who had caught up with them no longer hid themselves, but sprang forward on their chargers. Securely fastened in the stirrups, they sought them out and attacked, sending twenty-one to their deaths before they had issued the challenge. Terrified, the traitors shouted: "Betrayed! Betrayed!" But the attackers were not startled. So long as they found the traitors unarmed, they made an excellent test of their swords. Even three of those they found armed they put in such good order that of the eight, only five remained alive.

Count Angres rushed forward to strike Macedor on his gilded shield in sight of all; he hurled him to the ground dead. Deeply grieved to see his companion slain, Alexander went almost mad with grief, and his blood seethed with rage. Yet his strength and his daring doubled. Eager to avenge, if he could, his friend's death, he went and struck the count with such force that his lance broke. The count, however, was a very strong man and a fine and bold knight. Were he not a wicked traitor, there would be no finer man on earth. He prepared to deliver such a blow that his lance split, cracking and splintering completely. His shield, however, did not break. Since both men were strong, neither dislodged the other more than he would have budged a rock. But the fact that the count was in the wrong placed him in grave peril. Furious at each other, the men drew their swords, since their lances were broken. There would have been no escape had these two assailants wished to continue a long time. Now, at last, one or the other would be forced to his death.

The count dared not remain there when he saw his men, who had been unarmed when taken by surprise, lying dead around him. The other side pursued them savagely, cutting and slashing them, hacking them to pieces and spilling out their brains, and calling the count traitor. When he heard himself accused of treason, he raced for safety to his tower keep, his men fleeing with him. In fierce pursuit their enemies raced after them. Of all those they overtook, they let not one escape, slaying and killing so many that I do not believe more than seven reached safety.

When those fleeing had entered the keep, they paused at the entrance. Their pursuers had followed them so closely that they would have come inside had the entrance been open for them. The traitors, while awaiting help from their men who were arming themselves down in the town, managed a good defense.

On the advice of Nebunal, a most prudent Greek, access to the castle was blocked so that those below could not reach their men, having delayed too long out of laziness and cowardice. Ahead was only a single gateway into the fortress. If they blocked this opening, they would not fear the approach of forces bent on their harm. In his speech Nebunal proposed to them that twenty go to take up fighting at the outer gate, for forces, if they had the power and strength, could easily rush there and assault with a damaging attack. The twenty would go and hold that gate, while the other ten would fight before the entrance to the keep in order to prevent the count from shutting himself up inside.

Nebunal's advice was adopted. Ten stayed to fight before the entrance to the keep, while twenty went to the fortress entrance. They delayed almost too long because they saw a company approaching, inflamed with burning desire for battle, which included many crossbowmen and men-at-arms skilled in the various sorts of equipment they carried: some with poleaxes, others with Danish axes, lances, and Turkish swords, bolts and javelins and arrows. The Greeks would have paid dearly for their movements had this company attacked them, but it failed to arrive in time: thanks to Nebunal's wise advice, the Greeks blocked the company's advance and forced the men to remain outside. When the reinforcements noticed themselves shut out, they held back, realizing that they could accomplish nothing more by attacking. Then began the desperate cries of women and small children, of old men and young, so loud that the men in the castle could not have heard thunder in the heavens.

The Greeks rejoiced, assured now that the count would have no chance of escaping capture. Four of them rushed up to the battlements on the walls to keep watch lest those outside, by some trick or scheme, gain entrance to the castle and fall upon them. The other sixteen returned to join the ten still fighting. It was by now bright daylight, and the ten had already succeeded in penetrating the keep. The count positioned himself beside a pillar, defending himself fiercely with an axe and cutting in half those who came within his reach. In this final day's battle, his men, standing in ranks by his side, took vengeance with all the strength they could.

Alexander's men bemoaned the fact that only thirteen of them were left when but now there had been twenty-six. Alexander went nearly mad with rage when he saw the casualties, the number of his own men maimed and dead. Vengeance, however, he did not neglect. Finding a long and heavy crossbar hanging at hand, he went and struck a good-for-nothing whose shield and hauberk were worth not a button in preventing his fall to the ground. After dealing with this man, he went after the count. Raising the crossbar to deliver a fine blow, he dealt him such a stroke with the square bar that the axe fell from the count's hands. So stunned and weakened was he that had he not been leaning against the wall, his feet would have failed to support him. With this blow the battle ended. Alexander leapt toward the count and seized him. The count did not move. Nothing of the others need be said; on seeing their lord captured, they were easily defeated. The Greeks took them all prisoners along with the count and led them off in deep and deserved disgrace.

The Greeks outside knew nothing of all this. But the morning after the battle ended, they discovered their men's shields among the bodies. And so, by mistake, they made a heavy lament for their lord. Because they recognized his shield, they all gave themselves up to grief, swooning over his shield and exclaiming that life was too long theirs. Cornix and Nerius fainted. While reviving them, Tor and Acoriondes cursed their own lives, the tears streaming down from their eyes to their chests. Life and joy were objects of contempt for them. Parmenides, more than all the others, pulled and tore at his hair. No greater grief could these five have made for their lord, yet their distress had no cause: instead of their lord, they carried away another man, though it was their lord, they believed, whom they bore. They were also deeply distressed by the other shields, which made them believe that the bodies were those of their companions. Senseless with grief, they swooned over them. Yet all the shields deceived them, for only one of their force, a man named Neriolis, had been slain. Had they known the truth, they would have carried only him away. But they felt as much grief for the others as for him. They picked up and carried them all off, yet in every case except one they were mistaken. Like a dreamer who believes the illusion to be reality, they were deceived by the shields with their orna-mental bosses, which caused them to accept the illusion as reality. By the shields they were deceived.

Bearing the bodies, they moved away to their tents where many people were consumed by sorrow. While the Greeks made their laments, all the others remained silent. Because of their mourning, a large crowd was present.

When Soredamor heard the cries and laments for her beloved, she thought and believed the hour of her birth to be cursed. The laments and mourning made her turn so pale that she looked like a dead woman. And what caused her the greatest pain and distress was the fact that she dared not openly display her grief. She concealed her mourning within her heart. Anyone noticing her appearance and attitude would have seen the depth of her anguish. But each was so concerned with his own sorrow that he cared about no one else's. Each lamented his own bitter and heavy loss. There the son wept for his father; the father wept for his son. One man fainted on his cousin, another on his nephew. And so there was grief everywhere for fathers and brothers and relatives. But most conspicuous of all was the grief of the Greeks, though they could expect great joy from it. The deepest grief of the entire army would soon change to great joy.

While the Greeks outside continued their heavy lament, those within endeavored to let them know the news that would delight them. They disarmed and tied up their prisoners, who entreated and begged them to be beheaded immediately. But the Greeks did not wish or care for that. Instead, they would guard them, they said, until they delivered them to the king: he would repay their services with proper rewards. After they had disarmed them all, they forced them to stand on the openings so that they would be seen by their men below. This kindness displeased the captives. When those below saw their lord captured and bound, they felt no happiness. From the wall above, Alexander swore by God and the world's saints never to allow a single captive to remain alive, but to kill them all promptly unless all went and surrendered to the king before his own men could capture them.

"Go at once to my lord, I command you," he shouted, "and place yourselves at his mercy. None of you, except the count here, has deserved death. Never will you lose life or limb if you place yourselves at his mercy. If you do not save yourselves from death simply by begging mercy, you may have little hope for your bodies or your lives. Go forward, all disarmed, to my lord the king, and tell him for me that Alexander sends you there. You will not waste your journey, for my lord the king will dismiss all his anger and wrath against you, so kind and nobly born is he. If you intend any other course of action, you will be brought to death, for I shall never have mercy on you."

The entire group accepted this recommendation, not stopping until the king's tent, where they all fell at his feet. The story they related was immediately known throughout the camp. The king mounted, then all his men mounted, and they spurred to the castle without wasting a moment.

Alexander came out of the castle to meet the king, who was pleased to see him. He handed over the count to him, and the king did not delay in exercising his justice. Much did the king honor and esteem Alexander, and all the others welcomed him, offering him their high esteem and honor. There was no one who failed to rejoice. The joy ended the grief they had earlier displayed. Yet no joy could be compared to the joy of the Greeks.

The king presented to Alexander the magnificent cup which weighed fifteen marks, clearly and assuredly informing him that he had no object so precious, except the crown and the queen, that he would not give him were he but to ask for it. Alexander dared not utter his desire in this regard, though realizing that the king would not disappoint him were he to ask for his beloved. He was so afraid of displeasing her, who would have been delighted, that he would rather suffer than have her against her will. And so he asked for a little time, not wishing to make his request until he knew her pleasure in the matter. But he did not ask for a little time or delay in accepting the gold cup.

Soredamor was most pleased and delighted to hear the true news about Alexander. When she learned that he was alive, she was so happy that she thought she had never known a single hour of distress. But long, it seemed to her, was his delay in his usual practice of coming to see her. Soon she would have her desire, for the two competed with each other in eager rivalry for the same moment.

Alexander longed to feast his eyes on her if only with a tender glance. Although he had intended to come to the queen's tent much earlier, he had been detained elsewhere, and the delay disappointed him. As soon as he could, he came to the queen in her tent. The queen, who knew many of his thoughts, met him; without his even having spoken to her, she had perceived well. As he entered the tent, she greeted him and made every effort to welcome him. She realized the reason for his coming. Because she wished to do him favor, she beckoned Soredamor to come beside her, and the three engaged in private conversation some distance from the others.

The queen was the first to begin. She had no doubt that the two loved each other, he loved her and she him. Of this fact she was quite certain. And she realized that Soredamor might have no finer lover. Seated between the two, she began to address them with appropriate and timely words. "Alexander," the queen said, "Love is worse than Hate because he wounds and destroys his devotee. Lovers do not know what they do when they hide their feelings from each other. There are many grievous labors in loving, and often all turns to confusion. The man who does not begin boldly can scarcely reach an end. It is said that nothing is so difficult as crossing the threshold. I wish to teach you about Love, for I see Love torture you. For this reason I wish to place you in school. Take care not to hide anything from me. From the way you both behave, I am well aware that you have made one heart of two. Never hide your feelings from me. You behave too foolishly in not telling each other your thoughts, for by the concealment you are killing each other. You will be Love's assassins. Now I advise you never to resort to force or yield to the willfulness of loving. Join yourselves together in marriage and honor. In this way, I believe, your love will have the power to last a long time. If the idea pleases you, I venture to assure you, I shall arrange the wedding."

When the queen had disclosed her thoughts, Alexander responded with his own. "Lady," he answered, "I offer no defense against your reproaches. Rather, I agree with your words. Never do I seek to be free from Love so as not to devote myself always to his service. Your words—and I am grateful for them—fill me with pleasure and desire. Since you know my will, I do not know why I hide it from you. Long ago, had I dared, I would have admitted my feelings, since concealing them has been my torture. But it may somehow be possible that this maiden would not wish that I be hers and she mine. Even if she grants me nothing of herself, I still place myself in her power."

At these words the maiden shuddered since she did not refuse this gift. Her words and her appearance betrayed her heart's desire, for she trembled as she agreed with him. Her will, her heart, her body she would place entirely at the disposal of the queen to do all that pleased her. The queen embraced them both and presented each to the other. "I give you, Alexander, the body of your beloved," she said. "Well I know that you already have the heart. Let who will smile or scowl at this, I present you each with the other. You, Alexander, hold what is yours, and you, Soredamor, what is yours." She had what was hers, and he what was his: he all of her, she all of him.

At Windsor that day, with the complete consent and approval of Sir Gawain and the king, the marriage was celebrated. I do not believe anyone could offer an adequate description of the magnificence and the feasting, the joy and the pleasure, but that still more would be at the wedding. Because several would be displeased, I do not wish to spend or waste my words, but I intend rather to devote myself to the telling of something more useful.

On that one day at Windsor, Alexander had all the honor and joy he desired. Three joys and three honors were his. The first was the castle he had captured. The second was the finest kingdom in Wales, which King

Arthur had promised to give him after his war had ended; on that day in his halls he made him its king. The third was the greatest joy, that his beloved was queen of the chessboard on which he was king.

Before three months had passed, Soredamor found herself full with the seed of life, and she carried it until her time. The seed ripened until the fruit came in the form of a child. There could have been no more beautiful creature far or near, and they called the child Cliges. That is the Cliges in whose memory this story has been translated. Hear me now tell of him and his valor when he had come to the age at which he should grow in honor.

Time passed, and it came about in Greece that the emperor who ruled Constantinople reached his end. He died. He had to die, for he could not overstay his allotted time. But before his death, he had convened an assembly of all the great barons of his land in order to send for Alexander, who was in Britain where he stayed gladly.

The messengers left Greece and started on their voyage. A storm took hold of them and ravaged their ship and their men. All drowned at sea, except one scoundrel, a renegade who loved Alis, the younger son, more than Alexander, the older. After he escaped the sea, he returned to Greece with the report that all had perished in the storm at sea while conducting their lord back on his return from Britain, adding that only he had escaped the storm's peril. His lie was believed. Without objection or challenge, the people accepted Alis and crowned him, presenting to him the empire of Greece.

It was not very long, however, before Alexander learned the certain news that Alis was emperor. He took leave of King Arthur, unwilling to renounce his land to his brother without contest. The king did not deter him from his plan; in fact, he told him to take with him so large a force of men from Wales, Scotland, and Cornwall that his brother would not dare stand against him after seeing his assembled array.

Had it been his pleasure, Alexander might have led a large company. But he had no interest in exposing his men to harm, provided that his brother be inclined to answer him that he would do his will. Forty knights he led away, as well as Soredamor and his son, not wishing to leave behind these two, who were most deserving of love.

At Shoreham they took leave of the entire court and put to sea. The winds were favorable, and the ship raced far more swiftly than a fleeing stag. Within the month, as I believe, they had anchored before Athens, a most wealthy and powerful city. In fact, the emperor was in residence in the city, and with him was a large assembly of the country's great barons.

Immediately upon arrival, Alexander dispatched a trusted man of his to the city to know if he would be received, or if his claim to be their rightful lord would be disputed.

For this mission the messenger was a courteous and wise knight named Acoriondes, a man of eloquence and wealth highly esteemed in the country because he was a native of Athens. In the city he occupied a position of importance which his ancestors had held from ancient times. When he learned that the emperor was in the city, he wished to challenge him for the crown on behalf of his brother Alexander, refusing him pardon for holding it without right. Coming directly to the palace, he found many delighted to see him. But he made not a word of response to anyone who welcomed him, waiting instead to hear their attitudes and feelings toward their rightful lord. He stopped only when he came to the emperor. He did not greet him, bow before him, or call him emperor. "Alis," he declared, "I bring you a message from Alexander, who is out there in this harbor. Listen to what your brother commands you: he asks you for what is his and does not seek anything that is not his right. Constantinople, which you hold, should be his, and his it will be. It would not be right or proper that there be strife between the two of you. Make a pact with him, I advise you, and hand back the crown peacefully to him, for it is right indeed that you surrender it to him."

"Honored friend," Alis answered, "you devoted yourself to folly in bringing this message. You brought me no consolation, for well I know that my brother is dead. I do not believe he is in the harbor. That he lives and that I should know it, I will never believe until I lay my eyes on him. His death some time ago grieves me. I believe nothing you say. And if he is alive, why does he not come? He should never fear that I would fail to give him enough land. He is foolish to keep his distance from me. He will never be the worse for serving me. Against me, no one will ever hold the crown and the empire."

Acoriondes heard that the emperor's response was not appropriate. Fear did not stop him from speaking his mind in reply. "Alis," he said, "God destroy me if the situation rests in this manner! In the name of your brother, I defy you, and in his name, as I should, I advise all these men I see present to renounce you and come to him. It is right that they rally to his side. They should make him their lord. Let the man who will be loyal show himself now!" With these words he left the court.

The emperor summoned all his most trusted men. He asked their advice about his brother who challenged him, wishing to know if he could count on them not to help or support his brother in this attack. Thus he meant to test each of them. But there was not even one to rally to his side in the dispute. All told him to remember the war Polynices waged against his own brother Eteocles, where they killed each other with their own hands. "The same may befall you if he intends to pursue the war. And the land will be brought to ruin." Accordingly, they advised him to seek a reasonable and just peace without either party making excessive demands.

When Alis heard that all the men he had summoned would desert him if he did not make a reasonable pact with his brother, he said that he would respect their plea in drawing up a suitable agreement. In his pact, however, he did include that, whatever the outcome of the matter, the crown would remain his. To create a firm and lasting peace Alis sent word to Alexander through one of his constables that he come to him and rule the entire land, but do him the honor of leaving him the title of emperor as well as the crown. Thus, if Alexander were pleased, the situation might be happily resolved between the two.

After the report was related to Alexander, he and his men mounted and rode to Athens, where they were joyously welcomed. But Alexander was not pleased to hear that his brother would have the crown, unless his brother would pledge him his oath never to take a wife and that after him Cliges would be Emperor of Constantinople. With this addition, the brothers were reconciled. Alexander administered the oath to Alis, who agreed and swore never to take a woman in marriage during his lifetime. They were reconciled and remained friends.

The barons were delighted. Although they regarded Alis as emperor, the affairs of state, both great and small, came before Alexander. What Alexander said was done, and little was done except under his name. Alis held nothing except the title of emperor. It was Alexander who was served and loved. And those who did not serve him out of love were made to serve him out of fear. Through love and through fear, he governed the entire country according to his will.

She who is called Death spares no man, weak or strong, slaying and killing all. Alexander was fated to die, for a sickness gripped him from which he could not recover. Before Death carried him away, he summoned his son. "Dear son Cliges," he said to him, "you can never know the extent of your strength and valor unless you first go to the court of King Arthur to measure yourself against the Bretons and the English. If fate takes you there, conduct yourself with such deportment that your identity remains unknown until you test yourself against the finest members of the court. Trust me in this matter, I advise you. And if occasion arises, be not afraid of testing yourself against your uncle Sir Gawain. Do not forget this, I beg you.''

Alexander did not live long after giving this advice. So heavy was Soredamor's grief for him that she was unable to go on living after him. She died of grief at the time of his death. Both Cliges and Alis mourned them, as they should. In due course they ceased their mourning: it is wrong to continue grieving, for no good may come of it.

In time their mourning ended, and for long after, the emperor refrained from taking a wife because he wished to remain loyal to his word. But there is no court in the whole world free from wicked counsel. Barons are often led astray by wicked counsel they believe and so do not adhere to the principle of loyalty.

The emperor's counselors came to him often, besetting, exhorting, and urging him to take a wife. Every day they pressed him so hard that their strong insistence made him break his oath and accede to their will. But she who would be Lady of Constantinople should be beautiful and charming, wise, elegant, and noble. His counselors then said to him that they wished to make preparations for a trip to Germany to ask for the hand of the daughter of the emperor. They advised him to take her as his wife, for the Emperor of Germany was very wealthy and very powerful, and his daughter was so attractive that Christendom never knew a maiden of her beauty.

The emperor agreed with all they said, and they set out on their way. Properly attired, they rode all day every day until they found the emperor at Ratisbonne, where they asked him to give his eldest daughter in marriage to the emperor Alis. Delighted by these tidings, the emperor gladly presented his daughter to them, for the act in no way demeaned him or diminished his honor. But he indicated his earlier promise to present her to the Duke of Saxony. They could not lead her away, he added, unless their emperor came there himself with a force large enough to prevent the duke, on his return, from doing him harm or disgrace. After the messengers heard the emperor's reply, they took their leave and returned.

The messengers came to their emperor and gave him the answer. From among his men the emperor selected his most experienced knights, the bravest he found. And he also took along his nephew, for whose sake he had vowed never in his lifetime to take a wife. But were he able to reach Cologne, he would not keep this vow.

On the appointed day Alis departed Greece, making his way toward Germany. Neither blame nor reproach would prevent his taking a wife, although the act would debase his honor. He continued his journey until reaching Cologne, where the emperor was celebrating a great German feast.

Now the company of Greeks had arrived in Cologne, and there were so many Greeks and so many Germans that more than forty thousand had to find quarters outside the city. Great were the crowds of people and exuberant the great joy of the two emperors, who were delighted to meet each other. As soon as the barons assembled in the long palace, the emperor at once sent for his daughter.

Without a moment's delay the maiden immediately entered the palace hall. She was as beautiful and well formed as if she had been designed by God Himself, Who was able to devote all His efforts here in order to make people stand in awe. Never did God her Creator give a man power of speech to describe her beauty but that she had still more. Fenice was the maiden's name, and not without reason, for as the phoenix is the most beautiful of all birds—and at a given time there can be no more than one—so, I think, Fenice's beauty knew no equal. This was a marvel and a miracle, for never again could Nature succeed in creating her equal. As I would render less than an adequate portrait, I do not intend to describe head, arms, hands, or body, for if I were to live a thousand years, and my talent doubled every day, I would waste my efforts and fail to capture the truth with my words. I am certain that if all my talent I devoted, all my labor I would lose. The attempt would be in vain.

With her head uncovered and her face bared, the maiden hastened along until she arrived in the palace hall. The radiance of her beauty shed greater light in the palace than would have four carbuncles. With his cloak removed, Cliges was standing before his uncle the emperor. The day was somewhat cloudy, but he and the maiden were both so fair that their beauty, like that of the rising sun all bright and red, sent forth a ray of light that bathed the palace.

To describe the beauty of Cliges I wish to draw a portrait that will be brief. Since he was already almost fifteen years old, he was in the flower of his age. He was as handsome and comely as Narcissus, who saw his own image in the spring beneath the elm tree. So much did he love its sight, people say, that he died because he could not possess it. Much beauty did he have, and little wisdom. But just as gold surpasses copper, Cliges had much more wisdom, and still more than I have stated. His hair was like gold, his face like a fresh rose. His nose was well shaped, his mouth beautiful. And his excellent figure was the finest Nature could design, since she placed in him at one time all she generally bestows on her creatures separately. Nature was so generous to him that she placed all in one portion, providing him with all she had.

This was Cliges, who possessed wisdom and beauty, generosity and strength. He had the timber as well as the bark. He knew more about fencing and archery and about hawks and hunting dogs than Tristan, the nephew of King Mark. No good quality was lacking in Cliges.

Cliges stood in all his beauty before his uncle the king. Those who did not know him struggled to look on him, just as others who did not know the maiden struggled to see her. All gazed on her in awe. Yet out of love, Cliges directed his eyes discreetly toward her and as prudently directed them back so that neither in the going nor in the coming might any take him for a fool. Tender were the looks he cast on her, and the people there did not notice the maiden repaying him in kind. Not in deceit but in true love, she gave her eyes to him and accepted his. She liked this exchange, and would have liked it even more had she known something of his character. She knew nothing but his handsome appearance, which she saw, and if she were to love a man only for his beauty, she would be wrong to place her heart on another. She had set her eyes and her heart on him, and for his part he had promised her his heart. Promised? Who gives it completely! Gives? No, I swear I lie, for no man can give his heart. I must find a different expression.

I shall not talk as do people who speak of uniting two hearts in one body. That two hearts can lodge together in one body is not true, nor does it appear true. And if indeed they could come together, it would not seem to resemble truth. But if it be your pleasure to listen, I shall explain to you the true sense in which two hearts are one without coming together. They become one only insofar as the desire of each passes to the other. They have like desires, and because their desires are identical, some people are accustomed to saying that each possesses two hearts. But one heart is not in two places. Their desires may well be the same, but each has his own heart, just as many different men may sing verses and songs in unison. From this simile I present to you proof that one body is incapable of having two hearts. You may be absolutely certain of this, because even if one does know another's desires and loathings, a body can have but one heart, just as voices in unison that seem a single voice cannot come from one mouth. But there is no need to dwell on this, for another urgent task presses on me.

At this moment I must speak of the maiden and Cliges. You will hear of the Duke of Saxony, who had sent his own nephew to Cologne. This very young man informed the emperor that his uncle the duke sent him word not to expect truce or peace with him unless he sent him his daughter; he added that the man minded to take her away with him should not be confident about his journey, for he would not find the road empty, but rather it would be well defended against him, unless the maiden was handed over to him.

Although the young man was not at all arrogant or offensive in delivering his message, he received no response from the emperor or any knight. And when he saw them all observing quiet in scornful silence, he left the court defiantly. Youth and its foolhardiness compelled him, as he departed, to challenge Cliges to a joust.

Mounting their horses for the joust, the two men counted three hundred on each side; thus the forces were exactly the same in number. The great hall was deserted and empty, not a man or woman, knight or young lady remaining there, for all went up to the galleries, battlements, and windows to see and watch those who were to joust. Even the maiden who had been subdued by Love and won to his will had gone up there. She was seated at a window, delighted to sit there since this place afforded her a view of the man who had robbed her of her heart. She had no desire to take it away from him, nor would she ever love anyone but him. Still she did not know his name, who he was or from what family, and it was not proper behavior for her to inquire. And so she longed to hear some information to gladden her heart.

As she looked out the window at the shields with their gleaming gold, and the men carrying them by their necks and delighting in the joust, she focused all her glances and thoughts in one direction so that she reflected on nothing else. Straining to catch sight of Cliges, she followed him with her eyes wherever he went. And for her, in open view, he jousted at his best only that she might hear of his great skill and bravery, for it would be right in any case that she esteem him for his valor.

Cliges made his way toward the duke's nephew, who was riding along, breaking many lances and routing the Greeks. Deeply disturbed by this, Cliges braced himself securely in his stirrups and galloped at breakneck speed, delivering a blow that made the youth vacate his saddle in spite of himself. There was great commotion as he stood up again. The youth stood and mounted, expecting to avenge his shame, but many expect to avenge their disgrace, if permitted, and end up enhancing it. The young man galloped toward Cliges, who lowered his lance to meet him, striking him so forcefully that he carried him to the ground once again. Now the youth had doubled his disgrace. And all his men were distraught, clearly seeing now that they would not leave the battle with honor. Not a man among them was valiant enough to remain in his saddle if Cliges came at him.

Germans and Greeks alike were delighted to see their forces routing the Saxons, who were leaving discomfited. Their men pursued them with contempt until they overtook them at a river, where they plunged many in the water, making them bathe. In the deepest section of the ford, Cliges overthrew the duke's nephew and so many of the others accompanying him that, to their disgrace and their displeasure, they fled, miserable and mournful.

Joyous was Cliges' return. From both sides he carried away the honor. He proceeded directly to a gateway near the room where the maiden was staying, and as he entered the gate, she exacted the toll of a tender glance, which, as their eyes met, he delivered her. In this fashion they captured each other.

But there was no German of the north or south with the capacity of speech who did not exclaim: "God, who is this man? Such great beauty flowers in him. God, from where has he suddenly come? He has received such great honor." These were their questions, and then others: "Who is this youth? Who is he?" At last, throughout the city, all knew the facts about his name and that of his father and about the promise the emperor had made and sworn to his father.

Already the news was repeated, and spread so far that even the maiden heard tell of it, and the news delighted her heart. Because of this she could never say now that Love had scorned her, nor could she ever complain, for he had made her love the most handsome, the most courteous, and the bravest man to be found anywhere. But she was compelled by necessity to marry a man who could not please her, and so was anguished and distraught, not knowing where to turn for counsel about the man she desired, except to her reflection and her sleepless nights. These two states pressed on her to the point of overwhelming and exhausting her. By her loss of color, she saw clearly that she did not have what she desired. She played less than usual, laughed less, enjoyed herself less. But if anyone asked her about herself, she concealed well her trouble and denied it.

Her nurse Thessala, who had raised her from infancy, was most knowledgeable about black magic. She was named Thessala because she had been born in Thessaly, where the devilish arts were devised, taught, and practiced; the women of that country created charms and spells. Thessala noticed the languid pallor of the one held in Love's power, and addressed her privately. "God, is your face so pale, my dear sweet young lady, because you are bewitched?" she asked. "I wonder much about your trouble. Tell me, if you can, where this sickness aggravates you most. If anyone is to cure you, you may rely on me, for I shall know how to restore your health. I know how to cure dropsy, and I can cure gout, quinsy, and asthma. I have so much knowledge of the pulse and about urine that you would be wrong ever to seek another physician. And I know more about tried and true enchantments and spells, if I dare say it, than Medea ever knew. I never wished to say a word of this to you, even though I did raise you until now. Do not blame me for this. I would have told you nothing of this had I not clearly observed that the illness assailing you places you in need of my help. Tell me your malady before it takes stronger hold of you, my young lady, and you will act wisely. The emperor placed me in your service to take care of you, and my efforts have kept you in excellent health. Now my labor will be wasted if I fail to cure this sickness of yours. Now take care not to hide from me whether this is sickness or something else."

Strongly fearful that her nurse might reproach her or try to dissuade her, the maiden dared not openly display all her desire. Yet hearing her boast of her skill and mastery in enchantments, charms, and compounds, she would tell her why her face was pale and languid. But first she made her promise to keep her secret forever and never try to dissuade her.

"Nurse," she said, "without word of lie, I used to think I felt no pain, but I shall soon believe I do. Merely thinking on it makes me most distraught and ill. But how does one know what may be good or ill unless by experience? My sickness is different from all others, for to tell you the truth, it brings me pain and joy, and in my misery I find delight. If there is possibly a sickness that pleases, my distress is my desire, and my pain is my health. I do not know why I complain, for I feel my sickness comes only from my desire. My desire is sickness, perhaps, but I take such pleasure in my desire that the pain it brings me is pleasing. And I take such joy from my distress that my suffering is pleasing. Thessala, nurse, tell me, is not this sickness two-faced? After all, it seems pleasing to me yet causes me anguish. I do not know how to tell if it be infirmity or not. Nurse, tell me its name, character, and nature. But rest assured, I have no interest in any kind of remedy, for I treasure the pain."

Thessala was most informed about Love and all his practices. From Fenice's words she knew and understood that Love was her tormentor. Because the young lady called her sickness pleasing, there was no doubt but that she was in love, for all other sicknesses except love are bitter. Love changes its bitterness to sweet delight, and often changes it back again. Thessala understood the situation well. "Never fear anything," she answered her. "I shall tell you at once the name and nature of your sickness. You have informed me, and I do agree, that the pain you feel seems to you health and joy. You are in love, then, and I present to you proof, for I find sweetness in no other sickness but love. All other sicknesses are always, as a rule, horrible and cruel, but love is pleasing and agreeable. You are in love, I am absolutely certain. I do not consider you base on this account, but base I shall regard it if folly or laziness makes you hide your feelings from me."

"Lady, you waste your words. I shall ascertain that there is no chance of your relating this to any person alive."

"Young lady, the winds will certainly speak of this before I do, unless you give me leave to do so. And I shall give you my promise also to help you succeed in this matter in order that you realize that I shall do your will."

"Nurse, you will indeed have cured me. But the fact that the emperor is marrying me fills me with sorrow and anger, for the man who pleases me is nephew to the man I am to marry. If the emperor has his pleasure with me, then mine I have lost and ended with nothing. I would rather be torn limb from limb than have the two of us be reminiscent of the love of Tristan and Iseult. Many madnesses, shameful to recount, were spoken of them. I could never reconcile myself to the life Iseult led. Love debased himself too much in her, for her heart belonged to one man and her body was the property of two lords. Thus she passed all her life, never refusing the two. Unreasonable was that love. But mine will always be stable, for under no circumstance will my heart and my body ever be divided. My body will never be prostituted. It will never be possessed by two partners. The man who has the heart has the body too; I exclude all others. But since my father gives me to someone else, and I dare not oppose him, I have no idea how the man who receives my heart's surrender may have my body. And when my husband is lord of my body, even if he takes it against my will, it is not right for me to welcome another man there. And this man may not marry without being disloyal to his word. Provided Cliges is not wronged, the empire ought to be his upon his uncle's death.

"But if you could use your skill to prevent the man to whom I am promised and given from having any part of me, you would do me a great service. Nurse, devote all your efforts that this man not break his promise. Under oath he swore to Cliges' father never to take a wife. Since he will soon marry me, his oath will be violated. But I have not so little respect for Cliges that I would not rather be buried alive than ever be the reason for the loss of a penny of the honor rightfully due him. May I never be able to bear a child and so bring about his disinheritance. Nurse, see to it now that I am in your debt forever."

Her nurse agreed. She said that she would devise so many spells, potions, and enchantments that the young lady would never have any worry or fear about the emperor: they would both lie in bed together, but all the time she was with him, she could be as secure as if there were a wall between the two. He would cause her, she continued, only this much distress, that he would take his pleasure in his sleep; when he was fast asleep, he would enjoy her at will, believing fully that when he enjoyed her, he was awake. He would never imagine his joy was but a dream, a flattering deceit, a lie. Thus he would enjoy her always: in his sleep, he would think himself at play.

The maiden loved, esteemed, and praised this kind service. By her promise her nurse offered her good hope, assuring her that she would be true to her word. With this hope the maiden could expect to obtain her joy, however long the delay, for Cliges would never be so ill disposed, if he knew that she loved him, as not to take delight in this love of hers. She thought to preserve her virginity in order to save his inheritance for him, and it could not be that he would not take some pity on her, were he of an excellent nature and such a man as he should be. The maiden believed her nurse, placing her complete faith and trust in her. They promised and swore to each other to keep this plan so secret that it would never be known. Thus their conversation ended.

When morning came, the emperor summoned his daughter, who came at his command. Why should I continue with every detail of the story? The two emperors met and settled their business so that the marriage took place and gaiety ensued in the palace. But I do not wish to pause to speak of every detail. I wish to turn my story back to Thessala, who did not cease from making and mixing potions.

Thessala mixed her potion. She added a profusion of spices to sweeten and temper it, beating and blending them well, and filtering the preparation until it was entirely clear. Because of the sweet fragrance of the spices, the taste was not bitter or sharp. By the time the potion was prepared, the day had drawn to its end, the tables had been placed for supper, and the tablecloths laid. But I am setting aside details of the supper. Thessala had to discern what scheme or what messenger she would employ to deliver her message.

All were seated for the meal. There were more than ten courses, and Cliges was serving his uncle. When Thessala noticed him serving his uncle, she thought that he wasted his service by being a servant to his own disinheritance. Watching this filled her with anxiety and pain. Then, like the courteous lady she was, she devised a plan to have her drink served by the man who would know joy and advantage from it.

Thessala summoned Cliges. He went to Thessala promptly and asked her why she had sent for him. "Friend," she said, "at this meal I wish to honor the emperor with a drink he will treasure. By Saint Richier I tell you, tonight I wish him to have no other drink. I believe that he should love it, for never has there been so fine-tasting or so costly a drink. Be careful, I warn you, that no one else drinks it, for there is too little of it. And I advise you again, do not let him know where it came from. Tell him only that you happened by chance to find it among the presents, and poured it into his cup, having detected and recognized the fragrance of fine spices in the air, and seen the clarity of the wine. If he happens to inquire about it, you can be certain that this answer will put his mind to rest. But never have misgivings about what I have told you, for the drink is pure and wholesome, full of fine spices. Perhaps someday, as I believe, it will bring you happiness."

When he heard that good would come of this, he took the potion and carried it off. Unaware of any wrongdoing, he poured it into the crystal cup and placed it before the emperor. The emperor, who had great faith in his nephew, took the cup and drank a large draft of the potion. At once he felt its strength go from his head down his body and back up again to his head, circulating from top to bottom and saturating every part of him without causing pain. When the time came to remove the tablecloths, the emperor had drunk so much of the pleasing beverage that during the night he would be intoxicated in his sleep and never escape its effect, the potion making him so excited that he would imagine himself awake when asleep. Now the emperor was duped.

Many bishops and abbots were in attendance to bless and consecrate the nuptial bed. When it was time to retire, the emperor, as he should, lay beside his wife. As he should? That was my lie, for he did not kiss or caress her, though they did lie together in one bed. The maiden trembled with fear, disturbed and afraid that the potion might not be effective. But it worked such an enchantment on him that he would never have his desire of her or anyone else except in his sleep, and then would have the kind of ecstasy possible only in a dream, believing the dream to be reality. Yet she feared him, at the beginning keeping her distance from him, and he could not come near her, for sleep quickly took hold of him. He fell asleep and dreamed, while believing himself awake: he exerted great force and effort to flatter the maiden, who adopted an attitude of aloofness toward him and protected herself in the way of a virgin. And he entreated her, calling her his sweetheart with great tenderness. He believed that he held her, and he held her not. But he took much pleasure from nothing, for he received nothing, kissed nothing, held nothing, addressed nothing, saw nothing, embraced nothing, quarreled with nothing, struggled with nothing. The potion was most effective in disturbing and tormenting him. He exerted himself pointlessly, for he indeed believed, and so boasted, that he was weary and exhausted from capturing the castle. This was his thinking, this his belief.

All at once I have told you everything. Never did he have any other pleasure. And if he is able to take her away with him, he must thus spend all his days. But I fear great difficulties will befall him before he holds her securely, for on his return the duke will not rest, since she was given first to him.

The duke had a large force with him and stationed troops at all the frontiers. And his spies were at the court, informing him daily about the entire situation, all the preparations, the length of the Greeks' stay, the date of their departure, and the particular route of their return.

The emperor did not stay long in Cologne after his wedding. He left in happy spirits, and the Emperor of Germany, out of his deep fear and dread of the Duke of Saxony's strength, accompanied him with a powerful escort. The two emperors did not cease their journey until they had traveled beyond Ratisbonne, where they encamped one evening in the meadows along the Danube. The Greeks were in their tents in the meadows beside the Black Forest, and lying in wait for them were the Saxons, encamped on the other side. The duke's nephew rode up a hill to see if he could gain an advantage and do harm to those on the other side. From his vantage point he saw Cliges riding along with three young men sporting with the shields and the lances they carried for joust and play. The duke's nephew, if ever he could, would cause them injury and pain. He set out with two companions, and all three kept themselves couched in a valley beside the forest to prevent the Greeks from seeing them before they emerged from the valley. The duke's nephew made his way toward Cliges and delivered a blow that lightly grazed his back. Cliges crouched and avoided the lance, which bruised him a little as it passed. When Cliges felt his injury, he rushed at the young man, striking him so hard that he easily drove the lance through the body and struck him dead.

The Saxons, terrified of Cliges, then immediately took to flight, scattering through the forest. Ignorant of the ambush, Cliges behaved boldly and foolishly by separating from his companions. He pursued those fleeing in the direction of the duke's forces, where the entire army was already preparing to launch an assault on the Greeks. All alone and without support, Cliges pursued them. And the young men, totally distraught by the loss of their lord, came at a gallop before the duke. Amid tears they informed him of the loss of his nephew. Not considering the news a laughing matter, the duke swore by God and all the saints that his life would never know joy or good fortune so long as he knew his nephew's murderer lived. And he proclaimed that the man who brought him the murderer's head would be his dear friend and bring him great consolation. One knight then boasted that he would present him with Cliges' head if Cliges would do battle with him.

Cliges pursued the young men until he fell upon the Saxons. And the knight who intended to carry off his head caught sight of him and set out without a moment's pause. Cliges turned round to distance himself from his enemies and galloped back to the spot where he had left his companions. But since they had returned to the tents to recount their adventure, he did not find one of them there.

The emperor called Greeks and Germans alike to mount. Through the camp, the barons armed themselves quickly and mounted. Yet the Saxon, fully armed, his helmet laced, continued his galloping pursuit of Cliges. Seeing him coming alone and wishing to have nothing in common with a faithless wretch or a coward, Cliges verbally assailed him. The knight, who could not hide his feelings, spoke first, insolently calling him page. "Page," he exclaimed, "here will you leave the pledge for my lord whom you killed. If I fail to carry off your head with me, I am not worth a counterfeit coin. I wish to present the duke with your head. I will never accept any other pledge from you. I will offer you as restitution for his nephew. That will be a fine exchange for him."

Cliges heard his foolish and base insults. "Vassal," he said, "on guard now! I defy you to take my head. You shall not have it without my consent."

Then they charged at each other. The Saxon missed his blow, and Cliges struck him so hard that he made him and his charger fall in a heap. The charger fell backwards on top of him with such force that it broke one of his legs completely. Cliges dismounted on the green grass and disarmed his opponent. When he had removed his equipment, he donned the arms himself and beheaded the man with the man's own sword. After he cut off the head, he fixed it firmly to the end of his lance. He would present it, he said, to the duke, to whom the knight had pledged to present Cliges' own head if he might meet him in combat.

No sooner had Cliges placed the man's helmet on his head, taken his shield (not his own, but the shield of the man who had fought him), and mounted the man's charger, letting his own go free to alarm the Greeks, than he saw more than a hundred banners and large battalions, composed of Germans and Greeks alike, who were most wicked and cruel. As soon as Cliges saw them coming, he rode directly toward the Saxons. His own men, not recognizing him because of the arms, pursued him relentlessly. And his uncle, distressed by the head he carried at the end of his lance, thought and believed that it was the head of his nephew. Not surprising was his fear.

The entire army raced after Cliges. To open the fight, Cliges had his own men pursue him until the Saxons saw him approach. But his arms and equipment misled them all. He had deceived and tricked them, for when he approached with his lance in its rest, the duke and all the others exclaimed: "Our knight comes! He carries the head of Cliges at the end of the lance he holds. The Greeks pursue him. Now to horse to help him!"

They all then gave rein to their horses, and Cliges, his lance upright with the head at its end, spurred toward the Saxons, crouching and covering himself behind his shield. He had not the courage of Samson. He was no stronger than any other man.

The two forces, one composed of Saxons, the other of Greeks and Germans, believed that Cliges was dead. One side was happy, the other doleful. But in time the truth would be known, for Cliges no longer remained silent. Crying out as he rode, he galloped toward a Saxon and struck him in the very chest with his ash lance, the head still attached to it, so that he forced him to vacate his stirrups. "Barons, strike!" he then shouted. "I am Cliges whom you seek. On now, bold noble knights! Let there be no coward here. Ours is the first joust. A coward does not taste such a dish."

The emperor was overjoyed to hear his nephew Cliges exhorting and inciting the men. He was delighted and consoled. And the duke was bewildered to realize now that he was undone, unless his own forces were larger. He had his men press together in tight ranks. The Greeks were in close array not far from them, pricking and spurring hard. Both sides gripped their lances, charged, and received the impact, as they should on such an urgent occasion. At the first encounter shields were pierced, lances shattered, saddlegirths broken, and stirrups cut. Many chargers had lost their riders, who lay on the ground.

While the other men did their work, Cliges and the duke, their lances lowered, rode at each other. They struck each other on their shields with such force that the strong and well-made lances flew into splinters. A skillful rider, Cliges stayed fully upright in the saddle without fumbling or faltering, while the duke, against his will, quit his saddle and left his stirrups. Expecting to take him prisoner and lead him away, Cliges struggled and exerted himself mightily, yet his strength was not enough, for the Saxons gathered round and rescued the duke from the fray. Nevertheless Cliges left the battle unharmed and with a prize: he led away the duke's Arabian charger, which was whiter than wool and, to a worthy man, equal in value to the wealth of Octavian of Rome.

The Greeks and Germans, having observed the quality and worth of the Arabian steed, were delighted to see Cliges mounted there. They knew nothing, however, about a trap, and never would know until it inflicted heavy casualties upon them.

A spy had come to the duke with news that delighted him. "Sir," he said, "not a single Greek capable of defending himself remains in the tents. Now, if you believe me, you may have the emperor's daughter taken, while you watch the Greeks intent on the assault and battle. Give me some of your knights, and I shall present your beloved to them. I shall guide them so safely along an old secluded path that they will not be seen or met by Germans from the north or south until they can easily abduct the maiden from her tent without encountering resistance."

The plan pleased the duke. He sent a hundred judicious knights and more with the spy, who guided them so well that they captured the maiden. Because they could lead her away easily, they did not resort to heavy force. When they had brought her some distance from the tents, they sent her ahead under an escort of twelve, whom they accompanied but a short way. While the dozen led the maiden away, the others informed the duke of their successful exploit. The duke wanted nothing more, and so forged an immediate truce with the Greeks from that moment until the next day. The terms of the truce were settled and accepted. The duke's men returned, and the Greeks, without further delay, went back to their own tents.

Unnoticed by any, Cliges stayed alone on a hill until he saw the twelve riding along with the young lady, whom they led off at full gallop. Eager to win renown, Cliges raced at once toward them, for his mind and heart informed him that their flight had a reason. The moment he sighted them, he spurred after them. They saw him coming, and thought and believed that it was the duke who followed them. "Let us wait a little for him. He has set off from the host by himself and races after us." Not a single one failed to believe this.

They all wanted to go and meet him, but each wished to ride there alone. Cliges had to ride down a deep valley between two mountains. Had they not come to meet him or waited up for him, he would never have recognized their insignia. Six came to face him, but he met them individually. The others stayed behind with the maiden, leading her away gently and at a slow amble. The six spurred at full speed through the valley. The man with the fastest horse outstripped all the others, shouting out: "Duke of Saxony, God save you! Duke, we have rescued your beloved. Now the Greeks will not take her away, for she will now be handed over to you."

When Cliges heard the shouts of the man riding up, his heart knew no laughter. Rather, it was a wonder that he did not go mad with rage. There was never a wild beast—leopard, serpent, or lion—seeing the loss of its young, so furious, enraged, and keen for combat as Cliges, for without his beloved, life held no meaning for him. He would rather die than fail to rescue her. In his anxiety, the deep anger he felt emboldened him mightily. He pricked and spurred the Arabian steed and went to deliver such a forceful blow to the Saxon's painted shield that, without word of lie, he made his steel lancehead feel his opponent's heart. This gave Cliges confidence. He had spurred and driven his Arabian charger more than a full acre's measure before the next man drew near, as they all came along singly and fearlessly, and he jousted with each individually. One by one he engaged them without any receiving help from the others. He attacked the second, who, like the first, expected to make Cliges rejoice with news of his misfortune. Cliges, however, did not care to hear his talk and chatter. He went and thrust his lance into the body; when he removed it, the blood poured out. He deprived him of his speech and his soul.

After these two, Cliges encountered the third, who expected to find a fair welcome and make him happy about a subject which in actuality grieved him. He spurred his charger to meet him, but before he had a chance to utter a word, Cliges plunged his lance a fathom into the body. To the fourth in turn he delivered such a blow that he left him on the field in a faint. After the fourth, he rushed toward the fifth, and then, after the fifth, toward the sixth. Not one of them held his ground against him. He left all mute and silent.

With no further concern for these six, Cliges had less fear of the others and rode after them with more boldness still. Now that he was rid of these men, he rode off to present to the others, who were leading the maiden away, misery and disgrace. He overtook them, attacking like a ravenous and famished wolf leaping on its prey. Now he considered himself fortunate to have occasion to display chivalry and courage in open view of the one who was his intoxication. Now he was dead unless he freed her, and she too was dead, being, on his account, desolate. But she did not know that he was so near. His lance in its rest, Cliges made a charge that pleased him: he struck one Saxon and then another so that in a single charge he knocked both to the ground, breaking his ash lance. So painful was their fall that their wounds prevented them from standing again to do him injury or harm. Fiercely angry, the four others all rode together to attack Cliges. But he did not couch or tumble, and they failed to dislodge him from his stirrups. He quickly unsheathed his sword with its sharpened blade. To win the favor of the young lady for whose love he longed, he galloped hard against a Saxon and dealt him such a blow with his sharpened sword that he cut off his head at the very center of the neck. That was the entire extent of his mercy.

As Fenice saw and watched him, she was not aware that this was Cliges. She would have liked the man to be he, but because of the peril involved, she said that she would not have such a desire. She was, in two ways, a fine beloved: she feared his death, and she desired his honor.

With his sword Cliges attacked the other three, who offered him strong resistance. They punctured and broke his shield, though they could not gain the upper hand or pierce the meshes of his hauberk. Nothing that met the blows of Cliges' assault stood firm: he blasted and destroyed all. He turned round more than a top driven and chased by a whip.

Valor and the love that gripped him emboldened him and made him eager to fight. He dealt so cruelly with the Saxons that he defeated or killed them all, crippling some and slaying others. But one who was his equal he let escape, that through this man the duke would know of the disgrace that was his and be desolate. Learning of his misfortune filled the duke with anger and grief.

Cliges led Fenice away, his love for her troubling and paining him. Unless he confessed it to her now, he would long suffer the torment of love, as would she, if she kept silent, not revealing her own desire. Now they might speak in private of their deep feelings for each other, yet so fearful were they of rejection that they dared not disclose their hearts. He was afraid that she might refuse him, and for her part she would have revealed herself had she not been afraid of rejection. Yet their eyes betrayed their thoughts, had they but known how to read the signs. Their eyes spoke with glances, but their mouths were so cowardly that they dared not utter a word about the love that was their master.

It is no wonder that she dares not begin, for a maiden is to be simple and timid. But why does he wait? Why does he delay? After all, for her sake he is bold everywhere and cowardly to none but her. God, whence comes his fear of a single maiden, simple and timid, feeble and shy? This makes me think I see dogs fleeing before the hare, the turtledove chasing the beaver, the lamb the wolf, the dove the eagle. It is as though the peasant forsakes his hoe, the instrument of his livelihood, and the falcon flees from the duck, the vulture from the heron, and the pike flees from the minnow, and the stag chases the lion. This is the world inverted. But I long to offer some reason why true lovers happen to lack courage and wisdom to tell their thoughts when they have time, leisure, and occasion.

You who are learning about Love, who faithfully observe the customs and practices of his court, who have never broken his law regardless of the consequences, tell if you can see any pleasure from Love that does not cause trembling or paleness. I shall never fail to throw into confusion anyone disagreeing with me. Anyone who does not tremble and turn pale, who is not bereft of wit and memory, seeks and pursues, like a thief, what is not his by right. A servant who does not stand in fear of his lord should not be in his retinue, nor should he serve him. He who does not esteem his lord does not stand in fear of him, and he who does not esteem him does not love him, but devotes his time to deceiving him, and stealing his belongings. A servant ought to tremble with fear when his lord calls or summons him. And whoever commits himself to Love makes Love his lord and master. It is right that he remember this and honor and serve him if he wishes to be in good standing in his court.

Love without fear and dread is a burning fire without heat, day without sun, honeycomb without honey, summer without flowers, winter without frost, a sky without a moon, a book without letters. Thus refute your opponent by proving that Love is not to be mentioned where fear is absent. Whoever would love must know fear, or else he is incapable of loving. But let him fear only his beloved and be bold everywhere for her sake.

Therefore, if Cliges stood in fear of his beloved, he made no mistake or error. But this fear would not have stopped him from talking to her immediately and seeking her love, whatever the outcome, had she not been the wife of his uncle. Accordingly, his wound festered and caused him further suffering and pain because he dared not express his desire.

Thus they made their way toward their people, and if they talked of anything, the subject did not interest them. Each sat on a fine horse, and they galloped toward the camp, where deep sorrow held sway. All the men in the camp were beside themselves with grief. But they were wholly mistaken to talk of Cliges' death, which was the cause of their loud and heavy mourning. And they also worried about Fenice, not believing that she would ever again be with them. And so for her sake as well as for his, all the camp was weighted in grief. But their mourning would not continue much longer, and the entire situation would change.

The pair had already returned to the camp, and so the grief had turned to joy. Joy came back, grief took flight, and all the army came and gathered to welcome them. When the two emperors heard the news of Cliges and the maiden, they went together in the highest spirits to greet them. Everyone longed to hear how Cliges had found and rescued the empress. When Cliges told them the story, his astonished listeners were loud in their praise of his valor and his bravery.

On the other hand, the duke was enraged. He pledged, he swore, he proposed, if Cliges dared, single combat between them both with the following provisions: if Cliges won the combat, the emperor would depart in safety and take his maiden with him; if he defeated or slew Cliges, who had done him serious injury, there would be no truce or peace to prevent each side from pursuing its advantage. These were the duke's proposals, and through an interpreter of his who knew Greek and German, he informed the two emperors of his desire for such a combat. The messenger delivered his message in both languages so that everyone understood it.

An uproar ensued throughout the camp. If it was God's pleasure, men exclaimed, Cliges would never undertake the combat. The prospect terrified both emperors. But Cliges fell at their feet, begging them not to be upset, but to grant him this combat as reward and recompense for any favor he may have done them. And if he was denied, he added, there would never be a day when he would do anything to please or honor his uncle.

The emperor, who held his nephew as dear as he should, raised him by the hand. "Dear nephew, I am deeply pained to know your keen desire to fight, for I expect grief to follow joy," he said. "You have made me happy, I cannot deny that. But agreeing to send you to the combat pains me since I see you are too young. You are so noble-hearted, I know, that I dare not deny any request you are pleased to make. I would agree with you only at your wish, be certain. Yet if my entreaty held any value, you would never undertake this endeavor."

"Sir, you waste your words," Cliges answered. "God confound me if I were to abandon the combat in exchange for the whole world. I do not know why I should ask you for a postponement or a long delay." When he granted him permission to fight, the emperor wept with pity. And Cliges wept with joy. Many tears were shed there. No postponement or delay was taken: before six in the morning, the summons to combat was announced to the duke by his own messenger according to the conditions he had proposed.

Secure and firm in his conviction that Cliges would not hold out against him but would promptly suffer defeat or death at his hands, the duke had himself armed at once. Longing for the combat, Cliges felt no concern at all about the manner of defending himself against the duke. In his desire to be knighted, he asked the emperor for arms. The emperor graciously presented him with arms, and Cliges accepted them, his heart burning with keen desire for combat. He rushed to be armed, and when he was equipped from head to toe, the emperor, deeply saddened, went to gird the sword to his side. Fully armed, Cliges mounted the white Arabian steed. From his neck he hung by its straps a shield without color or design made from elephant bone that could not break or split. All his armor gleamed white, and the charger and harness were whiter than snow.

Cliges and the duke mounted and announced to each other that they would meet halfway and that all their men on both sides were bound by oaths and pledges not to carry swords or lances: so long as the combat lasted, no man would be so bold as to dare move in order to inflict injury any more than he would dare pluck out his eye. Under this agreement they came together, each impatient to win the glory and joy of victory.

Before the first blow was struck, the empress had herself escorted there out of concern for Cliges. She had resolved that were he to die, she would die. No one's aid could ever prevent her from dying with him, for without him life offered her no pleasure.

When all had ridden onto the field, highborn and low, young and old, and the guards had taken up their positions, the two men took their lances and attacked each other so brutally that each broke his lance. Unable to remain in their saddles, they fell from their horses to the ground. But because they were not wounded, they leapt to their feet at once and came at each other without delay. To the astonishment of their men, they played a lay with the swords on the resonating helmets. It seemed to the onlookers that the helmets were aflame and blazing, for glowing sparks shot from the rebounding swords as from a piece of smoking iron the blacksmith draws from his forge and hammers on the anvil.

The two vassals were generous in bestowing blows in abundance, and each was well intentioned about repaying immediately what he borrowed. Neither held back from promptly repaying capital and interest without count or measure. But the duke became hot with anger and most annoyed because he had not defeated and killed Cliges in the first attack. He dealt him such a marvelously strong and severe blow that Cliges fell on one knee at his feet. The blow that brought Cliges down astonished the emperor. Had he been behind the shield himself, he could not have been more dismayed. But Fenice was so bewildered that she could not stop herself, whatever the effect, from crying out as loudly as she could, "Holy Mary!" That was all she cried, for her voice immediately failed her and she fell forward in a faint, hands stretched out, and slightly injured her face. The great barons lifted her back up and supported her on her feet until she regained consciousness. No one who regarded her or her appearance knew why she had fainted. Not a single person blamed her; on the contrary, they all praised her, assuming that she would have acted the same way for them had they been in Cliges' position. But in that there was no truth.

Cliges heard Fenice's cry most clearly. Her voice restored his strength and courage. He leapt back to his feet quickly, came in fury to the duke, and confronted him with such an attack that the duke was completely stunned to find him stronger and more combative, more agile and keener to fight than he had been, he thought, in their first encounter. Because he feared his attack, he said to Cliges: "Vassal, so help me God, I see you are most courageous and brave. If it were not for my nephew, whom I shall never forget, I would gladly make peace with you and abandon the dispute without more concern for it."

"Duke, what is your pleasure?" Cliges asked. "Is it not necessary for the man who cannot recover his rightful claim to surrender it? When one is forced to choose between two evils, one should choose the lesser. Your nephew did not behave prudently in becoming vexed and angry with me. Now you can be certain that if ever I can, I shall deal with you in like manner, unless you accept my terms for peace."

The duke thought that Cliges' strength was steadily growing. He considered himself much better off, before he was completely exhausted, to stop in the midst, escaping a bad impasse and leaving a dangerous path. Yet he did not confess the entire truth so openly to Cliges. "Vassal," he said, "I see how noble, alert, and stouthearted you are, but you are too young. And so I feel certain that I would win no honor or renown by defeating or killing you. I would never see a man of valor, or any man, to whom I should admit I had fought you, for I would do you honor and myself disgrace. But if you know the value of honor, always to your great honor will be the mere withstanding of my two attacks. Now my heart and mind tell me to release you from the dispute and fight you no more."

"Duke, these words help you not," Cliges replied. "You shall say them in a loud voice in the hearing of all. It will never be said or reported that you did this out of kindness to me. No, but rather that I took mercy on you. You must confirm this publicly for all present if you wish to make peace with me."

The duke confirmed it publicly. And thus they established peace and accord. Yet whatever the form of the agreement, Cliges, to the delight of the Greeks, held the honor and renown from it.

The Saxons, on the other hand, had no cause for mirth, for all had seen their lord worn out and forced to admit defeat. There was no question that if he could have gained the upper hand, he would never have made this agreement, but would have ripped the soul from Cliges' body had he the strength to do so. The duke returned to Saxony dejected, depressed, and disgraced, for there were not two of his men who did not consider him a faithless coward and unfortunate wretch. In total shame the Saxons returned to Saxony.

Without further delay, the Greeks returned toward Constantinople, delighted and joyful that Cliges' valor had cleared the way for them. From then on, the Emperor of Germany provided them no further escort. Taking leave of the Greek men, his own daughter, Cliges, and finally the emperor, he remained in Germany. And the Emperor of the Greeks went away, most pleased and happy.

Cliges, the brave and the well-educated, pondered his father's command. He intended to go to ask and entreat his uncle the emperor for permission, if he would give him leave, to travel to Britain, where he would talk with his uncle and the king, for he wished to see them and make their acquaintance. Presenting himself before him, he petitioned the emperor, if the request met his pleasure, to allow him to go to Britain to see his uncle and his friends. Despite Cliges' prudent entreaty, his uncle, after listening and hearing his entire request, refused him. "Dear nephew," he said, "your desire to leave me pleases me not. You will never obtain permission or leave without causing me deep pain, for I find it most agreeable and pleasing that you be here as my companion and, with me, lord of all my empire."

Cliges heard nothing agreeable at that moment in his uncle's rejection of his request and entreaty. "Sir," he said, "it is not fitting that I accept this partnership with you or anyone else, for I have not attained sufficient wisdom or valor. Nor should I share in governing an empire. I am too young, and my knowledge is scant. For this reason, gold, to know if it is pure, is applied to the touchstone. In the same way I wish to measure and prove myself where I expect to find the test—that is the sum of the matter. If I am valorous, I shall be able, in Britain, to apply myself to the touchstone, the true and pure test, and prove my valor. In Britain are worthy men famed for their honor and valor. The man who wishes to gain honor should associate with them. Honor resides there, and whoever associates with a worthy man gains it. That is why I ask leave of you. If you do not grant my request and send me there, you can be certain that I shall go lacking your leave."

"Dear nephew, since you are so determined that no entreaty or force on my part could stay you, I give you leave. God grant you the desire and disposition to return soon. Since entreaty, prohibition, and force will not prevail, I wish you to take with you a full bushel of gold and silver. I shall also provide you with horses of your choice for your support."

He had scarcely finished speaking when Cliges thanked him. At once the emperor placed before him all he promised and planned for him. Cliges took as much wealth and as many companions as suited and pleased him. For his personal use he led away four chargers of different color, one fawn, one white, one black, and one chestnut brown. But I was about to omit for you that which should not be passed over.

Cliges went to ask leave of his beloved Fenice, wishing to commend her to God. He came and knelt before her, weeping tears that bathed all his ermine-trimmed tunic. He kept his eye fixed on the ground, not daring to look her in the face, as though ashamed of some crime or wrong he had committed against her. And Fenice gazed on him with timid shyness, not knowing the reason for his visit. Somewhat hesitant, she spoke to him. "Friend, dear brother, stand. Sit beside me. Cease your tears and tell me your desire."

"Lady, what shall I say? What shall I leave unsaid? I seek your leave, I beg your leave, for I must travel to Britain."

"Then before I give you leave, tell me what business summons you."

"Lady, on his deathbed my father implored me never to allow anything to prevent my going to Britain as soon as I became a knight. And there is nothing that would cause me to neglect his command. Nothing should prevent my going there from here. It is still quite a distance into Greece, and if I went to Greece, I would find the journey from Constantinople to Britain very long. But it is proper that I take my leave of you as of that person to whom I belong entirely."

Many were the sighs and sobs suppressed and hidden at his parting, though none there opened his eyes or looked clearly enough to discern, at his departure, the certain truth that the couple were in love with each other. Despite his sorrow, Cliges left as soon as permitted. Lost in his thoughts he departed, and the emperor and many others remained behind absorbed in thought. But Fenice was the most pensive of all. She found no bank or bottom to the thoughts that consumed her, so much did they increase and overflow inside her.

Lost in her thoughts, Fenice came to Greece, where she was revered as lady and empress. Her heart and soul, however, belonged to Cliges wherever he traveled. Never did she wish her heart to return to her unless it was he who brought it back, he who was dying from the same disease with which he had slain her. And if he recovered, she would recover. For this he would never pay dearly unless she too paid dearly.

Her illness was visible on her face. Her color had changed and become very pale. The pure, clear, fresh hue Nature had set on her face had vanished. Often she wept, often she sighed. From the moment Cliges set off, she was almost indifferent to her empire and the high honor that was hers. And the manner in which he took his leave of her, his altered expression, his paleness, his tears, his bearing, these she stored forever in her memory, and how he came before her weeping, lowly and humble on his knees as though he were to worship her. All this she found pleasing and sweet to recall and cling to. Then, to please her mouth, she placed a little spice on her tongue: a phrase that never, for all of Greece, would she have wished its speaker to have used for purposes of deceit, in the sense she understood, since no other delicious morsel gave her life and nothing else brought her pleasure. This phrase alone, which was her nourishment and sustenance, relieved all her suffering. She sought no other food to eat, no other liquid to drink, for, at the time of their separation, Cliges had said that he belonged to her entirely. She found these words pleasing and fine. And from the tongue they touched her heart. She placed them in her mouth and in her heart because of the greater degree of safety there. Under no other lock dared she store this treasure, nor might she dispatch it to a better place than her own heart. She had such fear of robbers and thieves that she would never remove it at any cost. But her fear came without cause; she had no reason to be afraid of birds of prey. Like a building that cannot be destroyed by flood or fire, and will never move from its location, this treasure was immobile.

Uncertain and worried, she struggled to find and know something to which she might cling. In several ways she explored the matter, in her self-analysis offering the responses and making the objections. "Why would Cliges have said, 'I belong to you entirely,' unless Love caused him to say it? Then what right have I over him? Why should he esteem me so highly that I become his lady? Is he not more beautiful than I? Is he not more noble than I? I see none but Love with the power to bestow this gift on me. I cannot escape this man. And from my own example I shall prove that unless he loved me, he would never claim to be mine entirely any more than I would be his entirely. And I should not say this unless Love had given me to him. There is no way in which Cliges ought to have said that he was mine entirely unless he was under Love's control, for if he does not love me, he does not fear me. Love gives me entirely to him, and I hope that, in return, he has given him entirely to me. But what distresses me most is the fact that this phrase is common in its expression. I may certainly be the subject of mockery, for there are people who use flattering terms in talking even to strangers. 'I am yours, and all I have is yours,' they say, but they chatter more idly than jays. I don't know what to believe, for he possibly spoke in that fashion to deceive me with words of flattery.

"But I did see him change color and weep piteously. I don't believe that deceit stood behind his tears and his piteous and dejected countenance. No, trickery and deceit were not present. The eyes whence I saw the tears falling did not lie to me. If I know anything on this subject, I was able to find much evidence of love there. Yes, with the result that my thoughts in this manner were to my own detriment. To my own misfortune I have learned and retained this experience, for a great misfortune befell me as a result. Misfortune? Yes, I swear I am dead because I don't see the man who stole my heart with deceitful words of flattery. By his smooth talk and his flattering terms, my heart is estranged from its lodging, and has no desire to stay with me, so much does it despise me and my home. On my word, then, this man who has my heart in his power treated me ill. I am certain that the man who robs me and carries off all that is mine loves me not.

"Do I know this? Then why was he weeping? Why? It was not in vain. There were many reasons. I should not assume that I am responsible, for deep anguish accompanies parting from people known and loved. It is no wonder that he felt distress and pain, and wept at leaving people he knew. But the man who counseled him to go and live in Britain could have found no better way to slay me. One who loses his heart is dead. One who loses his heart deserves misfortune. But I never deserved it. Alas, wretch that I am, then why has Cliges slain me when I am innocent? Yet I reproach him in vain, for I have no cause.

"I am convinced that Cliges would never have deigned to admit his heart was like mine. But his is not the same. My heart has taken his as companion and will never leave it. His will never go anywhere without mine since mine secretly follows him. This is the partnership they have formed. But to tell the truth, they are divergent and contrary. How are they divergent and contrary? His is lord and mine is servant, and the servant, even against his will, must perform all his lord's wishes and neglect all other matters. This is my care, though he has no care for my heart or my service. This division that makes one heart lord of two pains me deeply.

Why is mine alone not as powerful as his is when alone? Then both would have the same power. My heart is prisoner and may move only when his moves. Whether his wanders or stays still, mine readies itself and prepares to follow and travel close to him. God, why are our bodies not near enough that I might have some way of retrieving my heart? Retrieve it? Wretched fool that I am, then I would remove it from its comfort. I would be its death. Let it remain there! I have no wish to move it. No, I wish it to remain with its lord until he takes pity on it. He should have mercy on his servant sooner there than here since they dwell in a foreign land. And if my heart knows how to employ flattery in his service, as one must at court, it will be wealthy before its return.

"Whoever wishes to be in good favor with his lord and sit at his right, according to the practice in fashion, must cull the down from his head, even if none be there. But here is an evil dimension: the flatterer smooths down his lord's hair, and if his lord knows only wickedness and treachery, the flatterer will never have sufficient courtesy to address him, but will make him believe and understand that there could be none equal to him in wisdom and valor. And the lord believes that his servant tells the truth, for when a man is wicked and insolent, despicable and cowardly as a hare, niggardly, foolish, and deformed, base in words and deeds, many who mock him behind his back honor and esteem him to his face. In his presence, the flatterer praises his lord when he speaks of him to others, pretending his lord does not hear the conversation. But if he thought his lord were not listening, he would never say anything to please him. And if his lord wishes to lie, he is prepared to give complete assent. Whoever frequents courts and lords must serve by lying.

"And so my heart must do the same if it wishes to have its lord's favor. Let it be a fawning flatterer. But Cliges is such a knight, so handsome, so noble, and so true, that no matter how much my heart flatters him, it will never be guilty of falsehood or lie toward him since no aspect of him can be improved. And so I wish my heart to serve him. As the peasant says in his proverb, 'Anyone who serves a worthy man is evil unless he becomes better for his company.' "

This was the manner in which Love tormented Fenice, though she found the torment an untiring delight. As for Cliges, he had crossed the sea and reached Wallingford, where he took expensive lodgings in fine quarters. But all the while his thoughts were on Fenice, and he never forgot her for a single hour. While he was staying there, his men carried out his commands and made inquiries, finally receiving information that the barons of King

Arthur had organized a tournament at which the king himself would be present.

The four-day tournament was scheduled to take place in the open country below Oxford, which was near Wallingford. Because the tournament was more than two full weeks away, Cliges could take his time equipping himself in the interval if he was in need of anything. He had three of his squires hasten to London under orders to fetch three different sets of armor, one black, one vermilion, and the third green. In addition, he ordered that each set be wrapped in new canvas for the return journey so that anyone meeting them along the road would not know the color of the equipment they carried.

The squires set out at once. On reaching London, all they sought they found at hand. Soon they had completed their task, and soon they returned home, traveling as quickly as they could.

Cliges was delighted when they showed him the equipment they had brought. He had it placed aside and hidden along with the set the emperor had presented to him when, by the Danube, he dubbed him knight. If someone were to question me at this point as to why he had them set aside, I would not wish to answer here, for the reason will be told and recounted to you when all the great barons of the land, who come there to win honor, have mounted their horses.

On the day selected and appointed, the esteemed barons gathered. King Arthur, in company with the men he had selected from among his finest, took up positions on the Oxford side. The majority of knights took up positions on the Wallingford side. Do not expect me to extend my tale by telling you such and such a king was there, and such and such a count, and there were these here, and those ones, and these others.

When the time came for the barons to gather, a knight of great renown from the company of King Arthur, following the custom at that time, rode out between the two ranks to open the tournament. But none dared advance to come joust with him; all held back. And there were some who asked: "What are the knights waiting for that none leaves the ranks? One will start out soon."

And many on the other side said: "Do you not see the kind of opponent their side has sent us? Let the ignorant man know well that the knight in position is one of the four finest known."

"Who is he then?"

"Do you not see him? It is Sagremor the Unruly."

"Is that he?"

"Yes, without doubt."

Cliges was listening and heard their words. Clad in armor blacker than a ripe mulberry, he was seated on Morel; all his equipment was black. Leaving the ranks of the other side, he spurred Morel, who darted forward. All the spectators spoke among themselves. "This man rides well, his lance in its rest. This is a most proper knight. He carries his arms most properly. The shield hanging from his neck suits him well. But he may be considered a fool for engaging, of his own accord, in a joust with one of the finest men known in this entire country. But where is he from? Where was he born? Who recognizes him?" "Not I." "Nor I. But no snow has fallen on him."

Such conversation engaged the people, and the two men gave free rein to their horses, no longer hesitating in their burning impatience for the joust and combat. Cliges delivered such a blow that he pressed his opponent's shield hard against the arm and the arm against the body. Sagremor fell flat to the ground. Sagremor acknowledged himself his prisoner.

The combat began at once, with adversaries charging at one another in keen competition. Cliges threw himself into the contest, seeking to meet someone to joust with. He did not encounter a knight before him whom he failed to unhorse and take prisoner. From both sides he took the honor. Wherever he rode to joust, he brought the tournament to conclusion. Whoever rushed forward to joust with him was not without great valor; rather, that man won more renown just in waiting for him than in taking another knight prisoner. And if Cliges led his opponent away prisoner, the latter was still highly regarded simply for daring to await him in the joust. The honor and renown of the entire tournament belonged to Cliges.

Cliges departed secretly and returned to his quarters lest anyone speak to him on some subject or other. In case someone had a search made for the lodgings with the black armor, he locked his equipment in a room to prevent people from catching a glimpse of or discovering it, and had the green armor openly displayed at the door alongside the road for passersby to see. Anyone inquiring after him would not learn the location of his quarters. By such a trick, Cliges concealed himself in the town, while his prisoners went from one end of town to the other asking after the black knight. None, however, could instruct them. Although King Arthur himself had him sought everywhere, all replies were the same. "We have not seen him since we left the tournament. We do not know what has become of him."

More than twenty youths sent by the king searched for Cliges, but his method of hiding prevented them from discovering any trace of him. The king crossed himself when he was informed that no one, highborn or low, was found who could indicate the knight's dwelling any more than if he were in Caesarea, Toledo, or Crete. "On my word, I know not what to say," the king exclaimed. "This news astonishes me. Perhaps it was a phantom who came among us. Today he overthrew many knights and carried off the pledges of the finest. They will not see their gates, lands, or countries this year. Each one will have broken his pledge." And thus the king spoke his pleasure, though he might well have remained silent on the subject.

That night all the barons spoke at length of the black knight, for no other topic entered their conversations. The next morning, without need of summons or entreaty, they all took up arms again. Lancelot of the Lake, who was not fainthearted, dashed forward to engage in the opening joust. Lancelot was the first to await the joust. And Cliges, greener than meadow grass, came riding a fawn charger with a fine mane. Where Cliges rode his fawn steed, there was no one, with hair or without, who did not gaze on him with awe. Both sides exclaimed: "This man is much more noble and skillful in every respect than that man yesterday in black armor, just as the pine is more beautiful than the hornbeam and the laurel more beautiful than the elder. But we still have not learned the identity of yesterday's knight. Yet we shall know the identity of this one today. Let anyone who knows him tell us his name."

Each man declared not to know him or, he believed, ever to have seen him. But he was more handsome than yesterday's knight and more handsome than Lancelot of the Lake. Had he been dressed in a sack and Lancelot in silver or gold, this man would still be the more handsome. All sided with Cliges.

The two men came charging at each other, spurring as fast as they could. Cliges went and dealt Lancelot such a blow to the gold-trimmed shield with the painted lion that he knocked him from the saddle and swooped down on him to accept his surrender. Unable to defend himself, Lancelot acknowledged himself his prisoner.

Behold the tournament now begun with the clamor and commotion of lances. Those on the side of Cliges placed all their trust in him, for whoever he challenged and struck had never enough strength to prevent himself from falling from his charger to the ground.

Cliges performed well that day: he unhorsed and took prisoner so many that he took twice the honor and gave his men twice the pleasure he had the day before. In the evening he returned to his quarters as quickly as he could and had the vermilion shield and the rest of the armor promptly brought out. He ordered the arms he had carried that day set aside, and his host carefully put them away. That night the knights he had taken prisoner again undertook a long search for him, but heard no word of him. At the inns, many people expressed praise and esteem for him.

The following morning, the strong and agile knights donned their armor again. From the ranks on the Oxford side emerged a vassal of great renown named Perceval of Wales. When Cliges saw him advance and heard his identity, that he was called Perceval, he was anxious to challenge him.

Clad in vermilion armor, Cliges immediately rode forward from the ranks on a chestnut brown Spanish charger. Then all watched him with even more awe than before and exclaimed that they had never seen such a captivating knight. Without a moment's delay, the two men spurred on until they exchanged heavy blows on their shields. The short, thick lances curved and bent. Within sight of all the spectators, Cliges dealt Perceval such a blow that he knocked him from his horse and forced him to acknowledge himself his prisoner without much talk and without much ado.

After Perceval offered his pledge, the tournament then began and everyone charged. Cliges forced every knight he met to fall to the ground. That day he could not be seen absent from the combat for a single hour. In the tournament, all struck at him as they would at a tower, though not in twos or threes, for such was not the custom or practice at that time. His shield became an anvil because all pounded and hammered there, splitting and quartering it. But none struck without paying the price and vacating saddle and stirrups. None leaving could fail to admit, unless willing to lie, that the entire victory that day belonged to the knight with the red shield.

The finest and the bravest would have liked to make his acquaintance. That could not take place so soon, however, for he rode off secretly when he saw the sun setting. He had his vermilion shield and all the rest of the armor taken away and the arms in which he was dubbed knight brought out. The arms and the charger were placed at the door in front.

But now the men realized that they had all been defeated and routed by a single man, who disguised himself daily with a fresh horse and armor, thus appearing to be a different person. This was the first time they perceived this. Sir Gawain declared never to have seen such a jouster, and because he wished to make his acquaintance and know his name, he said that he would be first at the next morning's meeting of knights. He did not boast, yet he thought and believed that the knight would have all the advantage and glory when their lances struck, though perhaps in their sword exchange the knight would not be his master, since in this area Gawain himself could not find his master. Now it was his wish to measure himself the next day against the strange knight who had different armor and changed his horse and harness each day. If he continued his daily habit of taking off his old feathers and putting on new ones, he would soon molt for the fourth time.

In this fashion Cliges took off his armor and put on new equipment again. And the next morning Gawain saw him return, whiter than the lily-in-bloom, gripping his shield by the straps and riding his rested white Arabian steed, which he had harnessed during the night. Gawain, the brave and the renowned, did not stop on the field, but spurred and rode forward, doing the best he could to joust well if he found an opponent. Soon the two men would be on the field, for Cliges had no care to stay behind, hearing men uttering: "That is Gawain. He is no weakling on horseback or on foot. No one is his equal."

Hearing the words, Cliges rushed toward him in the center of the field. They advanced and sprang at each other faster than stags who hear dogs barking in pursuit. The lances struck the shields with such clanging blows that the lances split, cracked, and flew into pieces all the way to the butt ends, the cantles broke, and the saddlegirths and breaststraps snapped. Both knights fell to the ground at the same time, then drew their naked swords, while men gathered all around to watch the combat.

In order to separate the pair and bring about accord, King Arthur advanced in front of all. But before the slightest talk of peace, the two fighters had torn apart their polished hauberks and ripped the meshes to pieces, cleft through the shields and cut them to bits, and smashed the helmets.

When the king had watched them as long as it was his pleasure, as did many others who said that they esteemed the white knight's feats of arms no less than those of Sir Gawain, none could still declare who was better, who worse, or who should be the victor if they were permitted to fight to the finish. But it did not suit King Arthur that they do more than they had done. Stepping forward to separate them, he said to them: "Withdraw! I forbid more blows. Instead, make peace. Be friends. Dear nephew Gawain, I beg this of you, for it does not befit a worthy man to continue a battle or assault where no hatred or dispute exists. But were this knight willing to come to my court to sport with us, he should meet no pain or sorrow. Entreat him, nephew."

"Gladly, lord."

Having no desire to decline the invitation, Cliges, who had carried out his father's command to the fullest, agreed to proceed there at the end of the tournament.

The king expressed his will that the tournament not continue too long. At that moment they could well have ended it.

The knights had dispersed, following the will and command of the king. Since Cliges was to follow the king, he sent for all his equipment. He came to the court as fast as he could, although he first changed his attire and was now dressed in the French style.

The moment Cliges reached the court, none stayed back, but everyone rushed to meet him in a display of the greatest joy and festivity possible. All the prisoners he had taken in the tournament called him lord, yet wishing to disavow this title to all of them, he declared that they were all discharged from their pledges if they thought and believed that it was he who had captured them. Not a single one failed to exclaim: "It was you, we are certain of that. We place great value on your acquaintance. And we should love and esteem you and call you lord, for not one of us is your equal. Just as the sun outshines the small stars so that their light cannot be seen in the clouds where the sun's rays shine forth, so too our deeds of valor pale and fade in contrast with yours. And yet our deeds used to be much renowned throughout the world."

Cliges found all their praise more than he desired, and did not know how to reply. Their words pleased him, yet made him feel ashamed. Because the blood went to his face, the men observed his complete embarrassment. They escorted him through the great hall and led him before the king, all bringing their praise and flattering words to an end.

It was already the proper hour for the meal, and those in charge of such matters hastened to set the tables. The tables had been laid out in the palace hall. While some took towels, others held basins and gave water to those who came. All washed and sat down. The king took Cliges by the hand and seated him before him, anxious to learn of his identity that day, if ever he could. There is no need to speak of the meal, for the dishes were as plentiful as if beef cost a penny. Once all their courses had been served, the king did not remain silent. "Friend," he said, "I wish to know if pride was the reason you deigned not to come to my court the moment you entered this country. And do let me know why you kept your distance from us and changed your equipment. Tell me your name and the country where you were born."

"I shall hide this no more," Cliges answered. Then he told and recounted to the king all he wished to know. When the king learned who he was, he embraced him and rejoiced over him. And everyone delighted in his presence. When Sir Gawain knew the truth, he hugged and greeted him more than did all the others. Everyone embraced him in welcome, and all the people spoke of him, noting how brave and handsome he was. The king loved him and honored him more than he did any of his nephews.

Cliges stayed with the king until the beginning of the summer; by that time he had been all over Britain as well as to France and Normandy. He had engaged in many chivalric feats, proving himself well. But the love torturing him did not soften or abate. His heart's desire made him think always on one subject; he remembered Fenice, who, far from him, suffered in anguish. The urge to go back seized him; too long had he been deprived of beholding the most desirable lady a man could ever desire. No longer would he stay deprived of her sight.

He prepared to return to Greece. He took his leave and set out on the return journey, although the king and Sir Gawain, as I believe, were very sad not to be able to detain him longer. Yearning to reach the lady he loved and desired, he hastened over land and sea. He found the trip extremely long because of his deep desire to behold the lady who had seized and stolen his heart. But she presented to him fair return, paying him back with a fine recompense for the toll she had exacted from him: in exchange, she gave him her own heart, for she was no less in love than he. But he remained uncertain of this, never having pledge or promise in this regard. And so his pain was heavy. And she too was in deep pain, for Love was tormenting and killing her. She found no pleasure or satisfaction in anything she could see from the moment she lost sight of him. Not knowing if he was alive brought her heart heavy sorrow. But Cliges was steadily drawing near, fortunate in having fair winds and calm weather. With joy and delight, he came to anchor before Constantinople.

The news of his return reached the city. There could never be any doubt of the emperor's pleasure, and the empress knew a hundred times more pleasure. Cliges and his companions had returned to Greece and anchored in Constantinople harbor. The emperor and the empress went to the harbor to meet him, followed by all the greatest noblemen. In public view, the emperor rushed to welcome and embrace him. When Fenice greeted Cliges, they caused each other to change color. As they approached, it was a wonder they held back from embracing and kissing with the kind of kisses that please Love. But that behavior would have been folly and madness.

Attracted by the sight of his arrival, people rushed from all directions, some on foot, others on horseback, all escorting him through the city to the imperial palace. Of the joy present there, nothing will be related at this moment. Except for the crown, his uncle surrendered everything of his to Cliges. As a way of serving him, he wished him to take, at his pleasure, whatever money or treasure he desired. But Cliges had no interest in silver or gold. He dared not reveal his mind to the person who caused his loss of sleep. And were he not afraid of rejection, he had ample opportunity to speak to her: there was nothing to prohibit or hinder him from seeing her daily and sitting alone beside her, for no one saw or thought harm in that.

One day, a long time after his return, Cliges came by himself to the room of the lady by no means his foe. You can be certain that the door was not barred to his entrance. He took his seat beside her, and everyone there withdrew a distance so that no one sat near them who might hear their words. Fenice made him tell her first about Britain; she asked about Sir Gawain's character and upbringing. She then came to the subject she dreaded: she asked if he loved lady or maiden in the country. Cliges was not reluctant or slow to respond well to this question; he knew how to explain the situation to her the moment she addressed him on the subject.

"Lady," he said, "I was in love there, though not in love with someone from there. Like bark without timber, my body was without heart in Britain. Since I left Germany, I have not known what became of my heart, except that it followed you. My heart was here, and my body there. I was not away from Greece, for my heart had come there. For that reason I have come back here. Yet my heart does not come or return, and I cannot draw it back to me. I certainly do not wish to do this, nor am I able. And how have you been since you came to this country? What joy since then has been yours here? Do the people please you? Does the land please you? I should not ask you more except whether the country pleases you."

"Although it did not please me before, a joyous pleasure awakens in me now. You may be certain I would not wish to lose it for any prayer or entreaty, for from it I cannot detach my heart, and never shall I resort to force to do so. In me is nothing except the bark, for I live without a heart and exist without a heart. I was never in Britain, yet my heart stayed there a long while. I do not know whether it behaved well or ill."

"Lady, since your heart was there, tell me the time and season it went there, if it be fitting that you tell this to me or anyone else. Was it there when I was there?"

"Yes, but you did not know. It was there when you were there, and it departed with you."

"God, I did not know. I did not see it there. God, what did I not know? Certainly, lady, had I known, I would have offered it fine company."

"That would have been a great comfort to me. Friend, you should have done well, for I would have been most gracious to your heart had it been pleased to come where it knew I was."

"Lady, it certainly did come to you."

"To me? It did not suffer solitude too long since mine also went to yours."

"Lady, then from what you say, both our hearts are here with us, for mine belongs to you entirely."

"Friend, and for your part you have mine. We are in perfect agreement. So help me God, you may be certain your uncle never had any part of me, for that did not please me, nor was it permitted him. Never yet has he known me as Adam knew his wife. It is wrong to call me lady, though I realize people call me lady who do not know that I am a virgin. Your uncle himself is ignorant, for he drank a sleeping potion, which makes him believe himself awake when asleep. He imagines himself having all the pleasure he wishes of me as if lying in my arms. But I have kept him at a distance.

"My heart is yours. My body is yours. No one will ever learn base behavior from my example, for when my heart surrendered to you, it promised and gave you the body so that no one else would ever have part of it. Love dealt me such a wound on your account that I never expected to recover. You brought me deep anxiety and pain. If I love you and you love me, you will never be called Tristan and I shall never be Iseult, for then the love would be not honorable but base and subject to reproach. The pleasure you now derive from my body is all you will ever know unless you can contrive the seizure and theft of my person from your uncle in such a way that he can never again find me, nor be able to blame you or me, nor know anything to use in accusation. Tonight you must give thought to this, and tomorrow you may tell me the best plan you have devised. And I too shall consider the question. Tomorrow morning when I rise, come speak with me, and we shall exchange our ideas and act on the plan we consider best."

When Cliges heard her will, he agreed with her completely, saying that this course of action would be excellent. Happy was she as he departed, and happy he as he went away, and that night each lay awake in bed, delighting in plans that seemed good.

As soon as they rose the next morning, they met together in private to consider the necessary arrangements. The first to speak, Cliges recounted his thoughts from the night. "Lady, "he said, "I think and believe no better course of action could be available to us than setting off for Britain. I propose to escort you there. Now be careful not to object. Throughout the land of my uncle the king, there will be greater joy over your coming, over you and me, than the joyous welcome Helen received when Paris brought her to Troy. If this does not please you, tell me your plan. I am prepared, whatever may happen, to accept your advice."

"And I shall speak," she replied. "I shall never go with you in this fashion, for then the entire world would talk of us the way people do of the blonde Iseult and Tristan. After we had gone, men and women all over would censure our happiness. No one would tell the story as it is, and none would accept it as true. Who would then believe that I evaded your uncle and preserved my virginity? People would consider me most shameless and dissolute, and consider you a fool. It is good to remember and to observe Saint Paul's command. Saint Paul instructs anyone wishing to live chastely to behave prudently enough not to arouse outcry, censure, or reproach. It is good to stop a malicious tongue. And provided you are not opposed, I can accomplish this very well, for according to my plan, I shall feign death. Soon I shall make myself ill. And your task is to arrange the preparations for my tomb. Apply all your efforts to the design of the bier and the tomb so that I do not suffocate to death. Fashion it so that no one ever notices or suspects anything. The night you would take me from there, find me the kind of refuge where you are the only one to see me. Let none but you, to whom I present and give myself, furnish me with any necessity. I wish no other man to serve me as long as I live. You will be my lover and my servant. All you do for me will please me. I shall never be lady of any empire unless you are its lord. A poor place, dark and drab, will be brighter to me than all these halls.

"The plan, if ably executed, will never be described as wicked. None will ever be able to speak ill of it since people throughout the empire will believe my body to have rotted in the ground. And Thessala, my nurse, who raised me and has my trust, will be my loyal assistant, for she is most prudent and I rely on her completely."

Cliges, after hearing his beloved, replied: "Lady, if this be possible and you trust your nurse to give you proper advice, there is nothing left but to prepare quickly. But if we fail to act prudently, we are lost beyond recovery. I intend to make a request of a master artisan of mine, an extraordinary carver and sculptor. There is no country in which he is not recognized for the works he has designed, sculpted, and painted. John is his name, and he is my serf. If John wished to apply his efforts, there is no handicraft, however difficult, in which he would be equaled. Compared to him, all are novices, like infants at a nurse's breast. By imitating his works, the artisans of Antioch and those of Rome have learned whatever designs they can craft. Furthermore, a man more loyal is not known. Now I shall test him, and if I can find loyalty in him, I shall grant him and all his heirs freedom. Withholding nothing from him, I shall reveal your plan, provided that he gives me his oath and pledge to assist me loyally and never to betray me."

"Let that now be," she answered.

Then, with her permission, Cliges left the room and went off. And she called for her nurse Thessala, whom she had brought from her native land. Without a moment's delay, Thessala came at once, not knowing why she was summoned. When she asked her lady in private about her will and pleasure, Fenice did not keep silent or conceal from her any of her thoughts.

"Nurse," she said, "I realize that anything I say to you will never pass farther. By testing you thoroughly, I have found you to be most prudent. You have my deep love for all you have done for me. Whenever I am in trouble, I turn to you. Never do I seek advice elsewhere. You know well my thoughts and my desires and why I lie awake. My eyes can see nothing pleasing to me except one object, but never shall I know its comfort until I purchase it at a dear price. And now I have found my equal: if I desire him, he in turn desires me, and if I suffer, he in turn suffers for my sorrow and my anguish. Now I must confide in you my decision and my plan, which privately we both agreed to adopt."

She then explained and confirmed her intention of feigning sickness, adding that she would complain so much that in the end she would make herself appear dead, and on that night Cliges would steal her away, "and then we shall be together forever." There was no other way, she thought, for them to go on living. Were she assured of Thessala's aid, she should carry out this scheme as she wished. "But my joy and my good fortune are too far from me and too slow in coming."

Her nurse assured her of complete assistance, telling her never to have any doubt or fear. And from the moment she undertook the mission, she said, she would take special care that any looking upon her would be convinced that her soul was severed from its body, once she had given Fenice a potion that would make her cold and wan, pale and stiff, unable to speak or to breathe. Yet she would be alive and healthy, insensitive to good or ill. She would never suffer harm an entire day and night on the bier or in the tomb.

When Fenice heard all this, she responded to her. "Lady," she said, "I place myself in your hands completely. Trusting in you, I have no worry about myself. I am at your disposal. Take care of me. And tell the people I see here to leave. I am ill, and they disturb me."

"Gentlemen," Thessala addressed them courteously, "my lady feels ill and says that it is her wish that you leave, for you talk too much and make too much noise. The commotion is bad for her. She will have no peace or rest so long as you are in this chamber. My anxiety is all the greater because never do I remember hearing her complain of illness. Depart. Do not be angry. You will not speak with her this evening." They left the moment she requested.

And Cliges had summoned John privately to his lodgings. "John, do you know what I would say to you?" he asked him in confidence. "You are my serf. I am your lord. I may sell you or give you away. I may take your body and your possessions as though they were mine. But were I able to trust you concerning some business I am planning, both you and your heirs would have freedom forever."

In his immense desire for freedom, John answered immediately. "Sir," he said, "there is absolutely nothing I would not do at your will to see myself, my wife, and my children free. Tell me your command. Never will there be a task so difficult as to cause me toil or trouble. Never will it be a burden to me. Were this not the case, I would be forced to set aside all my own work and act on this, even against my will."

"That is true, John, but this is the kind of matter my mouth dares not utter unless you swear and pledge to me, with complete assurances, to assist me loyally and never to betray me."

"Gladly, sir," John replied. "You would be wrong ever to have any worry. I swear and pledge never, as long as I live, to say anything I think may cause you anxiety or pain."

"John, even were I to suffer martyrdom, there is no man I would dare speak to about the business that prompts me to seek your advice. I would first let my eye be plucked out. Through your help and your silence, you will, I believe, do my pleasure."

"Yes, sir, so help me God."

Cliges then gave him a straightforward and complete explanation of the plan. And when he had told him the truth, as you know it from hearing me tell it, John assured him of his best efforts in creating a tomb, and proposed to take him to see a house of his that no one, man, woman, or child, had ever seen. If it was his pleasure to go with him, by himself and without any other, he would show him the place he had built where he did his works, his sculpting and his painting. The location was the most beautiful and most attractive he had ever seen. "Then let us go there," Cliges answered.

In a secluded spot below the town, John had labored with great skill to construct a tower, and it was there that John led Cliges. Guiding him through rooms with beautiful and well-illuminated wall paintings, he took him everywhere, pointing out the rooms and the fireplaces. In this remote house, where no one stayed or resided, Cliges continued to look about as he went from one room to another until he thought he had seen everything.

Cliges found the tower very much to his liking, and said it was fine and beautiful. His young lady would be safe there all her life, since no man would ever know of it.

"Truly, sir, she will never be found. Do you now think you have seen the entire layout of my tower? There are still some hiding places no man could discover. And if you are allowed to test this by investigating as best you can, you would never find them. No one is wise and subtle enough to discover more rooms inside unless I clearly point them out to him. All is here, be certain, including everything a lady needs. There is nothing left to do but come here. This tower is comfortable and beautiful, and as you will see, there is a wide level underground. You will never be able to locate an entrance or opening anywhere. The door is made of solid stone with such skill and craft that you will never find the joints."

"What I hear is astonishing," Cliges said. "Lead the way and I shall follow. I am anxious to see this."

Then John started off, leading Cliges by the hand up to a smooth and even door painted all in colors. John leaned against the wall, holding Cliges by his right hand. "Sir," he said, "there is no man who knows of any door or window in this wall. Do you believe that there is any possible way of passing through without breaking it down or damaging it?"

Cliges replied that he did not believe this, nor would he ever believe it without witnessing it. John then said that Cliges would witness this, for he would open the door in the wall. John, who had designed the work, unlocked the door in the wall and opened it for him without break or damage. They passed through, one in front of the other, then descended a winding staircase into a vaulted room, which John had used, at his pleasure, as his workshop.

"Sir," he said, "of all the men created by God, we are the only two who have been here. As you will soon see, this place is most comfortable. Let this location be your home and your beloved's hiding place. Such a lodging is excellent for such a guest. There are chambers and bathrooms, and in the baths hot water that comes through underground pipes. The man who would seek a comfortable hiding place for his beloved would have far to go before discovering one so suitable. When you have been throughout, you will consider it most pleasing."

When John had shown him everything, Cliges said: "Friend John, I grant you and all your heirs freedom. My devotion to you is boundless. I wish my beloved to be alone here entirely, with none knowing but you, I, and she."

"Thank you," John replied. "We have now been here long enough. Let us return at once since there is no more for us to do."

"You are right," Cliges answered. "Let us depart."

They then left the tower and went back to the city. On their return they overheard people whispering among themselves. "Do you not know the incredible news about my lady the empress? She lies in bed gravely ill. May the Holy Spirit make the good and wise lady healthy."

When Cliges heard their whisperings, he rushed to the court. No joy or pleasure was there: all were sorrowful and dejected on account of the empress. The illness she complained of was pretense, causing her no suffering or pain. She told everyone that she wished no visitors in her chamber except the emperor, him or his nephew (she dared not refuse these two), so long as she was in the tight grip of this illness that disturbed her head and her heart. But were the emperor, her lord, not to come to her, she would have no concern. It was for Cliges that she was forced to place herself in grave peril and danger, and since seeing him was her only desire, she was distressed at his not coming.

Cliges would soon be in her presence and stay until he had told her what he had discovered and seen. He came before her and spoke to her. His stay was brief, for Fenice cried out so that people would think her annoyed by what pleased her. "Get out! Get out! You disturb me. You weary me. My illness is so grave that I shall never regain my health."

After hearing these words, Cliges left, feigning the most dejected countenance ever beheld. He could not display his feelings, but his very heart was delighted at the anticipation of its joy.

Although not ill, the empress complained and feigned sickness. Because the emperor believed her, he did not cease his lament. He summoned physicians to attend her, but she did not wish anyone to see her and would let no one touch her. The emperor was distressed to hear her say that there was but one physician who could easily restore her health should it be his will. That physician would be the source of her life or her death, and in his hands she placed her health and her life. People thought that she was referring to God, but her meaning was misunderstood. She meant none but Cliges: he was her god, with power to cure her or to cause her death. Thus the empress took care that no physician examined her. She would eat and drink nothing in order to deceive the emperor better, and so she turned pale and purplish-blue all over.

Her nurse remained near her. After secretly searching throughout the city to avoid attention, she had managed, through an amazing scheme, to obtain from an incurably ill woman a pot filled with urine. To carry out the deception still more effectively, she paid her frequent visits, promising her that she would cure her sickness. Every day she carried a bottle for examining her urine, until she saw that medicine could help the woman no further and that she would die that very day. She brought the urine back and kept it hidden until the emperor rose. Then she went before him at once.

"If, sir, it be your will to command, summon all your physicians," she said. "My lady, who is consumed by this sickness, has urinated. She wishes the physicians to examine it, provided they come not before her."

When the physicians entered the great hall, they saw the urine foul and colorless. After each stated his opinion, they agreed that she would never recover, nor live past three that afternoon. Were she to live that long, God would take her soul to Himself at that hour without further ado. This was the consensus they reached among themselves. To the emperor's request and entreaty that they tell him the truth, they replied that they held no hope at all for recovery: she would give up her soul by three that afternoon. When the emperor heard their words, he almost fainted on the ground, as did many others who heard them. Never did people display the kind of sorrow present at that moment throughout the palace.

I offer you no description of the grief. You know the end Thessala sought with the potion she mixed and brewed. Much earlier had she devised all she knew to be necessary for the potion, and had beaten and blended it. A little before three o'clock, she gave Fenice the potion to drink. And the moment she drank it, her vision blurred, and her face turned pale and white as though she had lost her blood. Had someone flayed her alive, she would not have moved a hand or foot. She did not stir or utter a word, yet she clearly heard and understood the grief of the emperor and the cries that filled the great hall.

Throughout the city, people wept. With tears in their eyes they exclaimed: "God, what grief and misery despicable Death has dealt us! Death, you are too evil and greedy, ravenous and envious. You are insatiable. Never could you give the world such a fatal bite. Death, what did you do? God confound you for extinguishing all beauty. Of all creatures God ever strove to create, you killed the one who was, had she but lived, the finest and most holy. God is too patient in allowing you power to destroy His creations. Now should God be angry and cast you from your battlement, for with all your arrogance and insolence, you have been too defiant."

All the people thus went mad with rage, wringing their hands and beating their palms. And the clerics read their psalters and prayed for the good lady that God take mercy on her soul.

Amid the tears and cries, as the book testifies, three elderly physicians had arrived from Salerno, where they had long resided. They stopped on account of the mourning and made inquiries about the reason for the tears and cries, and the cause of the people's grief and distraction. "God, gentlemen, do you not then know?" people exclaimed to them in reply. "At this the entire world should go mad, one place after another, if the heavy sorrow and anger, the pain and severe loss that have today befallen us were known. God, then whence did you come not to know what just now happened in this city? We shall tell you the truth, for we want you to join in the grief we suffer. Do you not know of wretched Death, who desires and covets all and lies in wait everywhere for the finest? Do you not know of the dread deed she enacted today following her practice? God had lit up the world with a radiant light. But He cannot stop Death from pursuing her habits. Her power always does away with the finest she can find. Now she wants to prove her might and has removed in one body more excellence than she has left behind. Had she taken the entire world, she would not have done worse. Death cheated and robbed us of beauty, courtesy, wisdom, and all the goodness a lady may possess, for she has destroyed all goodness in the person of our lady the empress. Thus Death has killed us."

"Alas, God, well we know Your hatred of this city since we failed to arrive here earlier," said the physicians. "Had we come yesterday, Death could have esteemed herself highly had she snatched anything from us by force."

"Gentlemen, by no means would our lady have wished you to see her or to trouble yourselves on her account. There were many fine physicians, but it never pleased our lady that any see her or concern himself with her illness. No, on our word, she would not have wished that at all."

The physicians then recalled Solomon, whose wife hated him so much that she deceived him by feigning death. Perhaps this lady had done the same. If they could somehow manage to examine her closely, no man alive could make them utter falsehood or prevent them from telling the entire truth, should they find deception operating there. At once they went toward the court, where God's thunder would have been inaudible, so much commotion and wailing were there. The master of these three, the most knowledgeable, approached the bier. No one told him, "Do not touch that," nor did anyone draw him back. He placed his hand on her breast and her side, and felt beyond doubt that there was still life in her body; this fact he realized and clearly understood. Before him he saw the emperor crazed and overwhelmed with grief. In a loud voice he cried out and exclaimed to him: "Emperor, comfort yourself. I see and know with certainty that this lady is not dead. Set aside your grief and take comfort. If I do not restore her to you alive, you may slay me or hang me."

All the commotion throughout the palace quieted down and died away immediately. The emperor told the physician that he might give orders and speak his will freely. If he restored the empress to life, he would be lord and commander over him. But he would be hanged like a thief had he told any lie.

"I gladly accept this," he replied. "Unless I make this lady speak to you, never have mercy on me. Have the palace hall emptied for me at once so that no one is left here. I must examine in private the illness causing the lady's suffering. Since these two physicians are my colleagues, they will be the only people to remain here with me. Let all the others go without."

Cliges, John, and Thessala would have opposed this plan, but all those present might have misinterpreted their opposition had they tried to dissuade them. As a consequence, they kept silent and gave the advice they heard the others offer. And so they left the palace.

The three physicians violently ripped off the lady's shroud without resort to knife or scissors. "Lady," they then said, "be not frightened or upset, but speak with confidence. We know with clear certainty that you are completely sound and healthy. But be wise and courteous. Do not despair. If you seek our help, all three of us assure you of all the aid we can offer. You should not refuse it."

By this talk they expected to trick and compromise her, but their words had no effect. To their promise of concern she showed no care or heed. All their endeavors amounted to nothing. When the physicians saw that they would not realize any success with her by entreaty or flattery, they took her off the bier, saying that if she did not speak, she would recognize her folly, for they would resort to extraordinary measures never before inflicted on the body of any unfortunate woman. "We realize that you are alive and care not to talk to us. We realize that you pretend and thereby deceive the emperor. Have no fear of us. But if anyone has angered you, tell us your pleasure before we harm you. Your behavior is very base. We shall aid you in any business, whether it be wise or foolish."

All was in vain; their words had no effect. They then lashed her back, leaving visible marks all the way down, and gave her tender skin such a thrashing that they made the blood spurt out. After their lashings succeeded in breaking the skin and sending the blood that came from the wounds streaming down her back, the physicians could still accomplish nothing, not make her utter a word or sigh, and she did not move or stir. They then declared that they had to fetch fire and lead, which they would melt and lay on her palms rather than fail to make her talk. After searching out fire and lead, they lit the fire and melted the lead. That was their method of abusing and torturing the lady, those dissolute wretches who took lead all boiling and hot from the fire and poured it into her palms. Still not satisfied with the lead passing through her very palms, the cowardly bastards declared that unless she spoke immediately they would place her at that very moment on the grill until she was entirely burned. And she maintained silence, not forbidding them to beat or injure her flesh.

They were already about to place her on the fire to be grilled and roasted when more than a thousand ladies separated from the other people and went their own way. They came to the door and saw through a tiny crack the cruel tortures being inflicted on the lady by those forcing her to suffer martyrdom on the flaming coals. With the axes and hammers they carried, they smashed and broke in the door. Mighty was the clamor of their assault as they battered and smashed down the door. If they could now take hold of the physicians, the latter would be repaid all they deserved without delay.

The ladies rushed into the great hall together. In the crowd was Thessala, whose only concern was to reach her lady. She found her entirely naked by the fire, severely mistreated and sorely injured. She placed her back on the bier and covered her with the shroud.

As for the ladies, they went to deliver the three physicians the wages they deserved. Having no desire to send or wait for emperor or seneschal, they hurled the physicians out the windows down into the center of the courtyard. All three had their necks and ribs, arms and legs broken. No ladies ever behaved better.

Now the ladies had paid the three physicians their dire due. But Cliges was upset and desolate to learn of the terrible suffering and martyrdom his beloved had endured for his sake. He almost went mad because he was terrified, and rightly so, that she might have been badly injured or killed by the torture inflicted on her by the three physicians who had come there. And so he was despondent and despairing.

Thessala came with a precious ointment which she gently applied to her lady's blows and wounds. For this second enshrouding, the ladies wrapped her again in a white Syrian shroud, leaving her face uncovered. All the night their wailings never abated, nor did they cease or conclude. Throughout the city, highborn and low, poor and rich were beside themselves with grief. Each seemed set on outdoing all in the mourning and never, of his own will, relinquishing it. The heavy lamentation continued all night long.

The next morning John came to the court, summoned by the emperor. The latter told him his request and command. "John, if ever you fashioned a fine work, now devote all your skill and invention to designing a tomb, the most beautiful and the most finely crafted to be found."

John, who had already made the tomb, said that he had prepared a beautiful and exquisitely designed one, though when he began its construction, he intended to reserve it for the body of a saint. "Now let the empress be placed inside as though it were a reliquary, for she is, I believe, a most holy creature."

"You are right," said the emperor. "She shall be laid to rest outside Saint Peter's Cathedral, where the other bodies are buried, for before she died, she earnestly begged and implored me to have her laid there. Now set about your task. Fix your tomb in the most beautiful location in the cemetery, where it is right and proper that it be."

"Gladly, sir," John answered.

John departed at once and carefully prepared the tomb as a master craftsman would. He placed a feather bed inside on account of the hard stone, and even more on account of the cold. And that it might be fragrant for her, he spread flowers and leaves beneath. A more important reason for doing this, however, was to prevent anyone from seeing the mattress he had placed in the tomb.

By this time all the services had ended in the chapels and parish churches, and the bells tolled continually as should be done out of respect for the dead. Orders were given to bring the body and lay it in the splendid and nobly proportioned tomb John had designed with such care. In all Constantinople there was none, highborn or low, who, in tears, failed to follow the body, cursing and reproaching Death. Knights and squires fainted, and ladies and maidens beat their breasts as they disputed with Death. "Death," each exclaimed, "why did you not take ransom for my lady? Your gain was certainly small, whereas our loss is immense."

To be certain, Cliges mourned so much that he became madder and more distraught than all the others. It was a wonder that he did not slay himself. But he postponed this act until the hour and moment came for him to disinter Fenice, to embrace her, and to know if she was alive or not. The barons were at the edge of the grave, laying the body in its position. They did not interfere with John as he arranged the tomb; they could see nothing because all had fainted on the ground. And so John had ample time to carry out his work. He set up the tomb so that nothing else was inside, sealing all the joints carefully, then shutting the tomb. Then could the man be proud of himself who knew how, without damaging or breaking something, to open John's work or separate the joints.

Fenice was in the tomb until the coming of night's darkness. Thirty knights stood watch, and ten burning tapers shed much bright light. Weary from their sorrow and exhausted from the strain, the knights ate and drank that evening until all fell asleep together.

At night's approach, Cliges stole away from all the people at the court, not a knight or man-at-arms knowing what had become of him. He rushed off until he found John, who gave him all the advice he could, and dressed him in a suit of armor he would never need. Once equipped, the two rode to the cemetery, spurring their horses.

The entire cemetery was encircled by a high wall. The knights thought themselves safe and had locked the gate from the inside to prevent anyone entering. Now they were asleep. Cliges did not see how he might enter because he could not proceed through the gate, and in truth he had to enter, for Love encouraged and urged him on. Being as brave and agile as he was, he gripped the wall and crawled up. Inside was an orchard with many trees, and one was planted so near the wall that it actually touched the wall. Now Cliges had all he desired, for he lowered himself by this tree.

His first act was to go and open the door for John. Seeing all the knights sleeping, he extinguished the tapers so that no light remained. John uncovered the grave at once and opened the tomb without doing any damage. Cliges climbed into the grave and lifted out his beloved, who was weak and lifeless. He hugged her, kissed her, embraced her, not knowing whether to mourn or to rejoice. She did not stir or utter a word. As quickly as he could, John again sealed the tomb so that there was no evidence that it had been touched.

They approached the tower as fast as possible. When they had placed her in the tower's underground rooms, they removed her shroud. Ignorant of the potion she had inside her body that prevented her movement or speech, Cliges believed her dead. Despondent and despairing, he sighed heavily and wept. But soon the time would come when the potion would lose its power.

Hearing the mourning, Fenice struggled and strained for power to comfort him with a word or glance. The lament she heard him make almost broke her heart. "Alas, Death," he said, "how base you are to spare and reprieve vile and contemptible creatures. These you allow to live on and endure! Death, you are drunk and mad to make my beloved die for me. What a wonder I behold: my beloved is dead, and I am alive. Alas, sweetheart, why does your lover live and see you dead? Now it might be rightly stated that I have slain and murdered you since you died in my service. Beloved, I am then the death who killed you. Is this wrong? I took my life away from you, and kept yours. Sweetheart, were your health and your life not my joy? And did my soul not belong to you? I loved none but you. We two were one being. Now I have done what I had to do! I keep your life in my body, and mine is no longer in yours. And the one should be companion to the other everywhere. Nothing should separate them."

At this, Fenice heaved a sigh and uttered in a low and weak voice: "Beloved, beloved, I am not completely dead, though nearly so. I have no further care for my life. I expected to pretend and to deceive, but now I ought to complain because Death did not appreciate my deceit. It will be a miracle if I escape alive. The physicians painfully wounded me. They tore and broke my skin. Yet were it possible for my nurse Thessala to be here with me, she would restore me to full health if any efforts should avail."

"Beloved, then have no worry, for this evening I shall bring her here to you," Cliges replied.

"Lover, John should be the one to go."

John went and searched until he found Thessala. He explained to her how important it was that she come and that no obstacle detain her, since Fenice and Cliges summoned her to a tower where they awaited her. Because of Fenice's grave condition, she was to come with supplies of ointments and medications. If she delayed and failed to bring her immediate aid, Fenice would die.

Thessala ran at once and took ointments, plasters, and remedies of her own devising; she then rejoined John. They left the city secretly, not stopping until they reached the tower. When Fenice saw her nurse, she thought herself cured completely, so deep was her love for her and so strong her faith and trust in her.

Cliges greeted and embraced her. "Nurse, how welcome you are," he said. "I love and esteem you so much. Now tell me your opinion of this young lady's illness. What do you think? Will she again be healthy?"

"Yes, sir, have no fear. I shall cure her completely. Within a fortnight I shall make her healthier and livelier than she ever was before."

Thessala set her mind to healing her, and John went to fit out the tower with every necessity. Boldly and in open view, Cliges repeatedly traveled to and from the tower, for he had placed a molting goshawk there, and mentioned that he went to observe it. None might suspect that he rode there for any reason other than the goshawk. He often stayed there night and day. And John, so that no one entered without his consent, stood guard at the tower. Because of Thessala's fine cure, Fenice had no sickness to complain of. If Cliges were now Duke of Almeria, or of Morocco, or of Tudela, he would not have valued such honors as highly as a hawthorn berry in contrast to his own joy. Love certainly did not debase himself in bringing these two together, for when they embraced and kissed each other, both thought the entire world better for their joy and happiness. Regarding this, never ask me more.

Fenice lived in the tower all that year and well into the next, three months, I think, and still more. With the reappearance of summer, when flowers and foliage blossom and small birds make merry and delight in their own tongue, Fenice happened to hear the nightingale sing one morning. Cliges was holding her tenderly with one arm around her side and the other about her neck, and she, at the same time, embraced him. "Dear sweet love," she said to him, "an orchard where I might frolic would do me so much good. For more than fifteen full months I have not seen moonlight or sunlight. Were it possible, I would gladly go out into the daylight, for this tower confines me. And were there an orchard nearby where I might go and enjoy myself, it would often do me much good." Cliges promised to seek advice from John the moment he saw him.

It then happened that John was on his way there, for he was in the habit of visiting frequently. Cliges spoke to him of Fenice's wish. "All she commanded is prepared and ready," John answered. "This tower is well fitted out with all she wishes and requests."

Fenice was then delighted, and asked John to take her there. "Nothing prevents me," John replied, and then went to open a door. I do not have the ability or knowledge to describe its design. None but John could have made it. Because it was so concealed and covered, no one could ever have suspected a door or window was there so long as the door was shut.

When Fenice saw the door open and the sunshine she had not seen for so long stream in, all her blood stirred with joy. Since she was able to leave her hiding place, she said that she had all her desires and sought no other lodging. She then entered a pleasant and agreeable orchard. In the center of the orchard was a grafted tree that spread out at the top and was covered with many leaves and flowers. All the branches were trained to hang down so that they almost touched the ground, all, that is, except the trunk from which they grew. The trunk rose straight up. Fenice desired no other location. The small lawn beneath the grafted tree was most delightful and beautiful. Never is the sun so hot in summer, when highest in the sky, that its rays might ever pass there. Such was John's skill in setting up the tree and arranging and training the branches. It was there that Fenice went to play, and made her bed beneath the grafted tree. It was there that the pair knew their joy and delight. And a high wall connected to the tower surrounded the entire orchard so that no one might come there without climbing first through the tower. Now Fenice was happy. There was nothing that displeased her. Lying on the flowers and the leaves, she had all she desired: she was free to embrace her lover.

In the season when people take sparrowhawks and hounds and go to hunt larks and wild ducks and track quail and partridges, a knight bachelor of Thrace, a lively youth esteemed for his chivalric feats, happened one day to have gone hunting very near the tower. The knight's name was Bertrand. His sparrowhawk had flown off when it missed a lark. Bertrand would now consider himself ill-befallen if he lost his sparrowhawk. Seeing it descend and settle beneath the tower in the orchard delighted him; now he did not expect to lose it. He went at once and scaled the wall until he managed to climb over. Beneath the grafted tree he saw, sleeping together, Fenice and Cliges, naked body beside naked body. "God! What has happened to me?" he exclaimed. "What kind of marvel is this I see? Is this not Cliges? I swear, yes. Is this not the empress with him? Of course not, but this lady resembles her. No one else ever resembled her so much. She has such a nose, such a mouth, such a forehead as my lady the empress had. Nature could never make two creatures so much alike. In this lady I behold every feature I saw in my lady. Were she alive, I would truly assert that this was she."

At that moment a pear came loose and hit Fenice on the ear. She awakened with a start. Catching sight of Bertrand, she screamed: "Lover! Lover! We are dead. See Bertrand here! If he escapes us, we are caught in an ill trap. He will report that he saw us."

Bertrand then realized that this was truly the empress. He had to flee, for Cliges had brought his sword with him into the orchard and laid it in front of them. Cliges jumped up and took his sword, while Bertrand made a hasty flight, scaling the wall as fast as he could. He was almost over safely when, pursuing him, Cliges at once raised his sword and dealt him such a blow that he cut off his leg below the knee like a fennel stalk. Maimed and badly abused, Bertrand still managed to escape. When his men saw him from the other side of the wall, they were almost mad with grief to behold him so crippled. They immediately asked him the name of his assailant. "Do not speak to me," he said, "but place me on my horse. This matter will be related only in the presence of the emperor. The man who did this to me should not be without fear, nor indeed is he, for he is in mortal danger."

They then placed him on his palfrey and, deeply dismayed and mournful, led him down into the city, followed by more than twenty thousand others who rode all the way to the court. All the people raced there, each person struggling to arrive first.

Already Bertrand had publicly uttered his lament and plea to the emperor. Yet he was considered an idle chatterer to say that he had seen, beneath a grafted tree in an orchard, the empress entirely naked with the knight Cliges. The entire city was thrown into confusion by the news the people heard. Some thought it nonsense; others advised and counseled the emperor to proceed to the tower. Huge were the outcry and the commotion from the men preparing to follow him. But they found nothing in the tower, for Fenice and Cliges had left, taking Thessala with them. She was their comfort and assurance, declaring that if they happened to sight men pursuing them with the intent of capture, they would have nothing to fear, for those bent on their injury and harm would never come closer to them than the distance of a strongly drawn crossbow's shot.

The emperor was in the tower and commanded that John be sought and summoned. He had him bound and guarded, and said that because of the humiliation he had suffered, he would have John hanged, burned, and his ashes scattered to the winds. John would receive his proper reward, the emperor continued, although that reward would be without honor, since he had hidden his nephew along with his wife in the tower.

"You tell the truth, I swear," John answered. "I shall never lie or conceal anything on your account. And if I did any wrong, it is right indeed that I be imprisoned. But I would offer this as my excuse, that a serf must refuse nothing his rightful lord demands of him. And it is certainly well known that I am his and the tower is his."

"No it is not, John. It belongs to you."

"Me, sir? Yes, after him. I do not even belong to myself, and I have nothing that is mine, except what he grants me. And if you wish to say that my lord wronged you, I am ready to defend him against this charge without his so ordering me. The certain knowledge that I am to die emboldens me to declare my mind and will openly according to the careful consideration I have given the matter. Now come what may, for if I die for my lord, I shall not die with dishonor. All well know, beyond doubt, the oath and pledge you promised your brother, that after you, Cliges, who goes away into exile, should be emperor. But if it be God's pleasure, he yet will be. In this regard you are subject to reproach because you should not have taken a wife. Nevertheless you took her and wronged Cliges. He did no wrong to you. If you punish me with death and I die wrongfully for his

[166]

sake, he will, if he be alive, avenge my death. Do the best you can, for if I die in this manner, you shall die."

When the emperor heard these words, he broke out in a sweat of anger. Well he knew what John had stated. "John," he said, "you will have a reprieve until your lord is found. He behaved treacherously toward me. I cherished him very much. I had no intention of cheating him. But you will be held in prison. If you know what happened to him, I command you, tell me immediately."

"And how should I commit so great a treason?" John replied. "Were the life to be drawn from my body, I would certainly give you no information concerning my lord, even if I knew it. Besides this, so help me God, I can say no more than you about the direction they took. But you have no reason to be jealous. Your anger does not fill me with such fear that I would not tell you the entire truth of how you were tricked. And I shall never be believed!

"You were duped and deceived by a potion you took the day of your wedding. Since that time you never enjoyed your wife unless you happened to dream during your sleep. The night caused you to dream, and you had as much pleasure in your dream as if she had chanced to hold you in her arms when you were awake. That was all the happiness that came to you from her. Her heart so clung to Cliges that she feigned death for his sake. And he had such trust in me that he told me of this and placed her in my house, where he is the rightful lord. You should not blame me for this. I should have been hanged or burned had I refused my lord and betrayed his will."

When the emperor recalled the potion he had been pleased to drink, and which was Thessala's means of tricking him, he knew and realized for the first time that he had never enjoyed his wife—he was certain of that— unless it had happened to him in a dream. That joy was an illusion, and he declared that unless he avenged the humiliation and insult the traitor had done him by stealing his wife away, he would never be happy so long as the traitor lived. "Now quickly," he exclaimed, "let him be sought in every castle, town, and city all the way to Pavia, and from there all the way to Germany. Dearer to me than any other man will be he who brings them both captive. Now go and search carefully. Hunt for them in all places, near and far."

All set out as the situation demanded and passed the entire day searching. But Cliges had such friends there that had they found him, they would have taken him to a place of safety rather than lead him back again. For an entire fortnight they pursued him with some difficulty. Thessala, however, who guided the pair, led them so safely by her skills in magic that they stood in no fear or dread of all the emperor's efforts. They did not pass a night in town or city. And they had everything they usually wished, or even more, for Thessala went off to obtain all they desired, and brought it to them.

None followed or pursued them more because all had started back. Cliges, however, did not rest, setting out for his uncle King Arthur and searching until he found him. Then he complained and protested about his uncle the emperor: he had unlawfully taken a wife with the effect of disinheriting him, and he should not have taken one because of his promise to Cliges' father never to have a wife as long as he lived. And the king announced that he would sail with a navy before Constantinople, filling a thousand ships with knights and three thousand with men-at-arms so that no town or city, castle or stronghold, however high or powerful, could withstand their assaults.

Cliges did not forget to thank the king at that time for the aid he offered him. The king sent out to find and summon all the great barons of his land, and had boats and warships, galleys and barques sought out and prepared. He had these boats loaded to their fill with shields, lances, bucklers, and knightly armor. The king embarked on such massive preparations for war that neither Caesar nor Alexander saw their equal. He had all England and all Flanders, Normandy, Brittany, and France, as well as all the men as far as the borders, summoned and assembled.

They were already prepared to cross the sea when messengers from Greece arrived, who detained the king and his men and delayed the crossing. Accompanying the arriving messengers was John, a man who deserved to be believed, for he would not be witness or messenger to anything that was untrue and that he did not know as a certainty. The messengers were noblemen from Greece who were searching for Cliges. They made inquiries until they found him; then they rejoiced very much. "God save you, sir, in the name of all the subjects of your empire," they addressed him. "Greece is handed over to you, Constantinople is presented, because of the right you hold to them. Your uncle, though you do not know this, is dead from his distress at being unable to find you. He was so distraught that he lost his senses. He never ate or drank, and died like a madman. Dear sir, come back now, for all your barons send for you. They want and ask for you. It is their will that you be made emperor."

Some who heard this announcement were delighted, while others would have gladly sent their guests away and taken pleasure in the host setting off for Greece. But the voyage was set aside completely, for the king sent his men away and the army disbanded and returned home.

Wishing no further delay, Cliges, in his eagerness to return to Greece, hurried his preparations. Once prepared, he took leave of the king and all his friends. He took Fenice with him, and they set off, continuing their travels until they were in Greece.

The people gave Cliges a joyous welcome, as they should their lord, and presented him with his beloved as his wife. They crowned them both together.

Cliges made his beloved his lady, for he called her beloved and lady, and she lost nothing in this, for he loved her as his beloved, and she loved him as one should love one's lover. And each day their love increased. He never doubted her or quarreled with her on any subject. She was never kept in seclusion as empresses from that time on have been. Since then there has been no emperor who did not fear being deceived by his wife after hearing the story of Fenice deceiving Alis, first with the potion he drank, and then with the other treachery. For this reason every empress, no matter who she was, no matter how highborn or noble, was guarded in Constantinople as though imprisoned. The emperor had no trust in her so long as he remembered Fenice. More out of fear than worry over

SUNBURN, HE HAD HER ALWAYS KEPT UNDER GUARD IN HER CHAMBER.

NEVER WOULD SHE HAVE A MALE IN HER COMPANY UNLESS HE

HAD BEEN CASTRATED IN CHILDHOOD. CONSEQUENTLY

THERE WAS NO DOUBT OR FEAR OF LOVE

BINDING THEM IN HIS FETTERS.

HERE ENDS CHRISTIAN'S

WORK.

THE KNIGHT OF THE CART

INCE MY LADY OF CHAM-
pagne wills me to undertake the making of a ro-
mance, I shall undertake it with great goodwill, as
one so wholly devoted that he will do anything in
the world for her without any intention of flattery.
But another man might begin this in order to flatter
her; he would say, and I could only agree, that she
surpasses all living ladies as the south wind blowing
in April or May surpasses all winds. On my word, I am not one who would
flatter his lady. Shall I say, "The Countess is worth as much in queens as
a precious gem is worth in brocades and semiprecious stones?" No indeed,
I shall say nothing of this, though it is true despite my silence. I shall say
only that her command is more important in this undertaking than any
thought or effort I may expend.

Christian is beginning his book of the Knight of the Cart. The Countess
presents him with the matter and the meaning, and he undertakes to shape
the work, adding little to it except his effort and his careful attention.

One Ascension Day, King Arthur held a court sumptuous and splendid
to his liking, sumptuous as becomes a king. After dinner the king remained
among his companions. There were many barons in the great hall, and also
the queen and, I believe, many courteous and beautiful ladies conversing
in elegant French. Kay, who had planned and overseen the feast, was eating
with the stewards.

While Kay was seated at his meal, behold there arrived at the court a
knight in armor, fully equipped for combat. Dressed like this, the knight

came before the king where he was seated among his barons; he addressed him directly without word of greeting. "King Arthur, in my prison I hold knights, ladies, and maidens of your land and your household. But I tell you the news not because I intend to return them to you. On the contrary, I simply wish to inform you and serve notice that you don't have the force or wealth to free them. You can be certain you will die before you ever bring them aid."

The king replied that he had to endure what he could not change, though it much grieved him to have to do so. Then, making as if to go away, the knight turned on his heels and left the king. He came to the door of the great hall, but did not go down the stairs; rather, he stopped there and called out, "Your Majesty, if your court has a single knight you would dare entrust with the queen to lead her into the forest following me, on my word I will wait there for him; for if he can win her in combat against me and succeed in bringing her back again, I will surrender to you at once all the prisoners I hold captive in my land."

Many in the palace heard the challenge, and the whole court was in an uproar. The news reached Kay as he was eating with the serving men. Leaving his dinner, he made his way directly to the king and began at once to address him with indignation. "Your Majesty, I have served you very well in good faith and loyalty. Now I take my leave. Because I shall attend you no longer, I shall depart. I have neither desire nor inclination to serve you more."

The king was pained by what he heard. As soon as he could respond properly, he asked him: "Do you speak in sincerity or in jest?"

"Lord king, this is no jesting matter," Kay replied. "I am sincere about taking my leave. I seek no other reward or recompense from you for my service. And so I wish to leave now without delay."

"Is it anger or contempt that makes you want to go?" the king inquired. "Seneschal, continue to stay at my court. You can be certain that if you stay, I have nothing in this world I would not give you at once."

"Lord, it is no use," he said. "I would not stay here for a daily barrel of fine pure gold."

Behold the king at a complete loss what to do. He went to the queen. "Lady," he said, "do you know what the seneschal asks of me? He seeks permission to leave and says he will stay at my court no longer. I don't know why. What he is unwilling to do for me, he will do at once at your request. Go to him, my dear lady. Since he will not even consider staying for my sake, beg him to stay for yours. Even throw yourself at his feet. If I were to lose his company, I would never be happy again."

The king sent the queen to the seneschal, and she went. She found him with the others. Approaching him, she said to him: "Kay, believe me, the news I have heard about you disturbs me very much. I am unhappy to hear you want to leave the king. Why do you do it? What is your reason? I don't see the wisdom or the courtesy you usually exhibit. I implore you to stay. Kay, I beg you, stay."

"Lady, you are very kind, but I would not stay," Kay replied.

Again the queen made her plea, and all the knights joined with her. Kay told the queen that she tired herself in vain. Then the queen, noble as she was, laid herself at his feet. She refused Kay's request that she rise, declaring that she would not, that she would never again rise until he gave in to her will. At last Kay agreed to stay, provided the king and the queen grant him in advance a demand he would make. "Kay," she said, "whatever it is, he and I will grant it. Come now and we shall tell him the condition of your stay." Kay left with the queen, and they came before the king. "Lord, with great effort I have detained Kay here," the queen said. "But I have had to promise that you will give him what he asks." The king sighed with joy and said he would do whatever Kay requested.

"Lord, then learn my desire, which you have promised to grant me," Kay said. "I consider myself most fortunate to gain such a favor with your consent. You have agreed to entrust the queen who is present here into my keeping. We shall go together after the knight who waits for us in the forest." Though dismayed, the king entrusted her to Kay, for he was never false to his word. But the demand caused his anger and unhappiness to be visible on his face. The queen as well was equally distraught. All those in the household agreed that Kay's demand was proud, presumptuous, and senseless.

The king took the queen by the hand. "Lady, you must accompany Kay without protest," he said to her.

"Hand her over to me now," Kay said. "There is nothing to fear. I shall bring her back perfectly safe and happy." The king gave her to Kay, who led her away. All the others went out after them. There was no one who was not upset.

You can be certain the seneschal was quickly armed. His horse was led into the middle of the courtyard along with a palfrey fit for a queen. The palfrey was not restive or stubborn, and the queen approached and mounted. Sorrowful and despondent, she sighed and spoke low lest she be heard: "Alas, alas, if only you knew, I believe you would never let Kay lead me a single step." She thought she had spoken softly, but Count Guinable, who was near her as she mounted, heard her. At their departure, all the men and women present assumed that she would never return alive, and they grieved as deeply as though she lay dead on her bier. In his impudence the seneschal was taking her to the spot where the other knight awaited her.

No one's grief was strong enough to prompt him to follow after her until Sir Gawain addressed the king, his uncle, in private. "Lord, you have behaved like a child, and I am astonished," he said. "But if you heed my counsel, then while they are still near, we shall follow them, you and I, along with any others who wish to come there. As for me, I could not hold back from racing after them. It would be wrong for us not to follow them, at least until we know what will happen to the queen, and how Kay will behave."

"Let us set off, dear nephew," the king replied. "You have spoken courteously now. Since you have taken this matter into your hands, have the horses bridled, saddled, and led out that we may mount without delay."

At once the horses were brought out, saddled, and harnessed. The king was first to mount; then Sir Gawain mounted, and then all the others, each eagerly trying to outdo the other. Though anxious to be part of the expedition, each man went as he pleased, some armed, many others without armor. Sir Gawain was armed, and had two squires lead two chargers on their right. As the men neared the forest, they sighted and recognized Kay's horse coming out, and noticed both bridle reins broken. The horse came all alone, the stirrup leather spattered with blood, the cantle broken and smashed to pieces. The knights were all angered at the sight and nudged one another in dismay.

Sir Gawain rode far in advance of the rest of the company. It was not long before he saw a knight slowly approaching on a horse panting and sore, exhausted and covered in sweat. The knight saluted Sir Gawain first, then Sir Gawain returned his greeting. Recognizing Sir Gawain, the knight stopped to speak. "Sir, do you not see how my horse is so soaked in sweat and in such a state that it is of no use? I believe these two chargers to be yours. I beg you now to lend or give me either on the promise that I will repay your kind service."

"Choose now which one you want," Sir Gawain replied.

Much in need of a horse, the knight did not waste time distinguishing which was better in beauty or in size, but promptly mounted the one nearer him and immediately galloped off. The horse he had abandoned fell dead, for its rider had overworked and exhausted it that day.

Clad in armor, the knight raced off through the forest at once, Sir Gawain following in full pursuit. Sir Gawain reached the bottom of a hill and continued a long way until he found, lying dead, the charger he had given the knight. He also noticed that horses had trampled the ground, which was strewn with broken shields and lances. It looked as if there had been a furious struggle among several knights. He was sorry and disappointed not to have been there. He did not stay long, but hurried on his way. Then he happened to see again the same knight, all alone on foot, fully armed, his helmet laced, his shield hanging from his neck, his sword buckled. The knight had overtaken a cart.

In those days carts served the function of our pillories. In every sizable town where there are now more than three thousand carts, then there was only one. Like our pillories, carts served for murderers and robbers, for those found guilty in trials by combat, for thieves who had stolen the property of others or seized it by force on the roads. The convicted criminal was placed in the cart and led through every street. Thus he had lost all honor. From then on all courts refused him hearing. He was neither welcome nor respected. This was the cruel significance of carts in those days. And so that time the proverb was first used: "When you meet a cart, make the sign of the cross and pray to God such dishonor not befall you."

On foot, without his lance, the knight hurried after the cart; he saw a dwarf sitting on the shafts and, like a carter, holding a long whip in his hand. The knight spoke to the dwarf. "In God's name, dwarf, tell me if you have seen my lady the queen pass this way," he said.

The miserable dwarf, ill-born and ill-bred, would give no information, but replied: "If you want to climb into the cart I am driving, you will learn by tomorrow what has happened to the queen." The dwarf continued on his way without waiting for him a moment. The knight, for just two steps, hesitated a little before getting in.

Woe that he did this, and woe that he was ashamed of the cart and so did not jump up at once, for he would later consider himself ill-befallen. Reason, which disagrees with Love, told him to refrain from climbing in and admonished and instructed him not to do or undertake anything that could bring him disgrace or reproach. Reason, which dared speak this way, spoke from his lips, but not from his heart. But Love, which was enclosed in his heart, urged and commanded him to climb into the cart at once. Love achieved his desire. The knight leapt up without concern for the disgrace because this was Love's will and command.

Sir Gawain galloped after the cart, and seeing the knight sitting in it, was amazed. Then he spoke. "Dwarf, if you know anything of the queen, tell me."

"If you have as little self-regard as this knight sitting here, jump, if you wish, into the cart alongside him. I shall drive you with him," the dwarf answered.

When Sir Gawain heard this, he thought the invitation mad. He would certainly not climb in, he said; it would be base in the extreme to trade a horse for a cart. "Go where you will, and I shall go where you wish," he replied.

And so they continued, one on horseback, two riding in the cart, and in this way they proceeded together. Toward dusk they reached a fortified town that was, you can be certain, very rich and beautiful. All three entered through a gateway. The people were astonished to see the knight riding in the cart. Not bothering to whisper, everyone, highborn and low, old and young, shouted and jeered at him in the streets. The knight heard them uttering many vile reproaches about him. All were asking: "To what punishment is this knight being delivered? Will he be flayed alive? Or hanged? Or drowned? Or burned in fiery thorns? Tell, dwarf, tell, you who draw him along, what crime was he committing when he was caught? Is he a convicted robber? Is he a murderer? Was he defeated in trial by combat?" The dwarf said nothing and answered none of them.

Followed by Gawain, the dwarf led the knight to the place where he would stay, a tower keep which was straight ahead on the other side of the town. The keep stood on a high granite cliff whose front formed a sharp precipice, and beyond the keep were meadows. On horseback Gawain followed the cart into the keep. In the great hall they met a finely dressed young lady whose beauty was unrivaled in the land and who was accompanied by two attractive and charming maidens. As soon as they saw Sir Gawain, they were overcome with joy. They greeted him and asked about the other knight. "Dwarf, what crime has this knight committed that you drive him as if he were crippled?" The dwarf would not answer their question. He made the knight get down from the cart, then went away. No one knew where he went.

After Sir Gawain dismounted, attendants came forward to relieve the knights of their armor. The young lady had two fur-lined cloaks brought for them to wear. When it was time for supper, a lavish feast awaited them. The young lady sat beside Sir Gawain at the table. The knights would not have changed their lodging in hope of finding a better one, for all evening long the young lady showed them great honor, providing them with fine and charming company.

When supper ended, two beds, high and long, were prepared in a chamber, with a third beside them even more beautiful and ornate than the others, for, as the tale affirms, that particular one had all imaginable comforts of a bed. When it was time to retire, the young lady took both her guests and showed them the two long, wide, and handsome beds. "For your comfort have been prepared the two beds nearest us. But in that bed over there no one undeserving has ever slept. It was not made for your body," she said.

The knight who came in the cart felt contempt and disdain for the young lady's prohibition. "Tell me the reason this bed is forbidden," he asked by way of reply.

Having already anticipated this question, she answered without reflection. "You have no right to ask such a question," she said. "Any knight is in disgrace throughout the world after he has been in a cart. He has no right to make a request such as yours, let alone desire to lie there; he would pay at once for that. I have not had such an ornate bed prepared just for you to sleep in. You would pay dearly even for holding such an idea."

"You will see that before long," he replied.

"Shall I?"

"Yes."

"Then let me see."

"On my life, I don't know who will pay the penalty," the knight replied. "But like it or not, I intend to lie in that bed and take my rest."

As soon as he had taken off his shoes, he lay down on the bed, which was longer and higher than the other two by half an ell. He lay on a rich quilt of yellow brocade starred with gold. The fur was not of sheared miniver but of sable; the bedclothes that covered him befitted a king; the mattress was not made of thatch, straw, or old matting.

At midnight from the rafters like lightning came a lance, head first, which almost pinned the knight's thighs to the quilt, to the white sheets, and to the bed where he lay. To the lance was attached a blazing pennon. The quilt, the sheets, and the bed all caught fire, and the lance-head grazed the side of the knight without doing any real harm to his flesh except for a small scratch. The knight jumped up, put out the fire, took the lance, and hurled it into the center of the hall without even leaving his bed. Then he lay down again and slept as soundly as he had before.

At dawn the next morning, the young lady of the keep had her guests awakened and dressed and arranged that mass be said for them. After mass was sung on their behalf, the knight who had sat in the cart walked pensively to the windows overlooking the meadow and gazed down on the fields below. The young lady had come to the neighboring window, where she talked in private a while with Sir Gawain. I do not know the matter of the conversation, nor have I any idea of the words they exchanged. But while they were leaning on the window ledge, they saw a bier being carried beside the river through the fields below. On it lay a knight, and alongside three young ladies made loud and desperate laments. They also noticed a crowd of people following the bier and a tall knight in front escorting a beautiful lady on his left.

From the window, the knight recognized the queen. He did not cease to gaze on her most attentively, happy to do this as long as possible. When he could not see her, he wished to hurl himself out onto the ground below. He was already sliding out the window when Sir Gawain noticed him. Pulling him back, Gawain said: "Stay still, sir, I beg you. For God's sake, never think of behaving so madly. You are quite wrong to despise your own life."

"But he is right," the young lady said. "Will the infamous news of his ride in the cart not be known everywhere? He certainly ought to want death, for he would be better dead than alive. From now on life for him is only shame, misery, and humiliation."

Thereupon the knights asked for their equipment and armed. The young lady behaved with gracious courtesy. To the knight she had earlier mocked and ridiculed, she now generously offered a horse and a lance as token of her affection and goodwill. With all the courtesy of their training, the knights took leave of the young lady and bade her farewell, making their way toward the crowd they had seen. And so they passed through the castle yard without a word from anyone.

In great haste the knights set off to the place where they had seen the queen; yet they did not overtake the crowd, for it moved along at full gallop. Beyond the fields they entered a thick forest where they came upon a beaten path. They had wandered so far through the forest that it could have been six in the morning when they met a young lady at a crossroads. Greeting her, both knights implored and begged her to tell them, if she knew, where the queen had been taken. Prudent was her answer. "If you would promise me enough," she said, "I could certainly set you on the right highway and tell you the country where she is going and the knight who takes her there. But anyone wanting to enter the country would have to endure extreme hardship. Much would he suffer before arriving there."

"Young lady," Sir Gawain said to her, "with God's help, I pledge to you that I will place all my strength at your service, to be used as you wish and whenever you wish, if you will tell me the truth."

He who had been in the cart did not say that he pledged all his strength to her but, like one whom Love has made rich, powerful, and bold in every enterprise, assured her that, without fear or hesitation, he would do her will and place himself completely at her command. "Then I shall tell you," she answered, and so the young lady told them the tale. "On my word, sirs, Meleagant, a tall and strong knight, the son of the King of Gorre, has captured her and taken her to the kingdom where all foreigners are forced to live in bondage and in exile with no hope of return."

He then asked her another question. "Young lady, where is this country? Where might we find the road there?"

"You will know it," she replied, "but your way there will be filled with difficulties and dangerous passages, you can be certain, for it is not easy to enter the country unless you have the permission of its king, Bademagu. You can gain access there, however, by two treacherous and hazardous routes. One is called the water-bridge, as the bridge is underwater. From the bridge down to the bottom is exactly as deep as from the bridge up to the water's surface; the bridge, only a foot-and-a-half wide and equally thick, is precisely in the middle. Certainly this course ought to be rejected, and this one is the less dangerous. But there is much involved in the two adventures that I do not mention. The other bridge, more menacing and much more dangerous, no man has ever crossed. It is sharp like a sword, and so everyone calls it the sword-bridge. I have told you the truth as best I can."

"Young lady, if you will, show us these two routes," he asked her further.

And the young lady replied: "This is the direct road to the water-bridge, and that one goes directly to the sword-bridge."

Then the knight who had been in the cart said: "Sir, I give you your free choice: take one of these two routes, and let me have the other. Take the one you prefer."

"On my word," Sir Gawain replied, "both crossings are treacherous and frightening. I have no skill in such choices. I hardly know which to take. Still it is wrong for me to hesitate since you have left me the choice. I take the water-bridge."

"Then it is right that I go off to the sword-bridge without complaint," the other said, "and I agree to that." All three then went their separate ways, commending one another to God with utmost courtesy.

When she saw them riding away, she said: "Each of you must grant me a favor of my choosing the moment I wish it. Take care not to forget that."

"We certainly shall not forget, dear friend," the two knights answered, and each went his way. Like one powerless and defenseless against Love's control, the knight of the cart fell into such thoughts that he lost thought of himself. He did not know if he was alive or dead, did not remember his own name, did not know whether he was armed or not, did not know where he was going or whence he was coming. He remembered nothing except one person, and for her he put everyone else out of mind. He thought so much about her alone that he heard, saw, understood nothing.

His horse was carrying him at a good pace, not along an indirect route but along the straightest and best, until it chanced to take him to open land. On this heath was a river and across it a ford. On the other side an armed knight stood guard; with him was a young lady who had come on a palfrey. It was by now late afternoon, but the knight still did not change or alter his thoughts. His horse was very thirsty and noticed the clear and beautiful ford. The moment it saw the water, it raced there.

The knight on the other side cried out: "I guard the ford, knight, and I forbid you to cross." Still preoccupied with his thoughts, the other did not hear or heed him, and all the while the horse galloped toward the water. The guard cried out to him to turn back. "Stay away from the ford, and you will act wisely. That is not the way to cross." By his very heart, he swore he would strike him if he went into the water. But the knight heard him not, and so he shouted to him a third time. "Knight, do not enter the ford against my command and my will, or on my word I will strike you as soon as I see you there!" So rapt in his thoughts was the knight that he did not hear him, and the horse immediately left the bank, jumped into the water, and began to drink in great gulps.

The guard declared that the knight would pay for this: his shield and the hauberk on his back would never offer him protection. Then he set his own horse at a gallop, and from the gallop coaxed it to a run. He struck the knight and laid him flat in the center of the ford he had forbidden him to cross, making the lance fly from his hand and the shield from his neck.

The knight shivered as he felt the water. Stunned completely, he jumped to his feet like someone roused from sleep. He listened and looked about, wondering who could have hit him. Catching sight of the knight, he cried out to him: "Vassal, tell me why you struck me. I did not notice you ahead of me, and had not wronged you."

"I swear you did," he answered. "Have you not treated me shamefully since I forbade you three times to cross the ford? I shouted to you as loudly as I could. Surely you heard me challenge you, at least two or three times," he continued. "And then in spite of me you entered. And I did say I would strike you as soon as I saw you in the water."

The knight then answered. "Damn the man, as far as I am concerned, who ever heard or saw you. You may well have forbidden me to cross the ford, but I was rapt in thought. You would regret the harm you did, you can be certain, could one of my hands but hold you by the bridle."

"What would happen?" the other replied. "You could hold me by the bridle at this moment if you dare grip me there. To my mind a handful of ashes is worth more than your threats and boasts."

"That is all I want. Whatever happens, I would like to get my hands on you," he answered.

Then the knight advanced to the center of the ford. The other knight gripped the reins with his left hand and with his right the man's leg. He dragged, pulled, and pressed so tightly that his opponent protested, thinking he was pulling the leg from his body. He begged him to let go. "Knight," he exclaimed, "if you wish to fight me on equal terms, take your shield, your lance, and your horse, and joust with me."

"I swear I will not," he answered, "for I believe you would run away as soon as I released you."

When the guard heard this, he was ashamed and spoke again. "Knight, be trusting and mount your horse. I promise you in full faith not to flee or escape. You have spoken shamefully to me, and it rankles."

The other man then answered yet again. "First, I want a guarantee of your promise. I want you to pledge me this, not to flee or escape, not to touch me or come near me, until you see me mounted. And for my part, I shall extend you this great kindness: having held you, I shall set you free."

There was nothing left for him to do but make the promise. When the other knight heard the pledge, he went to pick up his shield and his lance, which had been floating in the ford and had by this time drifted far downstream. Then he returned and took his horse. When he had taken hold of it and mounted, he lifted his shield by the armstraps and placed his lance in its rest. The two then spurred at each other as fast as their horses could carry them. The guard of the ford attacked first and struck him so hard that he shattered his lance to pieces. The other knight struck back, hurling the guard flat into the ford in the middle of the current, and the water closed over him. He then drew back and dismounted, believing that he could chase and drive before him a hundred such knights. He unsheathed his steel sword; the other knight jumped up and drew his own fine and flashing sword; they then came at each other again. In front they held their shields, which gleamed with gold, for protection, and continued to wield their swords relentlessly. They dared hurl such dreadful blows at each other that the struggle was protracted and the knight of the cart felt deep shame in his heart. He told himself how poor was his repayment of the debt he had incurred in undertaking this route, since he had spent so much time in defeating a single knight. If yesterday he had come upon a hundred such knights in a valley, they would not, he thought and believed, have offered him any resistance. Now he was angry and unhappy to be missing his strokes and wasting the day because of exhaustion. The knight then attacked and pressed his opponent so hard that he turned and fled. The guard, to his chagrin, granted the knight access to the ford.

The knight continued his chase until his opponent fell to his hands. Running up to him, the cart-rider swore by all he could see that damned was the guard for knocking him into the ford and damned too for disturbing his thoughts. When the young lady accompanying the guard heard the threats, she was terrified; she begged the knight for her sake not to kill him. Thus was he forced to act, he said, because of the great disgrace done him; he could show no mercy for her sake. Then, with sword drawn, he approached the knight, who cried out in despair: "For God's sake and my own, have mercy on me, I beg you."

"As God loves me," he replied, "I have always shown mercy to anyone who shamed me, if he seeks mercy from me in the name of God. I do this in God's name, as is right. And so mercy I shall show you too. Because of your plea, I should not refuse you this. But first you shall swear to me to be my prisoner whenever and wherever I summon you."

The guard made this pledge, though it distressed him. "Knight," the young lady spoke again, "since this prisoner has sought and received mercy from you, then by your nobility, if ever you released a prisoner, release him to me. Let this prisoner go free for my sake, with the understanding that when the occasion comes, I shall repay you to the best of my ability with a service to your liking."

He then realized who she was from her statement and released his prisoner to her. She was ashamed and embarrassed to think he might have recognized her, for she did not want that to happen. He was anxious to depart, and the lady and her knight commended him to God and asked his leave.

After granting them leave, he continued on his way until late in the evening, when he saw a young lady approaching whose fine attire enhanced her great beauty. As one with both wisdom and good training, the young lady greeted him. "Young lady, God grant you health and happiness," he replied.

"Sir," she said to him, "my nearby home awaits your company if you decide to accept the invitation. But you may lodge there only if you lie with me. On this condition I extend you my invitation."

Although several men would have thanked her five hundred times for this offer, he became sullen and answered her in a different way. "Young lady, I thank you for your hospitality, which I appreciate very much. But the offer of lying with you I would rather forgo, if you please."

"By my eyes, then I shall give you nothing," the lady replied.

Unable to do better, he acceded to her condition, though his heart was nearly broken with the consent. Since thus far he had only been wounded, at bedtime he would have much more displeasure. And the young lady who was leading him away would have much distress and anxiety, for perhaps she would love him so much that she would be unwilling to let him go free. When he had acceded to her will and desire, she took him to a fortified residence, the most beautiful from there to Thessaly, which was completely enclosed by high walls and a deep moat. And the only man inside was the one she was expecting.

For her home she had had constructed a large number of extremely beautiful rooms and a grand and spacious great hall. Going alongside the river, they rode until they reached the lodging. They crossed the drawbridge that had been lowered for their entrance, and found the tile-roofed hall open. Entering through the opened door, they saw a table covered with a long and wide tablecloth. Candles were already lit in the candlesticks, and dishes had been placed on the table along with gilded silver goblets and two pitchers, one filled with red wine and the other with a heavy white wine. On the end of a bench beside the table they noticed two basins full of warm water for washing their hands, and on the other saw a richly patterned towel, clean and white, for drying them. They did not see or find within any attendant, servant, or squire.

The knight removed his shield from his neck and hung it on a hook; he took his lance and laid it on a rack above. Then he jumped down from his horse, while the young lady dismounted from hers. The knight was quite content that she dismounted without any desire for his assistance. Just after dismounting, she hurried off to a room without a moment's delay and returned with a short cloak of rich wool which she placed on him. Although the stars were already shining, the great hall was far from dark, for many large and twisted candles burned, drenching the room in brightness.

"Friend," she said to him after placing the cloak around his neck, "here is the water and the towel. There is no one to present or offer them to you since, as you observe, I am the only person here. Wash your hands, then sit down when you wish. This, as you can see, the hour and the meal demand. So wash, then seat yourself."

"Most gladly," he replied, and sat down. And she was pleased to sit beside him. They ate and drank together until it was time to get up from the meal.

When they left the table, the young lady said to the knight: "Sir, if you don't mind, go outside and entertain yourself. Please stay there only until you think I am in bed. Have no worry or displeasure concerning this, for if you are minded to keep your promise, you will come to me."

"I shall hold to your agreement," he answered, "and return when I think it time." He then went outside into the courtyard, staying quite a while until it was necessary for him to return, for he had to hold to the agreement. When he reentered the hall, he did not find the lady who had presented herself as his mistress, for she was not there. "Wherever she is," he said, not seeing or discovering her, "I shall look until I find her."

Because of the promise he had made her, he did not stop his search. In the first room he entered he heard a young lady screaming, and it was the very person with whom he was supposed to lie. He then noticed the door to another room open. Going in that direction, he saw straight ahead of him a knight who had thrown the lady down and held her completely disrobed across the bed. She believed for a certainty that he would come to her aid and cried loudly: "Help! Help! Knight, you are my guest. If you do not take this man off me, he will shame me in front of you. It is you who are to lie with me. That was your promise. Will this man then force his will on me before your eyes? Exert yourself, noble knight, and help me at once!"

The knight saw that the brute held the young lady, who was stripped to the waist; yet his deep shame and anger in beholding the naked man touching her nakedness did not provoke in him any desire or make him jealous in the least. Moreover, two fully armed knights were guarding the doorway with their swords drawn. Behind them were four men-at-arms, each holding the kind of axe that could cut down a cow's spine as easily as through the root of juniper or broom. Hesitating at the doorway, the knight said to himself: "God, what can I do? The object of my great pursuit is no one less than the Queen Guinevere. Having embarked on this quest for her, I must not have the heart of a hare. If Cowardice gives me her heart and I follow her rule, I shall never reach my goal. I am disgraced if I stay here. Merely to have spoken of remaining brings deep shame upon me now. My heart is sad and dark. I am so shamed and dejected that I wish to die for hesitating here so long. May God never have mercy on me if I speak with pride and would not rather die with honor than live with disgrace. What honor would there be if my path were clear and these men let me pass unchallenged? The greatest coward alive would certainly pass in that situation. And still I hear this unfortunate lady imploring me with her constant cries, calling upon the promise I made, and hurling vile reproaches at me."

At once he went to the doorway and stuck his head and neck through. Looking up by the window, he saw swords coming at him. He had the good sense to stand back. The two knights could not check their forceful strokes, and both swords hit the ground, smashing into pieces. When these had been shattered, he had less concern about the axes, his fear and dread of them having diminished. He then rushed in among the men, striking one man-at-arms, then another, from the side. He jostled his way against the arms and sides of the two he found near to him so that he knocked them both flat to the ground. The third aimed his stroke badly, while the fourth assailant struck him, cutting through his cloak and shirt and ripping the white flesh all along his shoulder so that blood ran down from the wound. The knight did not hesitate, nor did he complain of his wound, but pressed forward even more quickly until he seized the head of the man assaulting his hostess. Before his departure, he would be able to keep his pledge and promise to her. The knight forced his opponent to stand whether he wanted to or not, while the one who had missed his last stroke was coming after him as quickly as he could, raising his arm again, expecting, with his axe, to smash the knight's head through to the teeth. But the other knew a good defense: toward the assailant he pushed the other knight in such a way that the latter met the axe's blow where the shoulder joins the neck so that they were split apart. The knight then quickly took hold of the axe and tore it from his fingers. He released the man he had been holding, for he had to defend himself, seeing that the two knights were coming toward him and the three with the axes made savage attack. With an agile leap, he placed himself between the bed and the wall. "All of you, come at me now!" he said. "If there were twenty-seven of you now, enough combat would still be yours since I am so well positioned. You will never exhaust me."

"By my eyes," the young lady said, looking at him, "from now on, you have nothing to fear wherever I am." At once she dismissed the knights and the men-at-arms. Without hesitation or objection, they all withdrew from there. "Sir," the young lady continued, "you have defended me well against my entire household. Come now, I shall take you inside." Hand in hand they entered the hall. Not at all pleased was he, for he would have been delighted to be free of her.

In the center of the hall a bed had been prepared, with wide, spotlessly white sheets amply spread out. The mattress was not of crumbled straw or coarse cloths, and for a covering two embroidered silk quilts had been laid out on the bed. As for the young lady, though she lay in bed, she did not remove her shift. The knight found it quite difficult to take off his shoes and undress, and was sweating from the exertion. Nevertheless, in the midst of his efforts his pledge overcame his reluctance and impelled him onwards. Was this, then, a forceful prodding? Yes, of course, for he was forced to lie with the young lady. The agreement urged and commanded him.

At once he lay down in bed. No less than she had done, he did not remove his shirt. Careful not to touch her, he lay on his back and kept his distance, maintaining absolute silence like a lay brother forbidden to speak when lying in his bed. He never turned his face toward her or to the other side. He could not make a fair appearance to her. Why? His heart did not move out to her because all his attention was focused elsewhere. What every man would regard as beautiful and charming held no pleasure or attraction for him. The knight had only one heart, and it was no longer his; he had entrusted it to another so that he could bestow it nowhere else. Love, who governs all hearts, made it stay in one place. All hearts? No, but only those he values. The man whom Love deigns to govern ought to esteem himself the more. Love held the knight's heart in such high regard that he governed it above all, and bestowed on it such supreme pride that I am not inclined to blame him if he loathes what Love forbids and concentrates all his attention on Love's will. The young lady understood this; she realized that he hated her company and would gladly excuse himself. With no desire to touch her, he would never woo her.

"If you don't mind, sir," she said, "I shall leave here. I shall go to bed in my own room, and thus you would find more comfort. It seems neither my pleasure nor my company pleases you very much. Do not reproach me for telling you my thoughts. Have a good sleep tonight. You have followed my agreement so well that I have no right to ask more of you. And so I wish to commend you to God. I shall then leave."

After these words, she rose to go. As a lover wholly devoted to another, the knight, far from displeased, gladly let her depart. The young lady saw and understood his behavior. And so she came to her room, undressed completely, and went to bed. "Ever since I first made a knight's acquaintance," she said to herself, "I have not known one I would value at a third of an Anjou penny, except him. From what I can see and surmise, he plans to embark on a great exploit more arduous and dangerous than any knight has dared undertake. God grant him success." Thereupon she fell asleep and lay until dawn.

At daybreak she rose quickly. The knight also rose promptly and dressed. Without waiting for assistance, he put on his equipment and readied himself. At that moment the young lady arrived and saw him already attired. "May this day that has dawned be good for you," she said when she saw him.

"And for you the same, young lady," the knight answered, adding that he was impatient for someone to lead out his horse to him. The young lady had it brought to him.

"Sir," she said, "I would like to accompany you quite a way along the route if you agree to escort and conduct me according to the manners and customs observed in the kingdom of Logres since before our time." In those days the practices and liberties were such that if a knight came upon a girl—be she lady or maid-in-waiting—he would no more treat her with dishonor than cut his own throat should a noble reputation concern him. If he assaulted her, he would be held in disgrace always and at every court. But if she was under the escort of one knight, another, anxious to fight for her and successful in winning her in armed combat, might do with her as he pleased without receiving censure or shame. Thus the young lady told him that if he wished and dared to escort her according to this custom so that no one could harm her, she would accompany him.

"I promise you," he told her, "no one will ever harm you without first harming me."

"Then I wish to accompany you," she said.

She had her palfrey saddled; at her word it was done at once. The palfrey was led out along with the knight's horse. Without aid from a squire, the two mounted and galloped away.

She addressed him, but he cared nothing for her words and made no response. Thinking pleased him; speaking pained him. Often Love reopens the wound he inflicted, and the patient never applies a dressing for his recovery and good health, for he has no intention or desire of seeking a remedy or doctor unless his wound grows deeper. There was someone, however, the knight would gladly seek.

They followed the route of the highway's path until they noticed in the middle of a meadow a spring with a stone slab beside it. Someone, I know not who, had forgotten a gilded ivory comb on the stone. Never since the time of the giant Ysoré has anyone, wise or foolish, seen such a beautiful comb. And she who had used it had left behind at least half a handful of hair in the teeth.

When the young lady noticed the spring and saw the stone, she took another route, not wishing that he see them. He was happily preoccupied in his most pleasing thoughts and did not notice at first that she was leading him away from the main road. But when he realized this, he feared some deception, thinking that she had turned off the main road to avoid some danger.

"Hold a moment, young lady," he said, "you go the wrong way. Come back. I do not think anyone ever took the right way by leaving this road."

"Sir, I am certain we shall travel better this way," the young lady answered.

"I do not know what you are thinking, young lady," he replied, "but you can clearly see this well-trodden road is the right one. Since I have embarked along this way, I shall not go off in some other direction. Please come along now, for I shall continue along this road."

They proceeded until they neared the stone and saw the comb. "Truly I never remember seeing such a beautiful comb as the one I see here," the knight said.

"Give it to me," the young lady exclaimed.

"Gladly, young lady," he replied.

Then he leaned over and picked it up. Long he stared at it in his hand and examined the hair. His companion began to laugh. Noticing this, he asked her to tell him the reason for her laughter.

"Be quiet," she said. "I shall tell you nothing for the moment."

"Why?" he asked.

"Because I do not care to."

Hearing her response, he begged her in the tone of one who believed lovers should never be false to each other in any way. "If you love anyone deeply, young lady, then by him I ask, I entreat, I beg you, conceal this from me no longer."

"To be certain, your appeal is too strong," she said. "I shall tell you this without word of lie. If I know anything, I know this comb belonged to the queen. Believe me, those strands of hair you see left behind in the teeth of the comb, those strands that are so beautiful, so shining, and so radiant, they were from the queen's head. In no other meadow did they ever grow."

"On my word, there are many queens and kings," the knight said. "Which queen do you mean?"

"On my word, sir, the wife of King Arthur," she answered.

When he heard this, he did not have enough strength to do anything but bend forward, where he was forced to lean against the pommel of the saddle. This sight amazed and terrified the young lady, who expected him to fall. Do not reproach her for her fear, for she thought that he had fainted, and indeed he had come close to fainting. His heart was so pained that he lost his color and his voice for some time. And the young lady dismounted and ran as quickly as she could to hold him back and help him, for she had no desire to see him fall to the ground.

He was ashamed to see her. "What urgency brought you before me here?" he asked her. Do not expect the young lady to tell him the reason. Imagine the shame and embarrassment that would have been his, the grief and the pain too, had she revealed the truth to him.

Taking pains not to speak honestly, she addressed him with great tact. "Sir, I dismounted only to come and pick up this comb. I was so anxious to have it that I did not think I could hold it soon enough."

Willing to let her have the comb, he first pulled out the strands of hair so carefully that not one was damaged. Then he gave her the comb. The eye of man will never behold anything accorded such honor as the strands when he began to adore them. To his eyes, his mouth, his forehead, his cheeks, he touched them a hundred thousand times. All his joy consisted in doing this. In these strands was his happiness; in them was his wealth. Between his shirt and his skin he placed them on his breast, next to his heart. A cart full of emeralds and rubies he would not accept in exchange for them. He did not believe ulcers or any other illness would ever afflict him. He had nothing but contempt for essence of pearl, medicine for pleurisy, and antidotes for poison, even for prayers to Saint Martin and Saint James. Such faith was his in this hair that he needed no other aid.

But what was the hair like? You will, if I tell you the truth, think me a liar and a fool. When the Lendit fair is in its fullness and the wealth of goods openly displayed, the knight would have no wish for all that—this is the proven truth—unless he had found these strands of hair. If you wish the truth from me, gold refined a hundred thousand times, then melted down as often, would be darker than night in contrast to the brightest summer day of the entire year, were you to see the gold and the hair placed side by side. But why should I lengthen the tale? With the comb in her possession, the young lady quickly remounted, and the knight felt pleasure and ecstasy from the hair he clutched to his breast.

Beyond the plain was a forest. They followed a short path until their way narrowed and they were forced to travel in single file, for it was impossible to ride two horses there abreast. Along the main route, the young lady kept a good pace in front of her escort. Where the route was most narrow, they saw a knight approaching. As soon as the young lady noticed him, she recognized him. "Sir knight," she said, "do you see the man coming to meet you fully equipped and ready for combat? He certainly expects to take me away with him without challenge. I know his thinking well, for he loves me, the fool that he is. For long now he has been wooing me both in person and through his messengers. But my love scorns him, for nothing could make me love him. I would rather die, God help me, than ever love him. I am certain he is overjoyed now and as pleased as though he had won me already. Now I shall see what you can do. Now it will be evident if you have bravery. Now I shall see, now it will be evident, should your escort guarantee my safety. If you can protect me, I shall proclaim in all honesty that you are valiant and brave."

"Go, go," he told her, his comment implying as much as though he had said, "I hardly care for your talk. You worry without reason."

While they continued in conversation, the knight, who came alone, galloped toward them. He eagerly made haste, not expecting his efforts to be wasted. He considered himself fortunate to see before him the object of his deepest desire. As soon as he neared her, he greeted her from his mouth as well as his heart. "May the object of all my affections, who has given me least joy and most grief, be welcomed from wherever she rides," he exclaimed. It was not right that she be so niggardly in her words to him as to fail to return his greeting, at least with her mouth. The knight attached great value to the young lady's greeting, which had not dirtied her mouth or been of cost. Yet had he jousted brilliantly in a tournament that very moment, he would not have congratulated himself so much, nor thought of winning so much honor or so much renown. Because he was even more confident, he grabbed the reins of her bridle. "Now I shall take you away," he said. "Today I have sailed well and straight ahead, and reached a fine port. I am no longer wretched. After danger I have reached a haven; after great anxiety, happiness; after much pain, good health. I have now achieved all my desires in finding you where, without incurring dishonor, I can take you away with me at once."

"With this knight as my escort, nothing helps you," she replied.

"An escort so wretched indeed that I shall take you away now," he said. "This knight would eat a barrel of salt, I think, before contending with me on your behalf. I do not think I have ever met a man from whom I could not win you. And since I find you in so timely a situation, I shall lead you away before his very eyes, though it may displease and disturb him. Let him prevent it as best he can!"

All the arrogance the other knight heard uttered did not move him to anger. Without reproof or boast, he began to challenge him for her. "Sir, do not rush so!" he said. "Do not waste your words. Be a little modest in your speech. Your right to her will be respected once you have it. Know for certain, this young lady has come here under my escort. Let her be. You have detained her too long. Now she has nothing to fear from you." The other acknowledged that he would be burned alive unless, in spite of her knight, he took her away. "It would not be right," the first continued, "to let you take her away. Be certain I would first fight you. But if we want combat, we cannot have it on this road. Let us ride instead to some level place, a meadow or open field."

The challenger replied that he could ask nothing more. "I certainly agree," he said. "You are quite right; this path is too narrow. My horse is already in such discomfort that I fear it would crush its flank before I could turn it round." Then, with the greatest difficulty, he did turn, without harm or injury to his horse. "Yes, I am angry we did not meet in a wide area with others looking on," he said. "I would have liked them to see which of us does the better. But come now, and we shall look for a place. Near here we shall find some stretch of open land that is long and wide."

They then rode until they reached a meadow. Because of the beauty of this locale, knights, young ladies, and maids-in-waiting played many games in the meadow. Their games were not idle pastimes: some were playing backgammon and chess, others were happily engaged in various games of dice. Most played these games. Still others there returned to childhood pastimes of singing and dancing; some sang, some tumbled, some leapt, and some tested themselves in wrestling.

Mounted on a sorrel-coated Spanish stallion with gold bridle and saddle, a knight, somewhat elderly and dressed in armor of gray mesh, rode up from the other side of the meadow. One hand hung at his side, and because of the fine weather he was in shirt sleeves as he watched the games and dances. Slung over his shoulders was a fur-trimmed cloak of rich wool. On the other side near a path were as many as twenty-three armed knights on fine Irish horses. As soon as the trio arrived there, all the people put a stop to their festivities and shouted across the field. "See the knight! See him who was driven here in the cart! Let none of us continue our play with him here! Damn any who would play! Damn any who would care to play so long as he is here!"

Meanwhile, behold the elderly knight's son. He was the one who loved the young lady and considered her to be already his. He approached his father. "Sire," he said, "I am overjoyed. Whoever wishes to know this, let him hear. God has granted me the gift that I always wanted most. If He had had me crowned king, He would not have shown me such favor, nor would I have profited so much, or been so grateful to Him, for this prize is splendid and beautiful."

"I still do not know if it is yours," the knight told his son.

"You do not know?" the young man answered immediately. "Then do you not see? In God's name, sire, seeing I have her, doubt no more. In that forest I came from, I met her as she rode along. I think God led her to me, and I have taken her as my own."

"I still do not know if the man I see following you will agree. I suspect he comes to challenge you for her."

During their talk, the dancing had ceased because of the knight. When the people saw him, they refrained from rejoicing and playing out of disgust and contempt for him.

The knight did not hesitate, but followed at once after the young lady. "Knight, let the young lady be!" he shouted. "You have no right to her. If you dare, I shall defend her at once against you."

The elderly knight then spoke. "Did I not know this well? Dear son, do not keep the young lady longer. Let her go."

This command did not please the son, who swore never to return her. "May God never grant me happiness should I hand her over to him," he said. "She is mine and will stay mine, as a possession of my own. The buckler strap and all armstraps on my shield will be smashed before I let her go. I shall lose all confidence in my strength and in my arms, in my sword and in my lance, before I surrender him my beloved."

"Say what you will, I shall not let you fight," his father answered. "You rely too much on your valor. Do as I bid you."

"Am I a child to be scared?" the son arrogantly replied. "I can truly boast: in all the land surrounded by the sea, there is not one of the many knights found there so fine that I would let him have her, and not expect to bring him quickly to his knees."

"I have no doubt you believe this, dear son, since you have such faith in your own strength," his father answered. "But today I do not and shall not consent to see you test yourself against this knight."

"What dishonor would be mine if I heeded your counsel!" the son replied. "Damn him who would believe that and become cowardly, because of you, and not present himself boldly in combat against me. It is true that a man is treated badly by close friends. I could make a better bargain elsewhere, for you want to mislead me. I realize I could display my valor more in a foreign land. No one who did not know me would interfere with my will. Yet you use this occasion to insult and offend me. I am the more upset because you have reproached me for this. When any person, man or woman, is faulted, as you well know, his passion and determination only increase. May God never grant me happiness if I relent at all for your sake. No, in spite of you, I shall fight."

"By my faith in Saint Peter the Apostle," his father said, "I see now it is useless to entreat you. I waste my time admonishing you. But soon I shall conduct such a case that you will be forced, against your will, to obey me. You shall be put in your place." At once he summoned all his knights who had accompanied him, commanding them to take hold of his son, whom he could not correct. "I shall have him bound before I let him fight," he said. "You are all my men, and to me owe loyalty and devotion. By all you hold from me, I entreat and command you to do this. He behaves indeed like a fool, it seems to me, and displays great arrogance in contradicting my will."

The knights said they would seize him, and once held, he would lose all desire for combat and, against his will, be forced to surrender the young lady. All then came together and fell upon him, seizing him by the arms and neck.

"Do you not think yourself foolish now?" his father asked. "Admit the truth: you have neither power nor strength to joust or fight, however distressing or offensive your displeasure. Agree to all I desire, and you will act wisely. Do you know my intent? In order to assuage your disappointment, we shall follow the knight together, you and I, if you wish, through field and forest today and tomorrow, ambling along on our horses. We may soon discover him to be of such bearing and character that I would let you prove yourself, and fight as you please."

Much against his will, his son agreed to the proposal, necessity compelling him. Like a man without alternative, he said that he would accept the situation for his father's sake, provided they both follow him.

When the people in the meadow saw the outcome of the scene, they all shouted: "Did you see? The man who was in the cart has won such honor today that he leads away the beloved of our lord's son. Now our lord is going to follow him. We can honestly say that he finds some merit in him since he lets him take her away. Damn a hundred times the man who interrupts play longer on his account. Let us return to our sports." They then resumed their games, songs, and dances.

The knight turned at once, making no further delay in the meadow, and the young lady under his escort stayed no longer than he. Both made great haste, followed from afar by the father and his son.

The knight and the young lady rode through a stretch of mowed fields until nearly three o'clock. Then, in a most beautiful spot, they came upon a church with a walled cemetery beside the chancel. While the young lady held his horse until his return, the knight acted courteously and wisely in entering the church on foot to pray to God. When he had prayed and was returning, he saw an elderly monk coming ahead to greet him. At their meeting, the knight asked him in a quiet voice to tell him what was within the walls. The monk replied that this was a cemetery.

"In God's name, take me inside," the knight said.

"Gladly, sir." And he led him within.

Following the monk into the cemetery, the knight came upon the most beautiful tombs to be found this side of Dombes or even Pamplona. On each were carved letters forming the names of those who would be buried there. From row to row, the knight began to read the names to himself, and found those that stated: "Here Gawain shall lie, here Louis, and here Yvain." After these three he read the names of many other chosen knights, the most esteemed and finest in this land or elsewhere. Among the rest he found one tomb of marble that seemed the most beautiful work of all. Calling to the monk, the knight asked: "These tombs that are here, whose are they?"

"You saw the inscriptions," he answered. "If you paid attention to them, then you know what the tombs say and signify."

"Tell me about the largest one over there. Whom is it for?"

"I shall answer your question," the hermit replied. "That is the largest tomb of stone ever built. Neither I nor anyone has ever seen one so well carved or of such noble proportions. It is beautiful without and more so within. But do not concern yourself. It is useless to you since you will never see the inside. To open it would require seven strong and large men willing to raise the lid, for the tomb is covered with a heavy slab. And be certain that raising it would require seven men stronger than you or I. The inscription reads, 'The man who lifts this stone by himself shall be liberator of all men and women imprisoned in the land, whence no one, nobleman or clerk, leaves from the moment he enters. No one has ever returned from there. Foreigners are held captive, while the people of the land come and go as they please.' "

At once the knight went to lay hold of the stone. Without the slightest effort, he raised it more easily than ten men would have done, had they used all their strength. The monk was astonished and almost fell down at witnessing this marvel, for he did not expect to see the feat during his lifetime. "Sir, now I am most anxious to know your name. Will you tell it to me?" he asked.

"On my word, not I," replied the knight.

"That certainly displeases me," he said. "If you were to tell me, you would act most courteously, and great advantage might be yours as a result. Where do you come from? What place?"

"As you see, I am a knight, and I was born in the kingdom of Logres. Now I would like to leave. For your part, please tell me who will lie in that tomb?"

"Sir, he who will free all those imprisoned in the kingdom whence no one escapes."

After the monk told him all this, the knight commended him to God and all His saints. Then, escorted out of the church by the old white-haired monk, he came to the young lady; he could not have left before this. The knight and the young lady resumed their journey. While she was mounting, the monk told her all the knight had done inside and begged her, if she knew, to tell him the knight's name. Although she avowed not to know it, she dared assure him of one fact for certain, that as far as the four winds blow, there was no such knight alive.

The young lady then left him and galloped after the knight. At that moment their two pursuers rode up and saw the monk standing alone in front of the church. The elderly knight in shirt sleeves addressed him. "Sire, tell us, have you seen a knight escorting a young lady?"

"I shall not hesitate to tell you all I know," he replied. "They have just left here. The knight was inside, where he performed the truly marvelous feat of lifting, by himself and without the slightest effort, the stone on the great marble tomb. He is going to rescue the queen, and no doubt he will rescue her and all the other people with her. You know this yourself, for you have often read the inscription on the stone. Certainly no knight born of man and woman, or one who has sat in a saddle, ever equaled this man."

The father then addressed his son. "What do you think of this, son? Is this man not brave to have accomplished such a feat? Now you realize who was wrong: well you know if it was you or I. Not for Amiens would I have wished you to fight him, and yet you balked so much before you could be turned from your purpose. Now we can return, for we would act most foolishly to follow him farther."

"I agree," the son replied. "It would be useless for us to follow him. Since you wish, let us turn back." He was wise indeed in his decision to return.

All the while the young lady continued to ride alongside the knight, wishing to make him give her his attention. And she wanted to learn his name. Again and again she begged and entreated him to tell her until, his patience exhausted, he said to her: "Have I not told you I am from King Arthur's realm? By my faith in God and His power, you shall never know my name."

She then asked him permission to turn back, and he cheerfully gave her leave.

Thereupon the young lady departed, and he rode on alone until very late. After dusk, at bedtime, he was still following his route when he saw a knight, a vavasor, riding from the woods where he had been hunting. His helmet laced, he approached, bearing on the back of his tall gray hunter the game God had granted him. The vavasor raced up to meet the knight and offered him hospitality. "Sir, night will soon be here," he said. "You should be sensible now and seek lodging for the evening. Near here is a manorhouse of mine where I shall take you. To the limit of my ability, I shall lodge you better than anyone has before. I shall be happy if this pleases you."

"I accept your invitation gladly," he answered.

The vavasor immediately dispatched his son to ensure a fine lodging and hasten the preparations for supper. The young man did not delay, but with a glad and loyal heart executed his command at once. He galloped off, while those not bent on speed followed along until they reached the house. The vavasor's family consisted of his wife, who had been well brought up, five sons—two knights and three younger lads—whom he cherished, and two beautiful and charming daughters who were still unmarried. Though not born in that country, they had long been detained and imprisoned there. Their birthplace was the kingdom of Logres.

When the vavasor led the knight into his courtyard, his lady ran to meet him, and his sons and daughters jumped to their feet, all offering him their service. They greeted him and helped him dismount. The sisters and their five brothers paid scarce attention to their sire, knowing that their father wanted them to behave in this manner. They joyously welcomed the knight and did him great honor. After they had relieved him of his armor, one of the host's two daughters took her cloak from her shoulders and placed it about his neck. Thus he was well served at the supper. I intend to speak no further on this subject.

At the end of the meal, there was no trouble in finding several topics of conversation. The vavasor began first to ask his guest who he was and from what country he came, though he did not ask his name. "I come from the kingdom of Logres, and have never been in this land before," he answered immediately.

When the vavasor heard this, he was completely amazed, as were his wife and all his children. They were all deeply distressed and began to address him. "What a pity you were ever there, dear sir, for such great misfortune is yours. Now you, like ourselves, will live in bondage and in exile."

"Then whence do you come?" he asked.

"We are from your country, sir. In this land are many worthy men of your country held in bondage. Damn such a practice! Damn those who uphold it! Every foreigner who comes here is forced to stay. The land becomes his prison. Anyone who wishes may enter, but he must remain. And now this too is your fate. I believe you will never leave."

"I will if I can," he said.

The vavasor addressed him again. "How? Do you think you can escape?"

"Yes, God willing, and I shall do all in my power."

"Then all the others would have nothing to fear and would leave freely. For when one person escapes this prison in the proper manner, all the others, without fail, will be free to leave unchallenged."

At that moment the vavasor recalled a story he had been told about a knight of great excellence who would force his way into the country to rescue the queen, being held by Meleagant, the king's son. "Yes," he said to himself, "I think and believe this is the man, and I shall tell him so." He then addressed him. "Sir, keep none of your business from me. In return I promise to give you the best advice I can. If you manage to succeed, I too shall profit. For your benefit and mine, tell me the truth. I am convinced you came into this land, among these pagan people who are worse than Saracens, to rescue the queen."

"That is the only reason I came here," the knight answered him. "I do not know where my lady is held captive, but I intend to rescue her. Thus I need counsel urgently. Advise me if you can."

"Sir," he answered, "you have pursued a most difficult path. The route you are taking leads you straight to the sword-bridge. You do need to heed advice. If you trust me, you will go to the sword-bridge by a safer route, and I shall have someone guide you."

The knight wanted the shortest way. "Is it as direct as the other route?" he asked him.

"No," he said, "it is a longer but safer route."

"I do not care for that one," he replied. "But advise me about the shorter one, for I am prepared to take it."

"Sir, to be honest, that will not be to your advantage. If you go the other way, tomorrow you will reach a dangerous spot where trouble may soon be yours. The place is called the stone pass. Do you wish me to tell you of the perils of the path? Only one horse may pass through at a time; two men abreast could not go there. The pass is guarded and defended well. As soon as you reached there, you would encounter resistance. You would receive many blows from swords and lances, and return just as many, before you reached the other end."

When he had explained all to him, one of the vavasor's sons, who was a knight, stepped forward and addressed his father. "Sire, if you do not object, I shall go with this lord."

Thereupon one of the young lads stood up and said: "I shall go too." And to both their father gladly gave leave. The knight would not now travel alone. He appreciated their company very much and thanked them.

The conversation then ended, and the knight was escorted to bed so that he might sleep, if he so desired.

As soon as the knight could see daybreak, he rose. Those who were to accompany him saw him and rose immediately. The knights armed, took their leave, and set off, the young lad going in front. They followed their route together until, at exactly six that morning, they reached the stone pass. In the middle was a palisade where a man stood always on guard. Before they came near, the man in the tower saw them and shouted: "Enemy coming! Enemy coming!"

Thereupon behold, on horseback, a knight in new armor on the palisade, flanked by men-at-arms carrying sharp axes. The knight, watching the stranger approach the pass, insulted him shamefully about the cart. "Vassal," he said, "how very bold of you to enter this land. You were born a fool. No man who has been in a cart should ever come here. May God never grant you joy for it."

Then the two spurred toward each other as fast as their horses could gallop. The man who had to guard the pass split his lance in two pieces and let both fall to the ground. His opponent struck him in the neck right beneath the lining of his shield, hurling him flat on the stones. With their axes in hand, the men-at-arms jumped up, but deliberately missed him, not wanting to hurt him or his horse. When the knight realized that they had no desire or intention of harming or injuring him, he did not bother to draw his sword, but passed on without further dispute, and his companions followed him. One of them told the other that he had never seen such a knight, and that none was his equal. "Has he not performed an astonishing feat in forcing his way through the pass?"

"Dear brother," the knight said to his brother, "in God's name, hurry until you reach my father, and tell him of this adventure." The young lad asserted and swore that he would never take the message or leave this knight until he had been armed and knighted by him. If, however, his brother was so concerned about the message, let him be the one to take it.

Then all three continued along the route together until about three o'clock, when they met a man who asked their identity. "We are knights going about our business," they answered.

To the knight who seemed to him lord and master of the others, the man said, "Sir, I would like to offer lodging now to you and your companions."

"I could not take lodging at this hour," he told him, "for a man is a coward to delay or rest when engaged in such an enterprise. The business I have undertaken prevents me from taking lodging for some time."

"My home is not near here, but some distance ahead," the man said, addressing him again. "You can come there knowing that you will take your lodging at a proper time. It will be late when you arrive."

"Then I shall go there," he said.

The man then rode in front as their guide, the others following him along the open route. When they had traveled a long distance, they met a squire galloping along the road on a packhorse as round and fat as an apple. "Sir! Sir! Come quickly!" the squire shouted to the man. "The men of Logres have come armed against the people of this land. The war and its strife and fighting have already begun. They say a knight who has been in many battles has forced his way into this country. No one, however discomfited, can prevent him from going where he wishes. All the prisoners in this land say he will defeat our men, and thereby rescue all of them. Now take my advice and hurry!" The man then moved to a gallop. The three others were delighted by the news they heard, for they wished to help their people.

"Sir," said the vavasor's son, "hear what this squire has said. Let us ride and help our people in their struggle against the inhabitants here." Without waiting for the others, the man who guided them rode off immediately, and quickly made his way to a fortress situated firmly on a hill. He galloped along until he reached the entrance, while the others spurred after him. A moat and a high wall surrounded the bailey.

They had scarcely entered when a gate was dropped on their heels to prevent their return. "Let's go! Let's go!" they called out. "We shall not stop here." And they raced after the man until they came to the exit, which was not barred to them. The others were very upset to find themselves locked within, for they thought themselves victims of some enchantment. But the knight, of whom I must tell you more, had a ring on his finger; its stone had such power that anyone looking at it could not be subject to enchantments. Holding the ring before his eyes, he gazed on the stone and said: "Lady, lady, so help me God, I have great need of your aid now."

This lady who had given him the ring was a fairy, who had raised him in his infancy. So great was his trust in her that he never doubted she would bring him aid and relief wherever he was. But because of his invocation and the stone in the ring, he realized that there was no enchantment here, and knew for certain that they were confined and imprisoned.

Then they came to a low and narrow postern gate, but the gate was locked. All together they drew their swords, and the strength of their strokes broke the bar. Once outside the tower, they saw that a very large and fierce battle had begun down in the meadows: on one side, and on the other too, were at least a thousand knights in addition to the crowd of commoners. On their way down to the meadows, the vavasor's son spoke with wisdom and moderation. "Sir, before we reach there, I think we would be wise to have one of us ride ahead to inquire and learn which side our men take. I don't know where they come from, but if you wish, I shall go and see."

"Yes, I agree," he said. "Go there quickly, and be sure to return promptly."

He went quickly and rode back at once. "We are very fortunate," he said. "I have seen for certain that our men are on the side nearer us."

The knight rode into the battle immediately. Meeting a knight coming at him, he jousted with him and struck him so hard in the eye that he knocked him down dead. Dismounting, the young lad took the slain knight's horse and the armor he was wearing and armed himself carefully and properly. When armed, he mounted promptly, took the shield and the long and straight painted lance, and buckled to his side the bright and gleaming sharp sword. Into the battle he followed his brother as well as his lord, who had excelled so long in the fighting by breaking, splitting, and smashing shields, lances, and hauberks. Wood or steel did not prevent any man this lord attacked from being injured or knocked dead from his horse. By himself he did so well that he defeated all his opponents. And also admirable was the conduct of his two companions.

Ignorant of the knight's identity, the men of Logres were astounded, and asked the vavasor's son about him. Several posed so many questions that he replied to them: "Sirs, this is the man who will release us all from exile and the cruel misery that have so long been ours. We should do him great honor since, to deliver us from captivity, he has passed through so many dangerous places and will pass through still more. He has done much, and he has much to do."

All were delighted. The news traveled until it was known everywhere, for all heard it and all spread it. Their joy then increased their strength and courage. They killed many of the others and, it seems to me, disgraced the enemy more because of a single knight and his exemplary conduct than because of all the others together. Had night not been so near, the enemy would have been completely routed, but the night was growing so dark that the men were forced to separate.

At the time to depart, all the captives pressed round the knight as if vying with one another. From all sides they grabbed the reins of his horse and began to call out to him: "Welcome, dear sir." And each was saying: "On my word, sir, you shall lodge with me. In the name of God, sir, do not lodge with any but me." One person spoke in this manner, and all echoed the words, for young and old alike wanted him to accept their hospitality. Each person exclaimed: "You will be more comfortable in my house than anywhere else," and that was the way they addressed him. Everyone wanted to have him as guest, and he was jostled from one person to the next, a dispute almost breaking out among them. He told them that foolish and useless was their bickering.

"Cease this squabbling," he said. "It helps neither me nor you. Quarreling among ourselves is wrong. We should help one another. My lodging should not become reason for your argument and dispute. No, you should concern yourselves with lodging me where I might be on the direct route. That would be to everyone's advantage."

Nevertheless everyone still maintained: "That is my house!"

"No, that is mine!"

"You still talk like fools," the knight said. "In my opinion the wisest of you is foolish because I still hear you quarreling. You should be furthering my cause, yet you want to inconvenience me. If each of you had taken his turn to pay me as much honor and service as possible, then by all the saints prayed to in Rome, I would be no more grateful to you in accepting your kindness than I am now for your goodwill. In the name of God, Giver of Joy and Health, your good wishes please me as much as if each of you had already done me the greatest honor and kindness. So let the wish take the place of the deed."

With these words he overcame and appeased them all. Then they guided him along the road to the home of a very well-to-do knight, where all the people did their utmost to serve him. The whole evening long until bedtime everyone honored him, served him, and rejoiced in his presence, for they all cherished him.

When it was time to leave in the morning, each man wanted to accompany him, and presented himself and his services. But the knight wanted no other companions except the two who had accompanied him there. With these two alone, he continued along his way. That day they rode from early morning till dusk without happening on any adventure.

Galloping at great speed they reached, quite late, the end of a forest, where they sighted a knight's manorhouse. And they saw his wife, who seemed a fine lady, sitting in the doorway. As soon as she could see them, she rose to meet them. Her face wore an expression of joy and happiness as she greeted them. "Welcome!" she said. "I want you to accept the hospitality of my home. Dismount and take lodging."

"Thank you, lady. As you suggest, we shall dismount and accept your hospitality for the night." They dismounted, and after they did, the lady had their horses led away, for she had a fine household. At her call, her sons and her daughters came immediately: courteous and comely youths and knights and beautiful daughters. She asked some of them to unsaddle and groom the horses. Not one dared contradict her, but they obeyed her most willingly. At her request her daughters rushed forward to relieve the knights of their armor. When they had been disarmed, they were given three short cloaks to put on and escorted at once into their splendid lodgings.

The lord of the manor was not at home, but off in the forest with two of his sons. He came back soon, and his well-trained household ran to meet him outside the gate. With great speed, they unloaded and unpacked the game he carried. They then told him the news. "Sir, sir, though you do not know, you have three knights as your guests," they said.

"God be praised!" he answered.

The knight and his two sons gave a most joyous welcome to their guests. No one remaining idle, every last member of the household set about doing what had to be done. Some ran off to hasten the supper preparations, others to light the candles which, when lit, glowed steadily. Still others fetched the towel and the basins and offered water unsparingly for washing their hands. All washed, then went to sit down. In that house there was nothing unpleasant or offensive to be found.

During the first course, a surprise appeared in the courtyard in the form of a knight prouder than a bull, and the bull is a very proud beast. Fully armed from head to toe upon his charger, he rested one foot in the stirrup, while his other leg he had thrown with careful elegance over the neck of his long-maned charger. Behold he had arrived in this manner without anyone noticing him until he came before them and said: "Who is the senseless person, I want to know, with the pride and folly to come into this country expecting to cross the sword-bridge? In vain has he come to tire himself out. In vain has he wasted his steps."

These words did not daunt the knight, who answered him confidently: "I am he who intends to cross the bridge."

"You? You? How dare you think that? Before embarking on such a course, you should ask yourself about your possible end. You should remember the cart you rode in. I do not know if you are ashamed of your ride; yet no man in his right mind would ever have undertaken such a great enterprise had he felt the disgrace of that behavior."

He did not care to answer these remarks. But the lord of the manor and all the others were rightly astounded. "Oh God! What great misfortune!" each said to himself. "How base and despicable a cart is! Damn the hour it was first imagined and made! Oh God, what was he accused of? For what crime or misdeed was he led in the cart? He will be rebuked for this forever. Were he free of that reproach, you would not find a knight in the whole world, test his valor how you will, to equal this knight. If you assembled all such knights, you would not see even one so handsome or so noble, if the truth be told." And that was the general sentiment.

Puffed up with pride, the other knight began to speak again. "Knight, you who go to the sword-bridge, hear this. If you wish, you will cross the water easily and safely. I shall have you taken quickly across the water in a boat. But if I wish to levy a toll once I have you on the other side, I shall take your head, if I want it, or if not, it will be at my mercy."

His listener replied that he did not look for trouble; never would he risk his head in this adventure.

Again his opponent answered him. "Since you do not care to follow my advice, you must come outside and fight me hand to hand. The result will be disgrace and pain for you or for me."

To scoff at him, the knight replied: "If I could refuse, I would gladly exempt myself, but I would certainly rather fight than suffer a worse fate."

Before rising from the table where they sat, the knight told the attendants waiting on him to saddle his horse promptly and to bring him his equipment. Obeying his order at once, some employed their efforts in arming him; others led out his horse. As he rode along slowly on his horse, fully armed and holding his shield by its armstraps, it was obvious, you can be certain, that he was not to be excluded from the number of the noble and the brave. His horse well suited him, and the shield he clutched by the armstraps seemed his by right. His head fitted his laced helmet so well that you would never have assumed he had borrowed it or received it in pawn. On the contrary, you would be so pleased that you would have claimed he had been born and raised wearing the helmet. For this I would like you to take my word.

The knight who demanded the joust was on a stretch of open land beyond the manorhouse where the combat was to take place. When they saw each other, they galloped together in a savage assault. Their lances gave such blows that they bent, curved, and flew off in pieces, and their swords hacked away at their shields, helmets, and hauberks. By splitting the wood and breaking the steel, they inflicted several wounds. Such were the blows they dealt each other, as if they had made a contract in their rage. Often their swords slipped through to the horses' croups, where they were soaked in blood, for the swords gashed the flanks of the horses until both fell dead.

When their horses fell to the ground, the knights rushed at each other on foot. Such was their deadly hatred that their sword exchanges could surely not have been more brutal. The shower of their blows was more rapid than the coins thrown by a dice player who doubles his bet with each loss. Yet they played a very different game, not of wasted throws but of assaults and fierce warfare, of savagery and cruelty.

Everyone had come out of the manorhouse, the lord and his lady, their sons and daughters. No man or woman, close friend or not, stayed within, but all came and formed a line to watch the combat on the broad heath.

The knight of the cart accused and reproached himself for cowardice when he saw his host watching him. Then he also noticed all the others watching him. His whole body shook with anger; he felt he should have defeated his opponent long before. Then he struck him, plunging his sword in near his head. He stormed after him, the pressure of his attacks forcing his opponent to draw back. Without relaxing his assault, he took away his ground. The other knight almost lost his breath and could scarcely defend himself. The knight of the cart then remembered the shameful reproaches about the cart his rival had hurled at him earlier. He went at him, delivering such a blow that he broke every strap and string around the neckband of his hauberk. He sent his helmet flying from his head and his chinguard falling to the ground. He pressed him so hard and twisted him so harshly that the challenger was forced to seek mercy. Like the lark that cannot hold out or protect itself against the hawk which flies past to attack it from above, so, to his utter shame, was he compelled to ask and beg mercy since he could not help himself.

When the knight heard him implore mercy, he ceased his attack. "Do you wish mercy?" he asked.

"With great wisdom you have spoken now as any fool should," he replied. "I never craved anything so much as I crave your mercy at this moment."

"Then you must climb into a cart," he told him. "Since you dared hurl shameful insults at me, all your words are wasted unless you get into the cart."

"May it never please God that I mount there!" the knight answered.

"No? Then you shall die," he said.

"Sir, you can kill me. But in God's name I ask and beg your mercy on the one condition that I am not forced to climb into a cart. With this single exception I shall do anything, however painful or difficult. I would rather be dead, I know, than have agreed to that misfortune. I shall undergo any other punishment you say in return for your mercy and pardon."

While he was imploring mercy, behold there was a maiden racing across the heath on a fawn mule. Disheveled and disarrayed, she whipped the mule with heavy lashes. And the truth is that no horse's full gallop was as fast as the mule's pace.

"Knight, God fill your heart with perfect happiness in all its wishes," the maiden said to the knight of the cart.

"God bless you, maiden, and grant you joy and health," he answered, glad to hear her words.

Then she told him her wish. "Knight, in urgent need have I come to you from afar to ask a favor," she said. "The recompense will be the largest I can offer, and I think there will be a time when you will need my help."

"Tell me what you want," he answered, "and if I have it, it shall be yours at once, provided it is not too difficult."

"That knight you have defeated, I want his head," she told him. "The truth is you have never met a man so wicked or so disloyal. You will do nothing sinful or evil, but rather you will perform a noble act of charity, for he is the most despicable wretch that ever was or ever will be."

When the defeated knight heard her desire his death, he shouted: "Do not believe her! She hates me. In the name of God, who is both Father and Son and who took as His mother His own daughter and handmaiden, I beg you, have mercy on me."

"Ah, knight, do not believe this traitor!" the maiden exclaimed. "God grant you all the happiness and honor you can desire, and may He grant you success in your enterprise."

The knight was so confused that he paused and stopped to reflect. Should he give the head to the maiden who begged him to behead his opponent? Or should he have compassion and show mercy to him? He wished to accede to both demands. Generosity and Pity ordered him to satisfy both petitioners, for he was both generous and compassionate. But if she carried off his head, then Pity would be defeated and dead. On the other hand, if she did not carry off his head, then Generosity would be defeated. In such a prison of anguish, Generosity and Pity confined him and brought him distress and torment. In her supplication, the maiden wanted him to give her the head. On the other hand, his opponent appealed to his noble nature and mercy. And since he had begged mercy, should he not have it? Yes, for only once when he defeated an enemy and forced him to beg mercy had the knight refused the request and taken up the attack again. And so he would pardon the man who was entreating and begging him, since that was his desire. As for the maiden who wanted the head, would it be hers? Yes, if possible.

"Knight," he said, "you must fight me again. If you wish to save your head, I shall have mercy on you and let you pick up your helmet and equip yourself again. You have time to arm yourself from head to toe as best you can. But be assured of your death if I defeat you again."

"I want no more than that. I ask you no other favor," he answered.

"I offer you a further advantage," the other said. "In our fight, I shall not move from where I now stand."

The other knight armed. At once they returned eagerly to the combat. But this time the knight defeated him more easily than the first. The maiden cried out immediately: "Do not spare him, knight, no matter what he tells you. Truly he would not have spared you had he defeated you even once. You can be certain, if you believe him, he will trick you again. Noble knight, behead the most disloyal man in the kingdom and the empire and give me his head. You ought to present it to me because there will be a time for me to repay you. If given the chance, that man's tongue will trick you again."

Seeing his approaching death, the knight begged mercy at the top of his voice. But neither his cries nor anything he might say was of any value. Dragging him by his helmet, the victor tore off all the fastenings and smashed the chinguard and the gleaming hood from his head. The defeated knight pressed his claims as much as he could. "Mercy, in God's name! Mercy, valiant knight!"

"On my soul's salvation," he replied, "I shall never have mercy on you. I have already given you a chance."

"Ah, you would sin if you heeded my enemy and killed me this way," he said.

The maiden, wanting his death, urged the knight to behead him promptly and pay no further attention to his words. He struck the blow. The head flew across the field, and the body fell. The maiden was pleased and satisfied.

Picking up the head by the hair, the knight presented it to the maiden, who was delighted. "May your heart receive from the object it most desires," she said, "happiness equal to mine now that I hold the object I despised most. Nothing caused me pain except that this man lived so long. A reward from me awaits you. You will receive it when an occasion demands. I promise you great advantage for this service you have done me. Now I shall go. I commend you to God that He keep you from harm." The maiden departed after they commended each other to God.

All who had watched the combat on the open field were overwhelmed with happiness. Amid great rejoicing, they removed the knight's armor immediately and honored him as best they could. Without further delay they washed their hands again, eager to take their seats at the meal. Now their mood was much happier than usual, and they ate with great cheer. After the dinner had gone on some time, the vavasor spoke to his guest seated beside him. "Sir, it has been a long time since we came here from our birthplace, the kingdom of Logres. We would like honor, great success, and joy to be yours in this country. We would profit along with you, and so would many others, should honor and success in this enterprise be yours in this land."

"May God hear you," he answered.

When the vavasor had lowered his voice and finished speaking, one of his sons followed his talk. "Sir," he said, "all the means at our disposal we should place at your service. We should give them to you, not simply promise them. Should you need our help, we should not wait till you ask. Sir, do not worry about your dead horse, for there are strong horses here. I wish all we have to be yours. Instead of your horse take our best one, for you have need of it."

"I shall do that gladly," he replied. They then had the beds prepared, and everyone went off to sleep.

The next morning the three companions rose early, dressed, and readied themselves to leave. Their departure was an example of perfect courtesy: they took leave of the lady, the lord, and all the household. But there is one detail I must recount lest I omit something. The knight would not mount the borrowed horse which had been presented to him at the gate. Instead, I would tell you, he had one of the two knights accompanying him mount the horse, while he rode that knight's horse. This exchange suited and pleased him. When all three were mounted, they began their journey with the leave and permission of their host, who had honored and served them as best he could. They rode along the highway until the day began to lean toward its decline. Late in the afternoon, just before dusk, they reached the sword-bridge.

At the foot of this treacherous bridge they dismounted and looked down at the menacing water, black and roaring, dense and swift. Its muddiness and terror made it seem like the devil's river. Anything in the whole world that fell into the perilously deep current would disappear as if it had fallen into the icy sea. The bridge spanning the water was unlike all others: to be honest, there never was, nor would there ever be, such a menacing bridge or footbridge. The bridge across the cold water consisted of only a brightly polished sword, though the sword, the length of two lances, was strong and stiff. Since the sword was fastened to a huge stump on each bank, there was no need to worry about falling off because of the sword's bending or breaking. But to the eye it seemed incapable of sustaining heavy weight.

The two knights accompanying the third were most upset, for they believed two lions or two leopards were tied to a rock at the other end of the bridge. The water, the bridge, and the lions put them in such a fright that they both trembled with fear. "Sir, you must carefully consider what you see," they said. "This bridge is badly constructed and fastened. It is a miserable structure. If you do not turn back now, you will be sorry later. You must pay close attention to your alternatives. Suppose you do reach the other side—but that is no more likely than your getting control of the winds and preventing them from blowing, or keeping the birds that sing from daring to warble their songs. No, it is no more likely than a man entering his mother's womb and being born again. All this is as impossible as the sea being emptied. Can you believe and ascertain that those two raging lions chained over there will not kill you, then suck the blood from your veins, eat your flesh, and finally gnaw on your bones? We feel bold even daring to watch them with our eyes. If you do not take care of yourself, they will kill you. Of that you can be certain. In no time at all they will rip you apart and tear you limb from limb without mercy. But now take pity on yourself and stay here with us. You would be wrong to expose yourself knowingly to the danger of certain death."

He laughed as he answered them. "Sirs," he said, "I am very grateful for your concern for me, which is an expression of your affection and your noble character. I am certain you do not want me to suffer misfortune.

But I have such faith and trust in God that He will protect me everywhere. This bridge and this water are no more terrifying to me than this solid land. Now I plan to ready myself for the adventure of crossing to the other side. I would rather die than turn back."

Unable to say more, his companions sobbed with pity and sighed heavily. The other prepared himself as best he could to cross the torrent. What a remarkable feat he performed! He removed the armor from his hands and feet; he would not be unharmed or free of injury when he reached the other bank. On the sword, which was sharper than a scythe, he would balance himself firmly on his bare hands and feet, having removed his toecaps, boots, and leggings. Little worried about injuries to his hands and feet, he would rather maim himself than fall from the bridge and bathe in water from which he would never escape.

In deep pain and distress, he managed to make the crossing. His hands, knees, and feet were bloodied. But Love, his leader and guide, offered him relief and medication; for this reason his suffering was sweet. On his hands, knees, and feet he succeeded in reaching the other bank.

Then the knight recalled and remembered the two lions he believed he had seen from the other side. When he looked around, he saw nothing to harm him, not even a lizard or any other animal. He raised his hand in front of his face, regarded his ring, then looked again. Ascertaining in this way that neither of the two lions he believed he had seen was there, he believed that some enchantment was present, yet no living creature was there.

When the men on the other bank saw how he had crossed, they rejoiced as they should, though ignorant of the extent of his injuries. For his part, he considered himself most fortunate not to have suffered worse. With his shirt he wiped the blood that dripped from his wounds.

The knight saw a tower ahead of him more massive than any he had ever seen; there could be no finer tower. Leaning on a window ledge was King Bademagu. Careful and exact in all matters of honor and right, he wished to observe and practice loyalty above all. Leaning next to him was his son, who always did the very opposite as best he could, for disloyalty pleased him. No cruelty, villainy, or treason ever worried or wearied him. From their position they had seen the knight cross the bridge in heavy pain and agony. Anger and resentment caused Meleagant's color to change; he realized that he would now be challenged for the queen. Yet he was the kind of knight who feared no man, however strong or fierce. Were he not disloyal and evil, there would have been no finer knight. But he had a wooden heart without a drop of kindness or compassion.

What brought the son deep pain brought the king pleasure and joy. The king knew for a fact that the man who had crossed the bridge had no equal, for no one would ever dare make such a crossing with a heart that lodged Cowardice, which is more prompt in disgracing her people than Bravery is in honoring her followers. Bravery, therefore, cannot accomplish as much as Cowardice and Laziness, for it is true beyond doubt that it is easier to do evil than good. I could tell you more about these two were it not for the time it would take. But my purpose lies elsewhere, and I return to my subject.

Hear the king's instructions to his son. "Son," he said, "it was by chance we came, you and I, to lean by this window. We have received such a reward in witnessing the greatest deed of daring ever imagined. Tell me now if you are not impressed by the man who performed such a marvelous feat. Make peace with him. Reconcile yourselves. Return the queen to him with no conditions attached. You will never profit from fighting him, though you could suffer badly. Now let yourself be held wise and courteous. Send the queen to him before he sees you. In your country, bestow on him this honor: give him what he has come to seek before he demands it from you. You know quite well that he seeks Queen Guinevere. Do not behave in such a manner that you are taken to be obstinate, foolish, or proud. If he is alone in your country, you should keep him company. One man of valor should not shy away from another man of valor; he should go to him and treat him with honor and attention. A man is honored in honoring another. You can be certain honor will be yours if you honor and serve this man, who is surely the finest knight in the world."

"God confound him," he answered, "if there is not one as good or better." The father had been mistaken in forgetting about the son, who held himself in no less esteem. "Perhaps you would like me," Meleagant continued, "to kneel before him with my hands folded and become his liegeman and hold land from him? So help me God, I would rather become his vassal than return her to him. I will never give her up. I will defend her in combat against all foolish enough to dare come and seek her."

The king then addressed his son again. "Son, you would behave courteously by abandoning this stubbornness. Make peace: that is my advice and my prayer. You can be assured of the knight's shame if he does not win the queen from you in combat. He would certainly prefer to rescue her in combat than through a gesture of kindness, for this would enhance his reputation. That is why, in my opinion, he does not ask that she be given back peaceably. He wants to win her in combat. Therefore, you would be wise to rob him of the opportunity for combat. Make peace: that is my advice and my prayer. If you scorn my counsel, it will not matter to me if worse befalls you. And great misfortune may happen to you. The knight need fear none here except you. On behalf of all my men and myself, I guarantee him complete protection. I have never committed an act of disloyalty, treason, or evil, and I shall no more begin to do so for you than for a stranger. I have no wish to deceive you. I promise that the knight will have all he needs, arms and a horse, since his coming here was so courageous a feat. He will be guarded and safely protected against all men except you. I want you to understand this clearly: if he can defend himself against you, he need fear no one else."

"I have listened and kept silent long enough," Meleagant answered. "Say what you will, your words mean little to me. I am not such a hermit, nor such a man of valor, nor such a man of charity. I don't wish to be so honorable as to give him what I love most. He will not accomplish his task as quickly and easily as you and he imagine. The opposite will be the case. We shall not reach accord on this if you help him against me. What does it matter to me if he enjoys peace and the guarantee of safekeeping from you and all your men? That does not cause my heart to tremble. So help me God, quite the contrary. That he should be concerned only with me pleases me the more. I want you to do nothing on my account that might be construed as disloyalty or treachery. For as long as you please, be a man of valor and allow me my cruelty."

"What? You will not change your mind?"

"Not at all," he answered.

"Then I have nothing more to say. I shall leave you to yourself. Do your best. I go to speak with the knight. I wish to offer him freely my advice and my aid, for my sympathies are entirely with him."

The king then came down from the tower and had his horse saddled. A large charger was led out to him. He placed his foot in the stirrup and mounted. Of his men, he took only three knights and two men-at-arms to accompany him. They rode downhill until they reached the bridge, where they saw the knight wiping the blood from his wounds. The king assumed that the knight would be his guest for a long time while his wounds healed, though he might as well have expected to drain the sea.

The king was quick to dismount. The grievously wounded knight immediately stood to meet him, though he did not recognize him. As though he were completely healthy, he paid no attention to the pain in his hands and feet. When the king saw him exert himself, he rushed at once to greet him. "Sir," he said, "I am astonished that you have forced your way into this country of ours. But be welcome here. No one else will ever undertake such a feat. Never has it happened, and never will it happen, that any man has displayed so much courage in exposing himself to such danger. Be assured that I esteem you the more because you have accomplished what no one ever dared imagine doing. You will find me gracious, loyal, and courteous toward you. I am king of this land, and I offer you as much of my counsel and my aid as you wish. The reason for your quest seems self-evident to me. You come, I believe, for the queen."

"Sir," he answered, "you presume correctly. No other duty brings me here."

"Friend," the king said, "you will have to suffer before she is yours. You are seriously injured; I see the wounds and the blood. You will not find the man who brought her here so noble as to surrender her to you without a struggle. But you must rest and have your wounds treated until they are healed. I shall give you some ointment of the Three Marys and some that is even better, if it can be found, for I am concerned about your comfort and your recovery. During her imprisonment, the queen has been treated properly: no lustful man may lay hand on her, not even my own son, who brought her here with him and who is most pained at my behavior. Never has a man been so obsessed by rage and fury as he. But I have only the highest regard for you, and so help me God, I shall be pleased to give you whatever you need. My son's fine equipment will be no better than the arms I give you, though this will cause him great anger toward me. And I shall also give you the horse you need. However indignant anyone may be, I place you under my safekeeping against all men. You need fear no man except the one who brought the queen here. No man ever threatened an-other as I threatened him. Because he did not hand her over to you, my fury almost caused me to drive him from my land. Yes, he is my son. But do not worry. Unless he defeats you in combat, he can never, against my will, cause you the least harm."

"Sir," he replied, "I am grateful to you. But I waste too much time here, which I do not wish to lose. I do not suffer; no wound gives me pain. Show me where I may find him, for with such arms as are mine now, I am ready at once to take some sport in the exchange of blows."

"Friend, you had better wait two or three weeks until your wounds heal. It would be good for you to stay here at least a fortnight. I could never allow you to fight in my presence, much less watch you fight in the arms and equipment you have."

"With your permission, only these arms would be used," he answered. "I would prefer to fight like this now than seek adjournment, postpone-ment, or delay. In deference to you, however, I shall agree to wait until tomorrow. No matter what is said, I shall wait no longer." The king agreed to comply precisely with his wishes, then had him led to lodgings. He entreated and commanded those escorting the knight to make every effort to serve his needs. Without the least hesitation, they obeyed him.

In his fervent desire to bring about accord if he was able, the king returned to his son, speaking to him like a man anxious for peace and harmony. "Dear son, reach an agreement with this knight without resorting to combat," he said to him. "He has not come here for amusement, for hunting or chasing in the woods. No, he has come to seek and increase his honor and renown. I have seen him, and he is in need of much rest. Had he heeded my counsel, he would not have sought, at least for a month or two, the battle he craves so desperately. Do you fear falling into disrepute by returning the queen to him? Never be afraid of that, for you cannot be faulted. But it is wrong to keep something not rightly and properly yours. Despite the condition of his hands and feet, slashed and wounded and as yet not healed, he would gladly have begun to fight at this moment."

"You are foolish to be upset," Meleagant told his father. "By my faith in Saint Peter, I shall not heed you in this matter. Were I to listen to you, I should certainly deserve to be drawn by horses. If he seeks his honor, so I seek mine. If he seeks his renown, I too seek mine. And if he wants combat at all costs, I want it too, and a hundred times more than he."

"I see you are intent on folly, and that is what you will find," the king said. "Tomorrow, as you wish, you shall test your strength against the knight."

"May no greater disaster than that ever come my way!" Meleagant said. "I would prefer it were today rather than tomorrow. Behold now my expression more downcast than usual, my eyes distracted, my face drawn. No joy, no satisfaction, no cause for happiness will be mine until the combat."

The king realized that it was useless to advise or plead with his son, and so with reluctance left him. He selected a fine strong horse and good equipment, and sent them to the knight, who well deserved them. An elderly man, most devoutly Christian and with more loyalty than anyone in the world, was also present; he had greater skill than all the men of Montpellier in the healing of wounds. That night, as the king commanded, he attended to the knight to the best of his ability.

Throughout the country and surrounding vicinity, knights and barons, ladies and maidens had already heard the news. In all directions, from as far off as a long day's travel, they came, friends as well as strangers, racing through the night until morning. By sunrise there was such a press of people before the tower keep that no one could turn about.

Early in the morning, the king rose. Distressed about the combat, he came again to his son, who had already laced his Poitiers helmet on his head. No delay or peace was possible; the king tried again with all his heart, but to no avail. In the square before the keep where all the people were gathered, the combat was to take place according to the king's will and direction.

The king immediately summoned the foreign knight, who was led into the square, filled with people from the kingdom of Logres. As people are used to going to church on the annual feasts of Pentecost or Christmas to hear the organs, so, in similar manner, they had all congregated there. For three days all the maidens in exile from King Arthur's realm had fasted, walked barefoot, and worn wool shirts so that God might grant the knight, who had to fight for the captives, strength and courage against his opponent. On the other side, the people of Gorre prayed for their lord that God might grant him victory and honor in the combat.

Early in the morning, before six o'clock, the two knights, fully armed, were led into the center of the square on their two iron-clad horses. Well-proportioned in his arms, legs, and feet, Meleagant was handsome and alert; his helmet and the shield that hung from his neck were most becoming and impressive. But all favored the other knight, even those who were eager for his disgrace, and all declared that Meleagant was worth nothing in comparison with him.

When both men had taken their positions in the center of the square, the king came and detained them as long as he could in an effort to make peace. Yet he could not move his son. "Hold on to the reins of your horses," he told them, "at least until I have climbed to the top of the tower. To delay that long for me will not be too great a kindness."

Then in deep dismay the king left. He proceeded directly to where he knew the queen would be. The night before, she had asked him to give her a place in full view of the combat, and he had granted her request. Now he was going to find her and escort her there, eager always to do her every honor and service. He placed her at one window, reclining himself by another window to her right. Along with them were gathered many others, knights, prudent ladies, maidens born in that country, and many captives absorbed in prayers and petitions. All the men and all the women imprisoned there were praying for their lord, placing their faith in him and in God for their aid and deliverance.

Then, without further delay, the combatants had all the people stand back. Drawing up the shields at their sides, they gripped them tightly by the armstraps. Rushing together, they spurred so hard that they plunged their lances two arms' length into each other's shields, causing the lances to splinter and crumble like brushwood. Their horses charged violently at each other and clashed, head to head, body against body. Shields and helmets collided with such a crash that you would have thought you heard claps of thunder. Breaststraps, saddlegirths, stirrups, reins, and the rest of the harnesses, all were broken, and the saddlebows, once strong, were smashed to pieces.

The knights felt no shame in falling to the ground the moment their equipment failed. They quickly jumped back to their feet and, making no bragging taunts, rushed together more fiercely than two wild boars. Without menacing threats, they delivered heavy blows with their steel swords like men who know only mortal hatred. Again and again, so savagely did they slash helmets and gleaming hauberks that blood spurted from the shock of the swords. They battled brilliantly, stunning and wounding each other with blows of cruel savagery. Their long exchange of hard and fierce assaults gave advantage to neither man. At no time did the spectators know which of the two fared well, which poorly. But it was inevitable that the knight who had crossed the bridge was much weaker because of the wounds to his hands. His supporters, distressed to notice his blows growing more feeble, feared that the combat would worsen for him. Already they thought that he was getting the worse of it and Meleagant the better, and talked of this among themselves.

At the tower windows was a wise maiden, who reflected and said to herself that the knight had not undertaken the combat for her or for those other commoners who had come into the square. If it had not been for the queen, he would never have undertaken this exploit. She believed that he would recover his strength and boldness if he knew the queen was at the window, looking out and watching him. Had she known his name, she would have eagerly called to him to look round a little. And so she came to the queen. "Lady," she said, "I beg you, in God's name, and for your welfare as well as ours, tell me the name of that knight, if you know it, that he might be helped."

"Young lady," the queen replied, "your question bears no trace of hatred or wrong, but only good. The name of the knight, as I know, is Lancelot of the Lake."

"God!" exclaimed the maiden. "What happiness and delight are mine! My heart is so content." She then leaned forward and shouted to him so loudly that all the people heard her. "Lancelot! Turn round and see who watches you."

When Lancelot heard his name, he turned round promptly. And when he did so, up in the tower galleries he saw seated the one he most desired to see in the entire world. From the moment he caught sight of her, he did not turn or take his eyes or his face from her, but defended himself from the back. Meleagant pursued him as closely as he was able, pleased at the thought that his enemy could never now withstand him. Although the people of the country were delighted, the foreigners were so distraught that they were scarcely able to stand. Many were forced to sink to the ground in despair, some on their knees, others prostrate. Thus great joy and great sadness prevailed.

The maiden then shouted again from the window. "Oh Lancelot, how can you act so foolishly? You once were the epitome of all valor and excellence. I do not think or believe God ever made a knight equal to you in courage and renown. Now we see you at such a loss. Turn round to the other side where you may always see this tower. Sight of it will help you."

Lancelot was so ashamed and disgusted that he despised himself. He knew well, as did all the men and women there, that he had been receiving the worst of the combat for some time. He then jumped backwards and turned round, forcing Meleagant into a position between him and the tower. While Meleagant made every effort to regain his former stand, Lancelot attacked and struck him, his full weight behind his shield, whenever Meleagant tried to move round him. In this way, without seeking his opponent's consent, Lancelot forced him to totter two or more times. Through Love's great assistance and because Lancelot had never hated anyone so much as this opponent, his strength and courage increased. Love, coupled with the most deadly Hatred, gave him such resolution and courage that Meleagant no longer considered their encounter a frivolous matter. Deep fear took hold of him. He had never known or faced such a fierce knight, nor had any knight ever injured or wounded him as did this one. Glad to move away from him, he drew back and stepped aside, abhorring and avoiding his blows. Lancelot did not merely threaten him, but with constant attacks chased him toward the tower where the queen reclined. Often had he served her and paid her homage. Directing his opponent now so close to her, he was forced to stop short; had he gone forward another step, she would not have been visible to him. Thus Lancelot continued to drive him back and forth wherever he pleased, always stopping before his lady the queen. She had ignited the flame in his heart, which made him continue to gaze up at her. This flame incited him against Meleagant so that he could chase and drive him wherever he wished. Despite his own efforts, Meleagant was driven like a man crippled or blind.

When the king saw his son too exhausted to help or defend himself, he knew grief and pity for him. He would help him if he could. But if he wished to do this, he must address his request to the queen. Therefore he began to speak to her. "Lady, after you came under my care, I was devoted to you and served you honorably. I was pleased to do all I could to enhance your honor. Now repay my behavior. I would ask you a favor you should not grant me, unless you do so out of affection. I clearly see that my son has indeed received the worst in this combat. Not out of grief over this do I beseech you, but rather so that Lancelot, who has him in his power, not kill him. Even though Meleagant has wronged you both, you yourself, in gratitude to me, should not desire this outcome. Tell him for my sake, I beg you, to stop his assault. In this way, if you see fit, you may repay my service."

"Dear sir, since you ask me, I agree willingly," the queen answered. "If I felt deadly hatred for your son—and I am without affection for him—still you have served me so well that, to show you my gratitude, I will Lancelot to halt."

These were not private words, for Lancelot and Meleagant heard them. A lover is obedient; when he is completely in love, he performs his beloved's pleasure eagerly and promptly. Thus Lancelot, who loved more than Pyramus—if love more any man could—was compelled to obey.

Lancelot heard the words of the queen. The last words she had uttered, "To show you my gratitude, I will Lancelot to halt," had scarcely left her lips when he would not lay a hand on his opponent or make any move, even if Meleagant were to kill him. Lancelot did not stir, nor did he touch his opponent.

Made mad with rage and shame at hearing that he had reached the point where intercession for him had become necessary, Meleagant struck at Lancelot with all his force. The king went down from the tower to reprove him. Coming into the area of the combat, he addressed him at once. "What? Is it right now to strike him when he does not touch you? Now you are too cruel, too savage. Now at a contemptible moment are you too brave. We all clearly see that he has overcome you."

Misled by his disgrace, Meleagant spoke to the king. "Perhaps you are blind. I think you see nothing. Anyone is blind to doubt that I am not better than he."

"Find someone now who believes you," the king answered. "All present know whether you tell the truth or not. We clearly see the truth."

The king then instructed his barons to restrain his son. They obeyed him immediately and pulled Meleagant back. To restrain Lancelot did not require great force, for Meleagant could have done him much harm before he would have raised a hand against him. "So help me God," the king told his son, "now you must make peace and surrender the queen. You must renounce your claim and abandon the entire dispute."

"What folly you have spoken. I hear you talking nonsense. Go away. Let us fight. Stay out of this."

The king insisted on such an action, certain that if he let the fight continue, Lancelot would kill him.

"He would kill me? No, I would defeat him quickly and kill him, if you would let us continue to fight and not restrain us."

"So help me God, all your words are wasted," the king said.

"Why?" he asked.

"Because I do not agree. I shall not place my faith in your folly or your pride and allow you to be killed. A man is foolish to desire his own death, as you do without knowing. I realize that you despise me because of my desire to protect you. Just as I would wish, God will never let me stand by and watch your death. That would distress me too much."

He talked to his son and reproved him until peace and harmony were established on these terms: Meleagant would surrender the queen on condition that Lancelot fight him again one year, and no more, from the day he was summoned. This arrangement did not distress Lancelot. With the accord established, all the people pressed about. The decision was made that the combat would take place at the court of King Arthur, who governed Britain and Cornwall. There, it was decreed, the combat should occur. The queen had to accept the agreement, and Lancelot had to consent that if Meleagant made him seek mercy, the queen would return with him and no one would detain her. This condition proved acceptable to the queen, too, and Lancelot added his consent. So when the accord was settled, both knights withdrew and disarmed.

It was the custom in this country that when one captive was liberated, all the others were free to leave. Everyone blessed Lancelot. You can be certain that great joy should have been his, and indeed it was. All the foreigners gathered there celebrated Lancelot, and all exclaimed so that he would hear: "Yes, as soon as we heard your name, sir, we rejoiced, for we were certain indeed that we would all soon be freed."

Such joy was there among the crowds of people. Each person pushed forward, trying, if he was able, to touch him. Anyone who managed to come near him was happy beyond the telling. There was much joy there, and anger too. Those who had been freed abandoned themselves to sheer delight. But Meleagant and his people had no reason for rejoicing; on the contrary, they were pensive, downcast, and depressed.

The king left the scene of the combat and did not neglect to lead Lancelot with him. When Lancelot begged to be taken to the queen, the king replied: "I shall do this, for it seems to me quite proper. And if you wish, I shall take you to see Kay the seneschal too." Lancelot was so overcome with joy that he almost threw himself at the king's feet. The king led him immediately into the great hall where the queen had come to await him.

When the queen saw the king leading Lancelot by the hand, she rose before the king, lowering her head and remaining silent in an appearance of anger. "Lady," said the king, "here is Lancelot, who comes to see you. This should suit and please you."

"Me? Sir, he is unable to please me. I have no interest in seeing him."

"What? Lady, what has taken control of your heart?" inquired the courteous and noble king. "To be certain, you have done this man a grave injustice. Consider the service he has done you. During his search for you, he often placed his life in mortal danger. He defended you and freed you from my son Meleagant, who was in a fury at having to surrender you."

"Sir, to be honest, he wasted his time. I shall never deny it. For what he did, I thank him not."

Behold Lancelot dumbfounded. His answer, nevertheless, was the graceful response of a true lover. "Lady, your behavior grieves me, yet I dare not ask its cause."

If the queen had listened to him, Lancelot would have prolonged his lament, but in order to hurt and confuse him, she had no desire to respond even with a word, but withdrew into another room. Lancelot escorted her to the door with his eyes and his heart. His eyes, however, had only a short trip, since the room was quite near; if they could, they would have followed her gladly. While the tearful eyes remained behind with the body, the heart, lord and master and much more powerful, passed through the door after her. The king spoke to him in private. "Lancelot, I am amazed. What does this mean? Why can the queen not bear the sight of you? Why will she not speak to you? If ever she enjoyed talking to you, she should not now adopt an imperious attitude toward you, or scorn your words. After all, consider what you have done for her. Tell me now, if you know, did you do some wrong? Why did she act this way?"

"Sir, until just now I suspected nothing. But she has no wish to see me or to hear my voice, and this disturbs and distresses me."

"To be certain, she is mistaken," said the king, "for you did face deadly perils for her. Come now, dear friend, and we shall go and talk to the seneschal."

"I desire to go there," he replied.

Both went to the seneschal. When Lancelot stood before him, the seneschal addressed his first words to Lancelot. "How you have disgraced me!"

"I? In what way?" Lancelot asked. "Tell me what disgrace I have done you."

"A dread one, for you have accomplished the feat I could not achieve. You did what I could not do."

The king then left the two and proceeded out of the room alone, and Lancelot asked the seneschal if he had suffered badly. "Yes, and I do still," he replied. "I have never known such pain as now I have. I would have been dead long ago were it not for the king now leaving here. In his mercy he showed me such attention and friendship. Each time I required anything for my recovery, he gave it to me the moment he learned of my need. But then there is his son Meleagant, who knows every device of evil. Each time his father did me a kindness, he treacherously summoned his physicians and ordered them to dress my wounds with ointments that would slay me. What a father and stepfather I have had! When the king, anxious to speed my recovery, had a fine dressing applied to my wounds, his treacherous son, desiring my death, had it removed and replaced with a deadly ointment. But I am completely certain the king knew nothing of this. He would never allow such treachery or murder. Furthermore, you do not know the king's noble behavior to my lady. Since the time Noah built his ark, no watchman has ever guarded a frontier tower with the care he has shown her. His son is miserable because his father will not let him see the queen unless he himself or a group of people is present. The noble king deserves gratitude for treating her with great honor until this very day, and he continues this by doing her every service she might imagine. She alone has seen to her well-being during her confinement, and the king's respect for her grew as he saw her loyalty. But is this story I hear true? That she is so angered at you that, in front of everyone, she refused to talk to you?"

"What you have heard is completely true," Lancelot answered. "But for the sake of God, can you tell me why she hates me?" He did not know the reason, Kay replied, though her behavior entirely amazed him. "Let it be as she wills," said Lancelot, who could only resign himself to the situation. "There is nothing left for me but to take my leave," he said. "I shall go and find Sir Gawain, who also entered this land. We agreed that he would proceed directly to the water-bridge."

Thereupon Lancelot left the room and came before the king to ask leave to depart in that direction. The king granted his request willingly. But the prisoners Lancelot had freed from captivity asked him what they were to do. "All of you wishing to accompany me may do so," he said. "Those wishing to stay with the queen may do so; there is no obligation to accompany me."

With more than usual joy, all who wished to accompany him did so. With the queen stayed many knights, ladies, and maidens, who also rejoiced. Nevertheless, rather than stay there, every one remaining behind would have preferred to return to his own country. The queen, however, detained them on account of the impending arrival of Sir Gawain, saying that she would not leave until she heard news of him.

Everywhere the news spread that the queen was freed and the captives were delivered; without fail, they would depart at their pleasure and convenience. When all the people of the land came together, they asked one another the truth about the report and talked of nothing else. They were not at all angry that the dangerous passes had been destroyed. Now people were coming and going at will; such was not as things had been.

When the people of that land who had not attended the combat learned of Lancelot's conduct, they all advanced toward the pass they expected him to take, hoping to please the king by leading Lancelot back a prisoner. All of Lancelot's men were unarmed. Consequently, they were outraged to see the men of the land advancing in armor. It was not surprising that these people captured Lancelot, who was unarmed, and led him back a prisoner, his feet tied beneath his horse, "Gentle sirs," the men of Logres explained, "what you do is wrong! The king assured us safe conduct; we are all under his protection."

"We know nothing of this," they answered. "But since you are our prisoners, you must return to the court."

Rumor, which flies swiftly and races, reached the king that his men had captured Lancelot and killed him. On hearing this, the king was grievously upset and swore by his own head—this was his slightest oath!—that his murderers would be killed. They could never justify such an act, and if he could seize and hold them, it would be their fate to die by hanging, burning, or drowning. And if they attempted to deny their act, he would not believe a word of it. They had inflicted so much pain and so much shame on his heart that he should be reproached if he did not exact vengeance from them. Without doubt he would have revenge.

This rumor continued to spread everywhere, and reached the queen, who was seated at dinner. On hearing the false story about Lancelot, she nearly took her life. Believing the rumor true, she was so deeply distressed that she almost lost her ability to speak. Because of those present, however, she spoke openly. "It is true that his death saddens me deeply. I am not wrong to feel such pain, for he entered this land on my behalf. Therefore, I should be grieved." Then, lest she be heard, she told herself quietly that none should ever ask her to eat or drink again if the report of his death was true, for in his existence she found her life. In her misery, she rose at once from the table and went where no one could hear her weeping. So distraught was she that she clutched at her throat continuously, desiring to kill herself. Still she first took time to confess herself. As she beat her breast, she repented. Full of self-reproach, she accused herself of the sin she had committed against him. She knew that he had been hers always and would be hers still were he alive. Her cruelty to him caused her such anxiety that her beauty was altered. Her remorse over her harsh treatment of him, complemented by her vigils and fastings, dulled the luster of her complexion.

The queen counted all her sins as they passed before her. Reviewing them all, she wept many times. "Alas, wretch that I am, when my lover came before me, why did I not think of welcoming him? Why would I not hear him? When I refused to look at him or talk to him, did I not conduct myself like a fool? A fool? No, God help me, I am guilty of fatal cruelty. I meant it as a jest, but he did not take it that way, and has not forgiven me. None but I delivered his death blow, this I know. When he came before me smiling and expecting my delight at the sight of him, I would not look at him. Then was that not his death blow? Yes, my refusal to speak to him, as I know, destroyed at once his heart and his life together. I believe the double blow killed him. No other pillaging troops murdered him. God, shall I ever atone for this slaying? for this sin? No indeed. All the rivers and the sea will dry up first! Alas, wretch that I am, how much better should I have felt, what comfort should I have known, had I but once held him in my arms before he died. How? Yes, naked body against naked body, of course, so I might know greater pleasure. Now that he is dead, only cowardice prevents me from taking my life. Seeing that the only pleasure I know is the pain I suffer for him, should it not wound me to go on with my life after his death? Since his death, such is my only pleasure. To be certain, my present pain would be pleasant did he but live. It is a wicked woman who would prefer to die rather than endure pain for her lover. But I find great enjoyment in mourning him a long time. I would rather live and endure the blows of fate than die and be at rest." Neither eating nor drinking, the queen continued to grieve two more days until all thought her dead.

Many people bear news, and usually bad news rather than good. The rumor reached Lancelot that his lady and beloved was dead. Believe me, he was driven to grief. All could clearly see his deep sorrow and anger. The truth is that his pain was so severe, if you would hear and know this, that he despised his own life. He plotted to kill himself at once, after uttering his lament. Tying a running noose from one end of his belt, he said to himself with tears in his eyes: "Alas! Death, how you have lain in wait for me! My health was good, but you have struck me down. I am crushed, yet the sole pain I feel is the grief in my heart. This grief is an illness, indeed a fatal one, and I wish it to be fatal. Please God I shall die of it. How? If this does not please the Lord God, might I not die another way? Yes, I shall die, if He lets me tighten this noose round my neck. Then I expect to force Death, even against her will, to kill me. Death, who covets only those who care not for her, will not come to me. But my belt will capture and bring her to me. Since I shall control her, she will do as I wish. Still she will come too slowly. Such is my desire to control her."

He then, without a moment's delay, slipped the noose over his head and tightened it round his neck. To be certain of doing himself harm, he fastened the other end of his belt tightly to the pommel of his saddle without anyone noticing. Then he let himself slip to the ground, intending his horse to drag him along until he expired; he did not wish to live another hour. When those riding with him saw him fall to the ground, they thought he had fainted, for none noticed the noose he had tied round his neck. They lifted him back up at once and, when they had raised him in their arms, discovered the noose he had placed round his neck, making him enemy to himself. At that very instant they cut the noose, though already it had had such effect on his throat that for a time he was unable to speak. All the veins in his neck and throat were nearly severed. Then, even if he wanted to, he could do himself no harm.

Lancelot was not happy to be so closely watched. His grief almost consumed him, for he would gladly have killed himself had no one been watching him. Because he could not injure himself, he cried: "Alas, Death! You are despicable! You are vile! In God's name, Death, why did you not have enough power and might to kill me before my lady? I suppose it was because you did not wish or deign to perform an act of kindness. Your wickedness stopped you from it. You can have had no other reason. Alas, what service! What kindness! How well you behaved here! Damn any man who feels gratitude to you or offers you thanks for this service. I don't know who hates me more: Life who wants me, or Death who has no desire to kill me. Thus I am killed from both sides.

"In living on against my will, so help me God, I have what I deserve. I should have killed myself the moment my lady the queen appeared full of hatred for me. Her behavior was justified. She had sound reason, though I am ignorant of it. But had I known the reason before her soul went into God's presence, I would have made reparations rich enough to please her that she might take mercy on me.

"God, what could this crime have been? Perhaps she knew that I climbed into the cart. I expect this to be the reason. I do not know any other cause she has to blame me. That has ruined me. God, if this is why she hated me, why am I hurt by the crime? Anyone who would reproach me on this account never knew Love. It is impossible to assert that any act inspired by Love deserves reproach. Any act a man may perform for his beloved is a sign of love and courtesy. Yet I did not do it for my beloved. Alas, I don't know how to refer to her. I don't know whether or not to call her beloved. I dare not give her this name. Yet in loving, I believe I have been instructed enough to know this: had she loved me, she should not have esteemed me less because of my ride. On the contrary, she should have called me her true love, since any act Love wished me to perform for her seemed to me an honor, even climbing into the cart. She should have attributed my act to Love. And this is the proven truth: thus Love tests his followers; thus he recognizes his followers. But judging by my lady's appearance, that service of mine did not please her. Nevertheless, her lover's action on her behalf earned him the censure and shameful reproach of many, who blame me for the role I played. Now my sweet happiness has turned bitter. I swear that such is the usual habit of those who know nothing of loving and wash honor in the flood of shame. Anyone who washes honor in shame does not wash it at all but soils it. Now those who go about despising all of this know nothing of Love, and those who do not fear Love's commands place themselves above Love. There is no doubt that he who obeys Love's commands grows in stature. Whatever he does is forgivable. The man is a failure who dares not perform Love's will." This was Lancelot's lament. At his side his people, who were holding him and watching over him, shared his grief.

During this time, news reached them that the queen was not dead. Lancelot's comfort was immediate. If before he had displayed deep sadness and despair over her death, now that she was alive his joy was a hundred thousand times greater still.

When they were within six or seven leagues of the fortress where King Bademagu was staying, the king learned that Lancelot was alive and approaching in perfect health. The king listened with attention and delight to the report. Like the well-mannered man he was, he went to tell the queen of this. "Since you say this, dear sir, I believe it," she said to him. "I solemnly assure you that were he dead, happiness would never again be mine. Had but a single knight been captured and killed in my service, joy would be a distant stranger to me."

At this moment the king left. The queen longed for the arrival of her lover and her joy. She now had no further desire to be angry with him on any account. Rumor, which never rests but always races about without cease, reached the queen again and informed her that Lancelot, had he been allowed, would have killed himself for her. This news, which she believed entirely, delighted her, though at no cost would she have desired such a misfortune to occur.

In the meantime, behold Lancelot had arrived in great haste. As soon as the king caught sight of him, he ran to embrace and kiss him. His joy made him so light that he thought he should take to flight. But the people who had captured and bound him ended the rejoicing abruptly. They had all arrived, the king informed them, at an unfortunate time, for they would meet their cursed deaths. They had thought, they answered, that they had done the king's will. "What suits you displeases me," the king said. "This matter has nothing to do with Lancelot. You did not disgrace him; you disgraced me, for he traveled under my protection. However it is, the shame is mine. But you will find no cause for laughter if you try to escape me."

When Lancelot heard the king's anger, he devoted all his efforts to setting matters right and making peace until he succeeded. The king then took him to see the queen. This time the queen did not lower her eyes to the ground, but went happily to greet him. Showing him all possible honor, she had him sit beside her. They then talked at leisure on subjects of mutual pleasure, not lacking topics since Love had given them so much to say. Lancelot was then at his ease, for none of his words displeased the queen. In a quiet voice he said to her: "Lady, I am bewildered. Why did you look at me so when you saw me the day before yesterday? You would not speak a word to me. The blow you dealt me almost killed me. At that time I did not have the courage to dare ask your explanation. I do ask now. Lady, I am ready to make amends if only you would tell me the crime that so much distressed you."

"What? Were you not afraid and ashamed of the cart?" the queen replied. "When you hesitated for two steps, you showed your great reluctance to climb in. To be honest, that is the reason I would not look at you or speak to you."

"God protect me from such a crime again," Lancelot said, "and may God never have mercy on me if you are not entirely right. Lady, in the name of God, accept reparation from me at this moment. And if you are to forgive me, in God's name tell me so."

"Friend, be forgiven completely," the queen answered. "With all my heart I pardon you."

"Lady, I thank you," he said. "But I cannot say to you here all I would like to say. Were it possible, I would gladly talk with you more at your pleasure."

With her glance rather than her finger, the queen pointed out a window to him. "Come tonight," she said, "and talk to me at that window when everyone within is asleep. Come through this garden. You will not be able to enter or make your lodging here. I shall be within, you without, and you will have no success in entering. The only way I shall be able to approach you is through words or the touch of hands. Because I love you, I shall, if you like, stay there until morning. We may not meet together, for Kay the seneschal sleeps in my room in the bed in front of me. He still suffers from wounds covering his body. The door is never open, but locked and well guarded. When you come, be careful no spy catches sight of you."

"Lady," he replied, "I shall do my best not to be seen by any spy who would conceive ill ideas or tell slanderous stories." With this agreement about meeting, they separated happily.

Lancelot left the room so pleased that he forgot all his past troubles. For him the night was too long in arriving. The day exhausted his patience and seemed to last longer than a hundred other days or even a whole year. Had night fallen, he would have gone with such eagerness to their meeting. At last the night, in its struggle with the day, took the victory, covering and wrapping the day under its cloak of heavy darkness.

When Lancelot saw night obscuring the day, he pretended to be tired and weary. His long vigils, he said, made rest a necessity. Those of you who have done this can understand and explain why he pretended to be tired and went to bed because of the others in his lodging. But his bed meant nothing to him; nothing could have made him rest there. He could not have slept; he could not have dared sleep; in fact, he did not even wish the power or the daring to sleep.

Quietly and quickly he rose from his bed. He was pleased to find the moon and stars not shining and the house itself without candle, lamp, or lantern burning. He went outside and looked about, making certain that no one noticed him. But the people expected him to be asleep in his bed all the night long. Without companion to escort him, he hurried toward the garden, along the way encountering no one. It was fortunate for him that a piece of the garden wall had recently fallen. He slipped quickly through this break and continued along to the window, where he stood quietly, making sure not to cough or sneeze.

Then the queen came, dressed only in a white shift. She had not put on a dress or a coat over it, wearing only a short cloak of rich wool trimmed with marmot. As soon as Lancelot saw the queen leaning against the window behind the thick iron bars, he addressed her with tender words of greeting. And she at once returned his greeting, a similar desire consuming them both, he wanting her and she him. There was nothing tedious or vulgar in their talk. They drew near and held each other's hands. Powerless to come closer, they became enraged and cursed the iron bars. Yet Lancelot boasted that if it were the queen's will, he would enter there with her, the bars never stopping him.

"Do you not see these bars?" the queen asked. "They are stout to bend and hard to break. You could never dislodge them. There is no way you can squeeze, pull, or wrench them."

"Lady, be not concerned," he said. "I believe these bars to be useless. Only you may prevent me from reaching you. If you grant me permission, my way is clear. But if my scheme does not suit you, then the way is so difficult for me that my entry is impossible."

"To be certain, I do want it. My will does not prevent you," she replied. "Yet you must wait till I am in my bed so that any noise may not cause you harm. It would be no laughing matter should the seneschal, asleep here, be wakened by our clamor. So it is right indeed that I retreat. No good would come if he saw me standing here."

"Then go now, lady," he told her. "But be not concerned about my making any noise. I believe I can pull out the bars gently without much trouble and without waking anyone."

The queen turned away at once, and Lancelot prepared to try and loosen the window. Gripping the bars, he pulled and tugged until he made them all bend; then he wrenched them from their position. But the iron was so sharp that the end of his little finger was torn to the nerve and the entire first joint of the next finger severed. Since his mind was elsewhere, he did not feel his cuts or the blood that dripped from them. Although the window was not at all low, Lancelot slipped through with great ease and speed. He found Kay asleep in his bed, then came to the bed of the queen. He adored her and knelt down before her; in no saint's relics did he place such faith.

The queen held out her arms to him, embraced him, and hugged him to her breast. When she drew him into bed beside her, she showed him every possible pleasure. Love and her heart transported him. It was Love that made her give him such a joyous welcome. If her love for him was great, his for her was a hundred thousand times more so, for in all other hearts Love is absent in comparison with Love's presence in his. So completely did Love establish himself again in his heart that for all other hearts he left little.

Now Lancelot had all he desired. The queen eagerly sought his company and his pleasure as he held her in his arms and she held him in hers. In the pleasure of loving, he tasted such rapturous happiness by kissing and caressing her that theirs was, without word of lie, a wondrous joy, whose equal has never yet been heard or known. But on this matter I shall always be silent. Every tale should pass it over in silence. The choicest and most pleasurable joys are those the tale keeps from us.

All night long Lancelot enjoyed great pleasure. But the day's approach pained him deeply since he had to rise from his beloved's side. Rising made him feel like a martyr, for he suffered the agony of martyrdom in the torture of departure. His heart was persistent in staying with the queen. He could not lead it away, for it knew such pleasure with the queen that it had no desire to leave her. His body departed; his heart remained.

Lancelot returned directly to the window. But much of his blood stayed behind, the blood that dripped from his fingers having spotted and stained the sheets. Full of sighs and full of tears, he went away distraught. The fact that no hour had been set for another meeting pained him, but such an arrangement was impossible. He reluctantly left through the window he had been glad to enter. His fingers, no longer whole, were seriously injured. Still he set the bars up again and placed them back in their position so that it was not evident from either side, behind or in front, that the bars had been pulled, bent, or removed. At his departure he behaved like a suppliant in the room, acting as if he were before an altar.

In deep anguish he went away. He reached his own lodging without meeting anyone who might recognize him. As he undressed and got into bed, he woke no one. Then, to his amazement, he noticed for the first time the cuts in his fingers. But he felt no concern, certain that he had hurt himself pulling the iron window bars from the wall. Therefore he was not angry with himself, for he would have preferred to have his two arms dragged from his body than not to have entered through the window. But had he been seriously wounded or hurt on any other occasion, he would have been upset and angry.

In the morning, the queen had fallen into a gentle sleep in her curtained room. She had not noticed that her sheets were stained with blood, but thought them still most clean, white, and presentable. As soon as Meleagant was dressed and ready, he went to the room where the queen lay sleeping. He saw her open eyes and noticed the drops of fresh blood that stained the sheets. Nudging his companions, he looked at the bed of Kay the seneschal, as though sensing some evil. There too he saw bloodstained sheets, for that night, you should know, Kay's wounds had opened up.

"Lady, now I have found the evidence I wanted," Meleagant exclaimed. "How true that a man is foolish to try and protect a woman's honor! He wastes his time and his efforts. By protecting her, a man loses her faster than the man who makes no efforts on her behalf. What a wonderful guard my father has been! He watched over you because of me. He protected you carefully from me. But last night, in spite of all his efforts, Kay the seneschal gazed on you and took all his pleasure with you. This will be easily proven."

"How?" she asked.

"Since I must speak, I have found blood on your sheets, which is clear proof. I know everything. I prove all from the fact that I find the blood that dripped from his wounds on your sheets and on his too. Here is reliable evidence."

Then, for the first time, the queen saw the bloodstained sheets on both beds. She was astonished and turned scarlet with shame. "As the Lord God is my witness, this blood you see on my sheets never came from Kay," she said. "No, last night my nose bled, and that blood is, I suppose, from my nose." She believed she was telling the truth.

"I swear you speak nonsense," Meleagant said. "There is no need for lies. You are firmly caught, and the truth will be proven." He then addressed the guards present. "Men, do not move. Make certain the bedsheets are not removed before my return. I want the king to do me justice when he sees this."

Then he went looking for his father and, finding him, fell at his feet. "Sire," he said, "come and see what you failed to protect. Come and see the queen. Your eyes will behold authentic marvels I have seen and discovered. But before you go there, I beg you not to fail to do me justice and right. You well know the perils to which I exposed myself on behalf of the queen; yet you are my enemy, and have her guarded because of me. This morning I went to gaze on her in her bed, and saw enough to recognize that Kay lies with her each night. Sire, in God's name, do not be angry if I complain and am upset. I find it most humiliating to be hated and despised by the woman who lies with Kay every night."

"Silence!" the king answered. "I do not believe this."

"Sire, come and see the sheets and the condition Kay left them in. Since you do not trust my words but believe I tell you a lie, I shall show you the sheets and bedcover bloodied from Kay's wounds."

"Let us go there now, and I shall look at this," the king said. "I wish to see it for myself. My eyes will judge the truth of the matter."

Without delay the king went off to the room, where he found the queen getting up. He saw the bloodstained sheets on her bed and also on Kay's. "Lady, if my son has told me the truth, the situation is dire."

"So help me God," she replied, "no one ever told such a wicked lie, no, not even in a nightmare. I believe Kay the seneschal to be so courteous and so loyal that it would be wrong to suspect him. I am not the kind of woman who sells her body or merely gives it away at some fair. To be certain, Kay is not the kind of man to proffer me such a despicable proposal. Never have I had such an inclination, and never will I."

"Sire, I shall be most grateful to you," Meleagant told his father, "if Kay atones for his outrage in a manner that also shames the queen. Justice rests in your hands. I ask you, I beg you, exercise it. Kay has betrayed his lord King Arthur, who had faith enough in him to entrust to him what he loved most in this world."

"Sir, allow me to respond, and I shall acquit myself," Kay answered. "May God never pardon my soul when I depart this world if ever I lay with my lady. Yes, I would rather be dead than have committed such a hideous offense against my lord. May God never grant me better health than I have now, but rather kill me this very instant if ever I had such a thought. But I do know that last night there was so much blood from my wounds that my sheets are soaked. That is why your son suspects me, though he certainly has no such right."

"So help me God," Meleagant answered him, "devils and demons have betrayed you. Too great a passion seized you last night, and because you exerted yourself too much, your wounds undoubtedly opened again. Of that there can be no doubt. It is useless for you to deny it. The blood in both beds is the proof. You see the obvious evidence. It is proper that a man, clearly convicted, should pay for his crime. Never before has a knight of your honor done anything so despicable. The disgrace is yours."

"Sir, sir," Kay said to the king, "I shall defend my lady and myself against your son's accusation. Although he has caused me anxiety and pain, he is certainly wrong in his declaration."

"You are in too much pain. You are not able to fight," the king answered.

"Sir, sick as I am, I shall, if you allow it, fight him and prove myself innocent of the crime he has accused me of."

The queen had sent word secretly for Lancelot, and she told the king that if Meleagant dared persist in the matter, she would produce a knight to defend the seneschal against him. At once Meleagant spoke out: "There is no knight I would not fight, even were he a giant, until one of us is defeated." At that very moment Lancelot entered, accompanied by a troop of knights that filled the entire room.

Upon his arrival, the queen explained the situation in front of all, young as well as old. "Lancelot," she said, "Meleagant has here accused me of this shame. Before all who heard him speak, he has placed me under suspicion unless you make him retract his statement. Because he noticed that my sheets as well as Kay's were stained with blood, he states that last night Kay lay with me. Kay, he says, stands clearly convicted unless he is able to defend himself against him or someone else will undertake the combat in his aid."

"You need not plead your case where I am present," Lancelot answered. "May it never please God that such suspicion fall on you or on Kay. If any power of defense is mine, I am ready to fight as proof he never had such a thought. To the best of my ability, I shall defend him and undertake the combat on his behalf."

Meleagant jumped up. "So help me the Lord God," he exclaimed, "what pleasure and satisfaction are mine! No one should ever think me unhappy."

"My lord king," Lancelot said, "I know about lawsuits and their rules, about cases and judgments. In a situation of such suspicion, there should be no combat unless there are oaths."

Without fear, Meleagant answered him promptly. "Oaths are fitting. Let the holy relics be now brought out, for I know right is with me."

"I call upon the Lord God," Lancelot answered. "No one who ever knew Kay the seneschal would suspect him of such an act."

At once they demanded their arms and ordered their horses led out. Their horses were brought out fully equipped, and with the help of attendants, the combatants put on their armor. The relics were then carried out. Meleagant stepped forward, Lancelot beside him, and both knelt. Meleagant placed his hand over the relics and made his oath in a clear voice: "I take God and this saint as my witnesses: last night Kay the seneschal was the queen's companion in her bed and took all his pleasure with her."

"I accuse you of perjury," Lancelot said. "I swear Kay did not lie with her or touch her. May it please God to reveal the truth and take vengeance on the man who has lied. Yet like it or not, I shall swear another oath. If I am allowed to defeat Meleagant today, I will have no mercy on him, as truly as I place my trust in God and the saint whose relics are here." When the king heard this oath, he felt no joy.

After the swearing of the oaths, their horses, fair and fine in every way, were led forward. Each knight mounted his and charged at the other as fast as his horse could carry him. With their horses galloping at top speed, the vassals struck each other so hard that there was nothing left of their two lances except the shafts they held in their hands. Each combatant dragged the other to the ground. Not downcast, however, they stood up immediately and attacked each other as best they could with their sharp swords drawn. Burning sparks from their helmets shot toward the clouds. They clashed with such savage fury, chopping with their unsheathed swords, that as they rushed forward and backed away, they met and struck their blows. They sought no time to rest, nor even time to catch their breath.

In his anxiety and deep grief, the king called to the queen, who had gone up to the tower galleries to lean out. In the name of God the Creator, he asked her to let them be separated. "In good faith, whatever suits and pleases you, you may do with my complete accord," the queen answered.

Lancelot clearly heard the queen's reply to the king's request, and from that moment sought no further combat but immediately abandoned the fight. Meleagant did not wish to stop, but continued to fight and strike at him. The king rushed between the two and restrained his son, who swore he had no desire for peace. "I desire the fight! I care not for peace!" he exclaimed.

"Silence!" the king said to him. "Trust me, and you will act like a wise man. If you trust me, disgrace and injury will not come your way. Behave properly. Do you not remember that the combat with him was to take place at the court of King Arthur? Do you doubt that great honor, if it comes to you, would be yours there more than anywhere?" The king, speaking in this manner to see if he might calm his son, succeeded in appeasing him and separating the fighters.

Lancelot had longed to go and find Sir Gawain. And so he came to the king and then to the queen to ask leave to depart. With their permission he hastened to the water-bridge, followed by a large troop of knights. He would have been pleased, however, had many of those accompanying him remained behind. They continued their long journey several days until they were a league from the water-bridge.

Before the bridge was within view, a dwarf, carrying a whip to prod and frighten his large hunting horse, rode up to meet them. As he had been ordered, he at once asked: "Which of you is Lancelot? Do not hide him from me. I am one of you. Speak with confidence, for my question is meant to help you."

"I am the very man you seek," Lancelot answered for himself.

"Ah, Lancelot, noble knight, leave these men, trust me, and alone come with me. I wish to take you to a fine place. Let no one follow you at any cost, but let them wait for you in this spot. We shall return in a moment."

Suspecting no evil, Lancelot made all his men stay there and followed the dwarf, who had deceived him. The men awaiting Lancelot would have long to wait, for those who had taken him prisoner were not inclined to give him up.

When Lancelot failed to return, his men were so distraught that they knew not what to do, all declaring that the dwarf had tricked them and brought them grief. It would be useless to ask after Lancelot. Sad as they were, they began to search for him, though not knowing where to look for him or where to find him. In their deliberations, the wisest and most reasonable agreed, I believe, to go to the nearby water-bridge. Should they find Sir Gawain in forest or field, they would consult with him before searching for Lancelot. Without any reservations, all adopted this plan.

On their arrival at the water-bridge, they caught sight of Sir Gawain. In trying to cross the bridge, he had stumbled and fallen into the deep water. One moment he reached the surface; the next he sank down. One moment they saw him; the next they lost sight of him. They came to the edge and caught him with branches, poles, and sticks shaped like hooks. Because he had endured many hardships and passed through many perils and many attacks, he had only his hauberk on his back, his helmet on his head, equal in value to ten others, and his steel greaves, rusty now from his sweat. On the other bank were his lance, his shield, and his horse. Because he had swallowed so much water, those who rescued him did not expect him to live. Until he brought up the water, they heard not a word from him.

As soon as his heart began to beat freely again and he recovered his voice so that he could be heard and understood, he spoke, asking those he saw if they had any news of the queen. She remained with King Bademagu, they answered, who served her with great honor. "Has no one come, then, to seek her in this land?" Sir Gawain asked.

"Yes," they replied, "Lancelot of the Lake, who crossed the sword-bridge. He rescued and freed her, and all of us along with her. But a goiter, a hunchbacked and snarling dwarf, tricked us. A wretched cheat, he lured Lancelot away from us. We do not know what harm he has done."

"When was this?" Sir Gawain asked.

"Today, sir, close to here. The dwarf did this to us as we came with Lancelot to meet you."

"And what has Lancelot been doing since his arrival in this country?"

They began to recount everything without omission of a single detail. They told him about the queen, how she had been waiting for him and declaring that nothing would make her leave the country until she saw him and heard his news.

"Shall we go and search for Lancelot after leaving this bridge?" Sir Gawain asked them in response. All thought they should first proceed to the queen. The king would have a search made for him, for they believed his son Meleagant, who had such hatred for Lancelot, had had him imprisoned by some treachery. If the king knew where to find him, he would have him released. They could therefore hold off their search.

All agreed with this plan. At once they set out on their course until they reached the court where the king and the queen were. There also was Kay the seneschal, as well as that scoundrel, consumed with treachery, who had villainously caused all those arriving to be sick with worry over Lancelot. Considering themselves fatally betrayed, they heavily lamented their misery. The news of this sorrow was scarcely welcome to the queen. Nevertheless she had to display the finest appearance she could. In honor of Sir Gawain, she had to rejoice somewhat, and did so. Yet her sadness was not so concealed that it did not appear even a little in her manner. Joy and sadness were hers: at the thought of Lancelot her heart was empty, and toward Sir Gawain she displayed extreme joy.

All were depressed and beside themselves to hear the news of Lancelot's disappearance. The arrival and sight of Sir Gawain would have brought great pleasure to the king, but such grief and sadness were his over Lancelot's betrayal that he was bewildered and dejected. The queen begged and beseeched him to have Lancelot sought without a moment's delay from one end of the country to the other. Sir Gawain and Kay implored him on their part, and not a soul there failed to join in the request.

"Leave this task to me," the king said. "There is no need for further talk. For long I have been resolved on this. Even without urgings and requests I would have this search made." All humbly bowed to him.

At once the king dispatched his messengers, wise and well-known men-at-arms, throughout his realm to seek news of Lancelot all across the country. They sought information in every place, but learned nothing. Not discovering anything, they returned to the court where the knights were staying, Gawain, Kay, and all the others, who said they would go, fully armed, their lances in readiness, to search for Lancelot. No one else would they send in their place.

One day after dining, they were all putting on their equipment in the hall; when they were about to ride out, a youth entered. He passed by everyone until he came before the queen. She had lost her rosy complexion, for, still without news of Lancelot, she knew such sorrow that her complexion had changed color. The youth greeted her as well as the king who was beside her, and then greeted all the others and Kay and Sir Gawain. He gave a letter he held in his hand to the king. Taking the letter, the king had it read for all to hear by a man who would make no errors; the reader knew how to speak clearly the words written on the parchment. Lancelot, he announced, greeted the king as his good lord and, as a man entirely at the king's command, thanked him for the honor and service he had done him; Lancelot was strong and healthy, be assured, and residing at King Arthur's court. He asked the queen to come there, and commanded Sir Gawain and Kay to do the same. The letter bore such seals as to make them accept its authenticity, and they did accept it.

The news brought much happiness and joy. The entire court was filled with the uproar of rejoicing. The people announced their intention to set out the next morning at daybreak. And so at dawn they prepared to depart. They rose quickly, mounted, and rode on their way. With much celebration and jubilation, the king escorted them a long way along their road until they reached the borders of his kingdom. Once they were outside his realm, he took leave of the queen, then of all the others together. In taking leave, the queen thanked him with great dignity for all his services. She placed both her arms around his neck and promised him the guarantee of her service and that of her lord. Nothing greater could she promise him. Sir Gawain also, followed by Kay and then all the others, made similar promises to him as their lord and their friend. Then they followed their road. Again the king commended these three to God, then gave a final salute to all the others, and at last returned home.

Not a single day in the whole week did the queen or the troop accompanying her pause. Consequently, news of the queen's approach reached the court. Delighted, King Arthur felt his heart rekindle with joy and happiness at the idea that his nephew's valor, as he believed, had rescued the queen as well as Kay and all the commoners. But the truth was quite different from their imagining.

The inhabitants emptied the entire town as all went out to meet them. Knights and peasants, all shouted as they greeted those returning home:

"Welcome, Sir Gawain, who rescued the queen and many other captive ladies and returned many prisoners to us."

"Sirs, you praise me for no reason," Gawain replied to them. "Cease your talk at once. The glory has nothing to do with me. This honor embarrasses me. I did not arrive in time. My delay caused my failure. But Lancelot did arrive in time, and greater honor befell him than any knight ever received."

"Where is he then, dear sir? We do not see him here at your side."

"Where?" Sir Gawain replied at once. "At the court of my lord the king. Is he not there?"

"No, we swear, not there or anywhere in this country. Since the time our lady was led away, we have heard no news of him."

Then, for the first time, Sir Gawain realized that the letter was a forgery. The letter had tricked them, deceived them, and betrayed them. They then plunged back into their sorrow, displaying their grief as they entered the court. At once the king demanded news of what had happened. Many were there who could recount Lancelot's work, how he had rescued the queen and all the prisoners, and how the dwarf had ridden up to them and led him away through deceit. This news deeply upset and grieved the king, but his joy at seeing the queen again lifted his spirits and put an end to his sadness with happiness. When he had the object of his greatest desire, he worried little about the rest.

It was during the time the queen was out of the country, as I believe, that the ladies and maidens without husbands met among themselves and decided that they wished to be soon married. At this gathering they also decided to hold a great tournament. For one party the Lady of Pomelegoi would be patroness, for the other the Lady of Noauz. To those who fared poorly, the women would say nothing, but on those who fared well, they promised to bestow their love. That there might be more people, they had the date of the tournament announced and proclaimed long ahead throughout neighboring and distant lands.

The queen came back before the date they had chosen. As soon as they learned of the queen's return, several of them set out for the court. Once they had come before the king, they earnestly exhorted him to accede to their wish by granting them a favor. Even before he knew what they wanted, he assured them that he would grant their desire. They then announced their wish that he allow the queen to come and watch their tournament. He did not like to refuse anything, and therefore said that the idea pleased him provided it was the queen's will. Delighted by his response, they went before the queen. "Lady, do not take back from us what the king has granted us," they at once said to her.

"What has he granted?" she asked them. "Do not keep it from me."

They then answered her. "If you wish to attend our tournament, the king will not interfere or stop you." She would come, she said, since he had given his permission. At once the young ladies sent word throughout the realm that they were to escort the queen there on the day announced for the combat.

Here and there, far and near, the news spread everywhere. It traveled so far that it reached the kingdom whence once none returned; now, however, any who wished could enter or leave freely. Through the kingdom, the news traveled from mouth to mouth until it reached the house of a seneschal of Meleagant. Would that the fire of hell consume him, the faithless traitor! This seneschal was standing guard over Lancelot. His home was where Meleagant had imprisoned Lancelot, his enemy, whom he continued to hate with a deadly rage.

When Lancelot learned of the day and time of the tournament, his eyes were no longer dry and his heart knew no happiness. Seeing Lancelot troubled and sad, the lady of the manorhouse spoke to him in private. "Sir, for God's sake and for your own soul, tell me truthfully why your mood has so altered," the lady asked him. "You do not drink; you do not eat; I never see you laugh or play. Do not fear telling me your thoughts and your worries."

"Alas, lady, if I am sad, in God's name be not amazed. It is true that I am in great distress because I cannot be where all that is good in the world will be: that is at the tournament where, I believe, all the people are gathering. But if God made you so noble that you would allow me to go there, you can be completely confident that I would give you my pledge to come back to your prison."

"I would certainly be glad to do it," she said, "if I did not see my destruction and my death in it. I would never dare do it for fear my lord, the strong and despicable Meleagant, would kill my husband immediately. Do not be surprised that I fear him. You know how evil he is."

"Lady, if you are afraid I shall not return to your prison the moment the combat ends, I shall take an oath I will never break: nothing will prevent my return to your prison the moment the tournament ends."

"I swear to agree on one condition," she said.

"What, lady?"

"Sir, on condition you swear and guarantee to return and give me your love," she answered.

"Lady, all I have I shall certainly give you on my return."

"Now I know I mean nothing to you," the lady exclaimed as she laughed. "I know you have bestowed the love I have asked of you on another. Nevertheless, I shall not scorn to accept all I may have. I shall be happy with what is given me. I shall accept your oath to bind yourself to me by returning to my prison."

As soon as Lancelot had sworn by Holy Church to return without fail, as the lady desired, she gave him her lord's vermilion armor and his fine horse, which was remarkably bold and strong. Armed magnificently in wholly new and gleaming equipment, he mounted and rode off, continuing until he reached Noauz. He placed himself in this camp and lodged outside the town. Never had a man of worth occupied such small and lowly lodgings, but he did not wish to stay where he might be recognized.

Fine and chosen knights had assembled within the castle, but there were even more outside, for so many had come because of the queen's presence that not a fifth of them could be accommodated within. Had the queen not been present, there would have been one person for every seven now there. The barons were bivouacked in tents, pavilions, and other shelters up to five leagues around the town. It was wondrous to see so many ladies and charming maidens gathered there.

Lancelot had hung his shield at the door to his lodging. To rest with more ease, he had taken off his equipment and was lying on an uncomfortable narrow bed covered with a thin quilt of coarse grey cloth. All disarmed, Lancelot reclined on his side on the bed.

Then behold a fellow in shirt sleeves, a herald at arms, who had left as a pledge at the tavern his shoes and his coat. Barefoot and unprotected from the wind, he came at full speed. Finding the shield outside the door, he examined it, but it was impossible for him to recognize the shield or its owner; he did not know who was to carry it. Noticing the door to the house open, he went inside and saw Lancelot lying on the bed. The moment he saw him, he recognized him and made the sign of the cross. Lancelot fixed his gaze on him and forbade him to speak of him wherever the herald traveled. Should he say that he knew him, it would be better had his eyes been plucked out or his neck broken.

"Sir, I have held you in the highest respect, and I still do," the herald said. "As long as I live, I will never do anything to displease you."

As soon as he left the house, he ran shouting at the top of his voice: "Now he has come, the man who will take the measure! Now he has come, the man who will take the measure!" He shouted this everywhere, and people came from all around to ask him the meaning of his cry. He was not so bold as to explain it, but continued along repeating the same words. You can be certain this was the first time they were uttered: "Now he has come, the man who will take the measure!" Our master was the herald, who taught us the phrase, for he was the first person to use it.

Throngs of people had gathered there: the queen with all the ladies, knights and others, and many men-at-arms everywhere, on the left as well as the right. In the space selected for the tournament were large wooden galleries since the queen, the ladies, and the maidens were to be there. Never before had anyone seen galleries so beautiful, so long, and so well constructed.

All the ladies followed the queen there, eager to see the tournament and judge who would fare better or worse. The knights arrived by tens, by twenties, by thirties, then eighty from one side and ninety from the other, then a hundred, then still more, and even twice that number. So vast was the crowd assembled before and round about the galleries that the combat was begun. Armed and unarmed, the knights came together. Their lances resembled a great forest, for those who wished to sport had brought so many that nothing appeared to be there but lances, banners, and ensigns. Those who were to joust found many of their companions who had also come to joust. Others prepared to perform various feats on their horses. The multitudes in the meadows, tilled fields, and fallow lands made it impossible to estimate the number of knights there. Lancelot, however, did not appear at this first assembly. But when he did come across the meadow, the herald caught sight of his approach and could not refrain from shouting: "See the man who will take the measure! See the man who will take the measure!"

"Who is he?" people asked the herald, but he would tell them nothing.

When Lancelot entered the combat, he alone was worth twenty of the best. He began to joust so well that no one could take his eyes off him wherever he was. In the Pomelegoi camp was a brave and valiant knight with a spirited horse that ran faster than a wild stag; the son of the King of Ireland, he handled himself with great dignity and style. Yet all liked the unknown knight four times the more and anxiously inquired: "Who is this man who does so well?"

The queen drew aside a prudent and wise young lady-in-waiting. "Young lady," she said, "you must carry a brief message, and be quick about it. Go down from the galleries and approach that knight with the vermilion shield. Tell him in secret that I command him to do his worst."

Promptly and prudently she carried out the queen's will. She rode off toward the knight, not stopping until she neared him. Like the prudent and wise person she was, she spoke to him so quietly that no neighboring ear overheard her. "Sir, through me my lady the queen commands you, as I tell you, to do your worst."

As soon as he heard her words, he said he would do this eagerly as a man who was hers entirely. He then charged against a knight as fast as his horse could carry him and missed his blow when he should have struck him. From that moment until evening he did his worst, following the queen's pleasure. His opponent's attacks never failed, but found him with such force that he received harsh treatment. Lancelot then took to flight. That day he never turned the neck of his charger toward any knight. Even at risk of his death, he would have done nothing unless he saw it as cause of his deep disgrace, shame, and dishonor. He pretended to fear all the knights who were coming and going. The knights who before had esteemed him highly now made him the butt of their jokes and laughter. And the herald, who had exclaimed, "He will defeat all of them in their turn," was most downcast and depressed by the taunts and insults he heard.

"Now, friend, be silent," people said. "This man will take no one's measure. He has measured so much that now his measuring stick, which you praised so highly to us, is broken."

"What is happening?" many exclaimed. "Just now he was so brave, but suddenly he is such a coward that he dares oppose no knight. Perhaps he performed so well because he had never before taken up arms. And when he came he was so strong that no knight, however skilled, could withstand him, for he attacked like one gone mad. Now his apprenticeship in arms has taught him so much that he will never wish to take them up so long as he lives. His heart can no longer endure the fact that he is the greatest coward in the world."

Far from being upset, the queen was pleased and delighted, certain, though she said nothing, that the knight was indeed Lancelot. Thus all day long until evening he played the part of a coward; then at nightfall he left the tournament. At his departure, a great argument arose over the identity of the finest participant. The son of the King of Ireland had no doubt in his mind that all the honor and renown were his without any possible opposition, but he was sadly mistaken, since many there were his equals. Even the knight with the vermilion shield had brought such pleasure to the most beautiful and charming ladies and maidens that they had gazed on him more than anyone that day, watching his bravery and courage in the first encounters, then his cowardice as he dared face no knight; in the end, the very worst knight, had he wished, could have defeated and captured him.

All the knights and ladies agreed that they would return to the tournament the next morning, and the young ladies would choose as their husbands those who won the honors that day. This arrangement pleased them, and they returned to their lodgings.

When they reached their lodgings, people in many places began to talk. "Where is the worst of the knights, the despicable wretch? Where did he go? Where does he hide? Where did he go? Where will we look for him? Perhaps we shall never see him again since Cowardice drove him away. She embraced him so firmly that there is no greater wretch in the world. And he is not wrong, for a coward is, after all, a hundred thousand times more comfortable than a brave fighter. What fine comfort Cowardice brings, for he has given her a kiss as a sign of peace and accepted all she offers. To be honest, Bravery never debased herself so much as to lodge in him or sit near him. But now it is Cowardice who fills him completely. Cowardice has found such a loving host to serve her so faithfully that he loses all his honor in order to honor her."

Thus all night long they slandered him with their malicious stories. But one man often slanders another, though he is far beneath the man he slanders and despises.

Everyone said what he pleased about him, and by sunrise all the people had prepared themselves and returned to the tournament. The queen took her place again in the galleries with the ladies and maidens. Many unarmed knights were also present who had been imprisoned or taken up the cross to go on a crusade, and they were identifying to the ladies the arms of the knights they most esteemed. Among themselves they said: "Now do you see the knight there with the gold band across his red shield? That is Governal of Roberdic. And do you see the man after him who placed an eagle and a dragon side by side on his shield? That is the son of the King of Aragon, who has come into this country to win honor and renown. And do you see the man beside him who thrusts and jousts so well? He bears a shield half green and half azure, with a leopard emblazoned on the green half. He is the covetous Ignaures, amorous and pleasing. And the man with the shield with the pheasants beak to beak? That is Coguillant of Mautirec. And do you see those two near him on dappled horses with grey-brown lions on their gilded shields? One is called Semiramis, the other is his companion; their shields are emblazoned with the same device. And do you see the man whose shield has a gate where a stag seems to be leaving? On my word, that is King Yder." This was the conversation in the galleries. "That shield was made in Limoges. Pilades brought it here. He burns always with excitement to engage in the fight. That shield, along with the bridle and breaststrap, came from Toulouse. Kay of Estral brought them here. The other shield came from Lyons on the Rhone; there is no finer on the face of the earth. For a great service, it was presented to Taulas of the Desert, who bears it handsomely and uses it as solid protection. That other one there is English work made in London. See its two swallows who, though motionless, look as if they should fly; they receive many blows from Poitiers steel. Young Thoas carries it."

That was how they pointed out and described the arms of those they recognized. But they saw nothing of the man they scorned, and assumed that he had slipped away since he had not returned to the combat. When the queen did not see him, she wished to send someone to search through the crowds and find him. There was no one better to send on the search, she knew, than the young lady who had gone with her message the day before. At once she called to her. "Go, young lady, and mount your palfrey," she said. "I send you to the same knight you met yesterday. Look for him until you find him. Delay on no account. Once again tell him still to act in this manner, to do his worst. And when you have given him this instruction, pay close attention to his response."

The young lady obeyed immediately. The night before, convinced that she would be sent again, she had carefully observed the direction he had taken when he left. She made her way through the ranks of the men until she found the knight. She at once advised him to act in this manner still, to do his worst, if he wished to have the love and favor of the queen, this being her command.

"Since this is her command, I am grateful to her," he answered. And the young lady departed immediately.

Then all the youths, men-at-arms, and squires began to shout. "See this miracle!" they exclaimed. "The knight with the vermilion armor has returned. But what is he doing? In the world there is no vile coward so worthy of scorn. Cowardice has such a hold on him that he is powerless against her."

The young lady returned and came to the queen, who hurried to her and detained her until she heard his response. The queen then was delighted in her certain knowledge that this was no other but the man to whom she belonged entirely and who belonged entirely to her. She told the young lady to return at once and tell him that she commanded and entreated him to do the best he could. And the young lady said she would go without delay and find him at once.

The young lady came down from the galleries to the spot where her boy, who tended her palfrey, awaited her. She mounted and rode off until she found the knight. She at once went to him and said: "Now my lady commands you, sir, to do the best you can."

"Tell her now that I find grief in no act that suits her, since her will is my pleasure," he replied.

The young lady was not slow to carry his message, for she knew it would bring the queen delight and joy. She made her way to the galleries as quickly as possible. The queen rose and went to meet her, though she did not descend the stairs, but waited for her at the top. The young lady arrived, delighted with the message she was to deliver. She started to climb the stairs and, nearing the queen, said to her: "Lady, I have never seen a knight with such a noble disposition. He is most anxious to do all you command. If you ask me the truth, he receives the good as well as the bad in the same manner without altering his expression."

"On my word, that may well be," the queen said. She then returned to her window to watch the knights.

Lancelot waited no longer. Burning with desire to show all his valor, he lifted his shield by the armstraps. Guiding his charger by the neck, he let it run between two lines of fighters. All those deceived and deluded men who had ridiculed him much of the day and night would soon be astonished. Long had they had all their japes and fun at his expense.

Gripping his shield tightly by the armstraps, the son of the King of Ireland rode against him at full speed from the opposite side. They struck each other so fiercely that the son of the King of Ireland sought no more jousting. His lance had split and shattered, for he did not hit moss but the hard, dry boards of the shield. In this joust Lancelot taught him one of his masterful thrusts: he pinned his shield to his arm and pressed his arm to his side, then pulled him from his horse to the ground. Knights at once rushed forward from both camps, spurring and pricking their horses, some eager to rescue the poor knight, others eager to bring him further distress. The former, planning to aid their lord, knocked many from their saddles in the fury of the onslaught.

All that day Gawain, there with the others, did not participate in the tournament. He took such pleasure witnessing the brave deeds of the knight with the vermilion arms that the deeds of the others seemed colorless and pale in comparison. And the herald became so excited that he shouted that all might hear: "Now he has come, the man who will take the measure! Today you will see his deeds! Today his valor will shine forth!"

Then the knight turned his horse in another direction and charged against a most splendid knight. He struck him so hard that he dragged him from his horse a hundred feet or more. Now he began to work with his sword and his lance so well that no knight bearing arms watched him without pleasure; indeed, many armed in the jousts took delight in his exploits. It was wonderful to watch him make horses and knights tumble and fall together. Scarcely a knight he encountered could stay in the saddle of his horse, and he gave the horses he won to all who desired them.

Those who had mocked him now exclaimed: "We are humiliated. We are mortified. How wrong we were to slander and scorn him. Surely he is worth a thousand of those on the field. Yes, he has overcome and surpassed all the knights in the world, for there is none left to stand against him."

With wondrous eyes the young ladies watched him, saying that he dashed their plans for marriage. They dared not trust in their beauty or their wealth, their power or their nobility, for neither for their beauty nor their fortune would this knight care to have one of them as his wife. His own worth was, in effect, too great. Nevertheless, almost all bound themselves by such vows that they declared that if they did not marry him, they would not be given to any lord or husband that year. The queen, hearing their boastful display, laughed merrily to herself, knowing that the knight beloved by all of them would not choose the best, the most beautiful, or the most charming, even if all the gold of Arabia were heaped before him.

The young ladies had one common wish: each yearned to have the knight for herself. Each was jealous of the other as if she were already his wife. Because they saw his splendid jousting, they did not think or believe that any other knight, however much he pleased them, could perform this knight's feats. So fine was his performance that at the end of the tournament, any from either camp could declare, without word of lie, that the knight with the vermilion shield had had no equal there. All asserted this, and it was the truth.

When the knight departed, he dropped his shield along with his lance and trappings where he could see the crowd was thickest, then galloped away. So secret was his departure that none in the crowd noticed it. Once on his way, he raced directly to the place he had come from in order to keep his oath.

At the end of the tournament, all were looking and asking for him, but he was not to be found. He had fled lest any recognize him. The knights were most sorry and disappointed; had he been there, they would have been delighted. But if the knights were saddened by his sudden departure, much greater was the dismay of the young ladies when they learned the news. By Saint John they swore not to marry that year; since they did not have the man they desired, they renounced their claim to all the others. Thus the tournament ended without even one taking a husband.

Lancelot did not delay, but returned quickly to his prison. Two or three days before his return, the seneschal had come back and asked where he was. His wife, who had given Lancelot the seneschal's vermilion armor, excellent in condition, as well as his harness and his horse, told him the truth of how she had sent him to take part in the tournament of Noauz. "Lady," the seneschal said, "the truth is that you could have done nothing worse. I shall suffer badly on this account, I believe, for my lord Meleagant will treat me worse than the giant would were I in distress. I shall be tortured and killed the moment he hears the news. He will have no mercy on me."

"Be not so upset, dear sir," the lady answered. "You need not fear. Nothing can detain him, for by the saints he swore to me to return as soon as he was able."

The seneschal mounted immediately and rode to see his lord. While recounting the entire story, he offered him strong assurances, telling him how his wife had taken Lancelot's oath to return to the prison. "He will never break his word," Meleagant said. "I know that well. Nevertheless, I am very unhappy with your wife's behavior. At no cost would I have wished him to be at the tournament. But return now, and when he comes, make certain he is properly imprisoned so that he may not leave the prison or know any freedom of movement. And notify me at once of his return."

"All will be done as you command," the seneschal said. He went home and found Lancelot returned, a prisoner again within his walls. A messenger dispatched by the seneschal raced back to Meleagant by the fastest route and informed him of Lancelot's return. When Meleagant heard this, he summoned and assembled masons and carpenters, the best in the world, who obeyed his orders, some of the men reluctantly, others willingly. He told them to build him a tower; their strongest efforts would be needed to draw the stone and construct the tower by the sea. Near Gorre, but on this side, a long, wide arm of the sea circled an island, as Meleagant knew well, and it was there that he ordered them to haul the stone and materials for constructing the tower.

In less than fifty-seven days the tower was completed, strong and thick-walled, broad and high. After the construction, Meleagant had Lancelot led there and imprisoned within. He then had the doorways sealed up and made all the masons swear never to utter a word about the tower. He wanted it kept secret and left no entrance or opening there except one small window. Lancelot was to live inside, and according to the orders of the treacherous scoundrel, at certain specified times he would be given some paltry morsels of food through this little window. Now Meleagant had accomplished all he wanted. Afterward he rode directly to King Arthur's court.

Then behold Meleagant had arrived there. When he came before the king, he was filled with arrogance and madness as he began to speak. "Your Majesty, I swore to hold combat here at your court in your presence, but I see no sign of Lancelot, who was scheduled to be my opponent. Nevertheless, in the hearing of all I see here, I present myself for combat, as I should. If he is here, let him come forward and declare himself ready to keep the agreement to meet me at your court one year from this day. I do not know if anyone ever told you the origin of this combat. But I see knights here who were present when we made our pact and who can inform you if they are minded to acknowledge the truth. If Lancelot wishes to repudiate me, I shall hire no mercenary. No, I shall prove his error in hand-to-hand combat."

Seated beside the king, the queen drew him near her as she began to speak. "Lord, do you know who this is? It is Meleagant, who took me prisoner when I was under the escort of Kay the seneschal. He brought him a great deal of shame and suffering."

"Lady, I understand that clearly," the king answered her. "I know very well that he is the man who held my people captive."

The queen had no more to say, and the king directed his words to Meleagant. "Friend," he said, "so help me God, we have heard no news of Lancelot, and that saddens us deeply."

"My lord king," Meleagant said, "Lancelot told me I would definitely find him here. I am not to demand this combat except at your court. I would like all the barons here to be witnesses: I demand combat here one year from this day, according to the pact we made when we agreed to the combat."

At these words Sir Gawain stood up, disturbed by what he heard. "Lord," he said to the king, "nothing is known of Lancelot anywhere in this land, but we shall undertake searches for him. God willing, someone will find him before the end of the year, unless he is imprisoned or dead. If he does not come, grant me the combat. I shall undertake it. On that day, if Lancelot has not returned, I shall arm myself in his place."

"Ah, in God's name, my lord king, grant him this," Meleagant said. "It is his desire, and I beg you for it. I know no other knight in the world, with the exception of Lancelot, against whom I would rather test my strength. But be absolutely certain, if I do not fight one of the two, I shall take no one else as substitute or exchange."

The king said that he would agree to this combat if Lancelot did not return within that time. Then Meleagant left the king's court and rode away, continuing until he reached his father, King Bademagu. In his presence he adopted an expression of marvelous happiness in order to appear a brave man of some importance.

At his city of Bath, on that day which was his birthday, Bademagu was holding a joyous and full court. Crowds of people of all stations had accompanied him. The entire palace was filled with knights and maidens, including the sister of Meleagant. I shall tell you later the role I intend to have her play. I do not wish to mention it here, however, for speaking of it now would not suit my matter. I do not wish to entangle, corrupt, or distort it, but to follow a good and straightforward path.

For the moment I shall tell you of Meleagant's arrival. In the hearing of all, highborn and low, he addressed his father in a loud voice. "Father," he said, "so help you God, please tell me the truth. If a man by his own arms can bring fear to King Arthur's court, should he not be very happy? Is he not very strong?"

Without listening more, his father answered his question. "Son," he said, "all good men should honor, serve, and keep company with the man who can merit such esteem." He then flattered him by inviting him not to hide longer the reason for this statement; he asked him what he wanted and whence he had come.

"Sire," his son Meleagant answered, "I do not know if you recall the terms of the agreement that were stated and recorded when you forced a treaty between Lancelot and me. At that time it was declared in front of several of us, you do remember this I think, that we two should present ourselves at Arthur's court at the end of the year. I went there at the proper time, fully prepared for the business that brought me. I did all I should. I asked for Lancelot. I demanded him. It was arranged that I should fight him. But I could not see or find him. He had fled and run away. I did not leave there without a pledge: Gawain promised me that if Lancelot was no longer alive or failed to come within the appointed time, there would be no further postponement; in place of Lancelot, he could fight me. Arthur has no knight of greater renown, this is a well-known fact. But before the eldertrees bloom again, I shall see, if we come to blows, whether his renown equals his deeds. I only wish all this could take place now."

"Son," said his father, "your behavior makes people rightly consider you a fool. Anyone ignorant before now of your folly learns of it from your own words. It is true that a noble heart humbles itself, but the fool and the braggart will never lack folly. Son, I tell you this for your sake. Your personal qualities are those of hardheartedness and cruelty without the least trace of kindness or affection. Your heart needs some mercy. You are too fired by folly. This is why my respect for you is so slight. This is what will cause your downfall. If you are brave, there will be many to bear witness in the hour of need. A man of valor need not praise his own courage to lend greater luster to his deed; the deed speaks for itself. The praise you heap on yourself does not help you increase your honor in anyone's eyes; in fact, I hold you in even less esteem. Son, I warn you, but have my words any value? The man who talks to a fool has little effect. The man who wants to rid a fool of his folly wastes all his strenuous efforts. Excellence explained and taught is worthless unless put into practice. It is scarcely taught before it vanishes."

Meleagant was then beside himself with rage. I can certainly assert the truth: you have never seen a man born of woman so full of fury as he was. Anger severed civility at that moment, for he showed no respect whatever as he addressed his father. "Do you dream? Or are you delirious to say that I am mad because I tell you of myself? I thought I had come to you as my lord and my father. But this does not seem the case, for you have insulted me more shamefully, in my opinion, than you have any right to do. Can you tell me why you used this tone of address?"

"Yes I can."

"Then why?"

"Because I see nothing in you but anger and madness. I know your state of mind well. It will yet bring you great harm. Damn the man who can believe that Lancelot, the well-trained knight, respected by everyone but you, would have fled in fear of you. Perhaps he is buried. Or perhaps confined in a prison with the gate so firmly locked that he can leave only with permission. To be certain, I would be deeply upset were he in trouble or dead. Such a skillful man, so handsome, so brave, yet so moderate in his behavior. His loss would truly be too severe were he to die before his time. Please God that not be true."

After these words, Bademagu said no more. But a maiden, a daughter of his, had heard all he said. And you can be certain it was she whom I mentioned earlier in my story. Hearing such news of Lancelot made her unhappy, and she realized that he was locked away, since no one had knowledge or word of him. "May God never look upon me," she said to herself, "if ever I rest until I have definite and accurate news of him." At once without delay and making no disturbance, not even a murmur, she ran off and mounted a most handsome mule, one that moved at a gentle pace. But when she left the court, I must tell you, she did not know which way to turn. Knowing nothing and making no inquiry, she entered the first road she found and hurried along at random—she knew not where—without the companionship of any knight or man-at-arms.

In her eagerness to reach the object of her search, she hastened away. Keen was her pursuit and keen her quest, but it would not soon be over. She could not stop anywhere or rest long if she wished to succeed in her undertaking, namely, to release Lancelot from prison, provided that she found him and could free him. But I believe that before she finds him, she will have searched through many countries, traveled to many places, and traversed many lands before hearing any news of him. But why bother relating her journeys by day and her rests at night? Through mountains and valleys she traveled everywhere along so many routes that a month or more passed, and still she knew no more than she had known before. All her travels accomplished nothing.

One day when she was pensively and sadly riding across a field, she noticed in the distance a tower by the shore of an arm of the sea. There was no other dwelling, cabin or house, within a league of the tower. This was the one Meleagant had had constructed for Lancelot's imprisonment, though she was ignorant of this. As soon as she saw it, she could not turn her eyes to anything else. And her heart gave her a firm promise that here was the object of her lengthy search. Now her quest was accomplished. After leading her through many travels, Fortune had brought her the right way.

Riding up to the tower, the maiden drew close enough to touch it. As she went round, she listened carefully with all her attention to see if she might hear some sign of life that would bring her joy. She looked at the bottom; she gaped up at the top; she saw the tower's height and thickness. She was astonished not to see any entrance or window except for one small, narrow opening. And the high, straight tower had no steps or ladder. Consequently, she believed that the tower had been deliberately designed this way and that Lancelot was within. But before taking sustenance, she would know whether this was true or not.

Resolving to call Lancelot by name, she was about to do so but stopped and kept silent when she heard a voice from within the tower making a heavy and dreadful lament, seeking nothing but death. Complaining of unbearable pain and begging death to come, the voice despised its own body and life. Feebly, in low and hoarse tones, it lamented: "Alas, Fortune, how wretched for me is the movement of your wheel. You have overturned me shamelessly, for I was at the top; now I am at the bottom. I used to know happiness; now I know misery. You used to smile on me; now your expression is bleak. Alas, wretched man, why did you trust her, seeing that she has abandoned you so quickly? In a short space of time she has brought me, to be honest, from such a height to this depth. Fortune, you were wrong to mock me. Have you no concern? You do not care what happens. Alas, Holy Cross! Holy Spirit! I am lost! I am destroyed! I have nothing left.

"Alas, Gawain, your worth is so great, your excellence unequaled. How amazed I am you have not come to my rescue. You have certainly waited too long; you have not acted with courtesy. The man whose devoted friend you once were ought to receive your assistance. I can honestly say that if I had known you were imprisoned, I would have sought you on every sideroad and hideaway on either side of the sea for at least seven or ten years until I found you. But why do I debate with myself? You do not care about me enough to go out of your way on my behalf. True is the peasant's proverb: in time of need you can easily test the true friend, and nowadays you can scarcely find a friend. Alas, it is more than a year since this tower became my prison. Gawain, I am hurt that you abandoned me. But perhaps you know nothing of this, and so perhaps I am wrong to accuse you. Yes, I agree with that. I committed an outrageous and terrible injustice to think that way. I am certain that nothing under heaven, had you known the truth, could have prevented you from coming with your men to rescue me from this misfortune and misery. Because of our love and companionship, if for no other reason, you should have done that. But these words are useless. None of this can be.

"Alas, may the curse of God and Saint Sylvester fall on the man who condemned me to such disgrace! May God give him a fitting fate! That man Meleagant is the worst creature alive. Out of envy he has done me every harm he could."

Wasting away his life in grief, he then ended his lament and became silent. But she who was lingering below had heard all his words. Now she knew that she had reached her goal. Waiting no longer, she sensibly called to him as loud as she could, and more. "Lancelot, friend, you up there, speak to a friend of yours."

But the man inside did not hear her. She shouted louder and louder until, even in his extreme weakness, he heard her. Who could have been calling him? he wondered. The voice reached him; he heard the call but did not know the caller. He thought this might be some phantom. He looked all about him to see if he might spy anyone, but saw nothing except the tower and himself. "God!" he said. "What is this I hear? I hear talking and see nothing. I swear this is more than miraculous, for I am awake, not asleep. Had this happened to me in a dream, I would probably have thought it an illusion. But I am awake, and so I am disturbed."

Then, with some difficulty, he stood, and little by little made his feeble way over to the narrow opening. Once there he leaned out, trying to look up and down, sideways, and off into the distance. When he had surveyed the area as best he could, he saw the maiden who had shouted to him. He did not recognize her, though he did see her. On the other hand, she recognized him immediately. "Lancelot," she said, "I have come a long way looking for you. Now, thank God, I have succeeded. I have found you. I was the person who asked you for a gift when you were on your way to the sword-bridge. You willingly granted my request for the head of the defeated knight I despised. I had you behead him. In exchange for that kind gift, I have put myself to great trouble, and I will free you from here."

"Thank you, maiden," the prisoner answered. "If I leave here, the service I did you will be well repaid. If you can release me from this place, then by Saint Paul the Apostle I promise you on my word to be at your service forever. I swear to God, a day will not pass when I fail to do all you wish to request. You could ask me for anything I have, and it would be yours at once."

"Friend, do not be afraid that you will not leave here. This very day you will be released and free. Not for a thousand pounds would I abandon the notion of seeing you free before daybreak. Then after my efforts a quiet sojourn, peace, and relaxation will be yours. Anything of mine you like will be yours if you want it. So let nothing distress you. But first I must look about on the ground here for some tool that will, if I find it, allow me to widen this opening and release you."

"God help you find it!" he exclaimed in complete agreement with her plan. "I have plenty of rope in here. The servants gave it to me for pulling up my food, stale barley bread and dirty water, which makes my heart and my body ill."

Bademagu's daughter then went searching and found a strong pickaxe that was square and sharp. She quickly handed it up to him. He banged and hammered, pushed and struck at the wall with exhausting efforts until he could get out easily. Now he was so relieved, now he was so happy, be assured, to break out and leave the prison where he had been confined so long. Now he was out in the open, breathing fresh air. Even if someone had piled up all the world's gold and offered and given it to him, you can be certain he would not have wished to be back inside.

Behold Lancelot released, but so feeble that he tottered from his infirmity and weakness. So as not to hurt him, the maiden placed him gently in front of her on her mule. Then they rode away quickly. She deliberately avoided the main roads so that they would not be seen. They took the secluded paths, for had she traveled in the open, someone she knew might soon have done them much harm. She did not wish this to happen. Thus she avoided the dangerous places, at last reaching a retreat whose beauty and charm had often made her stay and rest there. The people who lived there obeyed all her requests, and the site was enclosed with lush foliage that made it safe and private.

Lancelot had scarcely arrived there when the maiden had him disrobed and placed him softly to rest in a beautiful, high bed. Then she bathed him and took such care of him that I cannot describe the half of it. She rubbed and massaged him as gently as though he were her father. With such attention she managed to revive his health; indeed, with her efforts he was restored. Now he was as beautiful as an angel, no longer emaciated or weak but handsome and strong. Thus he left his bed.

The maiden had looked for the finest robe she could find for him, and dressed him in it when he rose. He put it on joyously, more easily than a bird in flight. He embraced and kissed the maiden, then, with great affection, spoke to her. "Friend," he said, "I have only God and you to thank for my safety and health. You rescued me from prison. Now my heart and my body, my service and my possessions, all you want is yours. You have done so much for me that I am yours. Yet long has it been since I was at the court of Arthur, my lord, who has done me great honor. Much work awaits me there. Now, dear gracious friend, I would beg you to let me go out of love. If it be your pleasure, I would gladly go there."

"Lancelot, dear kind friend, I agree," the maiden answered. "All I wish is your honor and your welfare here and in all places."

She then presented him with a marvellous horse of hers whose equal none has ever seen. Ignoring the stirrups, he jumped up; without so much as a word, he found himself in the saddle. Then with sincere hearts they commended each other to God the All-truthful.

As Lancelot set off on his way, he knew such happiness that, even were I to take an oath, I could convey no notion of his joy at having escaped from his confinement. But often he said to himself that the disgraceful traitor who had ridiculed, tricked, and imprisoned him would meet grief, "And I am free, in spite of him." Then he swore by the heart and body of the Creator of the Universe that all the riches from Babylon to Ghent would not let him leave Meleagant alive were he to hold him in his power. Too heavy were the misery and shame Meleagant had done him.

But soon events would take place to permit such an outcome, for this very Meleagant, whom Lancelot threatened and already eagerly sought, had reached the court that same day without being summoned. Once there, he continued to seek out Sir Gawain until he saw him. Then the evil man, the proven traitor, asked after Lancelot, whether he had finally been seen or found, as though knowing nothing of the situation himself. And in fact he did not know everything, though he thought himself well-informed. Gawain told him truthfully that Meleagant saw that Lancelot had still not come. "Since it is you I find," Meleagant said, "come now and keep my agreement, for I shall wait for you no longer."

"If it pleases God, in whom I trust," Gawain answered, "I will certainly keep your agreement in a moment. I expect to acquit myself well against you. But if it comes to throwing dice and I have the higher number, then by God and Saint Foy, I will not stop until I have carried off all the stakes."

Then waiting no longer, Gawain ordered a carpet laid down and spread out there before him. Prompt to carry out his command, the squires calmly executed his instructions without hint of annoyance or complaint. They took the carpet and laid it in the spot he had designated. Without pause, he took his place on it and asked to be armed by his attendants, who stood before him still without cloaks. Three of them were there, brave and well-trained, though I do not know whether they were his cousins or his nephews. They did such a fine job of arming him that no one could have criticized them for even the slightest fault in their work. After they had equipped him, one of them went to lead out a Spanish charger that could run through fields and woods, hills and valleys, faster than the good Bucephalus. On such a horse as that mounted Gawain, the most accomplished and renowed knight of those ever blessed with the sign of the cross.

At the very moment that Gawain was about to take up his shield, he saw Lancelot dismounting in front of him. Gawain stared at him in astonishment, for he had come so suddenly, and I do not lie when I tell you he was as astonished as if Lancelot had just fallen at his feet from the clouds. As soon as he saw that it truly was he, no urgent task he might have had could have kept him from dismounting and holding out his arms. He greeted him, embraced him, kissed him. He was overwhelmed with happiness to see his companion. I shall tell you the precise truth; do not imagine that I lie. Gawain would have refused the kingship at once if that position meant leaving Lancelot.

Already the king and everyone else knew that Lancelot, whom they had awaited so long, had come back safe and sound, and there was jubilation everywhere. One of them, however, was chagrined. The entire court gathered to honor the knight they had been expecting for so long a time. There was no one so old or so young that he failed to display his great delight, which dissipated and dispelled the grief that had been theirs before. Sadness fled, and joy appeared in its place and awakened their hearts.

And did the queen not take part in this general rejoicing? Yes, to be honest, she was the very first to rejoice. What? God, where, then, was she? Nothing gave her so much joy as his return. And did she not come to him? Of course she did, for she was so close to him, went so near him, that her body almost followed her heart. Where, then, was her heart? It was welcoming Lancelot with kisses and joy. And why did her body hide? Why was her happiness incomplete? Was anger or hatred there too? Certainly not, not even the slightest trace. But this might have happened: the king and the others there might have opened their eyes and discerned the entire situation had she publicly obeyed all the desires of her heart. Without Reason, which removed this mad fit of passion, everyone would have witnessed all her feelings. That, then, would have been too great a folly. Therefore, Reason contained and controlled her foolish heart and her mad passion. She regained a little control and resigned herself to wait until she might discover and see a more favorable and more private place. They would reach that haven, which would be better than their present situation.

The king accorded Lancelot great honor. After he had given him a most cordial welcome, he addressed him. "Friend, long has it been since I have heard news of any man more welcome than this news of you. I have been anxious to know in what country you stayed so long. All winter and all summer I had a search made for you everywhere, but no one could learn anything of you."

"Dear lord," Lancelot answered, "I can certainly tell you in a few words precisely what happened to me. Meleagant, the evil traitor, imprisoned me the day the captives were released from his country. He forced me to live in utter disgrace in a tower by the sea. That is where he had me confined and locked away, and that is where I would still endure a hard life were it not for a friend of mine, a maiden for whom I once did a small service. She gave me a huge reward for a very small favor; she did me great honor and great good. But as for him whom I hate, and who sought, devised, and bestowed on me such shameful treatment, I would like to repay him without the slightest delay. He has come to claim it, and he will have it. There is no need for him to wait longer. All is quite ready. As for me, I am again ready too. God grant him no reason to be happy!"

Then Gawain addressed Lancelot. "Friend," he said, "if I pay your debt to this creditor, I shall consider it but a slight favor. And as you see, I am already mounted and prepared for combat. Dear friend, do not refuse me this favor, which I desire and beg."

Lancelot replied that he would first let his eye be plucked out, indeed both his eyes plucked out, before he could agree to that. He swore that such a thing would never happen. The debt was his, and the payment would be his, for those were the terms of his oath. Gawain realized that nothing he might say could have any effect. So he loosened his hauberk and lifted it from his back, then removed all his other armor. Without a moment's delay Lancelot armed himself with this equipment. He thought the time would never come to discharge his debt and settle his account.

Meleagant would never again know good fortune; he would be repaid. Astonished beyond belief by what he saw with his own eyes, he nearly lost his mind and almost fainted. "Yes," he said, "I was a fool not to go back before coming here to see that he was still imprisoned within my tower. Now he has tricked me. Oh, God, why should I have gone there? How could I have imagined he might possibly escape? Is the wall not built solidly enough? Is the tower not strong and high enough? There was no hole or opening to let him depart without help from someone outside. Perhaps a secret place was revealed? Had the wall been worn away so that it collapsed and fell to pieces, would he not have been destroyed along with it? His bones broken? His body dead? So help me God, of course he would, for had the tower fallen, he would definitely be killed. But when the wall ceases to stand, I believe there will not be a drop of water in all the sea and the world will no longer exist, unless the tower is beaten down by sheer force. No, that is not what happened. Something else took place. He received help in his escape. There is no other way he could have left. I have been duped with my eyes open. Whatever happened, he is now free. But had I taken proper precautions at that time, nothing of this nature would have happened. He could never have come to court. But my regret is too late. With no thought of lying, the peasant asserts an eternal truth: it is too late to close the stable after the horse has been led out. I know that severe insult and humiliation, if not worse suffering, will be my lot. What, then, will be the extent of my endurance and pain? So long as I can last, I shall exert all my efforts in this struggle, if it pleases God, in Whom I trust."

In this way he bolstered his courage and sought nothing but to meet his enemy on the field. His wait would not be long, as I believe, for Lancelot, who expected to defeat him quickly, was seeking him out.

But before their assault took place, the king told them both to go down to the open field below the tower. From there to Ireland was no place of such beauty. They followed his command and went down there at once. The king as well went there, along with crowds of men and women pressing together. All moved there; none stayed behind. And many knights and beautiful and charming ladies and maidens went to the windows on account of Lancelot.

In that open field was a sycamore tree of unequaled beauty. Its thick foliage covered a large space, and round about it was a border of beautiful, fresh grass that was always new. Beneath this beautiful and attractive sycamore, which had been planted in the time of Abel, was a clear spring that ran off with great rapidity. Its gravel bed, also beautiful and attractive, gleamed like silver. The water flowed off through a pipe made, I believe, of fine pure gold, which stretched down the middle of the open field in a valley between two woods. The king was delighted to sit down near the spring, where nothing displeasing met his sight. Then he had the people draw back.

Lancelot rushed at Meleagant with a fury equal to his hatred. But before attacking, he shouted to him in a loud and fierce voice. "Come here, I challenge you. Be certain, I will not spare you."

Lancelot spurred his horse and drew back the distance of an arrow's flight. Then both let their horses race against each other as fast as they could, and at once struck each other so fiercely on their sturdy shields that they pierced and punctured them; this time, however, neither was wounded, and their flesh was not even grazed. Without a moment's wait, they rode past each other, then came back, at the fastest speed their horses could manage, to deliver heavy blows on their fine strong shields.

They continued to deploy great strength, these brave and valiant knights on their swift and strong horses. From the force of their assaults, their lances passed through the shields hanging from their necks without even breaking or shattering until the naked steel reached their flesh. With such terrible pressure, each attacked the other so that both were thrown to the ground. Breaststraps, waiststraps, stirrups, nothing could help them. They were forced to vacate their saddles and fall backwards onto the bare ground. In fright the horses were bucking and rearing; kicking and biting, they too wanted to kill each other.

The knights who had fallen jumped up as quickly as possible and drew their swords that were engraved with letters. With their shields before their faces, they now gave careful thought to the best method of wreaking havoc with the sharp steel swords. Lancelot stood in no fear at all; he knew twice as much as his opponent about swordplay, since he had learned the art in his childhood. Both delivered such savage blows to the shields hanging from their necks and the gold-barred helmets that they battered and smashed them. Lancelot's assault, however, was most severe. With one dreadfully strong blow, he severed Meleagant's right arm, which, though covered with steel, was unprotected in front of the shield. When Meleagant felt the painful loss of his right arm, he said that the loss would be dearly paid for; if he could have the chance, nothing would stop his revenge.

Almost mad with malice, pain, and rage, Meleagant could no longer hope to win without resort to some evil trick. Counting on capturing his opponent, he rushed at him. Lancelot had prepared himself carefully, however. With his sharp-cutting sword, he made such a gash in Meleagant's belly that he would not recover until after April or May. His assault smashed against his noseguard and broke three teeth in his mouth. Meleagant was so enraged that he could say nothing. He would not stoop to beg mercy, for his mad heart ensnared him in its tight clutches and offered him ill advice. Lancelot advanced, unlaced Meleagant's helmet, and cut off his head. Never again would Meleagant deceive him. He had fallen dead. His life had ended.

None of the spectators took pity on Meleagant, I assure you. The king and all the others there were unable to contain their great joy. They had never known such happiness. They relieved Lancelot of his armor and led him away amid great celebration.

Lords, if I were to say more, I would depart from the matter. Therefore, I draw to a close; here the tale finds its full conclusion. Godefroi de Leigni, the clerk, wrote the ending of *The Cart*. Let no one, however, fault him for pursuing the story farther than Christian, for he did this only with the consent of Christian, who began it. His section started at the time Lancelot WAS IMPRISONED IN THE TOWER, AND CONTINUED THROUGH UNTIL THE ENDING. THIS MUCH WAS HIS SHARE OF THE TALE. NOW HE WISHES TO ADD NO MORE AND TO INCLUDE NO LESS, LEST HE SPOIL THE TALE. ¶HERE ENDS THE ROMANCE OF LANCELOT OF THE CART.

THE KNIGHT WITH THE LION

ARTHUR, THE GOOD KING of Britain, whose valor teaches us that we too should be courteous and brave, was holding court with all kinglike splendor at Carlisle in Wales on that feast so worth its cost one has to call it Pentecost.

After dinner the knights gathered again here and there through the halls where the ladies, married or unmarried, called them. Some knights talked of recent events; others were speaking of love, the tribulations and the sorrows and the blessings that often come to the disciples of his order. At that time Love's order was still fine and flourishing. Now, alas, there are very few disciples; nearly all have deserted him so that Love is held in disrepute. In olden days Love's disciples were known for courtesy and bravery, generosity and honor. Now *love* has become an idle word. Those who know nothing of his order maintain they love, but they lie. They have no right to talk. In their boasting, love is but an idle tale and a lie.

But now let us speak of those who once were and leave aside those who still are, for a courteous man, though dead, is worth a great deal more, in my opinion, than a living churl. So it is my pleasure to relate a story worth listening to about the king whose fame spreads near and far. And I do agree with the belief of so many Bretons that his renown will last forever. Thanks to him, people will recall his chosen knights, fine men who strove for honor.

On that particular day, many were surprised to see the king rise so soon and take his leave. Some were saddened by his departure and discussed it at length. Never before at such a grand feast had they seen him retire to his chamber to rest or to sleep. But on this day the queen happened to detain him, and he stayed beside her so long that he forgot himself and fell asleep.

Outside the door to his chamber were Dodinel and Sagremor, Kay and Sir Gawain. And Sir Yvain was there, as well as Calogrenant, a most agreeable knight, who had begun to tell them a tale more to his shame than to his credit. Hearing him tell his tale, the queen left the king's side and came upon them without being noticed so that she appeared among them before any saw her except Calogrenant, who leapt to his feet to greet her. Kay, who was quarrelsome and mean, sarcastic and spiteful, addressed him. "By God, Calogrenant, now I see that you are brave and nimble! How it delights me that you are the most courteous of our group! I know that you have complete faith in yourself, lacking as you are in wisdom. How proper for my lady to believe you surpass all of us in courtesy and bravery! Perhaps we neglected to rise out of laziness or because we didn't care. By God, no, sir! We didn't because we did not see my lady, and you had already stood."

"Kay, I think you would have burst had you not been able to pour out the venom that fills you. You are malicious and ill bred to quarrel with your companions," said the queen.

"Lady, if we are not better for your company, take care we are not poorer for it," Kay said. "I don't believe I said anything subject to reproach. So please, let us keep quiet. There is no courtesy or wisdom in continuing an idle dispute. This argument should end; no one should pursue it further. Since there must be no dispute, have him return to the tale he had started."

Calogrenant spoke in response to these words. "Lady," he said, "I could not care less about this silly quarrel. What does it matter to me anyway? If Kay's taunts were directed against me, his words will never harm me. Sir Kay, you have insulted and offended men worthier and wiser than I. That is your usual pastime. The dung heap will always stink, gadflies always sting, bees always buzz, and a scoundrel will always be an annoying pest. But now, with my lady's permission, I shall not return to my tale today. I beg her, by her grace, not to insist I do something against my will."

"Lady, all those here will be indebted to you," said Kay. "They would like to hear the story. Don't do it for my sake, but by the loyalty you owe the king, your lord and mine, ask him to continue, and you will act well."

"Calogrenant, pay no attention to the attack of Sir Kay, the seneschal," the queen replied. "He has always had a vicious tongue no one can correct. I would urge and beseech you not to harbor anger in your heart on his account. If you would retain my affection, do not refrain from telling because of him a tale we shall enjoy hearing. Do begin the story again."

"Lady, what you tell me to do is very painful indeed. I would rather have one of my teeth pulled out than tell them any more of my story today, were I not afraid of angering you. But I shall do your pleasure however much it displeases me. Since you wish, hear me now. Give me your heart and your ears, for words are lost completely unless they are understood by the heart. There are people who hear but do not understand, although they praise what they hear. Now they are capable only of hearing because their heart does not understand. The words come like the blowing wind to their ears; they do not linger or stay there, but pass quickly unless the heart is alert and ready to receive them. When they are heard, the heart can receive and enclose them, and make them stay. The ears are the route and channel the voice takes to the heart, and the heart embraces, inside the body, the voice that enters through the ears. Whoever would hear me now must lend me his heart and his ears. I don't intend to speak of some dream, idle tale, or lie.

"More than seven years ago, alone as a peasant, I happened to be riding along in the full armor of a properly attired knight in search of adventures. I turned off the main road to a path on the right, full of thorns and briars, leading through a thick forest. The way was treacherous, but despite the great trouble and inconvenience, I followed the direction of this path. I rode on almost the whole day until I left the Forest of Broceliande and came to an open plain, where I saw a wooden tower not more than half a Welsh league away. At a pace faster than a walk, I rode there and beheld the wooden tower and the deep, wide moat around it. Standing on the drawbridge was the man who owned the fortress, a mewed goshawk on his hand. I scarcely had time to greet him before he came to hold my stirrup, and he invited me to dismount. I did dismount, for after all, what else could I do since I needed lodging. He repeated to me more than seven times that the road was blessed that had brought me there. Then we crossed the drawbridge, passed through the gateway, and entered the courtyard. God grant that vavasor the same joy and honor he extended to me that night!

"In the center of the courtyard a gong was hanging, made, I believe, not of wood or iron, but all of copper. The vavasor struck the gong three times with a hammer hanging on a nearby post. At the sound of the gong, those who were upstairs in the house left and came down into the courtyard. Some ran to my horse, which the good vavasor was holding.

"I then saw a beautiful and charming maiden coming toward me. Gazing on her consumed all my attention, for she was lovely, slender, and tall. Proper and fine was the skill she employed in removing my armor, and she dressed me in a short peacock-blue cloak of rich wool trimmed with fur. All the others left us there so that she and I were alone. This pleased me since I wanted nothing else but to look at her. She took me to a seat on the most beautiful lawn in the world, surrounded by a low wall. I found her so well mannered, so fair of speech and so well informed, with such a delightful appearance and presence, that merely to be there was a great pleasure for me. Nothing in the world would have made me anxious to leave. That night, however, the vavasor annoyed me much by coming for me when it was time for supper. Since I could delay no longer, I followed his bidding.

"My description of the meal will be brief. It was entirely to my liking because the maiden sat across from me. After supper the vavasor told me he did not know how long it had been since he had offered hospitality to a knight errant in search of adventures. It was a long time since he had lodged anyone. Later he asked me to be kind and grateful enough to return by way of his home. 'Gladly, sir,' I answered him. It would have been disgraceful to refuse him. I should have done little for my host had I denied this request.

"That night I was very well lodged. And my horse was stabled for the night as I had asked, for my request was done. At daybreak I commended my good host and his dear daughter to the Holy Spirit. I took leave of everyone and departed as soon as possible.

"I had not traveled far from the manorhouse when I came upon wild bulls on the loose, fighting among themselves in a clearing. They were making such a roar with their ferocious savagery that, if the truth be known, I drew back a little. There is no beast fiercer or wilder than a bull. A churl, who looked like a Moor, was sitting on a stump with a large club in his hand. He was exceedingly ugly and repulsive; in fact, no words could possibly describe such a hideous creature. I moved closer to the churl and saw that his head was larger than that of a packhorse or any other beast. His hair was in tufts, and his bare forehead was nearly two spans wide. He had big hairy ears like those of an elephant, heavy eyebrows and a flat face, the eyes of an owl and the nose of a cat, a mouth stretching wide like a wolf's, the sharp and yellowed teeth of a wild boar, and a red beard and twisted whiskers. His chin merged into his chest, and he had a large backbone, twisted and hunched. Leaning on his club, he stood there dressed in a strange cloak, made not of cotton or wool but of two hides of recently flayed bulls or oxen which hung from his neck.

"The churl rose to his feet the moment he saw me approaching him. I did not know if he intended to hit me or what he planned to do, but I prepared to defend myself until I noticed he was standing perfectly still, not moving at all. He climbed up on a tree trunk where he was at least seventeen feet tall. He stared at me and said not a word more than a beast would. I assumed that he did not know how to speak or lacked sense. Nevertheless I was bold enough to address him. 'Come, tell me now whether you are a good thing or not.' And he told me he was a man. 'What kind of man are you?'

" 'Such as you see. I am never any different.'

" 'What are you doing here?'

" 'I am standing here tending the beasts in these woods.'

" 'You tend them? By Saint Peter of Rome, they know no man's command. I don't believe anyone can tend wild beasts in an open field, in the woods, or anywhere else unless they are tied up or enclosed.'

" 'I watch over and control them so they will not leave this spot.'

" 'How do you do this? Tell me the truth.'

" 'Not one of them dares move when it sees me coming. For when I get hold of one, I squeeze its two horns together with my tough and strong hands so that the others shake with fear and gather round me at once as if to beg mercy. No one but I could be so confident here, for if someone else were to come among them, he would be killed at once. So I am lord of my beasts. And now you must tell me what kind of man you are and what you seek.'

" 'I am, as you see, a knight, seeking what I cannot find. I have searched long and found nothing.'

" 'What would you like to find?'

" 'Adventures to test my valor and my courage. Now I ask and beg you to advise me, if you know, of some adventure or marvel.'

" 'You will certainly fail in this,' he replied. 'I don't know anything about adventures, and I have never heard tell of such. But if you were to go to a nearby spring and observe its custom, you would not return without difficulty. Near here you will immediately find a path to take you there. If you don't want to lose time, go straight ahead; otherwise you could quickly go astray, for there are many other paths. You will see the bubbling spring whose waters are colder than marble. The most beautiful tree Nature could ever create covers it with shade, and its leaves last all year—even winter cannot take them away. A lead basin hangs from the tree by a long chain that reaches down to the spring. Beside the spring you will find a stone slab, as you will see, which I cannot describe to you because I have never seen anything like it. On the other side is a small but very beautiful chapel. If you wish to put some water in the basin and spill it on the stone, you will see such a storm there that no beast will stay in the woods. The roebucks, stags, does, wild boars, even the birds will flee. And you will see such lightning bolts, winds, and crashing trees, rain, thunder, and flashes of light that if you can leave without great harm and hardship, you will be more fortunate than any knight who has ever been there.'

"I then left the churl once he had shown me the way. It was probably past nine and might have been near noon when I saw the tree and the spring. I recognized the tree, which, and I am telling the truth, was the most beautiful pine ever to grow on earth. I do not believe it ever rained so hard that a drop of water penetrated, but only flowed over the outside branches. From the tree I saw hanging the basin, made of the purest gold ever yet for sale at any fair. As for the spring, believe me, it was bubbling like boiling water. The stone was a single emerald with a hole in it the size of a bottle, and it rested on four rubies more radiant and more crimson than the morning sun when it rises in the east. I will never lie to you about this, but say only what I know.

"I wanted to see the marvel of the storm and tempest, and that desire was folly on my part. The moment I sprinkled some water from the basin on the hollowed stone, I would have been glad to repent, had I been able. I am afraid I poured too much, for I then saw the sky break open with such force that lightning from more than fourteen directions blinded my eyes and the clouds let loose, all at once, rain, snow, and hail. The storm had such terrible force that a hundred times I thought I would be killed by lightning bolts falling about me and trees crashing to the ground. You can be certain that I was terrified until the storm abated. But God granted me such comfort that the storm did not last long and all the winds died down. As soon as God wished them to cease, they dared not blow.

"When I saw the clear, pure air, I felt safe and happy, for joy, if ever I knew it, causes great suffering to be soon forgotten. The moment the storm ended, I saw so many birds gathered on the pine that, if anyone will believe me, not a single branch or leaf was visible since they were all covered by birds. And so the tree had become more beautiful. The birds were singing sweetly in harmony, one with another; each was singing a different tune, and I never heard one sing another's tune. I rejoiced in their joy and listened until they had finished their service at their own measured pace. I have never heard such beautiful joy, nor do I think any man ever will, unless he goes and listens to what charmed and pleased me so much that I should have been taken for a fool.

"I stayed there until I heard knights approach, or so it seemed. I thought there were at least ten. Yet there was only a single knight whose approach caused so much noise and commotion. The moment I saw him coming by himself, I took hold of my horse and lost no time in mounting. As though bent on evil, he was riding up faster than an eagle and looking as ferocious as a lion. From as far off as he could make his voice heard, he began to challenge me. 'Vassal!' he shouted, 'without challenge you have insulted and offended me. If you had some cause, you should have challenged me or at least sought justice before you began this strife. But if I can, Sir Vassal, I shall repay you for the obvious injury you have done. Round me is the evidence, my ravaged woods. The man who has suffered ought to protest, and I protest with good reason, for you have driven me from my home by lightning and rain. You have caused me great trouble. Damn him who thinks such action fair! Within my own woods and my own town, you made such an attack that the aid of tall towers or high walls would not have helped me. Even in a fortress of solid stone or wood, no man would have been safe. But you can be certain that from now on you shall not have truce or peace with me.'

"With these words we rushed together, gripping our shields tightly to cover ourselves. The knight had a good horse and a stout lance, and without doubt, he was a whole head taller than I. And so I was in serious trouble, for I was smaller than he and his horse was better than mine. I am telling the truth, be certain of this, to cover up my shame. I mustered all my strength and dealt him the strongest blow I could; my effort was in no way halfhearted. I hit him on the top part of his shield, and my lance flew into splinters while his remained whole. His lance was not light but, in my opinion, weighed more than any knight's lance. I have never seen one so large. And the knight hit me so hard that he sent me over the crupper of my horse flat down on the ground, where he left me in defeat and disgrace. He took my horse and left me there without so much as a glance back at me. Then he returned to the road. As for me, having no idea what to do, I remained there, absorbed in thought and confused. I sat beside the spring a moment and rested, not daring to follow the knight for fear of acting foolishly. Even had I dared follow, I did not know what had become of him.

"At last I decided to keep my promise to my host and return to him. This thought pleased me, and so that is what I did. I removed all my equipment in order to travel more lightly. And I returned in disgrace.

"When I reached his lodging that night, I found my host just the same, as good-natured and as courteous as I had found him before. I saw nothing in his behavior or his daughter's to suggest they welcomed me less gladly or paid me less honor than they had the night before. They all showed me great honor in their house, and I was grateful to them. So far as they knew or had heard tell, no man, they said, had ever escaped the place from which I had come without being captured or killed.

"Thus I departed and thus I returned, and on my return I considered myself a fool. And like a fool, I have told you a tale I never wanted to relate again."

"On my life, you are my first cousin and we ought to love each other," Sir Yvain exclaimed. "But I think you are a fool for keeping this from me so long. If I have called you fool, I beg you not to take offense. If I can, and if I obtain leave, I shall go and avenge your disgrace."

"It is obvious the meal is over," said Kay, who could never keep quiet. "There are more words in a pot full of wine than in a barrel of beer, and people say a cat when drunk becomes merry. After dinner, without budging, everyone goes to slay Noradin, and you will go to avenge Forré! Are your saddlepads stuffed? your iron greaves polished? your banners unfurled? Now, by God, Sir Yvain, will you start out tonight or tomorrow? Let us know, dear sir, when you will go to this martyrdom since we would like to escort you. There is no magistrate or bailiff who would not be glad to escort you. I beg you not to go without our leave, no matter what. But if you have a bad dream tonight, stay here!"

"What? Sir Kay, are you mad?" the queen asked. "Does your speech never stop? Damn your tongue and its endless bitterness! Your tongue certainly hates you because it speaks the worst it knows to everyone, whoever he may be. Damn a tongue that never stops its vile talk! Your tongue's babbling makes you despised everywhere. Can it betray you more? You may be certain I would accuse it of treason if it were mine. Anyone who cannot profit from criticism should be tied like a madman before the choir screen in church."

"Lady," Sir Yvain replied, "his words matter to me not one whit. So great is the resourcefulness, the knowledge, and the worthiness of Sir Kay that he will never be deaf or dumb in any court. He knows how to answer baseness with courtesy and wisdom, and has never behaved in any other way. Now, you know well if I lie. But I do not wish to quarrel or resume our foolishness. The man who has revenge, not the man who strikes the first blow, wins the battle. The man who insults his own companion would quarrel with a stranger. I do not wish to be like the watchdog that stiffens and growls when another dog snarls at it."

While they were talking, the king came out of his chamber where he had been sleeping until this time. When the barons saw him, they all sprang to their feet. He made them all sit down again. Then he sat beside the queen, and she repeated to him, at once and word for word, Calogrenant's entire tale, for the queen was a skillful storyteller. The king listened intently, and then swore three solemn oaths, on the soul of Utherpendragon his father, and on that of his son, and on that of his mother: to go, within a fortnight, to see the marvel of the spring and the storm, and to arrive on the Eve of the Feast of Saint John the Baptist and take lodging there for the night. He added that all who wished to go might accompany him. The entire court thought highly of the king's plan, for the barons and the knights bachelor were eager to make the journey.

Despite the rejoicing and happiness, Sir Yvain was disappointed because he was expecting to go there all alone. He was distraught and distressed that the king was to go. He was upset only because he was convinced that Sir Kay would be granted, without fail, the right to combat first—if he asked, his request would not be denied. Or perhaps Sir Gawain himself would ask first. The favor would never be refused if either of these two asked. Since he did not want their company, he would not wait for them, but would go all alone, by his own will, be it to his joy or his sorrow. No matter who stayed behind, he intended to be in the Forest of Broceliande within three days, where he would try, if possible, to find the narrow wooded path, which he was yearning so desperately to see, and the open plain, and the fortified manorhouse, and the pleasure and delight of the courteous maiden, who was most beautiful and attractive, and the worthy man who, along with his daughter, strove to honor every guest, so noble and well born was he. Then he would see the bulls in the clearing and the tall churl who watched over them. He was impatient to see the churl, who was so large and stout, hideous and deformed, and black like a smith. Then he would see, if he could, the stone, the spring, the basin, and the birds on the pine, and he would make the wind blow and the rain fall. But he would never brag, nor, had he his wish, would anyone ever know of this until great shame or great honor was his. Let the tale then be told.

Sir Yvain left the court without meeting any man and went alone to his lodging. He found all his household, and so gave orders to have his horse saddled. He then summoned one of his squires, from whom he hid nothing.

"Look here," he said, "come out with me and bring me my arms. I shall be going at once through that gateway on my palfrey. Take care not to delay since I have a very long route to cover. Have my charger well shod and lead it at once after me. Afterwards you will bring my palfrey back. But be careful, I warn you, if someone asks about me, never to give him any news. Otherwise you would be foolish to rely on me more, no matter how you now trust me."

"Sir, have no concern now," he replied. "No one will ever learn anything from me. Go now, and I shall follow you there."

Sir Yvain mounted at once so that he would avenge, if he could, his cousin's disgrace before returning. The squire ran immediately to get a good charger, and since the horse was already shod, he mounted without delay. He followed his lord at a gallop until he saw him dismounted in a secluded spot to one side of the road, where he had been waiting a short while. He immediately brought him all his armor and equipment and dressed him. Once armed, Sir Yvain did not wait. He rode every day over mountains and through valleys, through long and deep forests, through strange and wild places, passing through many treacherous spots, many perils and many straits, until he reached the narrow path full of brambles and dark shadows. Then he felt confident he could not lose his way. He would not stop, whatever price he had to pay, until he saw the pine that shaded the spring and the stone, and the tempest of wind and rain, hail and thunder.

That night, you can be certain, he had the host he desired. He found the vavasor even more polite and honorable than I have told you, and he saw a hundred times more wisdom and beauty in the maiden than Calogrenant had related. You cannot enumerate all the good qualities of a fine woman or a worthy man. Once they devote themselves to virtue, you cannot begin to give an adequate description, for no tongue can tell the honorable deeds such a worthy person can do. To his delight, Sir Yvain was finely lodged that night.

The next morning he came to the clearing and saw the bulls and the churl, who pointed out the path to him. More than a hundred times he crossed himself in amazement at how Nature could have fashioned such a hideous and base creature. Then he rode to the spring and beheld everything he wanted to see. Without wasting a moment or sitting down, he poured out all the water filling the basin on the stone. The wind and rain began at once, and the expected storm did come. When God restored fine weather, the birds came to the pine and made a marvelous display of joy above the perilous spring. Before this joyousness stopped, a knight rode up, with anger more hotly burning than embers, and as much noise as if he were chasing a rutting stag. The moment they saw each other, they rushed together in a display of deadly hatred. With their strong and stout lances, they dealt such severe blows that they pierced both shields hanging from their necks and tore their hauberks. The lances split and splintered, the pieces flying into the air. They then attacked each other with swords, cutting their shield straps in the clash. The shields were hacked to pieces from end to end so that the shreds hung useless as covering or protection. They slashed them so that they freely tested the gleaming blades against their chests, their sides, and their hips. Savage was their assault, yet like two rocks they did not move from their positions.

Never were two knights more intent on hastening each other's death. Careful not to waste their blows, they laid them on as best they could. The helmets were dented and bent, the meshes from the hauberks went flying so that the men drew a great deal of blood. Their bodies were so hot that their hauberks provided no more protection than a frock. As each thrust at the other's face, it was a wonder that such a savage and bitter struggle was lasting so long. But both men were so stouthearted that neither would yield a foot of ground until he delivered a fatal blow. Yet they were men of honor: they did not wish to hit or harm their horses; they would not stoop to such an act. All day they sat astride their horses without setting foot on the ground. And so the combat was the more honorable.

At last Sir Yvain crushed the knight's helmet. The knight was dizzy and stunned from the blow, and he fainted, for he had never felt such a cruel stroke. Beneath his headpiece his head was split open to the brain, so that bloodied bits of brain stained the meshes of his gleaming hauberk. He suffered such intense pain from this that his heart almost stopped. Because of his fatal wound, he fled, and he was not wrong, for further defense was no help to him. As soon as he collected his thoughts, he fled galloping toward his town. There the drawbridge was lowered and the gate opened wide for him.

As fast as he could, Sir Yvain spurred after him impetuously, just as a gerfalcon swoops down on a crane spotted from afar and draws so near that it expects to seize it, but does not even touch it. So the knight was fleeing, with his pursuer chasing him so closely that he could almost touch him. Nevertheless he could not overtake him, though he was near enough to hear him groan from the pain he was suffering.

But all the while the flight continued. And the pursuer was exerting all his strength, fearing he had wasted his effort unless he captured him dead or alive, for he remembered the insults Sir Kay had hurled at him. He had not discharged the promise he made his cousin, and no one would believe in his deed unless he returned with proof. The knight led him at a gallop to the town gate, where they both entered. No man or woman was seen in the streets where they passed, and the two came galloping up to the palace gate.

The gate was very high and wide, and yet the entry was so narrow that two men or two horses could not pass through abreast, or meet in the middle of the gateway, without jamming and great harm. The entrance was constructed like a trap set to catch a rat bent on mischief. There was a blade hidden above which dropped, struck, and impaled, because it was released and fell the moment the slightest movement tripped the trigger. Similarly, there were two springs underneath the gate which propped up a sharp, well-ground iron portcullis. If anything stepped on these mechanisms, the portcullis would fall, catching and cutting to pieces whatever the gate hit below. And in the very center, the entry was as narrow as a beaten path.

The knight was very prudent and rushed straight through the passage. Sir Yvain galloped madly after him, coming so close to him that he held him by the cantle from behind. And how well for him he happened to stretch forward! Except for this stroke of luck, he would have been cut in two as his horse stepped on the beam that held the iron portcullis in place. Like a devil from hell, the portcullis dropped down unimpeded and fell without great harm. It cut off the back of the horse, but, thank God, it did not touch Sir Yvain, except that it grazed his back so closely that it clipped off the two spurs flush with his heels. Yvain fell, astounded.

The knight who had been fatally wounded escaped in the following manner: farther ahead was another gate like the earlier one; he escaped by fleeing through this gate, and the portcullis dropped behind him. And so Sir Yvain was caught. Disconcerted and distraught, he remained shut in the great hall, which had splendid wall paintings in costly colors and a paneled ceiling all speckled with gilded nails. He was less perturbed, however, by his own situation than by his ignorance of the knight's whereabouts. While in this confusion, he heard a narrow door open from an adjoining small room. A young lady, lovely and attractive in face and form, came out and closed the door behind her. When she saw Sir Yvain, she was at first quite startled.

"I am terribly afraid that you are not welcome, knight," she exclaimed. "My lord is fatally wounded, and I am certain you are his killer. If you stay inside here, you will be cut to pieces. My lady is in such deep mourning. And her people about her are crying so much that their grief almost kills them. They know that you are inside here, but their heavy grief has made them incapable of doing anything now. Once they decide to attack you, they cannot fail to slay or hang you, whichever their choice."

"Please God they never kill me, and I never fall into their hands," Sir Yvain answered her.

"No, for I shall do all I can for you," she said. "A worthy man does not fear too much, and so I believe you are a worthy man since you are not too much afraid. And you can be certain, if I can, I shall honor and serve you as you did me. Once my lady sent me on an errand to the king's court. Perhaps I did not show the courtesy, prudence, or fine behavior a maiden should; yet not a knight there bothered to say a word to me except you alone, who are now here. Out of your deep compassion you honored and served me, and for the honor you paid me, I shall reward you now. I know your name well, and I recognized you clearly. You are Sir Yvain, the son of King Urien. Now, be absolutely certain, if you are willing to trust me, you will never be captured or harmed. Take this little ring of mine, and return it to me, if you please, after I have delivered you."

She then gave him the little ring, telling him that it had the same power as the bark that covers the wood and prevents it from being seen. But the ring had to be worn with the stone facing the palm. Then whoever had the ring on his finger need fear nothing, for no man could see him, however open his eyes, any more than he could see the wood beneath the bark.

Sir Yvain put on the ring, and when she finished speaking, the maiden took him to a seat on a bed covered with a quilt so precious that even the Duke of Austria did not own one like it. She then proposed to bring him something to eat, if this was his wish, and he replied that that would be welcome. The young lady hurried quickly to her room, and soon returned with a roast capon and a pitcher covered with a white cloth and filled with wine from a good vintage. This was a meal she was happy to serve him, and since he was hungry, he was eager to eat and to drink.

By the time he had finished eating and drinking, the knights were already stirring about inside, looking for him. They wished to avenge their lord, who had now been placed on his bier. "Friend," she asked him, "do you hear them all looking for you? They are making so much noise and commotion. But whoever comes or goes, never let the noise stir you. You will not be discovered unless you leave this bed. Soon you will see this hall filled with ill-disposed and malicious people expecting to find you here. I think they will bring the body through here for interment. They will start the search for you under the benches and beds. It will be entertaining and funny for a fearless man to watch such blind men. They will all be so sightless, so upset, and so deluded that they will go mad with rage. I can say nothing more now, nor dare I stay here longer. Yet I thank God for granting me the occasion to do your pleasure, which I have been so eager to do."

She then went back, and after her departure all the people gathered on both sides of the gates, brandishing clubs and swords. What a huge crowd, what a dense throng of mean and angry people! In front of the portcullis they saw the half of the horse that had been severed. They were then certain that once the gates were raised, they would find within the man they intended to put to death. They had the gates that had killed many people drawn up, and since there were no traps or tents in this particular siege, they all came through together. On the inside, just across the threshold, they found the other half of the dead horse. Yet none of them could see Sir Yvain, whom they were anxious to kill. And he saw them going mad with rage and anger. "How can this be?" they exclaimed. "There is no gate or window through which anything might pass save a bird that flies, or some small animal like a squirrel or a marmot or one even smaller. The windows are barred, and the gates were shut the moment our lord went through. Dead or alive, the body is here, because there is no trace of it outside. More than half the saddle is inside, we see clearly, but we find no trace of him except the torn spurs that fell from his feet. Now let us put aside this useless chatter and search every corner, for it appears he is still here, or we are all bewitched, or else devils have snatched him from us."

Blazing with anger, they all searched round the hall for him, banging on the beds, benches, and walls, but the bed where he lay received none of their blows so that he was not touched or hit. They thrashed about the room with their clubs, raising a huge uproar like blind men groping in search of something.

While they went checking under the beds and stools, a lady, one of the most beautiful a mortal has ever seen, came in. Of so fair a Christian lady, no one has ever heard tell. But she was so distraught with grief that she was, at that moment, on the verge of suicide. She cried out at the top of her voice, then fell in a swoon. When she had been set back on her feet, she began, like a madwoman, to tear at herself and pull her hair, clawing her hands and ripping her clothing and fainting at every step. Nothing could comfort her when she saw her lord carried dead before her on the bier. Believing that she could never be consoled, she was screaming in anguish. Holy water, crosses, and candles went ahead with the nuns; then came missals, censers, and the clerics, who were to give the final absolution for the hapless soul.

Sir Yvain heard the cries of grief that could never be described, for no one could describe them, and no book has ever recorded them. Although the procession had passed by, a large crowd had gathered round the bier in the center of the hall because crimson blood, fresh and warm, was dripping from the dead man's wounds. This was clear proof that the man who had waged the combat and defeated and killed their lord was, without fail, still inside. Then they looked and searched everywhere. They overturned and ransacked everything until they were all drenched in sweat from their turmoil and distress over the crimson blood dripping before their eyes. Sir Yvain was hit and jostled a great deal where he lay, but he did not budge. And the people screamed louder and louder because of the wounds bursting open. Astounded by the bleeding, they did not know where to lay the blame. Each was saying to the other: "The murderer is among us, and we don't see him. This is astonishing, the work of the devil."

Maddened with grief, the lady screamed as though insane. "Oh God! Will no one find the murderer, the traitor who killed my good lord? Good? Indeed the best of good men! True God, it will be your fault if You let him escape from here. I should blame no one but You since You hide him from my sight. No one has ever known the abuse and injustice You do me in denying me the sight of this man, who is so close to me. Because I don't see him, I can declare that some phantom or evil spirit has come among us. And so I am the victim of a magic spell. Or else he is a coward and afraid of me. And what cowardice on his part not to dare appear before me. Ah, phantom, cowardly thing, why are you frightened of me when you were bold before my lord? Why don't I have you in my power now? Has your strength gone already? Why can I not get hold of you now? How could it happen that you killed my lord, unless by treachery? Surely you would never have defeated my lord had he seen you. In this world he had no equal. Neither God nor man knew one, and there is none like him now. Certainly, if you were mortal, you would not have dared stand against my lord, for no one could compare with him."

Thus the lady argued with herself; thus in her heart at every turn she fought; thus she tormented herself, and along with her, her people made the loudest outcry of grief possible. While the body was being carried out for burial, the men continued searching hard for the murderer until exhausted. Completely worn out, they abandoned their search, unable to see anyone in the least suspicious.

By this time the funeral service was over. The nuns and priests had returned from the church and were making their way to the tomb. But all this meant nothing to the young lady in her room. Her thoughts were on Sir Yvain, and she came to him quickly. "Dear sir," she exclaimed, "these people have been hunting in great numbers. They have stormed about searching every corner with more scrutiny than a hunting dog tracking down a partridge or quail. You have certainly felt some fear."

"On my word, you have spoken true," he replied. "I never thought I could be so afraid. Yet if possible, I would like to look through some opening or window at the procession and the corpse." Yet he had no interest in the corpse or the procession. He would gladly have seen them all go up in flames even if it cost him a hundred marks. A hundred marks? To be honest, more than a hundred thousand! But he made his request because of the lady of that town, whom he wanted to see. The young lady placed him at a small window, repaying him as best she could for the honor he had done her.

Through this window, Sir Yvain watched the beautiful lady as she spoke. "Dear sir, as God has mercy on your soul, so indeed, to my knowledge, there has never been a knight on horseback in any way your equal. Dear noble sir, no knight was ever as honorable or worthy as you. Generosity was your friend, courage your companion. May your soul be in the company of the saints, dear sweet sir." Then she struck herself and tore everything on her body her hands could grasp.

Sir Yvain could scarcely stop himself from running out to restrain her hands, whatever the consequences. But the young lady begged him, advised him, ordered and admonished him kindly and graciously to be careful not to behave foolishly. "You are well off here," she said. "Take care not to move for any reason until this grief abates and these men leave, as they soon will. If you follow the advice I offer you now, you will have much to gain. You can be quiet and sit watching the people inside and out as they go their way. Not one will ever see you, and thus great advantage will be yours. Take care also not to speak out recklessly. I think that man more stupid than wise who, when the occasion presents itself, gets carried away and acts recklessly, losing all self-restraint. If you contemplate folly, take care not to act on it. The wise man hides his folly and, if he can, puts good sense into effect. Take care now to act wisely and not risk your head, for the people would not take ransom for it. Watch out for yourself and remember my advice. Keep still until I return. I dare stay no longer. I might possibly stay so long here that I would be suspected, not being seen in the crowd with everyone else. If so, I would be severely punished."

She then went away, and he stayed behind, uncertain what to do. He was distressed because of the body he saw them burying: he had no evidence that he had slain and killed him. Without some form of proof he could show in council, he would be held in contempt. Kay was so mean and malicious, bursting with mockery and spite, that he would never be free of him: he would keep taunting him, flinging insults and abuse as he had the other day. The nasty taunts were still fresh and rankling inside him. But a new love had made a raid into Yvain's territory and gathered in all his prey, and with his sugar and honey he was soothing the knight. Yvain's enemy had his heart with her, and he was in love with the person who hated him most. Without knowing, the lady had avenged well her lord's death. She had obtained greater revenge than she ever would have accomplished had Love not avenged the death by attacking Yvain so gently, striking his heart through his eyes. This wound lasts longer than one made by lance or sword, for a sword cut is soon healed and made whole when a physician tends it. But the wound of Love worsens the nearer its physician.

This was Sir Yvain's wound, from which he could never recover, for Love had devoted himself wholly to him. Love went about searching the places he used to frequent and removed himself from them, wishing no lodging or landlord except this new one. And he acted prudently in leaving a poor lodging because he should be Yvain's entirely. He thought no part of himself should be elsewhere, and so he searched all those low lodgings.

It is a great pity that Love acts this way, conducting himself so basely that he dwells in the worst lodgings he finds as readily as in the best. But now he had come to a home of welcome where he would be cherished, and he did well to stay. This is the way Love should behave, such a highborn creature is he. How astonishing that he dares lower himself in shame to vile places! Love resembles one who sprinkles his fragrant balm on ashes and dust, who hates honor and loves reproach, who dissolves soot in honey and mixes sugar with gall. But now he behaved differently, taking a noble lodging beyond reproach.

When the body had been buried, all the people, clerics, knights, and men-at-arms, departed. Not a lady remained, except the one who made no concealment of her grief. She stayed there all alone, often clutching her throat and wringing her hands and beating her palms. She was reading psalms from a psalter illuminated with gold letters. And Sir Yvain was still at the window gazing at her. The more he looked at her, the more she delighted him and the more he loved her. Love, who caught him at the window, filled him with the desire that she stop weeping and reading and find pleasure in speaking to him. But he despaired of his desire, unable to think or believe that it might happen.

"I may consider myself a fool to desire what will never be mine," he said. "I fatally wounded her lord. And I expect to have peace with her? I have no such hope, I swear, because she hates me above all else at this moment, and she has reason. I am wise to say 'at this moment,' for a woman has more than a hundred moods. Perhaps she will soon change her present mood. No, she will change it without any 'perhaps.' I am a fool to despair. God grant that she change soon. By Love's decree, I am fated to be forever in her power. The man who does not welcome the approach of Love is guilty of misconduct and evil. And I assert, listen who will, that such a man has no right to any joy. But in this respect I shall not lose, for I will love my enemy forever. I must not hate her unless I want to betray Love. As Love decrees, so must I love. And is she to regard me as her lover? Yes, of course, since I love her. And I call her my enemy because she hates me, and she is not wrong, for she loved the man I killed. Am I then her enemy? No, I am not, but rather her lover, for I never desired to love anyone so much.

"I lament so deeply her beautiful hair, which shines more brightly than pure gold. I am tormented with anger and rage to see her tear and pull it out. The tears falling from her eyes can never dry. This is not at all to my liking. Although her eyes flow with an endless stream of tears, yet there were never eyes so beautiful, and her tears bring me agony. Still nothing distresses me more than to see her tear her face, by no means deserving of such treatment. I have never seen such a beautifully formed face, so fresh and so delicately colored. And this, that she is her own enemy, is what rends my soul. She cannot refrain from harming herself in the worst of ways, yet no crystal or mirror is so bright and polished. God, why is she so mad? Why does she not spare herself such pain? Why does she wring her beautiful hands? Why does she beat and claw her breast? Would she not be amazingly beautiful to behold were she happy? After all, she is, even now in her fury, so fair. Yes, I can certainly swear to that. Never again would Nature surpass herself in a work of beauty—she has already exceeded the limits. Or perhaps Nature never worked that way. How could this be, then? Whence would such great beauty have come? Surely God made her with His bare hands to cause Nature to stare. If Nature wished to duplicate her, she might spend all her time, and even then would fail. I doubt if God Himself could ever succeed, were He to try with all His efforts, in creating another like her.

And so Sir Yvain contemplated the lady who tortured herself with grief. I do not believe this could ever happen again, that a prisoner like Sir Yvain,

in danger of losing his head, would so madly love a woman whom he would never seek in marriage, nor, perhaps, would anyone do it on his behalf.

He remained at the window until he saw the lady depart and both portcullises lowered. Another man, who preferred his own freedom to staying there, might have grieved, yet Yvain did not care whether the portcullises were closed or open. Had they been open, he certainly would not have left, not even had the lady given him leave and freely pardoned him her lord's murder that he might depart in safety. Love and Shame assailed him from two sides and detained him. Since no one would ever believe in the success of his quest, he was ashamed to leave. On the other hand, he had such a yearning at least—if nothing more—to see the beautiful lady that his imprisonment meant nothing to him. He would rather die than leave.

The young lady returned, wishing to keep him company, to comfort and entertain him, and to obtain and bring him whatever he wanted. She found him preoccupied and languid from the love that had laid hold of him. "Sir Yvain, how has the world been treating you?" she asked.

"I have had a very pleasant time," he answered.

"Pleasant? For God's sake, do you tell the truth? How can anyone have a pleasant time when he sees himself hunted to death? That man desires and longs for his own death."

"My dear friend," he said, "I assure you I do not wish to die. As God is my witness, I was delighted the entire time by what I saw, I was delighted, and I will be delighted always."

"Let us talk no more of this," she said, realizing the meaning of his statement. "I am not so foolish or so mad as not to understand well your words. But follow me now. I am going to take immediate steps to release you from prison. If you wish, I shall set you free, tonight or tomorrow. Come now, and I shall lead the way."

"Be certain I shall never leave here secretly, like a thief," he answered. "More honor will be mine if I leave when the people are all gathered outside in the streets than if I go during the night."

With these words he followed her into the small room. The resourceful young lady, eager to serve him, lent him everything he needed. And when the occasion arose, she recalled what he had told her, that he was delighted by what he saw when his mortal enemies were searching the hall for him.

The young lady stood in such favor with her lady that she was not afraid to speak openly, even on matters of importance, for she was her adviser and her attendant. So why should she be afraid to console her lady and remind her of her welfare? At the first opportunity, she spoke to her privately. "Lady, I marvel to see your foolish behavior. Lady, do you expect to recover your lord with your grief?"

"Not at all," she replied, "but if I had my way, I would die of sorrow."

"Why?"

"To follow him."

"Follow him? God forbid! And may God give you as fine a lord again as He can."

"You never uttered such a lie. He could not give me so fine a lord."

"He will give you a better one, if you would accept him, and I shall prove this."

"Go away! Be quiet! I shall never find such a man."

"Yes you will, lady, if you agree. But tell me now, if you don't mind, who will defend your land when King Arthur comes here, for he is supposed to arrive at the spring and the stone next week? You have already heard of this in letters the Damsel of the Wilds sent you. Ah, how kind she was to you! Now you should be planning the defense of your spring, and yet you don't stop weeping. Please, my dear lady, you must not delay. As you well know, all your knights are certainly not worth a chambermaid. Even the best will not pick up a shield or lance. You have many cowardly men; not one would ever dare mount a horse. And the king is coming with so large a force that he will capture everything, without opposition."

The lady understood and realized the sincerity of the advice, but she had a foolish quality common to other women; in fact, nearly all women have it. They recognize their folly yet refuse to relinquish their desire.

"Get out!" she exclaimed. "Leave me alone! If I ever hear you talk that way again, it will be to your misfortune unless you flee. You talk so much you tire me."

"Very well, lady," she replied. "It is most obvious that you are a woman, for a woman becomes angry when she hears someone giving her good advice."

She then went away, leaving her alone. On reflection the lady realized that she had been quite wrong. She would have been delighted to know how the young lady could prove that a knight better than her lord could be found. She would have been glad to hear her speak, but she had forbidden it. With this thought in mind, she waited for her return. The command of silence had no effect, for the young lady began at once to speak again. "Ah, lady, is it now fitting to kill yourself with sorrow? For God's sake control yourself. Stop this, if only out of shame. It is not right for such a noble lady to continue mourning so long. Remember your honor and your great nobility. Do you believe all valor died with your lord? There are still other men in the world as fine as he was, or better."

"God confound me if you are not lying! And yet name a single man reputed to be as valiant as my lord was during his lifetime."

"If I did, you would be mad at me. You would be angry and threaten me once more."

"No, I promise you, I will not."

"May it be for your future benefit, if it would please you. And God grant that it does please you. Since no one is listening or overhears us, I see no reason why I should keep quiet. You will think me presumptuous, of course, but in my opinion I may assert: when two armed knights come together in combat, which man is better, do you think, when one defeats the other? I would award the prize to the winner. What would you do?"

"I think you are laying a trap for me, and you want to catch me in my words."

"I swear I am right, you can be certain, and I shall prove to you that, of necessity, the one who defeated your lord is better than he was."

"Now I have heard the most absurd statement ever made. Get out, you possessed creature. Never come before me again to say a word about him."

"I was certain you would not thank me, lady. That is what I said before I began. But you made with me an agreement not to be mad or angry, and yet you have held to my trust badly. Now that is precisely what has happened to me. You told me your pleasure, and I was foolish to speak."

The young lady then returned to her room where Sir Yvain was staying; she was providing him with the utmost comfort. But because he could not see the lady, nothing pleased him, and he paid no attention and closed his ears to the young lady's pleas to him.

All night long, worry about the defense of her spring deeply perturbed the lady. She began to feel shame for insulting and blaming her young lady so spitefully. Beyond a doubt, she knew that her young lady would never have mentioned him for reward or payment or for any love she herself felt for him. And she realized that the young lady loved her more than him and would never offer advice that would bring disgrace or embarrassment— she was too loyal a friend for that. Behold now the lady's altered attitude: she did not expect to regain the love of the young lady she had insulted. And as for the man she had repulsed, she pardoned him most fairly, by reason and by right of plea, since he had not wronged her. She was arguing as though he had come before her, and this was the way she began the case. "Then would you deny," she asked, "that you killed my lord?" "That," he replied, "I cannot deny. So I admit it." "Then tell me why you did it. To hurt me? Or out of hatred or spite?" "May death take me if I ever did it to hurt you." "Then you have not wronged me at all, nor did you wrong my lord, for if he could, he would have killed you. And so, to my mind, my judgment is fair and right."

And so by her own arguments she found justice, wisdom, and reason there so that she had no cause to hate him. She spoke as she would like the situation to be, and by her own efforts she was kindling her love like the smoldering fire that ignites without anyone blowing or stirring it. If the young lady had come at that moment, she would have won the argument in which she had pleaded so much and received such abuse.

The next morning the young lady returned and resumed her plea where she had left off. The lady bowed her head, feeling guilty that she had insulted her. Now, however, she wished to make amends and ask the name, the rank, and the family of the knight. Wisely she humbled herself. "I wish to beg your pardon for the arrogant and offensive words I foolishly spoke to you," she said. "I shall follow your counsel. If you know, tell me about the knight you spoke of at such length. What kind of man is he? From what family does he come? If he is worthy of me, and if he agrees, I shall make him, I promise you, lord of my land and of me. But he will have to behave so that no one can reproach me with the words: 'There she is, the one who married her lord's murderer.' "

"In God's name, lady, it shall be so. You will have the most noble, the most worthy, and the most handsome lord ever descended from Abel's line."

"What is his name?"

"Sir Yvain."

"On my word, he is not base-born. He is a most noble man, I know well. He is the son of King Urien."

"On my word, lady, you speak the truth."

"And when can we have him here?"

"In five days."

"That would be too long. It is my will that he come now. Let him come tonight or tomorrow at the latest."

"Lady, I doubt a bird can fly that far in one day. But I shall send the fastest servant I have. I expect him to reach King Arthur's court at the latest tomorrow night. He will not be found nearer than that."

"That is still too late. The days are long. Tell him to race faster than usual and be back here tomorrow night. If he wishes, he will exert himself and make two days' journey in one. Tonight the moon will shine; so let him turn night into day. On his return, I shall present him with any gift he wants from me."

"Leave this matter to me. You will have him here within three days at the latest. Tomorrow summon your men and seek counsel about the king's imminent visit. You should consult them about upholding the tradition of the defense of your spring. There will never be one, highborn as he may be, who will dare boast going there. Then you will have every right to declare that you must take a husband. A knight of great renown seeks your hand. Yet you dare not accept him without their unanimous agreement and approval. What cowards are they all! In order to pass to someone else a burden they find too heavy, they will all fall at your feet and thank you since they will be freed from great terror. The man who fears his own shadow eagerly avoids, if he can, facing a javelin or a lance, for that is an awful sport for a coward."

"On my word, that is my wish. So I agree," the lady answered. "I had already devised the plan you described, and that is what we will do. But why do you stay here? Go! Delay no longer! Do all you can to have him here, and I shall remain with my people." And so their conversation ended.

The young lady pretended to send for Sir Yvain in his land. Every day, however, she bathed him, and washed and groomed his hair. In addition she prepared for him a vermilion robe of rich wool trimmed with fur that still had the chalk marks. There was nothing she would not lend him to adorn his attire: for fastening at his neck, a gold clasp ornamented with precious stones, designed in that land with such elegance, and a belt with a purse made of costly brocade. She fitted him out fully, then informed her lady that her messenger had returned with his task prudently completed.

"What? When will Sir Yvain come?" she asked.

"He is here already."

"He is here? Then come alone and secretly when no one is with me. See to it no one else comes here, for I would hate the appearance of a fourth."

The young lady then departed. She came back to her guest, though her face did not reveal the joy in her heart. Instead she told him that her lady knew she had hidden him there. "Sir Yvain, by God, it is useless to hide anything," she exclaimed. "Your entire story is widely known. My lady knows about you and holds me responsible. Hateful are her reproaches to me. But she has assured me that I may bring you before her without risk of your injury or harm. None of this will displease you, I believe, except for this, and I must not lie to you or else I would commit treason. She wishes to have you in her prison, and she wants the whole body there so that not even the heart is outside."

"I certainly agree. That will bring me no displeasure, for I long to be in her prison," he answered.

"And so you will, by my right hand I promise you. Come now, but take my advice. Be meek in front of her so that your imprisonment may not be severe. Otherwise, do not be dismayed. I don't think you will find imprisonment too unpleasant."

And so the young lady led him away, alarming him, then reassuring him, speaking in veiled references of the place where he would be imprisoned, since every lover is in prison. She was correct in calling him a prisoner, for every lover is a prisoner.

The young lady led Sir Yvain by the hand to the place where he would be cherished. He feared an unfavorable reception, and his fear was not surprising. They saw the lady seated on a large vermilion bedcover. Great fear, I assure you, had Sir Yvain as he entered the room. When they beheld the lady, she did not utter a word. Her silence filled Yvain with dread. Terror seized him, for he thought he had been betrayed. He stood there motionless until the young lady finally spoke. "Five hundred curses on a person who brings to a beautiful lady's room a knight who does not draw near, who has not mouth or tongue or even the sense to introduce himself!" she exclaimed. Taking him at once by the arm, she added: "Step forward, knight. Have no fear that my lady will bite you. Implore her peace and accord. And I shall pray with you that she pardons you the death of Esclados the Red, who was her lord."

Without further delay, Sir Yvain joined his hands, knelt down, and spoke like a true lover. "Lady, in truth, I shall never implore your mercy. On the contrary, I shall be grateful to you for anything you would do to me. Nothing could displease me."

"Nothing, sir? And if I kill you?"

"Lady, I shall thank you. You will never hear me say anything else."

"I have never heard anything like this," she said. "You place yourself at my will completely without being compelled."

"Lady, in truth, there is no force so strong as the one compelling me to conform to your will completely. I am not afraid to do anything you are pleased to command me. And if I could atone for the death in which I have wronged you, I would atone without further ado."

"What?" she asked. "Tell me now and be free of the atonement. Did you wrong me when you killed my lord?"

"Lady, have pity," he said. "When your lord attacked me, was I wrong to defend myself? When one man in self-defense kills another who wants to capture or kill him, tell if he bears any blame."

"Not at all, if one judges rightly, and I think there would be no value in having you put to death. I am eager to know whence this force comes that commands you to assent to my will unquestioningly. I absolve you of all offenses and all misdeeds. Be seated, and tell me why you are so submissive."

"Lady," he answered, "the force comes from my heart, which is in your control. My heart has given me this desire."

"And what inspired your heart, dear friend?"

"Lady, my eyes."

"And what inspired the eyes?"

"The great beauty I beheld in you."

"Then is beauty at fault?"

"Lady, because it makes me lo ‹ .'

"Love? And whom?"

"You, dear lady."

"Me?"

"Truly indeed."

"In what way?"

"In such a way that my love cannot be greater. My heart will not stir from you, nor do I find it elsewhere. I cannot think of anything else. I give myself to you entirely. I love you more than I love myself. I shall gladly live or die for you according to your pleasure."

"And would you dare undertake the defense of my spring for me?"

"Yes of course, lady, against all men."

"Know then that we are in accord."

Thus they had reached a swift agreement. Before this the lady had held council with her barons, and so she declared: "From here we shall proceed to the great hall where the men are assembled. Because of the urgency they see, they have counseled and urged me to take a husband. Here and now I present myself to you. I shall never go back on my decision. I should not refuse as my lord a fine knight and a king's son."

Now all the young lady's wishes had been perfectly realized. Sir Yvain no longer suffered any pain. I can tell and relate this to you well, for the lady took him with her into the great hall, which was filled with knights and men-at-arms. Sir Yvain had such a noble bearing that they all gazed at him in awe and rose to their feet when the two entered. They all saluted and bowed to Sir Yvain. "This is the man who will marry our lady," they surmised. "Damn anyone who opposes him, for he seems a wonderfully worthy man. Certainly with him the Empress of Rome would have a fine match. Would that our lady were already engaged to him, and he to her, their bare hands joined, and the wedding occurring today or tomorrow." And thus they all spoke, one after the other.

The lady went to sit on a bench at the end of the hall where everyone could see her. When Sir Yvain seemed about to sit at her feet, she had him rise. She asked her seneschal to speak out so that everyone could hear. The seneschal, not arrogant or hesitant, then began. "Lords," he proclaimed, "we are at war. Every day the king prepares all the force he can muster to come and ravage our lands. Within a fortnight everything will be laid waste unless there is a good protector. When my lady married nearly six years ago, she did so on your advice. Now she is sad: her lord is dead. The man who held all this country and adorned it so well has now but a plot of earth. Such a shame that his life was so short. A woman is incapable of carrying a shield or striking with a lance. If our lady could marry a fine lord, she would improve and strengthen her position. Never was there greater need than now. Do you all advise her to take a lord before the tradition ends that has been observed in this town for more than sixty years?"

When he finished, everyone present agreed that such a course of action seemed proper, and they all came to her feet. Their attitude only increased her desire, and she let them urge her until, as though against her will, she agreed to do what she would have done even if all had opposed her. "Since this is your will, lords," she said. "This knight seated beside me has wooed me and asked my hand. He would attach himself as my liegeman and submit himself to my service. I am grateful for this, and you too should be grateful. I do not know him personally, it is true, but I have heard much said of him. He is a noble man, you can be certain, for he is the son of King Urien. Even beyond his high birth, he is a man of such great valor, and has such courtesy and wisdom that I should not be dissuaded. I believe you have all heard of Sir Yvain. It is he who asks my hand. I shall have a more noble lord than I deserve on the day when this happens."

"If you act wisely," they all exclaimed, "this day will never pass without the marriage taking place. It is a fool who delays a single hour acting for his own benefit."

Because of their entreaty, she agreed to do what she would have done anyway, for Love ordered her to take the action for which she asked counsel and advice. But there was much greater honor in her marriage because she had her people's permission. Far from displeasing her, their urging stirred and incited her heart to act as it desired. A fast-moving horse gallops even more quickly when prodded. Before all her barons, the lady offered her hand to Sir Yvain.

The next morning, from one of her chaplains, he received the Lady of Landuc [Laudine], the daughter of Duke Laududet, the hero of a lay. And so that very day, without further delay, he married her and they celebrated their nuptials. There were many mitres and croziers, for the lady had summoned her bishops and her abbots. Many people of great nobility attended. Joy and happiness were in abundance, more than I could recount to you even after further thought. I prefer to keep silent rather than say more.

From then on Sir Yvain was lord and the dead man completely forgotten. His killer was now the husband of his widow, and they lay together. The people loved and esteemed the living lord more than they ever did the dead lord.

Yvain was well served at the marriage celebrations, which lasted until the eve of the king's arrival with his company at the marvelous spring and the stone. And his entire household was on this expedition, for no one had stayed behind.

"In God's name, what has happened to Sir Yvain?" Sir Kay exclaimed. "After dinner he boasted of going to avenge his cousin's disgrace, and he has not come. It is obvious that he was drunk. He has run away, I suppose. He would not dare come at any price. What great arrogance to make such a boast! Bold indeed is the man who dares praise an exploit no one else praises, and who has no witness of his merit unless that of false flattery. What a difference between a coward and a man of valor! Round the fire the coward brags about himself; he regards all men as fools and believes that no one knows his true character. The brave man would be distressed to hear someone relate his valorous deeds. Yet I certainly agree with the coward, who is not wrong to boast. If he doesn't speak for himself, who will? The heralds pass over him in silence when they announce the names of the brave and discard those of cowards. No one can be found to lie for cowards. Foolish is the man who praises himself and brags."

These were Sir Kay's words; then Sir Gawain spoke. "Enough, Sir Kay, enough! If Sir Yvain is not here at the moment, you do not know what prevents him. To be certain, he never lowered himself to utter such insults about you. For his part, he has shown courtesy."

"Sir," he replied, "I shall keep quiet. Since I see you are offended, you will not hear me speak of him again today."

In order to see the rain, the king poured a full basin of water on the stone beneath the pine, and at once rain came down in torrents. The wait was not very long before Sir Yvain, fully armed, entered the forest without pause, galloping at breakneck speed on a tall and sleek horse that was strong, bold, and swift. Sir Kay resolved to request the right to combat, for whatever the outcome, he always sought to open the battles and combats; he would be furious if such were not the case. Before all, he came to the feet of the king to be granted this combat. "Kay," the king said, "since it is your desire, and since you have asked it ahead of all the others, you should not be denied." Kay thanked him, then mounted.

Sir Yvain recognized Kay by his armor. Could he disgrace him but a little, he would be pleased and do it gladly. He took his shield by the straps, and Kay took his, and they rushed at each other, spurring their horses and lowering their tightly gripped lances. They thrust them a little forward so that they held them by the leather-covered butts. When they came together, they strove to deliver such blows that the two lances broke in pieces and split to the butts. Sir Yvain dealt Kay such a powerful blow that he somersaulted from his saddle, hitting the ground on his helmet. Not seeking to do him further harm, Sir Yvain dismounted and took his horse. This outcome pleased the many spectators. "Ha, ha, you insulted others, and now look where you lie," several exclaimed. "Yet it is right indeed that you be forgiven this time since this has never happened to you."

In the meantime, Sir Yvain came before the king, leading the horse by the bridle with the intention of returning it to him. "Lord," he said to him, "have this horse taken away, for I would be wrong to keep anything of yours."

"Who are you?" the king asked. "For I should never know you by your speech, unless I saw your face or heard your name."

Sir Yvain then revealed his name. Kay was overwhelmed with shame, almost dying of humiliation since he had accused him of running away. In their delight the others felt great joy in Yvain's honor. The king himself rejoiced, and Sir Gawain, loving Yvain's company more than the company of any knight he knew, was a hundred times happier than anyone else.

Anxious to learn of Yvain's entire adventure, the king earnestly implored him, if he did not mind, to tell them how he had fared, and urged him to give an accurate account. Yvain recounted to them everything about the young lady's kind service to him, detailing all without omission. Then he invited the king and all his knights to come and stay with him, adding that they would give him joy and honor by taking lodging with him. The king replied that he would gladly give him such affection, pleasure, and company for a full week. Sir Yvain thanked him. Making no further delay, they mounted at once and proceeded directly to the town. Ahead of the party, Sir Yvain sent a squire with a crane-hunting falcon so that the company would not come upon the lady by surprise and her people would decorate their houses in the king's honor.

The lady was delighted with the tidings of the king's approach; in fact, everyone who heard the news was happy and elated. The lady summoned all her people and asked them to ride out to meet him. There was no grumbling or complaining; all were eager to do her will.

Mounted on their tall Spanish steeds, they all rode to meet the King of Britain. With great ceremony they welcomed first King Arthur, then all his company. "Welcome to this company composed of so many worthy men!" they exclaimed. "The man leading them and giving them such fine lodging is a great man!" In honor of the king, the town resounded in jubilation. Silk draperies were brought out and hung as decorations, tapestries were spread outside and draped along the streets for the king the people awaited. They prepared still more, stringing awnings over the streets to protect the king from the sun. Bells, horns, and trumpets made the town reverberate with their music so that no one could have heard God's thunder. Where they dismounted, maidens played flutes and viols, tambourines, pipes, and drums. Elsewhere nimble young men performed their acrobatics. All threw themselves into the festivity, and in this joy they offered their lord a fitting welcome.

The lady came forth, regally dressed in a robe with fresh ermine trim, a diadem on her head all adorned with rubies. Her face showed no trace of annoyance, only joy and laughter, so that, in my opinion, she was more beautiful than any countess. The crowd was pressing all around her, and everyone, one after the other, was calling: "Welcome to the king, the lord of kings and lords of this world!"

Before the king could reply to everyone, he saw the lady coming toward him to hold his stirrup. Not wishing to let this happen, he hastened to dismount the moment he saw her. "Welcome a hundred thousand times to my lord king," she addressed him in greeting, "and blessed be Sir Gawain, his nephew."

"May you and your person, creature of beauty, have joy and great good fortune," the king replied. Then, like the noble and courteous man he was, the king embraced her around the waist, and she embraced him with open arms. I am saying nothing more about the welcome she offered them, though no one ever heard tell of people who treated their guests with so much joy, honor, and service. I could relate to you a great deal about the joy were I not concerned about the waste of my words.

I do want to say a brief word about a private meeting that took place between the sun and the moon. Do you know of whom I would speak to you? The man who was the lord of knights, renowned above all, must be called the sun. I refer to Sir Gawain. His example enhances all chivalry as the morning sun casts its rays abroad and lights all the places where it shines. And I call her the moon, for there can never be but one of such great loyalty and strong support. I call her this, however, not only because of her high reputation, but because her name was Lunete.

Lunete, attractive and of dark-brown hair, was a wise, intelligent, and shrewd young lady. She came to know Sir Gawain, who loved and esteemed her very much. Because she had saved his friend and companion from death, he called her his beloved and placed himself at her service. She told him of her great trouble in persuading her lady to marry Sir Yvain, and described how she had protected him from those who searched for him. He was among them, and they did not see him. Her account made Sir Gawain laugh. "My young lady," he said, "such as I am, I present myself as your knight both when you need me and when you don't. Unless you think you will do better, do not replace me with someone else. I am yours, and from now on be my lady."

"Thank you, sir," she replied. And while these two were becoming acquainted, the others were flirting. There were about ninety other ladies, and each one was beautiful and charming, noble, intelligent, prudent, and wise, ladies of noble birth and high lineage. And so the men were able to amuse themselves by conversing with them, looking at them, and sitting beside them, as well as kissing and caressing them. At least that much pleasure was theirs.

Sir Yvain was gratified to have the king staying with them. His lady honored the guests so much, both individually and as a group, that some fool might think her courteous behavior was prompted by love. But such people are simple-minded who think they are loved because a lady is courteous enough to speak to some unfortunate fellow and make him happy by embracing him. A fool is pleased by pretty words, and is easily deluded.

Everyone had a full week of pleasure. For those who wished, there was sport in hunting in the woods and hawking by the river. Whoever wanted to see the country Sir Yvain had acquired by his marriage to the lady could go and enjoy himself by visiting the castles located within four, five, or six leagues.

When the king had sojourned there until he wished to stay no longer, he had preparations made for his departure. During that week, all the men had begged and pressed Sir Yvain, as insistently as they could, to let them lead him off with them. "What?" Sir Gawain asked. "Will you be like those men who are less worthy because of their wives? Holy Mary damn the man who marries and regresses! When a man has a beautiful lady as his beloved or his wife, he should lead a better life. It is not right for her to love him after his honor and his renown cease. Certainly you would be angry too if you grew soft from her love. A woman quickly withdraws her love—and has every right to do so—and despises the man, in the realm where he is lord, who regresses because of her. Now more than ever your renown should increase. Break loose from the bridle and the halter, and we shall go to tournaments, you and I, so that people will not call you jealous. You must not daydream now. You have to frequent and engage in tournaments and strike with all your force, whatever the cost. He is indeed in a dream who does not stir. You have to come, I assure you. Do not try to evade. Take care our companionship not lapse on your side, dear companion, for it is not going to end on my account.

"It is a wonder how a man values a life of never-ending ease. It is good to wait for joy. A small pleasure when delayed is sweeter than a large pleasure enjoyed at once. The joy of late love is like green firewood when set aflame, for the longer the wait in lighting, the greater heat it yields and the longer its force lasts. One may grow accustomed to habits that are hard to throw off. When the wish to do so comes, it is impossible.

"I grant you, if I had such a beautiful beloved as you do, dear companion, then by the faith I owe God and all the saints, I would leave her most reluctantly. I would be a fool, I know. But one offers good advice to another that he would not take himself, as preachers who are faithless and dissolute teach and proclaim what is right with no intention of practicing it."

Sir Gawain spoke so often, and with such strong insistence, that his companion promised to speak of this to his wife and then to set out if he could obtain her leave. Whether this was wise or foolish to do, he would not return to Britain without her permission. When he took his lady aside to discuss the matter, she was not expecting a request for permission to depart. "My dearest lady," he said to her, "you are my heart and my soul, my well-being, my joy, and my happiness. Grant me one favor for your honor and for mine."

Although the lady did not know what he wished to ask, she consented at once. "Dear sir," she replied, "you may ask me whatever you please."

Sir Yvain immediately asked her leave to accompany the king and attend tournaments so that he would not be called derelict in duty. "I grant you leave for a fixed time," she answered. "But be absolutely certain, the love I have for you will turn to hate if you outstay the term I tell you. Know that I will never fail to keep my promise. If you break your word, I will hold to mine. If you want my love and hold me dearest of all, plan to return again at the latest a year from now, that is, a week after the Feast of Saint John, for today is the octave of that feast. You will forfeit my love if you fail to return to me by that day."

Sir Yvain sighed and wept so heavily that he could scarcely speak. "Lady, that is a very long time. If I could at will be a dove, I would be here often at your side. I pray God that, if it be His will, He not keep me from you that long. But a man who does not know what lies ahead believes he will return with great dispatch. I do not know what will happen to me, for some hindrance, such as illness or imprisonment, may detain me. You have been most unjust not to make an exception at least for physical incapacity."

"Sir, I grant this exception," she answered. "And yet I promise you, if God keeps you from death, nothing will prevent your return so long as you remember me. Now slip this ring of mine on your finger. I lend it to you. I want to be very clear in my remarks about the stone. No true and loyal lover suffers imprisonment or loss of blood, nor can any misfortune befall him provided he wears and cherishes the ring and remembers his beloved. And so he becomes stronger than steel. This will be your shield and hauberk. Never before have I desired to lend or give it to any knight. But I give it to you because I love you."

Now Sir Yvain had leave to depart, and he wept as he took his leave.

The king had no desire to tarry longer, no matter what was said. He was eager that all their palfreys be bridled, harnessed, and brought out, and his will was heeded at once. After the palfreys were led out, there was nothing left to do but mount.

I do not know whether I should tell more about Sir Yvain's departure and the kisses mixed with tears and steeped in sweetness that were bestowed on him as he left. And what should I say of the king, how the lady escorted him, accompanied by her maids-in-waiting as well as all her knights? I would spend too much time here. Because the lady was weeping, the king urged her not to proceed farther, but to return home. He implored her so much that, escorted by her people, she turned back in deep sadness.

Sir Yvain was so distressed at departing from his beloved that his heart did not leave. The king could lead the body, but not the heart, which attached itself so strongly to the heart of the lady left behind that he did not have the power to draw it away. The body cannot possibly live without the heart, and no man has ever seen such a wonder as the body alive without the heart. Yet this wonder did happen. The body still held on to life without the heart, which, though accustomed to lodging there, had no desire to follow the body farther. The heart found a good home, and the body lived in hope of returning to its heart. In place of the heart, the body had, in a strange manner, created a substitute out of hope, which often proves the traitor and breaks promises.

I do not think Yvain will ever recognize the time when hope will play him false. If he overstays the appointed term a single day, he will find truce or peace with his lady only with difficulty. Yet I expect he will overstay the time, for Sir Gawain will not let him depart.

Both of them went jousting wherever tournaments were held. Meanwhile, the year was passing by, and all year Sir Yvain performed so well that Sir Gawain was at pains to honor him and prevailed upon him to stay so long that the entire year slipped past, and much of the next too.

It was mid-August now, and the king was holding court amid festivities. The two knights had returned from a tournament where Sir Yvain had been the day before, and the tale relates, as I believe, that they had won all the honor. They had their pavilion pitched outside the town, having decided not to stay in the town, and held court there. They never went to the king's court; instead the king came to theirs, for their company had the best knights, and the vast majority.

King Arthur was seated among them when Yvain began to be consumed by his thoughts, and none had disturbed him so much since the time he took leave of his lady, for he realized that he had broken his promise and overstayed the time. He was scarcely able to hold his tears, but did so out of shame.

He was still deep in thought when they saw a young lady directly approach at a gallop on a black piebald palfrey. She dismounted in front of their pavilion, where no one helped her down or went to take her horse. As soon as she could see the king, she let her cloak fall. Without a cloak she entered the pavilion and presented herself before the king. She announced that her lady sent greetings to the king, to Sir Gawain, and to all the others except Yvain, the liar, the hypocrite, the disloyal traitor, who had tricked and deceived her. "Well has she recognized the treachery of this man, who purported to be a true lover but was a fool, a deceitful scoundrel. This thief has betrayed his lady, who had no experience of baseness, and never imagined that he was about to steal her heart. Lovers do not steal hearts. There are some who call lovers thieves, yet these people are blind in matters of love and know nothing about it. The lover takes the heart of his beloved, not to steal it but to protect it against those thieves, who seem worthy men but are themselves the robbers. These men are hypocrites, traitors, and robbers, who compete in stealing hearts they do not care about. But wherever the lover goes, he cherishes the heart and brings it back. Sir Yvain has killed his lady, for she believed that he would guard her heart and bring it back to her before the year had passed.

"Yvain, how remiss of you! You could not remember that you were to return to my lady within a year. She gave you leave to be away until the Feast of Saint John, and you respected her so little that you never again gave mind to the agreement. In her chamber my lady noted every day and every moment. When you are in love, anxiety prevents real sleep, and all night long the true lover reckons and counts the days as they come and go, in this way enduring the time passing. My lady's complaint is not premature or unreasonable. I say nothing by way of indictment, but this much I do say: the man who broke his promise to my lady has betrayed us.

"Yvain, my lady no longer has care for you. Through me she sends you word to return to her never and to keep her ring no more. She commands you to send it back to her with me, whom you see here before you. Give it back to her, for you are bound to return it."

Yvain could not answer, for he found himself bereft of speech and sense. The young lady stepped forward and took the ring from his finger. She then commended to God the king and all the others, except the man she left in deep distress.

Yvain became constantly more wretched. All he saw tormented him; all he heard tortured him. He wanted to flee by himself to some wild land where no one would know or seek him, where man or woman would know no more of him than if he had fallen into a bottomless pit. He hated himself above all, and knew no one to console him in the death he had brought upon himself. He would rather go mad than be unable to take revenge on himself, robbed, as he was, of joy through his own fault. He left the barons for fear of going mad in their presence. For their part, they paid no attention to him and let him go off by himself, realizing he had little interest in their conversation or company. And so he went away, far from the tents and the pavilions.

So violent a whirlwind broke loose in Yvain's head that he went mad. He clawed his flesh and ripped his clothing; he fled across meadows and fields, leaving his men bewildered and wondering where he could be. They went searching for him to left and right, in the lodging of knights, through hedgerows and orchards; yet they looked for him where he was not to be found.

Yvain continued to flee until, beside a park, he came upon a boy carrying a bow and five sharp, barbed, broadheaded arrows. He approached the boy because he wanted to take the bow and arrows he held. Yet afterwards he remembered nothing he had done.

In the woods he lay in wait for animals, then slew them and ate their flesh raw. And thus he lived, like a man wild and savage, until he came upon a small, meager cottage belonging to a hermit. The hermit was clearing his ground, and when he saw the naked man, he was convinced the man was mad. Such, indeed, was the case, as he understood clearly. Out of fear he shut himself in his little cottage. Yet out of charity the good man took some of his bread and his fresh water and placed them on a narrow window ledge outside his cottage. The other, craving the bread, approached. He took the food and chewed it. I do not believe he had ever tasted such hard, bitter bread. The measure of barley in the bread had cost no more than twenty sous. Yet hunger is a well-mixed and well-prepared sauce for any food, and Sir Yvain devoured the hermit's bread, which tasted fine to him, and drank the cold water from the jug.

After Yvain had eaten, he rushed back into the woods and hunted stags and does. When the good man saw him leave, he prayed under his roof to God to defend him and protect him, lest the man ever come there again. But there is no one, however senseless, who does not return eagerly to the place where he receives good treatment. And so while Yvain was mad, not a week passed that he did not carry some wild animal to the hermit's door. Thus he lived, and the good man undertook to stretch out the skins for him and cook a large portion of the meat. There was always the bread and the water in the jug on the window ledge for the madman's nourishment: food and drink were his, venison without salt or pepper and cold spring water. And the good man also took it upon himself to sell the skins and buy bread made of barley and unleavened rye. In this way Yvain had an ample supply of bread and venison which the hermit provided him. The supply lasted a long time.

Finally, one day, Yvain was found sleeping in the forest by two maids-in-waiting, who were accompanying their lady. One of the trio dismounted and hurried to the naked man they had sighted. She examined him closely without finding any sign that made her recognize him. If he had been richly attired, as he often was, she would have easily recognized him, for she had seen him many times. But she was slow to recognize him and continued examining him until she finally noticed a facial scar. Sir Yvain, she knew well, had such a scar on his face, for she had seen him often. From the scar, she was absolutely certain of his identity. Yet she wondered a great deal about what had happened to him that she found him so, destitute and naked. In amazement she crossed herself many times. Yet she did not disturb or waken him. Taking her horse, she remounted and rode to the others. Amid tears she told them all that had happened to her. I do not know why

I should delay by telling you of her distress. She addressed her lady tearfully. "Lady, I have discovered Yvain, the most gifted and most distinguished knight on earth. But I don't know what misfortune has brought the noble man to such a plight. Perhaps some grief of his makes him act like this, for a man may go mad through grief. It is most evident that he is not in his right mind, for were he sane, he would not behave so indecently. If only God would restore his senses to what they once were, and then, that Yvain would be pleased to come to your aid! In his war with you, Count Alier has made too many heavy assaults. I see this war between you two ended to your great honor, if God were to favor Yvain so that he regained his sanity and undertook to help you in this time of need."

"Take care now," the lady replied. "If he does not take to flight, then certainly, with God's help, I believe we shall remove all the frenzy and insanity from his head. But we must set out immediately. I remember an ointment Morgan the Wise gave me, and she told me it would remove from the mind any grave illness."

They rode at once to the castle, which was within a half-league of the kind of leagues they have in that country. As compared with ours, two of their leagues equal one, and four equal two. So while Yvain remained there all alone and asleep, the lady went to get the ointment. She opened a chest of hers, took out the box, and gave it to her maid, telling her not to be too liberal in its use, but to apply it only to the temples and the forehead, as there was no need to apply it anywhere else. She should rub it into the temples and the forehead, then hold on to the remainder carefully, for there was nothing wrong with him except in his brain. She also had a fur-trimmed outfit, a jacket and a cloak of scarlet silk, brought out. She carried these and led a fine palfrey on her right. And to these supplies she added, from her own belongings, a shirt, some soft breeches, and fine black stockings.

The maid set out at once and found him still asleep where she had left him. She took her horses to a thicket where she tied them securely. Carrying all the clothing and the ointment, she came to the spot where he was sleeping. She had enough daring to approach the madman in order to touch and minister to him. She massaged him with the ointment until the box was empty, for she was so anxious for his recovery that she applied it freely all over his body. She paid no heed to her lady's warning, nor even remembered it. She applied more than was necessary, convinced that she was acting for the best. She rubbed the temples, the forehead, the entire body down to the toes; indeed, she rubbed so much on the temples and along the entire body in the hot sun that she drove the melancholy and madness from his brain. Yet she was foolish to rub the body, for that was unnecessary. If she had had five measures of ointment, I think she would have done the same. Then she took the box and rushed off to hide near her horses. She left the clothing there because she wanted him, if he revived, to see it laid out and take it and dress. She waited behind a large oak tree until he had had enough sleep.

When he awoke, he had regained his reason and his memory. Seeing himself naked as ivory, he was deeply shamed, and would have been more so had he known what had happened to him. But he had no idea why he found himself naked. When he saw the new clothes before him, he was astonished as to how and by what chance the clothing had come there. Disturbed and embarrassed by his nakedness, he admitted that he would be undone and dead if anyone discovered and recognized him in this condition.

He quickly dressed himself and looked toward the woods to see if anyone was approaching. He tried to get up and stand, but could not manage to move a step. Because his grave illness had the effect of making him scarcely able to stand on his feet, he needed assistance, someone to help him and to guide him.

Then the maid decided to wait no longer. She mounted and rode near him, pretending not to know he was there. He struggled to call to her. His need was so great that he did not care who helped him; he only wanted to be taken to a lodging where he would regain his strength to some degree. The maid looked round as though she did not know what was happening. As if bewildered, she rode here and there, not wishing to proceed directly to him. He then began to shout again. "Lady! Over here! Over here!" And the maid guided her soft-stepping palfrey toward him. Under this pretense she made him believe that she knew nothing about him and had never seen him before. In this way she showed courtesy and wisdom.

When she came before him, she addressed him. "Sir Knight, what do you want that you summon me so urgently?"

"Ah, wise young lady," he answered, "by some mishap, I know not what, I have found myself here in these woods. By God and your own faith, I beg you lend or give me outright, at any price, that palfrey you are leading."

"Gladly, sir. But do accompany me where I am going."

"Where?" he asked.

"Out of these woods to a castle near here."

"Lady, tell me now if you are in need of me."

"Yes indeed," she said, "though I do not believe you are in the best of health. You should rest for at least a fortnight. Take the horse I lead on my right, and we shall ride to lodging."

He wanted nothing more, and so took the horse and mounted. As they rode along, they came to a bridge over a turbulent, swift-flowing stream. The maid threw in the empty box she carried. She hoped to excuse herself to her lady about the ointment by saying that it was her misfortune that as she crossed the bridge, the box fell into the stream. Because her palfrey tripped, the box slipped from her hand. She nearly fell in after, but then the loss would have been greater. This was the lie she intended to tell when she came before her lady.

They continued along together until they reached the castle, where the lady was happy to welcome Sir Yvain. She asked her maid privately for her box of ointment, and the maid, not daring to tell her the truth, told her the lie she had made up in all its detail. Then the lady was very angry. "This is a dreadful loss. I am most certain the box will never be recovered," she exclaimed. "But once a thing is lost, there is nothing left but to do without it. Sometimes you think you seek your own good when you seek your undoing. And so I, who expected good advantage and joy from this vassal, as I believed, have lost the finest and rarest of my possessions. Now, however, I would urge you to serve him in every way."

"Ah, lady, now you speak well, for it would be too great a shame to turn one loss into two."

Not another word did they exchange about the box. They served Sir Yvain in every possible manner: they bathed him and washed his head; they had him shaved and clipped, since you could have held a fistful of the beard on his face. All he wished was done for him. If he wanted armor, they gave it to him. If he wanted a horse, they provided him with one handsome and tall, spirited and strong.

Yvain remained there until a certain Tuesday when Count Alier arrived before the castle with knights and men-at-arms, who had been looting and setting fires along the way. The men inside the castle mounted at once and took their weapons. Armed and unarmed, they rode out to meet the plunderers, who did not deign to move, but waited for them in a pass.

Sir Yvain had rested so long that his strength had returned, and he went striking into the press, hitting a knight on his shield with such force that, I believe, he sent down knight and horse together in a heap; the man never stood, for his backbone was broken and the heart inside him burst. Sir Yvain drew back a little to recover. Then he covered himself completely with his shield and rushed ahead to clear the pass. You could not count one-two-three-four as rapidly as you could see him strike down four knights easily and quickly. Those with him took great courage from his example, for the moment a fainthearted man witnesses a worthy man attack a dangerous undertaking, he is filled with shame and dishonor, which expel the timid heart from his body and replace it with the bold heart of a worthy man. And so the men became brave, each holding his ground in the assaults of combat.

High up in her castle tower, the lady observed the battle and the rush to take and hold the pass, and saw many lying on the ground, wounded and dead, her own men and her enemies, but more of the others than of her own. Sir Yvain, the courteous, the brave, the good, forced them all to seek mercy, as the falcon does the teal.

The men and women who had remained inside the castle cried out as they watched from the battlements. "Ah, what a valiant fighter! How he makes his enemies yield! How fiercely he attacks them! He sets on the men around him like a lion among deer when the torment of hunger provokes. And all our other knights are the more courageous and bold because of him. Were it not for him alone, no lance would have been splintered, no sword drawn to strike. A worthy man ought to be revered and loved when he is found. See now how this man proves himself! See how he holds his place in the line! Now see how he stains his lance and his drawn sword with blood! See how he presses his opponents! See how he pursues them, how he comes toward them, how he overtakes them, how he retires, how he advances again! He pauses only briefly in retiring, delaying but a little before again advancing. See when he comes to the fight, how little he values his shield, how he lets it be cut to pieces. He feels no trace of pity, but is keen to avenge the blows dealt him. If someone made lances for him from all the trees in the Forest of Argonne, I doubt if any would be left by nightfall, for he would shatter all lances placed in his rest and demand more. And see how he draws his sword and strikes with it! Roland with Durendal never wrought such a slaughter of Turks at Roncesvaux or in Spain. If Yvain had some such companions in his company, the scoundrel we despise would leave discomfited or remain disgraced."

And they declared that a woman would be fortunate indeed to be loved by a man so powerful in arms and so recognizable among all as a taper among candles, as the moon among the stars, as the sun in comparison with the moon. He won the hearts of all the men and women, and because of the valor they beheld in him, they all wished that he would marry their lady and govern her land.

These were the compliments from all the men and women, and their comments were the truth. His assaults made his enemies take to flight as fast as they could. He pressed them closely, and all his company followed, for when next to him, they felt as safe as though completely enclosed by a high, thick wall of hard stone. The pursuit continued a long time until the men who fled were exhausted, and their pursuers cut them to pieces and disembowelled all their horses. As they were wounding and killing one another, those living rolled over those already dead. Savage was the abuse they dealt.

Meanwhile the count took to flight. Not reluctant to follow him, Sir Yvain did not flee, but chased him until he trapped him at the bottom of a steep hill near the entrance to a fortress belonging to the count. There the count was stopped, with no one near to help him. Without too lengthy a negotiation Sir Yvain accepted his pledge of surrender. Inasmuch as he held the count in his power and they were all alone, man to man, with no method of defense, evasion, or escape, the count swore to go and surrender to the Lady of Norison, to be her prisoner, and to make peace on her terms. After accepting his pledge, Yvain made him remove his helmet, take the shield from his neck, and hand over his drawn sword. Thus he won the honor of leading the count away prisoner and handing him over to his enemies, who did not restrain their happiness.

The news reached the castle before they arrived. With the lady at their head, all the men and women came out to meet them. Sir Yvain led the prisoner by the hand and delivered him to her. The count accepted her will and her demands completely, assuring her of his agreement by his word, by oath, and by pledges. He gave sureties and swore to her to keep peace forever, to compensate her for whatever losses she could prove, and to rebuild anew the houses he had destroyed. When they concluded the agreement to the lady's satisfaction, Sir Yvain asked leave to depart. She would not have given it had he wished to take her as his beloved or his wife.

Forbidding the people to follow or escort him a single step, he left promptly. Entreating him was in vain. He now rode back along the road, leaving the lady he had made very happy now very angry. The more he had pleased her, the more she was distressed and grieved because he would not remain longer. She wanted to honor him and, were he so pleased, to make him lord of all her possessions, or else she would have given him, for his service, rewards so large that he would have wished to accept them. But he had no desire to hear further talk from man or woman. Thus he left the lady and her knights, despite his deep regret over his inability to stay longer.

Absorbed in his thoughts, Sir Yvain was riding through a deep forest when he heard a loud cry of pain from the trees. He turned in the direction of the cry. When he reached a clearing, he saw a lion and a serpent, which was holding the lion by the tail and scorching his haunches with burning fire. Sir Yvain spent little time looking at this strange sight. When he considered which of the two he would help, he decided to go to aid the lion, because a serpent with its venom and treachery deserved nothing but harm. The serpent was venomous, and fire was darting from its mouth, so full of evil was the creature.

Intending first to kill the serpent, Sir Yvain drew his sword and advanced. He held his shield before his face as a protection against the flames gushing from the serpent's throat, which was more gaping than a pot. If the lion attacked him later, there would be a fight; yet whatever happened after, he still wished to aid the lion. Pity urged him and pleaded that he help and support the noble and honorable beast.

With his keen-cutting sword he attacked the evil serpent, pinning it to the ground and slicing it in two. He then struck it again and again until he had cut and hacked it to pieces. But he had to sever a piece of the lion's tail because the head of the wretched serpent still gripped the tail. He cut off as little as necessary; in fact, he could not have removed less. When he had freed the lion, he expected that the lion would spring at him and he would have to fight, but to the lion such an idea never occurred. Hear what the lion did. In a manner befitting the worthy and nobly born, he began to show that he was surrendering. He stood on his hind legs, stretched out his forepaws together to the knight, and bowed his head to the ground. Then he knelt down, his whole face wet with tears of humility. For certain Sir Yvain realized that the lion was thanking him and humbling himself before him, since he had delivered him from death by killing the serpent. This adventure delighted Yvain. He cleaned the serpent's venomous filth from his sword, which he then placed back in its scabbard. Then he resumed his journey. The lion walked close beside him, never to leave him, but to accompany him always to serve and to protect him.

The lion went ahead on the road. Because he was in front, he caught in the wind the scent of wild beasts grazing. Hunger and his natural instinct urged him to go hunting prey for his own food. This was the way Nature intended him to act. He set out on the trail a little until he had shown his master that he had sniffed out and taken up the scent of a wild animal. He then stopped and looked at him, for he sought to please him and had no intention of acting against his will. By such behavior, Yvain realized that the lion was showing him that he awaited his direction. He understood and knew that if he held back, the lion would hold back, and if he followed him, the lion would catch the game he had scented.

He then incited the lion by his cries, as he would have done a hunting dog. Immediately the lion put his nose to the scent he had detected. He had not been deceived. Not beyond a bow's range had he gone when he saw a deer grazing all alone in a valley. If he had his way, he would seize the deer, and this he did on the first bound, and drank the still-warm blood. He laid the slaughtered deer on his back and carried it to his master, who then, because of the lion's deep devotion to him, held him in great affection.

It was almost nightfall, and Yvain was pleased to spend the night in that spot. In order to strip as much meat from the deer as he cared to eat, he began to flay the animal, splitting the skin along the ribs and cutting a slice from its loin. He drew a flame from a flint and set a dry log on the fire. He then put his slice on the roasting spit to cook quickly over the fire, roasting it until it was cooked. Yet there was no delight in the meal as there was no bread, no wine, no salt, no tablecloth, no knife, nor anything else. While he was eating, his lion lay completely still in front of him, watching him intently until he had eaten his fill of the large steak. The lion ate the rest of the deer to the very bones. All night long, Yvain rested his head on his shield to take such sleep as this offered. And the lion had sense enough to stay awake, careful to watch over the horse, which was grazing on grass of scant nourishment.

Together they set out again in the morning. The next night, as I believe, found them both leading the existence of the previous night, and indeed, for nearly a fortnight they followed this pattern until they chanced to reach the spring beneath the pine.

Alas, Sir Yvain almost lost sense when this time he neared the spring and the stone and the chapel. A thousand times he called himself wretched and miserable. He was so distraught that he fell in a faint; his sharp sword dropped from its scabbard and the point pierced through the meshes of his hauberk close to the neck below the cheek. There is no mail that does not break open, and the sword cut the skin of the neck beneath the gleaming mail and made his blood spill. The sight convinced the lion that his master and companion was dead. Greater than ever before was the anger he experienced, as the display of his grief commenced. Never have I heard told or described such grief. He threw himself about, clawing himself and screaming. He wanted to kill himself with the sword he thought had killed his good master. With his teeth he grabbed the sword from him, laid it on a fallen tree, and steadied it on a trunk behind, fearing it might slip when he hurled his breast against it. He had almost accomplished his desire when Yvain recovered from his swoon. The lion had been rushing at death like a wild boar, careless of where he impaled himself. Now, however, he took restraint.

Sir Yvain was stretched out in front of the stone. When he regained his senses, he reproached himself for the year he had overstayed, which had made his lady hate him. "Why does this wretch not kill himself?" he exclaimed. "He has lost his happiness. Alas, why do I not take my own life? How can I go on living when I see the things that belong to my lady? Why does the soul still stay in my body? What is the soul doing in such a miserable body? Had it gone away, it would not be in such agony. Truly I must hate and reproach and despise myself to see the way I am now, and indeed, so I do. Whosoever loses his joy and his happiness through his own fault and mistake ought to despise himself to the death. He should loathe himself and take his life. And now, when no one looks at me, why do I spare my life? Why do I not kill myself? Have I not seen this lion so grief-stricken on my behalf that he wanted to run my sword through his breast into his body? Why should I fear death when I have turned my joy to sorrow? Joy is a stranger to me, and all comfort too. I shall say no more of this, for no one could speak of it. I have asked an absurd question. I was assured of the greatest happiness of all, but it lasted briefly. The man who loses such joy through his own fault has no right to good fortune."

While he was bemoaning his fate, a wretched captive, unhappily imprisoned in the chapel, heard his lament and saw him through a crack in the wall. The moment he stood up from his faint, she called to him. "God, whom do I see there? Who makes this lament?" she asked.

And he answered her: "Who are you?"

"I am a wretched captive, the most miserable creature that lives," she said.

"Be quiet, silly creature," he answered. "Your grief is joy, your sorrow happiness compared with my misery. The more a man is accustomed to a life of pleasure and joy, the more distracted and bewildered he is than any other man when sorrow comes his way. Through habit and practice, the weak man bears a burden another man of greater strength would not carry at all."

"I swear I know the truth of your words," she said. "Yet for all that, there is no reason to believe you are worse off than I. I don't believe that, for it seems to me you can go anywhere you want, while I am imprisoned. And here is the fate reserved for me: tomorrow I shall be taken and sentenced to death."

"Ah, God, for what crime?" he asked.

"Sir Knight, may God never have mercy on my soul if I have deserved it in the least. I shall tell you the truth; I shall not lie. I am here in prison because I am accused of treason, and I cannot find anyone to save me from being burned or hanged tomorrow."

"Now I can certainly declare that my grief and woe are worse than your misery, because you may be delivered from this peril," he said. "Could that not happen?"

"Yes, but I do not know as yet by whom. There are only two men at the moment who would dare defend me in combat against three."

"What? By God, are there then three?"

"Yes, sir, I swear there are three who accuse me of treason."

"And who are the men who love you so much that each would be bold enough to dare fight three in order to be your champion and save you?"

"I shall not lie to you. One is Sir Gawain, and the other Sir Yvain, for whose sake I shall be unjustly delivered tomorrow to the agony of death."

"For whose sake? What did you say?" he asked.

"Sir, so help me God, for the sake of the son of King Urien."

"Now I have heard you clearly, but you shall never die unless he dies with you. I myself am that Yvain who is responsible for your fearful state. And you are the one, I believe, who protected me in the great hall. You saved my life and my very body when, between the two portcullises, I was confused and distraught, distressed and miserable. I would have been captured and killed had it not been for your fine aid. Now tell me, my dear friend, who are the men who have imprisoned you in this dungeon and accuse you of treason?"

"Sir, I shall conceal nothing since you wish me to speak. It is true I did not hesitate to aid you in good faith. On my advice my lady received you as her lord. She trusted my opinion and my counsel. And by the Holy Paternoster I did think, and still do, that I acted more for her welfare than for yours. This much I confess to you. So help me God, I sought her honor and your desire. As you happened to overstay the year when you should have returned to my lady, she became furious with me, and thought that I had abused her trust in me. The seneschal learned this—he is a wicked, deadly traitor, who has been very jealous of me because my lady trusted me more than him in many matters. He realized he could create deep enmity between her and me. In the full court, with everyone present, he accused me of betraying her for your sake. I had no counsel or help but my own, and I said I had never been treasonous in thought or deed against my lady. Sir, in God's name, like someone beside herself and without taking counsel, I immediately added that I would be defended by one knight who would fight three. He did not have the courtesy to refuse the challenge, and at no cost could I retreat or retract my statement. And so he took me at my word. I had to pledge that I would, within thirty days, present a knight prepared to fight against three. Since then I have been to many courts. I was at King Arthur's court, where I found no one to help me. Nor did I find any who could tell me of you to my satisfaction, for they had no news of you."

"And Sir Gawain, the noble, the gentle, I beg you, where was he then? No maiden in distress ever failed to receive his help."

"I would have been delighted to find him at court. He would have refused me no request. But a knight had led the queen away, I was told. The king was beside himself when he sent him off after her. Kay, I believe, escorted her to the knight, who took her away. In great distress Sir Gawain went in search of her. Until he has found her, he will never rest a single day. Now I have told you the entire truth of my adventure. Tomorrow I shall suffer a disgraceful death. In their defiance and contempt of you, I shall be burned without reprieve."

"God forbid that you be harmed on my account," he answered. "You will not die if I have the power to prevent it. You can expect to see me tomorrow, prepared, as best I am able, to present myself, as I should, to secure your deliverance. But take care not to tell the people who I am. Whatever the outcome of the combat, be careful no one recognizes me."

"Certainly, sir. Since this is your wish, no torture could ever force me to disclose your identity. I would rather die first. Still I beg you not to return for my sake. I do not want you to undertake such a desperate combat. Thank you for your willingness in this pledge, but consider yourself fully absolved. I prefer to die alone rather than see them rejoice over your death as well as mine. Even after they had killed you, I would never be released. It is better that you remain alive than that both of us die."

"Dear friend, what you have said perturbs me much," Sir Yvain said. "Perhaps you do not want to be delivered from death? Or else you scorn the comfort and aid I would give you. I do not want to argue with you more. You have certainly done so much for me that I must not fail you in your need. I realize that you are frightened, but God willing—and I do believe in Him—all three knights will be dishonored. There is nothing more for me to do now but go and find lodging in these woods, for I know of none near here."

"Sir, God grant you a fine lodging and a fine evening. May He protect you, as I wish, from all harm," she said. Sir Yvain then departed, the lion always behind him.

The two traveled along until they came within view of a strong fortress belonging to a baron, which was enclosed on all sides by thick, strong, and high walls. Because it was so solidly built, the castle lay in no dread of attack from catapult or storming machine. But the open space outside the walls had been so razed that not a house or hut remained standing. You will hear the reason for this later when the time comes. Sir Yvain made his way directly to the fortress. As many as seven pages rushed forward; they had lowered a drawbridge for him and gone to meet him. Terrified at the sight of the lion accompanying him, they asked him if he would be pleased to leave his lion at the gate lest the animal wound or kill them. "Say no more," he replied. "I shall never enter without him. Either we shall both be lodged, or I shall stay outside, for I love him as much as my own being. Yet have no worry about him, for I shall keep him so well in hand that you may feel perfectly safe."

"Let us hope so," they answered.

The pair then entered the castle and proceeded ahead. They met knights, ladies, attractive young ladies, and servants, who welcomed him, helped him to dismount, and set about to relieve him of his armor. "Welcome to our midst, dear sir," they said to him. "God grant that you stay here until, with great joy and great honor, you may depart." From the highest to the lowest, they all made every effort to celebrate his arrival. But after they had escorted him happily into the house and shown him their great delight, a sorrow overcame them and they forgot their gladness. They began once more to utter their cries, weeping and tearing at their faces in distress. Thus for a long time they rejoiced at one moment, at the next wept, rejoicing in honor of their guest even though they had no such inclination. They worried about an adventure they were expecting the next day, all absolutely certain that it would happen before noon.

Their frequent change of mood, their display of joy and grief, perplexed Sir Yvain, who addressed the lord of the castle and the house. "In God's name, dear noble sir," he asked, "will you please tell me why you have honored me with such a mixture of joy and tears?"

"Yes, if you wish to know, but you should be content with silence and ignorance. I would prefer to tell you nothing to cause your dismay. Leave us to our grief. Pay it no attention."

"I could never see you so distraught and not take your distress to heart. I want to know, whatever sorrow such knowledge costs me."

"Then I shall tell you," he replied. "A giant has been attacking me savagely. He wanted me to give him my daughter, who is more beautiful than all the maidens in the world. That vicious giant—God bring him down!—is called Harpin of the Mountain. There is not a single day that he does not take all he can seize of my possessions. No one has a better right than I to grieve, to lament, and to complain. I should go mad from grief, for I had six sons, all knights, the finest men I know in this world, and the giant has taken all six. Before my eyes he has killed two, and tomorrow he will kill the other four unless I find someone to fight him and set my sons free, or unless I agree to surrender my daughter to him. He said that when he has her, he will give her over to the pleasure of the foulest and filthiest serving boys in his household. He would not, he added, lower himself to take her for his own. Unless God helps me, this is the grief I may expect tomorrow. So, dear sir, it is no wonder we are in tears. On your account we struggle, for the time being, to show the happiest face we can. A fool is he who brings a worthy man into his home and fails to honor him. And you seem to me a worthy man. Now, sir, I have told you all about our grave plight. In place of this town and fortress, the giant has left us nothing except what is here inside. If you noticed tonight, you saw that he has left nothing worth a small plank except for these remaining walls. He has razed the entire area around the castle. When he had taken what he desired, he set fire to the rest. And thus he played a most wicked game with me."

Sir Yvain listened to his host's entire account, and when he had heard it all, he gave him his reply. "Sir," he said, "your distress makes me most angry and upset. But one matter amazes me. Have you not sought help at the court of the good King Arthur? No man has such great strength that some willing to test their strength against his could not be found at the king's court."

The noble man explained to him that he would have had great assistance had he known where to find Sir Gawain. "Not in vain would I have entreated him, because my wife is his own sister. But a knight from a foreign land went to the court to ask for the king's wife, and has led her away. Yet for all his efforts he would never have taken her had it not been for Kay, who tricked the king into entrusting him with the queen and placing her in his keeping. He was a fool, and she foolish to entrust herself to his escort. And I in turn endure such great pain and loss, for had the brave Sir Gawain known what was happening, he certainly would have raced here for the sake of his niece and his nephews. But he is ignorant of this, and I am so sad that my heart is almost breaking. Gawain has gone in pursuit of the knight. May the Lord God bring that knight great harm for leading away the queen."

While listening, Sir Yvain did not restrain his sighs. Moved by pity, he responded: "Dear noble sir, I would gladly undertake this dangerous adventure if tomorrow the giant comes with your sons early enough to prevent my delay, for to keep a promise, I will be elsewhere tomorrow at noon."

"Dear sir, I thank you a hundred thousand times at once for this," the worthy man answered. And in turn all the people in the castle said the same.

At that moment the maiden came out of a chamber. Her figure was graceful, her face beautiful and pleasing. She was modest, quiet, and silent as she came, for her sadness knew no limit. She kept her head bowed to the ground. Her mother accompanied her, for their lord, who had called for them, wished to present them to their guest. They came entirely wrapped in their cloaks to hide their tears, and he told them to open their cloaks and raise their heads. "You should not be displeased to obey my command," he said, "for God and good fortune have sent us a noble and well-born man who assures me he will fight the giant. Delay no more. Let yourselves fall at his feet."

"God never let me see that!" Sir Yvain exclaimed at once. "Truly it would not be right for the sister of Sir Gawain or his niece to fall at my feet. God keep me from such pride that ever I would let them fall at my feet. Never would I forget the shame that would be mine. But I would be most grateful if they would take courage until tomorrow, when they may see if God will help them. It is needless to ask more of me, provided the giant comes early enough that I need not break my promise elsewhere. There are no circumstances that would make me fail to be, by noon to-morrow, at an undertaking, indeed the most important I could ever face."

He did not wish to make them completely confident, for fear the giant might not come early enough to let him return in time to the young lady imprisoned in the chapel. Yet he promised enough to fill them with good hope. And all thanked him, placing great trust in the hope he gave. He was a worthy man, they believed, since his companion was a lion who lay beside him as gently as a lamb. Because of their hope in him, they were consoled and happy and put an end to their grief. At the proper time they led him to a brightly lit bedroom. Out of deep affection for him, the maiden and her mother accompanied him there, and that affection would have been a hundred thousand times larger had they known of his great valor and courtesy.

Yvain and the lion lay down in that room to rest. Not daring to sleep there, the others locked the door so tight that the two could not come out until dawn the next morning. When the room was unlocked, Yvain rose and went to hear mass. According to his promise, he stayed until six that morning. Then he publicly addressed the lord of the castle himself. "Sir, I can wait no longer," he said. "If you don't mind, I shall go now, for I cannot stay more. Be absolutely certain, if such an urgent obligation did not await me, I would willingly and gladly remain here for the sake of the niece and nephews of Sir Gawain, for I love him very much."

These words made the maiden, the vavasor, and his lady shudder with fear. The prospect of his departure terrified them so much that they were willing, noble as they were, to lay themselves at his feet. But he would not permit an act he considered displeasing and improper. The lord then offered to give him all his possessions, land or anything else that he would take, provided he would wait but a little longer. "God forbid I take anything," he answered.

Terrified, the maiden burst into tears. She begged him to stay. Fraught with anxiety and dread, she implored him in the name of the glorious Queen of Heaven and the Angels, and in the name of God, not to leave them, but to wait just a little longer. And she called upon the name of her uncle, whom he said he knew and honored and esteemed. Yvain felt great compassion when he heard her invoke the name of his most beloved friend, and of the Queen of Heaven, and of Him who is the honey and very sweetness of mercy. He sighed in deep anguish: not for the kingdom of Tarsus would he want the woman burned to whom he had promised aid. If he failed to arrive there in time, his life would not last long, or else he would go out of his mind. On the other hand, the great nobility of his friend Sir Gawain increased his other distress, and his heart almost broke at the thought of not staying. He still did not move, but remained and waited. At last, galloping along leading the knights came the giant. A huge, square stake with a pointed end hung from his neck, which he used often to jab them. As for the sons, they had no clothing worth a straw except for some soiled and filthy shirts; their feet and hands were tied tight with ropes; and they sat on four limping, decrepit packhorses that were emaciated and exhausted. A dwarf, a scoundrel puffed up like a toad, had tied the horses' tails together. He was walking beside the four young men as they came riding by the woods. He never stopped beating them with a six-knot whip, imagining that he was doing something splendid, and he beat them until they bled. Thus the giant and the dwarf together led them in shame.

The giant stopped on the open plain in front of the gate and cried out to the worthy man, threatening to kill his sons unless he handed over his daughter. Then, he shouted, he would give her to his rabble of knaves as their whore, for he did not love or respect her enough to consider descending to her level. All the time she would be in the company of a thousand naked, filthy fellows, vagrant scum and scullion boys, and they would all abuse her.

The worthy man almost went mad when he heard the giant declare that he would make the man's daughter a whore, or else his four sons would now be killed before his eyes. His distress was that of a man who would rather be dead than alive. Again and again, amid heavy sighs and sobs, he called himself a miserable wretch. Then Sir Yvain began to speak to him in a noble and gentle manner. "Sir, that is a most wicked and insulting giant who swaggers out there. May God never let him have your daughter at his mercy. He insults her. He demeans her. Too great would be the misfortune if a creature of such beauty and noble lineage were abandoned to his serving boys. Bring me my horse and my arms, have the drawbridge lowered, and let me cross. The fight must exhaust one of us; whether him or me, I know not. If I could humiliate your cruel and evil oppressor into releasing your sons and coming to you to make amends for the insults he has hurled at you, then I would commend you to God and go about my business."

The people went and led out his horse. They handed him all his equipment and worked hard in his service, taking as little time as possible in his preparation. He was soon armed. When they had readied him in fine and fitting fashion, there was nothing left but to lower the drawbridge and let him cross. When it was lowered, he departed, and nothing could prevent the lion from following him.

The people who remained behind commended Yvain to the Savior, for they dreaded that their devilish enemy, who before their eyes had slain so many worthy men on the field, would do the same to him. And so they beseeched God to protect him from death, to let him kill the giant, and to return him to them alive and safe. Each one prayed devoutly to God, following his own desire.

With bold arrogance, the giant strode up to Yvain and threatened him. "By my eyes," he shouted out, "the man who sent you here loved you not. He could certainly find no better way to take revenge on you. How well he chose his vengeance for all the wrong you did him."

"You begin your argument in vain," said the fearless knight. "Do your best now, and I shall do mine. Senseless talk bores me."

Because Sir Yvain was anxious to depart, he raced at the giant, striking him in the chest, which he was protecting with a bearskin. From his side the giant came rushing at him with his stake. Sir Yvain dealt him such a blow in the chest that he pierced the skin and wet the head of his lance in the giant's blood as though it were sauce. The giant beat him so hard with his stake that he forced him to bend. Skilled in delivering heavy blows, Sir Yvain drew his sword. He had found the giant unprotected, for the giant trusted so much in his strength that he would not arm himself. His sword drawn, he attacked, striking him, not with the flat side but with the cutting edge, so that he sliced a thick piece of flesh from the cheek. The giant gave him a blow in turn that made him sink in a heap to the neck of his charger.

At that stroke the lion bristled and made ready to help his master. Leaping in anger, he tugged and tore with all his might at the giant's hairy hide as though it were a strip of bark. From underneath he ripped off a huge piece of the thigh along with the flesh and the nerves. Like a bull, the giant roared and screamed as he escaped him, for the lion had mauled him badly. He lifted his stake in both his hands to hit the lion, but missed: the lion had leapt aside, and so the wasted blow landed harmlessly past Sir Yvain without touching either of them. Sir Yvain took aim and struck two blows. Before the giant could recover, Yvain cut off his shoulder with the edge of his sword; with the other blow he ran the entire blade of his sword under the chest and through the liver. The giant fell, embraced by death. Had a mighty oak fallen, I do not believe there would have been greater noise than the giant made in his collapse.

All those on the battlements were eager to see the effect of the blow. It then became obvious who was the quickest, for all sped to the spoils like dogs racing to a fallen animal after a long chase. Without sign of laziness, all the men and women raced in their excitement to where the giant lay, his mouth agape. The lord himself ran there, as did all the people of his court. The maiden ran there, as did her mother. Now the four brothers knew happiness after enduring so much torture.

Certain that they could not detain Sir Yvain at any cost, the people urged him, on the completion of the business to which he was going, to return and to stay and enjoy himself at that time. He dared assure them of nothing, he answered, since he could not foretell whether or not the outcome for him would be favorable. But this much he did tell the lord, that he would like his daughter and his four sons to take the dwarf and proceed to Sir Gawain, when they learned of his return, and that they should recount how the knight had conducted himself, for good deeds not known are worthless. "This good act of yours will not be kept secret, for that would not be right," they replied. "We shall do what you will. But one question we would ask you, sir. When we come before him, whom can we praise if we do not know your name?"

"When you come before him, you may say this much," he said, "that I told you my name was the Knight with the Lion. And I must also ask you to tell him on my behalf that he knows me well, and I him, and yet he knows me not. For more I ask you not. Now I must go. My greatest fear is that I have stayed here too long. I shall have much to do elsewhere if by noon I can arrive there."

He departed without further delay. The lord had implored him, as eloquently as he could, to take with him his four sons; each would, had the knight wished, devote himself to his service. But the idea of anyone accompanying him did not suit or please him. Leaving them, he rode off alone.

As soon as he was on his route, Yvain rode back in the direction of the chapel as fast as his horse could carry him. The road was good and direct, and he knew how to hold to it. But before he could reach the chapel, the maiden had been dragged out, clad only in her shift, and the pyre on which she would be placed had been prepared. The knights who had wrongly charged her with a crime she had never even considered held her bound in front of the fire.

Sir Yvain reached the fire on which they intended to throw her. What he beheld disturbed him deeply. A man doubting this would be without courtesy or wisdom. He was most upset, it is true, yet he had strong faith that God and right would be on his side to aid him. In these helpers he placed his trust, and his lion disliked him not. He rushed toward the crowd. "Leave the young lady! Let her be, you wicked people!" he shouted. "It is not right to throw her in a furnace or on a pyre. She has done nothing to deserve that."

All the people separated on both sides to make room for him. He was most impatient to see with his own eyes the lady, wherever she was, whose image was always in his heart. His eyes searched her out until he found her, and he put his heart under such stress that he had to restrain and subdue it, as with great difficulty you restrain an impetuous horse with a strong rein. Yet he was glad to gaze on her and sigh, though his sighs were hidden lest anyone notice them. Instead, he struggled to curb his anguish.

When he heard and saw the miserable women making laments strange to him, he was seized with great pity. "Alas, God, you have forgotten us," they cried out. "Now we shall be in such distress over losing so fine a friend, who gave us such counsel and such help, who interceded on our behalf at court. On her advice my lady dressed us in fur-trimmed clothes. Circumstances will alter for us because there will be no one to speak on our behalf. God's curse on the man who takes her from us! Damn him who causes us this loss! Too severe will be our sorrow. There will never be anyone to offer the advice: 'Dear lady, that jacket and that coat and that cloak, give to this noble woman. In truth, if you send them to her, she will put them to good use, for she is in desperate need of them.' These words will never be uttered again, for there is no one else so noble and courteous. Everyone asks always for herself rather than someone else, even though, for herself, no need exists."

Sir Yvain, in the midst of these ladies, heard their complaints and laments, which were neither groundless nor feigned. And he saw Lunete on her knees, stripped to her shift. She had already confessed herself, sought God's pardon for her sins, and made her contrition. In his deep love for her, he went and brought her to her feet. "My young lady," he said, "where are these men who reproach and accuse you? The offer of combat will be theirs immediately unless they refuse."

Not having seen or noticed him before, she said: "Sir, from God you come to help me in my need. All stand here who bear false witness against me. Had you tarried but a little, I would soon have been coals and ashes. You have come to defend me, and as surely as I am innocent of the charge brought against me, may God give you strength to do so."

The seneschal and his two brothers had heard these words. "Ha, woman," he said, "you are stingy with truth and generous with lies. That man is hardly wise to assume such a heavy burden on the strength of your statement. What an unfortunate knight to come here and die for you. We are three and he is one. I advise him to leave here before matters worsen for him."

Yvain, angered by this remark, answered: "Whoever knows fear, let him flee. I am not so frightened by your three shields that I would go away in defeat without striking a blow. I would be now most discourteous to yield you the field of battle when I am still all in health and without injury. As long as I am alive and sound, such threats will never make me flee. But I advise you to free the young lady you have falsely accused. She has given me her word, and since she says it, I believe it. She has sworn to me on peril of losing her soul that she never acted, spoke, or even considered treachery against her lady. Now I believe what she has told me, and I shall defend her if I can. The righteousness of her cause is with me. If the truth be known, God also stands on the side of right, and God and right stand as one. Since they come with me, then I have better company than you have, and better aid too."

The seneschal made a foolish response. His opponent, he said, might use anything he wanted against them, provided the lion not harm them.

Yvain replied that he had not brought his lion there as his champion, nor did he want any but himself in the combat. But if his lion attacked, let them defend themselves well against him, for he himself guaranteed nothing. "No matter what you say," they replied, "if you do not subdue your lion and have him stand still, then there is no reason for you to stay. Leave, and you will act wisely, for all in this country know how the maiden betrayed her lady. It is right that she receive her due reward in fiery flames."

"The Holy Spirit forbid it!" said he who knew the truth. "God grant that I never leave here until I have delivered her." He then told his lion to draw back and lie still, and the lion obeyed.

Once the lion retreated, the words of their dispute came to an end, and the men moved away from one another. Though the trio galloped together toward him, he went to meet them at a walk, not wishing to be upset or hurt by the opening blows. He let them split their lances while keeping his own whole, for he made his shield a quintain where each one broke his lance. He galloped off until he was about a furlong from them; then at once he came back to the pressing business, for he had no desire for long delay. On returning, he hit the seneschal ahead of his two brothers, breaking his lance against the body, and dealing him such a fine blow that he was carried to the ground against his will. For a long time the seneschal lay, stunned and incapable of harm. The other two attacked the knight with their swords drawn, delivering heavy blows, but they received even heavier from him. One of his blows equaled exactly two of theirs. So well did he defend himself against them that they gained no advantage until the seneschal stood again and did his best to injure him. The other two joined him in his struggle until they brought injury to Yvain and gained the upper hand.

The lion, who watched this, waited no longer to assist his master, for it seemed to him his aid was needed. All the ladies, who loved the maiden, called repeatedly upon God, beseeching Him from their hearts not to allow the man who had risked his life on her behalf to be defeated or killed. The ladies came to his aid with their prayers, their only weapons.

The lion's initial assault proved most helpful. The seneschal was on foot, and the lion attacked him with such fury that he sent the meshes of his hauberk flying as if they were straw. He dragged him down so hard that he tore the flesh off his shoulder and his side. Whatever he touched, he stripped away, leaving the entrails exposed.

The two others suffered for that injury. Now the sides were even on the field. The seneschal could not escape death; he was wallowing and weltering in the stream of crimson blood pouring from his body. The lion attacked the others. Neither by threats nor by blows could Sir Yvain restrain him, though he struggled hard to do so. The lion undoubtedly knew that his master did not disdain his aid but, to the contrary, loved him the more for it. He went savagely at the men until they, having reason to lament his blows, had wounded and maimed him.

When Sir Yvain saw his lion wounded, his heart was justifiably enraged. He strove to wreak revenge by pursuing the men with such boldness that he brought them to disgrace: unable to make further defense, they threw themselves on his mercy.

Because of the aid he had offered, the lion was in great pain, and he was rightly distressed by his two wounds. For his part, Sir Yvain was not at all free of injury himself, for his body was covered with wounds. Yet he worried more about his lion's suffering than about his own condition.

By this time, exactly as he wished, he had delivered his young lady, and her lady had willingly pardoned her, dismissing her own anger. The men were burned on the pyre that had been kindled for her. It is right and just that the man who accuses falsely die by the same death he ordained for his victim.

Lunete was joyous and happy to be reconciled with her lady. They both showed more joy than has ever been shown by any others.

All the people, including even the lady, who held his heart unknowingly, offered the knight their service for as long as they lived, without recognizing that he was their lord. The lady earnestly implored him that it be his pleasure to stay until both he and his lion had recovered. "Lady," he said, "I shall not stay here today, but only when my lady dismisses her anger and her displeasure with me. Then all my afflictions will end."

"This upsets me very much," she replied. "I think the lady whose heart harbors anger toward you knows little courtesy. She would not close her door to a knight of your honor unless he had sorely injured her."

"Lady," he said, "I am happy to do her will at any cost. But do not ask me about this. Nothing will make me talk about the offense or the crime, except with those who know about it."

"Does anyone know of it except you two?"

"Yes indeed, lady."

"Please tell us your name, dear sir. Then you will be free to go."

"Completely free, lady? No, not I. I owe more than I might pay. Yet I should not keep from you the name I give myself. You will never hear people talk about the Knight with the Lion unless they talk of me. By this name I would be known."

"By God, dear sir, what does that mean? We have never seen you before, nor have we ever heard your name used."

"Lady, from this you may know that renown is not mine."

Then again the lady spoke. "Once more, if you don't object, I would beg you to stay."

"No, lady, I would certainly not do that until I was assured of my lady's goodwill."

"Go then with God, dear sir, and may He be pleased to turn your grief and your sadness to joy."

"God hear you, lady," he replied. Then under his breath he softly said: "Though you don't know, lady, you carry the key. You have the lock and the safe that contain my joy."

He went away in deep sadness. No one there recognized him except Lunete, who accompanied him a long way. Lunete alone was aware of his identity, and so he kept beseeching her never to reveal who her champion was. "Never shall I, sir," she said. He then begged her again not to forget him and, if she had the occasion, to intercede on his behalf with her lady. And she told him to say no more about this, for she would never be neglectful, forgetful, or remiss. Then he thanked her a hundred times.

As he set off, Yvain was worried and upset about his lion. He had to carry him, since the lion was unable to follow. With moss and ferns, he made a litter for him on the inside of his shield. When he had fashioned the bed for him, he laid the lion down as gently as possible and stretched him out on the shield.

On his shield Yvain dragged him in this manner until he came to the gateway of a fine and strong castle. Finding the gate closed, he called out. The porter opened it so promptly that Yvain needed to shout but once. The porter, extending his hand to take the reins, said: "Dear sir, accept my lord's lodging here before you, if it be your pleasure to dismount."

"I wish to accept your invitation, for it is time to find lodging for the night, and I am in great need of it," Yvain replied.

He then passed through the gateway and saw the assembled household all coming to meet him. They welcomed him and helped him dismount. Some of them laid the shield carrying the lion on the pavement, others took his horse and stabled it, while the squires, as was their duty, disarmed him and removed his equipment. As soon as the lord of the house heard news of his guest, he came into the courtyard and greeted him. His lady followed with all her sons and daughters. And large numbers of others rejoiced over his arrival and offered him hospitality. Seeing that he was ill, they gave him a quiet room, and showed him further consideration by lodging the lion there also. Two maidens, daughters of the lord of the house, were knowledgeable in medicine and applied their skills to his recovery. I do not know how many days he remained there until he and his lion had recuperated and were ready to set out again.

During this time it chanced that the Lord of the Black Thorn struggled with Death. So fierce was Death's attack that the lord had to die. After his passing it happened that the older of his two daughters declared that she would hold all his land uncontested for her entire life and yield nothing to her younger sister. The latter said that she would go to King Arthur's court for aid in establishing claim to her share of the land. When the elder saw that her sister would not concede all the land without dispute, she was most upset and said that if she could, she would go to the court ahead of her sister. She made ready and prepared herself at once. Without a moment's delay, she rode off and continued traveling until she reached the court. Although her younger sister followed after her as fast as she could, the steps of her journey were wasted. The elder sister had already presented her case to Sir Gawain, and he had promised her his services, but with one stipulation, which she accepted: were she to tell anyone of it, he would never take up arms on her behalf.

Clad in a short cloak of rich wool trimmed with ermine, the younger sister reached the court three days after the queen's return from the prison where Meleagant had detained her and all the other captives. Lancelot alone was yet detained inside the tower, the victim of treachery. And on this same day of the maiden's arrival, news reached the court of the cruel and wicked giant whom the Knight with the Lion had killed in combat. In that knight's name, the nephews of Sir Gawain had greeted their uncle, and his niece had related the distinguished service and great bravery the knight had shown for their uncle's sake, adding that Gawain knew the knight well, though he was ignorant of his identity.

When the younger sister heard all this, she was disturbed, distraught, and confused, for she expected to find no support or aid at the court since the finest knight could not help her. She had appealed to Sir Gawain in every way, calling on affection and resorting to entreaties. "Friend, you entreat me in vain," he answered her. "I am unable to do anything. I have another undertaking which I would not abandon."

The maiden left at once and came before the king. "Your Majesty, I come to you and your court for aid," she said, "and find none. I am astounded not to receive help. But I would behave badly if I departed without your leave. My sister may always know that anything she wants of mine will always be hers out of love. But if I have the strength, I shall never relinquish my inheritance provided I can find aid and support."

"Your words are wise," the king said. "While your sister is present, I advise, urge, and entreat her to surrender to you what is rightfully yours."

Because of the support of the world's finest knight, her sister felt safe. "Lord, may God confound me if I ever give her a town, castle, clearing, woods, field, or any more of my land," she replied. "But if some knight dares arm himself on her behalf and defend her cause, let him step forward at this moment."

"Your offer is unacceptable," declared the king. "More time is needed. She has as many as forty days at most to provide herself with a champion, according to the principles recognized by all courts."

"Dear lord king," she answered, "you may at your will establish your laws as you please. Although they do not suit me or apply to me, it is not for me to oppose. I must accept the postponement if she asks for it."

The younger sister said that she did ask for it; such was her desire and request. She then commended the king to God. She would not stop searching through every land for the Knight with the Lion, who did all he could to aid women in distress.

And so she began her search, passing through many lands without ever hearing word of him. This made her so depressed that she became ill. But it was fortunate that she happened to come to the home of one of her friends whom she loved very much. Her poor health could be seen in her face. The people there strove to detain her until she told them of her mission.

And another maiden took up the journey she had begun and continued the search on her behalf. So one stayed behind to rest, and the other rode all day, galloping along by herself until the approach of evening. The night made her apprehensive, and her anxiety was doubled by the fact that rain, as heavy as God could make it, began to fall and she was deep in the woods. Both the night and the woods worried her a great deal, and what worried her even more than the night or the woods was the rain. The road was so bad that her horse was often up to its girth in mud. Alone without an escort, a maiden in the forest might be terrified in such bad weather and on a night so black that she did not see the horse she was sitting on. She constantly invoked, first of all, God, then His mother, and then all the saints, and made many prayers that night that God would find her shelter and lead her out of the woods. She was still praying when she heard the blast from a horn. She was delighted, expecting to find lodging if she could but come there. Turning in the direction of the sound, she came upon a paved road, and the road took her directly to the horn whose sound she had heard. The horn had made three long, loud blasts. She rode straight to the sound, and reached a crossing on the right of the road, where she thought the horn and the person who had blown it might be. She galloped in that direction until she neared a drawbridge and observed the white walls and the barbican of a small circular castle. Thus guided by the sound, she happened upon the castle.

A watchman was standing on the walls, and it was he who had blown the horn that attracted her attention. As soon as the watchman saw her, he greeted her and then came down. He took the key and opened the gate for her. "Welcome, maiden, whoever you are," he announced. "Tonight you will have a fine lodging."

"I ask for nothing more tonight," the maiden said. And he led her inside. After the cares and troubles of her day, she was fortunate to reach a lodging where she would know much comfort. After dinner her host spoke with her and asked her destination and what she sought there. She then answered him. "I search for a man whom, as I believe, I have never seen and do not know. But a lion accompanies him, and I am told that I can trust him completely if I find him."

"I can testify to that myself," he exclaimed. "Some time ago I had urgent need of help, and God sent him to me. Blessed be the roads that brought him to my home, for he brought me revenge on a mortal enemy of mine, and gave me such happiness by killing him before my very eyes. Tomorrow you can see the body of a huge giant by the gate out there. So quickly did he slaughter him that the knight scarcely had time to sweat."

"In God's name, sir, be honest with me. Do you know which way he went and if he stayed in any place?" the maiden asked.

"As God is my witness, I know not," he replied. "But tomorrow I shall set you on the road he took when he left."

"God lead me where I shall learn certain news of him," she said. "I shall be so happy if I find him." The two continued talking for a long time, until at last they went to bed.

The young lady rose at daybreak, most anxious to find the knight for whom she searched. The lord of the house and all his company rose and set her on the highway leading to the spring beneath the pine. She hurried along the road toward the castle, and when she arrived there, she asked the first people she met if they could give her news of the knight and the lion who were constant companions. They had seen them defeat three knights, they told her, on that very spot of ground. At once she exclaimed: "For God's sake, since you have told me this much, do not keep from me anything more you can tell."

"We cannot," they answered. "We know only what we have told you. We do not know what has happened to him. He came here for the sake of a young lady, and if she cannot tell you news of him, none here can. You need not travel far, if you wish to speak with her. She has gone to that church to hear mass and pray to God. Judging from the time she has stayed there, her prayers are probably now ended."

As they were talking, Lunete came out of the church. "There she is!" they shouted. The maiden went to meet her, and the moment they greeted each other, she asked her for the information she wanted. Lunete said she would have one of her palfreys saddled, desiring to ride with her and to take her to a thicket where she had accompanied him. The maiden offered her heartfelt gratitude.

The palfrey appeared immediately, and Lunete took it and mounted. As they were riding along, she told the maiden how she had been accused and charged with treason: the pyre on which she was to be placed had been kindled by the time he came, in her most dire need, to her rescue. This was the conversation as she escorted her to the road that went directly to the spot where Sir Yvain had left her. When she had accompanied her this far, she said: "Keep to this road until you reach a place where, God and the Holy Spirit willing, you will hear more recent news than mine. I remember well that I left him either exactly in this spot or quite near here. Since then we have not seen each other, and I don't know what he has done in the meanwhile. When he left me, he badly needed dressings for his wounds. Along this road I send you after him. May God permit you, if it be His pleasure, to find him in good health today rather than tomorrow. Go now. I commend you to God. I dare not follow you farther lest my lady become angry with me."

At once the pair parted, one turning back, the other riding along till at last she reached the house where Sir Yvain had stayed until he was fully recovered. In front of the door she saw people standing: knights, ladies, and men-in-arms as well as the lord of the house. She greeted them and asked for any news they might tell her of a knight for whom she searched. "I have heard said that he is never without a lion."

"On my word, young lady, he has just left us," the lord replied. "You will still overtake him today if you can follow his tracks. Be careful not to tarry too long."

"God forbid, sir," she answered. "Tell me now by what path I should follow him."

"Go straight ahead," they told her, and begged that she take their greetings to him. Their plea was of little consequence, as she hardly heard it. Setting out at full gallop, she thought her palfrey's pace slow, even though it traveled at top speed. She galloped through mud as if the road were smooth and flat until she caught sight of the man who had the lion as his companion. She felt joy and exclaimed: "God, help! I now see the man I have so long pursued. I have followed him and sought him out. But if I race after him and catch up with him, what good is it for me if I fail to take him? I swear, in truth, if he runs off and fails to come with me, then my efforts are wasted."

With these words she pressed on in haste, her palfrey heavy in sweat. She stopped and greeted the knight, and he answered her immediately. "God save you, fair maiden, and deliver you from grief and woe."

"And you too, sir, who are my hope, for you have the power to deliver me from them."

She then rode nearer him. "Sir," she said, "I have been searching for you. The great renown of your honor has caused me to struggle in pursuit of you and pass through many lands. I continued to look for you, thank God, until at last I found you here. If I brought pain upon myself, I am not concerned about it; I do not complain of it, nor do I remember it. My whole body is so relieved, for the pain left me the moment I met you. Mine is not the business at hand. A woman more noble and more worthy, a woman better than I, sends me to you. If you disappoint her, then your renown has deceived her, for she counts on no other aid or support but yours. The young lady has been deprived of her inheritance by her sister, and turns only to you to defend her claim. It is impossible to convince her that anyone else could help her. Understand the truth: if you take the victory, you will have won and regained the honor of the disinherited sister and increased your own valor. On her own she searched for you to establish her right to her inheritance, placing her hope in your kindness. Had grave illness not detained her and confined her to bed, no one else would have come here. Now answer me, please, will you dare come to her aid, or will you rest?"

"I care not for rest," he replied. "No man can win renown that way. I shall not rest, dear friend, but gladly follow you where you please. If the lady on whose behalf you have searched for me does need me, have no despair, for I shall do all I can. God now grant me grace and courage to establish her rights through His goodwill."

They continued talking together as they rode along until they approached the Castle of Most Ill Adventure. They had no desire to ride on because the day was almost over. As they neared the castle, all the people watching their approach called out to the knight: "Ill come, sir, ill come. This lodging was shown to you for your misery and disgrace. An abbot could swear to that!"

"Ah, foolish and base people, filled with every evil and every goodness, why have you assailed me like this?" he asked.

"Why? You will know soon enough if you proceed ahead a little. But you will never know a thing until you have been inside that tall fortress."

Sir Yvain immediately turned toward the tower, and all the people cried out. "Alas, alas, you unfortunate man," they screamed at him, "where are you going? If ever in your life you met one who did you injury or shame, you will receive so much of that where you are going that you will be powerless to relate it."

After listening to them, Sir Yvain said: "You people without honor or goodness, arrogant wretches, why do you assail me? Why do you attack me? What do you ask of me? What do you want of me? What makes you growl at me?"

"Friend, you have no reason to be angry," said a courteous and wise lady of some years. "I assure you they speak not to hurt you. No, they are warning you, if you could but understand, not to go and lodge up there. Although they dare not tell you why, they chastise and chide you only because they wish you to be alarmed. It is their practice to act like this to all strangers to prevent them from entering there. This is our practice because at no cost dare we give lodging to worthy men who come from without. Now the rest is yours. No one will stop you. If you wish, ride up there, though I would advise you to turn back."

"Lady, if I followed your advice, I believe honor and advantage would be mine," he replied. "Yet I would not know where to find accommodation today."

"I swear I shall be silent, for that is not my business," she answered. "Go where you want. And yet I would be delighted to see you come back from there without being too much shamed. But that is impossible."

"Lady," he said, "may God reward you! But my true heart draws me there, and I shall follow my heart's desire."

Then, accompanied by his lion and the maiden, he approached the gate. "Come quickly, come," the porter shouted at him. "You have arrived at a place where you will be detained. You have come here to your misfortune."

Pressured and provoked into coming up by the porter's rude insolence, Sir Yvain went straight past him without saying a word and came upon a great high hall that was recently built. In front of it was a courtyard enclosed by large, round, pointed stakes, between which he saw as many as three hundred maidens inside, engaged in different kinds of embroidery, sewing threads of gold and silk as best they could. They were so poor that many had nothing on their heads and no belts around their waists. Their jackets were torn at the breasts and elbows; the shifts on their backs were soiled. From hunger and pain their faces were pale, their necks thin. They all noticed him looking at them, and bowed their heads and wept. For a long time they remained there without the will to do anything. Wretched as they were, they were unable to raise their eyes from the ground.

When Sir Yvain had watched them a while, he turned and rode back to the gate. The porter barred the way. "It is no use, dear master, you will not go away now," he yelled at him. "You will want to be outside now, but wanting that, I swear, avails you not. Before you leave, you will have suffered so much shame that you will be unable to bear more. It was unwise of you to enter here, for there is no escape."

"Dear brother, I have no wish to escape," he replied. "But tell me, on your father's soul, the young ladies I have seen in this castle weaving cloths of silk and gold embroidery, whence have they come? I am delighted by their work. But I am disturbed by their thin bodies and the sad expressions on their pale faces. I believe they would be beautiful and charming if they had what pleased them."

"I shall say nothing to you," he replied. "Find someone else to tell you."

"So I will, since there is nothing more I can do."

Yvain searched until he found the entrance to the courtyard where the young ladies were working. He stood before them all and greeted them together. He saw the teardrops running from their eyes and falling as they wept. "May it be God's pleasure to take this sorrow from your hearts and turn it to joy," he said to them. "I do not know the cause of your sorrow."

"God hear your call!" one answered. "You shall know who we are and from what land. I suppose that is what you wish to ask."

"Yes, that is why I came here," he said.

"Sir, a long time ago it happened that the King of the Isle of Maidens was traveling through many courts and countries in search of news. He continued traveling, like a born fool, until he fell into this peril. It was an evil hour when he arrived here. We prisoners undeservedly suffer the misery and disgrace of it. You can be certain such awful shame will be yours too unless they agree to accept ransom for you.

"In any case, it happened that our lord came to this castle, which is the home of two sons of the devil. Do not think this an idle tale, for they are the offspring of a woman and a demon. They were to fight the king, who was exceedingly alarmed. He was not yet eighteen years old, and they would have cut him in half as though he were a gentle lamb. The king was terrified, and escaped as best he could, swearing to send here every year, as long as he lived, thirty maidens from his kingdom. This tribute brought about his release. And it was settled by oath that the tribute should last as long as the two demons were alive. On the day they were overcome and defeated in combat, he would be released from this duty, and we, who are subjected to painful lives of misery and disgrace, would be set free. We shall never have anything to please us. Now I chatter like a child in referring to being set free. We shall never leave here.

"Always we shall weave cloths of silk. Never shall we be better dressed. Always we shall be poor and naked, and always suffer hunger and thirst. Never shall we be able to earn enough to have better food. We have hardly any bread, a little in the morning and less in the evening. Never, for her handiwork, will any maiden earn more than four deniers from the pound to live on, and that cannot give us enough clothing and food. Those who earn twenty sous a week are still not without burden. The truth, be certain, is that every one of us does at least twenty sous' worth of work or more. That amount would make a duke wealthy. We are destitute, and our employer becomes rich from our earnings. We lie awake most of the night, and work all day to earn our living, for he threatens us with bodily harm when we rest. So we dare not rest. But why talk more? We have so much misery and disgrace that I cannot tell you the fifth of it. Still we are often furious and enraged at the sight of young and worthy knights dying in combat against the two demons; they pay much for their accommodation, as you will tomorrow. Whether you wish to or not, tomorrow you will have to fight entirely on your own and lose your reputation against two devils incarnate."

"May God, the true King of Heaven, protect me and give you honor and joy, if it be His will," Sir Yvain answered. "Now I must go and see the people inside and learn how they will receive me."

"Go now, sir. The Giver of All Goodness save you."

He then went away and entered the hall, where he found no one, good or evil, who would speak to them of anything.

Sir Yvain, the maiden, and the lion passed through the house and went out into a garden. They did not discuss or even mention stabling their horses, but it did not matter; those who expected to have the horses had done the stabling. I do not know if they were wise in their expectations, for in the end the knight will have a horse that is all rested. The horses had oats and hay and straw up to their bellies.

Sir Yvain entered the garden with his party following him. He saw a noble man reclining on his side on a silk rug. In front of him a maiden was reading from a romance—I do not know about whom. A lady had come to recline there and hear the romance. She was the maiden's mother, and the lord was her father. They enjoyed watching and listening to her very much, for they had no other children. Not more than sixteen, she was so beautiful and charming that the god of Love, had he seen her, would have become her servant and caused her never to love anyone but him. To be her servant, he would have set aside his divinity and taken on human form. He would have struck his own body with the arrow whose wound never heals unless an untrue physician tends it. It is wrong for anyone to recover unless treachery is discovered there, and anyone healed another way is not a true lover. If the story pleased you, I could go on telling you of these wounds until I reached some ending. But soon there would be someone who would say I was telling you of a dream. People today do not fall in love or love as they used to. They do not even have the desire to hear talk of love.

But hear now the way the people received Sir Yvain, how they welcomed and lodged him. As soon as those in the garden saw him, they leapt to their feet in greeting. "This way, dear sir," they said. "May all God's words and works bless you and all that is yours."

I do not know if they were deceiving him, but they joyfully welcomed him and acted as though they were happy that he was comfortably lodged. Even the lord's daughter served him and paid him great honor as one should a noble guest. She relieved him of all his armor, and that was not the least of her service, for with her own hands she washed his neck, his head, and his face. Her father wanted all honor paid to their guest, and this was done. From her chest she took a pleated shirt, white breeches, and a needle and thread, which she used to sew on his sleeves as she dressed him. God grant that this attentive service not cost him too dearly! She presented him with a new jacket to put on over his shirt, and placed round his neck a brand new cloak, made of rich wool trimmed with miniver. Her efforts to serve him caused him embarrassment and shame; yet the maiden was so noble, so well born, and so courteous that she still believed she had done little. And she knew her mother was pleased that she was not inattentive to anything she thought might flatter him.

That night he was served so many dishes that there was too much to eat. Merely serving the dishes could exhaust the waiters. During the evening the people paid him every honor, nor did they neglect a single comfort as they took him to his bedroom. Afterwards they never disturbed him once he was in his bed. And the lion, as usual, lay at his feet.

In the morning God, whose authority governs everything, rekindled His light through the world as early as He could. Sir Yvain and the maiden accompanying him rose promptly and went to a chapel for mass, which was soon said on their behalf in honor of the Holy Spirit.

After the mass, Sir Yvain received bad news at the moment when he expected nothing to prevent his departure. Events, however, could not turn out as he wished. "Sir, if it be your pleasure, I go with your leave," he announced.

"Friend, I shall not give you permission yet," the lord of the house replied. "There is a reason I cannot do it. This castle has a cruel and diabolical custom I am forced to observe. I shall have two of my men-at-arms come here now. Both are huge and strong, and rightly or wrongly, you must take up arms against the pair. If you can defend yourself against them and defeat and kill both, then my daughter wants you for her husband, and the honor of this castle and everything around it are yours."

"Sir, I seek none of that honor," he replied. "May God never grant me any, and may your daughter remain with you. Because she is so beautiful and well mannered, the Emperor of Germany would be indeed blest to marry her."

"Be silent, dear guest," said the lord. "I don't hear your refusal since it is impossible for you to escape. The man able to defeat on the field your future assailants ought to have my castle and all my land, and to take as his wife my daughter. There is no way of avoiding or rejecting the combat. But I realize that you refuse my daughter out of cowardice, expecting to avoid the battle this way. But you can be absolutely certain that combat must be yours. No knight who sleeps here can possibly escape. This is an established custom and rule that will continue for too long a time. My daughter will never be married until I see them dead or defeated."

"Then I must fight, even though against my will. But I assure you, I would forgo it, and gladly. Although I regret this, I shall engage in combat since it cannot be avoided."

Then the two hideous and black sons of the demon arrived. Each of the two carried a jagged club of cornel wood, covered with copper and then wound with brass. Though they were armed from their shoulders down to their knees, their heads and faces were unprotected and their huge legs bare. Equipped like this, they approached, and for protection they held before their faces round shields that were light and strong. The lion started to tremble the moment he saw them, for he noted their equipment and realized that they were coming to fight his master. Shaking with boldness and anger, he bristled, his hair and his mane standing on end. As he beat the ground with his tail, he resolved to rescue his master before they had the chance to kill him. But when the two saw him, they exclaimed: "Vassal, your lion threatens us. Take him from here! Follow our orders and place him where he cannot manage to hurt us or help you. Otherwise admit your defeat. If he could, the lion would gladly help you, and you must be on your own to sport with us."

"You are the ones who fear him; take him away yourselves," Sir Yvain answered. "I am pleased and satisfied for him to hurt you, if ever he can, and I am delighted to have his aid."

"We swear that is no good," they said. "You will never have his help. Do as best you can by yourself without anyone's aid. You have to be alone and we two together. If the lion joined you to fight us, then you would not be alone, and it would be two against us two. I assure you, you have to take your lion from here, even though you have no such wish at this moment."

"Where do you want him to be?" he asked. "Or rather, where do you want me to put him?"

They then pointed out a small room to him. "Place him there," they said.

"Since that is your wish, it will be done," he answered.

He then took the lion and shut him inside. At once his equipment was fetched. After he was armed, his horse was led out and given to him, and he mounted. Reassured that the lion was locked away in the room, the two champions came riding at him to injure and disgrace him. So hard were the blows from their clubs that shield and helmet were of little value. Their strokes battered and smashed his helmet to pieces, and the shield shattered and dissolved like ice. The holes in his shield were large enough for his fist. The blows they delivered were fearsome.

And what did he do to the two devils? Spurred on by fear and shame, he defended himself as best he could, mustering all his force and effort to deliver hard and heavy blows. His opponents had no lack of his gifts, for he returned their kind acts in double measure.

Shut away in the room, the lion felt deep distress in his heart as he recalled the great kindness of his noble master, who would already be in urgent need of his aid and support. If he could get out, he would repay his master's generosity in full force and measure without any omission in the reckoning. Although he continued to search in every direction, he found no way out. He heard the blows from the dangerous and despicable combat, which pained him so much that he went mad with rage. He went rooting around until he came upon the door sill, which was rotting near the ground. He dug and tore away at it, at last wedging himself in all the way to his haunches.

In the meantime Sir Yvain was hard pressed and soaked in sweat, for the two giants, he was discovering, were powerful and cruel as well as persistent. He had endured their blows and returned as many as he could, but had not done them any injury. They were too skilled in swordplay: no sword, however sharp or cutting, could dint their shields. As a result, Sir Yvain might well fear death. Still he was able to hold his own until the lion scratched and crawled his way out underneath the door. If the scoundrels were not defeated now, they never would be, for they would never have peace with the lion so long as he knew they were alive. He grabbed and hurled one to the ground as though he were a sheep. Now the scoundrels were terrified. And everyone in that entire area felt joy in his heart.

The demon the lion took to the ground would never stand again without support from his partner. The latter was running to help him and to protect himself, fearing that the lion would grab him after killing the one he had already dragged to the ground. Terrified more of the lion than of the lion's master, he turned his back on Sir Yvain and exposed his bare neck. The knight would have been stupid to let him continue living since the situation had turned favorable. When the scoundrel showed his unprotected head and his naked neck, Yvain brought down such a smooth blow that he cut off his head, the victim unaware of the act. At once he dismounted, anxious to rescue the other demon and take him from the lion's grasp. All was in vain. The demon was in such agony that a physician would never arrive in time, for the lion's ferocious assault had left him mortally wounded. Nevertheless Yvain did drag the lion back and saw that he had ripped away the entire shoulder from its place. He had no further fear of him, for his club had fallen. The demon lay there, motionless and still, almost like a man dead. Still he had enough strength to talk, and he spoke as well as he could. "Please, dear sir, take away your lion so he will do me no more harm. From now on you may do whatever you wish to me. Anyone who asks and begs mercy should not be denied his request, unless he faces a man without compassion. I shall not defend myself more. I shall never rise from here again by any strength of mine. I place myself at your mercy."

"Then say whether you admit that you have been overcome and defeated," Yvain said.

"Sir, it is quite obvious," he answered. "I am defeated against my will and I do surrender. I admit this to you."

"Then you need not fear me, and my lion will let you be."

All the people then raced out and gathered round him. The lord and his lady embraced him and rejoiced as they spoke with him of their daughter. "Now you shall be our lord and master," they announced. "And our daughter will be your lady, for we shall present her to you as your wife."

"And as for me, I give her back to you," he replied. "Let the man who desires her have her; I care not. There is no scorn behind my words. So don't be angry if I do not take her. I cannot. I must not. If you please, hand over your captives to me. As you know well, the pact provides that they go free."

"What you say is true," he said, "and I do release and hand them over to you without dispute. But take my daughter along with all my wealth, and you will act prudently. She is wise, elegant, and beautiful. You will never have so wealthy a marriage if you refuse this one."

"Sir, you do not know my situation and what holds me back, and I dare not relate it to you," he answered. "But I do realize that I am refusing what would never be turned down by any man with a free heart, able to devote himself to a beautiful and charming maiden. If I could, and if I should, I would gladly marry her—you can be certain of the truth of these words— but I cannot marry her or anyone else. So insist no more. The young lady who came with me is waiting for me. She has been my companion along the way, and I do not wish to lose her company under any circumstance."

"You wish to leave, dear sir? And how will you manage it? My gate will never be opened for you unless I so decide and order. Instead, you will stay in my prison. Your behavior is arrogant and unjust, since I ask you to marry my daughter and you scorn her."

"Scorn her? Sir, upon my soul, I do not. But I cannot marry or stay here at any cost. I shall follow the maiden who is my guide. There is nothing more that may be done. But if it be your pleasure, I shall pledge to you by my right hand so that you will believe me: I shall return as you see me here now, if ever I can, and then I shall marry your daughter."

"Damn him who seeks anything from you or demands your oath or pledge!" he exclaimed. "If you want my daughter, marry her because she is beautiful and charming. You will then return promptly. I do not believe any oath or promise would ever make you come back sooner. Go now. I free you from all pledges and all agreements. If you are detained by wind and rain or anything else, it matters to me not. I shall never consider my daughter so vile that I would force her on you. Now go about your business. I care not whether you stay away or return."

Sir Yvain stayed no longer in the castle but went away, taking with him the released captives, whom the lord had handed over to him, poor and ill-clad. But now they considered themselves wealthy. As they emerged in pairs from the castle before their rescuer, I do not believe they would have rejoiced so much if the Creator of the whole world had come from heaven down to earth.

The people who had shouted every possible insult at him all came and escorted him along his way, asking his pardon and mercy. But he told them he knew nothing of that. "I do not know of what you speak," he said, "and since, as far as I recall, you said nothing which struck me as malicious, I hold you entirely free of that."

Delighted by his response, they all extolled his courtesy and accompanied him quite a distance. Then they commended him to God. After asking leave to depart, the young ladies went away, and as they left, they all bowed to him, praying that God would grant him joy and good health and hoping that he would attain his desire wherever he went. And he whom the delay was very much troubling replied, "God save them." "Go," he said. "God bring you in health and happiness to your lands." At once they set on their way and departed amid much rejoicing, and for his part, Sir Yvain immediately rode off in another direction.

Each day of that week, Yvain galloped along without pause. The maiden was his guide, for she was certain of the route and of the place where she had left the disinherited sister unhappy and desolate. When that young lady heard news of the maiden's arrival with the Knight with the Lion, no joy could ever equal the joy in her heart. Now she expected that if she insisted, her sister would give her a share of her inheritance. The maiden had been lying ill in bed quite some time. Only recently had she recovered from her grave sickness, as was apparent in her face. She ran out immediately to be the first to meet them, and she greeted them with every honor she knew. There is no need to tell the happiness in the house that night. Never a word can be told of it, since there would be too much to tell. I am passing over everything and resuming the story for you the next day when they mounted and rode on their way.

They continued to ride along until they reached the town where King Arthur had been staying a fortnight or more. The young lady who had disinherited her sister was there, having stayed near the court to await the arrival of her sister, who was now approaching. Little did she worry, for she did not expect her sister to find any knight capable of withstanding Sir Gawain in combat. Now of the forty, only one day was left. If this one day had passed, the case would undoubtedly have ended in her favor according to right and judgment. But there was much more to do than she thought or imagined.

Yvain and the maiden stayed outside the town that night in a lowly and cramped abode where no one knew them. Had they stayed in the town, all the people would have recognized them, and that was not their desire. At first light they left their lodging promptly and remained out of sight until the day was full and clear.

I do not know how many days had passed since Sir Gawain had taken lodging away from the court. No one there knew anything of him except the maiden for whose cause he would fight. He had gone into hiding about three or four leagues from the court. And when he came to court, he was so fully armed that even his longstanding friends could not recognize him by the arms he was bearing. The young lady, whose wrong toward her sister was quite evident, presented him in view of everyone at court. With his support she intended to settle the dispute in her favor, though she was not in the right.

"Lord, time passes," she said to the king. "It will soon be late afternoon, and today was the last day. Now it is obvious I am ready. Now I must defend my claim. If my sister were returning, she would have no reason to wait so long. I may thank God that she is not coming back here again. It is evident that she cannot better her situation. And I have put myself to this trouble for nothing, prepared every day until this, the very last, to prove rightful possession of what is mine. Without combat I have settled my claim, and now it is right that I leave and hold my inheritance in peace. As long as I live I shall not answer to my sister about this. Her life will be wretched and miserable."

Well aware that the dishonest maiden had wronged her sister, the king spoke. "Friend, on my word, in a royal court one must wait until the king's justice has had time to deliberate and render a verdict. There is no use maneuvering here. Your sister still has time, as I believe, to come here."

Before the king finished speaking, he saw the Knight with the Lion and the maiden beside him. The two came by themselves, having slipped away from the lion, who remained behind where they had spent the night. The king did not fail to recognize the maiden when he saw her, and the sight of her filled him with pleasure and joy. In the quarrel he stood behind her because he always sided with right. He was so happy that he cried out to her as soon as he could: "God save you, fair lady. Come forward."

At these words the other sister turned round trembling, and saw her sister and the knight she had brought to defend her claim; she turned blacker than earth. Everyone welcomed the maiden, who went before the king where she saw him. When she stood in front of him, she addressed him. "God save the king and his company! Your Majesty, if my cause and my just claim can now be established by a knight, it will be done by this one, who has been kind enough to follow me here. Although this noble and well-born knight had much business elsewhere, he took such pity on me that he set aside all that for my sake. Now my lady, my very dear sister, whom I love as much as my own heart, would show goodness and courtesy by leaving me my rightful estate. Were she to do this, she would act well, for I demand nothing that is hers."

"It is true that I want nothing of yours," her sister answered, "for you have nothing and never shall have anything. From preaching you will never gain anything, no matter how much you preach. All you can do is dry up from grief."

The other sister, who was courteous and wise, knew what was proper and replied immediately. "I am sorry indeed that such worthy men as these two will fight on our behalf in so small a dispute," she said. "But I cannot abandon my claim, for I would suffer a great deal from that. This is why I would be more grateful if you would leave me what is rightfully mine."

"Anyone who would answer you now would be a fool," the other replied. "May the flames of hell burn me if I give you anything to better you life. The banks of the Danube and the Seine will meet before I give you anything, unless by combat."

"God and right are on my side. I trust them, and I have trusted them. May they aid my knight and protect him from harm. Out of loyalty and love he has offered me his service, without knowing who I am. He does not know me, nor I him."

They continued talking until they had nothing left to say. Then they led their knights into the courtyard, where all the people crowded about, as people usually do who are anxious to see the blows of joust and combat.

The two fighters did not recognize each other, though they had loved each other always. Then did they no longer love each other? Yes, I answer you, and no as well, and I shall prove both replies correct. In truth, Sir Gawain did love Yvain and called him his companion, and wherever he was, Yvain referred to Gawain in the same way. Even here, had he recognized him, he would have had a celebration for him and would have laid down his life for him. Each would have acted that way rather than permit harm to befall the other. Is that not true and perfect love? Yes, without a doubt.

Yet is Hate not equally evident too? Yes, because each would certainly have wished to smash the other's head or shame him so much that he would have been the worse for it.

I swear it is a proven wonder that Love and mortal Hate are found together. God, how can two such contraries inhabit the same house? It seems to me they cannot live together in one house a single night, for once each knew the other was there, they could remain only with dispute and discord. Yet in one house are several divisions with galleries and bedrooms. It may be the same in this situation. Perhaps Love had shut himself in some hidden chamber, while Hate had gone to the galleries on the street side to be seen. Now Hate is ready for the forward attack, spurring and pricking against Love whenever he can, and Love does not even stir.

Ah, Love, where are you hiding? Come out, and you will see what forces the enemies of your friends have brought out and set against you. The enemies are the very men who love each other with a sacred love, for a love that is not false or feigned is a rare and sacred thing. And so Love is entirely blind, and Hate sees nothing. If Love recognized the men, he would have to prevent them from attacking and injuring each other. Therefore Love is blind, deceived, and defeated, for though he sees them, he does not recognize the men who are his rightful subjects. And Hate, unable to say why they detest each other, desires that they fight a wrongful combat. They hate each other to the death, and each does not love, you can be certain, the man who wants to disgrace him and desires his death. What? Then did Yvain wish to murder his friend Sir Gawain? Yes, and the feeling was mutual. Would Sir Gawain have killed Yvain with his own hands, or done something worse than I have said? Definitely not, I swear and assure you. Neither would have hurt or shamed the other, not for all God has done for mankind or for the whole Roman empire.

Now I have told a disgraceful lie, for it is most evident that each wished to attack the other with lance raised high in its rest. Each was eager to wound and cripple the other, to humiliate him and reduce him to despair, for he would never feign such actions.

Tell me now, when one has received the worst of the blows and been defeated, of whom will he complain? If they do go so far as to exchange strokes, I am terrified they will continue the strife of combat until one is defeated. If Yvain loses, will he be able to say in all fairness that he has been harmed and humiliated by a man whom he numbers among his friends, and who has never called him by any name except friend and companion? Or if it happens by chance that Yvain manages to bring Gawain to defeat or some form of disgrace, will Gawain have the right to complain? No, for he will not know whom to blame.

Because the men failed to recognize each other, they drew back in readiness. At the first assault, their thick ash lances shattered. Each spoke not a word to the other, for had they conversed, their encounter would have been different: they would have gone not to attack with lances and swords, but to hug and kiss each other. Now they were assaulting and maiming each other. Their swords were not the better for this, nor were their helmets or shields, which were battered and split. The edges of their swords were becoming notched and dull: they were exchanging such severe shocks not with the flat ends, but with the sharp edges, and delivering with the pommels too on the noseguards, backs, foreheads, and cheeks that the skin was turning black and blue from the blood forming underneath. The hauberks were so tattered, the shields so broken to pieces that neither man escaped injury. The force of the struggle scarcely allowed them to catch their breath. In the fury of their bout, any jacinth or emerald attached to their helmets was smashed and crushed. Stunned from the hard blows of the pommels on the helmets, they almost knocked each other's brains out. Their eyes bulged from their heads. Their fists were huge and square, their muscles strong, their bones hard. Savage were the facial blows they delivered with their tightly gripped swords, which were of immense service to them in their violent strokes.

Their long encounter exhausted them. The helmets were crushed, the shields bent and broken. Although they had drawn back a little to catch their breath and slow their pulses, the pause did not last long. The assault resumed even more fiercely than before. All the spectators exclaimed that they had never seen two more courageous knights. "This combat is no game, but a very hard struggle. They will never be rewarded as they deserve."

As the two friends continued to maim each other, they heard these words as well as talk of reconciling the two sisters. Although the younger had submitted to the king's decision and would not contradict him, the elder could not be persuaded to make peace. She was so malicious that even Queen Guinevere, the authorities in legal matters, the knights, and the king supported the younger. Everyone came to the king, begging him to give a third or a quarter of the land to the younger sister despite the elder, and to separate the two knights who were displaying great courage. It would be too unfortunate, they said, if one injured the other or deprived him of any part of his honor. But the king refused to intervene to bring about peace, for the elder sister, he said, was so cruel a creature that she had no interest in it. All these words the two knights heard as they continued to exchange blows.

All were astonished that the battle was so equal; there was no way to tell who was better or worse. The two fighters themselves, who were buying honor at the expense of agony, were amazed and aghast. They were so evenly matched in their assault that each wondered about the identity of his opponent, who put up such fierce resistance. They continued their combat until day gave way to night. Their arms were tired, their bodies in agony, and their blood, hot and boiling, bubbled from many wounds and ran down under the hauberks. It is no wonder they wanted rest, for they were in severe pain. They paused to rest, each man thinking to himself that at long last he had met his equal.

Their pause lasted a long time. They dared not fight again, for they wanted no further combat: the night grew dark, and they stood in dread of each other. These two motives prompted them to maintain peace. Yet before they left the field, they would learn each other's identity and know compassion and joy.

Brave and courteous as he was, Sir Yvain was the first to speak. His good friend did not recognize him from his words, which were almost inaudible. His voice was weak, hoarse, and cracking, for he was badly shaken by the blows he had received. "Sir," he said, "night advances. I am certain you will not be reproached or blamed if it separates us. For my part, I admit that I both fear you and esteem you. I have never been in a battle that caused me so much discomfort. There has never been a knight I so wanted to see and to know. I have the highest admiration for you. I expected to see myself defeated. Well you know how to land your strokes to their full advantage. I never knew a knight so expert in delivering blows. I would have preferred to receive much less than you have given me today. Your blows have completely stunned me."

"I swear you are not so stunned and dizzy," answered Sir Gawain, "for I am just the same or perhaps more so. If I were to know who you are, I doubt that I would be displeased. If I lent you anything of mine, you have repaid the account well, principal and interest. You generously paid back more than I was ready to accept. But however that is, since you would have me tell you my name, I shall not keep it from you. I am Gawain, son of King Lot."

When Yvain heard these words, he was taken aback, and completely at a loss from anger and vexation. He flung his bloodied sword and his shattered shield to the ground and dismounted. "Ah, alas, such misfortune!" he cried out. "We have waged this battle in such shameful ignorance because we did not recognize each other. Had I known you, never would I have fought you. I would have surrendered, I assure you, before the first blow."

"What? Who are you?" asked Sir Gawain.

"I am Yvain, who loves you more than any man alive anywhere, and you have always loved and honored me in every court. So much do I wish to make amends to you for this situation and to honor you that I am going to declare that I was utterly defeated."

"Would you do that for me?" asked the gentle Sir Gawain. "I would certainly be most presumptuous to accept such amends. This honor will never be mine, it will be yours. I give it to you."

"Oh, dear sir, say no more. That could never be. I am so exhausted and hurt that I can endure no longer."

"You certainly waste your words," his friend and his companion answered. "I am the one who is defeated and exhausted. I say this not to flatter you. There is no one in the world so unknown to me that I would not say this to him rather than receive more of the blows."

With these words they got down and threw their arms around each other. They kissed, each continuing to declare that he had been defeated. They were still arguing when the king and the barons came running from all sides at the sight of their reconciliation. They were anxious to hear what had happened, and who the men were who greeted each other so joyfully. "Gentle sirs," the king asked, "tell us what has brought this accord and friendship between you two. All this day I have seen such strife and hate here."

"Lord, the misfortune and mishap that led to the battle will not be hidden from you," said his nephew Sir Gawain. "Since you have stopped to hear and learn the cause, it is well to tell you the truth. I, Gawain, your nephew, did not recognize my companion Sir Yvain, this knight here, until, thanks to him and the will of God, he asked my name. Only when one told the other his name did we recognize each other, and that was after we had fought well. Our combat has been fierce, and our struggle had already been too long. Had we continued even a little more, it would have gone badly indeed with me. I swear he would have killed me because of his valor and because of the wrongful cause of that woman who chose me as her champion. But I would rather my friend defeat me in combat than kill me."

Sir Yvain's blood stirred. "God help me, dear sir," he said, "but you are most mistaken in what you say. Well does my lord the king know that I am definitely the one who is defeated and beaten in this combat."

"I am," the other exclaimed.

"No, I am," each continued to say.

Both men were so noble and well born that each continued to concede and give the crown of victory to the other. Neither was willing to accept the honor. Each desperately sought to make the king and all his men believe that he was the one who was defeated and beaten. When the king had listened a while, he stopped the dispute. What he heard delighted him, as did the sight of the two, who were now embracing. And yet each had inflicted many grave wounds on the other. "Gentle sirs," he announced, "there is great love between you, and you prove this when each declares his own defeat. Now leave all in my hands. I believe I shall effect a reconciliation between them that will do you honor and win me everyone's praise."

Both promised to follow the king's exact will according to his decree. And the king said that he would settle the quarrel justly and in good faith. "Where is the maiden who expelled her sister from her land and cruelly disinherited her by force?" he asked.

"Lord, I am here," she answered.

"There, are you? Then come here. For long have I realized that you disinherited her. Her rights shall not be denied anymore, for you have just admitted the truth to me. Of necessity you must surrender her her rightful share."

"Alas, lord king, if I have said anything unwise or foolish in response, would you take advantage of my statement? In God's name, lord, do not wrong me. You are king and ought to protect me against wrong and injustice."

"Because of that, I wish to return to your sister her proper rights," the king answered. "I never had any desire to be unjust. You have heard that your knight and your sister's have left the matter in my hands. I shall not say what you would prefer to hear, for your injustice is most evident. In an effort to honor the other, each knight declares that he is the loser. Since the decision is mine, I need not wait. Either you will do exactly what I say and abandon your unjust claim, or I shall declare that my nephew was defeated in combat. In that case it will be worse for you. But I shall say that only reluctantly."

Under no circumstance would he have said that, but he spoke in this manner to see if he might frighten her into restoring to her sister her share of the inheritance. He knew too well that she would never return anything because of his words, but only because of force or fear. Anxious and afraid, she made her response. "Dear lord, I must do your will, though with a sorrowful heart. I shall do it however much it hurts me. My sister will have her share of my inheritance. I name you yourself as my pledge to her that she may be the more assured of it."

"Invest her with it at this very moment," the king ordered. "Then she will be your liegewoman and hold land from you. Love her as you should

your liegewoman, and let her love you as her lady and as her own sister."
The king settled the matter, the maiden being given possession of her land,
and she expressed her gratitude to him for this.

The king told his nephew, the brave and valiant knight, to let himself
be disarmed, and he asked Sir Yvain also to allow his arms to be set aside,
if it was his pleasure, for they now had no need of them. Disarmed, the
vassals kissed as equals. During their exchange they noticed the lion, who
came running to seek his master. As soon as the lion saw him, he began
to show his happiness. Then you would have seen the people draw back,
even the boldest taking to flight.

"Everyone, be still!" Sir Yvain exclaimed. "Why do you flee? No one is
chasing you. Do not fear harm from the lion you see approaching. Please
believe me. He is mine and I am his. We are companions."

All who had heard tell of the adventures of the lion and his companion
then knew the truth, that this was none other than he who had slain the
evil giant. "God help me, lordly companion," Sir Gawain said to him. "You
have made me so ashamed. How miserably I have repaid you for your
service to me in slaying the giant and rescuing my niece and my nephews.
For so long I have thought about you, but I was always confused. I could
not recall, nor had I heard tell of any knight I knew, in any land I had
been, by the name of the Knight with the Lion."

They were disarmed as they talked, and the lion stepped quickly to where
his master sat. When he came before him, he rejoiced over him as well as
a beast could who had no power of speech.

Both knights had to be taken to an infirmary or sickroom, for they
needed a surgeon and plasters to heal their wounds. King Arthur, who
loved the knights very much, had them brought before him. The king had
a surgeon summoned who knew more than any man about medicine. The
surgeon set about the work of healing the wounds, and did so as best and
as quickly as he could.

When he had cured both knights, Sir Yvain, whose heart was forever
set on Love, realized that he could not go on living and would finally die
for Love unless his lady took pity on him. Thus was he dying. He decided
to leave the court by himself, and go and wage war at his spring. He would
cause such lightning, wind, and rain that she would be forced to make
peace with him, or else he would never stop plaguing the spring and causing
wind and rain.

As soon as Sir Yvain felt healed and healthy, he departed without any-
one's knowledge. With him was his lion, who never wished to leave his
company as long as he lived. They traveled until they reached the spring

where they made the rain fall. Do not imagine I lie to you. The storm was so fierce that no one could relate the tenth of it. The whole forest looked as though it would fall into the pit of hell. The lady was afraid her entire town would also fall. The walls tottered and the tower trembled so that the castle nearly collapsed. The boldest of her men would rather be taken prisoner among the Turks in Persia than be shut up within those walls. So terrified were the people that they all cursed their ancestors. "Damn the first man who built his home in this country! Damn those who built this town! In the whole world they could not have found a more hateful place, for a single man can assault and ravage and lay it waste."

"You must obtain advice about this, lady," Lunete said. "You will not find anyone to aid you in this crisis unless you go searching far from here. It is true that we shall never rest in this town or dare go beyond the walls and the gate. Were all your knights assembled for this undertaking, you can be certain even the best would not dare make a move. The situation now is that you have no one to defend your spring, and you will look ridiculous and despicable. What fine honor will be yours if the assailant leaves without combat! Surely your plight is unfortunate unless you think of some solution."

"You know so much. Advise me of a plan, and I shall follow your advice," the lady replied.

"Lady, if I could, I would certainly be glad to advise you. But you desperately need a wiser counselor. Therefore I dare not interfere. Like the others, I shall endure the wind and the rain until, if it be God's pleasure, I see another worthy man in your court, who will assume the burden and responsibility of this combat. I do not expect this to happen today, and the situation will worsen for you."

"Young lady, say something else," the lady answered her at once. "There is no man in my household I could count on to defend the spring and the stone. But now, please God, we shall hear your advice and your wisdom. In time of need, it is always said, you must test your friend."

"Lady, if someone thought he could find the man who slew the giant and defeated the three knights, it would be well to go in search of him. Yet as long as he suffers the enmity, anger, and hate of his lady, I think there is no man or woman alive he would follow, unless that person would swear to him and promise to do all possible to appease his lady's deep enmity, which causes him to die of anxiety and pain."

"Before you begin this search, I am prepared to pledge my word and swear to you that if he comes to me, I shall do all I can, openly and honestly, to bring about his pardon," the lady said.

"Lady, I have not the slightest doubt that you can easily bring about the pardon if that is your will," Lunete answered her. "As for your oath, unless you object, I shall take it now before I go my way."

"I have no objection," the lady said.

Lunete, who was most courteous, had a very precious reliquary brought out promptly for her, and the lady knelt down. With utmost courtesy, Lunete had caught her in the game of truth. In administering the oath to her, she who received it did not forget anything that might be to her advantage. "Lady, raise your hand," she said. "I do not want you to blame me for anything that happens in the future, since it is not for my sake that you act. Your own good will be the reason for your action. Please, swear to do all in your power for the Knight with the Lion until he has his lady's goodwill exactly as he had it before."

The lady raised her right hand and swore on such exact terms. "As you have stated it, I say it. I swear by God and this saint, my heart will never fail to do all in my power. I shall return to him the love and the favor he used to have with his lady, since I have the power and the ability."

Lunete acted very well; she had achieved precisely what she wanted.

An easy-gaited palfrey was led out for Lunete, and she mounted happily and gladly. She rode off and traveled until, by the side of the pine, she found the man she did not expect to find so close. She had anticipated a long trip before meeting him. As soon as she caught sight of him, she recognized him by the lion. She galloped toward him, then dismounted onto the hard ground. Sir Yvain knew her the moment he saw her. He greeted her, and she him. "Sir," she said, "I am delighted to have found you so near."

"What? Were you looking for me?" asked Sir Yvain.

"Yes indeed, and I have never been so happy since the day I was born. I have brought my lady to this position that, unless she would perjure herself, she will be your lady and you her lord exactly as it was before. I assure you, this is the truth."

The miracle Sir Yvain heard, which he never had expected to hear, overwhelmed him with joy. He could not thank her enough for bringing this about. He kissed her eyes, then her face. "My dear friend," he said, "there is no way I can repay you. I doubt I shall have the ability or the occasion to do you honor and service."

"Do not concern yourself, sir, and do not let the thought worry you," she said. "You will have both the ability and the occasion to render service to me as well as to others. If I have paid back what I owed, no more gratitude is due me than to one who borrows another's goods and then repays the debt. I still do not believe I have repaid you what I owe you."

"As God is my witness, you have done that more than five hundred thousand times. Now we shall go quickly, for that is only right. But have you told her about me? Who I am?"

"No, I swear she knows only that your name is the Knight with the Lion."

As they were talking, they rode off with the lion always behind until all three reached the town. They spoke not a word to any man or woman in the streets. At last they came before the lady. As soon as the lady heard of her maiden's return with the knight and the lion, she was delighted. She was eager to see the knight, to meet him and make his acquaintance.

In full armor, Sir Yvain fell at the lady's feet. Lunete, who was beside him, said to her: "Lady, bring him to his feet, and use your efforts and power and wisdom to gain him the peace and pardon no one else in the entire world but you can secure for him."

The lady then had him stand. "My power is entirely his," she said. "I would gladly realize his will and his good insofar as I am able."

"Truly, lady, I would not speak if this were not true," Lunete said. "All this is in your power even more than I have stated. Now I shall tell you the truth, and you will know. You never had and you never will have so fine a friend as this man. God wants true peace and true love that will be unending between you and him, and He has caused me to find him today so close at hand. To prove the truth of this, there need be no further denial. Lady, forgive him your anger, for he has no other lady but you. This is Sir Yvain, your husband."

These words made the lady tremble. "God save me!" she exclaimed. "You have now trapped me neatly. In spite of myself you will make me love a man who does not love or esteem me. You have done very well for yourself. And what fine service you have done me! I would prefer to endure winds and storms all my life. If it were not too shameful and too base to break an oath, he would never find pardon or peace from me at any cost. Every day I would have brooded in my heart, like fire smoldering under ashes. But now I do not wish to hear mention of this pain, nor do I care to recall it, since I have to be reconciled to him."

Sir Yvain heard and understood that his cause was proceeding so well that he would find his pardon and his peace. "Lady, one should have mercy on a sinner," he said. "I have paid for my ignorant action, and I wish to pay for it still. Folly made me stay away, and I acknowledge my guilt and disgrace. I have been most bold to dare come before you. But if you would allow me to stay, I will never wrong you again."

"That is certainly my wish," she answered. "Otherwise I would perjure myself, unless I did all I could to make peace between you and me. If it be your pleasure, I shall grant your request."

"Lady, five hundred thanks," he answered. "God could not grant me more happiness in this mortal life, so help me the Holy Spirit."

Now Sir Yvain had his pardon, and you may believe that however great his distress had been, he had never been so happy. All had come to a fine end. He was cherished and loved by his lady, and she by him. Now he had no memory of anyone else, for the joy he had in his dear beloved made him forget.

And Lunete was filled with happiness. She lacked nothing that pleased her, since she had brought about unending accord between the true Sir Yvain and his dear and true lady.

AND SO CHRISTIAN BRINGS TO A CLOSE HIS ROMANCE ABOUT THE KNIGHT
WITH THE LION. I HAVE NEVER HEARD TELL MORE ABOUT HIM, AND
YOU WILL NEVER HEAR MORE TOLD UNLESS SOMEONE WANTS
TO ADD LIES. ¶HERE ENDS THE KNIGHT WITH THE
LION. IT WAS GUIOT WHO COPIED THE MAN-
USCRIPT; HIS SHOP IS LOCATED IN
FRONT OF THE CHURCH OF
OUR LADY OF THE
VALLEY.

THE STORY OF THE GRAIL

HE MAN WHO SOWS little reaps little, and the man who wants a good harvest should scatter his seed where it will yield him a hundredfold, for good seed withers and dies in poor soil. Christian sows and plants the seed of a romance he is beginning, and sows it on such good ground that it cannot but yield a fine harvest, for he does it on behalf of the worthiest man in the empire of Rome. This man is Philip, Count of Flanders, whose worthiness surpasses that of Alexander. People say that Alexander was so great, but I shall demonstrate that the count's worthiness surpasses that of Alexander, who embodied all vices and all evils from which the count is safe and free.

The count is one who does not listen to base buffoonery or silly chatter; slander about anyone disturbs him. The count loves righteousness and justice, loyalty and Holy Church, and despises all baseness. None knows the extent of his generosity, for he gives, without hypocrisy or guile, according to the Gospel, which says, "Let not thy left hand know the good thy right hand doth." His generosity is known only to its recipients and to God, who knows all the secrets of men's hearts and sees all the hidden recesses of their very being.

And why does the Gospel say, "Hide from thy left hand thy good deeds"? Because, according to Holy Scripture, the left hand signifies vanity that comes from base hypocrisy. And what does the right signify? Charity, which boasts not of its good works, but conceals them so that none knows of them except Him who is both God and Charity. God is Charity, and according to Scripture—Saint Paul says it, and with him I say it—the man who dwelleth in Charity dwelleth in God, and God in him.

Then you can be certain that this is true, that the gifts of the good count are gifts of charity, for none counsels him in this matter except his noble and generous heart, which advises him to do good. Is he not worthier than Alexander, who had no concern for charity or any good? Yes, never doubt this.

Therefore Christian's labor will not be wasted when, at the count's command, he endeavors and strives to put into rhyme the finest tale that may be told at a royal court. This is the Story of the Grail, from the book the count gave him. Hear how he performs his task.

In the season when trees bud, bushes leaf, and meadows turn green, when small birds sing their sweet morning songs in their own tongue, and everything is aflame with joy, the son of the widowed lady of the remote Desolate Forest rose, quickly saddled his hunting horse, and took three javelins in hand. Equipped in this manner, he at once left his mother's manorhouse, intending to go and see his mother's plowmen, who were sowing oats on her land; they had six plows and twelve oxen. And so he entered the forest, and his heart itself immediately rejoiced in the gentle season and the song he heard from the happy birds. All this pleased him.

The season was so gentle and calm that he unbridled his hunting horse and let it go graze on the fresh green grass. And since he knew how to hurl the javelins he carried, he walked about throwing them behind him, to the front, toward the ground, in the air, until he heard the sound of five knights in full armor riding through the forest. As they neared, their armor made a loud clamor since branches of oaks and hornbeams often struck against their equipment. All the hauberks jingled; the lances knocked against the shields; the wood of the lances resounded; and the steel of the shields and hauberks reverberated.

The youth heard but did not see those rapidly approaching. Marveling at this, he said: "On my soul, my lady my mother spoke truth to me when she told me that there is nothing in the world more terrifying than devils. She instructed me that one should make the sign of the cross to guard against them. But I shall scorn this teaching. Never will I cross myself. Instead, with one of the javelins I carry, I shall strike the strongest with such speed that none of the others, I believe, will ever come near me."

In this manner the youth spoke to himself before he caught sight of them. When he did see them in the open without the woods concealing them, and noticed the jingling hauberks and the bright shining helmets, and beheld the green and the scarlet and the gold and the azure and the silver gleaming in the sun, he found everything most noble and beautiful. "Ah, Lord God, have mercy!" he then exclaimed. "These are angels I behold here. Alas, truly, now I have sinned grievously, now I have behaved most badly to call them devils. My mother told me no idle tale when she said to me that angels were the most beautiful creatures there are except for God, Who is the most beautiful of all. Here I behold the Lord God, I believe, for one of them is so beautiful to behold that the others, so help me God, have not a tenth of his beauty. My mother said herself that one must believe in God and worship Him, honor and pray to Him. And I shall worship that one and all the others with him."

He threw himself to the ground at once, reciting his creed and all the prayers he knew, which his mother had taught him.

The leader of the knights observed him. "Stay back, for this youth saw us and fell to the ground in fear," he told the others. "If we all rode toward him together, I think that he would be terrified to death and unable to answer any question I put to him."

They stopped, and he galloped toward the young man. Greeting him reassuringly, he said: "Youth, have no fear."

"By the Savior I believe in, I have none," the young man answered. "Are you God?"

"No, I swear."

"Who are you then?"

"I am a knight."

"I never knew a knight before, and never saw one or heard talk of one," the young man said. "But you are more beautiful than God. I wish I were like you, so sparkling and so formed."

At these words the knight rode near him. "Have you seen five knights and three maidens on this heath today?" he asked him.

The youth was intent on seeking and asking other information. He extended his hand and took hold of the knight's lance. "Dear honored sir, you with the name of knight, what is this you hold?" he asked.

"Now am I well informed!" the knight said. "I expected to learn news from you, dear friend, and you would learn it from me. I shall tell you. This is my lance."

"Do you mean that it is thrown the same way I throw my javelins?" he asked.

"Not at all. Youth, you are most foolish. Rather you strike with it directly."

"Then one of these three javelins you see here is more valuable, because I kill anything I want with it, birds or beasts as need be, and I kill them from a crossbow's range."

"Youth, I care not about this. But answer me regarding the knights. Tell me if you know where they are. And did you see the maidens?"

The youth took hold of him by the edge of his shield. "What is this? And what is it for?" he asked with complete sincerity.

"Youth," he replied, "this is a ruse to avert me from the subject of my question to you. I expected you, so help me God, to instruct me rather than learn from me. And you wish me to teach you this! Happen what will, I shall tell you, for I am pleased to accommodate you. What I carry is called a shield."

"It is called a shield?"

"Yes," he replied. "I should not scorn it, for it is so dependable that if anyone draws or shoots at me, it withstands all blows. This is the service it does me."

At this moment the knights who had stayed behind rode up to their lord. "Sir, what does this Welshman tell you?" they asked him at once.

"So help me God, he is ignorant of all manners since he never makes proper answer to any question I ask," their lord replied. "Instead, whatever he sees, he asks its name and purpose."

"Sir, be certain beyond a doubt that all Welshmen are, by nature, more stupid than grazing cattle. This one is just such a beast. The man who stops beside him is foolish unless he would loaf and waste his time."

"So help me God, I don't know," he said. "But before proceeding farther, I shall tell him whatever he would know. This is the only way I shall ever leave here." He then asked him another question. "Youth," he said, "be not annoyed, but tell me of the five knights and the maidens, whether you saw or met them."

And the youth took hold of him by the edge of his hauberk and tugged it. "Now tell me, dear sir, what is this you wear?" he asked.

"Youth, then you don't know?" he exclaimed.

"No."

"Youth, this is my hauberk, and it is as strong as steel."

"Is it steel?"

"You see this well."

"I know nothing about it, though, so help me God, it is very beautiful," he said. "How is it used? How does it serve you?"

"Youth, that is easy to explain. If you wanted to hurl javelins or shoot arrows at me, you could not harm me."

"Sir knight, God keep the does and stags from such hauberks, for I could never race after and kill them."

Again the knight spoke to him. "Youth, so help you God, can you tell me about the knights and the maidens?"

And he who had little sense said to him: "Were you born like this?"

"No, youth. That is impossible, for no one can be born like this."

"Then who dressed you so?"

"Youth, I shall certainly tell you who."

"Then tell it."

"I am glad to. It has not been five full days since King Arthur dubbed me knight and presented me with all this armor. But now tell me what has become of the knights who passed by here escorting the three maidens. Did they go slowly? Or did they flee?"

"Sir, look now at the tall trees you see on the ridge of that mountain. That is the Valdone Pass," he said.

"And what of that, dear friend?" he asked.

"My mother's plowmen are there, plowing and harrowing her fields. If those people passed by there, the plowmen, if they saw them, will tell you."

The knights said that they would ride there with him if he would take them to the men sowing oats in the field.

The youth took his hunting horse and rode over to the plowmen, who were harrowing the plowed fields where the oats had been sown. When they saw their lord, all trembled with fear. And do you know why they did? Because of the armed knights accompanying him. They realized that if the knights had told him of their occupation and their way of life, he would wish to be a knight, and then his mother would be distraught, for she had expected to prevent him from ever seeing a knight or learning of their profession.

"Have you seen five men and three maidens pass by here?" the youth asked the ox drivers.

"They have been making their way through these woods all day," the ox drivers answered.

And the youth addressed the knight who had conversed so much with him. "Sir, the knights and the maidens did pass by here. But now tell me about the king who makes knights, and the place where he usually resides."

"Youth, I shall tell you," he replied. "The king stays at Carlisle. He was in residence there not five days ago, for I was there and saw him. If you do not find him there, there will certainly be people to tell you where he is. He will never have traveled so far that you will fail to learn news of him. But now I beg you to instruct me by what name I shall call you."

"Sir," he said, "I shall tell you. My name is darling son."

"It is darling son? I certainly imagine you still have another name."

"Sir, on my word, my name is darling brother."

"Yes, I believe you. But if you wish to tell me the truth, I would like to know your proper name."

"Sir," he said, "I can certainly tell you. My proper name is darling little lord."

"So help me God, that is a fair name. Have you any others?"

"Sir, not I. I certainly have no others."

"So help me God, I hear the greatest wonders I have ever heard and, I believe, the greatest I shall ever hear." The knight immediately galloped off, anxious to catch up with the others.

The youth was prompt to return to his manorhouse, where his mother, concerned about his lateness, was sad and gloomy. The moment she saw him, she rejoiced with a joy she could not conceal. Like a most loving mother, she ran to meet him, calling him "darling son, darling son," more than a hundred times. "Darling son, your lateness has plunged my heart into grief. I almost died of anxiety and worry. Where have you been so long today?"

"Where, lady? I shall certainly tell you without word of lie. Something I saw gave me such happiness. Mother, did you not often say that the angels of God our Lord are so very beautiful that Nature never made such beautiful creatures, and that there was nothing in the world so beautiful?"

"Darling son, I still say so. It was the truth I spoke, and I declare it still."

"Be silent, mother. Did I not just see the most beautiful creatures there are riding through the Desolate Forest? They are more beautiful, I believe, than God and all His angels."

His mother put her arms around him. "Darling son," she said, "I entrust you to God's keeping, for I am most frightened for you. You have seen, I believe, the angels people complain of, and who kill all they meet."

"Honestly, I have not, mother, I have not. No, they say they are knights."

His mother fainted when she heard him mention the word *knights*. And after she had straightened up again, she exclaimed as an angry woman does: "Alas, wretch that I am, how unfortunate I am! Sweet darling son, I expected to protect you so carefully from the world of chivalry that you would never hear or see any of it. You would have been a knight, darling son, had it pleased the Lord God that your father and your other relatives trained you. There was no knight so highly honored, so feared and dreaded in all the Isles of the Sea, darling son, as your father. You can well boast of having no cause for shame regarding his family or mine. I am descended from knights, the finest of this country. In the Isles of the Sea there was, in my time, no family better than mine. But the finest have fallen on bad times. And it is well known in many places that misfortunes befall worthy men who uphold high honor and valor. Wickedness, disgrace, and laziness do not decline, for they cannot. But the good are destined to fall on bad times.

"Your father—you do not know this—was wounded between the legs and his body crippled. His large lands and his huge treasures, won through his valor, went all to ruin, and he fell into dire poverty. After the death of King Utherpendragon, father of the good King Arthur, worthy men were unjustly disinherited, impoverished, and exiled, their lands ravaged, and the poor reduced to the lowest condition. All who could flee from there fled. Your father owned this manorhouse here in the Desolate Forest. Incapable of fleeing, he had himself quickly carried here on a litter, since he knew no other refuge to which to flee. And as for you, you were little, and had two beautiful brothers. You were little, hardly more than two years old, and sucking at my breast.

"When your two brothers were old enough, they heeded their father's advice and counsel and traveled to two royal courts to receive arms and horses. The older one went to the King of Escavalon and served there until he was dubbed knight. And the younger, who was then nine, served King Ban of Gomeret. On one and the same day, both young men were dubbed knights and presented with their arms, and that very day they set out on their return journey home, eager to bring happiness to their father and me. He did not see them again, for they were defeated in armed combat along the way. Deep pain and grief have been mine that the two were slain in combat. And something of wonder befell the older one: ravens and crows pecked out both his eyes. Thus the people found the dead bodies.

"Your father died of grief for his sons, and I have led a bitter life since his death. You were all my comfort and all my good because I was bereft of my entire family. God had left me no one else for my joy and happiness."

The youth hardly heard anything his mother said to him. "Give me some food," he said. "I don't know what you talk to me about. But I would love to go to the king who makes knights. And displease whom it may, I will go there."

His mother detained and delayed him as long as she could. She dressed and outfitted him in a large canvas shirt and breeches made in the Welsh fashion with, I believe, the breeches and leggings all of one piece. And he had a deerskin coat and hood which fastened about him. These were his mother's preparations for him. She compelled him to remain there only three days, no more, for her coaxing was of no further use.

Then his mother felt a strange pang of grief. She wept as she hugged and kissed him. "Darling son, seeing you leave pains me deeply," she said. "You will go to the court of the king and tell him to present you with arms. There will be no refusal, for I am certain he will give you them. But when the time comes to test your equipment, what then will happen? How could you accomplish what you have never done or seen any do? Badly indeed, I fear. You will have no skill. It is no wonder, to my mind, if one does not know what one has not learned. But it is a wonder when one does not learn what is often seen and heard.

"Darling son, I wish to offer you one sensible counsel that you should carefully heed. And if you care to remember it, great good might come to you from it. In just a little while, son, if it be God's pleasure, you will be a knight. And this is my counsel to you. If you meet, near or far, ladies in need of aid or maidens in distress, be ready to give them aid if they request it of you. This is the basis of all honor. He who fails to honor ladies must find his own honor dead. Serve ladies and maidens, and you will be honored everywhere. And if you beg a favor of any of them, take care not to be offensive. Do nothing to displease her. He who wins a maiden's kiss has a great deal. If she grants you the kiss, I forbid you the remainder. For my sake you will forgo that. And if she has a ring on her finger or a purse on her belt, and from love or entreaty she gives you it, I shall consider it fine and fitting that you wear her ring; I grant you permission to accept the ring and the purse.

"Darling son, I would still tell you more. On roadways or at inns, never have a companion for long without asking his name. Know the person's name, for by the name you know the man.

"Darling son, speak with worthy men, travel with worthy men, for worthy men do not give their companions misleading advice. Above all I would beg you to enter church and minster to pray to our Lord that He grant you joy and honor, and help you conduct your life so that you may come to a good end."

"Mother, what is church?" he asked.

"A place where the service is celebrated to the One Who created heaven and earth, and there placed men and beasts."

"And what is minster?"

"The same. A beautiful and sacred house filled with holy relics and treasures, where the sacrifice of the body of Jesus Christ occurs, the holy prophet whom the Jews treated so shamefully. He was betrayed and wrongly condemned and, for the sake of men and women, suffered the agony of death. Until that time, souls went to hell when they left their bodies. He was the one who delivered them from there. He was bound to the pillar, scourged, and then crucified, wearing a crown of thorns. I counsel you to go to the minster to hear masses and matins and to worship the Lord."

"Then I shall be delighted to go to churches and minsters from now on, I promise you," the young man answered. Without further delay, he took his leave while his mother wept. His saddle was already in place, and he was equipped in Welsh fashion and guise with large rawhide boots for his leggings. Wherever he traveled, he usually took three javelins, and though he wanted to carry his javelins, his mother made him leave two behind because he looked too much like a Welshman. Had it been possible, she would have been delighted to have him abandon all three. In his right hand he carried a stick for goading his horse.

At the time of his departure, his mother, who loved him dearly, was in tears as she kissed him. She prayed God to hold him in His keeping. "Darling son, God grant you, wherever you go, more joy than is left for me," she said.

The youth was a stone's throw away when he looked back and saw that his mother had fallen unconscious at the end of the bridge, lying as if she had dropped dead. As he lashed his hunting horse across the rump with his stick, his horse sprang forward without a stumble, bearing him along at full speed through the large dark forest. He rode from morning until end of day, and that night slept in the forest until the bright day dawned.

Early in the morning when small birds sing, the youth rose and mounted his horse. He continued to ride until he sighted a pavilion pitched in a beautiful stretch of meadow beside the source of a small spring. The pavilion was a marvel of beauty, one side vermilion, the other with an embroidered gold border, and on top was perched a gilded eagle. The sun, shining crimson and clear, struck the eagle, and the entire meadow glowed in the pavilion's illumination. Situated all around the pavilion, which was the most beautiful in the world, were two leafy bowers, lodges designed in the Welsh fashion. The youth rode toward the pavilion. "God, I see Your house," he exclaimed before reaching the spot. "What a mistake I would have made had I not gone to worship You. Yet my mother did speak the truth to me when she told me such a house was the most beautiful thing there is, and declared to me that if ever I came upon a minster, I must go there and adore the Creator, in Whom I believe. On my word, I shall go there and pray that He gives me this day some food, for I am in great need."

Then he reached the pavilion and found it open. In the center of the pavilion he saw a bed with a silk brocade covering, and on the bed a maiden lay sleeping, all alone without company. Her maids had gone to pick fresh little flowers, which, following their practice, they intended to strew through the pavilion. When the youth entered under the pavilion, his horse took such a heavy stumble that the maiden heard it and awakened with a start.

"Maiden, I greet you as my mother instructed me," the innocent young man said. "My mother gave me instructions to greet maidens wherever I meet them."

Fearful of the youth, whom she took for a fool, the maiden trembled, blaming her own folly that he had found her alone. "Youth, go your way! Flee lest my lover see you," she said.

"Not on my life, unless—displease whom it may—I kiss you first, for that is what my mother taught me," the young man replied.

"As for me, never shall I kiss you if I can avoid it," the maiden said. "Flee lest my lover find you, for if he finds you, you are dead!"

With his strong arms, the youth embraced her clumsily, since he knew no other way. He stretched her out beneath him, and although she defended herself as best she could and struggled to escape, her efforts were in vain. Whether she wished or not, the youth, according to the tale, kissed her twenty times without pause. He then noticed on her finger a ring with a bright emerald. "My mother also told me to take the ring on your finger, but to do nothing more to you," he said. "Now give me the ring there. I want to have it."

"You certainly will never have my ring, be assured of that, unless you use force to pull it from my finger," the maiden answered.

The youth took hold of her hand, stretched out her finger by force, then took the ring from her finger and slipped it on his own.

"Maiden, I wish you every blessing," he said. "Now I shall go, well satisfied. You are much better to kiss than any chambermaid in my mother's entire household since your lips don't taste bitter."

Amid tears she said to the youth: "Do not take away my little ring. If you do, I shall be ill treated, and sooner or later, I promise you, you will lose your life for it."

The youth took to heart nothing he heard. Since he had not eaten in a long time, he was dying of hunger. He discovered a leather keg filled with wine and beside it a silver goblet, and on top of a clump of reeds saw a fresh white towel. He lifted it up, and found underneath three fine, fresh venison pies. This fare did not displease him because of the torment of his hunger. He broke open and eagerly devoured one of the pies in front of him. He then filled the silver goblet with wine, which was not at all bad, and took frequent and large gulps. "Maiden," he said, "I shall not let these pies be wasted today. Come and eat. They are very good. Each of us will have a share, and a whole one will still be left."

Despite his prayers and entreaties, the maiden wept all this time. Not a word of reply did she offer him, but shed heavy tears and wrung her hands. He ate as much as he wished and drank his fill. He then covered the unused food and promptly took his leave, commending to God the maiden, who found no delight in his greeting. "God save you, dear friend," he said. "In God's name, fret not about the ring of yours I take. Before I die I shall repay you for it. With your leave I depart."

Amid tears she declared that she would never commend him to God, for it was on his account that she would be forced to endure more suffering and more shame than any wretched woman ever knew, and never, as long as he lived, have his help or aid. Let him realize, she said, that he had betrayed her.

And so she remained there weeping. Then, in hardly any time at all, her lover returned from the woods. He was upset to see the tracks of the youth, who had gone his way. When he found his mistress in tears, he said: "Maiden, from these signs I see, I think a knight has been here."

"No, sir, I swear to you, there has not. But there was a young Welshman here, an offensive and despicable fool, who drank his fill of your wine and ate of your three pies."

"Is that why you weep thus, dear lady? I would have been willing to let him drink and eat everything."

"There is more, sir," she said. "There was a struggle for my ring. He took it from me and carries it off. I would rather be dead than have him thus take it away."

Behold him dispirited and sick at heart. "On my word, this is an outrage!" he exclaimed. "And yet, since he carries it away, let him keep it. But I suspect he did more. If there was more, conceal it not."

"Sir, he kissed me," she replied.

"Kissed?"

"Yes, I tell you well, but he did it against my will."

"No, rather it was to your pleasure and satisfaction. There was never opposition," he said, tormented by jealousy. "Do you think I don't know you? I certainly do; I know you well. I am not so cross-eyed or blind as not to see your falsity. You have embarked on a bad route. You have embarked on hardship. Your horse will never eat oats or be bled until I am avenged.

Your horse, when it throws a shoe, will never be reshod. If it dies, you will follow me on foot. The clothes you are wearing will never be changed. No, on foot and naked you will follow me until I have taken his head. Never shall I take another form of justice." He then sat down and ate.

The youth continued riding until he saw a charcoal-burner approaching, driving an ass before him. "Peasant, you there driving the ass before you, tell me the most direct route to Carlisle. I wish to see King Arthur. I am told that he makes knights."

"Youth, in that direction stands a castle by the sea," he replied. "If you travel to that castle, dear friend, you will find King Arthur there happy and doleful."

"Now tell me my will. Why is the king happy and doleful?"

"I shall tell you at once. King Arthur with all his host fought against King Rion, the King of the Isles, who was defeated. For this reason King Arthur is happy. And he is angered by his companions, who departed for their castles, where they find better places to stay. And the king does not know how they fare. That is the reason he is doleful."

The youth did not value the information at a penny, except that he did follow the route the charcoal-burner had pointed out to him. He continued along until, by the sea, he saw a strong, handsome, and well-situated castle. He noticed an armed knight riding through the gateway carrying a gold cup in his hand; he held his shield and his lance and his bridle by his left hand and the gold cup in his right; his equipment, all vermilion, suited him well.

When the youth saw the beautiful arms, all new, he was delighted. "On my word, I shall ask the king for these arms," he said. "If he gives them to me, I shall be delighted. And damn him who seeks any others!"

Then, in his eagerness to reach court, he raced toward the castle until he neared the knight. And the knight detained him a moment. "Tell, youth, where go you?" he asked him.

"I intend to go to court to ask the king for those arms," he replied.

"Youth, now you speak well," he said. "Go then and come back quickly. And say this to the cursed king, that if he does not wish to hold his land from me, then let him surrender it to me, or send someone to defend it against me, for I declare that it is mine. And believe it on this evidence, this cup that I carry here, which, when it was filled with wine and he was drinking from it, I took from him."

Now let the knight find another to repeat his message, for the youth understood not a word of it. He did not stop until he reached the court where the king and his knights were seated at dinner. The great hall was level with the ground, paved, and as long as it was wide. The youth entered the hall on horseback. King Arthur was seated pensively at the head of a table, and all the knights were engaged in conversations, amusing themselves but not the man preoccupied and silent.

The youth came forward. Not recognizing the king, he did not know whom to greet. Yonet came over to him, holding a knife in his hand. "Young man," the youth said, "you approaching with the knife in your hand, indicate to me which man is the king."

Yonet was most courteous. "Friend, he is over there," he answered.

The youth rode over to him and greeted him as he had learned. The king remained silent, uttering not a word. The youth addressed him a second time. The king continued in his thoughts, speaking not a word to him. "On my word," the youth then said, "this king never made knights. Since a word cannot be drawn from him, how can he make knights?"

He immediately prepared to go back and turned the head of his hunting horse. But like a man lacking reason, he led it so close to the king that— and I am telling the exact truth—it knocked a cap from his head onto the table in front of him. The king raised his head and turned toward the youth, setting aside all his own ponderings.

"Welcome, dear sir," he said. "I pray you not to take amiss my silence at your greeting. Anger prevented me from answering you. The greatest enemy I have, the man who hates me most and alarms me most, has disputed me for my land. He is such a fool that he declares he will hold everything free of claim, be I willing or not. He is called the Vermilion Knight of the Forest of Quinqueroi.

"The queen had come to sit here in front of me to see and comfort these knights who are wounded. The knight's words would have scarcely angered me, but he took my cup from in front of me and lifted it with such arrogance that he spilled all the wine it contained on the queen. This was a hideous and despicable affront. The queen has gone into her chamber, where she dies of burning anger and deep sorrow. So help me God, I do not believe that she can ever survive this."

The youth did not care a chive for anything the king said or related to him, nor did he care about the queen's sorrow or her shame. "Make me a knight, lord king, for I wish to set out," he said. Bright and laughing were the eyes in the head of the wild youth. None looking on him thought him wise, yet all looking on him thought him handsome and imposing.

"Friend," the king said, "dismount and hand over your hunting horse to this squire. He will look after it for you as you wish. I vow to the Lord God, your will shall be done for my honor and for your gain."

"The men I met on the heath never dismounted, and yet you wish me to dismount," the youth replied. "On my word, I will never dismount. But act quickly, and I shall set out."

"Ah, dear friend, I shall do it gladly for your gain and for my honor," the king replied.

"By the faith I owe the Creator, dear lord king," the youth said, "I shall never be a knight unless I am a vermilion knight. Give me the arms of the man I met outside the gate, who carries away your gold cup."

The seneschal, who was one of the wounded, grew angry at what he heard. "You are right, friend," he said. "Go at once and take the arms, for they are yours. You did not behave foolishly to come here for them."

"Kay, for the mercy of God, you are too anxious to insult, and you care not whom," the king said. "For a man of worth, that behavior is disgraceful. If the youth is silly and foolish, he may yet be of noble birth. And if his manners come from a churlish teacher's instructions, he may yet be worthy and wise. It is despicable to mock another and to promise without giving. A man of worth does not embark on a promise not in his power or intention to fulfill. Otherwise he alienates himself from that person, who is his friend without the promise, and, the moment the promise is made, expects the promise honored. Therefore it would be better, you can be certain, to refuse a man than have him hope in vain. To tell the truth, a man who makes a promise and fails to honor it deceives and mocks his friend, and loses his affection." Thus the king spoke to Kay.

As the youth was leaving, he noticed a beautiful and charming maiden. He greeted her, and she returned his greeting with laughter. And as she laughed, she said: "Youth, if you live long enough, I think and believe in my heart that in the entire world there never was nor will be a finer knight than you, nor will such be known. Such is my thought, belief, and expectation."

The maiden had not laughed in more than six years, and spoke in such a loud voice that all heard her. Deeply upset by her words, Kay jumped up and, with the palm of his hand, slapped her across her soft face so insolently that he knocked her flat to the floor. On his way back after hitting the maiden, he noticed a fool standing by a hearth. Out of anger and spite he kicked him into the blazing fire, for it was the fool's custom to say, "This maiden shall not laugh until she beholds that man who is to have supreme mastery of chivalry." The fool screamed; the maiden wept; and the youth did not stay but, without seeking counsel, rode after the Vermilion Knight.

Yonet knew all the highways and was glad to report news back to the court. All alone without companion, he ran through a garden in front of the hall, left through a postern gate, and continued to ride until he reached the highway where the Vermilion Knight awaited armed combat and adventure. The youth was rushing toward him to seize his arms. While awaiting him, the knight had set down the gold cup on a grey stoneblock. When the youth had come near enough that they might hear each other, he cried out to him: "Lay down those arms. Carry them no farther. This is King Arthur's command to you."

"Youth, does no one dare come here to uphold the king's right?" the knight asked him. "If no one is coming, conceal it not."

"What the devil, do you jest with me now, Sir Knight? Have you not carried away my arms? Remove them at once, I command you."

"Youth, I ask you if anyone is coming here on behalf of the king to fight me," he said.

"Sir Knight, remove your arms at once lest I remove them from you. I shall not allow you them longer. Be certain that I will strike you if you make me say another word about them."

In his anger the Vermilion Knight then raised his lance with both hands and, with the butt end, dealt him such a heavy blow across the shoulders that he made him crouch over the neck of his horse. The youth was enraged when he felt the wound he had received from the blow to his neck. As best he could, he aimed at his opponent's eye and sent a javelin hurling forward. He struck him through the eye into the brain; blood and brains oozed out the other side at the nape of his neck, and his opponent saw, heard, understood nothing more. From pain the knight's heart failed him, and he turned and fell outstretched on the ground.

The youth dismounted, set the knight's lance to one side, and removed the shield from his neck. But he could not manage the helmet on the knight's head, for he did not know how to take hold of it. Although he wished to unbuckle the sword, he did not know how, nor could he draw it from the scabbard. He continually took hold of the scabbard, pulling and tugging at it. Yonet, seeing the youth so busy, began to laugh. "Friend, what is this? What are you doing?" he asked.

"I don't know. I thought your king had given me these arms. But I shall have chopped the corpse all to pieces before removing any of these arms. They so adhere to his body that the inside and the outside seem to me all one in the way they cling together."

"Now don't be all upset. I shall separate them easily, if you wish," Yonet answered.

"Then act quickly now, and give them to me at once," the youth said.

Yonet immediately stripped the body, removing the leggings as far as the toes, and leaving not hauberk, leggings, head helmet, or any other piece of armor.

Despite Yonet's urgings, the youth had no wish to abandon his own garments. He would not take a comfortable tunic of padded silk, which the knight had worn under his hauberk while alive. And Yonet could not take the rawhide boots from the youth's feet. Instead the youth said: "What the devil, do you now jest with me that I trade my fine garments, which my mother just made for me, for this knight's clothes? Would you wish me to leave my heavy canvas shirt for his thin one? My little waterproof tunic for that one which would not withstand a drop of water? Damn the man by the entire throat who would now or ever exchange his good clothes for the bad ones of another."

It is a hard task to enlighten a fool. No entreaty had any effect on him. He wished nothing but the armor. Yonet laced the leggings for him, then placed the hauberk on him so that no one ever looked better, and set on his head the helmet, which suited him well. As for the sword, he taught him to gird it so that it hung loosely. He then placed the youth's foot in the stirrup and had him mount the charger. The youth had never seen a stirrup before, and he had not the slightest knowledge of spurs, but knew only of whips and sticks. Yonet brought the shield and the lance and handed them to him.

Before Yonet departed, the youth said: "Friend, accept my hunting horse and lead it away with you. It is a fine horse, and I give it to you because I need it no longer. Take the king his cup and greet him on my behalf. And tell the maiden whom Kay slapped on the cheek that, if I am able before I die, I intend to prepare him such a dish that she will consider herself avenged."

Yonet replied that he would deliver the king his cup and relay his message faithfully. They at once parted and went their ways.

Bringing the cup back to the king, Yonet entered through the door into the hall where the barons were. "Lord, rejoice now. Your knight who was here returns your cup to you," he said.

"Which knight are you talking to me about?" asked the king, still deeply angered.

"In God's name, lord, I refer to the youth who just left here," Yonet replied.

"Do you mean the Welsh youth, who asked me for the vermilion-painted arms of the knight who shamed me as best he could?" the king asked.

"Lord, I do indeed speak of him."

"And my cup, how did he have it? Did the other man like or esteem him so much that he was willing to hand it over to him?"

"No. From him the youth exacted heavy payment, for he killed him."

"How was that, dear friend?"

"Lord, I do not know. But I did see the knight strike him with his lance and cause him severe discomfort. The youth struck him back with a javelin through the face so that he made blood and brains ooze out behind his neck, and hurled him dead to the ground."

The king then addressed the seneschal. "Ah, Kay, what harm you did me today! Through your vicious tongue, which has uttered so much nonsense, today have you driven from me the youth who served me so well this very day."

"Lord," Yonet addressed the king, "on my life, he sends word through me to the queen's maiden, whom Kay struck out of anger, scorn, and spite at him. He says that if he lives and the occasion comes his way, he will avenge her."

The fool, who was beside the fire, heard the words. He leapt to his feet and came happily before the king. He was so delighted that he was skipping and jumping. "Lord king," he said, "so help me God, adventures now come your way, and you shall behold treacherous and harsh acts happening frequently. And Kay, I pledge to you, can be completely certain of regretting the hour he first saw his hands and his feet and his foolish and despicable tongue. Before the week ends, the knight will have avenged the kick Kay gave me, and the slap he gave the maiden will be repaid and avenged at a high price, for between the elbow and the armpit will he break Kay's right arm. For half a year Kay will support his arm in a sling from his neck. Let him carry it well there! He can escape this no more than dying."

These words so upset Kay that he almost exploded out of anger and malice. He could hardly restrain himself from killing the fool in front of all. But he held back from assaulting him lest he incur the king's displeasure.

"Ah, Kay, alas, how you angered me today," said the king. "The man who would have trained and taught the youth in use of shield, lance, and arms to the point where he could handle them a little by himself would doubtless be an excellent knight. But the youth is as totally ignorant of arms as of everything else. In time of need, he could not even draw his sword.

"Now he sits armed on his horse. He will encounter some vassal not reluctant to maim him in order to win his horse. Quickly will that vassal wound or slay him, for the youth is so silly and clumsy that he will not know how to defend himself. He will soon have exhausted his capabilities."

Thus the king, his expression downcast, lamented and mourned for the youth. But, unable to accomplish anything in this manner, he let his speech end.

The youth spurred through the forest without pause until he reached an open stretch of land alongside a river, which was wider than a crossbow shot. All the water round about flowed through its large bed. Crossing a meadow, he rode toward the great river he beheld. Seeing that the river was deep, black, and much more rapid than the Loire, he did not enter, but rode along the bank.

Across the river was a tall rocky cliff, and the water beat against its base. On the cliff side, which sloped down toward the sea, stood a strong and splendid castle. The youth turned to the left where the water flowed into a bay and saw the towers of the castle being given birth, for he thought that they were being born and were issuing from the castle.

In the center of the castle stood a massive and mighty keep. Facing the bay where the river opposed the tide was a strong barbican, and the sea beat against its base. At the four corners of the wall, which was built of heavy quarry stones, were four low turrets, handsome and strong. In addition to being well situated, the castle was also comfortable within. In front of the round castelet, a bridge built of stone, sand, and lime spanned the river. The bridge, solid and high, was flanked by battlements all across; midway along the bridge was a tower, and at the end a drawbridge, fashioned and fitted to serve its function: a bridge by day and a gate by night. The youth made his way toward the bridge.

A worthy man, dressed in an ermine cloak, was walking along the bridge enjoying himself while waiting for the person riding toward the bridge. In his hand the worthy man held a short walking stick for his leisure. Two attendants not wearing cloaks followed him. The youth approaching remembered his mother's teaching, for he greeted the man. "Sir, this is what my mother taught me," he said.

"God bless you, dear friend," said the worthy man, who recognized and knew from the youth's speech that he was foolish. "Dear friend, whence do you come?" he asked.

"Whence? From King Arthur's court."

"What did you do there?"

"The king made me a knight. May good fortune be his!"

"A knight? God bless me, I did not suppose that he could remember such things at this time. I thought the king would be concerned with matters other than making knights. Now tell me, nobly born friend, those arms, who gave them to you?"

"The king gave them to me," he answered.

"Gave? How?"

And he related the tale to him as you have heard it. It would be pointless and tedious to tell the tale a second time, for no tale wants repetition.

The worthy man then asked him what riding skills he knew. "I can ride uphill and down just as I did on the hunting horse I had at my mother's house."

"Tell me more about your arms, dear friend. What can you do with them?"

"I can put them on and remove them, just like the squire who armed me after disarming the knight I had slain before my eyes. And the armor is so light for me to wear that I feel no pain."

"By the soul of God, I esteem this highly, and I am delighted," the worthy man said. "Now tell me, if you do not mind, what need brought you here?"

"Sir, my mother told me to go to worthy men for their counsel, trusting in their words, for those who trust worthy men have much to gain."

"Dear friend, blessed be your mother for giving you good advice," the worthy man said. "But is there anything more you wish?"

"Yes."

"And what?"

"This and no more, that you lodge me the rest of the day."

"Gladly, on condition that you do me a favor, which, as you will see, will be to your great advantage," the worthy man replied.

"What?" he asked.

"That you take your mother's advice and mine."

"On my word, I promise that," he said.

"Then dismount." And the youth dismounted.

One of the two attendants who had come there took his horse, and the other relieved him of his armor. The youth was left in his foolish outfit with the rawhide boots and the badly made and badly cut deerskin tunic his mother had given him.

The worthy man had the sharp steel spurs which the youth had brought with him fixed to his own heels. He mounted the youth's horse, hung the shield from his neck by the strap, and took the lance. "Friend," he said, "now take a lesson in arms. Watch how one should hold a lance, and spur and check a horse."

He then unfurled his banner and by example instructed the youth how to take his shield. He made it hang a little forward so that he had it touching the horse's neck, then placed the lance in its rest and spurred the horse, which was worth a hundred marks, for no horse moved with more desire, vigor, or speed. The worthy man was skilled in handling shield, lance, and horse, for he had learned it from childhood.

All the worthy man did satisfied and pleased the youth. When he had excellently performed all his maneuvers in front of the youth, who had paid close attention, he returned to the youth, his lance raised. "Friend, would you too know how to handle shield and lance and to spur and direct your horse?" he asked him.

He answered at once that he would be happy not to live another day, or hold lands or wealth, on condition that he too could learn to do the same.

"If willing to make the effort and apply himself, dear friend, a man may learn what he does not know," the worthy man said. "Every skill requires desire, effort, and practice. All knowledge comes from these three. And since you have never performed these activities, nor seen anyone perform them, no blame or shame is yours if you do not know how."

The worthy man then had him mount. And the youth began to bear shield and lance as skillfully as if he had spent all his life in tournaments and wars, and traveled throughout the world in search of battles and adventures. All this came to him naturally. And when nature is the teacher and the heart lends full attention, nothing can be difficult to accomplish with nature and the heart devoting their efforts. With these two he performed so well that the worthy man was delighted, telling himself that had the youth applied himself and devoted his whole life to deeds of arms, still his display would have been masterful. When the youth had carried out his exercises, he rode back before the worthy man, his lance raised, as he had seen him do. "Sir," he asked, "did I do well? Do you think the effort will help me if I am willing to apply myself? My eyes have seen nothing they desired more. I would love to know as much as you do."

"Friend, if you have the desire, you will know what you must. No need to worry," the worthy man answered.

Three times the worthy man mounted, and three times he taught the youth all he could show him about arms until he had shown him much. And three times he had him mount and follow. "Friend," he said to him at the end, "if you met a knight and he struck you, what would you do?"

"I would strike him back."

"And what if your lance shattered?"

"After that there would be no more for me to do but run and attack him with my two fists."

"Friend, that is not what you should do."

"Then what should I do?"

"You should go and attack with the sword."

The worthy man then desired to instruct and teach him in arms as to how to defend himself with the sword if anyone attacked him or to attack with it when occasion demanded. He planted his own lance upright in the ground before him, then took his sword in his hand. "Friend, this is how you should defend yourself if attacked," he said.

"God save me," the youth said, "no one knows as much about this as I do. At my mother's house I learned so much about this, using cushions and wooden shields, that I was often exhausted."

"Then let us go inside the castle now, for there is nothing left to do," the worthy man said. "Dismay whom it might, your lodging for the night will have every mark of honor."

Then, as they went off side by side, the youth said to his host: "Sir, my mother taught me never to travel with a man or bear him company for long without knowing his name. Since she instructed me to learn this, I would like to know your name."

"Dear friend, my name is Gornemant of Gohort," said the worthy man.

Thus the two walked hand in hand together into the castle. At a flight of stairs, an attendant came unsummoned carrying a short cloak. He ran up to place the cloak on the youth lest a harmful chill seize him after the heat. The worthy man had sumptuous lodgings, beautiful and spacious, and fine servants. The dinner was set out, and the food was excellent, well prepared and attractively served.

After the knights washed, they sat down to the meal. The worthy man seated the youth next to him, and had him eat from the same platter. I have no more details as to the nature of the dishes or their number, and I make no idle tale of this, except that they had sufficient food and drink.

After they had left the table, the worthy man, who was most courteous, asked the youth who had sat next to him to stay a month. Were the youth willing, he would gladly detain him an entire year; during that period the youth might learn skills, if he so desired, that would aid him in time of need.

"Sir," the youth said to him, "I don't know if I am near the manorhouse where my mother lives, yet I pray God that He guide me to her and that I see her again. I saw her fall unconscious at the end of the bridge before her gate. I don't know if she is living or dead. When I left her, she fell unconscious out of grief for me, I realize that. And so it would be impossible for me to stay here long without knowing her condition. No, I shall set off tomorrow at dawn."

The worthy man heard that entreaty was useless; the words failed. And so since the beds were already made, there was no more pleading, and they went to bed.

Early in the morning the worthy man rose. He went and found the youth lying in bed. He had gifts carried to him: a shirt, linen breeches, leggings dyed with brazilwood, and a silk tunic woven and made in India. He sent them to him that he might dress. "Friend, if you trust me, you will wear these clothes you see here," he said to him.

"Dear sir, you might improve your words," the youth replied. "Are not the garments my mother made me better than these? And yet you want me to wear these?"

"I swear on my life, youth, no, they are worse than these," the worthy man said. "When I brought you here, dear friend, you told me you would do all I asked."

"And so I will," the youth replied. "I shall never oppose you in any matter."

He hesitated no longer in putting on the clothes, setting aside the ones his mother had given him. The worthy man stooped and fastened his right spur for him. It was the custom at that time that whoever dubbed a man knight should fasten for him his spur. Many other attendants were present, and each, as occasion permitted, devoted himself to arming the youth. The worthy man took the sword and girded it on him, then kissed him and said that with the sword he had conferred on him the highest honor God had created and ordained. This is the order of chivalry, which must be free of all baseness.

"Dear brother," he said, "in case you must enter combat with a knight, remember what I would say and entreat you to do. If you overcome him, forcing him to beg mercy because he can no longer defend himself or hold his ground against you, do not deliberately kill him.

"And take care not to be too talkative or too inquisitive. No one can talk too much without often telling stories that will turn to his discredit. The wise man says and repeats: 'The man sins who speaks too much.' Therefore, dear brother, I warn you not to speak too much.

"And I also advise you that if you come upon a young lady or woman in any kind of distress, be she married or unmarried, give her aid if you know how to help her and have the means in your power. In doing this you will do well.

"One other matter I tell you, and treat it not with disdain, for it is not to be disdained. Go eagerly to the minster to pray to the Creator of all that He have mercy on your soul and protect you in this earthly life as His Christian."

And the youth said to the worthy man: "All the apostles of Rome bless you, dear sir, for I heard my mother say the very same."

"Now, dear brother, never again say that your mother instructed and taught you," said the worthy man. "I do not blame you for saying this until now, but henceforth, by your grace, I entreat you to stand corrected. If you repeated it, people would consider you foolish. Therefore, I entreat you, be careful."

"Then what shall I say, dear sir?"

"You may say that the vavasor who fastened your spur instructed and taught you."

And he promised the worthy man that so long as he lived, he would never again utter the phrase unless in regard to him, for he thought his teaching to him good. The worthy man then made the sign of the cross over him, raising his hand high and saying: "God save you, dear sir. Since staying here troubles you, go with God as your guide."

The new knight left his host, anxious to reach his mother and find her alive and well. Being much better acquainted with the woods than the open country, he entered the lonely forests, and continued riding until he sighted a strong and well-situated town. Outside the walls he saw nothing but river, sea, and deserted land. He galloped in the direction of the town until he arrived in front of the gateway. But before reaching the gate, he had to cross a bridge so feeble that he thought it could scarcely support him. The knight rode across the bridge without evil mishap or disgrace. When he reached the gate, he found it securely fastened. He knocked but not gently, called out but not softly, then banged until a gaunt and pale maiden hurried to the windows of the hall. "Who is it calling there?" she asked.

He looked up toward the maiden and saw her. "Dear friend, I am a knight who begs you to let me enter and have lodging for the night," he said.

"Sir, you shall have it, although you will never be thankful for it," she said. "Nevertheless we shall offer you as good a lodging as we can."

Then the maiden withdrew, and the man waiting at the gate feared that he would be left standing there too long. And so he began to bang again. Immediately came four men-at-arms with huge axes on their shoulders and swords girded at their side. After they released the gate, they said: "Sir, come inside."

Had life been kind to the men-at-arms, they would have been handsome. But they had known so much hardship from vigils and hunger that they were pitiful to behold.

The knight found the land outside barren and deserted. Nothing inside was an improvement. Everywhere he went he found the streets empty and the houses old and fallen down, not a man or woman about. In the town were two minsters, which had both been abbeys, one of frightened nuns, the other of helpless monks. He found no fine decorations or tapestries in the minsters, but beheld only split and cracked walls and roofless towers. And the buildings stood open night as well as day. Throughout the town there was no mill grinding or oven baking, and he saw no bread, cake, or anything for sale, not even a penny's worth. The town was so desolate, he discovered, that there was no bread, pastry, wine, cider, or ale.

The four men-at-arms led him to a slate-roofed palace where they had him dismount, and then disarmed him. At once an attendant came down the stairs to the hall carrying a grey cloak. While he placed it round the knight's neck, another attendant stabled his horse in a stall where there was no wheat or hay, but only a little straw; there was nothing else in the house. Other attendants had the knight ascend the stairs ahead of them into the beautiful great hall, where two worthy men and a maiden came to meet him. The worthy men were old, though still not completely white-haired. Had they not known anxiety and distress, they would have been in the full vigor and strength of their fine age.

The maiden approached, more gracious, more elegant, and more adorned than sparrowhawk or popinjay. Her cloak and her gown were of black silk starred with spotted fur; the cloak, neither too long nor too wide, had ermine lining that showed no sign of wear and a black-and-white sable collar. If ever I described the beauty God bestowed on a woman's form or face, I now wish to attempt another description where there will be no word of lie. Her hair fell freely, and anyone who saw it would certainly think that it was, were this possible, all fine gold, so golden and bright was it. Her fore-head was white, high, and smooth as though a man's hand had sculpted the work from stone, ivory, or wood. She had brown eyebrows with a wide space between her eyes; the eyes themselves were laughing and grey, clear and wide apart, the nose long and straight; the crimson hue set on the white of her face was more becoming to her than vermilion on silver. To ravish men's hearts and minds, God had made her a marvel surpassing marvels. Never before had he created such, nor done so ever since.

When the knight saw her, he greeted her, and she him, as did the two knights present. With gracious dignity the maiden took his hand. "Dear friend," she said, "your lodging tonight will certainly not befit a worthy man. But were you informed this moment our entire state and condition, you might perhaps believe that I spoke this way out of malice in order to make you leave. But please stay and accept such lodging as there is. God grant you a better one tomorrow."

And so she led him by the hand to a beautiful, long, and wide room with a vaulted ceiling. The two sat on a bed covered with a samite quilt. Knights entered in groups of four, five, and six, and sat down together, not uttering a word, their eyes on the man sitting in silence beside their lady. Mindful of the worthy man's advice, the young knight refrained from speaking. All the knights began to whisper among themselves. "By God! I wonder if the knight is mute. That would be a great shame, for never was there so handsome a knight born of woman," each said. "Most becoming is he, seated beside my lady, and most becoming too is she at his side. If only both were not speechless! He is so handsome and she so beautiful that knight and maiden never suited each other so well. From their appearance it seems that God created them for each other that He might unite them."

The maiden kept waiting for the young man to say something to her. Finally she saw clearly and understood that he would never address a word to her unless she first spoke to him. "Sir, whence did you come today?" she asked in a most noble manner.

"Young lady, I spent the night at the castle of a worthy man, where fine and handsome accommodation was mine," he answered. "The castle has fine, strong, and well-constructed towers, one tall and four small. I do not know how to sum up all the work, nor do I know the name of the castle, but I do know that the name of the worthy man is Gornemant of Gohort."

"Ah, dear friend," the maiden said, "fine are your words and courteous your speech. God the King reward you for calling him a worthy man. You never spoke a truer word, for he is a worthy man, by Saint Richier, I can swear to that! Know that I am his niece, though I have not seen him in a long time. I am certain that you have met no worthier man since you left your home. He gave you a happy and joyous reception, which he knew well how to provide, being a nobly born and worthy man, powerful, prosperous, and rich. But inside here are only six small loaves which an uncle of mine, who is a prior, a holy and religious man, sent me for tonight's supper, along with a small keg filled with mulled wine. There is no other food here except a small deer one of my servants killed this morning with an arrow."

At once she ordered the tables set up. And when they were placed in position, the men were seated for supper. Although they ate with eager appetites, they spent but a short time seated at dinner.

After the meal, the men separated: those who had stood watch the night before stayed and slept, while those who were to watch over the town that night departed. There were fifty men-at-arms and squires who kept watch that evening. The others devoted their attentions to their guest's comfort. Those attending to his bedding spread fine sheets and an expensive quilt for him and placed a pillow at the top. That evening the knight had all the comfort and all the delight possible in a bed, with the single exception of the pleasure of a maiden, if it had pleased him, or of a lady, if it had been allowed him. But of this pleasure he was ignorant. And therefore I am right in telling you that he fell asleep quite quickly, free of all cares.

But his hostess did not sleep. She was shut in her room, and while he slept comfortably, she was absorbed in her thoughts, helpless against a war raging inside her. Often she turned over, often she gave a start, often she tossed and turned restlessly. Over her shift she threw a short cloak of scarlet silk and decided, boldly and courageously, to place all at risk, though her decision was no trifling matter. She resolved to go to her guest and tell him something of her situation. She then left her bed and went out of her room. She was so frightened that all her limbs trembled and her body perspired. In tears she left her room and came to the bed where he slept. Weeping and deeply sighing, she bent and knelt down; she was crying so much that her tears dampened his entire face. She did not have the courage to be more forward with him.

She wept so much that she awakened him. Amazed and bewildered to feel his face moist, he saw her kneeling before his bed, embracing him tightly round the neck. He behaved with such courtesy that at once he took her in his arms and drew her toward him. "Fair lady, what is your pleasure? Why have you come here?" he asked her.

"Alas, noble knight, have mercy! For the sake of God and His Son, I beg you not to think ill of me for coming here. Although I am nearly naked, I never intended anything foolish, sinful, or base. In this world there is no creature alive so sad or so wretched but that I am not sadder still. Nothing I have pleases me. I have never known a day without misfortune. Thus I am in misery. Never shall I look at another night except this one now, or another day except tomorrow. Instead, with my own hand I shall kill myself. Of the three hundred and ten knights who garrisoned this town, only fifty remain. A cruel knight, Anguiguerron, the seneschal of Clamadeu of the Isles, has led off and imprisoned or killed two hundred and sixty. I grieve as much for those imprisoned as for those killed; I realize that the prisoners will die there, for they will never be able to leave. Because of me, many worthy men are dead. It is right that I grieve over this.

"All winter and summer Anguiguerron besieged the town without ever drawing back. All that time his forces increased and ours diminished. Our provisions are exhausted; not enough remains to feed a bee. We have been brought to the point that, unless God intervenes, this town will tomorrow be surrendered to him and I handed over as prisoner. The town can be defended no longer. But certainly I will kill myself before he takes me alive. He will then have only my corpse, and I shall not care if he carries me off. Clamadeu expects to have me. He will never have me. He will have my body without life or soul. In a chest of mine I keep a fine steel knife, which I shall plunge into my heart. This much I had to tell you. Now I shall go my way again and let you rest."

The knight, if he had the courage, could soon win fame, for she came weeping on his face for no other reason, no matter what she made him hear, than to inspire him to battle, if he dared, to defend her and her land.

"Dear friend," he said to her, "show a more cheerful face tonight. Take comfort. Weep no more. Come near me here and wipe the tears from your eyes. If it be God's pleasure, He will grant you a better end tomorrow than you describe to me. Lie down beside me in this bed, which is wide enough for the two of us. Do not leave me the rest of the night."

"I would do that if it pleased you," she replied.

He held her clasped in his arms and kissed her. Then, with every gesture of tenderness and comfort, he placed the quilt over her. She allowed him to kiss her, and I do not think he was displeased. Thus, all night long until the approach of morning, they lay beside each other, their mouths touching. That night she knew this much consolation: arm clasped in arm, their mouths touching, they slept until daybreak.

Unescorted, the maiden went back to her room at dawn. Unaided by any chambermaid, she dressed and made herself ready without waking anyone.

As soon as the guards who had stood watch that night could see the day, they awakened those sleeping, rousing them from their beds, and the men rose quickly.

The maiden returned to her knight without delay. "Sir, God give you a good day this day!" she said to him in a noble manner. "I realize that you will stay here no longer. There would be no value in staying. You will leave, and I do not object, for I would be discourteous to object to your departure. We have done nothing here for your ease and comfort. But I pray God to prepare you better lodging, with more bread, wine, and salt than you found here."

"Dear lady," he said, "this will not be the day I go and seek other lodging. No, if ever I can, I shall bring peace to all your land. If I find your enemy without, I shall be angered if he stays there longer. He has no reason to cause you grief. But if I defeat and kill him, I ask that my reward be your intimacy. I would accept no other recompense."

Clever was the maiden's response. "Sir, you have asked me now for a poor and miserable thing. But if I refused to give it to you, you would consider my behavior arrogant. Therefore I do not intend to deny it to you. Yet do not say that I become your lover on the promise and condition that for my sake you go to your death. That would be too great a pity. Be certain that you are not strong or old enough to hold your ground or endure combat or strife against such a hardened knight."

"That is what you will see today, for I shall go and fight him. No warning will stop me," he said.

She had constructed such a scheme for him that she reproached him for his plan, all the while wanting him to execute it. But it often happens that on seeing a man intent on doing one's will, one hides one's wishes in order to make him more eager to carry it out. Thus she behaved cleverly, rebuking him severely for the plan she had set in his heart.

He asked that his armor be fetched for him, and it was brought out. The gate was opened for him. The men armed him and had him mount a horse they had harnessed for him there. No one present failed to show his worry and say: "Sir, God help you today, and grant heavy misfortune to Anguiguerron the seneschal, who has ravaged all this country."

All the men and women were in tears as they escorted him to the gate. When they saw him outside the town, all exclaimed together: "Dear sir, may that True Cross, on which God permitted His own Son to die, protect you today from misfortune, imprisonment, and deadly peril, and bring you back safely to a place where pleasure, delight, and comfort may be yours." This was their prayer for him.

The men in the besieging host saw him coming and pointed him out to Anguiguerron, who was sitting before his tent, convinced that the town would be surrendered to him before nightfall, or that someone would come forward to fight him in bodily combat. Already he had laced his leggings, and his men rejoiced, believing that they had overcome the town and the entire country. The moment Anguiguerron sighted the knight, he had himself promptly armed and trotted toward him on a strong and robust horse. "Youth, who sends you here?" he asked. "Tell me the reason for your journey. Do you come in peace? Or do you seek combat?"

"But you, what are you doing in this land?" he replied. "First you tell me this. Why have you been slaying the knights and ravaging the entire country?"

With disdainful arrogance he answered him. "I want the town emptied and the keep surrendered to me today. Too long has it been defended against me. And my lord shall have the maiden."

"Damn those words and damn their speaker," the youth said. "No, you must renounce all claim to her."

"Now, by Saint Peter, you offer me lies. Often it happens that the innocent man pays the penalty," said Anguiguerron.

Annoyed by his words, the youth placed his lance in its rest, and the two spurred against each other without word of challenge, holding thick but not unwieldy ash lances with sharp heads. The horses raced forward. The strong knights felt mortal hatred for each other. With such impact did they strike that they cracked the boards of their shields, splintered their lances, and brought each other to the ground. But they quickly leapt back up again and, as fast as their horses could carry them, without exchanging word of insult, charged at each other more fiercely than two wild boars. They struck each other in the middle of their shields and through the tightly meshed hauberks. From the violence of their anger and the force of their arms, they sent pieces and splinters from the lances flying in two directions.

Anguiguerron alone fell, feeling the pain from the wounds in his arms and his sides. The youth dismounted, not knowing how to pursue him on horseback; after jumping from his horse to the ground, he drew his sword and attacked him. I do not know what more to describe to you, all the blows one by one or how each man fared. Savage were the blows, and the combat lasted a long time until Anguiguerron fell. The youth assailed him fiercely until his opponent begged mercy of him; he answered him that there was not a drop of mercy. Yet he remembered the worthy man, who had taught him not to kill a knight deliberately once he had defeated him and gained the upper hand.

"Dear honored sir," Anguiguerron said to him, "do not be so haughty as to deny me mercy. You have the best of it now, I grant and assure you. You are a very fine knight, but not so fine that people who knew us both and had not witnessed this would believe that you had killed me single-handedly in armed combat. If I bear witness for you, before my men, in front of my tent, that you vanquished me in combat, my word on this will be believed, and your honor will thereby increase. No knight ever had greater honor. Take care, and if you have a lord who has done you service or good without being repaid, send me to him. On your behalf I shall go there and tell him how you defeated me in armed combat. I shall yield myself prisoner to him to do his will with me."

"Damn him who would ask more of you! And do you know, then, where you will go? To that town. And you will tell the fair lady who is my beloved that you will place yourself at her mercy and never harm her your whole life long."

"Then kill me, for she would also have me killed," he replied. "She desires nothing more than my torment and my death, since I was one of those who killed her father. And I have borne her so much enmity that this year I imprisoned or killed all her knights. Dire would be the imprisonment given me by the man who made me her prisoner. I could never receive worse treatment. But if you have any other friend, man or woman, not intent on my harm, send me there, for if she held me, this lady would certainly take my life."

The youth then told him to go to a castle belonging to a worthy man, and gave him the lord's name. No mason in the entire world could describe the design of the castle better than the youth did. He extolled to him the river, the bridge, and the turrets, the tower keep and the strong walls encircling it, until the man understood and realized that the youth wished to send him as prisoner to the place where he was hated most.

"I see no safety for me where you send me, dear sir," he said. "So help me God, you intend to set me on a fatal route and place me in evil hands, for I killed one of his own brothers in this war. Kill me, dear friend, rather than force me to go to him. If you drive me there, I shall meet my death."

"On my word, then you shall go to King Arthur's prison," he said. "You shall greet the king on my behalf and tell him from me that he should point out to you the young lady Kay the seneschal slapped for laughing when she saw me. You shall make yourself her prisoner and tell her at once that under no condition whatever will I enter any court King Arthur holds until I have avenged her."

Anguiguerron replied that he would do this service very well. The knight who had defeated him then turned in the direction of the town, while Anguiguerron went away to the prison, after having his standard carried off. The besiegers left; no one, brown-haired or blond, remained there.

The townspeople came out to meet the knight as he returned. Though quite upset at his not beheading the knight he had defeated or handing him over to them, they joyfully welcomed him and relieved him of his armor as he stood on a horseblock. "Sir, since you did not bring Anguiguerron inside here, why did you not behead him?" they asked.

"On my word, sirs, that, I believe, would not have been good for me to do," he replied. "In spite of me you would have slain him, since he killed your relatives and I could not guarantee him protection. I would have been worth little had I not taken mercy on him once I had the upper hand. And do you know what mercy? If he honors his pledge to me, he will place himself in King Arthur's prison."

At that moment the young lady arrived, rejoicing over him, and led him to her chambers to relax and rest. She did not hold back from embracing and kissing him. Instead of food and drink, they enjoyed themselves with kisses, caresses, and gracious words.

But foolish were Clamadeu's thoughts as he came expecting to have the town at that time without opposition. A youth displaying deep grief met him midway along the road and recounted to him the news of Anguiguerron his seneschal. "In God's name, sir, it goes very badly now," exclaimed the young man, who made such a lament that he tore out his hair with his hands.

"What goes badly?" Clamadeu asked.

"On my word," the young man replied, "your seneschal is defeated in armed combat and goes to yield himself prisoner to King Arthur."

"Who did this, youth? Come tell, how could this happen? Whence could the knight come capable of compelling so worthy and so valiant a man to surrender in armed combat?"

"Dear sir," he answered, "I don't know who the knight is, but I do know that I saw him leave Beaurepaire in vermilion armor."

"And so, youth, what do you advise me?" said Clamadeu, almost out of his mind.

"What, sir? Go back, for you would gain nothing, I believe, if you proceeded ahead."

At these words a knight came forward, somewhat white-haired, who was Clamadeu's counselor. "Youth," he said, "your words are not good. He ought to heed wiser and better counsel than yours. He will act foolishly if he heeds you. I advise him to proceed ahead." He then continued. "Sir, do you wish to know how you could have the knight and the town? I shall tell you clearly, and it will be easily done. Within the walls of Beaurepaire is no food or drink, and so the knights are weak, while we are strong and healthy. Not suffering from hunger or thirst, we could sustain a heavy onslaught if those inside dare come forward to engage us in battle out here. We shall send before the gateway twenty knights to do battle. The knight who enjoys himself with his sweetheart Blancheflor will wish to perform more deeds of chivalry than he will be able to endure. And so he will there be captured or killed, for his weakened knights will offer him little help.

And all our twenty will do nothing but engage them in a deceitful manner until through the valley we come upon them so unexpectedly that we surround them on all sides."

"On my word, I do propose this action you present to me," said Clamadeu. "Chosen men we have here, five hundred armed knights and a thousand well-equipped men-at-arms, and so we shall take the enemy as though they were dead men."

Clamadeu sent before the gateway twenty knights, who unfurled to the wind their many-colored pennons and banners. As soon as the men inside the town saw them, they opened the gate wide, as the youth wished, and he rode out at their head to join battle with the knights. Bold, strong, and proud knight that he was, he attacked them all together, appearing no apprentice in arms to any he encountered. That day many a gut felt his lancehead. One man he pierced in the chest, another in the breast; he broke one man's arm, another's collarbone; this man he killed, that one he wounded. He handed over the prisoners and presented the horses at once to those who needed them.

Then the men of the town, occupying a large section of the field before the open gateway, noticed the large battalions coming up the entire valley, by count five hundred knights as well as the thousand men-at-arms approaching. Their opponents saw the defeat of their men, who had been wounded or slain; as a result they proceeded directly to the gateway in close and ordered ranks. The men of the town stationed themselves close together at their gateway and received them boldly. Yet they were weak and few in number, and the strength of their opponents increased with their troops who had followed them. At last the men of the town did not have the strength to withstand their attack, and fell back inside their town. Above the gateway were archers shooting into the large and dense throng of men rushing ardently to gain access to the town. In the end, a troop of attackers forced their way inside. On to those below, the men above knocked down a portcullis, which, as it fell, crushed and killed all the men it hit. Never could Clamadeu have witnessed a sight that grieved him so much: the portcullis had killed many of his men and shut him outside. He was forced to remain idle: a hasty assault would be but wasted effort.

His adviser counseled him. "Sir," he said, "it is no wonder if misfortune befalls a worthy man. According to the Lord God's pleasure and will, good and evil, we well know, befall everyone. You have lost some of your men, yet there is no saint without a feast day. Disaster has come down on you: your men have suffered much, and the men inside have won. But be certain of this, their time to lose will come. If they remain within for five days, pluck out both my eyes. The town and the keep will be yours, for all the men will come out for mercy. If you would remain only today and to-morrow, the town will be yours. That same lady who has refused you so long will beg you in God's name that you be willing to take her." Then all those who had brought tents and pavilions there had them set up, while the others camped and lodged as best they could.

Those inside the town disarmed the knights they had captured. They did not place them in towers or in irons, provided that, as loyal knights, they pledged to remain prisoners on their word and never to seek their captors' harm. Thus were they all together inside the town.

That same day a high wind had driven over the sea a barge carrying a full cargo of grain and other provisions, arriving, as God pleased, safe and intact before the town. When the people inside the town caught sight of it, they sent to inquire and know the identity of the arrivals and their purpose in coming. Thereupon they came down from the town to go and meet the people and learn who they were, where they came from, and what they sought.

"We are merchants, carrying provisions for sale: bread, wine, and salted pork, and if there be need, we have enough cattle and pigs to sell," they replied.

"Blessed be God, who gave the wind the force to bring you drifting here. Welcome to you. Disembark, for you have sold your goods at as high a price as you wish to charge. So come and take your payment. You will not be able to avoid accepting and counting bars of gold and silver we shall offer you for the wheat. And for the wine and the meat, we shall present a cart filled with riches, and more if need be."

The buyers and sellers then performed their duties well. They set about unloading the ship and had all its goods carried ahead to the people in the town for their relief. You can imagine the great delight of the townspeople on seeing the arrivals carrying the provisions. As quickly as they could, they had the food prepared.

Now Clamadeu, who passed the time outside, could take a long rest, for the townspeople had cattle, pigs, and salted pork in abundance as well as bread, wine, and venison. The servants lit the fires in the kitchens to cook the food, and the cooks were not idle.

The youth could now enjoy himself in complete comfort at the side of his beloved. She embraced him, and he kissed her, and so each found joy in the other.

The great hall, not at all quiet, rang with the din of the rejoicing. All had craved food so long and, since it was now there, were jubilant. And the cooks hastened the preparations until they had the famished people sit at the meal. When the people had finished the meal, they left their places at the table.

Clamadeu and his men, having learned the news of the townspeople's good fortune, were infuriated. They declared that since the town could not be reduced to starvation, they were forced to move back. In vain had they besieged the town.

Mad with rage, Clamadeu, without seeking any advice or counsel, sent a message to the town that if the vermilion knight dared, he could find him alone on the plain until noon the next day ready to do combat with him. When the maiden heard the message announced to her lover, she was distressed and angered, for he sent word back to Clamadeu that, happen what might, combat, since he sought it, would be his. The grief the maiden felt then grew heavier and heavier, though her grief, I believe, would never make him stay. All the men and women begged him not to go into combat against a man no knight had ever overcome in battle. "Sirs," said the youth, "be quiet now, and you will act well. Not for any man or anything in the world will I ever abandon the combat."

Thus they broke off their words, not daring to say more to him on the subject. Instead they went to bed and rested until sunrise the next morning. But for their lord they were deeply grieved, and regretted that their pleas were futile. That night his beloved implored him insistently not to go into combat, but to be at peace, for the people had no further worry about Clamadeu or his men. All her words, however, were in vain, and that was a wondrous marvel, for he found her attentiveness to him deliciously sweet since with each word she kissed him so tenderly and so softly that she put the key of love into the lock of his heart. Yet there was no way possible for her to dissuade him from going into combat.

The youth called for his equipment, and the man to whom he had entrusted it fetched it for him as quickly as he could. There was heavy mourning at his arming, for all the men and women were in grief. He commended them all to the King of Kings, mounted his Norwegian steed, which had been led out for him, then scarcely stayed among them but, leaving them to their laments, rode away immediately.

When Clamadeu saw the man who was to fight him approach, he foolishly expected to force him to vacate his saddlebows quickly. The plain was level and attractive, and there was none there but the two, Clamadeu having dismissed and dispersed all his forces. Without word of challenge, each man, his lance placed in its rest in front of the saddle, charged at the other. The ash lances they held were thick and not unwieldy and with sharp heads.

The horses raced forward. The strong knights felt mortal hatred for each other. With such impact did they strike that they cracked the boards of their shields, splintered their lances, and brought each other to the ground. But they quickly leapt up again and charged firmly at each other. For long they battled as equals with their swords. If I wished to recount the story in detail, I would be able, but I do not wish to exert effort in this matter, for one word is as good as twenty. In the end Clamadeu was forced against his will to beg mercy.

As had his seneschal, Clamadeu accepted all the youth's terms, except that under no circumstance would he be imprisoned inside Beaurepaire, any more than his seneschal would, nor, for the whole empire of Rome, would he go to the worthy man who had the well-situated castle. But he did agree to place himself in King Arthur's prison, and to deliver to the maiden whom Kay had insolently slapped with such brutality the message that the youth would achieve his wish and avenge her if God would grant him strength. After this the youth made him pledge that the next morning before daylight all imprisoned in his towers would be freed and permitted to return; that as long as he lived, he would disperse, if ever he could, any army before the town; and that the young lady would never be troubled by him or his men.

And so Clamadeu returned to his own land. When he arrived there, he commanded that all the prisoners be released from prison and permitted to leave unhindered. As soon as he spoke the word, his command was carried out. Behold the prisoners already released. They departed immediately, carrying all their equipment, since nothing belonging to them was kept from them.

All alone, Clamadeu made his way in another direction. It was the custom at that time, as we find written in the source, that a knight defeated in combat had to yield himself prisoner in all the equipment he wore at the time he left combat, not adding or removing any piece. Thus equipped, Clamadeu followed the route of Anguiguerron, who was proceeding directly to Dinasdaron, where King Arthur was holding court.

On the other hand, there was great jubilation in the town where all those had now returned who had long stayed in confinement too vile. The entire great hall and the lodgings of the knights resounded with joy. In the churches and minsters all the bells rang out gaily, and there was no monk or nun not offering prayers of thanksgiving to the Lord God. Through the streets and through the squares, all the men and women danced their rounds. The townspeople celebrated now that no one was besieging them or waging war.

Anguiguerron was still on his way. Behind him was Clamadeu, who spent three successive nights in the same lodgings where Anguiguerron had stayed. He followed his tracks well until he came to Dinasdaron in Wales, where King Arthur was holding high court in his halls. All alone, Clamadeu entered, equipped as he had to be. He was recognized by Anguiguerron, who had already delivered a full account of his message at court since his arrival the day before, and been retained at court as part of the household and council. When he saw his lord covered in crimson blood, he did not fail to recognize him. "Sirs, sirs, behold marvels!" he immediately exclaimed. "Believe me, the youth with the vermilion armor sends here this knight you see. He has defeated him, I am completely certain, since this man is covered in blood. From here I recognize the blood and the man himself as well, for he is my lord and I his liegeman. Clamadeu of the Isles is his name, and I once believed there was no finer knight in the empire of Rome. But misfortune befalls many a worthy man." Thus Anguiguerron spoke, and then Clamadeu arrived there. Each ran to the other, and they met in the court.

All this took place one Pentecost. The queen was seated beside King Arthur at the head of a table. Many counts and kings were present, and many queens and countesses too. The knights and the ladies had come from the minster after all the masses ended. Without a cloak, Kay came through the great hall, a cap on his head, his blond tresses twined in a single braid, and a stick in his right hand. In the world there was no knight more handsome, but his malicious jests marred his beauty and his valor. He wore a tunic of costly colored silk, and around his waist an embroidered belt whose buckle and all the links were of gold. This I remember well, and so the story testifies. Everyone moved out of his way as he walked through the hall; afraid of his malicious jests and his wicked tongue, all made way for him. Unwise is he who does not fear maliciousness too publicly displayed, whether in seriousness or in jest. All present were so frightened of his malicious jests that none spoke a word to him. Before all he walked up to where the king was seated. "Were it your pleasure, lord, you could eat now," he said.

"Kay," the king replied, "let me be. By the eyes in my head, with such a high court assembled, I have no intention of eating on so great a feast day until some news reaches my court."

While they thus talked, Clamadeu entered the court. He had come to yield himself prisoner at court, equipped as he had to be when he came. "God save and bless the finest king alive, the most noble and the most well born, as all bear witness who have heard accounts of the great deeds of valor he has performed," he said. "Listen now, dear lord," he continued, "for I wish to give you my message. Though grieved to do so, still I acknowledge that a knight who defeated me has sent me here. I am forced to yield myself prisoner to you on his behalf, for I can do nothing else. But to any who would ask me if I know his name, I would reply that I do not. But I do tell you this information about him, his arms are vermilion and, he declared, you presented them to him."

"Friend, the Lord God help me!" the king said. "Tell me the truth, if he is vigorous and fit, healthy and well."

"Yes, dear lord, he is, be completely certain of that," Clamadeu replied. "He is the most valiant knight I have ever known. And he told me to speak to the maiden who laughed when she saw him. Kay did her such disgrace by slapping her. But the knight will avenge her, he declared, if the Lord God so grants him."

When the fool heard these words, he danced for joy, exclaiming: "God bless me, lord king. Now the slap will be avenged. And don't regard this as mockery, for Kay will be unable to prevent his arm from being broken and his collarbone dislocated."

When Kay heard these words, he considered them very silly. Be certain that he refrained from hitting the fool over the head, not out of cowardice, but only because of the presence of the king and his own shame. The king shook his head. "Ah, Kay," he said, "I am much chagrined that the knight is not present with me. He left here because of that foolish tongue of yours, and I am saddened."

At these words Girflet rose to his feet on the king's command, as did Sir Yvain, who enhanced all those who bore him company. The king commanded them to take the knight and conduct him to the chambers where the queen's maidens played among themselves. The knight bowed to the men, and, following the king's command, they led him to the chambers and pointed out the maiden to him. He told her the news she wished to hear. She was still upset over the slap she had received; although she had recovered from the blow itself, she had not forgotten or outlived its shame. Cowardly indeed is the man who forgets shame or injury done him. In a strong and vigorous man, pain passes, and shame endures; in the coward, shame grows cold and dies. After Clamadeu had delivered his message, the king retained him for life in his household and court.

The youth who had fought him for the land of the lady named Blanchefleur, his beautiful beloved, enjoyed her presence at his side. She and her land would have been entirely his had his thoughts not been elsewhere. But another matter occupied him; he remembered his mother, whom he had seen fall unconscious, and more than anything else, he wanted to go and see her. He dared not take leave of his beloved. She refused and forbade him, commanding all her people to entreat him to stay. But their words had no effect, except that he promised them that if he found his mother living, he would bring her back with him and, from then on, govern the land; they could be assured of this. And if she were dead, he would come back. And so, with the promise to return, he went his way, leaving in sorrow and anger his nobly born beloved as well as all those with her.

As he left the town, he encountered the kind of procession that occurred on Ascension Day or on a Sunday. All the monks had come there, dressed in rich silk copes, and so too all the nuns in their veiled hoods. "Sir," they all cried out, "you delivered us from exile and brought us back to our homes. It is no wonder if we weep when you would leave us so soon. Our grief ought to be great, and indeed it cannot be greater."

"Be assured, you should fear nothing," he answered them. "Do you not believe it would be good for me to see my mother, who lives all alone in the woods called the Desolate Forest? Whether she lives or not, I shall return, for under no circumstance will I renounce my word. If she is living, I shall have her take the veil of a nun in your church; if she is dead, you will hold a service for her soul each year that God may place her along with the souls of the good in Holy Abraham's bosom. And you, sir monks, and you, ladies, grief should not be yours, for if God leads me back, I shall donate a great deal to you for the repose of her soul." Thereupon the monks, the nuns, and all the others departed, and the youth went away, his lance in its rest, all equipped as he had been on his arrival there.

All day long the youth continued his journey without encountering any mortal—Christian man or woman—who might show him his route. He did not cease praying to the King of Glory, his true Father, that He grant him the sight of his mother. He still was praying when he came to a river flowing down a hill. He examined the deep, swift current, not daring to enter. "Ah, powerful Lord God, he who crossed this water would, I believe, find my mother on the other side, alive and healthy."

Thus he traveled along the bank until he approached a rocky cliff whose base was washed by the water so that he could proceed no farther. He looked up the rushing river and saw a boat coming downstream. Inside the boat were two men, one of them rowing while the other fished with his hook. He stopped and waited for them, expecting them to come down to him. The pair stopped and dropped anchor securely where they were in the middle of the river. The man in the bow was fishing with his hook, baiting the hook with a small fish scarcely larger than a minnow. The youth, not knowing what to do or where to find a crossing, greeted them. "Instruct me, sirs, if there is a ford or bridge across this river," he addressed them.

And the man fishing answered him. "No, dear brother, by my faith. Nor is there for twenty leagues upstream or down, believe me, a boat larger than the one we are in, and this would not carry five men. It is impossible, then, to cross on horseback. There is no ferry, bridge, or ford."

"In God's name, tell me now where I may find lodging," he asked.

"You will need that and more, I believe," he answered him. "I shall lodge you tonight. Ride up there by that cleft in the rock. When you reach the top, you will see in the valley ahead of you, near rivers and woods, a house where I live."

At once he rode off and reached the top. And when he came to the summit of the hill, he looked out beyond and saw nothing but sky and earth. "What did I come in search of? Folly and nonsense!" he said. "God today give evil mishap to the man who sent me here! He set me certainly on a good route when he told me that I would see a house once I was here at the top. Fisherman who told me that, you were too deceitful if you spoke to me with evil intent."

In a valley ahead of him, he then caught sight of the top of a tower emerging. From here to Beirut could be found no tower so beautiful or so well situated. Constructed of grey stone, it was square and flanked by turrets. The great hall stood in front of the tower, and the living quarters in front of the hall. The youth rode down in that direction, declaring that the man who had sent him there had set him on a good route. Thus he proceeded toward the gate.

Before the gateway he found a drawbridge lowered. As he rode across the drawbridge, four young attendants came to meet him. Two relieved him of his armor; the third led his horse off to give it hay and oats; the fourth placed on him a new cloak of fresh rich wool. They then led him to the living quarters. From here to Limoges, be certain, anyone in search of living quarters would find or see none so splendid. The youth stayed there until the lord sent two attendants for him. He accompanied them into the hall, which was square, being as long as it was wide.

In the center of the hall he saw, seated on a bed, a man of worth, handsome and with greying hair. A sable cap, black as a mulberry with a silk band around the top, covered the man's head, and his robe was of the same material. Before the man, in the middle of four columns, brightly blazed a great fire of dry logs. Four hundred men could have been comfortably seated around the fire. The high and wide solid columns that supported the hood of the chimney were made of heavy bronze. Before the lord came the attendants, one on each side, leading the guest to him. The moment the lord saw his guest approaching, he greeted him. "Friend," he said, "take no offense if I do not rise to meet you, for I cannot move without pain."

"In God's name, sir, do not speak of it," he answered. "God grant me joy and health, I take no offense."

The worthy man made such an effort for the youth that he managed to lift himself up. "Friend, have no fear. Come near me," he said. "Take a seat here at my side, as I bid you."

The youth seated himself next to him, and the worthy man asked him: "Friend, where did you come from today?"

"Sir," he replied, "this morning I left Beaurepaire, as it is called."

"So help me God, you traveled a long distance today," exclaimed the worthy man. "You must have left this morning before the watchman had blown his horn to mark the dawn."

"No, the six o'clock bell had already rung, I assure you," replied the youth.

While they thus talked, a young attendant entered at the door, a sword hanging by the rings from his neck. He handed it to the wealthy man. The latter, drawing it out halfway, clearly saw where it had been made, this being engraved on the blade. He also noticed that it was made of such fine steel that it could not break into pieces except by a singular peril known only to the man who had forged it. The attendant who had brought it spoke. "Sir, the blonde maiden, your niece who is so beautiful, sends you this gift. You have never seen so noble a sword of its length and width. Bestow it on whomever you please. But my lady would be most happy if it were given to one who would use it well. The man who forged the sword made only three, and since he is about to die, he can never again forge another sword like this one."

The lord invested the young stranger with the sword, holding it by the rings, which were worth a treasure. The sword's hilt was of the finest gold of Arabia or of Greece, the scabbard of gold brocade from Venice. The sword, thus richly decked, the lord presented to the youth. "Dear sir, this sword was appointed and destined for you. And I wish you to have it. Buckle it on and test it," he said.

The youth thanked him for it and buckled it on, not fastening it too tight. He then unsheathed the naked blade and, after holding it a little, put it back into its scabbard. You can be certain that it greatly suited him at his side and, even more, in his grasp. In time of need, it surely seemed, he would use it as a nobleman might.

Behind him, around the brightly blazing fire, he noticed a knight bachelor, and recognized him as the one guarding his armor. He entrusted him with his sword, and the knight kept it for him. The youth then took his seat again at the side of the lord, who showed him great honor. And about them was light as bright as candles may furnish in a hall.

While they talked of this and that, a young attendant entered the room, holding a shining lance by the middle of its shaft. He passed between the fire and those seated on the bed, and all present saw the shining lance with its shining head. A drop of blood fell from the tip of the lance, and that crimson drop ran all the way down to the attendant's hand. The youth who had come there that night beheld this marvel and refrained from asking how this could be. He remembered the warning of the man who had made him a knight, he who had instructed and taught him to guard against speaking too much. The youth feared that if he asked a question, he would be taken for a peasant. He therefore asked nothing.

Two more attendants then entered, bearing in their hands candelabra of fine gold inlaid with niello. Handsome indeed were the attendants carrying the candelabra. On each candelabrum ten candles, at the very least, were burning. Accompanying the attendants was a beautiful, gracious, and elegantly attired young lady holding between her two hands a bowl. When she entered holding this serving bowl, such brilliant illumination appeared that the candles lost their brightness just as the stars and the moon do with the appearance of the sun. Following her was another young lady holding a silver carving platter. The bowl, which came first, was of fine pure gold, adorned with many kinds of precious jewels, the richest and most costly found on sea or land, those on the bowl undoubtedly more valuable than any others. Exactly as the lance had done, the bowl and the platter passed in front of the bed and went from one room into another.

The youth watched them pass and dared not ask who was served from the bowl, for always he took to heart the words of the wise and worthy man. I fear harm may result, for I have often heard it said that there are times when too much silence is the same as too much speech. Whether for good or ill, he did not ask them any question.

The lord ordered the attendants to spread tablecloths and offer water for washing. Those whose duty and practice it was to perform such service obeyed. While the lord and the youth washed their hands in warm water, two attendants carried in a wide ivory table, which, as the story relates, was of one solid piece. They held it for a moment before the lord and the youth; then two more attendants came with two trestles. The wood of the trestles had two virtues that caused the pieces to last forever: since they were made of ebony, no one ever feared the wood's rotting or burning; these two dangers did not affect this wood. The table top was positioned on the trestles, and the tablecloth laid. What can I say of the tablecloth? No legate, cardinal, or pope ever ate on one so white.

The first course was a haunch of venison peppered and cooked in fat. There was no scarcity of clear wines of varied quality to drink from gold cups. An attendant who had brought out the peppered haunch of venison carved it before them on the silver platter, and placed the slices on a large piece of flat bread for the two men.

Meanwhile the bowl passed before them again, and the youth did not ask who was served from the bowl. He was afraid because of the worthy man, who had gently warned him against speaking too much, and, remembering this, had his heart always set on it. But he kept silent longer than was necessary. As each course was served, he saw the bowl pass before them completely uncovered, but did not know who was served from it, and he would have liked to know. Yet he would definitely inquire of one of the court attendants, he said to himself, before his departure, although he would wait until morning, when he took leave of the lord and his entire household. The matter was thus postponed, and he set about drinking and eating.

Pleasing and delicious courses and wines were brought to the table. The meal was sumptuous and splendid. That evening both the worthy man and the youth with him were served with food usually on the table of counts, kings, and emperors. After supper the two passed the evening in conversation, while the attendants readied the beds and prepared some very costly fruit for the night: dates, figs, and nutmegs, pears and pomegranates, and, for the end, sweet digestives and Alexandrian ginger. Later they drank many fine drafts of sweet wine made without honey or pepper, good mulberry wine, and clear syrup. The youth, unaccustomed to all this, was astonished.

"Friend, it is time this evening to go to bed," the worthy man said to him. "I shall, if you don't mind, go and lie in my chamber. And you will lie down outside here when you wish. I do not have use of my body, and so must be carried."

Thereupon four strong and agile servants came from one chamber, took hold of the corners of the bedspread where the worthy man lay, and carried him where they were told, into his chamber. Other attendants had stayed with the youth to attend his needs and serve him. When he wished, they removed his leggings, undressed him, and placed him on a bed fitted with delicate white linen sheets.

The youth slept until daybreak the next morning, by which time the household had risen. He opened his eyes and looked about, and seeing no one there, had to get up alone. However upset he was, he rose, having no alternative. Without waiting for aid from anyone, he put on his leggings, then went to fetch his arms, which he found at the head of the table where they had been brought for him. When he had donned all his armor, he walked toward the doors of the chambers he had seen open the night before. But he set out in vain, for he found them firmly shut. He shouted and knocked hard; no one opened up for him or made reply. After all his shouts, he walked to the door of the great hall, discovered it open, and went all the way down the stairs. He found his horse saddled, and saw his lance and his shield leaning against the wall. Then he mounted and rode all about, not meeting or seeing squire, attendant, or servant. He went straight to the gateway, where he found the drawbridge lowered. It had been left in this position so that nothing would stop him from crossing unhindered when he arrived there.

Because he saw the drawbridge lowered, he thought that the attendants had gone into the forest to examine traps and snares. Having no wish to stay longer, he decided to follow them to learn if any of them would tell him, this not being indiscreet, why the lance was bleeding and where the bowl was being carried. He then passed through the gateway. Before he was across the drawbridge, he felt the feet of his horse spring up. It made a great leap, for had the horse not jumped, both it and its rider would have been ill-befallen. The youth turned back to see what had happened, and noticed that the drawbridge had been raised. He shouted, and no one answered him. "Come speak!" he exclaimed. "You who raised the drawbridge, speak to me! Where are you? I don't see you. Come forward, and I shall see you and ask you for the information I would like to have." Thus he made a fool of himself by his talk, for no one would answer him.

Making his way toward the forest, he entered upon a path where he discovered fresh tracks of horses that had passed there. "I believe the men I seek rode in this direction," he said. He then galloped through the woods, following the tracks as long as they continued, until by chance he noticed a maiden under an oak tree, who was lamenting and moaning like a sorrowful wretch.

"Alas, miserable am I!" she cried out. "At what an evil hour was I born! What an evil fate is mine! Nothing worse could have happened to me! Would to God I should not be holding my lover dead. Death, who devastates me, would have done much better were my lover alive and I dead. Why did he take his soul and not mine? What means life to me when I behold dead the creature I loved most? Without him, certainly, I care nothing for my body or my life. Death, cast out the soul from my body and let it be hand-maid and companion to his, should his design to accept it."

This was her lament over the body of a headless knight she embraced. Having noticed her, the youth did not stop until he was before her. He approached and greeted her. Her head bowed, she returned his greeting without interrupting her lament. "Maiden, who killed the knight lying in your lap?" the youth asked her.

"A knight killed him this morning, sir," the maiden answered. "But I am amazed by something marvelous I behold. God save me, one could ride, as people attest, twenty-five leagues in the very direction you came from without finding a lodging place that was good, clean, and honest. And yet your horse has flanks so smooth and mane so brushed that had the horse been washed, brushed, and provided with a bed of hay and oats, it would not have a belly more filled or face and neck more sleek. And you yourself have spent, it seems to me, a comfortable and restful night."

"On my word, dear lady, I was as comfortable as possible," he replied. "And if this is evident, it is as it should be. Were anyone here to call out loudly, he would be clearly heard where I lodged last night. You have not thoroughly explored nor become well acquainted with the country. I had, without doubt, the finest lodging I ever had."

"Ah, sir, then you spent the night at the home of the wealthy Fisher King?"

"By the Savior, maiden, I don't know if he is a fisherman or a king, but he is courteous and wise. I know nothing more to tell you, save that last night I met two men seated in a boat, gliding along gently. One of the two men was rowing, the other fishing with his hook. The latter directed me to his house last evening and gave me lodging."

"Dear sir, he is a king, I dare tell you," said the maiden. "But he indeed was wounded in a battle and crippled so that he does not have use of his body. He was struck by a javelin in the buttocks. He still suffers such dis-comfort that he cannot mount a horse. But when he would sport or un-dertake some pleasant pastime, he has himself placed in a boat and goes fishing with his hook; for this reason he is called the Fisher King. And thus he finds pleasure since he could not suffer or endure any other sport. He is unable to hunt in the fields or along the riverbanks. But he has his fowlers, his archers, and his huntsmen, who pursue game in his forests. Therefore he is delighted to live in this house here, for in the entire world there is no more comfortable a place for him, and he has had constructed a house worthy of a wealthy king."

"On my word, maiden, what I hear you say is true," he said. "Last night, as soon as I came before him, I marveled at this. I stood back from him a moment, and he told me to come and sit next to him and, as he was incapable, not to regard as arrogance that he did not rise to meet me. Since I saw his infirmity, I went and sat beside him."

"He certainly showed you great honor by seating you next to him. And tell me now if, when you sat down beside him, you saw the lance with its bleeding tip, though no flesh or vein be there."

"If I saw it? Yes, on my word."

"And did you ask why it bled?"

"I never spoke of it."

"So help me God, know then that you behaved very badly. And did you see the bowl?"

"Yes indeed."

"And who held it?"

"A young lady."

"Whence did she come?"

"From a room. And she went into another, passing in front of me."

"Did anyone walk ahead of the bowl?"

"Yes."

"Who?"

"Two attendants, no one else."

"And what did they hold in their hands?"

"Candelabra filled with candles."

"And who came after the bowl?"

"A young lady."

"And what did she hold?"

"A small silver platter."

"Did you ask the people where they were going thus?"

"Not a word left my mouth."

"So help me God, that is worse. What is your name, friend?"

And the youth, ignorant of his name, had a sudden inspiration and replied that his name was Perceval the Welshman. He did not know whether or not he spoke the truth. And though he did not know, he spoke the truth. When the maiden heard him, she stood up opposite him and told him angrily: "Your name is changed, friend."

"How?"

"Perceval the wretched! Oh, unfortunate Perceval, what a hapless man you were not to have asked these questions. You would have cured the good king who is infirm. He would have regained use of his limbs and been capable of governing his land. But now be certain that harm will befall you and others. This has happened, know well, because of your sin against your mother, for she died of grief for you. I know you better than you know me, since you do not know who I am. For a long time I was brought up with you in your mother's house. I am your first cousin, and you are my first cousin. I grieve no less for your misfortune in not learning what is done with the bowl and to whom it is carried, than for your mother who is dead, or for this knight, whom I loved and cherished for calling me his sweetheart and escorting me like a noble and true knight."

"Ah, cousin, if what you told me is true, tell me how you know it," Perceval said.

"I know it as truly as one who witnessed her burial."

"God in His goodness have mercy on her soul!" said Perceval. "You have told me a cruel tale. And since she is buried, for what would I continue? Only on her account was I proceeding there; I wanted to see her. I must take another route. But if you were willing to accompany me, I would be pleased. He who is here dead, I swear to you, will be worth nothing to you. The dead with the dead, the living with the living! Let us proceed together, you and I. I consider it folly on your part to stand watch here all alone over this dead body. Let us pursue his killer. And I tell you and promise you: if I can overtake him, either he will compel me, or I him, to beg mercy."

The lady, unable to repress the grief in her heart, spoke to him. "Sir, under no circumstance would I go with you or leave him until I have buried him. If you take my advice, you will follow this paved road from here. The evil and insolent knight who robbed me of my sweetheart rode off on this road. I have not said this, so help me God, because I would have you pursue him. Yet from where was the sword taken that hangs at your left side? It never spilled man's blood, nor was it ever drawn in need. I well know where it was made, and I well know who forged it. Be careful never to place your trust in it. Without fail it will betray you when you go into battle, for from you it will fly into pieces."

"Dear cousin, one of my host's nieces sent it to him last night. He gave it to me, and I consider it a fine present. But if what you told me is true, I am deeply dismayed. Now tell me, if you know, should it be broken, would it ever be repaired?"

"Yes, though only with great difficulty. If anyone knew the route to the lake above Cotatre, he could have it repaired there, beaten and tempered again. If chance takes you there, go to a smith named Trabuchet, not to any but him, for he made it and will repair it; no other man attempting the task will ever accomplish it. Be careful no one else tries his hand, for he would not succeed."

"I would certainly be most upset if it broke," said Perceval.

He then rode off, and she stayed behind, not wishing to leave the body of her lover, whose death was the cause of her deep grief.

Perceval rode along the path, following the tracks, until he came upon a thin and weary palfrey moving ahead of him at a walk. The palfrey's thin and wretched appearance made him think it had fallen into ill hands. It seemed to have been subjected to hard work and little food, like a hired horse, which has hard work by day and poor care by night. Such seemed the case with the palfrey: it was so thin that it shivered as though benumbed by cold. All its hair had been shorn, and its ears drooped. Since the palfrey had nothing but hide covering its bones, all the mastiffs and watchdogs were there expecting to make a meal of the spoils. On its back was a saddlecloth and on its head a bridle, both befitting such an animal. And riding it was a maiden, the most wretched ever seen. Still, had life been kinder to her, she would have been beautiful. But so dreadful was her life that not a palm's breadth of the dress she wore was whole, her breasts protruded through the rips, and everywhere the material was tied together with knots and coarse stitchings. Her skin was scratched as though by a lancet, for it was cracked and burned by frost, hail, and snow. Her hair was not bound; she wore no cloak; and her face showed many ugly traces of the unending tears that flowed down to her bosom and over her dress, falling as far as her knees. Anyone in such distress might well have a heavy heart.

As soon as Perceval saw her, he galloped toward her. She pulled her clothing round her to cover herself better. More holes then began to open, for when she covered herself further, every hole she closed opened a hundred more. In her pale, wan, and wretched state, Perceval rode up to her and, when he caught up, heard her doleful lament about her misery and her pain.

"God, may You never be pleased that I live longer in this condition!" she exclaimed. "Too long have I been wretched, too much misfortune have I endured, and all without cause. God, since You well know I have deserved none of this, send me, if You will, someone to release me from this pain, or else deliver me Yourself from the one who forces me into such a shameful life. I find no mercy in him. I cannot escape him with my life, and yet he will not kill me. I don't know why he wants the companionship of a wretch like me unless he cherishes my disgrace and my misfortune. If he was certain that I deserved it, even if I was not at all pleasing to him, he should have had mercy, for so dearly have I paid him. But certainly he has no love for me when he forces me to drag after him in such a harsh life, and cares not."

Then Perceval, who had reached her, said to her: "God save you, fair lady."

When the maiden heard him, she bowed her head and spoke in a subdued voice. "Sir, you who greeted me, may your heart have all it desires. And yet it is not right that I say this."

Perceval blushed with shame. "Wait, maiden, why not?" he asked her. "I certainly do not think or believe that I ever before laid eyes on you or did you wrong."

"Yes you did," she said, "so that I am so wretched and grief-stricken that none should greet me. I sweat in distress when anyone stops me or looks on me."

"To be honest, I was unaware of wronging you," Perceval said. "I certainly did not come here to harm or shame you; rather, my route brought me here. And the moment I saw you, so scorned, so destitute and naked, my heart could know no joy unless I knew the truth. What adventure brought you to such sorrow and such pain?"

"Ah, sir, mercy," she said. "Say no more, flee from here, and let me be. Your sin makes you stop here. Flee, and you will act wisely."

"This I would know: what fear or what threat makes me flee when no one chases me?"

"So that the Proud Knight of the Heath, who seeks nothing but battle and combat, not come upon us together. If he found you here, he would be certain to kill you at once. He becomes so furious at anyone stopping me that, provided he arrives there in time, no one who speaks to me or detains me can save his head. It is but a little time since he killed a man. But he first tells each one why he delivered me into such vile wretchedness."

While they thus talked, the Proud Knight rode out of the woods and came like a thunderbolt, raising the sand and the dust and shouting: "Cursed be you for halting here, you standing beside the maiden. Know that your end is at hand for stopping and detaining her a single step. But I would not kill you without recounting to you what disgraceful offense caused me to have her live in such deep shame. Listen now, and you will hear the tale.

"One day I had gone into the woods and left this maiden in a pavilion of mine. I loved none but her alone. Then, by chance, a Welsh youth happened to come there. I do not know what route he traveled, but this much he did: he kissed her by force, and she admitted this to me. What harm to her if she lied? Since he kissed her against her will, did he not have all he desired afterwards? Yes. No one will ever believe that he kissed her without doing more. The one act leads to the other. If a man kisses a woman when both are alone together, and does nothing more, then I think that the decision is his. A woman who surrenders her mouth easily grants the remainder, if the man earnestly requests it. She may indeed defend herself. Yet it is well known, beyond doubt, that a woman wants to win everywhere, except in that one contest where she holds the man by the throat, and claws, and bites, and struggles, yet wants to be overcome. She defends herself against this, yet longs for it. She has such cowardice about surrendering, yet wants to be taken against her will, never then showing goodwill or thanks. I therefore believe that he lay with her. He took from her a ring of mine she wore on her finger, and carried it away; I am distressed at this. But he first drank his fill of some strong wine and ate from three pies I was having stored for myself. Yet now my beloved has a courteous reward for this, as is obvious. Let anyone who does folly pay for it that he may take care not thus to fall again. When I returned and learned this, my anger was evident. I was furious, as I had right to be. I declared that her palfrey would have no oats, nor be reshod, nor be freshly bled, nor would she have coat or cloak other than the one she wore at the time, until I should overcome the man who violated her, and kill and behead him."

After listening, Perceval answered what pleased him. "Friend, know beyond doubt that she has done her penance. I am the one who kissed her by force and, by my act, distressed her. And I took her ring from her finger. But that was all: I did nothing more. I did eat, I assure you, one of the pies and half of another, and drank my fill of your wine. I did nothing foolish."

"On my life, you have now told a remarkable tale," the Proud Knight exclaimed. "Now you have deserved death since you have confessed the truth."

"Death is still not so near as you think," Perceval said.

Then, without more words, they let their horses race at each other. They clashed with such fury that they splintered their lances and both vacated the saddles, each bringing the other to the ground. But they quickly leapt up again, drawing their naked swords and exchanging savage blows.

The combat was stern and fierce. I have no desire to relate more, since that seems to me effort wasted, except that their struggle continued until the Proud Knight of the Heath admitted defeat and begged mercy of him. The youth never forgot the worthy man's entreaty that he not kill a knight who had begged mercy of him. "On my faith, knight," he said, "I shall never have mercy on you until you have it for your beloved. She has not deserved the cruel life you have forced her to endure, I can swear to that."

He who loved her more than his own eye answered him. "Dear sir, I am willing to make amends to her as you wish. I am ready to do whatever you command. My heart is sorrowful and black for the cruel life I have caused her to lead."

"Go then to the nearest manorhouse of yours in this region," he said, "and have her bathe and rest until she is recovered and healthy. Then clothe her and take her, well-adorned and well-attired, to King Arthur. Greet him on my behalf, and place yourself at his mercy, equipped just as you are when you leave here. If he asks on whose behalf, tell him on behalf of the youth he made vermilion knight upon the advice and agreement of Sir Kay the seneschal. You are to recount to the king the penance and the cruel life you forced your maiden to endure, and tell it publicly to all present so that all the men and women hear you, including the queen and her maidens, who possess great beauty. One I esteem above all. Because she laughed when she saw me, Kay slapped her, totally stunning her. Seek out this maiden, I command you, and give her this message from me: under no condition will I enter any court King Arthur holds until her injury is avenged to her joy and happiness."

The Proud Knight replied to Perceval that he would willingly go there and relate all he had commanded. And there would be no delay, he continued, except for the time necessary for his maiden to rest and ready herself. He would gladly have taken Perceval as well to rest, and to tend to his cuts and wounds.

"Go now, and may good fortune be yours," Perceval said. "I ponder other things, and so shall seek other lodging." The conversation then ended. Neither man waited there longer, but without more words they parted.

That evening the knight had his beloved bathed and richly dressed. He brought her such comforts that her beauty was restored. Afterwards, they both took the highway to Caerleon, where King Arthur was holding court. The celebration was intimate, only three thousand esteemed knights being present. In sight of all, the knight, bringing his maiden with him, went to yield himself prisoner to King Arthur. When he was before the king, he said: "Lord, I am your prisoner to do your will. And it is right and reasonable that I do so, for such was the command given me by the youth who asked and obtained vermilion arms from you."

As soon as the king heard this, he understood what the knight meant. "Disarm, dear sir," he said. "May joy and good fortune be his who presented you to me. And you yourself be welcome. On his account you will be honored and cherished in my house."

"Lord, he gave me another command. Before I am disarmed, I would request of you that the queen and her maidens come to hear the news I have brought you. The news may be recounted only in the presence of the maiden who was slapped on the cheek for a single laugh she uttered. That was her sole offense." He thus ended his words.

When the king heard that he was to summon the queen into his presence, he sent for her. And she came there, along with all her maidens, hand in hand, walking in pairs.

When the queen was seated beside her lord King Arthur, the Proud Knight of the Heath addressed her. "Lady, a knight I esteem, who defeated me in armed combat, sends you greetings. I do not know what more to tell you of him, except that he sends you my beloved, this maiden here."

"Friend, many thanks be his," said the queen. And to her he recounted all the foul disgrace he had long visited on his beloved, the suffering she had endured, and the reason he had acted in this manner; he told her all details, concealing nothing. Afterwards, the maiden whom Kay the seneschal had struck was pointed out to him.

"Maiden," he said to her, "he who sent me here commanded me to greet you on his behalf, and never to move a foot farther before telling you this. So help him God, under no condition will he enter any court King Arthur holds until he has avenged the buffet and blow you received on his account."

When the fool heard this, he leapt to his feet. "God bless me, lord Kay, you truly will pay for it, and very soon," he cried out.

The king spoke after the fool. "Ah, Kay, most courteously you acted toward the youth in your mockery of him! By your mockery you robbed me of him so that I expect to see him never again."

The king then had his prisoner knight sit before him. He pardoned him from imprisonment, then commanded that he be disarmed. Sir Gawain, who sat beside the king on his right, inquired: "In God's name, lord, who can this man be who, by himself, defeated in armed combat a knight as fine as this? In all the Isles of the Sea I have not seen, known, or heard named a knight to compare with him in feats of arms and in chivalry."

"Dear nephew, I do not know him, yet I did see him," the king replied. "When I saw him, I thought it not important to make any inquiry of him. And he bade me make him knight at that very moment. I saw that he was fine and handsome, and so said to him: 'Gladly, brother. But dismount until gilded arms are fetched for you.' And he declared that he would never take them, nor dismount, until he had vermilion arms. He made further astonishing remarks, wishing no arms but those of the knight who had carried off my gold cup. Kay, who was, is still, and always will be insulting, never wishing to say a good word, spoke to him. 'Brother, the king presents the arms to you. They are yours. Go at once and take them!' The youth, not understanding the joke and believing Kay to tell the truth, followed the knight and, by hurling a javelin at him, slew him. I do not know how the dispute and confusion began. All I know is that the Vermilion Knight of the Forest of Quinqueroi had the arrogance to strike him, I know not why, with his lance. And the youth struck him in the eye with a javelin, killed him, and took his arms. Since then he has served me so well that, by my lord Saint David, who is worshipped and prayed to in Wales, never will I lie two successive nights in the same chamber or hall until I see him, if he is living, on sea or land. Rather, I shall set out at once in search of him."

As soon as the king had sworn this oath, all were certain that there was nothing to do but go.

Then you would have beheld pillows and bedcovers packed, chests filled, packhorses saddled with their burden, and a long trail of carts and wagons loaded with various sizes of tents and pavilions. In a full day, a wise and well-educated clerk could not record all of the equipment and all the provisions that were quickly prepared. Thus, as if setting off to war, the king left Caerleon, with all his barons following him. Befitting her honor and majesty, the queen took with her all her maidens, leaving behind not a single one.

That evening, in a meadow beside a forest, the men pitched camp. During the night, as the country was cold, there was a heavy snowfall. The next morning Perceval rose early, as was his custom, eager to seek and encounter adventures and deeds of chivalry. He rode directly to the frozen, snow-covered meadow where the royal host was camped. Before reaching the tents, he heard and saw a flock of wild geese flying over, blinded by the bright snow. The geese fled a falcon in fast pursuit of them. The falcon at last found one of them alone, separated from the others. Pouncing, the falcon struck at it, knocking it to the ground. It was too late for the falcon, however, which flew away, not caring to plunge after or attack it.

Perceval galloped to the spot where he had seen the fall. The goose, struck in the neck, had shed three drops of blood, which, like a natural color, spread on the white snow. Not so seriously injured that it was unable to leave the ground, the goose had flown from there by the time of Perceval's arrival.

Seeing the trampled snow where the goose had lain and the still visible blood, Perceval leaned on his lance to gaze on the image. The blood and the snow together reminded him of the fresh hue on his beloved's face, and he mused until he forgot himself. He thought that the rosy hue stood out against the white of her face like the drops of blood on the white snow. Gazing gave him such pleasure that he believed he was beholding the fresh hue on his beloved's face.

All the early morning long, Perceval was lost in his contemplation. In time, squires emerging from the tents saw him musing and thought him dozing. Before the king, still lying in his pavilion, had awakened, the squires met Sagremor in front of the king's pavilion. Sagremor was named the Unruly because of his unruliness. "Come, speak. Don't hide it from me," he said. "Why do you come here so quickly?"

"Sir, outside this camp we have seen a knight dozing on his charger," they answered.

"Is he armed?"

"On our word, yes."

"I shall go speak with him, and lead him back to court," he said.

Sagremor immediately hastened to the pavilion of the king and awakened him. "Lord, there on that heath is a knight sleeping," he exclaimed.

The king commanded him to go, telling and urging him to lead the knight to him without fail.

Waiting not a moment, Sagremor ordered his horse led out and his arms fetched for him. The command was executed as soon as issued, and he had himself armed quickly and well. Fully equipped, he left the camp and rode on until he reached the knight. "Sir," he declared, "you must come to court."

The youth did not stir, acting as though he had not heard him. Sagremor began again to address him, and still the youth did not stir. Furious, Sagremor exclaimed: "By Saint Peter the Apostle, you will come there, willing or not. I regret my request of you, for I did waste my words." He then unfurled his ensign, took his position on one side, and told him to be on guard, for he would strike him if he did not defend himself.

Perceval, looking in his direction, saw him charge at a gallop. He then abandoned his thought altogether and spurred against him. As they met,

Sagremor splintered his lance; Perceval did not bend or break his, but thrust at him with such force that he hurled him from his horse. Sagremor's horse, head raised high, at once fled toward the tents at a gallop.

The sight of the horse distressed the barons, and Kay, never able to refrain from words of cruelty, mocked Sagremor in his address to the king. "Dear lord, behold now how Sagremor returns! By his grasp of the reins he holds the knight and leads him back against his will!"

"Kay, it is not good that you mock worthy men," the king said. "Proceed there yourself, and we shall see if you fare better than he."

"Lord," said Kay, "I am delighted it be your pleasure that I go there. Without fail I shall bring him by force, be he willing or not. And I shall have him give his name."

He then went to arm fully. Once equipped, he mounted and rode off toward the youth, who, so absorbed in contemplating the three drops, noticed nothing else. From a distance Kay shouted to him: "Vassal, vassal, come to the king! On my word, you shall come there at once, or pay dearly."

Hearing the threat, Perceval turned the head of his horse, and with his steel spurs goaded the animal, which did not move slowly. Each knight was eager to do his best, and they charged in full earnest. Kay struck him and, since he had mustered all his strength, broke and shattered his lance as though it were a piece of bark. Neither was Perceval halfhearted: he struck Kay under the boss of his shield and hurled him onto a rock so that he dislocated his collarbone and, between the elbow and the armpit, broke the bone of his right arm as though it had been a splinter of dry wood. Such had the fool often foreseen and related, and accurate indeed was the fool's prediction.

Kay fainted from the pain, and his horse fled at a gallop toward the tents.

The Britons saw the horse returning without the seneschal. Attendants rushed to mount, and knights and ladies set out. When they found the seneschal unconscious, all believed him dead. On Kay's account the king was in deep distress, and all the men and women in mourning. And over the three drops, Perceval leaned on his lance again to gaze on the image.

The king, most upset about his wounded seneschal, was told not to be dismayed, for Kay would recover, provided he had a physician who could set the broken bone in the arm and reset the collarbone. The king, who held Kay dear and cherished him in his heart, sent to him a wise physician and three maidens trained at the physician's school. They set the broken bone in the arm, reset the collarbone, and bound the arm; they then carried him to the royal pavilion and made him comfortable, informing the king that he had no reason to worry since Kay would recover.

"The Lord God help me," Sir Gawain addressed the king, "it is not right, lord—well you know, as you yourself have always declared and rightly judged—that one knight distract another from his thoughts, whatever they be, as the two have done. I do not know if they were in the wrong, but misfortune is certainly theirs. Perhaps the knight mused on some loss he had suffered, or was distressed and pained because his beloved had been stolen from him. But if it be your pleasure, I would go and observe his behavior, and if I should find that he has abandoned his thought, I would ask and urge him to come here to you."

These words angered Kay. "Oh, Sir Gawain, you will lead the knight by the hand despite his displeasure!" he exclaimed. "You will succeed if you possess—and he permits you—the power. Thus have you taken many prisoners. When knights are exhausted from much armed combat, then someone proceeds to the king to request leave to go and conquer! Damn my neck, Gawain, if you are not so wise that one can still learn from you! You are able to employ words of beauty and polish. Will you speak to him in abusive language, using malicious insults? Damn whoever believed or will believe that! You can certainly undertake this combat in a silk tunic, and never need to break a lance or draw a sword. You may take pride in the fact that if your tongue does not fail to utter, 'Sir, God save you and grant you life and health!' he will do your will. I don't speak to instruct you. Well you know how to coax him just as one strokes a cat. And people will declare, 'Now Sir Gawain fights fiercely!' "

"Oh, Sir Kay, you might have spoken to me in fairer words," he replied. "Do you now expect to avenge your anger and your rage on me? On my word, dear friend, I shall bring him, if ever I can. Never will this cost me a broken arm or a dislocated collarbone, for such wages are not to my liking."

"Proceed there now on my behalf, nephew, since you have spoken courteously," said the king. "If possible, bring him here. And take all your equipment, for you will not go unarmed."

Gawain, honored and renowned for all virtues, had himself armed at once and mounted a strong and proper horse. He rode straight to the knight, who was leaning on his lance, still not weary of his pleasing thought. But the sun had melted two of the drops of blood that stood out on the snow, and the third was disappearing. As a consequence, the knight was not so absorbed in his thought as he had been. Sir Gawain rode toward him at a quiet amble, showing no hostility. "Sir," he said, "I would have greeted you had I known your heart as well as I do my own. But I can tell you this much, that I am a messenger of the king. Through me he sends word, commanding you to go and speak with him."

"There have been two here already," said Perceval, "who drove away my joy, wishing to lead me off as if I were their prisoner. And I had been musing on a most pleasing thought. Anyone wishing me to leave here did not seek my good. For before me, in this place, were three drops of fresh blood that illumined the white snow. In gazing on them, I thought I beheld the fresh hue on the face of my beautiful beloved. I wanted never to take my eyes away."

"Certainly that thought was not base, but courteous and sweet," said Sir Gawain. "And he who took your heart from it was foolish and presumptuous. But I am anxious and eager to know your plans. If you should not object, I would gladly take you to the king."

"Now tell me truly, dear sir, if Kay the seneschal is there," asked Perceval.

"Yes, truly he is there, and be certain that it was he who now jousted with you. Although you may not know, the joust cost him dearly, for you broke his right arm and dislocated his collarbone."

"Then avenged is the maiden Kay struck," replied Perceval.

When Sir Gawain heard this, he gave an astonished start. "Sir, so help me God, it was you for whom the king has been searching," he said. "Sir, what is your name?"

"Perceval, sir. And yours?"

"Sir, know truly that my baptismal name is Gawain."

"Gawain?"

"Yes, dear sir."

Perceval was delighted. "In many places, sir, I have heard tell of you," he said. "And should you not mind, I would like to make your acquaintance."

"I am certainly pleased no less than you, but rather more, I believe," Sir Gawain replied.

"Then on my word, I shall gladly go where you wish, for it is right," Perceval said to him. "And I shall now have higher regard for myself because I am your companion."

Then they rushed to each other and embraced. Both began to unlace their helmets and chinguards, pulling down the mail from their heads. They then returned happily.

Their joy in their own company was seen by attendants from a hilltop who ran at once to the king. "Lord, lord," they exclaimed, "on our word, Sir Gawain brings the knight back, and both show great delight in each other." There was no one who heard the news who did not leave his tent and go to meet them.

Kay addressed his lord the king. "Now Sir Gawain, your nephew, has the esteem and the honor. The combat, difficult and perilous, involved no risk, for he returns in as good condition as he left. He never received a blow, nor did any feel a blow from him. And he never uttered word of challenge. Thus it is right that the praise and the honor be his. And people will say that he has accomplished what two others of us could not, although we used all our strength and effort." Thus, rightly or wrongly, Kay had his say, as he usually did.

Sir Gawain wanted to bring his companion to court, though not in his armor but completely disarmed. And he took him to his tent, where he had him relieved of his arms. One of his chamberlains brought clothes from his chest, a most becoming and splendid tunic and cloak, and gave them to Perceval to wear; he was thus appropriately dressed. The two knights then proceeded, hand in hand, to the king, who was sitting in front of his pavilion. "Lord, lord," Sir Gawain addressed the king, "I bring you the knight whom, as I believe, you have been anxious to see the past fortnight. It is he of whom you spoke often, and he for whom you have searched. I present him to you. Behold him here."

"Many thanks, dear nephew," said the king, who rose to his feet at once to welcome him. "Welcome, dear sir," he exclaimed. "Inform me, I pray you, what I should call you."

"On my word, I shall never conceal my name from you, dear lord. It is Perceval the Welshman," answered Perceval.

"Oh, Perceval, dear friend, now that you have entered my court, should I have my way you will never leave it again. Since first I saw you, I have regretted not knowing the great destiny God had ordained for you. Yet it was clearly foretold by the maiden and the fool Kay the seneschal struck so that all the court knew it. You have fulfilled the prediction in all its detail. None doubts this now. I have heard the truth about your knightly exploits."

As he spoke, the queen arrived, having heard news of Perceval's coming. As soon as Perceval saw her and learned who she was, and noticed, following the queen, the maiden who had laughed when she saw him, he went at once to meet them. "God grant joy and honor to the most beautiful and the best of all ladies living. So say all who see her and all who have seen her," he said.

"Be welcome as a proven knight of high and noble valor," the queen replied to him.

Perceval then greeted the maiden who had laughed for him. He embraced her and said to her: "Dear lady, if ever you are in need, I would be the knight never to fail to aid you." And for this the maiden thanked him.

The king, the queen, and the barons joyously welcomed Perceval the Welshman, and led him to Caerleon, returning there that evening. All night long they rejoiced, and their rejoicing continued through the next day. On the third day they saw a maiden approaching, riding a tawny mule and holding a whip in her right hand. The maiden's hair was twisted in two large black braids, and if the book is accurate, there never was a creature so totally foul, even in hell. You have never seen iron as black as her neck and her hands, yet these, compared with her other features, were the least repulsive. Her eyes were two holes small as rats' eyes; she had the nose of a cat or monkey, and the ears of a donkey or cow. Her teeth were so yellowed that in color they resembled the yolk of an egg. She had a beard like a goat. In the middle of her chest she had a hump, and her spine was like a crook. Her shoulders and her hips were shaped well for leading a dance. With her hunched back and twisted legs moving like two branches, she was ideal for the dance.

The maiden made her mule trot directly toward the knights. Never before had such a maiden appeared in a royal court. She greeted the king and all the barons together, except for Perceval. Still seated on her tawny mule, she exclaimed: "Oh, Perceval! Fortune is in front hairy and bald behind. Damn him who greets you or wishes you well. Why did you not seize Fortune when you found her? You went to the Fisher King's, and saw the bleeding lance. Was it for you, then, such a great effort to open your mouth and speak that you could not ask why that drop of blood gushed from the gleaming point of the lancehead? You saw the bowl, and did not ask or inquire what wealthy man was served from it. Wretched is he who sees favorable opportunities that may not be more favorable, yet waits for fairer opportunities to come along. It is you, wretch, who saw that it was the time and place to speak, yet remained silent. Unfortunate was your foolish mind! Unfortunate your silence! Had you asked, the wealthy king, so sorely afflicted, would have been cured of his wound and would have held his land in peace, land he will never hold again. And do you know what will befall the king if he is not cured of his wounds, and does not hold his land? Ladies will lose their husbands; hapless maidens will be orphans; many knights will die; and lands will be laid waste. All these ills will result because of you."

The maiden then addressed the king. "Be not annoyed, Your Majesty, I am leaving. I yet have to take lodging this evening far from here. I do not know if you have heard of the Proud Castle. That is where I must go. In the castle are five hundred and sixty six esteemed knights, and each, be assured, has with him his beloved, a lady noble, courteous, and beautiful. I tell you this information because no one goes there without meeting joust and combat. Whoever would perform deeds of chivalry will not fail to have them if he seeks them there. And whoever would desire to have the greatest glory in the world, I think I know the piece of ground, the very place, where he, if he dares, may best win it. On the hill below Montesclaire is a maiden under siege. Whoever could raise the siege and deliver the maiden would win great honor. All praise would be his. And the man to whom God grants such good fortune might gird on, without fear, the Sword with the Strange Baldric." Thereupon the maiden, having spoken her will, fell silent and left without further word.

Sir Gawain leapt up, exclaiming that he would go and do his best to rescue her. Girflet, the son of Do, said in turn that he would go, with God's help, before the Proud Castle. "And as for me," exclaimed Kahedin, "I shall go and climb the Perilous Mount, and not halt until I arrive there."

Perceval in his turn spoke differently. He declared that never, his whole life long, would he stay in the same lodging two successive nights, nor, hearing of any perilous passage, fail to cross it, nor fail to go and fight in combat any knight superior in valor to any other, or any two knights together. No anguish would make him abandon the quest until he knew who was served from the bowl, and until he had found the bleeding lance and discerned the true cause of its bleeding.

As many as fifty men had risen, all vowing and pleading to one another not to fail to search out any combat or adventure they heard of, no matter how treacherous the land.

As they spoke thus, behold they then saw Guinganbresil coming through the door of the great hall, carrying a gilded shield with an azure stripe. Guinganbresil recognized the king and greeted him as he should. He did not greet Gawain; rather, he accused him of treason. "Gawain," he declared, "you slew my lord, and did so without ever challenging him. For that, dishonor, reproach, and blame are yours. So I charge you with treason. May all the barons realize that I have uttered no word of lie."

At these words Sir Gawain, totally indignant, leapt to his feet. Agravain the Proud, his brother, jumped up and pulled at him. "For the love of God, dear sir," he exclaimed, "do not dishonor your lineage. I will defend you, I promise you, against the outrageous insult this knight hurls at you."

"Sir, no man but I will ever come to my defense against it," he answered. "I must defend myself, for he accuses none but me. If I knew of any wrong I had done the knight, I would be glad to seek peace with him and offer him reparation to the satisfaction of all his friends and mine. But since he has uttered this outrage, I shall defend myself here, there, or where he wishes. Behold my gage."

Guinganbresil declared that he would prove his charge before the King of Escavalon, who, in his mind and opinion, surpassed Absalom in beauty.

"I pledge to you that I shall follow you at this very moment," Gawain declared, "and there we shall see who has the right."

At once Guinganbresil departed, and Sir Gawain readied himself to follow without delay. Whoever had a good shield, a good lance, a good helmet, or a good sword offered it to him, but he had no wish to carry equipment belonging to another man. He took with him seven squires, seven chargers, and two shields. Before he left court, there was, on his account, heavy mourning: many beat their breasts; many tore their hair; many clawed their faces. There was no lady, however sensible, who did not display her grief for him. As Sir Gawain set out, many men and women wept for him.

You will now hear me tell you of the adventures he encountered. He first came upon a troop of knights riding across a heath and, following them, a lone squire, a shield hanging from his neck, leading on his right a Spanish steed. "Squire, tell me, who are these men passing here?" Gawain asked.

"Sir, this is Meliant of Lis, a brave and courageous knight," he answered.

"Are you in his service?"

"Not I, sir. My lord, no less worthy than he, is Traez of Anet."

"On my word, well I know Traez of Anet," Sir Gawain replied. "Where does he go? Hide nothing from me."

"He rides to a tournament, sir, where Meliant of Lis is to contend against Tiebaut of Tintagel. You too would go there, had I my wish, to aid those within the castle against those without."

"God! Was Meliant of Lis not raised in Tiebaut's household?" Sir Gawain asked.

"Yes, sir, God save me. His father loved Tiebaut as his liegeman and had such faith in him that on his deathbed he commended his little son into his keeping. With all the care he could provide, Tiebaut protected and raised him. In time Meliant came to entreat and beg love of one of Tiebaut's daughters, who declared that she would never grant him her love until he was a knight. Meliant, wanting to hasten the procedure, had himself knighted, then returned to his plea.

" 'On my word,' the maiden answered, 'until you have performed before me so many feats of arms and so many jousts that you have paid for my love, it can never be. Things obtained for nothing are not so pleasant and sweet as those paid for. If you wish my love, arrange to tourney against my father, for I want to ascertain whether my love, if I granted you it, would be well bestowed.'

"And so, as she dictated, he undertook the tournament, for Love has such great mastery over those in his power that they dare not refuse any of Love's commands. And you would do nothing were you not to go and give aid to those inside."

"Friend, go and follow your lord, and you will act wisely," Sir Gawain said to him. "Let your words end."

The squire immediately departed, and Sir Gawain continued traveling along in the direction of the town, since there was no other road.

Tiebaut had all his barons and his neighbors assembled, and summoned all his relatives. Highborn and low, young and old, they had all arrived there. But Tiebaut's counselors in the town, terrified that Meliant wished to destroy them all, advised him in private not to tourney against him.

Tiebaut then had all the entrances to the town walled and sealed. The gates were firmly closed up with solid brick and mortar so that only one entrance, a small postern gate that had been left open, remained unblocked. The postern gate was made not of alderwood but of copper, reinforced by an iron bar so thick that it contained a whole cartload of iron.

Sir Gawain came to the gate, all his equipment in front of him. He had to travel by the town or turn back again, for there was no other road or path within a seven-day journey. When he saw the postern gate closed, he rode on to a meadow, all fenced in with stakes, below the castle tower. He dismounted beneath an oak, where he hung his shields within sight of the townspeople.

Several of the townspeople were delighted that the tournament had been abandoned. In the town was an elderly vavasor, a wise man feared by all, who was powerful in land and lineage. His very opinion on an action, regardless of the action's outcome, was taken for truth. As the men had been pointed out to him in the distance before they had entered the enclosed meadow, he had seen them coming, and had gone to speak to Tiebaut. "So help me God, sir," he said, "I believe I have sighted two knights, companions of King Arthur, coming here. Two worthy knights demand

[399]

attention, for even one may win a tournament. For my part I advise and affirm that you go in all confidence to this tournament. You have good knights, good men-at-arms, and good archers, who will kill their opponents' horses. I am certain that the enemy will come to tourney before this gate. If their arrogance brings them here, ours will be the gain, theirs the loss and misfortune."

On the vavasor's advice, Tiebaut permitted all who wished to arm and ride out. Thus the knights were pleased. The squires raced for the equipment and saddled the horses. The ladies and maidens came to sit at the top of the tower to watch the tournament. Below them they saw in full view Sir Gawain's equipment, and because they noticed two shields hanging from the tree, they believed there were two knights. After they had walked up, the ladies said that they considered themselves fortunately born to see these two knights arming before them.

While they thus spoke, there were others saying: "God! Lord! This knight has with him harness and horse enough for two, yet no knight accompanies him. What will he do with two shields? No such knight was seen carrying two shields at one time." They were therefore astonished that the knight, who was alone, would carry both shields.

While they thus conversed, the knights set out. The older daughter of Tiebaut, who had brought about the tournament, had climbed to the top of the tower. Accompanying the older was her younger sister, who wore sleeves of such refinement that she was called the girl with small sleeves, so fitted had they been to her arms. Along with Tiebaut's two daughters, all the ladies and maidens had climbed to the top. The tournament now assembled in front of the town.

There was none so handsome as Meliant of Lis, according to the testimony of his beloved. To all the ladies around her, she said: "Truly, ladies, no knight I have ever seen has pleased me so much as Meliant of Lis. I do not see why I should lie to you about this. Is there not pleasure and delight in beholding so handsome a knight? Well should he sit his horse and carry lance and shield, so fine is his deportment."

But her sister, seated beside her, declared to her that there was one more handsome. This statement angered the other, who rose to strike her. The ladies restrained her, anxious to prevent her from hitting her young sister. The older daughter was in a fury.

The tournament commenced. Many lances were shattered, many sword blows struck, many knights unhorsed. You can be certain that whoever jousted with Meliant of Lis paid dearly. None lasted before his lance, for he hurled any opponent to the hard ground. And if his lance broke, he struck heavy blows with his sword. Thus none from one camp or the other surpassed him.

His beloved was so delighted that she could not contain herself. "Ladies, ladies, behold wonders!" she exclaimed. "Never before have you seen or heard tell of his equal. Behold the finest knight bachelor your eyes might see. He is more handsome and more valorous than all in the tournament."

"I see one perhaps more handsome and more fine," said her young sister.

Her sister at once stood before her and, seething with rage, spoke. "Are you so impudent, sour child, that you dare criticize anyone I praise? You do so to your misfortune. So take this slap, and another time be wary."

She then struck her, leaving the mark of all her fingers on her face. The ladies near the older sister reproved her and pulled her back.

They then spoke again among themselves about Sir Gawain. "God!" exclaimed one of the young ladies. "That knight, there under the hornbeam, why does he wait? Why does he not arm?"

Another maiden, still younger, told them that he had pledged peace.

A third spoke in turn after her. "He is a merchant. Say no more."

"No, he is a moneychanger," said a fourth. "He has no wish to share today with poor knights the wealth he carries with him. Don't think I lie to you. Those boxes and those bags hold money and silverplate."

"Truly, you have evil tongues," said the younger sister. "You are wrong. Do you think a merchant carries as heavy a lance as he carries? You have certainly slain me today with these devilish words of yours. By my faith in the Holy Spirit, he looks more like a jouster than a merchant or a moneychanger. From his appearance, he is a knight."

The ladies replied to her together. "Although he appears as one, dear sweet friend, he is not one. He has given himself such an appearance to evade the customs and the rights of passage here. He is a fool to think himself so clever, for like a thief he will be captured for this cleverness and charged with foolish and base thievery. As a result he will have the noose around his neck."

Hearing the words of the ladies clearly and understanding that they spoke of him, Sir Gawain was annoyed and ashamed. But he believed, and rightly, that thus accused of treason, he was obliged to continue on in order to defend himself. If he did not ride into combat as he had agreed, he would disgrace first himself, then all his lineage. Fearful of being wounded or taken prisoner, he did not enter the tournament, and he was anxious to enter, seeing the tournament steadily increasing in force. And Meliant of Lis called for a heavy lance that he might strike harder.

All day long until nightfall, the tournament continued before the gate. Whoever had won spoils carried them off where he thought they would be safe.

The ladies saw a squire, tall and baldheaded, holding the shaft of a lance and coming with a headpiece round his neck. One of the ladies called him foolish, then said to him: "God help me, lord squire, you are a senseless fool to ride into that press and snap up headpieces and lanceheads, broken butts of lances and ensigns. Do you act like a good squire? He who rushes in thinks little of himself. He is a fool who does not think of his own profit when he is able. Behold the most noble knight ever born, for were you to pluck out all the hairs of his mustache, he would not stir. Now do not have the cheap plunder. But take all the horses and all the wealth, and you will act wisely, for no one will ever prevent you."

At once the squire entered the meadow and struck one of the horses with the butt of his lance. "Vassal," he exclaimed to the knight, "are you unhealthy and ill that you here keep watch all day, doing nothing, not piercing shields or breaking lances?"

"Look here," the knight said, "what does it matter to you why I stay here? It is possible that you will sometime learn. But on my life, it will not be now, for I care not to tell you. Flee from here, and follow your route. Go and attend your own business."

The squire left him at once, not being one to dare say anything to annoy him.

The tournament ended. Many knights had been taken prisoner, and many horses slain. Meliant's men had the honor of the day, but the men from the town carried off the spoils. On separating, the camps swore to one another to reassemble the next day and to tourney all day long.

Thus they separated for the night, and all who had left the town rode back inside. Sir Gawain was there, and entered at the back of the crowd. Before the gate he met the vavasor, the worthy man who had advised his lord that day to begin the tournament. In a fine and noble manner, the vavasor invited Gawain to lodge with him. "Sir, in this town is lodging all prepared for you," he said. "Please stay here tonight. Should you travel farther, you would not this day find good lodging. For this reason I urge you to stay."

"Thank you, dear sir, I shall stay," replied Sir Gawain, "for I have heard worse suggestions today."

The vavasor led him to his lodging, asking him, among questions of this and that, why it should be that he had not borne arms with them that day in the tournament. And Gawain told him the full cause: that, accused of treason, he had to avoid risk of wound, injury, or imprisonment until he could clear himself of the charge laid on him. By his tarrying, he might dishonor himself and all his friends, if he could not in time reach the combat he had undertaken. In admiration, the vavasor said that he approved of his action, that he had acted correctly in refraining from the tournament for this reason. The vavasor then led him to his house, where they dismounted.

Intent on harshly denouncing Gawain, the townspeople held discussion on how their lord might go and seize him. And his older daughter did all she could to spite her sister. "Sir," she said, "well I know that you have lost nothing today. Rather, I believe you have won much more than you know, and I shall tell you how. You would act wrongly not to order men to go and seize that man. The vavasor who led him into the town will not dare defend him, for that man lives by evil trickery. He has shields and lances carried and horses led on the right, passing himself off as a free man while going about his merchant's trade. But now give him what he deserves. He is at the house of Garin, the son of Berte, who offered him lodging. He passed here just now, for I saw Garin leading him there." Thus she did her best to bring Gawain to shame.

The lord mounted immediately. Wishing to go there himself, he rode directly to the house where Sir Gawain was. When his young daughter saw him proceeding there in this fashion, she left by a back door, wishing not to be seen, and followed the fast and straight route to Sir Gawain's lodging at the house of Lord Garin, the son of Berte. Garin had two beautiful daughters, and when the maidens saw their little lady coming, they could not conceal their joy, displaying it sincerely. Each took her by the hand, and happily they led her inside, kissing her on the eyes and the mouth.

Lord Garin, who was not destitute or poor, had remounted, along with his son Bertrand, and the two rode to the court, as they often did, intending to speak to their lord. They met him on the street, and the vavasor greeted him and asked him where he was going. Their lord told him that he was intending to go to the vavasor's house for recreation. "This should not upset, annoy, or displease me," Lord Garin replied. "And there you could now behold the most handsome knight on earth."

"On my word, that is not my reason for going," the lord replied. "I shall have him seized. He is a merchant intent on selling horses, and he pretends to be a knight."

"Oh no! These words of yours I hear are too base," said Lord Garin. "I am your liegeman, and you are my lord. In my name and that of all my family, I here return you your homage. Rather than allow you to shame that man in my house, I challenge you here and now."

"So help me God, I had no such desire," replied the lord. "Your guest and your lodgings will have nothing but honor from me. Yet on my word, that is not how I have been advised and admonished to act."

"Many thanks," the vavasor said. "You will do me honor in coming to see my guest."

They drew alongside each other at once, and rode until they reached the house where Sir Gawain was. On seeing them, Sir Gawain, who had been well brought up, greeted and welcomed them. The two returned his greeting, then sat beside him.

The worthy man, who was lord of that country, then asked him why, since he had come to the tournament, he held himself back and did not joust that day. Gawain did not deny to him that shame and disgrace were his, yet he related to him that a knight had accused him of treason, and he was thus on his way to defend himself at a royal court.

"You had a lawful reason, sir, without doubt," the lord said. "But where will this combat take place?"

"Sir," he said, "I must go before the King of Escavalon, and I believe I follow the highway there."

"I shall give you an escort to guide you there," the lord said. "And because you must pass through poor country, I shall give you provisions to take and horses to carry them."

Sir Gawain replied that he had no need to take them. If he might find any for sale, he would have food in plenty, good horses, and all he needed where he traveled. For that reason he required nothing of him.

With these words the lord departed. As he was leaving, he saw his younger daughter coming from the other direction. She immediately threw herself at Sir Gawain's feet and held him by the leg. "Listen, sir," she said, "I have come to you to make an appeal against my sister who struck me. So please do me justice."

Sir Gawain remained silent, not knowing of what she spoke, and placed his hand on her head. The girl tugged at him. "To you I speak, dear sir," she said. "To you I make an appeal against my sister. I don't love or cherish her, for today, with little cause, she disgraced me."

"Fair one, why does it involve me? What justice may I do you?" he asked.

The lord, who had taken his leave, heard his daughter's request. "Daughter, who orders you to come and appeal to knights?" he asked.

"Dear sir, is she your daughter then?" Gawain inquired of him.

"Yes, but take no heed of her words," the lord answered. "She is a child, a silly fool."

"Certainly I should then be too despicable if I did not discover her will," Sir Gawain said. "Tell me now, my sweet and noble child," he continued, "how might I do you justice regarding your sister?"

"Sir, for tomorrow only, please, for love of me, bear arms in the tournament."

"Tell me then, dear friend, did you ever entreat a knight in time of need?"

"Never, sir."

"Pay no attention," said the lord. "Whatever she says, do not heed her folly."

"So help me God, sir, she has spoken fine little words for so small a girl, and I shall never refuse her," Sir Gawain said to him. "Since this is her pleasure, tomorrow I shall be, for a time, her knight."

"Thank you, dear sir," said the girl, so happy that she bowed to the ground.

Thereupon, without more words, father and daughter departed. The lord carried his daughter away on the neck of his palfrey, and while bringing her back, asked her why this dispute had arisen. She told him the truth from beginning to end. "Sire," she said, "I was distressed to hear my sister testify that Meliant of Lis was the most handsome and finest knight of all. I had seen a knight down in that beautiful meadow, a knight more handsome than he, and could not stop myself from contradicting her. Because of that my sister called me a foolish, sour child and pulled my hair. Damn any who approved of this! I would let both my braids be cut to the nape of my neck—to my distress!—on agreement that tomorrow at daybreak that knight defeat in combat Meliant of Lis. Then would end the cries of praise my lady my sister utters of him. She talked of him so much today that she exhausted all the ladies. But a great gust drops little rain."

"Dear daughter," the worthy man said, "I permit and command you to send him as a courtesy some token of esteem, your sleeve or your wimple."

And she who was naive said: "Gladly, sire, since you say so. But my sleeves are so small that I dare not send him one. Were I to send him it, he might esteem it not at all."

"Daughter, I shall look into this matter," her father said. "Now be quiet, for I am satisfied with this." Speaking thus, he carried her away in his arms, delighting in holding and hugging her until they arrived before the palace.

When the other daughter saw him coming with her little sister in his arms, her heart was troubled. "Sire," she asked, "from where does my sister, the girl with small sleeves, come? She knows already how to connive and deceive, given to that at a tender age. From where have you now brought her?"

"What does it matter to you?" he said. "You should be silent. She is worth more than you. You pulled her braids and struck her. Your discourteous behavior distresses me."

She was then deeply distraught by this reproach and this insult from her father. He had a piece of crimson samite taken from his chest and immediately cut into a long, wide sleeve. He then called his daughter. "Daughter," he said to her, "rise early tomorrow morning, and go to your knight before he sets out. As a token of love, offer him this new sleeve, and he will carry it when he rides to the tournament."

She answered her father that she wished to be awake, ready, and dressed as soon as she saw the bright dawn.

At these words her father departed, and the girl, delighted, begged all her companions, if they wished her love, not to let her sleep long in the morning but to awaken her promptly as soon as they saw day. They were pleased to do so: the moment they saw the dawn break in the early morning, they had her rise and dress.

The girl rose early and went by herself to Sir Gawain's lodgings. But she did not go early enough, for they had already risen and gone to the minster to hear mass sung for them. For a long time they prayed and heard what was to be heard, and all the while the girl stayed at the vavasor's house. When they returned from the minster, the girl jumped to her feet to meet Sir Gawain. "God save you and grant you joy today!" she said. "As a token of my love, wear this sleeve I have here."

"Gladly, friend, and thank you," Sir Gawain replied.

The knights then armed without delay and, in their equipment, assembled outside the town. The maidens and all the ladies of the town went back up on the walls, where they watched the troops of brave and bold knights assemble. At the head of all his men came Meliant of Lis, arriving at a gallop and leaving his companion two and a half furlongs behind. At the sight of her lover, the older sister could not restrain her tongue. "Ladies, see the approach of him who has the renown and mastery of chivalry," she exclaimed.

As fast as his horse could carry him, Sir Gawain rode out toward Meliant, who feared him little. Meliant shattered his lance to pieces. Sir Gawain dealt him such a blow that he severely wounded him and brought him immediately to the ground. Reaching out his hand to Meliant's horse, he took hold of the reins and handed the horse to a squire. He told him to go to the girl on whose behalf he was in the tournament and inform her that he was sending her his first spoils of the day, for he desired that she have them. The squire took the horse, all saddled, to the girl.

From the tower window where she was, the girl had seen Lord Meliant of Lis fall. "Sister," she said, "now you can see Lord Meliant of Lis, whom you praised so highly, lying on the ground. You do know how to judge right! What I told you yesterday is now evident. Now one clearly sees, God save me, that there is one of greater worth than he."

Thus she deliberately contradicted her sister until she drove her from her senses. "Shut up, sour child!" her sister exclaimed. "If I hear you say another word of him today, I shall give you such a blow that your feet will not support you."

"Hold back, sister! Remember God!" said the little girl. "You should not strike me for telling you the truth. On my word, I did see him defeat Meliant, and you did too, as clearly as I. I don't believe he has the strength left to stand again. And even were you to burst, I would still say that there is no lady present who does not see him stretched out flat, his legs in the air."

Had she been allowed, her sister would then have slapped her, but the ladies round her would not let her strike her sister. At that moment they saw the squire approach, leading on his right the horse. He found the girl seated at a window, and presented the horse to her. After thanking him more than sixty times, the girl had the horse led away. The squire went to express her gratitude to his lord, who appeared to be lord and master of the tournament.

There was no knight, however skilled, who could face Gawain's lance and not vacate his own stirrups. Never before had Gawain been so keen to win charges. This day, by his own hand, he took four in spoils and presented them as gifts: the first he sent to the little girl; out of respect he gave the second to the wife of the vavasor, who was delighted by the gift; the third, one of his two daughters had, while the other had the fourth.

The tournament disbanded, and the men came back through the gate. From one camp and the other, Sir Gawain carried away the honors; it was not yet noon when he left the combat, and on his return, he had such a crowd of knights following him that the entire street was filled. All who saw him wished to inquire and ask who he was and of what country. At the door to his lodgings he met the girl. She at once took hold of him by the stirrup, nothing else, then greeted and addressed him. "Thank you, sir," she said.

He realized what she wished to say and answered her in a noble manner. "Little lady, I will be old and white-haired before I, no matter where I be, am remiss in your service. I shall never be so far from you that, should I learn of your need, anything would prevent me from coming to your aid at the first word."

"Many thanks," the girl replied.

The two were thus speaking when her father arrived. He implored Sir Gawain, as best he could, to stay the night and lodge with him. Sir Gawain excused himself from staying, telling him he could not. The lord begged him to tell him, if he pleased, his name. "Sir, my name is Gawain. Never before has my name been withheld when it was inquired of me. Never yet have I offered it without first being asked."

When the lord heard that he was Sir Gawain, his heart was filled with joy. "Sir," he said, "come now and accept my lodging for the night. I have not yet served you, and, I can swear to this, never in my life have I seen a knight I would like to honor so much."

He begged him to stay, but Sir Gawain refused all his entreaties. The little girl, who was not foolish or evil, took hold of his foot and kissed it, then commended him to the Lord God. When Sir Gawain asked the meaning of her act, she told him that she had kissed his foot so that wherever he traveled, he would remember her.

"Have no fear, dear friend," he told her. "However far from you I be, so help me God, I shall never forget you." Thereupon he departed, taking leave of his host and the others, and all commended him to God.

Sir Gawain spent that night at an abbey, where he had all he needed. Early the next morning he continued to follow his route until, as he rode along, he saw animals grazing at the edge of a forest. He told Yonet, who led one of his horses—the best of all—and carried a strong and stout lance, to stop and to pass him the lance and saddle him the horse he led on his right. Yonet handed over to him his horse and the lance without delay, and Gawain turned in pursuit of the does. After many twists and turns along the trail, he overtook one of them beside a briar patch and stretched his lance across its neck. But the doe darted to the side and escaped after the stags. He chased it until he was just about to stop it and catch it, but his horse lost a shoe. When he could not capture the doe, he ordered Yonet to dismount, for his horse was limping badly. Following his command, Yonet lifted its foot and discovered a shoe missing. "Sir," he said, "it needs to be shod. There is nothing to do but proceed gently until a smith is found to fit a new shoe."

They then continued their travels until they sighted people issuing from a town and setting off on an excursion. At the front were people in short coats, boys on foot leading dogs; then came hunters carrying sharp spears, followed by archers and servants carrying bows and arrows; then came knights. At the back of all the knights came two on chargers, one a youngster more handsome than all the others. He alone greeted Sir Gawain and took him by the hand. "Sir, I am detaining you," he said. "Ride to where I came from today and dismount at my house. This is the proper and correct time of day to take lodging if such be your pleasure. I have a courteous sister who will make you welcome. And this lord you see here in front of me will take you there. Sir," he then said to the lord, "I send you, dear companion, with this lord. Lead him to my sister. First greet her; then tell her that I send her word, by the love and the trust that should exist between her and me, that if ever she loved a knight, she should love and cherish this one and treat him as she would me, her own brother. Until our return, let her give him such comfort and such company that he will know no displeasure. After she detains him at her side in such noble fashion, return promptly, for I would like to go back to keep him company as soon as I can."

The knight then departed and conducted Sir Gawain to where all held him in mortal hatred. But none there recognized him, for no one had ever seen him before, and so Sir Gawain suspected no danger.

Gawain regarded the site of the town, which sat on an arm of the sea, and noticed that the walls and the tower were so strong that they feared no assault. He looked at the entire town, peopled with beautiful men and women, and the tables of the moneychangers all covered with gold and silver and other coins. He saw the squares and the streets all filled with every type of workman engaged in every possible activity: one fashioning helmets and another hauberks, one lances and another blazons, one bridles and another spurs. Some furbished swords, while some fulled cloth and others wove it; still others combed it, and others sheared it. Some melted down gold and silver; others fashioned them into fine and beautiful works: cups and bowls, enameled jewelry, and rings, belts, and buckles. One might well believe and declare that the town held a fair every day, filled as it was with so much wealth: wax, pepper, grain, spotted and grey furs, and all kinds of merchandise. He gazed on all this, pausing here and there along his way.

They continued on until they reached the tower, where attendants came and took all their equipment and their baggage. The knight entered the tower alone with Sir Gawain, and led him by the hand to the young lady's chamber. "Dear friend," he addressed her, "your brother sends you greetings, and commands you that this lord be honored and served. Act not unwillingly, but as gladly as if you were his sister and he were your brother. Be careful not to be niggardly in granting all his wishes. Be generous, gracious, and noble. Attend to this now, for I depart. I must follow your brother to the forest."

The lady was delighted. "Bless him for sending me such company as this!" she exclaimed. "He who lends me such a handsome companion does not despise me. Thanks be his! Dear sir, come and sit here at my side," she continued. "Because I see you to be handsome and noble, and for my brother, who makes this request of me, I shall bear you good company."

The knight rode off at once, staying with them no longer. Sir Gawain remained, not lamenting at being left alone with the beautiful and attractive young lady. So well had she been brought up that she did not believe any would watch her on account of her being alone with him. The couple talked of love, for had they spoken of anything else, they would have wasted their time in sheer folly. Sir Gawain sought and begged her love, telling her that he would be her knight his life long. She did not refuse, but willingly granted his wish.

In the meantime, a vavasor entered there who would do them much harm, for he recognized Sir Gawain. He found them kissing and taking such joy in each other. The moment he beheld their joy, he could not restrain his tongue but cried out at the top of his voice, "Woman, be shamed! God confound you and destroy you! The man in the entire world you should hate most, and you allow him the pleasure of you, letting him embrace you and kiss you. Wretched, foolish woman, how well you behave in following your nature! You should have torn out his heart with your hands rather than kissed his mouth. If your kisses touch his heart, you have drawn his heart from his breast. But you would have done much better to tear it out with your hands. This is what you should have done, if a woman is to act well. But there is no trace of woman in one who despises evil and loves good. It is wrong to call her woman, for she loses her name where she loves only good. But you are a woman, this I clearly see. The man sitting at your side killed your father, and you kiss him! When a woman can have her pleasure, she cares little for the rest."

With these words he turned and left before Sir Gawain could say a word to him. And the lady collapsed on the stone floor, where she lay unconscious a long time. Sir Gawain took her in his arms and lifted her up, pale and green at the fear that was hers. When she had recovered, she said: "Alas, now are we dead! Because of you I shall now die an unjust death, as, I know, will you because of me. Now, I believe, the commoners in this town will come here. You will behold more than ten thousand assembled before this tower. But there is enough equipment here for me to arm you quickly. A man of worth could defend this tower against an entire enemy."

Frightened, she ran immediately to fetch the equipment. When she had equipped him well with the armor, both she and Sir Gawain felt less fear, save for the misfortune that no shield could be found. And so he made a shield of a chessboard and said: "Friend, I do not need you to go and find me another shield." He then tipped onto the ground the chess pieces, which were made of ivory and of harder bone, and were ten times heavier than ordinary chess pieces. From now on, whatever might happen, he would expect to defend the door and the tower entrance, for he had girded on Escalibor, the best sword that there was, which could cut steel as easily as wood.

Coming down from the tower, the vavasor discovered an assembly of men from the locality seated side by side: the mayor, the aldermen, as well as many other townsmen. They had taken no purgatives so that they were bloated and heavy. He raced to them, crying out: "Now to arms, men! Let us go and seize the traitor Gawain, who slew my lord!"

"Where is he? Where is he?" said one and another.

"On my word," he said, "I found him, Gawain the proven traitor, in that tower, where he takes his pleasure, caressing and kissing our lady. And she denies him nothing. On the contrary, she is pleased and willing. But come now, and we shall go and seize him. If you can hand him over to my lord, my lord will be most pleased with our service. The traitor has deserved disgraceful treatment. All the same, take him alive, for my lord would rather have him alive than dead, and rightly so, for a dead man fears nothing. Do your duty and alert the entire town."

Thereupon the mayor got up, as did all the aldermen after him. You would then have seen enraged peasants seize axes and halberds; one man took a shield without shoulder straps, another took a swinging door, and another a wicker basket. The town crier proclaimed the summons, and all the people assembled. The bells of the community rang out so that none might stay away. There was none so wretched who did not take a pitchfork or flail, pickaxe or mace. Killing a snail never raised such commotion in Lombardy. There was none so cowardly who did not go there bearing a weapon. Behold Sir Gawain dead unless the Lord God comes to his aid.

The young lady prepared to assist him boldly and shouted to the commoners. "Away! Away! Base people, mad dogs, vile serfs!" she exclaimed. "What devils summoned you? What do you seek? What do you want? God never grant you joy! So help me God, you will not lead away this knight here. But, God willing, there will be, I know not how, many of you wounded and killed. This knight did not fly here, nor come along some secret path. My brother sent him to me as his guest and begged that I treat him just as I would my brother himself. Do you think me a peasant for bearing him company and showing him joy and comfort at my brother's urging? Who wishes to hear, let him hear: there was no other reason I rejoiced over him, nor did I have any foolishness in mind. For this reason, I bear you greater ill will because of the terrible affront you do me, drawing your swords on me at the door to my chamber. And you cannot say why. Or if you have a reason, you did not tell me it. You display utter contempt for me." Thus she spoke her mind.

Meanwhile, the men broke down the door with forceful blows from their axes and managed to split it in two. The porter inside had barred their passage well: with his sword in his hands, he gave such payment to the first man to present himself that those following him were frightened and none dared advance. Each took thought for himself, afraid for his own head. None was bold enough to approach this fearsome porter; none would raise his hand against him or proceed a step farther.

The young lady picked up the chess pieces lying on the ground and hurled them with fury at the assailants. She tightened and gathered up her skirt, swearing like a madwoman that if ever she could, she would have them all destroyed before she died.

The commoners drew back, declaring that they would tear down the tower on the pair of them if they failed to surrender. The two defended themselves better and better with the large chess pieces they threw at them. Many of the men retreated, unable to withstand their assault, then began with steel pickaxes to undermine the tower in the hope of tearing the tower down. They dared not attack or fight at the door, which was securely barred against them. That door, please believe me, was so narrow and low that only with great difficulty could two men have entered together. For this reason a man of worth could easily hold and defend it. And as for the unarmed men, there was no need to summon a finer porter than the one there to split their heads down to the teeth and smash their brains.

Of all this, the lord who had lodged Sir Gawain knew nothing; he was riding back as quickly as he could from where he had gone to hunt. All the while the men continued to assault the tower with their steel pickaxes. Behold now Guinganbresil—by what chance I know not—come galloping into the town. He was astounded by the din and hammering he heard the commoners raise. He knew nothing of Sir Gawain's presence within the tower, but on learning of this, he forbade anyone there who held his life dear to be so bold as to dare dislodge a single stone. And they declared that they would not cease on his account, but would that day tear down the tower on top of his own body too had he been inside the tower with Gawain.

Seeing that his command had no effect, he decided to go and find the king and lead him to the upheaval the townsmen had begun. The king was just coming from the forest, and Guinganbresil addressed him at their meeting. "Sir, the mayor and the aldermen have caused you great shame. Since this morning they have been assailing and destroying your tower. Unless they pay dearly for their act, I shall bear you ill will. I had accused Gawain of treason, be certain of this, and it is he whom you have had lodge at your house. Since you made him your guest, it would be only right and fitting that there he never come to harm or disgrace."

"He shall not, adviser, once we arrive there," the king replied to Guinganbresil. "I am most upset and angry that this happened to him. I should never be surprised that my people bear him deadly hatred. But if I can, I will protect him from imprisonment or harm. Because I lodged him, I shall treat him with great honor."

And so they reached the tower, where a great uproar was being made. The king told the mayor to leave and have the commoners disperse. They departed, not a man remaining there, since this was the mayor's will.

In the town was a vavasor, a native of the town, whose advice was heard throughout the country, for he was a man of great wisdom. "Sir," he said to the king, "now you should have good and loyal counsel. It is no wonder if the man who committed treason in slaying your father has been attacked. He is hated to death, and rightly so, as you know. But the fact that you lodged him must be his protection and guarantee that he will not suffer imprisonment or harm here. To speak without word of lie, Guinganbresil, whom I see here, should guarantee and protect him, for he rode to the court of the king to accuse him of grievous treason. The fact is not to be hidden: Sir Gawain has come to defend himself at your court. My counsel is to postpone this combat and for Sir Gawain to go in search of the lance with the bleeding tip—even if you wipe it, a drop of blood will always be falling from it. Let him hand over that lance to you, or else place himself here again in such imprisonment as is now his. You would then have a better chance of holding him captive than you have at this moment. You could never, I believe, inflict so severe an imprisonment on him that he could not overcome it. One should inflict harm on one's enemy in every manner imaginable. You know no better counsel for torturing your enemy."

The king adhered to this counsel. He went to his sister in the tower and found her indignant with rage. She rose to meet him, as did Sir Gawain, who knew no fear; he did not tremble or turn pale. Guinganbresil stepped forward and said a few words in vain. "Sir Gawain, Sir Gawain, I had guaranteed your safety, but warned you never to be so bold as to enter any castle or town belonging to my lord, but rather that you avoid it. As for what has been done to you here, now is not the time to make your complaint."

The wise vavasor spoke. "Sir, so help me the Lord God, all this can be put right. From whom may reparation be demanded for the commoners' attack on him? The dispute would not end until the great day of judgment. But it will be done according to my will. My lord the king, who is here, has given me the command, and I declare it: provided both you and Sir Gawain do not object, he declares that you both postpone this combat one year, and that Sir Gawain go in search of the lance whose tip constantly bleeds, shedding tears of the clearest blood. And it is written that the time will yet be when all the kingdom of Logres, once the land of ogres, will be destroyed by that lance. For this reason my lord the king wishes to have assurances and oaths."

"To be certain, I would let myself die or languish here eight years rather than give you the oath or even offer my pledge," answered Sir Gawain. "I am not so afraid of dying that I would not prefer to suffer and endure death with honor than to perjure myself and live in disgrace."

"Dear sir," the vavasor said, "dishonor will never be yours, nor, on my word, will you ever be the worse for it. I would explain to you my meaning. You will swear to do all in your power to search for the lance. If you do not find the lance, return to this tower, and be absolved of your oath."

"Thus as you say it, I am ready to take the oath," he replied.

A precious reliquary was immediately brought to him, and he made his oath to spare no effort in searching for the bleeding lance. Thus the combat between him and Guinganbresil was postponed one year.

Sir Gawain had escaped great peril. He took leave of the lady and told all his attendants to return to his land, leading back all his horses except Gringalet. Amid tears, the attendants turned from their lord and set off. Of them or their grief, I have no wish to tell more. Of Sir Gawain, the tale is silent here at this point. And so we shall speak of Perceval.

Perceval, so the story says, had so lost his memory that he no longer remembered God. Five times April and May had passed; five whole years had gone by since he worshipped God or His cross in church or minster. Thus had he lived the five years.

Yet he did not stint in his pursuit of chivalric deeds. He searched for strange adventures, savage and stern ones, and came upon so many that he tested himself well. Never did he encounter a task so severe that he failed to succeed in it. Within the five years he had sent as prisoners fifty thousand esteemed knights to King Arthur's court. Thus had he passed the five years and never remembered God.

At the end of five years, he happened to be making his way through a wilderness, fully armed as he usually was, when he met five knights escorting as many as ten ladies, their heads hidden within their hoods. All were walking barefoot in woolen rags. The ladies were astonished to see a man coming in armor bearing shield and lance. As penance for their sins, they were themselves proceeding on foot for the salvation of their souls. One of the five knights stopped him and said: "Stay back! Do you not believe in Jesus Christ, Who wrote down the new law and gave it to Christians? It is surely neither right nor good, but most wrong to bear arms on the day Jesus Christ died."

And he who had given no thought to day, hour, or time, so distressed was his heart, answered: "What is today then?"

"What, sir? Do you not know? It is Good Friday, when one should venerate the cross with a pure heart and weep for his sins. This is the day when He Who was sold for thirty pieces of silver was hung on the cross. Free of all sin Himself, He became man for the sins of the entire world, be certain of this, for the entire world was corrupt. It is true that He was God and man, and was conceived by the Holy Spirit and born of the Virgin. In Him God took on flesh and blood, and His divinity was clothed in the flesh of man. This is a certainty, and he who will not believe it will never look on His face. He was born of the Virgin Lady and took on both the form and the soul of man with His holy divinity. Truly on such a day as this was He put on the cross. He then delivered all His friends from hell. Most holy was that death which saved the living and the dead, bringing them from death to life. In their hatred the wicked Jews, who should be killed like dogs, forged their own evil and our great good when they raised Him on the cross. They damned themselves and saved us. This is the day all those with faith in Him should do penance."

"And where do you now come from like this?" Perceval asked.

"Sir, from over there, from a good man, a holy hermit, who lives in the forest. Yet such is his holiness that he lives only by the glory of God."

"In God's name, sir, what did you seek there? What did you ask? What did you do?"

"What, sir?" replied one of the ladies. "We asked counsel there for our sins and made our confession. We did the greatest work that may be done by a Christian who would please God."

What Perceval heard made him weep, and thus he wanted to go and speak with the good man. "I would like to go there to the hermit if I knew the pathway," he said.

"Whoever would go there, sir, let him follow the straight path and look for the branches we knotted with our hands when we came. We made such signs there that no one going to this holy hermit would lose his way."

Then, without further questioning, they commended each other to God.

As Perceval started on the path, he felt his very heart sighing because he knew he had sinned against God and was sorry. In tears he made his way toward the forest, and when he reached the hermitage, he dismounted and disarmed. He tied his horse to a hornbeam, then entered the hermit's dwelling. In a small chapel he found the hermit and a priest and a young cleric, this is the truth, who were beginning the service, the sweetest and most beautiful that may be said in holy church.

Perceval fell to his knees the moment he entered the chapel. The good man called to him, seeing his innocence and his weeping, and noticing the tears running down from his eyes to his chin. Deeply afraid of having offended the Lord God, Perceval first grasped the hermit's foot, then bowed to him and, with hands joined, begged him to counsel him in his great need. The good man bade him make his confession, for unless he confessed and was repentant, he would never receive communion.

"Sir," he said, "it has been five years since I have known where I was. I have not loved God or believed in Him. Since that time I have done nothing but ill."

"Oh, dear friend," said the worthy man, "tell me why you have done so. I beg God to have mercy on the soul of His sinner."

"Sir, I was once at the home of the Fisher King. I saw the lance with the head that does truly bleed. And about the drop of blood I saw falling from the tip of the shining head, I made no inquiry. Since then, to be certain, I have done nothing to make amends. I saw the bowl there, but do not know who was served from it. Since then such heavy sorrow has been mine that I would gladly die. Thus have I forgotten the Lord God, for since then I have never implored His mercy or, to my knowledge, done anything to obtain mercy."

"Oh, dear friend, tell me now your name," the worthy man said.

And he answered him: "Perceval, sir."

At this word the worthy man, recognizing his name, sighed. "Brother," he said, "misfortune has befallen you for a sin of which you are ignorant. This is the grief you caused your mother when you left her. She fell to the ground unconscious at the end of the bridge outside the gate, and died of that grief. Because of the sin you committed there, it came to pass that you did not ask about the lance or the bowl. Thus evils have befallen you. You would not have survived so long, be certain, had she not commended you to the Lord God. Her prayers had such power that for her sake God watched over you and protected you from imprisonment and death. Sin cut off your tongue when you did not ask why the lancehead you saw pass before you never ceases to bleed. Foolish were you not to learn who was served from the bowl. The man who is served from it was my brother. My sister and his was your mother. And as for that rich Fisher King, he is, I believe, the son of this king who has himself served from the bowl. Do not imagine that it holds pike, lamprey, or salmon. With a single host carried to him in the bowl, we know, he sustains and nourishes his life. Such a holy object is the bowl, and so pure in spirit is he himself that his life requires no further nourishment than the host that comes in the bowl. For fifteen years now he has been served in this manner, never leaving the room where you saw the bowl enter. Now I would instruct you and give you penance for this sin."

"Dear uncle, I agree to this, and with all my heart," said Perceval. "Since my mother was your sister, you should call me nephew, and I should call you uncle and love you the more."

"That is true, dear nephew. Now repent. Since Pity takes hold of your soul, have in you Repentance as well. Every day go as a penitent to the minster before you go anywhere else. This will be for your benefit. Let nothing deter you. If you are in a place with minster, chapel, or church, proceed there when the bell rings, or earlier if you have risen. This will never be to your disadvantage, but for your soul's benefit. And if mass has begun, to be there will be all the better. Stay there until the priest has finished all his prayers and his chants. If you do this willingly, you may yet rise in merit and have a place in paradise. Believe in God, love God, worship God. Honor worthy men and good women. Stand in the presence of priests. These are observances that cost little, and God truly loves them because they spring from humility. And if a widow, maiden, or orphaned girl seeks your assistance, help her, and you will be the better for it. This is the highest act of charity. So assist them, and you will do well. Take care never to fail in this on any account. It is my wish that you do this for your sins if you would have the graces of God that once were yours. Now tell me if this be your will."

"Yes, most gladly," he answered.

"Now I pray you stay here with me two full days, and in penance eat such food as is mine."

Perceval agreed to this, and the hermit whispered a prayer in his ear, repeating it until Perceval learned it. This prayer contained many of the names of Our Lord, all the highest and the greatest which the tongue of man never dared pronounce except when in peril of death. When he taught him the prayer, he forbade him to utter it except in times of grave danger.

"I will not, sir," he said.

So with delight Perceval stayed and heard the service. After the service he venerated the cross and weeping for his sins humbly repented. Thus was he there a long while.

For food that night he had what pleased the hermit, nothing but beets and chervil, lettuce, cress and millet, bread made from barley and oats, and clear spring water. His horse had straw and a full trough of barley, and was properly stabled and groomed as it should be.

Thus Perceval came to know that God was crucified and died on the Friday. On Easter, Perceval received communion with a pure heart.

Here the tale says no more of Perceval. And before you hear me tell more of him, you will have heard much told of Sir Gawain.

After Sir Gawain escaped from the tower where the commoners had attacked him, he continued his travels. One day between nine in the morning and noon, he rode up toward the slope of a hill where he saw a tall and massive oak tree with thick foliage offering a great deal of shade. He noticed a shield hanging on the oak and a straight lance alongside. He hastened toward the oak and saw a small Norwegian palfrey beside the tree. He was astonished by this, for it did not seem right to him to see shield, arms, and small palfrey together. Had the palfrey been a charger, he would have thought that some vassal, traveling through the country to win his honor and his renown, had climbed this hill. He then looked beneath the oak and saw a maiden seated there who would have been beautiful and attractive had joy and happiness been hers. But she had wedged her fingers into her tresses to tear out her hair, and was going mad in a display of her grief. She grieved for a knight whom she was kissing constantly on the eyes, the forehead, and the mouth. When Sir Gawain approached her, he did not know if the knight was dead or alive. "Young lady," he asked, "is this knight you hold your lover?"

"Sir," she replied, "you can see that he is in grave peril from his wounds, for from the least of them he might die."

"My sweet friend," he said to her, "wake him up. Do not let him be. I want to ask him news of this land."

"Sir, I would not wake him," the maiden replied. "I would rather allow myself to be flayed alive! Never have I so cherished a man, and never will

I so long as I live. What a wretched fool I would be if I did anything to make him upset with me when I see him resting and asleep."

"I shall awaken him, I swear."

With the tip of his lance, Sir Gawain lightly touched the knight's spur so as not to distrub him but to awaken him. He had nudged the spur so gently that he did not harm him. On the contrary, the knight bowed his head and said: "Sir, I thank you five hundred times for having touched and awakened me so graciously, causing me no discomfort. But for your own sake, I beg you, do not pass beyond here, for you would act too foolishly if you did. Take my advice and stop."

"Shall I stop, sir? And why?"

"On my word, sir, I shall tell you if you would listen to me. No knight who traveled there on field or road has been able to return. Here is the border of Galloway, a most harsh and cruel land whose people are faithless. No knight can ever pass beyond here and return alive. No one ever escaped from there alive except me, and I am in such wretched condition that I believe I shall not see night. I met a knight, brave and bold, strong and proud. Never have I encountered one so bold, or tested myself against one so strong. Therefore, I advise you, it is better to turn back than to ride down this hill."

"On my word, to turn back would be despicable," said Sir Gawain. "I did not come for rest. Since I have undertaken this route, I should be thought too foul a coward if I turned back from here. I shall proceed until I see why no one may return."

"I see well that it must be so," said the wounded knight. "Since this is your will, you will ride there. But I would gladly make a request of you. If you have good fortune—which no knight in any era could nor, I believe, will ever have, neither you nor another in any way—return this way and see, in your mercy, if I am alive or dead, or if I fare better or worse. If I am dead, out of charity and in the name of the Holy Trinity, I beg you to have pity on this maiden that shame or misery not be hers. And may it please you to do so, for God never created or wished to create a maiden more noble or more well born, more courteous or better educated. She seems to me distressed now on my account, and she is not mistaken, for she sees me near death."

Sir Gawain granted his request, promising to return by this route unless prevented by imprisonment or some other misfortune, and to give the maiden the best counsel he could.

He then left the pair and continued his journey across plains and through forests, not stopping until he sighted a strongly fortified town. The stately town was of but little less wealth than Pavia. On one side was a large seaport with deep anchorage, on the other the vineyard and a beautiful and attractive forest with lush undergrowth. Lower down flowed the river that all around girded its walls and followed its course down to the sea. On all sides the town and the castle were firmly walled.

Sir Gawain crossed a bridge and entered the town. When he had ridden up to the most fortified section of the entire town, he found a maiden all alone in a meadow beneath an elm admiring in a mirror her face and her throat, which were whiter than snow. With a thin circlet of gold brocade, she had fashioned a coronet round her head. Sir Gawain spurred his horse at an amble toward the maiden.

"Go easy, go easy, sir!" she cried out to him. "Gently now, for you ride too foolishly. Foolish is he who hurries for nothing."

"God bless you, maiden," said Sir Gawain. "Now tell me, dear friend, what thought prompted you to tell me so quickly to go easy? You had no reason."

"Yes, knight, I had reason, on my word, for I know well your thought."

"And what is it?" he asked.

"You wish to pick me up and carry me down from here on the neck of your horse."

"You do speak the truth, maiden."

"I knew it well," she replied. "Damn the man who ever had such a thought! Take care never to think of placing me on your horse. I am not one of those silly girls knights take pleasure in carrying off on their horses when they ride away on chivalric exploits. Me you shall not carry off! Yet if you have the valor, you might take me with you. If you would make the effort to bring me my palfrey from that garden, I would ride with you until misery and hardship, grief, shame, and affliction befall you in my company."

"Is anything else needed, dear friend, but courage?" he asked.

"To my knowledge, nothing, vassal," said the maiden.

"Oh, dear friend, where will my horse stay should I go there? It could not cross this plank I see."

"No indeed, sir, hand it over to me and cross on foot. I shall take care of the horse for you so long as I can hold it. But hurry back, for it might escape me or be taken away before you return."

"You have spoken the truth," he said. "It will not be your fault if it is taken from you, nor, likewise, if it escapes you. Never will you hear me say more on this subject."

And so he handed it over to her and passed by. He determined to carry with him all his equipment in the event that he found someone in the garden who wanted to refuse him the palfrey or forbade him to take it. Then would there be commotion and strife before he brought it back.

Thereupon he crossed the plank and saw a huge throng of people looking at him in astonishment. "May devils burn you, maiden, for doing such evil!" they all exclaimed. "May your body have ill fortune, you who never esteemed a worthy man and had so many beheaded. This is a dreadful disgrace. Knight, you who wish to lead away the palfrey, why do you not know the ills that will befall you if you lay a hand on it? Oh, knight, why do you approach it? Surely you would never touch it if you knew the great dishonor, the terrible ills, the grievous pains that will befall you should you lead it away."

Such were the words of all the men and women, for they wished to warn Sir Gawain not to approach the palfrey but to turn back. Although he heard and understood them well, he would not abandon his plan. He rode on, greeting the crowds, and all the men and women returned his greeting, but in such a fashion that they all seemed accustomed to lives of distress and anguish. Sir Gawain rode toward the palfrey and extended his hand, intending to take it by the reins, for the palfrey had bridle and saddle. But a tall knight, seated beneath a verdant olive tree, exclaimed, "Knight, in vain have you come for the palfrey. Even to extend your finger toward it would be most presumptuous on your part. Yet I have no intention of forbidding or stopping you if you are anxious to have it. But I advise you to depart, for should you take it, you will encounter perilous obstacles elsewhere."

"Not for that shall I give up, dear sir," Sir Gawain replied. "The maiden admiring herself beneath that tree sends me for it. And if I did not take it back to her now, what would I have come here for? I would be shamed throughout the world as a worthless coward."

"Taking it will bring you misfortune, dear brother," said the tall knight. "In the name of God the Sovereign Father, to Whom I would like to surrender my soul, I have never seen a knight take it as you intend to lead it away without encountering such misfortune that his act cost him his head. Such is the evil fate I fear for you. And if I have warned you against it, I intended no harm. Lead it away if you wish; neither I nor any man you see here will prevent you. But if you dare lay a hand on it, the roads you follow will be perilous. I advise you not to undertake this, for you would lose your head."

These words did not deter Sir Gawain in the slightest. He made the palfrey, whose head was black on one side and white on the other, cross the plank ahead of him. It knew how to cross easily: carefully taught and trained, it had crossed often. Sir Gawain took it by its silk reins and proceeded directly to the elm where the maiden admired herself. She had let her cloak and her wimple fall to the ground so that her face and her body were open to view.

Sir Gawain handed her the palfrey, all saddled. "Come here, young lady," he said, "and I shall help you mount."

"May God never, in any place you go, allow you to recount that you held me in your arms," the maiden exclaimed. "If your naked hand touched or felt anything of me, I would hold myself shamed. My fate would be too cruel if it were told or known that you had touched my flesh. I would rather have my skin and flesh flayed to the bone, I dare well say this here and now. Leave me the palfrey at once, and on my word, I shall mount without seeking your help. God grant that I may see today what I expect to see. Great joy will be mine this night. Go where you wish, for your hand will come no nearer my body or my clothing. And I shall follow you constantly until on my account some great setback, shame, or misfortune befalls you. I am completely certain I shall see you ill-befallen. You cannot escape this any more than death."

Sir Gawain heard all that the haughty maiden told him, but spoke to her not a word. He gave her the palfrey, and she let him have his horse. Sir Gawain bent down, intending to pick up her cloak and place it over her shoulders. The maiden, not reluctant or afraid to insult a knight, watched him. "Vassal, what does my cloak or my wimple matter to you?" she said. "In God's name, I am not half so simple as you think. I have no desire for your service. Your hands are not clean enough to touch anything I place on my body or around my head. You should not lay hand on anything that touches my forehead, my eyes, my lips, or my face. May it please the Lord God the Son that I never be inclined to accept your service."

And so the maiden mounted, after putting on and fastening her clothes. "Knight," she said, "now go where you wish, and I shall follow you along every road until I see you disgraced on my account. And that, God willing, will be today."

Sir Gawain kept silent, answering her not a word. Completely shame-faced, he mounted, and they set off. His head lowered, he rode back toward the oak where he had left the maiden and the knight who was in urgent need of a physician for his wounds. Sir Gawain knew, better than any man, how to heal a wound. In a hedgerow he spotted an herb that was effective for taking the pain from a wound, and went to pluck it. After gathering the herb, he set off and continued to ride until he reached the maiden displaying her grief. The moment she saw him, she addressed him. "Dear sir, I think this knight is now dead, for he hears and understands nothing."

Sir Gawain dismounted and found that the knight's pulse was very strong and his cheeks and lips not overly cold. "Lady, this knight is alive, be absolutely certain of this," he said, "for he has a strong pulse, his breathing is good, and his wound not fatal. I bring him an herb that will help him, I think, and relieve some of the pain from his wounds as soon it touches him. No better herb can be applied to a wound, and the book states as proof that the herb has such power that if it were applied to the bark of a tree that was infected but not entirely dried up, its roots would take hold again, and the tree would become so healthy that it would be covered with leaves and flowers. Your lover, my maiden, would then have no fear of dying were this herb applied to his wounds and fastened with a bandage. But a very fine wimple would be necessary for a secure bandage."

"I shall immediately give you the one on my head," the maiden said without reluctance, "for I have brought no other here."

She removed from her head her white and delicate wimple, and Sir Gawain cut it, as he had to do, then applied the herb he held to all the knight's wounds, the maiden assisting him as best she could. Sir Gawain did not move until the knight sighed and spoke. "God reward him who restored to me the power of speech," he said, "for I was terrified of dying without confession. Already devils had come in procession, seeking my soul. Before my body is buried, I would like to make my confession. I know a chaplain near here; if I had something to mount, I would go and confess my sins and receive communion. I would never fear death once I had confessed and taken communion. But do me a service now, if it should not trouble you. Give me that squire's nag which approaches here at a trot."

Hearing this, Sir Gawain turned and saw an ugly squire riding along. What was he like? I shall tell you. He had tousled red hair that stood stiff and on end like the bristles of a porcupine; the same were his eyebrows, and they covered all his face and his nose down to his whiskers, which were twisted and long. His mouth was a large slit, his wide beard forked and then curled back, his neck was short, his chest protruding. Sir Gawain was anxious to go to meet him and learn if he could have the nag. But first he addressed the knight. "So help me the Lord God, sir, I do not know who the squire is, but I would rather give you seven chargers, if I had them here on my right, than his horse, whoever he may be."

"Sir," he said, "know well that he is intent only on harming you if he can."

Sir Gawain set off to meet the squire who was approaching, and asked him where he was going. The squire, who was not nobly born, said to him: "Vassal, what business is it of yours where I come from or where I go? Whatever road I follow, may your body have ill fortune!"

Sir Gawain immediately paid him his proper reward, striking him with his open palm. Since his hand was covered in armor and he was eager to strike him, he knocked him over and emptied the saddle. When the squire attempted to rise, he staggered and fell back, fainting nine times or more. When he did manage to stand again, he exclaimed: "Vassal, you struck me!"

"This is true, I did strike you, but scarcely hurt you," he replied. "Nevertheless, before the eyes of God, I regret hitting you, but you spoke with great stupidity."

"Now I shall not fail to tell you what you will pay for it," he said. "The hand and arm with which you struck me you will lose, for you will never be pardoned your blow."

While this took place, the knight, whose head had been very weak, found words to address Sir Gawain. "Let this squire be, dear sir. You will never hear him say a word to your honor. Let him be, and you will act wisely. But bring me his nag, then take this maiden you see here beside me, tighten the girths on her palfrey, and help her mount, for I have no wish to stay here longer. If ever I can, I shall set off on the nag and look for a place where I may make my confession. I do not intend to stop until I have confessed myself, taken communion, and received the final anointing."

At once Sir Gawain took the nag and handed it over to the knight, whose sight was now restored and cleared, and he looked at Sir Gawain and recognized him for the first time. Sir Gawain took the maiden and, like a noble and courteous knight, set her upon the Norwegian palfrey. While he helped her, the knight took Gawain's own horse, mounted it, and began to make it prance about in all directions. Sir Gawain laughed in astonishment to see him gallop all over the hill and, while laughing, said to him: "Sir knight, on my word, you are foolish to make my horse prance about as I now behold. Dismount and hand him back to me. You might easily hurt yourself and make your wounds break open."

"Gawain, be quiet," he replied. "Take the nag and you will act wisely, for you have lost your horse. I have taken it for myself, and will lead it away as my own."

"Wait! I came here for your benefit, and you would do me such ill? Do not lead my horse away. That would be treachery."

"Gawain, whatever should befall me, I would now like to rip your heart from your belly with my two hands."

"This reminds me of the oft-repeated proverb 'Help some men, and break your own neck'," Gawain replied. "But I would like to know why you take my horse from me and why you would hold my heart. Never did I wish to harm you, and never in all my life did I. I do not believe I have deserved this treatment from you. So far as I know, I have never before seen you."

"Yes, you have, Gawain. You saw me in a place where you disgraced me. Do you not remember the man you tormented by forcing him against his will to eat for a month with the hounds, his hands tied behind his back? Know that you acted foolishly, and disgrace is now yours for it."

"Are you then that Greoreas, who abducted the maiden and had your pleasure with her? Yet you well knew that in King Arthur's land, maidens are protected. The king gave them safeguards, granting them protection and safe conduct. I do not think or believe that you hate me or seek my harm for what I did to you, for I acted according to the true justice that has been instituted and established throughout the king's land."

"Gawain, you applied the justice to me, I remember that well, and so now you must suffer what I shall inflict. I shall lead away Gringalet, being unable for the moment to exact further vengeance. You must exchange it for the nag from which you knocked the squire, for no other exchange will be yours."

Greoreas then left him and raced after his beloved, who was galloping away, and followed her at full speed. The evil maiden laughed, saying to Sir Gawain: "Vassal, vassal, what will you do? It may now indeed be said of you that wicked fools are not dead. I well know, so help me God, that my fate is to follow you. Nowhere will you ever turn without my gladly following you. If only the nag you took from the squire were a mare! That would please me, know this, for your humiliation would be worse!"

Sir Gawain immediately mounted the trotting nag, knowing he could do no better. The nag was an ugly beast, with its thin neck, thick head, and wide, floppy ears. All the failings of old age were evident: one lip drooped the length of two fingers below the other, eyes troubled and dim, hooves marked with sores, hard flanks slashed all to pieces by the spurs. The nag was long and thin, with a lean croup and a long spine. The reins and the headpiece of the bridle were made of slender cord; the saddle, far from new, had no covering. He found the stirrups so long and fragile that he dared not settle himself in them.

"Oh, things certainly go well now!" exclaimed the insulting maiden. "Now I shall be pleased and happy to go where you wish. Now it is indeed right and fitting that I gladly follow you a week, a fortnight, three weeks, or a month. Now are you well equipped. Now do you sit on a fine charger. Now do you look like a knight who should escort a maiden. From now on, I wish to take my pleasure in seeing your misfortunes. Spur your nag a little and test it. Never be frightened, for it is strong and nimble. I shall follow you, as agreed, and never leave you until disgrace befalls you, as certainly it will."

"Dear friend," he replied to her, "say what you please, but it does not befit a maiden beyond the age of ten to be so ill-tongued. On the contrary, she should be polite, well-trained, and well-mannered."

"I care not for your lessons, knight of ill fortune. Ride on and be quiet, for you now have such comfort as I wished to see."

And so they rode on until evening, both remaining silent. He rode in front, and she behind him. He did not know what to do with his packhorse, unable, despite all his efforts, to make it trot or gallop. Whether he liked it or not, the packhorse moved at a walk, and if he goaded it with his spurs, he urged it into so loathsome a trot that the packhorse's insides so shook that he could bear riding no faster than a walk. Thus he rode on the packhorse through desolate and deserted forests until he reached flat land alongside a deep river of such width that no mangonel or catapult could have sent a stone across, and it was wider than a crossbow's range. On the other side of the river stood a most well appointed castle, strongly fortified and very majestic. I have no desire to lie in this matter. The castle stood on a cliff with such splendor that no eyes of living man ever beheld so splendid a fortress. In a palace well situated on natural rock and built entirely of dark-grey marble were at least five hundred open windows, a hundred filled with ladies and maidens gazing at the flowering meadows and gardens before them. Many of the maidens were dressed in samite, and most wore silk dresses of different colors, all brocaded with gold. Thus the maidens stood at the windows, their beautiful bodies, from their waists up to their golden hair, visible from without.

The maiden who accompanied Sir Gawain was the most evil creature in the world. She rode directly to the river, then halted and dismounted from her small dappled palfrey. On the bank was a boat locked and secured to a stone block. Inside the boat was an oar, and on the stone was the key that locked the boat. The maiden, whose very heart was evil, climbed into the boat, her palfrey after her, as she had done many times before.

"Vassal," she said, "dismount and climb in behind me. Bring with you your packhorse, which is thinner than a pullet. Cast off the anchor to this barge. Unless you cross the river swiftly, or can flee quickly, misfortune will befall you."

"Wait, maiden. Why?"

"Do you not see what I see?" she asked. "If you saw it, knight, you would flee quickly."

Sir Gawain immediately turned his head and saw a knight, fully armed, riding across the plain. "Now, if you don't object, tell me who this is who rides my horse," he asked the maiden. "The traitor whose wounds I healed this very morning robbed me of it."

"By Saint Martin, I shall tell you," replied the maiden with delight. "But know truly that I would never tell you if I thought it would be to your advantage. Since, however, I am certain that he comes for your misfortune, I shall not hide it from you. He is the nephew of Greoreas, who sends him here after you, and because you asked me, I shall tell you why. His uncle commanded him to pursue you until he had killed you and presented to him your head. For this reason I advise you to dismount, unless you wish to await your death there. Embark here and flee."

"I will certainly never flee on his account, maiden, but rather await him."

"I will certainly never say more to you, but rather keep silent," said the maiden. "You will display fine spurring and fine charging before the beautiful and attractive maidens leaning there at those windows. Because of you their position delights them, and because of you they have come here. The moment they see you stumble, they will rejoice. You now look like a knight who ought to joust with another whatever the toll."

"Maiden, never will I steal away. I will go out to meet him. And if I might recover my horse, I would be pleased."

He rode back at once toward the plain and turned the head of his horse toward the man galloping across the sandy riverbank. Sir Gawain awaited him, bracing himself in the stirrups with such force that he broke off the left one and had to abandon the right. Thus he awaited the knight, for the packhorse never stirred, and his spurring could not move it. "Oh God," he exclaimed, "how ill a knight feels when, eager to engage in feats of arms, he finds himself mounted on a nag."

All the while the other knight galloped toward him on his horse, which was not one that limped. He dealt him such a blow with his lance that it bent back and shattered all across, leaving the tip in the shield. Sir Gawain struck him on the top of his shield, running at him with such strength that his lance smashed through both shield and hauberk and knocked him to the fine sand. Sir Gawain extended his hand, caught his horse, and leapt into the saddle. He found this adventure so pleasing, and his heart felt such joy, that never in his entire life had he known more happiness.

He returned to the maiden he had brought there, but found no sign of her or the boat. He was deeply disappointed to have thus lost her without knowing what had become of her.

While thinking of the maiden, he saw a skiff driven by a boatman coming from the bank where the castle stood. When the boatman arrived at the landing, he said: "Sir, I bring you greetings from those maidens across there. They request that you not deprive me of my rightful property. Deign to hand it over to me."

"God bless all the company of maidens and you as well," he replied. "Through me you will lose nothing where you can lay rightful claim. I have no desire to wrong you. But what property do you ask of me?"

"Sir, here at this crossing you defeated a knight. His charger ought to be mine. Unless you would wrong me, you should hand over the charger to me."

"Friend," he replied, "it would be too painful for me to forfeit this property, for I would be forced to travel by foot."

"Wait, knight. Those maidens you see think you now most disloyal and hold your act most wicked in not returning to me my property. Never has it happened before, nor has it ever been said, that at this landing a knight was unhorsed and, learning of it, I failed to have the horse. Or had I not the horse, I could not fail to have the knight."

"Friend," Sir Gawain said to him, "without argument take the knight and hold him."

"On my word, he is not yet so crippled," said the boatman. "You yourself would have much trouble in capturing him, I think, if you dared await him. Yet if such be your courage, go take him and bring him to me. Thus will you be cleared of your debt."

"Friend, if I dismount, can I in good faith trust you with my horse?"

"Yes, certainly," he said. "I shall guard it faithfully for you and gladly return it to you. I shall never wrong you in any way so long as I live. This I pledge and promise."

"And I in turn trust you on your pledge and your oath," he replied.

Immediately he dismounted and entrusted the boatman with his horse, and, saying he would guard it in good faith, the boatman took it. His sword drawn, Sir Gawain set out toward the man who needed no further injury, for he had lost much blood from a gash in his side. Sir Gawain approached him. "Sir," said the knight, frightened, "I cannot conceal this from you. I am so sorely wounded that I need suffer no more. I have lost eight pints of blood, and so place myself at your mercy."

"Then rise from there," Gawain replied.

The knight rose with some difficulty, and Sir Gawain led him to the boatman, who was deeply grateful to him. Sir Gawain begged the boatman to tell him if he knew of a maiden he had led there and of her whereabouts.

"Sir, give no thought to the maiden or her whereabouts," he answered. "No maiden is she, but worse than Satan, for she has had many knights beheaded at this landing. Were you to follow my advice, you would come and lodge now in a dwelling such as mine. It would not be to your advantage to remain on this side of the river, for this is a savage land abounding in great wonders."

"Since this is your advice, friend, I am willing to heed your counsel whatever may befall me."

He followed the boatman's advice, and his horse was led on board behind him. They boarded and set off, sailing to the other shore. Near the water stood the boatman's house, so comfortable and splendid that a count might disembark there. The boatman led his guest and his prisoner inside, and treated them to every possible comfort. For supper, Sir Gawain was served with all befitting a worthy man: plover, pheasant, partridge, and venison as well as strong and clear wines, new and old, whites and reds. The mariner was delighted with his guest and his prisoner.

Their meal ended, the table was taken away, and the men washed their hands. That night Sir Gawain was glad to accept the boatman's service, which pleased him. He had a host and a house to his liking. As soon as he could see the break of the next day, he rose, as he should, following his habit. The boatman, out of affection for him, rose as well. The two leaned at the windows of a turret, and Sir Gawain gazed out on the country, which was very beautiful, looking at the forests and the plains and the castle on the cliff.

"Host," he said, "I would like to ask and inquire of you, if you don't mind, who is lord of this land and of that castle up there?"

"Sir, I do not know," his host at once answered him.

"You do not know? This is remarkable, for you told me you were a sergeant of the castle, a position bringing you substantial revenue. Yet you do not know who is its lord?"

"I can assure you, I know not, nor have I ever known," he said.

"Dear host, then tell me now who guards and defends the castle."

"Sir, it is guarded very well. There are five hundred bows and crossbows always ready to shoot. Were the castle ever attacked, the guard would shoot ceaselessly without ever tiring, so skillfully are they stationed. This much I shall tell you of the situation. There is a queen, a noble and wise lady of high rank from a most exalted family. With all her treasure of silver and gold, the queen came to reside in this country and, as you can see here, had this strong manorhouse constructed. She brought with her another lady, whom she loves very much and calls queen and daughter. And that lady also has a daughter, who does not disgrace or debase her family; I do not believe that under the heavens there is a more beautiful or better-mannered lady.

"The great hall is well protected by magic and enchantment, as, if you wish me to tell you, you will next learn. A clerk, wise in astronomy, whom the queen brought with her, installed in this fine palace such great marvels that never before have you heard tell of their like. No knight can remain alive and well an hour there who is a coward or has any trace of the evil vices of slander or greed. No coward or traitor survives there, nor any man forsworn or perjured. Thus such men die there quickly, unable to survive or live.

"But many squires are assembled there from many lands, who serve those inside in their training at arms. There are up to five hundred of them, some bearded, others not. A hundred have no beard or mustache; a hundred have beards beginning to grow; a hundred shave and trim their beards each week; a hundred have hair whiter than wool; and a hundred have hair turning grey.

"There are also elderly ladies without husbands or lords, who have been unjustly disinherited of their lands and their honors after the death of their husbands. And orphaned maidens are there with the two queens, who show them great honor. Such people come and go through the castle in expectation of a great occurrence that could never be, and this is folly on their part. They await the coming there of a knight to support them, giving the maidens lords, restoring to the ladies their homes, and making knights of the youths.

"But the sea will turn to ice before a knight is found capable of staying in the palace, for he would have to be perfectly wise and generous, noble and handsome, loyal and bold, free of villainy and vice, and without a trace of covetousness. Such a knight, if he came, could be lord of the palace: he would restore to the ladies their lands and bring many wars to their peaceful end; he would marry off the maidens and dub the youths knights; without delay he would rid the palace of the enchantments."

These tidings pleased and delighted Sir Gawain. "Host," he said, "let us go down. Have my arms and my horse immediately brought to me. I do not wish to stay here longer. I shall set off."

"Where, sir? Stay, God save you, today, tomorrow, even longer."

"Host, now is not the time. Blessed be your house. But I shall go, so help me God, to see what the ladies do and what these marvels are."

"Sir, keep silent! God willing, you will not be so foolish. Follow my advice and stay here."

"Host," he said, "you take me for a faithless coward. God abandon me wholly if ever I accept such advice."

"On my word, sir, I shall be silent, for saying more would be an effort wasted. Since you take so much pleasure in going, proceed there. I am deeply troubled, yet it is right that I take you there, since no other escort, know this well, would be worth more to you than mine. But I would have a favor of you."

"Host, what favor? I wish to know."

"Not until you have promised me it."

"Dear host, I shall do your will, provided it shames me not."

He then commanded that his charger be brought from the stable, all harnessed for riding, and asked for his arms, which were carried to him. Then he armed, mounted, and set off. And the boatman prepared to mount his palfrey, willing to guide him faithfully to where he unwillingly proceeded. They rode along until they reached the foot of the steps in front of the palace. There they came upon a one-legged man, seated all alone on a bundle of rushes. His false leg was silver or silver-plated, inlaid with gold and precious stones. The one-legged man's hands were not idle, for he used a small knife he held to carve a stick of ashwood. The one-legged man did not address a word to those who passed in front of him, and they did not address him.

The boatman drew Sir Gawain to him and said: "Sir, what do you think of this man with one leg?"

"On my word, his false leg is not made of spruce," said Sir Gawain. "It looks very beautiful to me."

"In God's name, the one-legged man is wealthy; he has large and handsome revenues," said the boatman. "You would hear news that would deeply upset you were it not that I guided and accompanied you."

The two then proceeded along until they arrived at the palace with its very high entrance. The doors were magnificent and beautiful, and all the hinges and bolts, as the story testifies, were pure gold. One of the doors was beautifully carved ivory, the other door ebony with equally fine carving, and each door was illuminated with gold and precious jewels. The stone floor of the palace was a carefully worked and polished mosaic of many different colors, green and crimson, indigo and greenish-blue.

In the center of the palace was a bed without trace of wood, every section made of gold except for the cords, which were all silver. I am not making up an idle tale about the bed. Hung from each of the cord knots was a small bell, and across the bed was spread a samite cover. On each bedpost was mounted a carbuncle, and they gave off more light than four burning candles. The bed rested on four grotesque dogs with puffy cheeks, and the dogs themselves were on four wheels of such mobility and speed that but a slight push with a single finger to any part of the bed could roll it from one end of the room to the other. Such was the bed that, if truth be told, no count or king ever had or would have a bed such as this. And the bed rested in the very center of the palace.

The palace—and I wish to be believed in this—had no section made of chalk: the walls were marble, and the windows above were so clear that anyone looking through the glass could see all who entered the palace once they passed through the door. The windows were painted in the richest and finest colors that could be created or described. For the moment I have no wish to recount and depict everything.

In the palace were at least four hundred closed windows and a hundred that were open. Sir Gawain walked all about the palace, gazing in earnest throughout. When he had finished looking, he called to the boatman. "Dear host," he said, "I see nothing here in this palace to make one fearful of entering. Say now what you meant in warning me with such vehemence not to come here and see it. I intend to sit on this bed and rest a while, for I have never seen so magnificent a bed."

"Oh, dear sir, God keep you from going near it. If you approached it, you would die the worst death any knight ever died."

"Host, what shall I do then?"

"What, sir? I shall tell you since I see you disposed to saving your own life. At my house, when you were about to come here, I asked you a favor, though you did not know what it was. Now I would ask the favor. Return to your own land and tell your friends and the people of your country that you have seen the most magnificent palace that you and the others have ever known."

"Then I shall say that God hates me and I am altogether disgraced. Nevertheless, host, it seems to me that you say this for my benefit. But on no account would I abandon my resolve to sit on the bed and see the maidens I noticed yesterday evening leaning out these windows."

The host backed away in order to make his point the better. "You will behold none of the maidens you speak of," he replied. "Return just as you came here, for under no circumstance will you see them. But, so help me God, the maidens, the ladies, and the queens, who are in the chambers on the other side, are now watching you through the glass windows."

"On my word," said Sir Gawain, "if I do not see the maidens, at least I will sit on the bed, for I do not think or believe that there should be such a bed unless someone, a noble man or a lady of high rank, reclines there. On my soul, whatever may happen to me, I shall certainly sit on it."

The boatman, seeing that he could not stop him, ceased speaking. But he had no desire to stay in the palace and see him sit on the bed. So he took his leave, saying: "Sir, I am deeply troubled and distraught about your death. Never has a knight sat on this bed and not died, for this is the Bed of Marvels, where no one ever sleeps or slumbers, rests or sits, and rises healthy and well. It is a great pity that you will leave your head in pawn without possibility of ransom or redemption. Since I cannot lead you away from here by argument or by affection, God have mercy on your soul."

He immediately left the palace, and Sir Gawain sat down on the bed, armed as he was with his shield hanging from his neck. When he sat, the bed cords clanged and all the little bells sounded. The entire palace reverberated. All the windows flew open, the marvels were uncovered, the enchantments appeared. Arrows and crossbow bolts flew in through the windows; I do not know how many struck Sir Gawain's shield, and he did not know who hurled them. Such was the enchantment that no man could see where the bolts came from or the archers who fired them. You can well understand that there was a mighty uproar at the release of the bows and crossbows. Not for a thousand marks would Sir Gawain have wished to find himself there at that hour.

But soon the windows shut again by themselves, and Sir Gawain pulled out the bolts that had fixed in his shield and wounded his body in several places where blood spurted out. Before he had removed all of them, another test confronted him: a churl knocked open the door with a stake, and a wondrous lion, fierce and proud and famished, leapt through the door of the room and attacked Sir Gawain with violent fury and savagery. It planted all its claws in his shield as if it were wax, and knocked Gawain down, forcing him to his knees. He leapt up at once, unsheathed his fine sword, and struck the lion so hard that he cut off its head and two of its paws. Sir

Gawain was then pleased, for the paws still hung by their claws from his shield, one yet dangling outside and the other visible on the inside.

After he slew the lion, he sat down again on the bed. His host, a happy expression on his face, came back at once into the palace and found Sir Gawain sitting on the bed. "Sir," he said, "you have nothing more to fear, I promise you. Remove all your equipment. Your coming here has forever dispelled the enchantments from the palace. Young and old will honor and serve you within. God be praised!"

Thereupon a crowd of attendants arrived, all well dressed in tunics. They all fell to their knees, all saying: "Honored sir, we present our services to you, as to one we have long desired and awaited. The time you delayed seemed long to us." One of them immediately took him and began to relieve him of his arms, while others went to stable his horse, which was outside. As he was being disarmed, a beautiful and comely maiden entered, a gold diadem on her head, her hair as bright as gold or more so. Her face was white and illumined by Nature with a pure crimson hue. The maiden was most proper, beautiful and well shaped, tall and slender. Behind her came other beautiful and charming maidens. An attendant came there all alone, draping from his neck a set of clothes—a cloak, a tunic, and a jacket. The cloak was lined with ermine and with sable black as a mulberry, and the cloth itself was a rich scarlet wool. Sir Gawain marveled at the maidens he saw approaching, unable to stop himself from jumping to his feet to meet them. "Be welcome, maidens!" he exclaimed.

The first bowed to him. "Honored sir," she said, "my lady the queen sends you greetings, and commands all of us to treat you as our rightful lord and to come and serve you. I am the first to promise you my service in all sincerity, and the maidens coming here all regard you as their lord and have long desired your arrival. They are delighted to see you, the finest of all worthy men. There is nothing more now to say, except that we are ready to serve you."

All immediately bowed to him and knelt down, committing themselves to honor and to serve him. He had them rise at once and take seats. He took pleasure in their sight, partly because of their beauty, but more so because they made him their prince and lord. His joy at the honor God had done him was greater than any he had ever felt.

The maiden who had arrived first then stepped forward and greeted Sir Gawain. "My lady sends you this robe to wear before she sees you," she said. "In her wisdom and courtesy, she believes that you have suffered great toil, pain, and hardship. Put on this robe and see if it fits you. After being in the heat, the wise protect themselves against the cold, for many suffer from congealed blood. Therefore my lady the queen sends you an ermine cloak so that the cold not harm you, for just as water turns to ice, the blood congeals and hardens when a man shivers after being in the heat."

Sir Gawain responded, befitting the most courteous knight in the world. "May that Lord in Whom no good is lacking save my lady the queen and you too for your courteous and becoming words. Most wise is the lady, I believe, since her messengers are so courteous. She well knows what a knight needs and must have since, by her grace, she sends me here a robe to wear. Thank her on my behalf."

"On my word, sir, I shall gladly do so," said the maiden. "Meanwhile you may dress and look through these windows at the condition of this land. You may then, if it be your pleasure, climb that tower to gaze on forests, plains, and rivers until my return."

Thereupon the maiden left, and Sir Gawain dressed in the robe, which was very splendid, and fastened his neck with a clasp hanging at the collar. He was then eager to go and explore the tower. He and his host went there together, and climbed a winding staircase at the side of the vaulted palace. When they reached the top of the tower, they viewed the surrounding land, more beautiful than any could describe. Sir Gawain beheld the rivers, the plains, and the forests filled with wildlife. He looked at his host and said to him: "In God's name, host, it is my great pleasure to stay and go hunting and shooting in these forests before us."

"Sir, you may as well say no more about that," said the boatman. "For I have often heard it said that anyone so beloved by God as to be hailed here as lord, master, and protector would never leave this house. Thus, rightly or wrongly, is it laid down and established. Therefore, you must not speak of hunting or shooting, for here have you your abode. There will never be a day when you leave here."

"Host, be quiet," he replied. "If I heard you say more, you would drive me out of my mind. So help me God, I could not live inside here seven days any more than I could sevenscore years were I unable to leave whenever I wanted."

Thereupon he left the tower and went back into the palace hall. Angry and absorbed in his thoughts, his face sad and mournful, he sat on the bed until the maiden who had been there before returned. Angry as he was, Sir Gawain, on seeing her, rose to meet her and immediately greeted her. Noting his altered color and countenance, she perceived from his appearance that something had angered him but dared make no show of it. "Sir, at your pleasure my lady will come to see you," she said. "The meal is ready. You may eat, if you wish, either down here or up there."

"Dear lady," Sir Gawain replied, "I have no desire for food. May ill fortune befall me if I eat or enjoy myself before hearing news I desperately need to hear, news that can bring me joy."

Much dismayed, the maiden at once returned. The queen summoned her and asked her for news. "Dear young lady," said the queen, "in what frame of mind did you find the good lord whom God has given us here?"

"Oh, honored noble queen, I am wounded and dying from grief for the noble and well-born knight. One can draw from him only words of anger and rage. I cannot tell you why, for he did not tell me, and I do not know, nor dared I ask him. But of him I may certainly tell you that the first time I saw him today, I found him a man of such fine manners, so pleasant in his speech and so well educated that one could not tire of listening to his words or gazing on his handsome face. Now suddenly he is so altered that he would like, I believe, to be dead, for there is nothing that does not trouble him."

"My young lady, be not dismayed now, for he will be appeased the moment he sees me. Never will he lodge such deep anger that I shall fail to dispel it and put delight in place of anger."

The queen then set out and came into the palace hall, and with her was the other queen, who was pleased to go there. With them they took a hundred and fifty maidens and at least as many attendants. As soon as Sir Gawain saw the queen coming, holding the other by the hand, his heart surmised and told him that here was the queen of whom he had heard. But he could easily guess this from the sight of her white tresses hanging down to her hips and her white mottled silk dress delicately embroidered with gold threading. When Sir Gawain saw her, he did not delay in going to meet her. He greeted her, and she him.

"I am, after you, sir, lady of this palace," she said to him. "I leave you its lordship, for you are most worthy of it. But are you of King Arthur's household?"

"Yes indeed, lady."

"And are you, I wish to know, of the Knights of the Watch, who have performed many deeds of prowess?"

"No, lady."

"I do believe you. Are you, tell me, of those of the Round Table, the finest in the world?"

"Lady," he said, "I would not dare say I am one of the most esteemed. I do not consider myself one of the finest, nor do I think myself one of the worst."

"Dear sir," she replied to him, "I hear you speak with great courtesy, not claiming the honor of the finest or the reproach of the worst. But tell me now of King Lot. How many sons did he have by his wife?"

"Four, lady."

"Now tell me their names."

"Lady, Gawain is the eldest. The second is Agravain the Proud with hard hands. Gaheriet and Guerehet are the names of the final two."

The queen spoke to him again. "Sir, so help me God, such are, I think, their names. Please God they were all here together with us! Tell me now, do you know King Urien?"

"Yes, lady."

"And has he no son at the court?"

"Yes, lady, two of great renown. One is named Sir Yvain, the courteous and the well-mannered. I am in a happier disposition all day when I can see him in the morning, such wisdom and such courtesy do I find in him. The other is also named Yvain, who is not his own full brother, and is therefore called the Bastard. He surpasses all knights who do combat with him. Both are at the court, most wise, most courteous, and most brave."

"Dear sir," she said, "how is King Arthur now?"

"Better than he has ever been, healthier, happier, and stronger."

"On my word, that is not wrong," she said, "for King Arthur is a child. He is a hundred years old, certainly no more, nor can he be. But I wish you still to tell me, if you do not mind, one thing more: how is the queen?"

"Truly, lady, she is so wise, so courteous, and so beautiful that God created no language or religion wherein so wise a lady could be found. Not since the time God formed the first woman from Adam's side has there been a lady so renowned, and she should be so, for just as the wise teacher instructs the little children, so my lady the queen instructs and teaches the entire world. From her descends all virtue, for she is its origin and source of movement. No one leaving my lady may go away disconsolate, for well she knows each person's worth and what she should do to please him. No man performs any good or honorable deed unless taught it by my lady, nor will any man ever be so unhappy who goes away in anger from my lady."

"Nor will you do so, sir, from me."

"Lady, I do believe you," he said, "for before I saw you, I cared not what I did, so sorrowful and dejected was I. Now I feel so happy and so joyous that more so I could not be."

"Sir, by God who gave me birth," said the queen with the white tresses, "your happiness will yet double. Your joy will always increase and never fail you. Since you are so happy and joyous, the meal is ready, and you may eat whenever and wherever you please. If it be your pleasure, you may eat up here, or if you prefer, you may come to eat in my chambers below."

"Lady, I have no wish to exchange this palace hall for any chamber, for I have been told that no knight ever sat or ate here."

"No, sir, none who left again alive or survived here an hour or even half an hour."

"Lady, then I shall eat here, should you grant me leave."

"Sir, I grant you that willingly. You will be the very first knight to eat here."

Thereupon the queen departed, leaving with him a hundred and fifty of the most beautiful of her maidens. They dined beside him in the hall, serving and attending to all his wishes. More than a hundred attendants served at the meal, some with hair turning grey, others not, and some entirely white-haired. Still others had no beards or mustaches, and two knelt before him, one cutting meat, the other serving wine.

Sir Gawain had his host dine at his side. The dinner, by no means brief, lasted longer than one of the days around Trinity Sunday, for it was a foul dark night, and many large torches had burned out before the meal ended. After supper they all exhausted themselves rejoicing over their lord, whom they cherished, and then retired to bed.

When Sir Gawain wished to go to sleep, he lay on the Bed of Marvels. One maiden placed a pillow beneath his ear for his slumber there. When he awakened the next morning, a robe of ermine and samite had been prepared for him. And in the morning the boatman came before his bed and had him rise, dress, and wash his hands. As he rose, Clarissant was there, the wise and worthy, beautiful and attractive, fair-spoken maiden. She then went into the chamber and knelt before the queen, who asked her as she embraced her: "Little girl, by the faith you owe me, has your lord yet arisen?"

"Yes, lady, some time ago."

"And where is he, my dear little girl?"

"Lady, he went to the tower. I don't know if he has come down yet."

"Little girl, I wish to go to him, and God willing, he shall have nothing today but joy, pleasure, and good."

The queen then stood, anxious to go to him. She finally found him high up at the windows of a turret watching a maiden and an armed knight riding down a meadow.

Behold from the other direction the two queens, side by side, arriving at the place where he stood looking out. They came upon Sir Gawain and his host at two windows. "Happy be your rising, sir," said both the queens. "May today be happy and joyous for you. May the Glorious Father Who made His daughter His mother grant this!"

"May He Who sent His son to earth to honor Christianity grant you great joy, lady. But if you will, come over to this window and tell me who this maiden might be who comes here. She is accompanied by a knight carrying a quartered shield."

"I shall tell you gladly," said the queen as she looked at him. "This is she who brought you here yesterday evening. May evil fire burn her! But do not worry about her, for she is too wicked and too base. And, I beg you, do not concern yourself with the knight she brings with her, for he is, without doubt, the most courageous of all knights. Combat with him is no jest, for at this landing he has defeated and killed many knights before my eyes."

"Lady," he said, "I wish, if you grant me leave, to go and speak to the maiden."

"Please God, sir, I not grant you leave that will cause your harm. Let the troublesome and evil maiden go on about her own business. Never, God willing, shall you leave this palace on such futile labor. Unless you would wrong us, you are never to leave here again."

"Oh, nobly born queen, now have you dismayed me. I would consider myself ill paid were I unable to leave this town. Please God I not be a prisoner here so long."

"Oh, lady, let him do all he wishes," said the boatman. "Do not hold him back against his will, for he might die of grief."

"I shall allow him to leave," said the queen, "on condition that, if God saves him from death, he return again tonight."

"Lady," he said, "be not distressed, for if I can, I shall return. But I request and beg of you a favor. If it be your pleasure and command and you do not object, do not ask my name for eight days."

"Since this is your wish, sir, I shall allow it," said the queen, "for I do not desire your hatred. Had you not forbidden me, the first thing I would have asked you would have been your name."

So they came down from the tower, and attendants ran up and handed him his arms to equip his body. They had brought out his horse for him, and he mounted, all armed, and rode to the landing, accompanied by the boatman. They both embarked, and oarsmen rowed strongly until they reached the other shore, where Sir Gawain disembarked.

The other knight spoke to the pitiless maiden. "Beloved, this knight riding in arms toward us, tell me, do you know him?"

"No," the maiden answered, "but I do know that it was he who brought me here yesterday."

"So help me God, none other was I seeking!" he replied. "I was deeply afraid he had escaped me. No knight born of a mother who ever crossed the borders of Galloway boasted elsewhere of returning from this country if I happened to see him or find him before me. Since God has allowed me to see him, this man shall be captured and held."

At once, without challenge or threat, the knight rushed forward, his arm through his shield, spurring his horse. Sir Gawain charged toward him, dealing him such a blow that he wounded him severely in the arm and side. But the wound was not fatal; the hauberk resisted so well that the lancehead could not pierce through, except for a full finger's length of the tip that passed into the body and bore him to the ground. The wounded knight stood and saw, much to his dismay, his blood, for blood ran along his arm and side. He rushed at Sir Gawain with his sword, but was so quickly exhausted that he was unable to stand. He was forced to beg mercy. Sir Gawain received his pledge, then handed him over to the boatman, who awaited him.

The evil maiden had dismounted from her palfrey. Sir Gawain approached and greeted her. "Remount, dear friend," he said. "I shall not leave you here, but take you with me across the river where I must go."

"Oh, knight, how bold and fierce you act now!" she exclaimed. "Had my lover not been exhausted from his old wounds, you would have faced heavy combat. Your boasts would have ended; you would not utter such chatter. You would have been more mute than the player checkmated in a corner. But admit the truth to me now. Do you consider yourself more worthy than he because you defeated him? It often happens, as you well know, that the weak defeat the strong. But if you left this landing and rode with me to that tree, and performed one exploit that my lover, whom you placed in the boat, did for me at my will, then I would testify that you are more worthy than he and no longer hold you in contempt."

"To go only that far, maiden, I shall never refuse to do your will," he said.

"Please God I never see you return from there," she said.

They then set out on their way, she in front and he following. The ladies and the maidens in the palace pulled their hair and tore and ripped their clothes, exclaiming: "Alas, miserable wretches that we are, why do we yet live when we see this man who was to be our lord going to his sorrow and his shame? The evil maiden is at his right, the base-born girl, leading him to the place from which no knight returns. Alas, we who were born at a lucky hour are heartbroken, for God had sent us the man who knew all good, who lacked nothing, neither courage nor any other virtue."

Thus they lamented for their lord as they watched him follow the evil maiden. She and Sir Gawain came beneath the tree, and when they arrived there, he called out to her. "Maiden," he said, "tell me now if I am free of my duty, or if it be your pleasure that I do more. If ever I can, I shall do it rather than lose your favor."

The maiden then said to him: "Do you see that deep ford where the banks are so steep? My lover used to cross there."

"But I do not know where the ford is. It is too deep all the way along to ford, and the bank is too steep, I fear, so that no one could descend."

"You would not dare enter there, I know that well," said the maiden. "Certainly I never thought you had the courage to dare cross, for this is the Perilous Ford where no one, unless he be most extraordinary, dares cross on any account."

Thereupon Sir Gawain led his horse down to the bank. He saw the deep water below and the steep bank above. But the river was narrow. Seeing this, Sir Gawain told himself that his horse had jumped across many wider ditches and thought that he had heard it told and related in many places that he who could cross the deep water of the Perilous Ford would have all the renown in the world. He then drew back from the river, and returned at a gallop for the jump. But the horse failed, not taking the jump well, and fell into the middle of the ford. His horse swam until its four feet touched ground, then readied itself for a leap. It shot out so well that it leapt onto the steep bank. After reaching the bank, the horse stood completely still on its feet, incapable of movement.

Finding his horse exhausted, Sir Gawain was forced of necessity to dismount. He immediately dismounted, then planned to take off its saddle. He removed it and turned it on its side to dry. After he had removed the saddlegirth, he wiped the water from the horse's back, sides, and legs. He then saddled the horse again, mounted, and rode at a walk until he saw a knight by himself hunting with a sparrowhawk. In the meadow before him, the knight had three hunting dogs. The knight was more handsome than any tongue could tell. Sir Gawain approached and greeted him. "Dear sir," he said, "may God who made you more handsome than any other creature grant you good fortune today."

The knight was prompt to reply. "You are the good man. You are the handsome man. But tell me, if you don't mind, how you left the evil maiden alone over there. Where did her companion go?"

"Sir," he said, "a knight carrying a quartered shield was escorting her when I met her."

"And what did you do?"

"I defeated him in armed combat."

"And what became of the knight?"

"The boatman, who told me that he should have him, took him away."

"He certainly told you the truth, dear sir. The maiden was once my beloved, but she did not agree, never deigning to love me or call me lover. I never had pleasure of her, even by force, for I loved her against her will. I took her from a lover of hers whose company she shared. I killed him and led her away, devoting myself to her service. But my service was worth nothing, for she sought the occasion to leave me as soon as she could, and took as her lover that one from whom you have just now taken her. That knight was no jester. No, so help me God, he was very brave. Yet he never dared come where he thought to find me. But today you performed an act no knight dared undertake. And because you dared it, you acquired the honor and the renown of the world through your great valor. It took immense courage for you to leap the Perilous Ford, and know that for a fact no knight has ever come out of it."

"Sir," he said, "then the maiden lied to me when she told me and had me believe as truth that her lover crossed it once a day out of love for her."

"Did she say that, the liar? Oh, would that she had drowned there, so possessed by the devil is she to tell such an idle tale. She hates you, I cannot deny that, and this devil—God confound her!—wanted you to drown in the depths of the hideous water. But give me your word now—you will pledge to me, and I to you—that if you wish to ask me anything, be it to my joy or my sorrow, I shall never conceal the truth if I know it. And likewise you will tell me in turn all I wish to know, for on no account will you lie to me if you can tell me the truth."

Both made this pledge, and first Sir Gawain began to question. "Sir," he inquired, "I ask you about a town I see there. Whose is it and what is its name?"

"Friend," he answered, "I shall tell you the truth about the town. The town you see belongs to me. There is no man born to whom I owe any of it. I hold it only from God. It is called Orquelenes."

"And your name?"

"Guiromelant."

"Sir, you are most brave and valiant, I have often heard said, and you are lord of a great land. And what is the name of the maiden of whom no good is spoken near or far, as you yourself bear witness?"

"I can well testify that she is much to be feared, so evil and scornful is she," he replied. "For this reason she is called the Haughty Maiden of Logres, the place where she was born and taken from as a child."

"And her lover who has gone, willing or not, as the boatman's prisoner, what is his name?"

"Friend, know about the knight that he is an extraordinary knight and is called the Proud Knight of the Narrow Passage. He guards the borders of Galloway."

"And what is the name of the castle over there, so fine and so fitting, which I came from today and where last night I ate and drank?"

At these words Guiromelant turned in sadness and started to leave. Gawain called to him. "Sir, sir, answer me. Remember your pledge!"

Guiromelant stopped, turned his head toward him, and said: "Curse and damn the hour I saw you and gave you my pledge! Go your way. I declare you free of your pledge, and you free me of mine. I expected to ask you news of the land over there. But you know as much about the town, I believe, as you know about the moon."

"Sir," he said, "I lay there last night and slept on the Bed of Marvels. No bed is like it, and no one has ever seen its equal."

"Sir," he said, "I marvel much at the news you tell me. It is a pleasure and delight for me to hear your lies, for listening to you is like listening to a teller of idle tales. You are a minstrel, I see this well. But I thought you were a knight and had performed some feat of arms there. Yet inform me now if you did any act of prowess there. And what did you see there?"

"Sir," Sir Gawain answered him, "when I sat on the bed, there was great commotion in the palace hall. Do not think I lie to you. The bed cords clanged, little bells hanging from the bed cords sounded, windows that were closed flew open by themselves, crossbow bolts and smooth arrows struck my shield, and also fixed there were the claws of a mighty lion, proud and bristling, which had long been chained in a chamber. The lion was brought out against me and struck against my shield with such force that it was held there by its claws, which it could not withdraw again. If you do not believe this happened, see the claws still here. I cut off its head, thank God, and its feet too. What do you think of these proofs?"

At these words Guiromelant dismounted as fast as he could. Bowing to Gawain, his hands joined together, he begged him to forgive the foolish words he had uttered.

"I forgive you completely," he said. "Remount."

Deeply ashamed of his foolish words, he remounted. "Sir, so help me God," he said, "I did not believe that anywhere, near or far, could there be a knight who could have the honor that is yours. But about the white-haired queen, tell me if you saw her, and if you asked her who she was and where she came from."

"I did not think to ask that, though I saw her and spoke to her," he replied.

"I shall tell you," he said. "She is the mother of King Arthur."

"By the faith I owe God and His power, King Arthur, so I believe, lost his mother a long time ago, sixty years or still more, to my knowledge."

"It is true, sir. She is his mother. After his father Utherpendragon was buried, it came to pass that Queen Ygerne arrived in this country with all her treasure, and constructed on that cliff the castle and the rich and beautiful palace I have heard you describe. You saw, I am certain, the other queen, the other noble and beautiful lady. She is the wife of King Lot and the mother of the one to whom I wish all possible evil. She is the mother of Gawain."

"Gawain, dear sir? I know him well, and so I dare say that this same Gawain lost his mother at least twenty years ago."

"She is his mother, sir, never doubt that. She followed her mother there, and was bearing a child. And that child is the noble and beautiful maiden who is my beloved and also sister—I would not lie—to that one to whom God grant deep disgrace! If I held him and he were as near me as you are, he would certainly not leave with his head. I would behead him in this very place."

"You do not love as I do," said Sir Gawain. "On my soul, if I loved maiden or lady, I would love and serve all her family out of love for her."

"You are right, I agree. But when I remember Gawain, how his father killed mine, I cannot wish him well. And Gawain himself, with his own hands, killed a brave and valiant knight, one of my own cousins. I never had occasion to take revenge. But do me now a service. Proceed to that castle, bearing this ring on my behalf, and present it to my beloved. I wish you to go there for my sake, and tell her that I trust and believe that her love is such that she would rather her own brother Gawain die a bitter death than that would I hurt the smallest toe on my foot. Send my beloved my greetings and give her this ring on behalf of me, her lover."

Sir Gawain then slipped the ring on his smallest finger. "Sir," he said, "by the faith I owe you, you have a beloved who is wise and courteous, noble and well born, beautiful and charming, if she agrees with what you have told me here."

"Sir," he said, "you will do me a great kindness, I assure you this, if you bear this present of my ring to my dear beloved, for I love her very much. To express my gratitude to you, I shall tell you the name of this castle, as you asked me. The castle, if you do not know, is called the Rock of Canguin. Many fine cloths, bright reds and deep ones, and many rich wools are dyed there, which are sold and brought in abundance. Now I have told you what you wished, without word of lie, and well have you spoken in return. Would you ask me more?"

"No, sir, only leave to go."

"Sir, tell me your name, if you do not mind, before I allow you to leave me," he said.

And Sir Gawain answered him. "Sir, so help me the Lord God, my name will never be hidden. I am the one you hate so much. I am Gawain."

"You are Gawain?"

"Yes, the nephew of King Arthur."

"Then on my word, you are very bold or else very foolish to tell me your name, knowing that I hate you to the death. Now I am deeply pained and troubled that my helmet is not laced and the shield not braced and hanging from my neck. If I were armed as you are, be certain that I would behead you here and now. Nothing would make me spare you. But if you dared wait for me, I would ride and fetch my arms, then return to fight you, bringing three or four men to observe the combat. Or if you wish another alternative: we shall wait seven days and come back fully armed on the seventh day to this place. You will send for the king, the queen, and all his men, and I shall summon my troops from all my land. Then our battle will not be undertaken in secret, but all those who wish to see it will see it, for combat between two worthy men, as we two are said to be, should not be held in private. No, it is right indeed that many knights and ladies be present. And when one is worn out and all know this, the victor will be honored a thousand times more than he would be if none but he knew."

"Sir," said Sir Gawain, "I would gladly forgo this if, with your agreement, it were possible that there be no combat. If I did you wrong, I shall willingly make amends, to the satisfaction of your friends and mine, so that all is right and fair."

"I do not know what right there can be if you dare not fight me," he said. "I have proposed two alternatives. Act upon the one you prefer. If you dare, wait for me and I shall go fetch my arms. Or summon all your forces from your land to be here in seven days. At Pentecost King Arthur will be holding court, I have heard, at Orcanie, but two days' journey from here. Your messenger could find the king and his men ready to set out. Send him there and you will act wisely, for a day's delay is worth a hundred sous."

"So save me God, the court will definitely be there. You do have all the information," he replied. "And I shall dispatch there those I wish."

"Gawain," he said, "I wish to take you to the finest landing in the world. The water is so swift and deep that no living thing can cross it or spring to the other bank."

Sir Gawain answered that he would never seek bridge or ford, whatever might happen. "Lest the wicked maiden consider me cowardly, I shall keep my promise and ride directly back to her."

Then he spurred his horse, and it jumped easily across the water without encountering difficulty. When the maiden who had so maligned him with her words saw that he had crossed to her, her heart and her intentions changed, for she immediately greeted him, saying that she had come to him to beg mercy for her misdeed since he had endured great hardship on her account." "Dear sir," she said, "hear now why I have been so haughty to all the knights in the world who have taken me in their company. If you don't object, I shall tell you. This knight on the other shore who spoke to you—God destroy him!—was wrong to bestow his love on me, for he loved me and I hated him. He caused me bitter pain by slaying—I shall not lie about it—the man whose beloved I was. The knight then expected to do me so much honor in his scheme to win me to his love. But his efforts were wasted. At the first opportunity given me, I stole away from his company and joined the knight from whom you in turn took me today. This knight means less to me than a bootstrap. But ever since the time death parted me from my first lover, I have been mad, speaking so haughtily and acting so basely and so foolishly that I had no care whom I opposed. I acted deliberately, wanting to find someone so irritable that I could anger and enrage him into cutting me into pieces. Long have I wished for death. Sir, now do me such justice that no maiden hearing of me will ever speak shamefully to a knight."

"Dear one," he said, "why should I care to do you justice? May it never please the Son of the Lord God that you come to harm from me. But mount without delay, and we shall ride to that mighty castle. Behold the boatman at the landing waiting to carry us across."

"I shall do all your will, sir," said the maiden. She then climbed into the saddle of her little long-maned palfrey. And they rode to the boatman, who ferried them across the water without effort or trouble.

The ladies and the maidens who had been bitterly lamenting for him saw them coming. All the palace attendants were beside themselves on his account. Now their rejoicing was the greatest ever seen. The queen was seated in front of the palace hall waiting for him. She had all her maidens join hands to dance and begin the celebrations. They commenced their joy to welcome him, singing and dancing in rounds, and he arrived and dismounted in their midst. Amid great festivity they removed the equipment from his legs and arms, chest and head. They also rejoiced over the maiden he had brought, all the men and women serving her for his sake, since they did nothing for her own sake. In celebration, all entered the hall and sat down. Sir Gawain took his sister and seated her beside him on the Bed of Marvels. In a low voice he whispered to her: "Young lady, from beyond this landing I bring you a little ring with a deep-green emerald. A knight sends it to you out of love, greeting you and saying that you are his sweetheart."

"Sir, I believe it," she replied. "But if I have any love at all for him, it is from afar that I am his beloved. He never laid eyes on me, nor I on him, except that I saw him from across the water. He has long given me his love, and I thank him. He never came from there, but his messengers entreated me so much that I granted him my love. I would not lie about this. Only to this degree am I his beloved."

"Oh, dear maiden, he already boasted that you would much prefer your own brother Sir Gawain dead than that he hurt his toe!"

"What! Sir, I marvel much how he uttered such great folly. In God's name, I did not think his manners so ill. Now he has been most imprudent in sending me this message. Alas, my brother does not even know of my birth, nor has he ever seen me. Guiromelant spoke wrongly. On my soul, I would not have my brother suffer any more than myself."

While the two thus talked and the ladies heard them, the elderly queen spoke to her daughter seated beside her. "Dear daughter, what do you think of that lord sitting beside your daughter, my little girl? He has been speaking privately to her a long time. I do not know the subject, but I am delighted. And it is not right that I be displeased, for it is a sign of high nobility that he is drawn to the wisest and most beautiful in the palace, and he is right. Please God he marry her and she please him as much as Lavinia did Aeneas."

"Oh, lady, may God so incline his heart that they be as brother and sister," said the other queen, "and that he love her and she him so much that they may be as one flesh."

By her prayer the lady meant that he should love her and take her as his wife; she had not recognized her own son. They would be like brother and sister, with no other love between them, when they learned that she was his sister and he her brother. And their mother would rejoice, but not for the reason she expected.

After Sir Gawain spoke to his beautiful sister a long time, he stood and called to an attendant he saw on his right, the one who seemed most worthy, diligent, and helpful, the wisest and most sensible of all the attendants in the hall. He went down to a chamber, only the attendant accompanying him. When both arrived there, he said to him: "Attendant, I think you are clever and bright. If I tell you a secret of mine, I advise you to keep it hidden that you may profit from it. I wish to send you to a place where you will be joyously welcomed."

"Sir, I would rather have my tongue torn from my throat than have one word you wish hidden fly from my mouth."

"Friend," he said, "then go to my lord King Arthur, for I am Gawain, his nephew. The route there is not long or difficult, for the king set up his court for Pentecost in the city of Orcanie. If the journey there costs you anything, rely on me for the expense. When you come before the king, you will find him deeply angered, and yet when you greet him on my behalf, great joy will be his, nor will there be a single person hearing the news who is not delighted. To the king you will say, by the faith he owes me (since he is my lord and I his liegeman), that no reason should prevent him from appearing before me below this tower by the fifth day of the feast, that he should encamp in the meadow, and that he should bring with him such company of nobility and commoners as has come to his court. I have undertaken a combat with a knight who esteems neither me nor the king, whom he considers a man of little worth. The knight is assuredly Guiromelant, who hates me to the death. Speak also to the queen that, by the great faith that should exist between her and me, she should come there, for she is both my lady and my friend. When she learns the news, she will not refuse, bringing with her, out of love for me, the ladies and the maidens who will be at court that day. But one thing concerns me. Have you a good hunting horse to bear you there swiftly?"

He answered him that there was a fine one at his disposal, tall, swift, and strong, that he could take.

"Then I have no worry," he replied.

The attendant led him quickly to a stable, where he brought out strong and well-rested hunting horses. One was harnessed for riding and travel, for he had had it newly shod, and it lacked neither saddle nor bridle. "On my word, attendant, you are well equipped," said Sir Gawain. "Go now, and may the Lord of Kings grant you good travel there and back, and keep you on the right road."

Thus he sent the attendant on his way, escorting him to the water and commanding the boatman to carry him across. The boatman had him ferried across, and he did not become weary, for he had many oarsmen.

The attendant made the crossing and took the right road to the city of Orcanie, for a man who can ask directions can travel anywhere in the world.

Sir Gawain returned to his palace, where he stayed amid great joy and delight, all the men and women rejoicing over him.

The queen had hot baths prepared in five hundred tubs, and had all the squires wash and bathe. Robes made for them were ready when they left the baths: the cloth was woven silk and the lining ermine. All the night the squires remained in the chapel until after matins, standing and never kneeling. In the morning Sir Gawain, with his own hand, fastened the right spur to each squire, girded the sword, and dubbed him knight. He then had a company of at least five hundred new knights.

The attendant continued to travel until he reached the city of Orcanie, where the king was holding a court appropriate to such a feast. The sick and the lame, seeing the youth, said: "He comes in urgent need. I think he bears news for the court from afar. Whatever his report, he will find the king deaf and dumb, so consumed is he by sorrow and anger. And who will there be now to counsel him when he has heard the messenger's news?"

"Stay! What business is it of ours to speak of the king's counsel?" said others. "We ought to be frightened, dismayed, and dejected since we have lost the one who dressed us all in God's name, and from whom all good came to us through alms and charity." Thus, throughout the city, the poor lamented for Sir Gawain whom they loved very much.

The attendant passed by, riding until he reached the palace where he found the king seated, a hundred counts palatine, a hundred dukes, and a hundred kings sitting around him. The king was absorbed in mournful thoughts, seeing his great barony but not his nephew, and in his deep DISTRESS HE FELL IN A FAINT. THE FIRST TO ARRIVE WAS NOT HESITANT TO LIFT HIM UP AGAIN, FOR ALL WERE RUSHING TO HIS AID. ¶FROM HER SEAT IN A GALLERY, LADY LORE HEARD THE GRIEF THROUGH- OUT THE HALL. FROM THE GALLERY SHE RAN DOWN AND, LIKE ONE TOTALLY DISTRAUGHT, CAME TO THE QUEEN. WHEN THE QUEEN SAW HER, SHE ASKED HER WHAT SHE HAD

. . .

WILLIAM OF ENGLAND

 HRISTIAN WISHES TO BE-
gin the telling of a tale—without omission or ad-
dition—in matching rhymes or leonines, and in a
straightforward manner. So long as he pursues his
tale, he will never follow any digression; he will
take the most direct path available to him in order
to reach the end as soon as possible. The man who
would search out and consult the stories of England
will discover one at Saint Edmund's that is most credible because of its
truth and delight. Should someone ask for proof of this, let him go there
if he wishes and see for himself.

Christian, experienced in storytelling, tells of a king who lived in En-
gland. This king loved God and his faith and revered Holy Church. Each
day, according to a vow he had made, he heard the services, never failing
to attend matins or mass so long as he was healthy and able. The king, who
embodied charity and exemplified humility, governed his realm in peace.
The king's name was William.

The king had a wise and beautiful wife, herself of a royal family, but
the story tells no more about her, and I have no wish to falsify the tale.
The queen's name was Gratienne, and she was a most excellent Christian.
King William loved her very much and always called her his lady. The lady
loved her lord with equal or greater love. If the king loved and believed
in God, no less did the queen. If he embodied charity, no less did she. If
humility dwelt in him, I have read and discovered in the story that just as
much dwelt in the queen. So long as prosperity was his, he never failed to

attend matins. And, in truth, the queen also attended as often as she was able. Such was the goodness of these two people.

For six years the couple lived together without being able to have a child. In the sixth year the queen conceived. When the king learned of this, he had her cared for and well attended. He undertook this responsibility himself, for nothing mattered so much to him. So long as she was able—the fruit in her womb as yet not too burdensome—she went to matins daily, as was her custom, at the hour when the king rose. But when the king saw the time approach for her confinement, he no longer allowed her to attend, fearing that it might be injurious to her. He ordered her to remain at home. She did remain, while he attended, for he had no wish to fail in the observance of his vow.

One night he awoke as usual at the proper hour and wondered why he was not hearing the bell for matins. At the very moment it should have sounded, he heard a clap of thunder and jumped up. He raised his head, looked about the room, and beheld such a brilliant brightness that he was dazzled. At the same instant he heard a voice speak to him: "King, go into exile. From God and His Son, I tell you this, that He so commands you and through me so orders you."

Amazed at this event, the king consulted his chaplain the following morning after matins. This man gave him loyal and wise counsel according to his understanding of the matter. "Sir, about this vision you have beheld," he said, "I do not know, nor do you, if it has come from God. But I do know that many goods are yours that are not yours rightfully. Have it proclaimed at once that you are prepared to make amends if duly requested. This is my counsel. There is no other. Do not retain the belongings of others, but offer redress on all accounts. I fear that this vision comes from some phantom."

Not inclined to scorn what the chaplain counseled and commanded him to do, the king immediately summoned to his court all the people whose goods he knew he held wrongfully. To each he returned his due; to each, as best he could, he gave his pledge and his belongings according to the full measure of the claims against him.

When the king was in bed that night, at the very same hour he heard the noise, saw the brightness, and heard the voice; he crossed himself. Be certain that he was startled at this marvel. Deeply afraid of what he heard, he rose as quickly as he could, and went to the church to pray, confess his sins, and beg God's mercy. After the king had heard matins sung, he called the chaplain aside in the chapel and again sought his counsel, telling him that God had ordered him to go with all haste into exile. Though not such a person as to dare find fault with the king, the chaplain answered him.

"If you do not mind, sir, wait again tonight, and if this happens to you a third time, be assured that both the noise and the brightness come from God. I tell you this and I repeat it: wait still for the third time. And if God calls upon you a third time, then seek no further counsel, but hold the world in contempt and despise your own person. Love God alone and pray to God. Out of love for God hold everything in contempt. Withholding nothing, give away all your wealth. Distribute all your money to the poor, to hospitals, and to churches. These are the places for alms-giving. Give away cups, give away rings. Give away coats, give away cloaks. Give away jackets and quilts. Give away gerfalcons, give away goshawks, and give away chargers and palfreys. Give away everything at this time so that nothing worth a chestnut is left to you of your belongings. Carry nothing worth a straw except the clothes you wear. When the time comes, God will restore your fortune a hundredfold. Your belongings will not diminish, for you will be rewarded and recompensed a hundredfold."

The king recognized the truth in his words and said to him: "In the name of God in Heaven, dear sir, keep this matter a secret. Just as if this were confession, never disclose a word."

"May absolution never be mine, sir, if I make known anything that should be kept secret."

The king then left the church, as did the chaplain. The king, however, did not forget. He immediately ordered all his treasure brought before him. He summoned the abbots and the priors of poor houses that lacked resources. He summoned abbesses and prioresses, summoned the poor, summoned the sick. Unburdening himself of his treasure, he freed himself of his goods, giving up and handing over all in the name of God. And the queen did the same, giving away her spotted and grey furs and her ermine, as well as her rings and her finery, for on both nights she too had heard the thunder and the voice. Of all her belongings, she kept nothing worth so little as a glass cup. And so day had passed into night, and they had distributed and given away everything.

That night the two of them scarcely slept, for both were listening attentively, impatient to hear the noise and outcry and to see the brightness again. At the proper hour they heard the noise, and both, praising the Lord God for this, beheld the brightness together. And the voice spoke: "King, leave here. Go away with all haste, and you will act wisely. I am a messenger to you from God. It is His will that you go into exile. This delaying of yours angers and vexes Him."

The king rose at once, unclad, and crossed himself. Not disdaining God's will, he rose quietly and quickly put on his clothes and his shoes. And the queen also rose. The king was deeply upset to see this, for he had expected to steal away from her. But he was obliged to keep her with him, no matter what he himself wished, for he would not leave her or go anywhere without her.

Seeing her rise, the king asked her the reason. "Lady," he said, "why are you getting up? By the faith you owe me, what is your purpose?"

"But what is yours?"

"Lady, I have to go to matins. I rise because I want to go there, and I shall do as I usually do."

"To matins? Do you jest?"

"Not at all, lady," answered the king.

"Yes you do, sir, so help me God. It is no use trying to conceal it. You will not leave here so easily. I will tell you myself if you do not speak."

"Tell, then, if you know."

"Gladly, sir. Nothing you saw tonight escaped my eyes. I heard the noise, I saw the light, and I heard the voice, which still haunts me. The voice ordered you to go, without resistance, and to pass your life in exile."

"Lady, I dare not deny it. I cannot. I should not. God will have His way with me, and as best I can, until the hour of my death, I will strive to do His will."

"Sir," said the nobly born queen, "God grant you the power to do His will. But you act the fool in wishing to go without my agreement and my knowledge. What bad counsel is yours! Know then that I am astonished that you ever dared think or plan to go into exile without my counsel. What distress would then be mine! You would surely have betrayed me and brought about my death if you had abandoned me. Certainly happiness would never have been mine."

"Happiness? Why not? What would be the reason when you would want for nothing except me?"

"Except you, dear sir. Without doubt such penance would be too heavy for me. This separation would grieve me too much. My soul will be parted from my body before I depart from you."

A second, a third, and a fourth time the king begged her that it be her pleasure to let him depart. "Lady," he said, "accept without quarrel that I go away with your leave, and never speak a word of this. I must wander the world from end to end to follow God's will."

"Sir, I have no intention of being silent for your sake," replied the lady, who was most wise. "We shall make this journey together, and this is, I think, as it should be. Together we have known much joy, wealth, honor, and comfort. Together we must endure sorrow, poverty, shame, and discomfort. In the most equal measure I can devise, I want to share with you joy and sorrow, good times and bad."

"Ah, lady, you have my thanks," said the king. "On my counsel you will remain here, for you are too heavy with child. Not even for one hundred thousand gold marks would I want some harm to befall you in these woods. The time is near, and will soon come, when you will have to take to bed and give birth to your child. To whom could you entrust it? to what attendants? to what nurses? As for you yourself, with what morsels would you be served and nourished? Your life would be very short. Your discomfort and suffering would very soon be ended, and in no time you would be dead. And even if your courage leads you to have no thought for yourself, to fear no misfortune, and to be dismayed by nothing, have pity on your baby to whom you will soon give birth. At least let your baby live, for if he dies through your fault, you will be guilty of his death. As for me, then what could I do? After you two, I would die of grief, incapable of living on. Thus you would be, I believe, the death of your infant, yourself, and me. Through your doing, all three of us would be dead. Why do you want to kill yourself? It would be better to perfume your beds and your chambers with laurel and myrrh and keep in comfort your body and the baby to whom you will soon give birth. He is wrong who, accepting advice, does not heed good counsel. It is fitting that he suffers who hears counsel but does not believe it. If I do not counsel you rightly, never again trust me in anything."

"Sir, you speak very well, but I firmly believe that anyone trusting in God cannot be without help. Never part from me or my company. God will not forget you but will watch over me and you and the baby who will be born to us. Let us now set out together confidently, as God commanded. May He take us under His protection!"

"Lady, whatever may befall me, I must abide by your will since you will not stay here. Then let us go, and God be with us."

They stepped out through one of the room's windows. At that time the moon was not shining, and the night was very dark indeed. They hurried out of Bristol, where they had been staying, and entered a forest. Accompanied by his pregnant wife, the king walked along, his sword girded at his side. They carried nothing else with them, rejoicing, however, in the goodness and purity of their own hearts.

They followed neither roads nor paths, lest people approaching from some direction ahead or behind might detain them. They followed neither roads nor regular routes, but turned off through the forest where they saw it was most dense. And so all night long they fled, and if they had pain, they rejoiced in it, for it seems sweet to those whose hearts God inspires and illumines, but it would be bitter to all those with little sense of loving God.

In the morning when the people awoke, those at the court were amazed: What was happening? Why was the king not rising, he who usually rose early? For many, this could have been a matter of concern, and they would have been more upset had they known the truth. They suspected nothing upsetting, but kept waiting for him to rise. And they waited a very long time, until midday had passed. They waited so long that they were deeply worried. When they saw that he was not rising, they went to the door to his chamber and found it closed. For a long time they stood and listened, then called at the door and knocked. After a long period of listening, they knocked and pounded until they smashed the bolt and the hinges and forced the door open. They rushed into the room, found neither the king nor the queen inside, and marveled that it could be so. Discovering the window open through which the couple had let themselves down, they then thought that the two had departed.

But before uttering a word, they rummaged through whatever they found in the chamber: chests, lockers, boxes, and trunks. They emptied all the rooms and chambers of everything they found there, but their searching was in vain: they found nothing there, nor was there anything. A small child noticed an ivory horn under the bed, which the king, this story relates, was accustomed always to carrying in the woods. The child took the horn home for amusement and kept it a very long time.

There was then no need to hide the truth: the news spread everywhere that King William had disappeared. The entire realm was in mourning, and everyone lamented no less the disappearance of the queen. All the people searched afar: they had searches made across sea and land, in every place except where the couple was.

The two always held to their journey and lived like wild animals on acorns and beechnuts, fruits of the forest, pears, and wild apples. They ate mulberries and hawthorn berries, buds from plants, wild plums, and service berries, where they found them. For want of any other drink, they drank the rain from the clouds. Nevertheless they accepted with patience all their discomfort and their distress.

They traveled so much from day to day, as chance led them, that they went down toward the sea. They followed no road or path before they emerged from the forest. Finally they came down to the sea. There they found a hollow rock that formed a cave, and they entered the rock for their lodging that night. They took what shelter they could, their lodging offering much discomfort: a hard bed and cold nourishment.

The queen was exhausted, and so she fell asleep—it was no wonder—the moment she lay down. When she awoke, her time came and she went into labor. Severe was her agony, and she called upon God and the glorious Virgin. She implored Saint Margaret. She loved all the saints and all the virgins, for she feared them all and trusted them all, and she prayed to them all, as she should, to beseech All-powerful God for her deliverance. But she was terrified that she had no woman to assist her, for she had great need of one, a woman knowing better than a man how to aid her. The two, however, were so remote from any human presence that no woman could arrive there in time to help. And so the king had to fill the role.

With deep humility and true nobility, the king did whatever she instructed him to do, showing no disdain or displeasure at any task, until she delivered a beautiful little boy. The king cherished the baby and gave thought to making a bed for him. He then drew his naked sword, cut down the right side of his coat, wrapped the infant in it, and laid it on the ground. He himself then sat down. Because he wanted to ease his queen's discomfort, he placed her head on his knees, nobly, gently, pityingly, until the queen, who had suffered a great deal in her labor, fell asleep. And when she awakened, she again entered labor and cried out loudly: "Glorious Holy Mary, at the same time daughter and mother, you who gave birth to your son and your father, look, glorious lady, with your beautiful eyes, upon your woman." She kept calling again upon the Virgin until she gave birth to a baby boy.

The king was so caring that with his own sword he cut down the other side of his coat, and laid the infant inside. He then sat down again, and placed the queen's head upon his own knees in place of a pillow. Again she began to fall asleep, and slept until morning. When she awoke, she felt greater hunger than any woman has ever felt. "Sir," she said to her lord, "if I don't have something to eat soon, you will see me faint. My hunger is so severe and so intense that, whatever the cost, I shall be forced to eat at least one of my babies, to satisfy my craving for food."

The king immediately started up. This hunger distressed him, and he did not know what he could do, except, he thought, give her pieces of his own flesh to eat until he could do something better. Clutching his sword, he took hold of his thigh. Tortured by hunger, the lady watched his compassion and his nobility, and pity seized her. "What would you do?" she said. "Satisfy me with some other meal. By Saint Peter of Rome, whom one travels to Rome to beseech, never will my flesh eat yours, by the faith I owe the Holy Paternoster."

"Ah, lady, do so," he answered. "By my own flesh and my own blood, I want to save my son from death. So long as my heart beats and I have flesh on my bones, never, I dare tell you for certain, will my babies be eaten unless I have completely lost my mind. Eat my flesh as you will, for God will restore my health. I can easily recover from my wound. But I am frightened for my child. There would be no recovery for him, and God would never forgive you for your mortal sin of eating your own children."

"Sir," she said, "be quiet now. Calm yourself a little. I shall endure my pain and my hunger as best I can. As for you, go seek and ask if you might find some people who would, for the love of God, agree to help you. And return again soon."

"Gladly, lady," replied the king. "I shall come back as quickly as I can, I promise you."

He immediately set out on the road, praying God to be with him. Looking to the sea, he noticed merchants in port, heartily and happily loading their merchandise onto a ship in the harbor. The ship was nearly ready for its journey by the time the king reached the merchants. He was so poor and destitute that he looked like a beggar. He greeted them, and in God's name implored them to hear him a moment until he told them his need.

"Sirs," he said to the merchants, "God be kind to you here, and God grant you all profit! If you have any food at all, give me some that God may repay you for it, protecting you all from difficulty, and thus grant profit to you all."

One of them, as though angered, spoke to him. "Beggar, get out of here, get out of here! Believe me, you will be beaten or thrown into the sea today to pay for this fare."

"Oh," said one of the others, "don't concern yourself. Let this beggar, this tramp be. Don't bother with him at all. Whatever they may have, the poor, the wretched have to live off the earnings of worthy men. Let his request and begging be. It is his profession to go begging up and down the world. Not here did he begin it, and not here will he end it, for he knows no other trade."

"Ah, noble sir, thank you," said the king. "In truth, I did begin here, but it will not finish here. It has been forejudged upon me and destined, and I have to carry out my fate. Nevertheless my begging would end at this moment were I not distressed more about another's discomfort than about my own. My wife gave birth tonight, be certain of this, to two children. I am apprehensive and frightened for them. So severe a hunger has gripped my wife that she is about to take back into her belly the children to whom she has given birth."

"Ah, mister beggar, how you lie now!" retorted the merchants, who were most suspicious. "Now you have uttered an enormous lie. Never has there been such a devil incarnate, a woman who ate her own children. Such a thing has never been, nor will it ever be. Yet take us there, provided it be not too far from here. And so let us go to the place where the children lie."

About fifteen of them declared their intention of going, and they all set out following the king. With all speed the king led them along the most direct route to the spot where the queen was lying. When one of the men, who thought most highly of himself, beheld the queen, he said, "This lady wears no make-up. There is no fake hair or painted face here. Beggar, where did you get her? Where did you find so beautiful a lady?"

"Friend, be assured in all truth that I am her husband."

"Ah, now I am in a fine state indeed, since you dare lie to me still. It will be too late for you to repent if another word escapes your lips. She has had enough of you. The lady asks for nothing more. Too long has she led a life of begging with you, and too long has she been led across the land. Such a lady is wise indeed to rely on such a scoundrel! Tell us no more lies today, but speak only the truth. There certainly was no priest present when you were first joined together. Confess where you stole her."

"Ah, sir," said the king, "don't say that! Would to God I had been so free of all other sins! Never indeed have I been accused or charged with theft. You wrong me in imputing this to me. But why should I justify myself, since I shall never be believed?"

"Beholding such a great beauty, the very devils would question you, because she could not have such a companion unless she had been abducted."

The lady herself spoke. "Indeed, sirs, I am his wife, given in marriage by the priest."

"You are now so given over to lying that you do so shamelessly. You two have nothing in common. He never married you. What a pity that you are his, and have been for so long. You have escaped his clutches, for now we shall carry you away gently to our ship. You will be treated with all comfort, though this may bother and displease some. And the fool who brought you has no further right to you. But the two babies will stay with him, for they will help him in his begging. If he takes good care of them, he will act wisely, for they will win back for him whatever he pays out. As long as he cares for them, he will never die of hunger or thirst."

When the king heard their offensive words, he showed no semblance of wisdom, so overwhelmed was he with anger. He wanted to take hold of his sword, which lay at his feet on the ground. But when they saw him extend his hand, one of them pushed him back, the second struck him in the face, and the third grabbed the sword. The fourth instructed and explained to the others to cut two poles for a litter to carry the lady. Some of them rushed into the woods, and felled and cut two poles. As soon as they had cut them and tied them together with strong cord, they laid boughs, leaves, and ferns all across for a litter. When they had made everything ready, they returned to the cave and, according to their will and pleasure, but contrary to the will of the king and of the queen, carried the lady away on the litter.

Although deeply grieved by this, the king, all alone against them, could offer no resistance. Yet he was struck and cudgeled, jostled and rebuffed so much as they departed that one of them, who was a worthy man, took pity on him and spoke to him. "My dear friend, take heed. I shall give you five besants of fine red gold if you desist, for you pursue us in vain. Friend, I beg you, take the besants and the purse, for you will need them."

"Sir, I care not for your property. I value not your gift. Keep your besants, for I would not take them for anything."

"Vassal, are you too courageous, or too foolish, or else too haughty to deign to accept five besants when you are in need? Before this day is over, your anger will abate. I shall leave them here, and so you come and take them when you wish."

The merchant threw the purse with all the besants as far as he could toward the cave, and the purse caught on a tree's crooked branch, and there it hung. Without further ado, the men carried the lady to the ship. The king remained behind, maddened by grief and by rage. Once out to sea, the mast hoisted, the mariners raised the sail without delay.

While the men went on their way, the king remained there, lamenting and mourning. Heavy was his mourning, heavy his lamenting, and he had no desire to do anything. He returned to the cave planning what he might do. If he stayed in England, all the barons would continue their search for him until he was discovered. He then thought of two boats he had noticed by the sea when he came there. He would embark with his twins in one of the boats, he said, and they would sail on the high seas wherever God would guide them. He then set off with one of his children, leaving the other in the cave, and came to the sea, where he found one of the boats all fitted out. He placed the baby inside, then went in haste, without resting, to get the other. He did not pause until he reached the cave. But there he discovered a large animal like a wolf, and a wolf it was. He saw that animal holding the infant in its mouth. Behold now the king wild with grief to see his infant held by the wolf. And he did not know what might happen. Such was his grief that he did not know what he was doing. The wolf fled, and he pursued it as fast as he could. But he followed in vain, for he could not catch up with it. He did not restrain himself on that account, but pushed himself onwards until he wore himself out, and still he saw no trace of the wolf. Thus exhausted, he was unable to move one more step, and of necessity he had to sit by the side of a large rock and lie down. There he stretched out, and there he fell asleep.

The wolf, with the baby in its mouth, did not bruise or harm him. It was fleeing in the direction of a road where merchants were traveling. The moment they spotted the wolf, they screamed and shouted, and threw sticks and stones at it until the wolf gave up its prey to them in the middle of the road. It abandoned its prey and took to flight.

All the merchants rushed forward, running until they reached the infant. The moment they took him in their hands, they unwrapped and untied his garments. Delight and laughter were theirs to behold the child all unscathed and laughing. They believed and understood this to be a miracle.

One of the men openly declared to all the others that the child would be his. Each of them would agree, he said, that the infant be his alone. "We grant you this," they replied.

"Sirs, I shall make him my own son."

The merchant then took him, and straightaway the men reached the boat where the king had placed the other child. The man who was first to discover and see him asked and urged all the others to renounce any claim to the child and thereby to incur his deep gratitude. And he said that if the child lived and sought to be a worthy man, he would cherish him as much as he would his own cousins and his own nephews.

"Let him be yours," they all said to him. "The gift is well placed. He will be entirely yours. No one will ever reproach you."

Now the two infants had good fathers, but they were not known to be brothers, though it was said that the two looked as alike as if they had been born together. The merchants departed immediately, with the least possible delay. They were ready very quickly, having spent little time in the harbor.

But I have told you enough about them. Listen then to what the king did when he awoke. So maddened was he with grief and anger that he did not know what counsel to take. On waking, he was inconsolable. "Ah, God," he said, "how the base-born merchants have betrayed me! They have taken the queen from me. Wolf, you renewed my grief by carrying off my child. Ah, wolf, damn the day you were born! Now have you had a fine meal of my child whom you have eaten. Now are you stronger and stouter! Ah, wolf, vile hated animal, what a splendid attack of yours in killing an innocent! As for the other child, I shall set off to the harbor, for, whatever distress has been mine, I shall consider myself fortunate if God allows me to recover him."

As best he could, he hastened to the sea, where he expected to find his child. His heart nearly broke when he found no trace of the child. Then all his sorrow began again, his pain increasing and doubling. His heart stopped; his blood surged. His misfortune, however, never caused him to fall into evil despair. On the contrary, he worshipped God and gave Him thanks, always grateful to Him for whatever misfortune befell him. In the end, he remembered the merchant's purse, and now, he said, he was inclined to go to take it and keep it. He then went in that direction. And when he was just about to take hold of it, his hand already stretched out to it, an eagle caught sight of the vermilion purse and came in a wondrous way: it seized the purse from his hands, and delivered him such a blow across the face with its two wings that he fell to the ground.

When the king stood up again, he said, "God is angry with me. Well have I perceived it, and well have I known it. I have been craven in my heart. Out of love for God I have given up the honor and dominion of a realm. Sin took me by such surprise that it blinded me and I became covetous of a bit of wealth. It almost betrayed and killed me. Ah, disloyal Covetousness, you are the root of all evil, you are its source and its well. Covetousness is vile indeed: the man she attacks and captures, the more he has, the more he wants. In such torment is the covetous man, who suffers in abundance, just as Tantalus does, who suffers a wretched existence in hell. There he endures a wretched existence indeed, for the sweet ripe apple hung so near him that his nose touched it, water was up to his mouth, and yet he was languishing of thirst and dying of hunger. He struggled and stretched, extending himself to take the apple. Never could he reach the apple but it escaped his grasp, making him only the more desirous. In such torment and such punishment are many because of Covetousness, who have basketfuls more than they could ever use. He has too much who neither honors nor serves anything. However much he has, it will be of no value to him. Not he who locks away possessions, but he who dispenses and distributes them is the true possessor. This is the person, and so should he be, who has friends, honor, and wealth."

Thus the king reproached and blamed Covetousness, and often he fainted at the thought of his wife and his children. Such was his anger, such was his sorrow, that he could not stay in one place. He did not know where to stop, for his grief led him at random, at one moment retracing his route, at another moving forward. And whatever he did, he always knew grief. Now he sat, now he stood up, now he entered the woods, now he returned. Thus he behaved all day long. And at night he knew no repose, for there was no place he could see where he wished to take rest. Now he wanted to go, now he wanted to sit, now he wanted to go, now he wanted to return. He did not know where to set his mind.

He traveled along by chance up and down, here and there, until he came upon a large crowd of merchants eating off white tablecloths in the meadow; they had made tables with their cloaks, their sacks, and their trunks. The king, pale from grief and hunger, came where he saw them gathered. But it would have been better for him to have fallen among dogs, for he was very likely to be beaten there. Nevertheless he greeted them. "To death! To death! This living devil, this thief!" they cried out. "Let no stick be spared! Let him be beaten and thrashed! Break his arms and legs! Don't let him get away from you! He is, I believe, the master of the order of killers, of murderers. He is its abbot or its cellarer; he is the one who leads all the others. He spies our gold and our silver. If he could join us, he would expect to steal everything from us. Now, quickly, at him!"

The servants leapt forward. With no desire to leave himself in their hands, the king fled—he had no desire to stop—as far as his feet could carry him. Not until daybreak the next morning did he return in their direction. At daybreak the men were about to depart, ready now to lift anchor. The king fell at their feet and begged them, out of love for the true God, to let him board their ship. And he begged them until they agreed. Out of love for God, in Whom they believed, they received him aboard their ship.

They immediately sailed out of the harbor. They crossed the high seas until they safely reached port at Galloway. A wealthy citizen there, who was not a dice player, retained the king as his serving man. The citizen wanted to know his name. The king replied that he would tell the truth, but told him the beginning of his name, speaking in a hidden manner, and left off the ending. "Sir," he said, "I must tell you the truth, and so I tell you. In my land people call me Will."

"Now tell me, Will, what do you know how to do? Can you draw water from the well and skin my eels? Can you groom my horses? Can you stuff my birds? Can you look after my house? If you can take proper care of it, and if you can lead my cart, then you will surely merit the wages I shall pay you."

"Sir," said Will, "I do not refuse any of this, and I will do still more. You will never find me reluctant to do you service."

The king gladly became a servant in the townsman's house, and he never refused any job commanded of him. He did everything without any anger or resentment. He refused no task, no matter how lowly or contemptible it might be. If someone hurled insults at him, neither the abuse nor the insults made him less zealous in his services; rather, he bowed and removed the man's shoes. "Who humbles himself shall be exalted," so it is said, and this is the truth. Humility exalts a man, and elevates him to a position of great honor.

Through his service, the king met with such success that he became steward of the household. Everything was under his control, bread, wine, and all else. The citizen entrusted him with his keys, and the king acted according to his own will. But now I wish to be silent about the king, for it is fitting that I tell you once again about the queen and her life.

The merchants who led away the queen did not stop until they reached Sterling. They dropped anchor and harbored there, staying until the queen recovered. Amid much clamor, a quarrel over her then broke out among the merchants, for she was a source of such pleasure and delight to each of them that each one wanted to have her either by force or by money. But not one of them could explain why he, more than the others, should be her lord. And so the quarrel among them grew until the matter was brought before the country's lord, whose name was Gleolais. This man was not a king, duke, or count, but he was a very fine knight. Roland himself did not excel him! By now he was so elderly and feeble that scarcely a word was said of him, for long years and old age utterly destroy and undermine a man's beauty, strength, and valor. When Gleolais learned of this business, he went to bring among them an accord that treated them all equally; not one of them gained anything. Nor was this all: he had the best and most valuable of their possessions carried away, and he had the queen conducted into his chambers with his wife.

Both the lord and his lady were elderly, and the queen was very beautiful, and shamefaced as a maiden. Because of the queen's openness, the lady held her in great affection, and because of her wisdom and beauty, Gleolais loved her in his heart and concealed his love. So long as he and his wife were together, he never spoke to the queen, so I believe.

The lady died before her lord, and he was left without son or daughter, for they had been childless. Now he believed that things were working out well for him, for he could marry the woman who had been the pleasing object of his attention. For a long time he thought about it without saying anything to her. No longer would his love be concealed from her.

Gleolais called her aside and asked her to be his beloved and his wife: as long as he lived, she would be his sweetheart and his beloved. "Lady," he said, "I give you all my land free and clear as well as myself. My land will be yours more than it will be mine. When I am gone, you will lose nothing, for I do not have an heir who could deprive you of it after my death. Once it is handed over to you and affirmed by my people, there will not be a man on earth to raise a challenge. I do not know what more to promise you. But, I beg you, behold in me your lord and your lover."

The lady bowed to the ground. She remembered that she was a queen. Now she would be the wife of a baron: too debased would be her name! She then pondered how she might respond. She would rather be burned or flayed alive than ever in this way—by force or by entreaty, for land or for property—to have as her lord and lover any man unless it was he who was already hers. She did not know if she would ever have him again; in this matter she had no belief or hope. But for now, she would not agree.

"Dear sir," she said, "listen to me calmly for a moment. May God hear your prayers and recompense you for the kindnesses you did me in your house. Dear sir, now consider carefully whether one should make a lady of a manor out of a serving girl and a peasant. You are a baron and lord of a manor, and my father was a peasant. I am so foolish and wretched that it is a sin for me to be alive. I have done nothing useful or joyous in my life. Listen, if you will, to the truth, but let it be kept secret. Sir, I was a nun who had taken vows. I then left my convent and led a perfidious life. Across the land I made my living on my back, a base, common whore who refused no passerby. But in God's name don't reproach me for telling you my confession. I am a low wanton, and I am contemptible. I should not have such a noble lord. And there is still a graver fault to reveal, if I dared speak, but what I have said should satisfy you."

"Beloved, then keep the rest silent, and know that you are so pleasing in my eyes that for your wisdom and your beauty, I would have you as my wife. Never be dismayed by your past actions, for I have been sullied myself by follies and sins. Often I pursued my own desires. Neither your sins nor your parentage will stop me marrying you. Do you not know that the chestnut, sweet and pleasant as it is, comes from a husk that is painfully prickly and bitter? I do not know who your father was, but were he a king or an emperor, you could not be more worthy. Often one cannot tell from the heir who the father was. Many bad folk come from good stock, and good come from bad stock. Sweetheart, behold your lover, and be my own sweet sister. I am so entirely and wholeheartedly yours that nothing else matters. Never will I cherish you any less. It is honorable to repent of wickedness and folly. The person who fails to repent and reform should be in disgrace. You have repented and reformed. Now God has elevated you to such a height that it is His will that you be my wife."

Tears from the queen's eyes drenched her entire face, and she did not know what to say or do. But though she could not deceive him, she could neither belong to him nor ally herself with him as his wife. She would be pleased to be lady of the land, for better or for worse, and then to hold it after his death, for he was already old and white-haired. On the other hand, she would prefer to be burned alive or drawn by horses than have any carnal relationship with him. The one she wanted, the other she did not. The land she wanted, but she had no care for him. Yet she did give him assurance: he was to grant her a respite of but one year (that was as long as she could delay him), and within the year assure her of his lands by oath.

She then spoke so that he, who loved her so much that he believed everything she told him, would grant her wish. "Dear sir, this is why I ask you for a respite of one year. When I came to repent, I was instructed to do three years of penance, a penance that forbade me the companionship of any man for those three years. Sir, the Apostle of Rome imposed such penance on me. You shall never touch my flesh until these years have all passed. Thus I shall love you ten times more. I have held to this rule for two years, and I have now reached the third. You are able to wait for me until the end of this year. Nevertheless, had God not borne me ill will and my soul not been burdened, you would, by my will, have already married me. But I am a fool to believe you. You are, I believe, making fun of me. Are you mocking me? Don't hide it from me. Don't talk to me of it in jest, for you will win no honor by making fun of a foolish serving girl."

"Ah," he replied, "dear sweetheart, in God's name, do not malign yourself, nor think my words mock you. This matter is so certain that you will know before long whether or not I made fun of you."

"Sir, then grant me the delay I ask of you, for it cannot be otherwise."

"I grant it to you," he answered her. "But be certain that I have no desire to delay the wedding."

And she who was very wise said, "Dear sir, so be it, since this is your will. But do not be displeased about the rest."

Immediately, without seeking delay, he sent word throughout his land that he had resolved to take a wife, and that it was his will that she be honored and served by all. Any worthy man or knight, he added, absent from his wedding feast would be summoned by law. At once diverse people little suited to meeting together, knights, men-at-arms, jugglers, falconers, huntsmen, members of religious orders, and secular canons, assembled at the court. The man who had vowed to wed Gratienne led her before them all. No one laid eyes on her without saying, "This lady is no fool, but my lord acts foolishly. Certainly, if ever I knew a woman, she is taking his land but not him. And he takes her for herself alone, for she has a smooth white neck, a bright face, and a fresh complexion. This sets my lord's heart on fire. She has aroused and excited him, and he has swallowed the bait. But my lord has done a poor job of bird hunting. Who counseled him to wed this unfortunate creature? She will become merry, noble, and arrogant, for she is not yet twenty-six. She will want to fulfill all her own wishes, and my lord will have little of his own. She will consider my lord, as I well know, of less value than a dead dog. What does it matter? Let him do as he pleases. Because of his advanced age, I do not believe that he will see out the year." Thus did they speak among themselves. Others were dancing in rounds, and so joy engulfed the palace.

And then the lord received his wife from the hands of an abbot. There was abundant jeering and laughter, for the marriage was treated with mockery and derision. But there was much joy at the wedding feast. All the court bustled with excitement, and all night long there was dancing and merrymaking.

Be assured that the lord and his lady did not consummate their relationship that night. To tell the truth, neither of them even touched the other. She was pleased, and he was pained. But before the people departed, he wanted them all to do homage to his lady, and they did so since they saw it was his will. All of them paid her homage, and swore to be loyal to her all her life and, if it pleased her, also to love her. This was her wish, and she worked hard to achieve it: she acted with such wisdom and behaved with such kindness that she made all love her. Her gentleness and her nobility won her everyone's love. Each one declared himself happy to do her pleasure. All of them, rivals in their eagerness, believed the time never too soon to honor and serve her. Now, however, I do not wish to spend more time on this subject. I have told you as much as I should at this time about the queen.

Now it is right that you know what happened to the two children. The merchants who raised them had landed in Caithness, where they had had them taken to the church and baptized. They called one Lovel, naming him after the wolf who had been carrying him away in its mouth when the merchants came upon it on the road. And so the wolf was his godfather. They called the other Marin because he had been found on the sea.

After their baptism, the children grew in strength and stature. By the time they were ten, nowhere in the world were there such beautiful children, none more courteous and none more comely, for Nature, which does more than nurture can, gave them these qualities. Nature never fails. She always carries sauces with her, but one is sweet, the other bitter; one murky, the other clear; one is old, the other fresh. In one are cloves, cinnamon, cardamom, and nutmeg blended with pomegranate juice and pure balsam. The other is a dreadful blend, without sugar or honey, but with scammony, bile, venom, and poison; no remedy can cure or save the person whom Nature obliges to consume it. Such nature as is in a man, such is the man. That is the sum of it.

Nature, then, has such great influence that she makes a person good or evil. If a nature could change, the children under the authority of the two churls raising them would have grown in churlishness so that they themselves would have been churls, were Nurture able to combat Nature. But Nature had such a good origin and so gave them such good instructions that they disdained to do evil. The two were unable to imitate the churls who gave them their education. They adhered to their own nobility and improved themselves on their own. From Nature they had all the equipment to exalt and refine themselves. Never did any bad influence germinate, take hold, or root in their hearts, for they immediately severed, eradicated, and uprooted it. But their greatest fortune was to have been raised near each other, and so they knew each other from infancy; there was, though, no other knowledge: they did not know they were brothers. They believed it true that their fathers were those with whom they lived, and they had no suspicion they were related to each other. Yet they were always delighted to be in each other's company.

"Doesn't this child closely resemble the other one?" people said. "Look at his hair. Doesn't the other one have the same hair? And don't they have the same eyes, the same nose, the same mouth, and the same chin? They both behave the same way, and their voices are the same, for if you heard each child separately without seeing them, you would think and believe when you had heard the two of them that only one voice had spoken. And they have such deep affection for each other that they almost call each other brother. There is a marvelous thing about these children: each gives the other counsel, and they do not care for the friendship of other children. This attitude comes, I think, from their nature. And I believe that they scorn others, for they allow none in their company. Damn me by the throat if they were ever forged by Master Foukier or Master Gosselin. And so each man cherishes his own, and they love the children very much, and this is only right, for they are very beautiful and proper. Indeed they seem like twins, and that is how they are. They seem noble and highborn."

Such were the conjectures about the two children among the people, who wished them well for the future. "In truth," they said, "these children no more resemble Master Foukier or Master Gosselin than the evening does the morning."

Despite what was said in the community, the merchants were planning which occupation they would have the children learn, for they would be better at buying and selling if they knew some trade. Master Gosselin wished to make Lovel a skinner of furs, and told him this. But Lovel firmly refused and swore that he would never go to learn unless Marin went with him. And Master Foukier chose the same trade for Marin and informed him so. But the latter replied that, whatever might happen, he would never go to the workshop unless Lovel came with him. Thus both children refused. And the churls, who expended their efforts in vain, threw both children to the ground, and struck them and kicked them, each one in his own house. But such were the children that they dared not utter a cry. One should no more trust a churl when he is angry than a male or female bear. An angry churl is a living devil.

Master Foukier was so furious with Marin, who stood up to him and refused to do his will, that he called him a miserable boy. He had found him on the road, he said, for a serving girl had wrapped him in an old piece of a threadbare coat and placed him on the sea within sight of the forest of Yarmouth. And he had been found in a boat. Now has the churl shown himself! Now have you found the sauce made of scammony! Shamed be the churl's tongue, and God curse his nature! Shamed be his heart and his mouth!

When Marin heard these reproaches, he knew deep shame and deep anguish. Like a base-born scoundrel, the churl beat and battered him. Out of rage and spite, he raced to his chest and took out the piece of cloth that he had put away. He brought it to him and gave it back to him. Marin gladly took it and stuffed it under his cloak, all wrapped up tight; he had put on his cloak so that he might escape from him more quickly. And he fled through the main gate, wiping the tears from his face and his eyes.

Marin knew nothing of Lovel, his dear friend, his companion, whom Master Gosselin had beaten like a mongrel dog, dragged, and, worst of all, insulted as foully as he could: he had taken him from a wolf, he said, wrapped in a piece of an old coat. The churl taunted him in every way; with his foul mouth he said and did the worst he could, as his own nature dictated. Nevertheless, without realizing it and without intending to do good, he did him kindness in returning to the child the piece of cloth in which he had found him wrapped.

Thus the churl's conduct was both good and bad. He acted badly according to his intention, for his sole intent was to do harm. And he acted well in that he pleased the child. Thus he performed a kind act unknowingly. Lovel, who wept so hard that the tears from his eyes wet his face all the way down to his chin, fell to his knees before the merchant and, as he cried, said to him: "Dear sir, you have raised me—God reward you for this!—and until now with much kindness. Now I beg you, by your kindness, that since I must go away, you grant me leave for this parting without anger. For certainly I am entirely yours; I am and I shall be, and as well I ought to be. One should not hate one's master, or despise him, or disdain him, if he beats one for the sake of instruction. It reveals a wicked nature to condemn, for one misdeed alone, the man whose kindness one has tested and from whom one has often received kindness. You, who have done me so much kindness, owed me nothing except out of generosity. And you took such pains with me that you have returned me to myself, as for the first time I now know. Because of you, then, I have my life, for you took me from the wolf when it had snatched me away. My life and all that I am, I am because of you—I acknowledge this—since your efforts on my behalf removed me from such peril. No father could do more for his real son. Now it saddens me to leave you. But rest assured that all the same I will be yours wherever I am, for you should love more the person on whom you have no claim than the person who has a natural right to you, since his is the superior service who knows no obligation to serve."

When the churl had heard the child acknowledge with such kindness the goodness he had shown him, he said to him: "Now be at peace, dear son, for I lied to you. I had hardly uttered the lie when I repented of it. But you should forgive me since I was angered. My words have not hurt you, for tongue lashings do not wound. Be at peace, and stay near me, and learn to earn your livelihood as I did. The wealthy man finds many friends. And the man who has nothing is regarded as nothing: no one will ever associate with him, no one loves him, and no one respects him. If you enter the service of others and you are poor, all those who see you will scorn you, for in these days the wise man who is poor is held a fool in all courts, and the rich man who is a fool is held a wise man. This is the universal practice, and that is why I advise and recommend never to worry about how you amass wealth if you wish to seem a wise man."

The child had no concern for this advice. He had no interest in usury, for his nature rejected it. "Sire," he said, "whether your words be lies or the truth, it is right that you be excused. Never will I bear you ill will. But be assured, I shall obtain leave of you without further delay, or else I shall go without your leave. If you do not give me your leave, I shall depart secretly and stealthily some morning."

[469]

"My dear son, stay this night at least until the morning."

"I have no need of these words. I have no care for your urgings. Were I to leave here now, I would still travel quite a distance today."

"You are not yet ready or equipped as I would wish."

"You do not know what you are talking about. I don't lack anything I am aware of."

"Yes you do: a pair of cowhide boots, spurs, and a coat for the rain. I shall give them to you, although I can ill afford to, as well as a packhorse and a palfrey. My loss of you will then be the greater!"

"Ah sire, God keep you and grant me the power to repay you before I die!"

The merchant gave the child a sackcloth coat, which pleased him, as well as a pair of boots and old spurs. He then had him bridle and saddle two iron-grey packhorses that were large, fast, and good for travel. And for his squire he gave him a servant named Rodain. Lovel had no reason to be annoyed with this—quite the opposite, for he was pleased. He had a bow and arrows, and so he asked the servant to take them, and the latter carried his bow and his arrows. Master Gosselin lent them some coins to the value of one mark, then said to them: "Never stop at any place, I advise and instruct you, unless you see there the chance for your profit. And return to me."

Now Lovel was equipped, and so he took his leave and departed. He was deeply saddened not to see Marin as he left. He thought Marin was in town, just as Marin imagined him to be. The two of them had one and the same thought, ignorant as they were of the adventure that had befallen each of them.

The two boys took the same route. Lovel, who was on horseback, had ridden to the bottom of a hill and saw Marin ahead of him but, not paying close attention, did not recognize him. Still, to make his horse move more quickly, he spurred with such zeal that he made the blood spurt out the sides. Marin saw Lovel galloping down, followed by Rodain, who stayed near him as best he could. He marveled at who the people were but, because of their gallop, feared that they were coming to do him harm, or that they wanted to capture him and lead him back again. He thought he should make every effort to flee as fast as he could. If possible, he would run and take refuge in a forest he saw ahead of him. If he could reach there before they did, they would lose track of him forever and never know his whereabouts, since he was small and slender. If he reached the bushes, he would take shelter there and never be found. Thus, without knowing, Marin sought his own misfortune in his impatience to take cover in the woods. Had he committed a theft, he could not have come there more quickly, even had he seen the provost arriving to take him prisoner.

Lovel was on such a mount that he overtook Marin in no time at all. When the latter saw him, shame immediately colored his face, for he feared that his friend knew the whole truth about the reason for his flight. And Lovel was overjoyed to see that it was his companion. He was not reluctant to dismount quickly, but leapt to the ground and kissed his friend. "Companion," he said, "at this moment I was going my way, deeply discomfited because I did not have you with me. By Saint Peter, I thought you were at your father's house. Now tell me, my dear friend, your father, Master Foukier, is he angry with you?"

Marin then raised his eyes, which he had fixed upon the ground, for he heard that Lovel knew nothing of his adventure. He dared not tell him the whole truth for fear of being shamed. He did tell and recount to him that his father had beaten him and driven him from his house, threatening to pluck out both his eyes, for he had wanted to make him a skinner.

"A skinner? May God never laugh at this! Curses on the craft of skinners, friend, by the faith I owe you. My father, Master Gosselin, wanted to make me do the same. He wanted to make me prepare polecats or sables, I don't know which. Because I dared refuse, he beat me so hard that I am still in pain. Yet according to my wish, I left there of my own free will, thus dressed and thus equipped. If I had had you with me, or if I had known that you were ahead of me, I would have wanted nothing."

"To be honest, my father's angry outbursts would have meant nothing to me if I had only thought to have your company. But now it would be good to know where we should travel."

"Friend, I cannot guess where chance may lead us. We have enough money for this week. Before seven days have passed, chance will have us meet a lord who will retain us in his service. We cannot fail in this."

At that moment they saw a young small deer jump out of a hedge. Marin told Lovel to draw. "And so I shall," he replied, "without fail." Rodain, his squire, gave him an arrow and the curved bow. The deer, which was grazing in a field of oats, awaited the blow. Lovel hit it in the main artery of its heart, and the deer grunted. Marin rejoiced over the blow. Without a swoon, the deer dropped dead.

The boys raced so fast to their game that they became winded. They loaded it on one of their packhorses, and mounted in delight. They were kind enough to have Rodain mount behind one of them. To amuse himself, Lovel shot off showers of arrows through the forest.

They rode along until they reached the base of a fresh spring with pure, clear water. Surrounding it was a beautiful meadow of green grass. And the stream ran along fine gravel that was more brilliant and beautiful than pure shining silver. Noticing a recently built lodge nearby, Lovel and Marin stopped and dismounted. They entered the lodge, where they saw a hunting horn hanging from a beam. Marin looked around and searched everywhere but found no other object. The lodge was well protected against the rain by a thick covering of branches. Neither the spring nor the lodge was unwelcome to the two boys. "My advice is that we take our lodging here," said one of the boys. "Rodain knows the countryside. He will go into a town and get bread, salt, and a flame for the fire."

"I shall be glad to go," he answered. "This path leads straight to an abbey, where I shall find assistance. The monks, I know for certain, will give me bread, salt, and wine."

"Go, and God grant that your words prove true."

He rode off and did not stop until he reached the monk's gate. He asked for all he needed, and it was given to him. He found the cellarer to be most generous, for he denied him nothing. Rodain forgot nothing: he carried a ewer full of wine, a flame for the fire to cook the meat, and a lap full of bread and salt.

The boys had already skinned the deer and cut their steaks when one of them looked around and saw the squire racing up: he traveled at no languid pace. As soon as they caught sight of him, they ran to meet him and cried out to him their welcome. They did not flinch from taking and unloading the wine he brought them to drink, the bread, the salt, and the flame for the fire. All three were cooks and serving boys as they prepared their venison.

It would have pleased them to remain in the forest if they had had time. But before it was the hour to eat, a forester whose duty and office was the surveillance of the forest arrived at the lodging. No one, however rich or powerful, stranger or familiar, dared draw a bow or shoot there. He was angry to find the children inside his recently built lodge. When he entered, Lovel and Marin stood and greeted him. They saw that he was hot and sweating with anger and rage. He did not reply a word to their greeting, but said to them: "Fatal is your capture. By that God in Whom I believe, you have reached a bad port! I shall take you before the king, and for his deer that you have taken, he will have you hanged or dismembered, your hands cut off or your eyes plucked out."

"My dear friend," Lovel replied, "God can defend us against that! We have, I believe, done nothing for which we should hang. Now grant us a truce for tonight, and tomorrow at dawn we shall proceed where you wish. To have this truce and peace, we will give you all our possessions. We have silver to the value of a mark; if you desire it, we will give it to you. Take it now out of your kindness, for we have nothing more here. If we could give you more, there would be no need to demand it."

"I grant you this," he answered, "but put the money in my hand. Then the truce will be properly concluded."

Rodain, who had kept the purse, took it out and opened it. He gave him all the coins. The forester, filled with covetousness, was delighted to have them. He then said to them: "I promise you, you have nothing to fear from me today."

The boys were now reassured, and all night long they made merry as they drank and ate their fill. Since there was no straw or hay, they lay on the ground upon their saddle cushions.

The forester woke them as soon as he caught sight of the dawn. Rodain harnessed the horses for them and had them mount. Having traveled there frequently, the forester took the lead, for he knew the way. They kept straight to their route until, late in the afternoon, they came before the King of Caithness. All three greeted him together. The forester made known to him the truth, which it was his duty to relate. "Sir," he said, "yesterday these boys I have led back to you passed through the woods and shot one of the deer in your forest. That is the reason I have led them to you. If it be your will, exercise your justice. But one should exact no punishment from such children. I would never have taken them, be certain, had I not feared violating my oath and loyalty to you. I took them only out of respect for my oath."

"You have said enough," the king answered, "and you have done as you should. I see that the boys are comely and handsome, and it is my will to retain them at my court. If they are wise and courteous, great advantage could be theirs."

"My lord king," Lovel replied, "nothing else do we seek. Our thanks to you. We are delighted that you have taken us into your care."

"Child," he said, "you are welcome, you and your brother with you. Brothers you are, I believe."

"In God's name," Lovel answered, "dear lord, I do not speak to contradict you, but I invoke Him as witness: we are not brothers or relations."

"Be silent," said the king. "That cannot be. Two children can never be so alike in all ways. You are brothers, but you dare not declare it. No matter. Whether you are brothers or not, tell me your names."

"Sir," he said, "I have no desire to conceal this. My name is Lovel. My companion, whom I love very much, has the name of Marin."

The king asked them no more questions, but commanded one of his serving men to take care of the children and to be their teacher in hunting and hawking in the woods and along the rivers. And this man taught them all concerning hounds and hawks.

Because the king saw the wisdom and bravery of the children, he held them in such affection that at his court they had presents as sumptuous as they wished. He had them furnished with as many horses and clothes as they desired. And the children accompanied the king into the forest. Staying in the woods to shoot their arrows and hunt gave them such delight that they desired never to leave. They hunted deer, doe, and other animals of the forest.

From the boys I return to the king, whom I left at the townsman's home. I have recounted to you so much about the lads that I ought not to tell you more. And so let us begin again with the king. The townsman had put him to such tests that he had found him to be a loyal man. The king was so much in charge of the household that he made no justification or account for any of his spending. The townsman never asked him to render an account, for he had such trust in him since he had witnessed his loyalty.

One day, drawing him aside, the townsman said to him: "Will, if you would, I shall be glad to lend you three hundred pounds from my funds. Travel to buy and to sell in Flanders or England, Provence or Gascony. If you know how to achieve your purpose at Bar, Provins, or Troyes, you cannot fail to grow rich. And I seek no share, but only to have my own back again. Keep all the profit for yourself. The legacy of poverty is harmful, and you have been deeply harmed by it. Were you to make a profit of two hundred marks, I would not take a penny of it."

"Thank you," the king answered. "I wish we already had all the money ready. Since this is your advice to me, I ought to heed your counsel. I shall not miss a market or fair where I can be this year. I know much about leather, alum, and red dye, as well as fox pelts. I shall soon gain a great deal."

The townsman, who had collected all the funds, gave them to him. The king then readied himself to go to markets and fairs. He put all of his money into acquiring catskins that were motley-colored or black. He haunted fairs and markets until he had earned much more than the townsman had lent him, for he was more adventurous and fortunate than all the other merchants.

When the king returned from the fairs, the townsman was astonished at the enormous extent of his earnings, and the king had been away but such a short time! Because the king had been so fortunate in his trading, the townsman esteemed him still further. He loved and respected him even more, and honored him more than he had before. He told the king that he wanted him to accompany his two sons. They would travel together to earn money. His sons would go with him, and both of them would serve him. And he said that he would give them his ship with a freight worth a thousand marks, indeed three thousand. They would travel to Puy and Saint-Gilles, but for their first trip he sent them to England, for a great fair was to take place the following week in Bristol. The townsman wanted his ship to sail there first, and he entrusted his two sons into his care. He ordered his sons to trust Will and never to be so bold as to contradict him. They assured and promised their father that they would always act in exact accordance with his command.

The king, who was impatient to go, and the townsman's sons prepared to travel to Bristol. The ship had a rich cargo, the sea was calm and still, and they were jubilant as they set sail. The skipper's name was Therfes, and he knew a great deal about navigation and about the sea and the stars. With ropes they hoisted the sails, and the ship set on its way, beating and breaking the waves under a heavy wind so that they reached their destination very quickly. The king ordered all their cargo unloaded from the ship, including the gently ambling horses, for these gentle amblers were excellent horses, swift and strong. The men hurried to unload the ship, spending and losing the entire day in the task. The following day they arrived in Bristol.

The land was under the rule of a young man, a nephew of King William. He had been given the realm and the crown, and they had crowned him king because there was no heir closer to the throne who ought to hold the land. The young king had come into the town with a large company of Englishmen the day before King William was to sell his merchandise in another area of the town. And he was a good seller, extolling his wares to those who bargained with him. They did not cheat him in any way, for he was well informed about the value of each article and its proper price.

At the time of his heaviest selling, the king noticed a youth holding a horn and ordered him to approach. The man came over at the first call. The king, ignorant of the man's thinking, asked him what he intended to do with the horn he held. After hearing him, the youth said that he wanted to sell it.

"Then sell it to me."

"Gladly."

"How much do you want?"

"Five pounds exactly."

"Five pounds?"

"Yes."

"And you will have them on condition that you tell me where the horn was found."

"Since you ask me, sir, I shall tell you how I have it. It once happened, I know this well, that King William, my lord, a worthy man I dare declare, disappeared, he and his wife, who was renowned for her goodness, and no one knew what became of them. The servants in their household ransacked the entire hall and took whatever they found there. At the time when this happened, I was very small, still a young child, and I was raised in the king's house. No one pursued me or stopped me, and so I went searching and rummaging all through the house as the adults were doing, and I found the horn under a bed. I stooped down and took it. I do not know if I did anything amiss, but I have guarded it well until this day. Now I want to go in God's name on a pilgrimage to Saint-Gilles. I shall give to the poor in this town what I obtain for this horn. I shall realize no other reward from it."

"You will do well," he answered him. "Perhaps you shall profit still. You may still be rewarded by one you are unaware of."

The king immediately ordered a serving man to pay him the five pounds, and not a penny less. The man at once gave the money to him, though reproaching the king for this transaction. The young man walked through the market distributing all his money wherever he found need.

The people who saw their lord, those who had always known him, were passing in front of him, collecting and gathering there in order to look at him at some length. All day long they came together in front of his stall to see him. They then went off to the king to report that a merchant had been observed in the town who looked so completely like King William that they were very anxious to know whether he was the king or not.

"What is his name?" asked the king. "Have you as yet inquired who he is and from what country?"

"We know nothing, sir, and we made no inquiries of him."

"Then I intend to go there," he said. "I want to speak with the merchant. If he looks like my uncle, we shall be together, and if he believes me, from now on I shall beg him to be with me. I would retain him, for he will make me remember my uncle when I see him. Now let us go, and I shall ask him about his business and his personal situation. I should have been there already, for I am most eager to see this man."

The king then set on his way, mounted on a large Castilian charger. A grand crowd followed him, for they all desired to see the king whom they once loved. But none knew that it was he, for he had been in exile twenty-four years, and no one had had news of him. Had they known the truth, that it was he, they would have been jubilant.

The king did not cease or desist, but spurred ahead of the entire throng following him until he spotted his uncle. When he saw him, he dismounted and hugged him around his neck. He greeted him and embraced him. "Friend," he said, "by Saint Nicholas, how I have longed to see you! Now you must sit beside me, for I want to commune with you and receive your wise counsel."

The king knew him well. "As you wish. But I shall never be at your side. I would sit at your feet, for you seem to me a man of great nobility."

"Do not be afraid. Do not tremble. Seat yourself with confidence beside me. I am king, and you seem a king. You look like an uncle of mine, just as the ruby resembles the carbuncle, and the flowers of the rosebush the rose, for they are one and the same. Because of him, be certain, I love you so much that I nearly call you uncle, lord, and even king. Never have we beheld such a marvel. Never has it happened, nor will it happen. Friend, there will be enough merchants to sell scarlet, alum, red dye, and wax. I have come to tell and entreat you to stay at my court. Your dominion will extend from the source of the Thames all the way to its opening into the sea, so help me God. Unless the idea displeases you, I shall make you my seneschal."

"Seneschal! What good fortune! In truth, sir, I have no desire for this. I could soon climb so high that I would be led to miscount all the steps and to come down. I would be compelled to take such a fall that I would die of grief. One has certainly seen people elevated who fall back down in ignominy and return whence they came. Therefore I have no wish to become involved in this. Now you can make this promise to someone else, for I desire to keep my own occupation. And might it not happen that the king who vanished would return? I would then be forced to take a fall, and so be a merchant again. I have no desire for such a result. You yourself, who are a king, now tell me courteously, what would you do if he returned?"

"I would certainly be very happy, and, so God have mercy on my soul, I would give him back the realm and the crown that I have kept for him, and I would never ask anyone's opinion about it, for I am but vicar, provost, alderman, or mayor. For his sake I wish—and so I beg you—that we be good friends. Never go away from me. Dine each day at my court with all the people who are in your company. When at court, take hay and oats, and when you go your way, your expenses will be paid. Throughout my realm you will be exempt from the duties and tolls the other merchants pay on all their purchases and sales. Now, if you do not mind, tell me your home and your name, for this will be only to your advantage."

"Sir, I am Will of Galloway. Over there I have blue pastel, red dye, alum, and scarlet to color my clothes and my wool."

Like the noble and worthy man he was, the nephew then took leave of his uncle: he offered him good service, and served him even better than he had promised him, and held him in great affection and great honor while he stayed in the town. And the other people loved him so much and showed him such kindness that he could easily see that if he were to acknowledge the truth, things might be just as they once were, that he would have recovered the entire realm of England unencumbered, and there would be no dispute or war. Well he perceived this, and well he knew it. But he stayed in the town without ever revealing his identity.

He did not take leave of his own nephew when it was time to depart the town. One morning he set off. At daybreak Therfes had prepared the ship. Already it was carefully loaded with the finest merchandise available from here to Aleppo. The ship had scarcely left the harbor, and the men were just on the open sea, when the wind began to blow. The sea became choppy, and the wind grew. "Back to the harbor! To the harbor!" the men cried out. But the waves roared, pounding and battering the ship so that both its sides cracked, and the beams nearly broke. The sea, which just before had been smooth, was now full of mountains and valleys. Already the waves were so high and the valleys so deep that the ship could not hold its course but rose and fell with the swell. Everywhere the day was becoming dark, and the wind growing in force. The sky was murky, the darkness thick. The sea now seemed to expand, now seemed to contract. The master mariner was terrified to behold all four winds struggling with one another, and the sea and the air at war, as the thunder roared and the lighting flashed. He abandoned the ship to itself and let it drift. One wave threw it against another, just as one tosses a ball, at one time the ship rising up to the clouds, the next moment plunging into the depths. "Let go the sails! Let go the sails!" shouted Therfes. But all four winds erupted, and snapped and ripped all the ropes and the sail. The canvas flew into a thousand pieces, the sail was in shreds, the mast in splinters.

On board the ship, the men were in utter terror. They invoked God and the cross, and all cried out at the top of their voices: "Saint Nicholas, help! Help! Intercede for us with God that He may take pity on us and bring peace among these winds that war without reason. In their warfare they are killing us. The winds rule this sea, as we can clearly see. They are the masters, as is evident. Whoever pays the price for their discord will never have recompense. To our misfortune do we witness their excess. Shall we be destroyed and killed for their sport? These winds now make war as do lords of the land who burn and ravage castles for their pleasure. Thus we, poor wretches, will pay for the wars of these noble barons. One can compare the sea to the land and the winds to these barons, who devastate the world, just as the winds devastate the waves. Ah, God, calm these winds that are our terror. Before we die, God, guide our ship to harbor, abate this torment for us, and lessen the fury of these winds. If it be Your will, now have they blown enough." Thus did they all call upon the Lord God, but they still wallowed and drifted along their course on the waves. For three days the tempest lasted, and with such violence and such excess that the men never knew where they were, nor did they ever eat or drink. On the fourth day, at the appearance of dawn, the weather became clear, the sea was settled and still, and the winds had made peace. Only one gentle breeze was blowing all alone, which was left to sweep away the clouds and clear the air. Now Therfes was able to get his bearings and identify the country where chance had brought their boat, for they were near a foreign land.

The king called him and addressed him courteously. "Master," he said, "where are we? Do you recognize this town?"

"Sir, I know it well. I will never lie to you about anything. But if you want to take port there, a heavy cost will be exacted from you, and it will be necessary to pay the price. First the lord and then his lady will come to search through the ship. No jewel will ever be so dear, no object so precious, that the lord cannot have it if it delights and pleases him. It is then the lady's turn to choose, and she will take what pleases her. And then the seneschal, without caring whom he grieves, takes his choice. This toll is heavy indeed. But afterwards, from that time on, the merchant can sell what he has at the highest price possible. Never need he fear that someone might steal from him the least valuable object, for the lord would offer him full recompense."

The king said to him that they would take harbor. Whatever the cost, they would never forgo disembarking at once. The master mariner worked very hard, so that through their efforts the men brought the ship into the harbor safe and sound and turned toward the castle. But all this would not be without cost.

When those inside the castle saw the ship, they sent a man-at-arms to inquire if this was a merchant ship. He went there quickly and asked who the people were and from what land. The king himself answered him. "We are merchants from Galloway."

The man-at-arms asked them nothing more but returned to the castle. "Now quickly! Do not delay, for merchants have come to the harbor," he said.

Not another word was said, for the lady of the land—there was no longer a lord—immediately mounted and went to ask for her customary rights. Th seneschal spurred after her, for he had his rights to take at the harbor. The lady arrived there, and when the king saw her, he came at once to greet her. But he was disappointed not to behold her completely, for she had covered her face. Nevertheless he greeted her and said: "Be welcome, my dear lady. Dismount now. I know well what you seek. I know well the custom of this harbor. I carry a richer cargo than any merchant has ever had. I shall be happy if I have objects that are most pleasing to you."

"Friend, I must look over all your belongings one by one. When I have carefully examined each, I shall then take the one that is, to my eyes, the best of all."

The lady then boarded the ship. Her heart beat hard in her breast as she looked carefully at the king, for it was telling her that she had seen him elsewhere. The king had all the most expensive and finest merchandise displayed for her, fabrics fit for an emperor, cloth of gold, quilts, sables, plumes, and ermine furs, silver backgammon boards and gold chessboards. But she was looking at the horn hanging from the ship's mast, and gazed steadily at the horn. No other object did she like as much as the horn she saw. Closely examining both the horn and the king consumed all her attention. She was unable to fix her eyes elsewhere. She made her eyes go from the king to the horn, and brought them back from the horn to the king. She did nothing but look until she came to the foot of the mast. With no desire to go farther, she took the horn and kissed it, showing how much it pleased her. After contemplating it a long time, she returned it without saying a word, then walked back toward the king.

The day had been beautiful, and the queen was now pleased and happy. She sat down beside the king on the ship, and then saw on his little finger a small ring that belonged to his wife: out of love for her, he was still wearing it. On the day he went into exile, he had overlooked it, for it had been tied to his belt by a silk thread. When the lady saw the ring, she did not fail to recognize it. "Dear sir," she said, "I want nothing my eyes behold except that ring you wear. With that, you will have paid in full."

"Ah, lady," answered the king, "do not speak so. I shall never settle my account for so little. The ship's cargo could bring one hundred marks. Take that if you wish. Do not take my ring from me, for the gold and the jewel together are worth no more than an ounce. But by the faith I owe you, I prefer it to everything else. My entire life is on my finger since it wears this ring. Take it from me, and you will kill me."

"Ah, sir merchant, be quiet! It will be very easy for you to buy a similar ring. If I wanted to demand it, you could not refuse me. I am not asking for very much. Since I take so little of your wares, I act foolishly and mistakenly, for this capital is so poor. Such is the practice here that you cannot refuse me anything of yours I would take, provided it be a single possession."

"Lady, it is not wise of you not to take something else. You will have the ring. Keep it now. But I have made you a great gift, for against my will I have torn it from my heart, for it was not on my finger. Now I have given you my life. God grant me and you joy!"

The lady was delighted with his words. She thanked him, then took the ring and put it on her own finger. "Friend," she said, "in return for this ring you shall have no lodging but my castle. You and all your companions shall spend the night under my roof. You shall all come with me, for this is my will and my request."

"Thank you," the king answered.

Those accompanying the lady considered it great folly that she had taken the ring when, had she been wise, she could have had a hundred marks' worth of wares. The seneschal did not leave an apple's worth of his tolls, his customary rights, and his dues, but took the finest of the merchandise there when he could identify it. The lady then returned, leading the king, whom she wished to celebrate, serve, and please with her kindnesses, and his entire company into dinner along with her.

The king had a great desire to see the lady's face. She ordered the tables set up, and this was done; there was no scarcity of servants, and they hurried with the preparations. The lady lowered her veil from her face down to her chin. She was not pale of complexion, and allowed herself to be seen. Water was presented for her beautiful white hands. When the king came to hold the sleeves for her, she spoke to him laughingly: "This merchant is too wealthy to serve so poor a lady. I have nothing to merit your attention to me. Sir merchant, wash now, and place your order with as much authority as if you had reached the place where you would expect to be the most desired guest."

After they had washed, they went and sat down. The lady had her guest sit at her side next to her, and the two dined together. She looked at him, and he at her, until the king recognized for the first time that this was his wife herself who was eating there, and indeed it was she. Each concealed his identity from the other, and so it happened that they did not reveal themselves. They talked about many other subjects until the king saw hounds entering and began to recall his former love of hunting. How willingly and often had he ridden behind the hounds in pursuit of a stag. Nothing had brought him so much pleasure as hunting and shooting in the woods. He entered so deeply into these thoughts that while awake he was beginning to dream.

Do not think me a liar, nor marvel at this. One does indeed dream while awake. Dreams, like thoughts, are of true things as well as of lies. This then is the truth, never doubt it, that the king dreamed while awake. In his dream he seemed to be beside a river, chasing through a forest a stag with sixteen points. Absorbed in his thoughts, he forgot himself completely so that he was calling and urging the hounds to pursue the stag. And all the nobles and the servants in the room heard him call out: "Go! Go! Bliaut, this stag is getting away!"

And they all laughed and joked about this, saying among themselves: "This merchant is a born fool. Look at his bewilderment!"

But the lady, who was more caring of him, drew him toward her, and he gave a start as if he had been sleeping. Tenderly the lady called him by the names of lord and friend, as one whom she loved very much; she put both her arms about his neck and implored him to tell her why he had cried out so loudly. "Lady, I have not forgotten. And since you have asked me, I shall tell you. I was absorbed in my thoughts. The truth is that I was lost in thought, and seemed to be chasing the largest stag I have ever seen. I was so near catching it, the hounds had come so close to it, that it seemed to me they had hold of it. Had I been asleep and dreaming, I could not have believed it with more certainty."

The lady was wise and shrewd. She did not take lightly what her lord had thought, for she perceived well and knew that he would be glad to go hunting. And so she began to embrace him. Her people thought her a fool for hugging her lord, but they were ignorant of the matter. And whatever might be said, she intended to fulfill all his desires if she could. "Sir," she said, "you must go into the woods immediately. Would you thank me if I accompany you there?"

"Would I, lady? Yes indeed, very much. I have not had such a pleasure for more than twenty-four years. Since then I have had hardship enough."

"Sir, I swear to you by Saint Paul and these arms with which I embrace you that if I can do anything, you will see your dream come true before night falls."

The lady immediately gave the command to leash the hounds in pairs and saddle her hunting horses, and she had the hunters prepare themselves.

Soon they were ready to set out, each with all his necessary equipment. They had all taken their horns and their bows, and rode until they reached a clearing where they found the stag of sixteen points. All the hounds started after it, and when the stag took to flight in great leaps, they went hallooing in pursuit. The stag fled, the hounds bayed and darted forth through the forest, the woods reverberated, and the field resounded. The lady spoke to the king and told him of her own adventures, and he told her of his too. Out of love, they both wept tears of joy and compassion. There is no man who, had he heard them confide to each other the tale of their wanderings, would have been so hard of heart that he would not have taken pleasure in the hearing and felt both joy and compassion.

The queen was the first to speak. Without interruption she told him how Gleolais had taken her and made an agreement with her, how he had died within the year, and how the land and the harbor remained in her power uncontested. She continued to speak. "Sir, a king, a neighbor of mine, wanted to marry me and asked for my hand. Because I had no wish to marry him, he issued me a challenge, and since then there has been a hard and desperate war. And this is why I have told you the story: these woods lie between his land and mine. Therefore I would tell, entreat, warn you above all else about a river that divides these woods. If the stag runs in that direction and swims across the water, I advise, counsel, beg you to turn back. Never cross the river, for our enemies are over there."

The king said that if he had not captured the stag before he reached the river, he would, if he remembered, turn back at once. "Dear lord, with this agreement," said the queen, "I grant you leave to chase after the stag. You chase it. I will not join in the chase. I shall amuse myself by ambling along after you at a walk."

The king then left her side. The horn hanging from his neck, the king heard the baying of the hounds in their heated pursuit of the stag. They all pressed forward with such eagerness that the stag dreaded their pursuit, and so fled until it was all hot from its panting and sweating. It rushed toward the river, and all the hunters stayed back. The hounds continued toward the river in furious pursuit of the stag. The king let his hunter gallop freely after the hounds. He did not fear to enter the water, for he saw the stag crossing the water and all the hounds swimming after it. Thus he forgot the queen's instruction and warning, for she had told, entreated, warned him above all else not to cross the river. This was a wasted entreaty. He rushed straight after the stag without looking for another route. The stag made its way across, and all the hounds pursued it so closely that they completely encircled it, caught hold of it by its sinews and thighs, and brought it by force to the ground. When the king saw that the stag was taken, he began to blow his horn to signal the capture. Three times he took breath and blew it, and the sound carried so far that two knights in the forest, who were at war with the lady, heard it. When they heard the sound, they rode at once in that direction as fast as their horses could carry them. Both were equipped in the trappings of war: kneeguards and coats of mail, lances, swords, and shields. In their eagerness, both were coming with one intention: to kill the man or else to take him prisoner and deliver him to their lord. When the king saw them approach, he began to remember, and in his thoughts he recalled that he had violated the order the queen had given him. He saw one knight coming, his sword drawn, and the other clutching his shield. They delivered him a menacing challenge. "Vassal," they said to him, "why, on what counsel, on what authority, have you dared come hunting here?"

The king had dismounted and, hearing their threatening words, did not wait for them in the open field but fled for refuge to an oak tree, leading his horse after him. There he made the oak tree his shield. The two knights shouted, "You have lived too long, vassal, unless you surrender now. Do not defend yourself against us, for you must now die or beg mercy."

The king, who saw his own death facing him, said to them, "Sirs, I wish nothing but mercy. I seek mercy. And I tell you this with all certainty, were you to slay me now, it would soon be the worse for you."

"How? Sir vassal, in what manner? Is this a threat with your entreaty? By delivering a threat, you have asked mercy foolishly."

One of the knights then spoke to the other. "Strike! I don't wish to have mercy, since he threatens me that after his death he will do me the worst he can."

Both then fell upon him. The king, afraid for his life, took cover behind the oak tree and his horse. "Sirs," he called out, "you would do an evil deed in killing me, for you would have slain a king."

"A king?"

"Yes."

"Of what land?"

"Of England."

"Then what have you come here to seek? What adventure brings you here?"

The king told them the entire tale of his exile and his hardship, and the knights dismounted to hear the tale. They listened to him as he told them how he had gone into exile, how soon thereafter his wife and his two sons were taken from him. Both sighed and wept so heavily that it seemed they would never stop. He told them first of the queen whom the merchants had carried away from him, and of the injury they had done him. Their sighs and tears increased when he began to tell them how he had lost his children, how he had ripped the cloth of his coat to wrap them, and how he had carried one to the boat. When he expected to pick up the other one, he saw it carried away by a wolf. For a long time he chased it until, exhausted by fatigue, he found himself forced to sit down on the ground, where he fell asleep. When he returned to the boat, he found no trace of the other child. He did not forget to tell them about the coins and the purse which the merchant had thrown to him, and how the eagle had snatched it from him and knocked him to the ground.

And now miracles happened. From the clouds came the purse with the coins. God sent them as a gift. They were startled when the purse fell among them. The king did not leave it at his feet, but stooped down to pick it up. "Sir, your forgiveness," said one of the knights. "Truly God has shown us in His mercy and His goodness that your tale is true."

The other knight then addressed him. "My dear lord, so help me God, I have never known my father. My father you are, your son I am, for the worthy man who raised me told me that he had taken me from a wolf, and he told me at what time. In an angry outburst of spite, he gave me a strip from the coat in which he had found me wrapped. I still have it. If you wish, you will then know for certain whether or not I am your son. And on account of the wolf, I have the name of Lovel. I have no need to say more since the truth is the witness."

These words overjoyed the other knight, who was stunned and incredulous and said that nothing like this had happened to any mortal man. "God," he said, "has brought me here, for now I know what I did not know. I had my brother here with me without even knowing it. For a very long time we have been companions in good friendship. Now be certain we are companions and brothers. And you, dear sir, are my father. For I was found in the boat, and the truth will be proven when I show you the piece of cloth which I shall find at my lodging. I have kept it to this day."

"Sirs, may God be the source of my finding you," said the king. "I must see and touch both pieces I cut from my coat if you would have me believe you."

"Come along then, and you will see them. Otherwise it would be dangerous to come looking for us by yourself."

"So it shall be," said the king. "Let us cut up our deer first."

"You have spoken well."

They then cut it up. After they had dismembered it, they set off and in time reached their home. They had no desire to do anything until they had seen the pieces of cloth. The king recognized them easily and declared that they were his. Both his sons then rejoiced over him, hugging and kissing him often. Be certain that this delighted the king, who, in his great joy, continued kissing them both and showering them with affection.

Thus all three knew such joy together that their host said that it seemed that they had found a purse. "Dear host, your words are the absolute truth," Lovel said. "A new guest has accompanied us into your house. Him we must honor and celebrate, and rightly so. If you would hear the true story of this, he is the king and lord of England. Therefore I would urge you to have your lord and mine enter at this moment, and thus you will do well. He will be delighted to meet him and make his acquaintance when he comes to see him here."

Without a moment's delay, their host went off to the King of Caithness and told him the news. Astonished by this development, the king mounted and rode along until he reached the lodging. The young men ran to meet him, and taking their father by the hand, they brought him before the King of Caithness. To him they revealed the entire adventure in all its details without omitting anything. And they showed him the sign, the two pieces of cloth, at which the king crossed himself and said that the truth was evident. "What a fine adventure you have found!" he said. "Joy should be yours. Even before I knew anything of your parentage, I had seen such valor in you that I had no hesitation in making you both knights. Well have you deserved this, for many times did you serve me willingly in my war. Many times have you angered the proud lady, the wretch, who will never have peace with me as long as I live unless she marries me or surrenders her land to me. But she evades this, so let her go away."

The king answered, "Without doubt, I promise you, she will surrender it to you tomorrow. Never will there be further strife. If my two sons have helped you, such is their duty, as you know, for you cared for them. But had they known the lady, they should not have done it, for it is a sin and a crime to wage war against your own mother. It is a cruel and bitter war when a son makes war against his mother. When he vexes and angers her, he sins against mankind and against God. Mankind blames him, and God hates him. But such a man may do evil in ignorance. You have done evil, but you did so in ignorance. You acted rightly and reasonably, for you did not know her and you were aiding your lord. Sirs, your mother is the lady whose lands you have ravaged many times with fire and flame. And so in one and the same service you were treacherous and loyal, for you did deeds both good and evil. Neither praise nor blame do I extend to you, ascribing both to you at the same time."

Beside themselves at the revelations they heard, Marin and Lovel wiped their eyes, the tears streaming down their face, for both of them wept from joy. "God! When will it be day?" they said. "Long and annoying will be our wait until tomorrow. Tomorrow she will see both of us, and we shall go and beg mercy. But we must never forget the merchants who raised us. They did so much more for us than they had to, for they owed us nothing. It is right that they see us again. Then they will know what they found. They proved their good worth indeed in caring for us."

Talking on many subjects, they detained the King of Caithness that night at their lodging. Their conversations whiled away much of the night while the servants hurried to prepare and cook the supper.

From here I would like to return to the queen, who was so aggrieved that she wanted to die. "Alas, unfortunate woman," she exclaimed, "the great joy I had in my lord was mine for but a short time. But the joy only increases my grief. The loss of the joy Jesus Christ had given back to me deepens and intensifies my grief. Now I must renew the war against my enemies who have captured and killed my lord. Now quickly, sirs!" she said. "Now quickly! Tomorrow we will march against them. Have it proclaimed that our entire army be assembled at daybreak. Let no one, highborn or low, cavalry or infantry, who can carry lance or bow stay behind. Tomorrow shall I find them all at the crossing."

Already the order was proclaimed throughout the land so that no one, freeman or serf, if he valued his own life, was to fail to cross the ford at the border by six in the morning. There they assembled the next morning, and the queen came there too. None holding back, they set off without delay. Before long, however, they would have an encounter other than the one they were expecting.

In scarcely any time they caught sight of the two kings followed by their people. The two groups were approaching so near that they recognized each other. On seeing the king, the queen was astonished, and her anger softened. She had her men stay back. But the king had no desire to halt, so filled was he with delight and joy. "Lady, welcome!" he said to her.

"Sir, and welcome to you. How have you been held in this land? Tell me this. Are you their prisoner? Or have they set you free? If they seek ransom for you, have no worry, for I have come to give it to them if their people dare wait for mine."

The king laughed at what he heard. He was accompanied by his two sons and the king who had cared for them. "Ah, God," said he, "You smile on us now! How You show us Your favor now! Do you not know, my dear lady, what I have found on this road? Truly, I found your joy and mine in this place yesterday. Happy the time we set out chasing the stag! Happy the time it was found! Happy the time it started off! Happy the time it was overtaken and surrounded! Happy the time it was captured, and happy the time it was slain! We have defeated those at war with you. Here is the King of Caithness. He has come to place himself at your mercy. And do you know who these two are who have caused you so much distress?"

"Do I know, sir? Damn the day these men I behold were born. These men killed all my men. These men have harassed me to the point of death. These men have ravaged and leveled my land to such a degree that outside the walls and fortifications, they have left me nothing worth six pennies. These men were the first messengers who expected to make me marry their lord. These men were the destroyers who took my men and held them for ransom. What can I say in sum? They waged the entire war. They are the most evil on earth. They have caused me so much vexation and anger that I know for certain that they, more than all others, are my mortal enemies."

"No, they are your friends in the flesh."

"Friends? How?"

"They are your sons."

"God," said the lady in response, "is this possible?"

"Yes, without doubt."

Both groups then advanced toward each other when they heard the marvelous news. Immediately the queen took her sons in her two arms, for her heart was sparked with joy, and she hugged and kissed them both. She had no words to express her joy. And the two of them, beside themselves with joy, threw themselves at her feet and together begged her: "Lady, if it seems right to you, forgive us all our misdeeds that we have done against you. We know now that we were wrong, but until now we were ignorant. We thought we were entirely right. Thus we sinned through ignorance, but whoever sins through ignorance does not deserve heavy penance."

"You have won your pardon, for you wanted to do me much greater honor than I ever had. Because of my own interests, I resented you."

The King of Caithness then approached the queen. "Lady," he addressed her, "well I know that in no way did I wrong you. My intention of making you a queen did not warrant your hatred. But I resented what was told me, and I believed them that you were a very lowly woman. I did not know that you were my lady. And so I come at your mercy."

"Your Majesty, it is I who thank you with all my heart for my two sons. With this first word of thanks, you have won from me all over which I have been the lady for a long time. But I add one condition: that my lord the king agrees."

"Agree, lady? But I will this and advise the same, and it still seems to me too little."

"Sir," she said, "I hand it over to you." She then bestowed the land on him, and he accepted it. And immediately, without a moment's delay, they left this area where such joy had been displayed. The queen led both companies with her. No one accompanying her did anything to disturb her pleasure, but they granted all her wishes, and escorted her all the way to Sorlinc in an open display of joy.

Marin and Lovel now wished to send for their merchants. They had only to command, and they gave the order. Messengers set out and searched for them until they found them, and then told and recounted everything to them. The merchants, joyously happy, mounted and rode without delay, night as well as day, following the most direct road. They did not cease galloping until they reached the castle of Sorlinc, where the court had assembled. Nevertheless the place was scarcely to their liking, for they would have much preferred to be at London or Winchester, York or Lincoln. Without making too long a story, know that the court was large indeed, as was the merchant's joy, too. As soon as they reached the court, Marin ran to meet them. And Lovel, who was very astute, made every effort to welcome them, leading them straight before the kings while exerting himself to do them honor. In the hearing of all, Lovel told the tale without feeling any shame in the telling.

"Sirs, sirs, because of these worthy men whom you see here, we are safe and sound. This one snatched me from the cruel wolf and raised me in his house. That one found Marin on the ship and raised him fair and fine. They raised us in kindness, holding nothing back from us, but giving us free access to all their possessions. Now they will have their reward for this. And anyone who does not love them, be certain of this, will not be a good friend of mine."

Scarcely had the queen heard these words than she greeted the merchants. She led them aside away from the crowd. It seemed that she would never sufficiently rejoice over them or honor them. At once she had ermine robes and fur-lined coats given to them that had been in her wardrobe. Very pleased with these clothes, the men considered themselves well recompensed and said that they would sell them and obtain silver and money for them. This made the queen laugh, and as she laughed she said to the merchants: "Sirs, do not worry now. I want you to have these clothes. Wear them with the understanding that ones just as good will often be yours. This is the down payment I offer you. Never will you need anything that will not be freely yours. For the rest of your life, you need never go in search of fairs. I intend to make you and your families wealthy. Samite, purples, reversible cloths, ermine, sable, or fine furs, none of these will you lack, Master Gosselin, nor you either, Master Foukier, for I cherish both of you."

"Lady, do not consider us fools. If these clothes are ours, we could have fourteen pairs of lambskins and woolens made from each one."

"Be silent!"

"Lady, by God's body, we shall never ask to take your clothes, for we shall not be able to sell them."

The queen was very courteous: she took no offense at what she heard, for she could only laugh at the folly of the two peasants. The peasant is a very foolish animal. But before giving them the clothes, she had the idea of giving them the money for the clothes, then giving the clothes back to them. "Sirs," she said, "now sell me these clothes, then take them back again. But the bargain will be concluded on condition that you must wear them afterwards."

They replied that they would be glad to sell them to her for thirty marks, and no less.

"I would not wish to lower the price by a penny, be absolutely certain of that."

"So be it!" they replied. "And we shall be glad to wait one week or even a fortnight."

Then they put on the costly clothes. So foolish and so silly were their appearances and their expressions that they seemed outfitted in borrowed fur-lined clothes and robes.

The two kings, of England and of Caithness, celebrated together for an entire week at Sorlinc. And the land was handed over to the King of Caithness. On the ninth day, without delay, the ships were readied in the harbor. There was no desire for further entertainment, further comfort, or further lingering. Without further ado, having sighted a fair wind, they boarded the ships.

The king had not forgotten to summon his townsman to come to him in England. Therfes had already set out on this matter. And the king had retained with him the townsman's two sons. As king, he promised to give them castles and keeps. Their sea crossing was straightforward, for this time the sea, not agitated, vexed, or angry, caused them no fear or worry.

The king began to speak. "God! How quickly comes joy or grief according to Your wish and will. Ah, God, since I was here, how much grief and distress have I had, and now I have joy and happiness."

He then set out toward the cave, followed by Lovel and Marin. And Master Foukier and Master Gosselin as well as the townsman's two sons were also with them. The king and the queen owed these men greater kindness and greater attention, greater joy and honor than all the others in the company. And so, without doubt, did they behave.

When the king reached the cave, he took the King of Caithness by the hand and said to him: "Sir king, see the bed here, see the bed and the room here—how well I recall and remember!—where the queen was in labor when she delivered her two sons. In that direction I ran after the wolf, chasing it until I was exhausted. Marin was left behind in a boat among the ships. Now I find it so pleasant to recount the heavy hardships and the harm that came to me in this dwelling. The desire has seized me now not to leave here, not to travel to castle or town, until the arrival of my nephew, who is now regarded as king."

They had soon set up their lodging by the cave, and at once news of their arrival spread across the country. His nephew came and gave back to him the crown and all the land.

With a large entourage, the king entered London, where everyone, eager to see him, jubilantly welcomed him. The king stayed in London until the citizen from Galloway, whom he had summoned, arrived. He commanded his men to serve him, love him, and honor him above all others. And the king did as he should and loved and trusted him above all men and made him his first councilor. He knighted both his sons and married them, as the tale tells, to daughters of two wealthy counts, and they both were castellans. As for the young boy who had taken the coins at the Bristol fair for the horn and distributed them, for the good of his soul, to the poor, the king made him his chamberlain and presented him with a most wealthy lady who brought with her a yearly income of a thousand marks. And as

FOR THE TWO MERCHANTS, HE SETTLED ON THEM A YEARLY INCOME OF A
THOUSAND STERLING MARKS. ¶SUCH IS THE CONCLUSION OF THIS
TALE. I KNOW NO MORE OF IT, NOR IS THERE ANY MORE.
ROGER LE COINTE, A COMPANION OF MINE,
WHO IS FRIEND TO MANY WORTHY
MEN, RECOUNTED THE MAT-
TER TO ME.

1. Editions of *William of England*

There are two editions of *William of England:*

(A) Wilmotte, Maurice, ed. Paris: Les Classiques Français du Moyen Age, 1978. This edition follows the text of B.N. fr. 375, the oldest manuscript copy of the romance, dating from the late thirteenth century. The preceding translation follows the Wilmotte edition.

(B) Holden, A. J., ed. Geneva: Droz, 1988. This edition follows the text of Saint John's College, Cambridge, B9, a more recent manuscript copy than B.N. fr. 375, dating from the beginning of the fourteenth century. The same text was printed in Foerster's editions of Chrétien de Troyes.

2. Critical Studies of *William of England*

Francis, E. A. "*Guillaume d'Angleterre.*" In *Studies in French Language, Literature, and History Presented to R. L. Graeme Ritchie.* Cambridge, England: Cambridge University Press, 1949. Pp. 63–76.

Gerould, Gordon Hall. "Forerunners, Congeners, and Derivatives of the Eustace Legend." *PMLA* 19 (1904):335–448.

Legge, M. Dominica. "The Dedication of *Guillaume d'Angleterre.*" In *Medieval Miscellany Presented to Eugène Vinaver by Pupils, Colleagues, and Friends,* ed. F. Whitehead, A. H. Diverres, and F. E. Sutcliffe. Manchester, England: Manchester University Press, 1965. Pp. 196–205.

Lonigan, Paul R. "The Authorship of *Guillaume d'Angleterre:* A New Approach." *SFr* 47–48 (1972):308–314.

Mickel, Emanuel J., Jr. "Studies and Reflections on Chrétien's *Guillaume d'Angleterre.*" *KRQ* 33 (1986):393–406.

———. "Theme and Narrative Structure in *Guillaume d'Angleterre.* In *The Sower and His Seed: Essays on Chrétien de Troyes,* ed. Rupert T. Pickens. Lexington, Ky.: French Forum, 1983. Pp. 52–65.

Robertson, Howard S. "The Authorship of the *Guillaume d'Angleterre.*" *RomN* 4 (1962):156–60.

———. "Four Romance Versions of the William of England Legend." *RomN* 3 (1962):75–80.

Sturm-Maddox, Sara. " 'Si m'est jugie et destinee': On *Guillaume d'Angleterre.*" In *The Sower and His Seed: Essays on Chrétien de Troyes,* ed. Rupert T. Pickens. Lexington, Ky.: French Forum, 1983. Pp. 66–80.

Williams, Harry F. "The Authorship of *Guillaume d'Angleterre.*" *SAR* 51 (1987):17–24.

VARIANT READINGS OF THE MANUSCRIPT

Although the base text for the translations is MS B.N. 794, I have rejected a few readings and substituted from B.N. 1374, B.N. 1433, B.N. 1450, B.N. 12560, B.N. 12576, the Annonay fragments, and Vatican Library 1725. The rejections are comparatively few, and I include here only substantive variant readings that alter the translation. The rejected reading is listed in parentheses and preceded by the reading adopted. For the sake of convenience, the numbering of the lines follows the numbering in the Classiques Français du Moyen Age texts.

EREC AND ENIDE

352	mues	(mue)
408	cotes	(costez)
1290	vavasors	(chevaliers)
1321	dun	(dui)
1322	valt mie	(ualent pas)
1369	vair	(bai)
1571	la vert porpre	(lautre robe)
1648	or	(qui)
1711	mervoille	(uermoille)
1858	li messagier	(tot maintenant)
1949	seignorie	(conpaignie)
2075–79	mesire G. savanca qui dune part le fianca antre Evroic et Tenebroc et Melis et Meliadoc lont fiancie daltre partie	(antre Erec et Tenebroc et Melic et Meliadoc mes sire Gauvains savanca de lautre part le fianca ensi fu fete lanhatie)
2200	tant	(molt)

2419	ot	(a)
2438	queroit	(quierent)
2819	point	(joint)
2824	joindre	(poindre)
3202	denor	(damor)
3266	acote	(acointie)
3299	seoir	(joer)
3662	les	(le)
3774	blesse et anpire	(sache et detire)
3778	les escuz	(li escu)
3935	sot	(et)
3954	despee	(despees)

after 4002, add:
se mes consax en est creus
si bien ni estes conneus

4203	le roi	(.e.) [Erec]
4204	Erec	(le roi)
4205	lavees	(bandees)
4206	rebandees	(relavees)
4306	ses mains et ses crins descirant	(et ses dras trestoz desirant)
4322	de mort	(.e.) [Erec]

after 4488, add:
Cadoc de Tabriol ai non
sachiez quensi mapele lon
mes quant de vos partir mestuet
savoir voldroie sestre puet
qui vos estes et de quel terre
ou vos porrai trover ne querre
ja mes quant de ci partirai
ja ce amis ne vos dirai
fet Erec ja plus nan parlez
mais se vos savoir le volez

4577	descirer	(dessirier)
4998	mar	(car)
5527	gaster	(haster)
5682	vet	(vont)
6049	me fainsisse	(mespreisse)
6167	a cui que il desabelisse	(a cui quil onques abelisse)
6393	borc	(bois)

6669	don et	(de lun)
6684	lune i portraist geometrie	(an fu louraigne establie)
6685	ele	(il)
6710	son de corde	(sanz descorde)
6724	consoillent	(consoille)
6725	les	(li)
6735	cos	(cors)
6755	Gavoie	(Savoie)
6767	Gavoie	(Savoie)
6839	textes	(teptre)

after 6878, add:

que a raconter le mangier
asez an orent sanz dangier
a grant joie et a grant plante
servi furent a volante
qant cele feste fu finee
li rois departi lasanblee
des rois et des dus et des contes
don asez estoit granz li contes
des autres genz et des menues
qui a la feste sont venues
molt lor ot done largemant
chevax et armes et argent
dras et pailes de mainte guise
por ce quil iert de grant franchise
et por Erec quil ama tant
li contes fine ci a tant

CLIGES

64	il ne deigna	(il deigna)
526	lor	(li)
559	que	(car)
568	celi qui por samor	(celui por qui amor)
590	cil plus	(cil qui)
592	que cil	(est cil)
625	que je veul	(que veul)
728	luevre de fors quex	(la lumiere queus)
800	el front	(le front)
1025	despoir	(mervoil)
1034	ferai	(serai)

1155	esprover	(escouter)
1251–52	loz est sor Tamise logiee tote la pree est herbergiee	(loz est sor la pree logiee tote Tamise est herbergiee)
1253	verz	(viez)
1398	quil eust non	(quil mapelast)
1518	mout	(mon)
1951	li vint	(li .x.)
1957	li vint	(li dis)
2060	refont	(refet)
2144	se	(et)
2219	tre	(tref)
2321	perdre	(perdrer)
2406	li mois	(la nuiz)
2658	an	(ab)
2749	darc	(dart)
2822	qui a lempereor	(qui la besoigne li)
2842	a trois canz	(a .iii.)
2877	il est preuz	(il preuz)
2922	cil li rant	(cil le part)
4198	vos	(moi)
4418	tant het et	(tant et)
4451	mes	(car)
4470	cors	(cuer)
5017	en un panser	(en volente)
5124	vos	(moi)
5450	lose	(toche)
5500	la torz	(le jor)
5607	li	(la)
5684	an	(ne)
5730	quonques Dex	(que onques)
5755	desver toz li mondes	(desirrer toz li monz)
5811	cort	(tor)
5960	mander	(mandre)
6010–11	or soit en leu de saintuaire lempererriz dedanz anclose	(quan ni meist fors saintuaire lempererriz i est anclose)
6169	ma vie	(mamie)
6293	torz	(corz)

6384   trape   (trace)

after 6464, add:

> mais par ce me vueil rescuser
> que sers ne doit rien refuser
> que ses droiz sires li coment
> ce set an bien certainement
> que je suis suans et la tor soe
> non est Johans ancois est toue
> moie sire vere apres lui
> ne je meismes miens ne sui
> ne je nei chose qui soit moie
> sil meismes ne la motroie
> [et] se ce vos voliez dire
> que ver vos est mespris mesires
> je suis prez quil vos en defande
> sanz ce que il nos me comande
> mais ce me done hardement
> de dire tout seurement
> ma volante et ma gorgiee
> tele com lai fete et forgiee
> car bien sai que morir mestuet
> or soit ainsins com estre puet
> que se je mur por mon seignor
> ne morrei pas a desennor
> car bien sevent tuit sen dotance
> lou seremant et [la] fiance
> que vos plevites vostre frere
> apres vous seroit amperere
> Cliges qui sen vet en essil
> mais se Deu plaist ancor liert il
> et de ce fetes a reprendre
> que fame ne deviiez prendre
> mais totes voies la preistes
> et vers Cliges vos meffeites
> il nest de rien vers vos mefez
> et se je sui por lui desfez

6621   retorne   (atorne)

after 6638, add:

> et chascun jor lor amors crut

THE KNIGHT OF THE CART

209   ha ha   (ha rois)

290   besoigne en est   (besoigne nest)

484	tient	(taint)
686	ces deus voies	(ces voies)

after 752, add:

mes li chevaliers ne lot mie
et cil tierce foiz li escrie
chevalier nentrez mi el gue
sor ma desfense et sor mon gre
que par mon chief je vos ferrai
si tost come el gue vos verrai

792	le feistes	(me feristes)
859	antrevienent	(antrevient)
961	travail	(orguel)
1128	si regarde amont vers la feste	(et garde amont par la fenestre)
1468	sain	(soing)
1871	autres	(autre)
1888	defors et dedanz	(dedanz et defors)
2327	vont tant quil	(tant que il)
2329	que cil fu fors	(quil furent fors)
2330	li lessierent apres le cors	(lor lessierent apres les cors)
2537	trois corz	(ii. corz)
2550	trois ostes	(ii. ostes)
2555	li mandre	(li miaudres)
2798	besoing	(besoig)
2961	a maint autre	(au moins autrui)
2971	se mestier aviez	(boen mestier avriez)
3097	desarme	(desire)
3316	tarir	(garnir)
3675	laparcut	(saparcut)
3857	set que cist locirroit	(sai que cist tocirroit)
3858	les	(vos)
3913	presse	(feste)
4275	ocirra	(ocirrai)
4276	morz qui onques ne desirra	(comant nautrement nen porrai)
4443	prindrent	(pristrent)
4641	once san creva	(ongle san crena)

after 4762, add:

molt a or bele garde feite
mes pere qui por moi vos gueite

4891	mamet	(mamez)
4921	loent	(losent)
5220	jen sui priez	(jen preiez)
5349	li prison	(si prison)
5362	les dames et les	(li dameisel les)
5394	venist	(venir)
5586	la se sont les dames atraites	(la si se sont landemain traites)
5704	tot le jor	(tote nuit)
5810	Keus	(cuens)
5861	mervoilles	(vermoilles)
5876	pucele	(pucel)
5924	esbai	(esbaudi)
5984	et cil qui gaber le soloient	(et cil chevalier le suioient)
6044	en ont	(en a)
6222	rachat	(rabat)
6320	a lore	(luevre)
6343	resvez	(resbez)
6382	quan	(quant)
6474	ti fioies	(le feisoies)
6522	redi je mie	(redi mie)
6589	toz jorz mes	(toz mes)
6614	a plante corde	(plante de corde)
6670	nest mie moins	(nest moins)
6794	detenant	(decevant)
6807	ja set	(va san)
6891	quil san lot	(quil lot)
7041	lautres	(lautre et)

THE KNIGHT WITH THE LION

166	voie	(voiz)
222–23	li un correrent au cheval que li bons vavasors tenoit	(je descendi de mon cheval et uns des sergens le prenoit)
278	espaarz	(lieparz)
358	ce voiz	(fet il)
373	tu li	(ne li)

after 422, add:

quele boloit com iaue chaude

543	puis	(nus)
683	savoit	(savroit)
701	lande	(bande)
708	les tors	(la tor)
713	de ferron	(desperon)
717	fera	(ferai)
796	mes plus de cent	(mes de cent)
906	jusqua	(parmi)
921	desoz*	(desus)
949	fors que tant	(maintenant)
1063	mes qui que	(mes qui)
1088	aunee	(atornee)
1225	devant moi	(devant)
1275	antancion	(en la meison)
1311	diaus	(dist)
1360	cucre et de ses bresches	(cuer et de ses lermes)
1507	nes Deus	(nus daus)
1530	eles	(ele)
1535	retienent	(retient)
1536	vienent	(vient)
1590	ce que il	(ce quele)
1591	quant	(que)
1664	molt	(se)
1671	que	(qui)
1673	laissiez seviax	(lessesiez viax)
1793	amander	(comander)
1888	quele ne li	(quele li)
2019	cuers	(cors)
2114	contredeist	(contreist)
2159	dame i ot	(dameisele ot)
2173	durerent	(durererent)
2220	la pluie	(sanuie)
2346	le roi que il	(la joie quil)

*I have followed Foerster's reading.

2444	et li autre santredonoient	(li uns a lautre se donoient)
2445	car dames	(que dautres)
2446	dont chascune	(que aucune)
2497	samor	(senor)
2600	atant	(desfant)
2654	la vie	(lame)
2661	sovant	(se vant)
2662	traiste	(traite)
2705	honte	(hont)
2768	trespassa	(tresposa)
2840	siaue nete	(sa porrete)
2850	sauce	(force)
2851	bien destanpree et bien confite	(desatranpree et desconfite)
3015	rot	(tot)
3084	desor .i. pont	(a oripont)

after 3115, add:

tele hore cuide an desirrer

3117	son	(sot)
3169	povre cuer et lasche	(poinne ovrer antasche)
3170	antasche	(alasche)
3179	lestor	(la tor)
3228	quil nes pecoit et demant autre	(com il pecoie devant autre)
3336	plus	(plust)
3374	en terre	(enz terre)
3435	un brachet	(uns brachez)
3508	qui	(quil)
3575	diax quant il la	(de qanquil a)
3595	dirai	(dira)
3606	oil	(cil)
3773	si rese	(remese)
3808	menor	(greignor)
3819	talant nen	(parole en)
3918	que il	(qui il)
4066	que il	(quele)
4068	miax	(moiax)
4145	vos	(nos)
4192	vint	(mut)

4283	et il	(et il li)
4421	seroie or mal afeitiez	(feroie ore quafeitiez)
4438	retient	(retint)
4458	pais	(paist)
4545	tort	(tor)
4563	dame	(dameisele)
4768	ving	(vieng)
4797	.xl.	.xiiii.
4819	amee	(acointe)
4853	pria	(cria)
4873	adreca	(asena)
5008	ses	(sel)
5195	cotes	(codes)
5197	as dos sales	(as cos pales)
5280	que	(et)
5309	.xx.	(.v.)
5349	les cuidoient	(lun an cuident)
5362	acoter	(acoder)
5379	nest droiz que nus garir en	(nest que nus pener i)
5425	en a honte	(en la bote)
5428	poi	(preu)
5466	soit droiz ou	(soit ou)
5470	fille a seignor	(fille et senors)
5482	fille a per	(fille avrez)
5483	doit avoir	(et ma fille)
5484	cil qui porra	(se cez porrez)
5485	caus qui	(que ja)
5507	au	(dun)
5606	si anserre	(et desserre)
5742	man maine	(molt maime)
5838	quarantaine	(quinzainne)
5879	en apert	(desapert)
5880	cort	(cor)
6041	ont	(sont)
6042	a tes amis	(a celamis)
6044	sentraimment	(santremet)
6047	avugle tote	(asez trop glote)

6070	jur et afi	(jur afi)
6238	mervoilles	(merevoilles)
6266	ansanglantee	(ansanglante)
6279	qui	(que)
6344	sanc	(san)
6423	por ce	(force)
6568	a ton los	(an toz leus)
6586	que	(qui)

THE STORY OF THE GRAIL

31	qui	(et)
70	fueillent	(fuelles)
97	lancant	(lancent)
187	sire	(amis)
299	erent	(herent)
414	si haut	(vostre)
442	la	(sa)
443	rois	(morz)
447	foir	(poir)
450	ne poit foir	(foir car a)
477	li	(lor)
549	a sa ceinture	(sa ceinture ou)
580	cui	(que)
639	biax	(granz)
640	vermoille	(mervoille)
641–42	et lautre fu dorfois bandee desus ot une aigle doree	(lune partie fu doree et lautre fu dorfois bandee)
813	cui	(qui)
992	al	(le)
1025	veer	(doner)
1113	el	(del)
1145	ses	(sest)
1153	mout	(avoit)
1178	le hiaume	(la coiffe)
1196	la meissele	(la memele)
1248	li fos	(li feus)

1250	mout liez	(iriez)
1266	le cote	(le col)
1276	por ce que au roi despleust	(que au roi por ce despleuz)
1336	dedanz	(devant)
1401	si	(se)
1463	us	(ialz)
1507	ancontriez	(ancotriez)
1516	an	(a)

after 1624, two lines have been deleted:

> et li prodom sest abeissie
> se li a lesperon chaucie

1648	puet	(doit)
1649	ne	(li)
1745	quan san poist	(quan poist)
1836	mes se	(mes qui)
1909	qui est prieus	(mout glorieus)
1917	mises	(mise)
1971	sent	(voit)
2018	len	(se)
2053	lez	(lons)
2132	quele li a mis en corage	(qui li a mis el cors la rage)
2161	cuidoit bien	(cuidoient)
2169	tantost quAnguinguerrons	(tant que Anguinguerrons)
2245	mes non pas tant quil	(non pas tant que il)
2246	ne leust	(nos eust)
2308	la iert ma morz se	(einz moci tu que)
2414	qui se deporte	(devant la porte)
2438	la porte	(les portes)
2465	porte	(portes)
2510	font tres et paveillons	(ont fet son pavellon)
2527	devant	(desor)
2572	li vaslez	(longuement)
2625	einz	(an)
2661	devant	(desor)
2684	quil	(qui)

After 2918, add:

> plus grant que de nule autre chose
> congie prendre a samie nose

2920	sa gant	(gent)
3024	fete	(ferte)
3041	peschierres	(chevaliers)
3060	quatre	(troi)

After 3092, add:

cil qui li amainent son oste
si que chascuns li fu dencoste

3106	que je le vos comant	(jel vos lo bonement)
3156	destinee	(destine)
3164	et sachiez que	(mout lesgarde)
3182	entre	(delez)
3183	et ces qui el lit	(de ces qui leanz)
3191	ert	(est)
3215	quausi	(ausi)
3228–29	tot ausi com passa la lance	(tot autresi com de la lance
	par devant le lit sen passerent	par de devant lui trespasserent)
3236	si	(se)
3240	ou bien lan	(bien lor an)
3242	as vallez	(au vaslet)
3302	qui	(einz)
3313	mugates	(mugaces)
3314	grenates	(grenaces)

After 3354, two lines have been
removed and placed after 3376:

por ce que riens nel retenist
de quel ore que il venist

3412	quil i ot une trace	(que il i ot une tor)
3413	chevax	(chastiax)
3428	quasez mialz esploitie eust	(que de mort garanti leust)
3429	la morz qui si	(sa mort trop fort)
3436	en giete	(regiete)
3474	cleremant	(hautemant)
3488	najant	(naigent)
3536	char	(sanc)
3672	ce me seroit mout	(fet il ice mest)
3678	tant quil	(que il)
3679	dun	(un)
3685	sanbloit ·	(sanble)

3705	estoit	(estest)
3706	quele vestoit	(que ele vest)
3709	rotures	(costures)

After 3712, add:

ausi com sil fust fait de jarse
que ele avoit crevee et arse

3719	sain li avaloient	(manton li coloient)
3832	galois i vint	(del bois revint)
3853	rue	(tue)
3871	reving	(le vi)
3971	sejorner	(atorner)

After 4100, add:

que maintenant les ailles prendre
cil qui ne sot le gab antandre

After 4177, add:

por esgarder cele sanblance
que li sans et la nois ansanble

4178	la fresche color li resanble	(que la fresche color li sanble)
4189	les gotes	(la gote)
4291	qui maintes foiz devine lot	(si con li fos devine)
4404	assises	(remises)
4530	la vostre	(fet il)
4544	que	(qant)
4600	crot	(croit)
4606	bos	(los)
4614	les chevaliers	(le chevalier)
4643	et si	(a lui)
4697	Do	(Nut)
4719	lautre et dit	(lautre dit)
4734	seignor	(pere)
4777	.vii. escuz	(.ii. escuz)
4781	mainte	(maint)
4817	comanda	(demanda)
4844	sor	(qua)
4898	ot	(ont)
4932	.ii.	(.vii.)
4933	.ii.	(.vii.)
4937	.ii.	(.vii.)

4985	nan	(san)
4986	lor	(li)
5047	bien le	(ce me)
5106	mes	(me)
5174	del chastel	(de la tor)
5180	por	(de)
5188–90	car cil ne losera desfendre	(un chevalier qui sanz desfandre
	qui la amene en la vile	sert ceanz de malvese guile
	quil vit de molt malvaise guile	sa amene an ceste vile)
5272	li	(lor)
5299	sa petite	(li sires sa)

After 5320, add:

> est ele vostre fille donques
> oil mais ne vos en caille onques
> fait li sires de sa parole
> enfes est niche chose fole
> certes fait mesire Gavains
> dont seroie je tro[p] vilains
> se sa volente ne savoie
> dites moi fait il tote voie
> mes enfes dols et debonaire
> quel droit je vos porroie faire
> de vostre seror et coment
> sire demain tant solement
> se vos plaist por amor de moi
> porterez armes au tornoi
> dites moi dont amie chiere
> sonques mais feistes proiere
> a chevalier por nul besoing
> nenil sire nen aiez soing
> fait li sire que quele die
> nentendez pas a se folie
> et mesire Gavains li dist
> sire se Damediex mait

5328	que	(qui)
5393	et cest	(tot)
5419	crever	(lever)
5539	qui	(dom)
5608	Yvonet	(Yvonez)
5616	cheval	(escu)
5638	dun	(del)
5709	joiax	(oisiax)

5719	tor	(cort)
5779	quil	(qui)
5800	arriere	(a terre)

After 5820, add:

cele qui nestoit pas seure
quant ele lot de larmeure
bien armé si douterent mains
et ele et mesire Gavains
mais que tant de meschief i ot
que descu point avoir ne pot
si fist escu dun eschequier
et dist amie je ne quier
que vos mailliez autre escu querre
lors versa les esches a terre
divoire furent dis tans gros
que autre eskec de plus dur os
or mais qui que doie venir
cuidera bien contretenir
luis et lentree de la tor
quil avoit cainte Escalibor
la meillor espee qui fust
quele trenche fer com fust
et cil fors sen fu avalez
et trove seant lez a lez
une assamblee de voisins
le maieur et les eschevins
et dautres borjois grant fuison
qui pas navoient pris poison
quil estoient et gros et cras
et cil vint la plus que le pas
criant or as armes seignor
salons prendre le traitor
Gavain qui mon seignor ocist
ou est ou est fait cil et cist
par foi fait il je lai trove
Gavain le traitor prove
en cele tor ou il saaise
nostre pucele acole et bese
ne ele nel contredist rien
aincois li plaist et sel velt bien
mais or venez si lirons prendre
sa mon seignor le poez rendre
molt lares bien a gre servi
li traitres a deservi
quil soit a honte demenez
et neporoec vif le prenes

quil lameroit mix vif que mort
me sire et si naroit pas tort
que chose morte rien ne doute
estormissiez la vile toute
si faites che que vos devez
tantost sest li maires levez
et tot li eschevin apres
lors veissiez vilains engrez
qui prenent haces et gisarmes
cist prent un escu sanz enarmes
cist prent un huis et cist un van
li crieres crie le ban
et trestoz li pules aune
sonent li saint de la comune
por che que nus nen i remaigne
ni a si malvais qui ne praigne
forche ou flael ou pic ou mache
onques por tuer la limace
not en Lombardie tel noise
ni a si malvais qui ni voise
et qui alcune arme ni port
hez vos monseignor Gavain mort
se Damediex ne le conseille
la damoisele sapareille
por lui aidier come hardie
et a le commune sescrie
hui hui fait ele vilenaille
chien esragie pute servaille
quels dyables vos a mandez
que querez vos que demandez
que ja Diex joie ne vos doint
si mait Diex nen menrez point
del chevalier qui est caians
ainz en i avra ne sai quans
se Dieu plaist mors et affolez
il nest pas caiens avolez
ne venus par voie reposte
aincois le menvoia a hoste
mes frere et molt proie en fui
quautretant feisse de lui
com del cors mon frere demaine
et tenez vos ment a vilaine
se por sa proiere li faz
compaignie joie et solas
qui oir le volra si loie
conques por el ne li fis joie
nautre folie ni pensai

por che plus mal gre vos en sai
que vos si grant honte me faites
qui vos espees avez traites
a luis de ma chambre sor moi
si ne savez dire por coi
et se vos dire le savez
araisonne ne men avez
si me vient molt a grant despit
que que cele son talent dist
et cil luis a force pechoient
a cuignies que il tenoient
si lont en deus moitie[s] fendu
et molt lor a bien desfendu
li portiers qui dedens estoit
a lespee que il tenoit
a si le premerain paie
que li autre en sont esmaie
ne nus avant traire ne sose
chascuns garde la soie chose
que chascuns de sa teste crient
nus si hardis avant ne vient
qui le portier tant [ne] redout
ja niert teus qua la main i tout
ne que il voist avant un pas
le damoise[le] les eschas
qui jurent sor le pavement
lor rue molt ireement
si sest estrainte et secorchie
et jure come correchie
quele les fera toz destruire
sele onques puet, ains quele muire
mais le vilain arriere vont
si safichent quil abatront
sor aus la tour sil ne se rendent
et cil mix et mix se desfendent
de gros esches que il lor ruent
li pluisor arriere sen fuient
qui lor assaut soffrir ne puent
et a pis dacier la tor fuent
ausi com por la tor abatre
quasalir nosent ne combatre
a luis qui bien lor est vees
de luis se vos plaist me creez
quil estoit si estrois et bas
quensamble ni entraissent pas
doi home sa molt paine non
por che le pooit uns preudom

bien contretenir et desfendre
por homes desarmez porfendre
dusques dens et escerveler

Delete lines 5821–23

5873	menuie	(me mervoil)
5874	se	(et)
5901	qui nan revoldroit	(cil qui nan voldroit)
5916	il est ci	(ge vos di) ·
5932	manbre	(tranble)
5945	li	(uns)
5962	sest	(ert)
5988	un mout	(a un)
5989	fors tret	(fet traire)

After 5989, add:

et il a le seremant fet

6016	demora	(anplea)
6053	nul	(an)
6131	un	(le)
6146	li prie	(prie Dieu)

After 6162, add:

et de cele gote de sanc
que de la pointe del fer blanc
vi pandre rien nan demandai
onques puis certes namandai

6241	montrer	(entrer)

After 6248, add:

se pucele aide te quiert
aiue li que miex ten iert
ou veve dame ou orfenine
iceste almosne est enterine

After 6278, add:

mes il ni ot se betes non
cerfueil laitues et cresson
et mill et pain dorge et davaine
et iaue de clere fontaine

6294	la tor	(prison)

After 6298, add:

trop bien foillu por onbre randre
au chasne vit un escu pandre

6299	delez une lance droite	(une lance tote droite)

6309	et	(ou)
6311	eust montee cele angarde	(et eust montee langarde)
6321	es ialz el front et an la boche	(les ialz et le front et la boche)
6360	nan pot	(ne pot)
6393–94	que ja aveigne que nus lait ne vos ne autres por nul pleit	(que se il avient por nul pleit que vos ne altres ne nus leit)
6436	an un prael	(ot un pomel)
6476	doels	(ire)
6508	deable tardent	(que deable ardent)
6532	que	(et)
6685	si na pas	(se il na)
6752	forchiee	(tondue)

After 6812, add:

> tant que ge soie anhuliez
> et confes et comeniez

6918	tos	(tex)
6921	lons	(durs)
6923	durs	(lons)
6930	foibles	(foible)
6966	chevauchent	(chevauche)
6973	sil	(cil)
6974	an un si felon	(e an un si dur)

After 7020, add:

> et sor le perron fu la clef
> de coi fermee fu la nef

| 7045 | gehui | (gehuir) |

After 7069, add:

> qui de la sont cointes et beles
> apoiees a ces fenestres

7228	et san demeinne	(grant joie an meinne)
7248	autresi	(avoec li)

After 7320, add:

> lor barbes chascune semainne
> san i a .c. plus blans que lainne

7377	iroiz	(eroiz)
7428	verdeles	(verdes)
7464	tot enmi	(toz coverz)
7468	au chief desus avoit verrieres	(de bone oevre et de colors chieres)

7469	cleres	(clere)
7470	le voirre	(livoire)
7473	li voirres	(lyvoires)
7523	ferir	(foir)
7546	mes il	(et quil)
7692	eles	(ele)
7724	li	(si)
7746	vont	(mont)
7785	dolante	(pansive)
7806	autres	(autre)
7884	quanz	(quant)
7905	ra	(a)

After 7985, add:

       tuit blanc et li altre mesloient

7987	de chenes	(tuit chenu et)
7997	la trinite	(Natevite)
8004	et quant il volt aler	(encois que il salast)
8130	de mere nez	(ne passa mer)
8172	bordes	(jengles)
8273	peitrax	(preitrax)

After 8284, add:

       sel salua et si li dist
       biaus sire cil Dex qui vos fist

8285	bel sor tote autre criature	(biax fu sor tote creature)
8286	il vos	(Dex vos)
8289	si	(se)
8298	mene	(mena)
8408	gi	(ge)
8410	nus liz ne	(nule ne)
8650	pucele	(puce)
8675	gehui	(gehuir)

After 8770, add:

       que par mame je ne voldroie
       plus sa pesance que la moie

After 8790, add:

       et quil laint tant et ele lui
       quil soient come frere et suer

8796	li uns de lautre	(ele de fi le)

| 8805 | vistes | (hunbles) |
| 8905 | panes | (robes) |

A Bibliography of Texts and Critical Studies

This bibliography, designed to accompany the translations, falls into two natural divisions. The first, "Editions of Chrétien de Troyes," includes the major editions of the romances as well as selected important studies of the manuscript traditions and related editorial considerations. The second, "Critical Studies in English of Chrétien de Troyes," lists all studies of Chrétien, first, the general studies that focus on his writings and at least two of the romances, and second, a list of critical writings on each of the five romances.

Douglas Kelly's *Chrétien de Troyes: An Analytic Bibliography* (London: Grant and Cutler, 1976) is the standard bibliographical introduction. Annual annotated bibliographies of work on Chrétien are included in the Modern Language Association International Bibliography (1921–   ), published first in *PMLA* and now separately by the Modern Language Association of America, and in the International Arthurian Society Bibliography (1949–   ), published in *BBSIA*. Some attention is paid to Chrétien in *Arthurian Legend and Literature: An Annotated Bibliography*, vol. I: *The Middle Ages*, ed. Edmund Reiss, Louise Horner Reiss, and Beverly Taylor (New York: Garland, 1984).

Essays on medieval Arthurian writings that both precede and follow Chrétien's romances appear in *Arthurian Literature in the Middle Ages*, ed. Roger Sherman Loomis (London: Oxford University Press, 1959). There are also detailed entries on medieval and postmedieval Arthurian literature in *The Arthurian Encyclopedia*, ed. Norris J. Lacy (New York: Garland, 1986).

1. Editions of Chrétien de Troyes

There are two major editions of the romances of Chrétien de Troyes, the editions of Wendelin Foerster, completed by Alfons Hilka, which are based on all manuscripts known at the time, and the editions under the general supervision of Mario Roques, which use MS B.N. 794 as the base text.

(A) Christian von Troyes. *Sämtliche Werke*, ed. Wendelin Foerster. Halle: Max Niemeyer, 1884–99; repr. Amsterdam: Rodopi, 1965. (*Cliges*, 1884; *Der Löwenritter*

[*The Knight with the Lion*], 1887; *Erec und Enide*, 1890; *Der Karrenritter und das Wilhelmsleben* [*The Knight of the Cart and The Life of William*], 1899.) *Der Percevalroman (Li Contes del Graal) von Christian von Troyes*, ed. Alfons Hilka. Halle: Max Niemeyer, 1932.

(B) Chrétien de Troyes. *Les Romans de Chrétien de Troyes*, ed. Mario Roques. Paris: Les Classiques Français du Moyen Age, 1952–75. (*Erec et Enide*, 1952; *Cliges*, ed. Alexandre Micha, 1957; *Le Chevalier de la charrete*, 1958; *Le Chevalier au lion (Yvain)*, 1960; *Le Conte du graal (Perceval)*, ed. Félix Lecoy, 1973–75.)

There are also separate editions of the following romances:

EREC AND ENIDE

Erec et Enide, ed. and trans. Carleton W. Carroll. New York: Garland, 1987. The base text is MS B.N. 794.

THE KNIGHT OF THE CART

Lancelot, or The Knight of the Cart, ed. and trans. William W. Kibler. New York: Garland, 1981. The base text is MS B.N. 794.

THE KNIGHT WITH THE LION

Yvain (Le Chevalier au Lion), ed. T. B. W. Reid. Manchester: Manchester University Press, 1942; repr. with minor corrections, 1967. This edition follows Foerster's text.
Yvain ou Le Chevalier au Lion, ed. Jan Nelson, Carleton W. Carroll, and Douglas Kelly. New York: Appleton-Century-Crofts, 1968. The base text is MS B.N. 794.
The Knight with the Lion, or Yvain, ed. and trans. William W. Kibler. New York: Garland, 1985. The base text is MS B.N. 794.

THE STORY OF THE GRAIL

Le Roman de Perceval ou Le Conte du Graal, ed. William Roach. Geneva: Droz; Paris: Minard, 1959. The base text is MS B.N. 12576.

Some of the more important studies of the manuscript traditions of Chrétien's writings, related editorial problems, and the dating of the romances include:

Foulet, Alfred. "On Editing Chrétien's *Lancelot*." In *The Romances of Chrétien de Troyes: A Symposium*, ed. Douglas Kelly. Lexington, Ky.: French Forum, 1985. Pp. 287–304.
———. "On Grid-Editing Chrétien de Troyes." *ECr* 27, 1 (1987):15–23.
Hult, David F. "Lancelot's Two Steps: A Problem in Textual Criticism." *Speculum* 61 (1986):836–58.
———. "Steps Forward and Steps Backward: More on Chrétien's *Lancelot*." *Speculum* 64 (1989):307–316.
Hunt, Tony. "Chrestien de Troyes: The Textual Problem." *FS* 33 (1979):257–71.
———. "Redating Chrestien de Troyes." *BBSIA* 30 (1978):209–237.
Janssens, Jan. "The 'Simultaneous' Composition of *Yvain* and *Lancelot*: Fiction or Reality?" *FMLS* 23 (1987):366–76.

Micha, Alexandre. *La Tradition manuscrite des romans de Chrétien de Troyes*. Paris: Droz, 1939; repr. Geneva: Droz, 1966.

Misrahi, Jean. "More Light on the Chronology of Chrétien de Troyes?" *BBSIA* 11 (1959):89–120.

Mullaly, Evelyn. "The Order of Composition of *Lancelot* and *Yvain*." *BBSIA* 36 (1984):217–29.

Pickens, Rupert T. "Towards an Edition of Chrétien's *Li Contes del Graal:* Hilka vv. 1869–2024." *ECr* 27, 1 (1987):53–66.

Reid, T. B. W. "Chrétien de Troyes and the Scribe Guiot." *MAE* 45 (1976):1–19.

Roques, Mario. "Le Manuscrit fr. 794 de la Bibliothèque Nationale et le scribe Guiot." *Romania* 73 (1952):177–99.

Shirt, David J. "How Much of the Lion Can We Put before the Cart? Further Light on the Chronological Relationship of Chrétien de Troyes's *Lancelot* and *Yvain*." *FS* 31 (1977):1–17.

Uitti, Karl D., with Alfred Foulet. "On Editing Chrétien de Troyes: Lancelot's Two Steps and Their Context." *Speculum* 63 (1988):271–92.

Woledge, Brian. *Commentaire sur Yvain (Le Chevalier au lion)*. 2 vols. Geneva: Droz, 1986–88.

——. "The Problem of Editing *Yvain*." In *Medieval French Textual Studies in Memory of T. B. W. Reid*, ed. Ian Short. London: Anglo-Norman Text Society, 1984. Pp. 254–67.

——. "Un Scribe champenois devant un texte normand: Guiot copiste de Wace." In *Mélanges de langue et de littérature du Moyen Age et de la Renaissance offerts à Jean Frappier*. Geneva: Droz, 1970. Vol. 2, pp. 1139–54.

2. CRITICAL STUDIES IN ENGLISH OF CHRÉTIEN DE TROYES

Part One: General Studies

Artin, Tom. *The Allegory of Adventure: Reading Chrétien's "Erec and Yvain."* Lewisburg, Pa.: Bucknell University Press, 1974.

Benson, Larry D. "The Tournament in the Romances of Chrétien de Troyes and *L'Histoire de Guillaume Le Maréchal*." In *Chivalric Literature*, ed. Larry D. Benson and John Leyerle. Kalamazoo, Mich.: Medieval Institute Publications, 1980. Pp. 1–24.

Benton, John F. "Collaborative Approaches to Fantasy and Reality in the Literature of Champagne." In *Court and Poet: Selected Proceedings of the Third Congress of the International Courtly Literature Society*, ed. Glyn S. Burgess. Liverpool: Francis Cairns, 1981. Pp. 43–57.

——. "The Court of Champagne as a Literary Center." *Speculum* 36 (1961):551–91.

Blaess, M. "The Public and Private Face of King Arthur's Court in the Works of Chrétien de Troyes." In *Chrétien de Troyes and the Troubadours: Essays in Memory of the Late Leslie Topsfield*, ed. Peter S. Noble and Linda M. Paterson. Cambridge, England: St. Catherine's College, 1984. Pp. 238–48.

Brogyanyi, Gabriel John. "Plot Structure and Motivation in Chrétien's Romances." *VR* 31 (1972):272–86.

Bruckner, Matilda Tomaryn. *Narrative Invention in Twelfth-Century French Romance: The Convention of Hospitality (1160–1200)*. Lexington, Ky.: French Forum, 1980.

Busby, Keith. "The Characters and the Setting." In *The Legacy of Chrétien de Troyes*, ed. Norris J. Lacy, Douglas Kelly, and Keith Busby. Amsterdam: Rodopi, 1987. Vol. 1, pp. 57–89.

———. "Chrétien de Troyes English'd." *Neophil* 71 (1987):596–613.

———. "Medieval French Literature: Recent Progress and Critical Trends." In *The Vitality of the Arthurian Legend*, ed. Mette Pors. Odense: Odense University Press, 1988. Pp. 45–70.

Carasso-Bulow, Lucienne. *The Merveilleux in Chrétien de Troyes' Romances*. Geneva: Droz, 1976.

Colby, Alice M. *The Portrait in Twelfth-Century French Literature*. Geneva: Droz, 1965.

Collins, Frank. "The Terms *cortois, cortoise,* and *corteisie* in the Works of Chrétien de Troyes." *VR* 36 (1977):84–92.

Cook, Robert G. "The Structure of Romance in Chrétien's *Erec* and *Yvain*." *MP* 71 (1973):128–43.

Dembowski, Peter. "Monologue, Author's Monologue and Related Problems in the Romances of Chrétien de Troyes." *YFS* 51 (1974):102–14.

Duggan, Joseph J. "Ambiguity in Twelfth-Century French and Provençal Literature: A Problem or a Value?" In *Jean Misrahi Memorial Volume: Studies in Medieval Literature*, ed. Hans R. Runte, Henri Niedzielski, and William L. Hendrickson. Columbia, S.C.: French Literature Publications, 1977. Pp. 136–49.

Ferrante, Joan M. "The Problem of Lyric Conventions and Romance Form." In *In Pursuit of Perfection: Courtly Love in Medieval Literature*, ed. Joan M. Ferrante and George D. Economou. Port Washington, N.Y.: Kennikat Press, 1975. Pp. 135–78.

Finnie, W. B. "The Structural Function of Names in the Works of Chrétien de Troyes." *Names* 20 (1972):91–94.

Frappier, Jean. "Chrétien de Troyes." In *Arthurian Literature in the Middle Ages*, ed. Roger Sherman Loomis. Oxford: Clarendon Press, 1959. Pp. 157–91.

———. *Chrétien de Troyes: The Man and His Work*, trans. Raymond J. Cormier. Athens: Ohio University Press, 1982.

Goetinck, Glenys W. "Chrétien's Welsh Inheritance." In *Gallica: Essays Presented to J. Heywood Thomas by Colleagues, Pupils, and Friends*, ed. R. H. Spencer. Cardiff: University of Wales Press, 1969. Pp. 13–29.

Green, D. H. "Irony and Medieval Romance." *FMLS* 6 (1970):49–64.

———. *Irony in the Medieval Romance*. Cambridge: Cambridge University Press, 1979.

Grimbert, Joan Tasker. "Misrepresentation and Misconception in Chrétien de Troyes: Verbal and Nonverbal Semiotics in *Erec et Enide* and *Perceval*." In *Sign, Sentence, Discourse: Language in Medieval Thought and Literature*, ed. Julian N. Wasserman and Lois Roney. Syracuse, N.Y.: Syracuse University Press, 1989. Pp. 50–79.

Grimm, Charles. "Chrestien de Troyes's Attitude towards Woman." *RR* 16 (1925):236–43.

Guyer, Foster E. "The Influence of Ovid on Chrétien de Troyes." *RR* 12 (1921):97–135; 216–47.

———. *Chrétien de Troyes: Inventor of the Modern Novel*. New York: Bookman Associates, 1957.

———. *Romance in the Making: Chrétien de Troyes and the Earliest French Romances*. New York: S. F. Vanni, 1954.

Haidu, Peter. *Aesthetic Distance in Chrétien de Troyes: Irony and Comedy in "Cliges" and "Perceval."* Geneva: Droz, 1968.

————. "Narrativity and Language in Some Twelfth Century Romances." *YFS* 51 (1974):133–46.

————. "Romance: Idealistic Genre or Historical Text?" In *The Craft of Fiction: Essays in Medieval Poetics*, ed. Leigh A. Arrathoon. Rochester, Mich.: Solaris Press, 1984. Pp. 1–46.

Hanning, Robert W. *The Individual in Twelfth-Century Romance.* New Haven: Yale University Press, 1977.

————. "The Social Significance of Twelfth-Century Chivalric Romance." *M&H* 3 (1972):3–29.

Holmes, Urban Tigner. *Chrétien de Troyes.* New York: Twayne, 1970.

Hunt, Tony. "Chrestien and the *Comediae*." *MS* 40 (1978):120–56.

————. "Rhetoric and Poetics in Twelfth-Century France." In *Rhetoric Revalued*, ed. Brian Vickers. Binghamton, N.Y.: Center for Medieval and Early Renaissance Studies, 1982. Pp. 165–71.

————. "The Rhetorical Background to the Arthurian Prologue: Tradition and the Old French Vernacular Prologues." *FMLS* 6 (1970):1–23.

————. "The Structure of Medieval Narrative." *JES* 3 (1973):295–328.

————. "Tradition and Originality in the Prologues of Chrestien de Troyes." *FMLS* 8 (1972):320–44.

Jackson, W. T. H. "Problems of Communication in the Romances of Chrétien de Troyes." In *Medieval Literature and Folklore Studies: Essays in Honor of Francis Lee Utley*, ed. Jerome Mandel and Bruce A. Rosenberg. New Brunswick, N.J.: Rutgers University Press, 1970, Pp. 39–50.

————. "The Nature of Romance." *YFS* 51 (1974):12–25.

Kellogg, Judith L. "Economic and Social Tensions Reflected in the Romance of Chrétien de Troyes." *RPh* 39 (1985):1–21.

Kelly, Douglas. "The Art of Description." In *The Legacy of Chrétien de Troyes*, ed. Norris J. Lacy, Douglas Kelly, and Keith Busby. Amsterdam: Rodopi, 1987. Vol. 1, pp. 191–221.

————. "Chrétien de Troyes: The Narrator and His Art." In *The Romances of Chrétien de Troyes: A Symposium*, ed. Douglas Kelly. Lexington, Ky.: French Forum, 1985. Pp. 13–47.

————. "Gauvain and *Fin' Amors* in the Poems of Chrétien de Troyes." *SP* 67 (1970):453–60.

————. "The Logic of the Imagination in Chrétien de Troyes." In *The Sower and His Seed: Essays on Chrétien de Troyes*, ed. Rupert T. Pickens. Lexington, Ky.: French Forum, 1983. Pp. 9–30.

————. "Romance and the Vanity of Chrétien de Troyes." In *Romance: Generic Transformation from Chrétien de Troyes to Cervantes*, ed. Kevin Brownlee and Marina Scordilis Brownlee. Hanover, N.H.: University Press of New England, 1985. Pp. 74–90.

————, ed. *The Romances of Chrétien de Troyes: A Symposium.* Lexington, Ky.: French Forum, 1985.

Krueger, Roberta L. "Contracts and Constraints: Courtly Performance in *Yvain* and the *Charrete*." In *The Medieval Court in Europe*, ed. Edward R. Haymes. Munich: Wilhelm Fink, 1986. Pp. 92–104.

————. "Reading the *Yvain/Charrete*: Chrétien's Inscribed Audiences at Noauz and Pesme Aventure." *FMLS* 19 (1983):172–87.

Lacy, Norris J. *The Craft of Chrétien de Troyes: An Essay on Narrative Art.* Leiden: Brill, 1980.

————, Douglas Kelly, and Keith Busby, eds. *The Legacy of Chrétien de Troyes.* 2 vols. Amsterdam: Rodopi, 1987–88.

Laurie, Helen C. R. "Chrétien and the English Court." *Romania* 93 (1972):85–87.
———. "The 'Letters' of Abelard and Heloise: A Source for Chrétien de Troyes?" *SM* 27 (1986):123–46.
———. *Two Studies in Chrétien de Troyes.* Geneva: Droz, 1972.
Liborio, Mariantonia. "Rhetorical *Topoi* as 'Clues' in Chrétien de Troyes." In *Rhetoric Revalued,* ed. Brian Vickers. Binghamton, N.Y.: Center for Medieval and Early Renaissance Studies, 1982. Pp. 173–78.
Loomis, Roger Sherman. *Arthurian Tradition and Chrétien de Troyes.* New York: Columbia University Press, 1949.
———. *Celtic Myth and Arthurian Romance.* New York: Columbia University Press, 1927.
Luttrell, Claude. "The Figure of Nature in Chrétien de Troyes." *NMS* 17 (1973):3–16.
Maddox, Donald. "The Awakening: A Key Motif in Chrétien's Romances." In *The Sower and His Seed: Essays on Chrétien de Troyes,* ed. Rupert T. Pickens. Lexington, Ky.: French Forum, 1983. Pp. 31–51.
Michener, Richard L. "Courtly Love in Chrétien de Troyes: The 'Demande d'Amour.' " *SN* 42 (1970):353–60.
Moorman, Charles. "Chrétien's Knights: The Uses of Love." *SoQ* 1 (1963):247–72.
Morris, Rosemary. "Aspects of Time and Place in the French Arthurian Verse Romances." *FS* 42 (1988):257–77.
Nitze, William A. "The Character of Gauvain in the Romances of Chrétien de Troyes." *MP* 50 (1953):219–25.
Noble, Peter. "The Character of Guinevere in the Arthurian Romances of Chrétien de Troyes." *MLR* 67 (1972):524–35.
———. "Chrétien's Arthur." In *Chrétien de Troyes and the Troubadours: Essays in Memory of the Late Leslie Topsfield,* ed. Peter S. Noble and Linda M. Paterson. Cambridge, England: St. Catherine's College, 1984. Pp. 220–37.
———. *Love and Marriage in Chrétien de Troyes.* Cardiff: University of Wales Press, 1982.
———, and Linda M. Paterson, eds. *Chrétien de Troyes and the Troubadours: Essays in Memory of the Late Leslie Topsfield.* Cambridge, England: St. Catherine's College, 1984.
Nolan, E. Peter. "Mythopoetic Evolution: Chrétien de Troyes's *Erec et Enide, Cligés,* and *Yvain.*" *Symposium* 25 (1971):139–61.
Norden, Ernest E. "The Figure of the Father in the Romances of Chrétien de Troyes." *SCB* 38 (1977):155–57.
Nothnagle, John T. "Chrétien de Troyes and the Rise of Realism." *ECr* 5, 4 (1965):202–207.
Nykrog, Per. "The Rise of Literary Fiction." In *Renaissance and Renewal in the Twelfth Century,* ed. Robert L. Benson and Giles Constable. Cambridge: Harvard University Press, 1982. Pp. 593–612.
———. "Two Creators of Narrative Form in Twelfth Century France: Gautier d'Arras—Chrétien de Troyes." *Speculum* 48 (1973):258–76.
Ollier, Marie-Louise. "The Author in the Text: The Prologues of Chrétien de Troyes." *YFS* 51 (1974):26–41.
Owen, D. D. R. "Profanity and Its Purpose in Chrétien's *Cligés* and *Lancelot.*" *FMLS* 6 (1970):37–48.
———. "Themes and Variations: Sexual Aggression in Chrétien de Troyes." *FMLS* 21 (1985):376–86.
Pickens, Rupert T. "*Estoire, Lai* and Romance: Chrétien's *Erec et Enide* and *Cligés.*" *RR* 66 (1975):247–62.

———, ed. *The Sower and His Seed: Essays on Chrétien de Troyes*. Lexington, Ky.: French Forum, 1983.

Press, A. R. "Death and Lamentation in Chrétien de Troyes's Romances: The Dialectic of Rhetoric and Reason." *FMLS* 23 (1987):11–20.

Robertson, D. W., Jr. "Some Medieval Literary Terminology, with Special Reference to Chrétien de Troyes." *SP* 48 (1951):669–92.

Runte, Hans R. "Initial Readers of Chrétien de Troyes." In *Continuations: Essays on Medieval French Literature and Language in Honor of John L. Grigsby*, ed. Norris J. Lacy and Gloria Torrini-Roblin. Birmingham, Al.: Summa Publications, 1989. Pp. 121–32.

Sargent-Baur, Barbara Nelson. "Old and New in the Character-Drawing of Chrétien de Troyes." In *Innovation in Medieval Literature: Essays to the Memory of Alan Markman*, ed. Douglas Radcliff-Umstead. Pittsburgh, Pa.: Medieval Studies Committee of the University of Pittsburgh, 1971. Pp. 35–48.

———. "Promotion to Knighthood in the Romances of Chrétien de Troyes." *RPh* 37 (1984):393–408.

Stevens, John. *Medieval Romance*. London: Hutchinson, 1973.

Thompson, Raymond H. "The Prison of the Senses: *Fin' Amor* as a Confining Force in the Arthurian Romances of Chrétien de Troyes." *FMLS* 15 (1979):249–54.

Topsfield, L. T. *Chrétien de Troyes: A Study of the Arthurian Romances*. Cambridge: Cambridge University Press, 1981.

Uitti, Karl D. "Chrétien de Troyes and His Vernacular Forebears: The City of Women, I." *FrF* 11 (1986):261–88.

———. *Story, Myth, and Celebration in Old French Narrative Poetry, 1050–1200*. Princeton: Princeton University Press, 1973.

Vance, Eugene. *From Topic to Tale: Logic and Narrativity in the Middle Ages*. Minneapolis: University of Minnesota Press, 1987.

Varty, E. K. C. "On Birds and Beasts, 'Death' and 'Resurrection,' Renewal and Reunion in Chrétien's Romances." In *The Legend of Arthur in the Middle Ages*, ed. P. B. Grout, R. A. Lodge, C. E. Pickford, and E. K. C. Varty. Woodbridge, Suffolk: D. S. Brewer, 1983. Pp. 194–212.

———. "The Giving and Withholding of Consent in Late Twelfth-Century French Literature." *RMSt* 12 (1986):27–49.

Vermette, Rosalie. "*Terrae Incantatae*: The Symbolic Geography of Twelfth-Century Arthurian Romance." In *Geography and Literature: A Meeting of the Disciplines*, ed. William E. Mallory and Paul Simpson-Housley. Syracuse: Syracuse University Press, 1987. Pp. 145–60.

Warning, Rainer. "Heterogeneity of Plot—Homogeneity of Narration: On the Constitution of Chrétien de Troyes' Romances." *ECr* 18, 3 (1978):41–54.

Williams, Harry F. "A Note on Chrétien's Virtuosity." *USFLQ* 22 (1984):49–50.

Woods, William S. "The Plot Structure in Four Romances of Chrestien de Troyes." *SP* 50 (1953):1–15.

Zaddy, Z. P. "Chrétien de Troyes and the Epic Tradition." *CN* 21 (1961):71–82.

———. "Chrétien de Troyes and the Localisation of the Heart." *RPh* 12 (1959):257–58.

———. *Chrétien Studies*. Glasgow: University of Glasgow Press, 1973.

Part Two: Studies of Individual Romances

EREC AND ENIDE

Adler, Alfred. "Sovereignty as the Principle of Unity in Chrétien's *Erec*." *PMLA* 60 (1945):917–36.

Archambault, Paul J. "Erec's Search for a New Language: Chrétien and Twelfth-Century Science." *Symposium* 35 (1981):3–17.

Bogdanow, Fanni. "The Tradition of the Troubadour Lyrics and the Treatment of the Love Theme in Chrétien de Troyes' *Erec et Enide*." In *Court and Poet: Selected Proceedings of the Third Congress of the International Courtly Literature Society*, ed. Glyn S. Burgess. Liverpool: Francis Cairns, 1981. Pp. 79–92.

Bradley-Cromey, Nancy. "The 'Recraeantise' Episode in Chrétien's *Erec et Enide*." In *The Study of Chivalry: Resources and Approaches*, ed. Howell Chickering and Thomas H. Seiler. Kalamazoo, Mich.: Medieval Institute Publications, 1989. Pp. 449–71.

Brogyanyi, Gabriel John. "Motivation in *Erec et Enide*: An Interpretation of the Romance." *KRQ* 19 (1972):407–431.

Brumlik, Joan. "Chrétien's Enide: Wife, Mistress and Metaphor." *KRQ* 35 (1988):401–414.

Buckbee, Edward J. "*Erec et Enide*." In *The Romances of Chrétien de Troyes: A Symposium*, ed. Douglas Kelly. Lexington, Ky.: French Forum, 1985. Pp. 48–88.

Burgess, Glyn S. *Chrétien de Troyes: "Erec et Enide."* London: Grant and Cutler, 1984.

———. "The Theme of Beauty in Chrétien's *Philomena* and *Erec et Enide*." In *An Arthurian Tapestry: Essays in Memory of Lewis Thorpe*, ed. Kenneth Varty. Glasgow: French Department of the University of Glasgow, 1981. Pp. 114–28.

——— and John L. Curry. " 'Si ont berbïoletes non' (*Erec et Enide*, l. 6379)." *FS* 43 (1989):129–39.

Clark, S. L., and Julian N. Wasserman. "Language, Silence, and Wisdom in Chrétien's *Erec et Enide*." *MichA* 9 (1976–77):285–98.

Coghlan, Maura. "The Flaw in Enide's Character: A Study of Chrétien de Troyes' *Erec*." *RMSt* 5 (1979):21–37.

Collins, Frank. "A Semiotic Approach to Chrétien de Troyes's *Erec et Enide*." *Interpretations* 15 (1984):25–31.

Cropp, Glynnis M. "Count Caloain's Courting of Enide." *Parergon* 3 (1985):53–62.

Goulden, Oliver. "*Erec et Enide*: The Structure of the Central Section." In *Arthurian Literature*, vol. ix, ed. Richard Barber. Woodbridge, Suffolk: D. S. Brewer, 1989. Pp. 1–24.

Harris, R. "The White Stag in Chrétien's *Erec et Enide*." *FS* 10 (1956):55–61.

Hart, Thomas Elwood. "Chrestien, Macrobius, and Chartrean Science: The Allegorical Robe as Symbol of Textual Design in the Old French *Erec*." *MS* 43 (1981):250–96.

———. "The *Quadrivium* and Chrétien's Theory of Composition: Some Conjunctures and Conjectures." *Symposium* 35 (1981):57–86.

Hunt, Tony. "Chrestien and Macrobius." *C&M* 33 (1981–82):211–27.

Huppé, Bernard F. "The Gothic Hero: Chrétien's *Erec*." In *The Twelfth Century*, ed. Bernard Levy and Sandro Sticca. Binghamton, N.Y.: Center for Medieval and Early Renaissance Studies, 1975. Pp. 1–19.

Iyasere, Marla W. Mudar. "The Tripartite Structure of Chrétien's *Erec et Enide*." *Mediaevalia* 6 (1980):105–121.

Kelly, Douglas. "The Source and Meaning of *conjointure* in Chrétien's *Erec* 14." *Viator* 1 (1970):179–200.

Lacy, Norris J. "Narrative Point of View and the Problem of Erec's Motivation." *KRQ* 18 (1971):355–62.

———. "Thematic Analogues in *Erec*." *ECr* 9, 4 (1969):267–74.

Laidlaw, J. C. "Rhyme, Reason, and Repetition in *Erec et Enide*." In *The Legend of Arthur in the Middle Ages*, ed. P. B. Grout, R. A. Lodge, C. E. Pickford, and E. K. C. Varty. Woodbridge, Suffolk: D. S. Brewer, 1983. Pp. 129–37.

Laurie, Helen C. R. "The Arthurian World of *Erec et Enide*." *BBSIA* 21 (1969):111–19.

———. "Chrétien's *bele conjointure*." In *Actes du XIVe Congrès International Arthurien*. Rennes: Presses Universitaires de Rennes, 1985. Vol. 1, pp. 379–96.

———. "The Testing of Enide." *RF* 82 (1970):353–64.

Le Goff, Jacques. "Vestimentary and Alimentary Codes in *Erec et Enide*." In *The Medieval Imagination*, trans. Arthur Goldhammer. Chicago: University of Chicago Press, 1988. Pp. 132–50.

Luttrell, Claude. "Chrestien de Troyes and Alan of Lille." *BBSIA* 32 (1980):250–75.

———. *The Creation of the First Arthurian Romance: A Quest*. London: Edward Arnold, 1974.

Maddox, Donald L. "Nature and Narrative in Chrétien's *Erec et Enide*." *Mediaevalia* 3 (1977):59–82.

———. "The Prologue to Chrétien's *Erec* and the Problem of Meaning." In *Jean Misrahi Memorial Volume: Studies in Medieval Literature*, ed. Hans R. Runte, Henri Niedzielski, and William L. Hendrickson. Columbia, S.C.: French Literature Publications, 1977. Pp. 159–74.

———. *Structure and Sacring: The Systematic Kingdom in Chrétien's "Erec et Enide."* Lexington, Ky.: French Forum, 1978.

———. "The Structure of Content in Chrétien's *Erec et Enide*." In *Mélanges de philologie et de littératures romanes offerts à Jeanne Wathelet-Willem*, ed. J. De Caluwé. Liège: Marche-Romane, 1978. Pp. 381–94.

Mandel, Jerome. "The Ethical Context of Erec's Character." *FR* 50 (1977):421–28.

Mickel, Emanuel J., Jr. "A Reconsideration of Chrétien's *Erec*." *RF* 84 (1972):18–44.

Murphy, Margueritte S. "The Allegory of 'Joie' in Chrétien's *Erec et Enide*." In *Allegory, Myth, and Symbol*, ed. Morton W. Bloomfield. Cambridge, Mass.: Harvard University Press, 1981. Pp. 109–127.

Mussetter, Sally. "The Education of Chrétien's Enide." *RR* 73 (1982):147–66.

———. "The Fairy Arts of *Mesure* in Chrétien's *Erec*." *KRQ* 31 (1984):9–22.

Nelson, Deborah. "Enide: *amie* or *femme*?" *RomN* 21 (1981):358–63.

———. "The Role of Animals in *Erec et Enide*." *KRQ* 35 (1988):31–38.

Nelson, Jan A. "A Jungian Interpretation of Sexually Ambiguous Imagery in Chrétien's *Erec et Enide*." In *The Arthurian Tradition: Essays in Convergence*, ed. Mary Flowers Braswell and John Bugge. Tuscaloosa: University of Alabama Press, 1988. Pp. 75–89.

Newstead, Helaine. "The *Joie de la Cort* Episode in *Erec* and the Horn of Bran." *PMLA* 51 (1936):13–25.

Niemeyer, Karina H. "The Writer's Craft: *La Joie de la Cort*." *ECr* 9, 4 (1969):286–92.

Nitze, William A. "Conjointure in *Erec*, vs 14." *MLN* 69 (1954):180–81.

———. "Erec and the Joy of the Court." *Speculum* 29 (1954):691–701.

———. "Erec's Treatment of Enide." *RR* 10 (1919):26–37.

———. "The Romance of Erec, Son of Lac." *MP* 11 (1914):445–89.

Ogle, M. B. "The Sloth of Erec." *RR* 9 (1918):1–20.

Owen, D. D. R. "Reward and Punishment in Chrétien's *Erec* and Related Texts." In *Rewards and Punishments in the Arthurian Romances of Mediaeval France*, ed. Peter V. Davies and Angus J. Kennedy. Cambridge, England: D. S. Brewer, 1987. Pp. 119–32.

Patterson, Lee. "Virgil and the Historical Consciousness of the Twelfth Century: The *Roman d'Eneas* and *Erec et Enide*." In *Negotiating the Past: The Historical Understanding of Medieval Literature*. Madison: University of Wisconsin Press, 1987. Pp. 157–95.

Plummer, John F. "*Bien dire et bien aprandre* in Chrétien de Troyes' *Erec et Enide*." *Romania* 95 (1974):380–94.

Sargent-Baur, Barbara Nelson. "Erec's Enide: 'sa fame ou s'amie'?" *RPh* 33 (1980):373–87.

Scully, Terence. "The *Sen* of Chrétien de Troyes's *Joie de la Cort*." In *The Expansion and Transformations of Courtly Literature*, ed. Nathaniel B. Smith and Joseph T. Snow. Athens, Ga.: University of Georgia Press, 1980. Pp. 71–94.

Sheldon, E. S. "Why Does Chrétien's Erec Treat Enide So Harshly?" *RR* 5 (1914):115–26.

Shippey, T. A. "The Uses of Chivalry: 'Erec' and 'Gawain'." *MLR* 66 (1971):241–50.

Sturm-Maddox, Sara. "Hortus non conclusus: Critics and the *Joie de la Cort*." *O&C* 5 (1980–81):61–71.

———. "The *Joie de la Cort*: Thematic Unity in Chrétien's *Erec et Enide*." *Romania* 103 (1982):513–28.

———, and Donald L. Maddox. "Description in Medieval Narrative: Vestimentary Coherence in Chrétien's *Erec et Enide*." *MedR* 9 (1984):51–64.

Sullivan, Penny. "The Education of the Heroine in Chrétien's *Erec et Enide*." *Neophil* 69 (1985):321–31.

———. "The Presentation of Enide in the *premier vers* of Chrétien's *Erec et Enide*." *MAE* 52 (1983):77–89.

Uitti, Karl D. "Vernacularization and Old French Romance Mythopoesis with Emphasis on Chrétien's *Erec et Enide*." In *The Sower and His Seed: Essays on Chrétien de Troyes*, ed. Rupert T. Pickens. Lexington, Ky.: French Forum, 1983. Pp. 81–115.

Whitehead, F. "The *Joie de la Cour* episode in *Erec* and Its Bearing on Chrétien's Ideas on Love." *BBSIA* 21 (1969):142–43.

Wittig, Joseph S. "The Aeneas-Dido Allusion in Chrétien's *Erec et Enide*." *CL* 22 (1970):237–53.

Woodbridge, Benjamin M. "Chrétien's Erec as a Cornelian Hero." *RR* 6 (1915):434–42.

Zaddy, Z. P. "The Structure of Chrétien's *Erec*." *MLR* 62 (1967):608–619.

Zak, Nancy C. *The Portrayal of the Heroine in Chrétien de Troyes's "Erec et Enide," Gottfried von Strassburg's "Tristan," and "Flamenca."* Göppingern: Kümmerle Verlag, 1983.

CLIGES

Blumenfeld-Kosinski, Renate. "Chrétien de Troyes as a Reader of the *Romans Antiques*" *PQ* 64 (1985):398–405.

Bullock-Davies, Constance. "Chrétien de Troyes and England." In *Arthurian Literature*, vol. I, ed. Richard Barber. Woodbridge, Suffolk: D. S. Brewer, 1981. Pp. 1–61.

Chase, Carol J. "Double Bound: Secret Sharers in *Cligés* and the *Lancelot-Graal*." In *The Legacy of Chrétien de Troyes*, ed. Norris J. Lacy, Douglas Kelly, and Keith Busby. Amsterdam: Rodopi, 1988. Vol. 2, pp. 169–85.

Curtis, Renée L. "The Validity of Fénice's Criticism of Tristan and Iseut in Chrétien's *Cligés*." *BBSIA* 41 (1989):292–300.

Ferrante, Joan M. "Artist Figures in the Tristan Stories." *Tristania* 4,2 (1979):25–35.

Freeman, Michelle A. "Chrétien's *Cligés*: A Close Reading of the Prologue." *RR* 67 (1976):89–101.

———. "*Cligés*." In *The Romances of Chrétien de Troyes: A Symposium*, ed. Douglas Kelly. Lexington, Ky.: French Forum, 1985. Pp. 89–131.

———. *The Poetics of Translatio Studii and Conjointure: Chrétien de Troyes's "Cligés."* Lexington, Ky.: French Forum, 1979.

———. "Structural Transpositions and Intertextuality: Chrétien's *Cligés*." *M&H* 11 (1982):149–63.

Hanning, R. W. "Courtly Contexts for Urban *Cultus*: Responses to Ovid in Chrétien's *Cligés* and Marie's *Guigemar*." *Symposium* 35 (1981):34–56.

Harris-Stäblein, Patricia. "Transformation and Stasis in *Cligés*." In *An Arthurian Tapestry: Essays in Memory of Lewis Thorpe*, ed. Kenneth Varty. Glasgow: French Department of the University of Glasgow, 1981. Pp. 151–59.

Lacy, Norris J. "*Cligés* and Courtliness." *Interpretations* 15 (1984):18–24.

———. "Form and Pattern in *Cligés*." *OL* 25 (1970):307–313.

Levine, Robert. "Repression in *Cligés*." *Sub-stance* 15 (1976):209–221.

Lloyd, Heather. "Chrétien's Use of the Conventions of Grief Depiction in a Passage from *Cligés*." *FMLS* 20 (1984):317–322.

Lonigan, Paul R. "The *Cligés* and the Tristan Legend." *SFr* 53 (1974):201–212.

Maddox, Donald L. "Critical Trends and Recent Work on the *Cligés* of Chrétien de Troyes." *NM* 74 (1973):730–45.

———. "Kinship Alliances in the *Cligés* of Chrétien de Troyes." *ECr* 12,1 (1972):3–12.

———. "Pseudo-historical Discourse in Fiction: *Cligés*." In *Essays in Early French Literature Presented to Barbara M. Craig*, ed. Norris J. Lacy and Jerry C. Nash. York, S.C.: French Literature Publications, 1982. Pp. 9–24.

McGrady, Donald. "The Hunter Loses His Falcon: Notes on a Motif from *Cliges* to *La Celestina* and Lope de Vega." *Romania* 107 (1986):145–82.

Nelson, Deborah. "The Public and Private Images of *Cligés*' Fénice." *RMSt* 7 (1981):81–88.

Noble, Peter. "Alis and the Problem of Time in *Cligés*." *MAE* 39 (1970):28–31.

Owen, D. D. R. "Chrétien and the *Roland*." In *An Arthurian Tapestry: Essays in Memory of Lewis Thorpe*, ed. Kenneth Varty. Glasgow: French Department of the University of Glasgow, 1981. Pp. 139–50.

Polak, Lucie. *Chrétien de Troyes: "Cligés."* London: Grant and Cutler, 1982.

Robertson, D. W., Jr. "Chrétien's *Cligés* and the Ovidian Spirit." *CL* 7 (1955):32–42.

———. "The Idea of Fame in Chrétien's *Cligés*." *SP* 69 (1972):414–33.

Rubey, Daniel. "The Troubled House of Oedipus and Chrétien's *Néo-Tristan*: Rewriting the Mythologies of Desire." *PsyR* 75 (1988):67–94.

Shirt, David J. "*Cligés*: Realism in Romance." *FMLS* 13 (1977):368–80.

———. "*Cligés*: A Twelfth-Century Matrimonial Case-book?" *FMLS* 18 (1982):75–89.

Staines, David. "*Cligés*: Chrétien's Paradigmatic Experiment." In *Courtly Romance*, ed. Guy Mermier. Detroit: Michigan Consortium for Medieval and Early Modern Studies, 1984. Pp. 251–72.

THE KNIGHT OF THE CART

Adams, Alison. "Godefroi de Leigni's Continuation of *Lancelot*." *FMLS* 10 (1974):295–99.

Adler, Alfred. "A Note on the Composition of Chrétien's *Charrette*." *MLR* 45 (1950):33–39.

Baron, F. Xavier. "Love in Chrétien's *Charette*: Reversed Values and Isolation." *MLQ* 34 (1973):372–83.

Bogdanow, Fanni. "The Love Theme in Chrétien de Troyes's *Chevalier de la Charrette*." *MLR* 67 (1972):50–61.

Botterill, Steven. "Re-reading Lancelot: Dante, Chaucer, and *Le Chevalier de la charrette*." *PQ* 67 (1988):279–89.

Brault, Gerard J. "Chrétien de Troyes' *Lancelot*: The Eye and the Heart." *BBSIA* 24 (1972):142–53.

Brewer, Derek. "The Presentation of the Character of Lancelot: Chrétien to Malory." In *Arthurian Literature*, vol. III, ed. Richard Barber. Woodbridge, Suffolk: D. S. Brewer, 1983. Pp. 26–52.

Bruckner, Matilda Tomaryn. "*Le Chevalier de la Charrette (Lancelot)*." In *The Romances of Chrétien de Troyes: A Symposium*, ed. Douglas Kelly. Lexington, Ky.: French Forum, 1985. Pp. 123–81.

——. "An Interpreter's Dilemma: Why Are There So Many Interpretations of Chrétien's *Chevalier de la Charrette?*" *RPh* 40 (1986):159–80.

Brumlik, Joan. "Illusory Duality in Chrétien's *Lancelot*." *KRQ* 36 (1989):387–99.

Burrell, Margaret. "The *sens* of *Le Chevalier de la charrette* and the Court of Champagne." *BBSIA* 37 (1985):299–308.

Clark, Susan L., and Julian N. Wasserman. "Putting the Cart before the Horse: Excess, Restraint, and Choices in Chrétien's *Chevalier de la Charrette*." *ELWIU* 11 (1984):127–35.

Condren, Edward I. "The Paradox of Chrétien's *Lancelot*." *MLN* 85 (1970):434–53.

De Looze, Laurence N. "Chivalry Qualified: The Character of Gauvain in Chrétien de Troyes' *Le Chevalier de la Charette*." *RR* 74 (1983):253–59.

Diverres, A. H. "Some Thoughts on the *Sens* of *Le Chevalier de la Charrette*." *FMLS* 6 (1970):24–36.

Fowler, David C. "Love in Chrétien's *Lancelot*." *RR* 63 (1972):5–14.

Fullman, Sally. "*Le Jeu de miroirs*: The Role of the Secondary Women Characters in *Le Chevalier de la Charrete* of Chrétien de Troyes." *ISSQ* 31, 1 (1978):18–28.

Hult, David F. "Lancelot's Shame." *RPh* 42 (1988):30–50.

Kelly, Douglas. *Sens and Conjointure in the Chevalier de la Charrette*. The Hague: Mouton, 1966.

——. "Two Problems in Chrétien's *Charrette*: The Boundaries of Gorre and the Use of *novele*." *Neophil* 48 (1964):115–21.

Krueger, Roberta L. "Desire, Meaning, and the Female Reader: The Problem in Chrétien's *Charrete*." In *The Passing of Arthur: New Essays in Arthurian Tradition*, ed. Christopher Baswell and William Sharpe. New York: Garland, 1988. Pp. 31–51.

——. " 'Tuit li autre': The Narrator and His Public in Chrétien de Troyes' *Le Chevalier de la Charrette*." In *Courtly Romance*, ed. Guy R. Mermier. Detroit: Michigan Consortium for Medieval and Early Modern Studies, 1984. Pp. 133–50.

Lacy, Norris. J. "Spatial Form in Medieval Romance." *YFS* 51 (1974):160–69.

——. "Thematic Structure in the *Charrette*." *ECr* 12, 1 (1972):13–18.

Laurie, Helen C. R. "Chrétien de Troyes and the Choice of Hercules." *RLR* 80 (1972):147–56.

——. "*Eneas* and the *Lancelot* of Chrétien de Troyes." *MAE* 37 (1968):142–56.

Love, Nathan. "Why *Tu*, Rather Than *Vous*, in Chrétien de Troyes' *Le Chevalier de la charrete?*" *LingInv* 11 (1987):115–27.

Lyons, Faith. "*Entencion* in Chrétien's *Lancelot*." *SP* 51 (1954):425–30.

Mandel, Jerome. "Elements in the *Charrette* World: The Father-Son Relationship." *MP* 62 (1964):97–104.

———. "Proper Behavior in Chrétien's *Charrette*: The Host-Guest Relationship." *FR* 48 (1975):683–89.

Mickel, Emanuel J., Jr. "The Theme of Honor in Chrétien's *Lancelot*." *ZRP* 91 (1975):243–72.

Morgan, Gerald. "The Conflict of Love and Chivalry in *Le Chevalier de la Charrete*." *Romania* 102 (1981):172–201.

Raabe, Pamela. "Chrétien's *Lancelot* and the Sublimity of Adultery." *UTQ* 57 (1987):259–69.

Shirt, David J. *"Le Chevalier de la Charrette*: A World Upside Down?" *MLR* 76 (1981):811–22.

———. "Chrétien de Troyes and the Cart." In *Studies in Medieval Literature and Languages in Memory of Frederick Whitehead*, ed. W. Rothwell, W. R. J. Barron, David Blamires, and Lewis Thorpe. Manchester: Manchester University Press, 1973. Pp. 279–301.

———. "Chrétien's *Charrette* and Its Critics, 1964–74." *MLR* 73 (1978):38–50.

Soudek, Ernst. "Structure and Time in *Le Chevalier de la charrette*: An Aspect of Artistic Purpose." *Romania* 93 (1972):96–108.

———. "'The Tragic Qualities of Guenièvre and Meliagant in *Le Chevalier de la charrette*." *RomN* 13 (1971):363–68.

Southward, Elaine. "The Unity of Chrétien's *Lancelot*." In *Mélanges de linguistique et de littérature romanes offerts à Mario Roques*. Paris: Bade, 1953. Vol. 2, pp. 281–90.

Speyer, Marian F. "The Cemetery Incident in Chrétien and Its Celtic Original." *RR* 28 (1937):195–203.

Topsfield, Leslie T. *"Fin'Amors* in Marcabru, Bernart de Ventadorn, and the *Lancelot* of Chrétien de Troyes." In *Love and Marriage in the Twelfth Century*, ed. Willy van Hoecke and Andries Welkenhuysen. Leuven: Leuven University Press, 1981. Pp. 236–49.

———. "Malvestatz versus Proeza and Leautatz in Troubadour Poetry and the *Lancelot* of Chrétien de Troyes." *ECr* 19, 4 (1979):37–53.

Webster, K. G. T. "The Water-Bridge in Chrétien's *Charrette*." *MLR* 26 (1931):69–73.

White, Sarah Melhado. "Lancelot on the Gameboard: The Design of Chrétien's *Charrette*." *FrF* 2 (1977):99–109.

———. "Lancelot's Beds: Styles of Courtly Intimacy." In *The Sower and His Seed: Essays on Chrétien de Troyes*, ed. Rupert T. Pickens. Lexington, Ky.: French Forum, 1983. Pp. 116–26.

Williamson, Joan B. "Suicide and Adultery in *Le Chevalier de la charrete*." In *Mélanges de littérature du Moyen Age au xxᵉ siècle, offerts à Mlle Jeanne Lods*. Paris: Collection de l'Ecole Normale Supérieure de Jeunes Filles, 1978. Vol. 1, Pp. 571–87.

Zaddy, Z. P. *"Le Chevalier de la Charrette* and the *De amore* of Andreas Capellanus." In *Studies in Medieval Literature and Languages in Memory of Frederick Whitehead*, ed. W. Rothwell, W. R. J. Barron, David Blamires, and Lewis Thorpe. Manchester: Manchester University Press, 1973. Pp. 363–99.

THE KNIGHT WITH THE LION

Adler, Alfred. "Sovereignty in Chrétien's *Yvain*." *PMLA* 62 (1947):281–305.

Arthur, Ross G. "The Judicium Dei in the *Yvain* of Chrétien de Troyes." *RomN* 28 (1987):3–12.

Auerbach, Erich. "The Knight Sets Forth." In *Mimesis*, trans. Willard R. Trask. Princeton: Princeton University Press, 1953. Pp. 123–42.

Bogdanow, Fanni. "The Tradition of the Troubadours and the Treatment of the Love Theme in Chrétien de Troyes' *Chevalier au Lion*." In *Arthurian Literature*, vol II, ed. Richard Barber. Woodbridge, Suffolk: D. S. Brewer, 1982. Pp. 76–91.

Brodeur, Arthur Gilchrist. "The Grateful Lion." *PMLA* 39 (1924):485–524.

Brown, Arthur C. L. "Chrétien's *Yvain*." *MP* 9 (1911):109–128.

———. *Iwain: A Study in the Origins of Arthurian Romance*. Cambridge, Mass.: Harvard University Press, 1903.

———. "The Knight of the Lion." *PMLA* 20 (1905):673–706.

Brown, George Hardin. "Yvain's Sin of Neglect." *Symposium* 27 (1973):309–321.

Brugger, E. "Yvain and His Lion." *MP* 38 (1941):267–87.

Burrell, Margaret. "The Fountain and Its Function in *Yvain*." *AUMLA* 52 (1979):288–95.

Busby, Keith. "The Reception of Chrétien's Calogrenant Episode." In *Tussentijds: Bundel Studies Aangeboden aan W. P. Gerritsen*, ed. A. M. J. van Buuren, H. van Dijk, O. S. H. Lie, and F. P. van Oostrom. Utrecht: HES Publishers, 1985. Pp. 25–40.

Carter, M. L. "The Psychological Symbolism of the Magic Fountain and the Giant Herdsman in *Yvain*." *Mythlore* 11, 3 (1985):30–31.

Chaitin, Gilbert D. "Celtic Tradition and Psychological Truth in Chrétien's *Chevalier au lion*." *Sub-stance* 3 (1972):63–76.

Clark, Susan L., and Julian N. Wasserman. "Conflict and Resolution: Implications of Enclosure in Chrétien's *Yvain*." *ELWIU* 8 (1981):63–72.

Combellack, C. R. B. "The Entrapment of Yvain." *MS* 37 (1975):524–30.

———. "Yvain's Guilt." *SP* 68 (1971):10–25.

Cook, Robert G. "The Ointment in Chrétien's *Yvain*." *MS* 31 (1969):338–42.

Curtis, Renée L. "The Perception of the Chivalric Ideal in Chrétien de Troyes's *Yvain*." *ArthI* 3 (1989):1–22.

Diverres, A. H. "Chivalry and *fin'amor* in *Le Chevalier au Lion*." In *Studies in Medieval Literature and Languages in Memory of Frederick Whitehead*, ed. W. Rothwell, W. R. J. Barron, David Blamires, and Lewis Thorpe. Manchester: Manchester University Press, 1973. Pp. 91–116.

———. "Yvain's Quest for Chivalric Perfection." In *An Arthurian Tapestry: Essays in Memory of Lewis Thorpe*, ed. Kenneth Varty. Glasgow: French Department of the University of Glasgow, 1981. Pp. 214–28.

Duggan, Joseph J. "Yvain's Good Name: The Unity of Chrétien de Troyes' *Chevalier au lion*." *OL* 24 (1969):112–29.

Edwards, Robert. "The Problem of Closure in Chrétien's *Yvain*." In *The Twelfth Century*, ed. Bernard Levy and Sandro Sticca. Binghamton, N.Y.: Center for Medieval and Early Renaissance Studies, 1975. Pp. 119–29.

Eichmann, Raymond. "Yvain's Lion—A Recapitulation." *PAPA* 2 (1976):26–32.

Fogg, Sarah. "The Function of Split Personality in Chrétien's *Yvain*." In *The Twenty-seventh Annual Mountain Interstate Foreign Language Conference*, ed. Eduardo Zayas-Bazan and Manuel Laurentino Suarez. Johnson City, Tenn.: Research Council of East Tennessee State University, 1978. Pp. 114–21.

Foulet, Alfred, and Karl D. Uitti. "Chrétien's 'Laudine': *Yvain*, vv. 2148–55." *RPh* 37 (1984):293–302.

Gale, John E. "*Le Chevalier au Lion*: Chrétien's Warning of Decadence." *RomN* 16 (1976):422–29.

Grimbert, Joan Tasker. "Adversative Structure in Chrétien's *Yvain*: The Role of the Conjunction *mes*." *MedR* 9 (1984):27–50.

———. "On the Prologue of Chrétien's *Yvain*: Opening Functions of Keu's Quarrel." *PQ* 64 (1985):391–98.

Haidu, Peter. "The Hermit's Pottage: Deconstruction and History in *Yvain*." In *The Sower and His Seed: Essays on Chrétien de Troyes*, ed. Rupert T. Pickens. Lexington, Ky.: French Forum, 1983. Pp. 127–45.

Hall, Robert A., Jr. "The Silk Factory in Chrestien de Troyes' *Yvain*." *MLN* 56 (1941):418–22.

Halligan, G.J. "Marriage in Chrétien's *Yvain*." *AUMLA* 34 (1970):264–85.

Hamilton, George L. "Storm-making Springs: Rings of Invisibility and Protection—Studies on the Sources of the *Yvain* of Chrétien de Troies." *RR* 2 (1911):355–75; 5 (1914):213–37.

Harris, Julian. "The Rôle of the Lion in Chrétien de Troyes' *Yvain*." *PMLA* 64 (1949):1143–63.

Hartman, Richard. "The Disinherited Damsel: The Transformation of a Convention in Chrétien's *Yvain* and the *Queste del Saint Graal*." *MichA* 12 (1979):61–67.

Heffernan, Carol F. "Chrétien de Troyes's *Yvain*: Seeking the Fountain." *RPLit* 1 (1982):109–121.

Hibbard, Laura. "The Sword Bridge of Chrétien de Troyes and Its Celtic Original." *RR* 4 (1913):166–90.

Hunt, Tony. "Beginnings, Middles, and Ends: Some Interpretative Problems in Chrétien's *Yvain* and Its Medieval Adaptations." In *The Craft of Fiction: Essays in Medieval Poetics*, ed. Leigh A. Arrathoon. Rochester, Mich.: Solaris, 1984. Pp. 83–117.

———. *Chrétien de Troyes: "Yvain."* London: Grant and Cutler, 1986.

———. "The Dialectic of *Yvain*." *MLR* 72 (1977):285–99.

———. "The Lion and Yvain." In *The Legend of Arthur in the Middle Ages*, ed. P. B. Grout, R. A. Lodge, C. E. Pickford, and E. K. C. Varty. Woodbridge, Suffolk: D. S. Brewer, 1983. Pp. 86–98.

———. "*Texte* and *Prétexte*: *Jaufre* and *Yvain*." In *The Legacy of Chrétien de Troyes*, ed. Norris J. Lacy, Douglas Kelly, and Keith Busby. Amsterdam: Rodopi, 1988. Vol. 2, pp. 125–41.

Knight, Stephen. " 'Prowess and Courtesy': Chrétien de Troyes' *Le Chevalier au Lion*." In *Arthurian Literature and Society*. London: Macmillan, 1983. Pp. 68–104.

Kratins, Ojars. *The Dream of Chivalry: A Study of Chrétien de Troyes's "Yvain" and Hartmann von Aue's "Iwein."* Washington, D.C.: University Press of America, 1982.

———. "Love and Marriage in Three Versions of *The Knight of the Lion*." *CL* 16 (1964):29–39.

Krueger, Roberta L. "Love, Honor, and the Exchange of Women in *Yvain*: Some Remarks on the Female Reader." *RomN* 25 (1985):302–317.

Lacy, Norris J. "Organic Structure of Yvain's Expiation." *RR* 61 (1970):79–84.

———. "Yvain's Evolution and the Role of the Lion." *RomN* 12 (1970):198–202.

Laidlaw, James. "Shame Appeased: On the Structure and the *Sen* of the *Chevalier au Lion*." In *Chrétien de Troyes and the Troubadours: Essays in Memory of the Late Leslie Topsfield*, ed. Peter S. Noble and Linda M. Paterson. Cambridge, England: St. Catherine's College, 1984. Pp. 195–219.

Laurie, Helen C. R. "Beasts and Saints: A Key to the Lion in Chrétien's *Yvain*." *BBSIA* 39 (1987):297–306.

Lonigan, Paul R. "Calogrenant's Journey and the Mood of the *Yvain.*" *SFr* 58 (1976):1–20.

———. *Chrétien's "Yvain": A Study of Meaning through Style.* Ann Arbor, Mich.: University Microfilms International, 1978.

Loomis, Roger S. "Calogrenanz and Crestien's Originality." *MLN* 43 (1928):215–22.

Luria, Maxwell S. "The Storm-making Spring and the Meaning of Chrétien's *Yvain.*" *SP* 64 (1967):564–85.

Luttrell, Claude. "From Traditional Tale to Arthurian Romance: *Le Chevalier au Lion.*" *NMS* 22 (1978):36–57.

———. "King Arthur's Solemn Vow and the Dating of *Yvain.*" *FMLS* 13 (1977):285–87.

Morgan, Louise B. "The Source of the Fountain-Story in the *Ywain.*" *MP* 6 (1909):331–41.

Murtaugh, Daniel M. "Oïr et Entandre: Figuralism and Narrative Structure in Chrétien's *Yvain.*" *RR* 64 (1973):161–74.

Newstead, Helaine. "Narrative Techniques in Chrétien's *Yvain.*" *RPh* 30 (1967)431–41.

Nitze, William A. "The Fountain Defended." *MP* 7 (1909):146–64.

———. "A New Source of the *Yvain.*" *MP* 3 (1905):267–81.

———. "Yvain and the Myth of the Fountain." *Speculum* 30 (1955):170–79.

Noble, Peter. "Irony in *Le Chevalier au Lion.*" *BBSIA* 30 (1978):196–208.

Press, A. R. "Chrétien de Troyes's Laudine: A *Belle Dame sans Mercy?*" *FMLS* 19 (1983):158–71.

Reason, Joseph H. *An Inquiry into the Structural Style and Originality of Chrestien's "Yvain."* Washington, D.C.: Catholic University of America Press, 1958.

Ryding, William W. "Narrative Structure, Free Association, and Chrétien's Lion." *Symposium* 23 (1969):160–63.

Sargent-Baur, Barbara Nelson. "The Missing Prologue of Chrétien's *Chevalier au lion.*" *FS* 41 (1987):385–94.

———. "With Catlike Tread: The Beginning of Chrétien's *Chevalier au Lion.*" In *Studies in Medieval French Language and Literature Presented to Brian Woledge in Honour of His 80th Birthday*, ed. Sally Burch North. Geneva: Droz, 1987. Pp. 253–75.

Schweitzer, Edward C. "Pattern and Theme in Chrétien's *Yvain.*" *Traditio* 30 (1974):145–89.

Severin, Nelly H. "The Function of the Magic Fountain in Chrétien's *Yvain.*" *Chimères* 1976, pp. 27–37.

Shirt, David J. "Was King Arthur Really 'Mad'? Some Comments on the *Charrete* References in *Yvain.*" In *An Arthurian Tapestry: Essays in Memory of Lewis Thorpe*, ed. Kenneth Varty. Glasgow: French Department of the University of Glasgow, 1981. Pp. 187–202.

Uitti, Karl D. "*Le Chevalier au Lion (Yvain).*" In *The Romances of Chrétien de Troyes: A Symposium*, ed. Douglas Kelly. Lexington, Ky.: French Forum, 1985. Pp. 182–231.

———. "Chrétien de Troyes' *Yvain*: Fiction and Sense." *RPh* 22 (1969):471–83.

———. "Intertextuality in *Le Chevalier au Lion.*" *DFS* 2 (1980):3–13.

———. "Narrative and Commentary: Chrétien's Devious Narrator in *Yvain.*" *RPh* 33 (1979):160–67.

Vance, Eugene. "Chrétien's *Yvain* and the Ideologies of Change and Exchange." *YFS* 70 (1986):42–62.

Whitehead, F. "Yvain's Wooing." In *Medieval Miscellany Presented to Eugène Vinaver*, ed. F. Whitehead, A. H. Diverres, and F. E. Sutcliffe. Manchester: Manchester University Press, 1965. Pp. 321–36.

Woledge, B. "Notes on Rhythm in Chrétien's *Yvain*." In *The Legend of Arthur in the Middle Ages*, ed. P. B. Grout, R. A. Lodge, C. E. Pickford, and E. K. C. Varty. Woodbridge, Suffolk: D. S. Brewer, 1983. Pp. 213–26.

Zaddy, Z. P. "The Structure of Chrétien's *Yvain*." *MLR* 65 (1970):523–40.

———. "Yvain as the Ideal Courtly Lover." In *Studies in Medieval French Language and Literature Presented to Brian Woledge in Honour of His 80th Birthday*, ed. Sally Burch North. Geneva: Droz, 1987. Pp. 253–75.

THE STORY OF THE GRAIL

Adolf, Helen. "A Historical Background for Chrétien's Perceval." *PMLA* 58 (1943):597–620.

———. "Studies in Chrétien's *Conte del graal*." *MLQ* 8 (1947):3–19.

Armstrong, Grace. "The Scene of the Blood Drops on the Snow: A Crucial Narrative Moment in the *Conte du Graal*." *KRQ* 19 (1972):127–47.

Bogdanow, Fanni. "The Mystical Theology of Bernard de Clairvaux and the Meaning of Chrétien de Troyes' *Conte du Graal*." In *Chrétien de Troyes and the Troubadours: Essays in Memory of the Late Leslie Topsfield*, ed. Peter S. Noble and Linda M. Paterson. Cambridge, England: St. Catherine's College, 1984. Pp. 249–82.

Buettner, Bonnie. "The Good Friday Scene in Chrétien de Troyes' *Perceval*." *Traditio* 36 (1980):415–26.

Burns, E. Jane. "The Doubled-Question Test: Mystic Discourse in Chrétien's *Perceval*." *RomN* 23 (1982):57–64.

———. "Quest and Questioning in the *Conte du graal*." *RPh* 41 (1988):251–66.

Crow, A.D. "Some Observations on the Style of the Grail Castle Episode in Chrétien's *Perceval*." In *History and Structure of French: Essays in the Honour of Professor T. B. W. Reid*, ed. F. J. Barnett, A. D. Crow, C. A. Robson, W. Rothwell, and S. Ullmann. Oxford: Blackwell, 1972. Pp. 61–87.

Fowler, David C. *Prowess and Charity in the "Perceval" of Chrétien de Troyes*. Seattle: University of Washington Press, 1959.

Groos, Arthur. "Perceval and Parzival Discover Knighthood." In *Magister Regis: Studies in Honor of Robert Earl Kaske*, ed. Arthur Groos. New York: Fordham University Press, 1986. Pp. 117–37.

Ham, Edward B. "The Blancheflor-Perceval Idyll and Arthurian Polemic." *KFLQ* 6 (1959):155–62.

———. "Ecclesia-Synagoga in Chrétien's *Perceval*." *KFLQ* 7 (1960):201–206.

Hoffman, Stanton de V. "The Structure of the *Conte del graal*." *RR* 52 (1961):81–98.

Holmes, Urban T., Jr. "A New Interpretation of Chrétien's *Conte del Graal*." *SP* 44 (1947):453–76.

———, and M. Amelia Klenke. *Chrétien, Troyes, and the Grail*. Chapel Hill: University of North Carolina Press, 1959.

Hunt, Tony. "The Prologue to Chrestien's *Li Contes del graal*." *Romania* 92 (1971):359–79.

Kahane, Henry and Renée, and Angelina Pietrangeli. "On the Sources of Chrétien's Grail Story." In *Festschrift Walther von Wartburg zum 80. Geburtstag*. Tübingen: Max Niemeyer, 1968. vol. 1, pp. 191–233.

Klenke, M. Amelia. "The Blancheflor-Perceval Question." *RPh* 6 (1952):173–78.

———. *Chrétien de Troyes and "Le Conte du Graal": A Study of Sources and Symbolism*. Madrid: José Porrùa Turanzas, 1981.

———. "Chrétien de Troyes and Twelfth-Century Tradition." *SP* 62 (1965):635–46.

———. "Chrétien's Concept of Charity: Perceval versus Gawain." *KFLQ* 9 (1962):219–30.

———. "'Chrétien's Symbolism and Cathedral Art." *PMLA* 70 (1955):223–43.

———. *Liturgy and Allegory in Chrétien's "Perceval."* University of North Carolina Studies in Romance Languages and Literatures 14 (1951).

———. "Some Mediaeval Concepts of King Arthur." *KFLQ* 5 (1958):191–98.

———. "The Spiritual Ascent of Perceval." *SP* 53 (1956):1–21.

Lacy, Norris J. "Gauvain and the Crisis of Chivalry in the *Conte del graal.*" In *The Sower and His Seed: Essays on Chrétien de Troyes*, ed. Rupert T. Pickens. Lexington, Ky.: French Forum, 1983. Pp. 155–64.

Laurie, Helen C. R. "Chrétien at Work on the *Conte du Graal.*" *Romania* 107 (1986):38–54.

———. "Further Notes on Chrétien's *Conte du Graal.*" *Romania* 95 (1974):284–308.

———. "Some New Sources for Chrétien's *Conte du Graal.*" *Romania* 99 (1978):550–54.

———. "Towards an Interpretation of the *Conte du graal.*" *MLR* 66 (1971):775–85.

Loomis, Roger S. "The Grail Story of Chrétien de Troyes as Ritual and Symbolism." *PMLA* 71 (1956):840–52.

Luttrell, Claude. "The Prologue of Crestien's *Li contes del Graal.*" In *Arthurian Literature*, vol. III, ed. Richard Barber. Woodbridge, Suffolk: D. S. Brewer, 1983. Pp. 1–25.

Mahler, Annemarie E. "The Representation of Visual Reality in *Perceval* and *Parzival.*" *PMLA* 89 (1974):537–50.

Mahoney, John. "The Name *Chrétien* and the Perspectives on the Grail." *RomN* 6 (1964):209–214.

Newstead, Helaine. "The Blancheflor-Perceval Question Again." *RPh* 7 (1953):171–75.

Nitze, William A. "Arthurian Names in the *Perceval* of Chrétien de Troyes, Analysis and Commentary." *UCPMP* 38 (1955):265–97.

———. "The Fisher King and the Grail in Retrospect." *RPh* 6 (1952):14–22.

———. "The Guinganbresil Episode in Chrétien's *Perceval.*" *Romania* 72 (1951):373–80.

———. "Perceval and the Holy Grail." *UCPMP* 28 (1949):281–332.

———. "The Sister's Son and the *Conte del Graal.*" *MP* 9 (1912):291–322.

Olschki, Leonardo. *The Grail Castle and Its Mysteries*, trans. J. A. Scott. Manchester: Manchester University Press, 1965.

Owen, D. D. R. "The Development of the Perceval Story." *Romania* 80 (1959):473–92.

———. *The Evolution of the Grail Legend.* Edinburgh: Oliver and Boyd, 1968. Pp. 102–164.

Pickens, Rupert T. *"Le Conte du Graal (Perceval)."* In *The Romances of Chrétien de Troyes: A Symposium*, ed. Douglas Kelly. Lexington, Ky.: French Forum, 1985. Pp. 232–86.

———. *The Welsh Knight: Paradoxicality in Chrétien's Conte del Graal.* Lexington, Ky.: French Forum, 1977.

Potters, Susan. "Blood Imagery in Chrétien's *Perceval.*" *PQ* 56 (1977):301–309.

Rutledge, Amelia A. "Perceval's Sin: Critical Perspectives." *O&C* 5 (1980):53–60.

Sargent-Baur, Barbara Nelson. " 'Avis li fu': Vision and Cognition in the *Conte du Graal.*" In *Continuations: Essays on Medieval French Literature and Language in Honor of John L. Grigsby*, ed. Norris J. Lacy and Gloria Torrini-Roblin. Birmingham, Al.: Summa Publications, 1989. Pp. 133–44.

Shell, Marc. "The Economy of the Grail Legends." *CRCL* 5 (1978):1–29.

Spensley, Ronald M. "Gauvain's Castle of Marvels Adventure in the *Conte del graal.*" *MAE* 42 (1973):32–37.

Sturm-Maddox, Sara. "King Arthur's Prophetic Fool: Prospection in the *Conte du Graal.*" *MRom* 29 (1979):103–108.

———. " 'Tenir sa terre en pais': Social Order in the *Brut* and in the *Conte del Graal.*" *SP* 81 (1984):28–41.

Weinraub, Eugene J. *Chrétien's Jewish Grail.* Chapel Hill: University of North Carolina Press, 1976.

Williams, Harry F. "The Hidden Meaning of Chrétien's *Conte du Graal.*" In *Diakonia: Studies in Honor of Robert T. Meyer,* ed. Thomas Halton and Joseph P. Williman. Washington, D.C.: Catholic University of America Press, 1986. Pp. 145–57.

———. "Interpretations of the *Conte del graal* and Their Critical Reactions." In *The Sower and His Seed: Essays on Chrétien de Troyes,* ed. Rupert T. Pickens. Lexington, Ky.: French Forum, 1983. Pp. 146–54.

———. "The Numbers Game in Chrétien's *Conte du Graal* (Perceval)." *Symposium* 31 (1977):59–73.

JOURNALS AND SERIES

ArthI	*Arthurian Interpretations*
AUMLA	*Journal of the Australasian Universities Language and Literature Association*
BBSIA	*Bulletin Bibliographique de la Société Internationale Arthurienne/ Bibliographical Bulletin of the International Arthurian Society*
C&M	*Classica et Mediaevalia*
Chimères	*Chimères: A Journal of French and Italian Literature*
CL	*Comparative Literature*
CN	*Cultura Neolatina*
CRCL	*Canadian Review of Comparative Literature*
DFS	*Dalhousie French Studies*
ECr	*L'Esprit Créateur*
ELWIU	*Essays in Literature* (Macomb, Ill.)
FMLS	*Forum for Modern Language Studies*
FR	*French Review*
FrF	*French Forum*
FS	*French Studies*
Interpretations	*Interpretations* (Memphis, Tenn.)
ISSQ	*Indiana Social Studies Quarterly*
JES	*Journal of European Studies*
KFLQ	*Kentucky Foreign Language Quarterly*
KRQ	*Kentucky Romance Quarterly* (later *Romance Quarterly*)
LingInv	*Lingvisticae Investigationes*

MAE	Medium Aevum
M&H	Medievalia et Humanistica
Mediaevalia	Mediaevalia: A Journal of Mediaeval Studies
MedR	Medioevo Romanzo
MichA	Michigan Academician
MLN	Modern Language Notes
MLQ	Modern Language Quarterly
MLR	Modern Language Review
MP	Modern Philology
MRom	Marche Romane
MS	Mediaeval Studies (Toronto)
Mythlore	Mythlore
Names	Names: Journal of the American Name Society
Neophil	Neophilologus
NM	Neophilologische Mitteilungen
NMS	Nottingham Medieval Studies
O&C	Oeuvres & Critiques
OL	Orbis Litterarum
PAPA	Publications of the Arkansas Philological Association
Parergon	Parergon: Bulletin of the Australian and New Zealand Association for Medieval and Renaissance Studies
PMLA	Publications of the Modern Language Association
PQ	Philological Quarterly
PsyR	Psychoanalytic Review
RF	Romanische Forschungen
RLR	Revue des Langues Romanes
RMSt	Reading Medieval Studies
Romania	Romania
RomN	Romance Notes
RPh	Romance Philology
RPLit	Res Publica Litterarum: Studies in the Classical Tradition
RR	Romanic Review
SAR	South Atlantic Review
SCB	South Central Bulletin
SFr	Studi Francesi
SM	Studi Medievali
SN	Studia Neophilologica
SoQ	Southern Quarterly
SP	Studies in Philology
Speculum	Speculum: A Journal of Medieval Studies

BIBLIOGRAPHY OF TEXTS AND CRITICAL STUDIES

Sub-stance	*Sub-stance: A Review of Theory and Literary Criticism*
Symposium	*Symposium*
Traditio	*Traditio: Studies in Ancient and Medieval History, Thought, and Religion*
Tristania	*Tristania: A Journal Devoted to Tristan Studies*
UCPMP	*University of California Publications in Modern Philology*
USFLQ	*USF Language Quarterly* (University of South Florida)
UTQ	*University of Toronto Quarterly*
Viator	*Viator: Medieval and Renaissance Studies*
VR	*Vox Romanica*
YFS	*Yale French Studies*
ZRP	*Zeitschrift für Romanische Philologie*

An Index of Proper Names

Dolorous Mount. *See* Yder of the Dolorous Mount

Dombes [in France]: *Cart*, 193

Dover [in England]: *Cliges*, 100

Durandel, Roland's sword: *Lion*, 295

Easter: *Erec*, 1; *Grail*, 418

Eglimon. *See* Menagormon

England/English, xiv, xxiii; *Erec*, 82; *Cliges*, 87, 90, 118, 168; *William*, 450, 474–75, 478, 484, 486, 490

Enid, xi–xiii, xv–xvii; *Erec*, 6–12, 17, 19–23, 26–27, 29–48, 51–54, 57–73, 76–82, 84–85; *Cliges*, 87

Erec, xi–xii, xv–xvii, xix, xxiv, xxvii; *Erec*, 1–86; *Cliges*, 87

Escalibor, Arthur's sword: *Grail*, 411

Escavalon, King of, xxiii; *Grail*, 345, 398, 404, 413–14

Esclados the Red, Laudine's husband: *Lion*, 263, 266–68, 280

Eteocles, son of Oedipus, King of Thebes: *Cliges*, 118

Evrain, King of Brandigan: *Erec*, 67–72, 75, 78

Fenice, xvi–xviii, xx; *Cliges*, 120–28, 133–42, 149–53, 156–66, 169

Fernagu, Saracen warrior: *Erec*, 72

Ferolin of Salonica, companion of Alexander: *Cliges*, 103

Finisterre. *See* Greslemeuf of Finisterre

Fisher King, xxiii–xxiv; *Grail*, 376–80, 382, 396, 416–17

Flanders: *Cliges*, 168; *William*, 474. *See also* Philip, Count of Flanders

Forré, legendary pagan monarch ["To avenge Forré" is a proverbial phrase meaning "to make vain boasts."]: *Lion*, 264

Foukier, Master: *William*, 466–68, 489–91

France/French, ix, xiii–xiv, xx; *Erec*, 67; *Cliges*, 87, 148–49, 168; *Cart*, 170

Franchegel, companion of Alexander: *Cliges*, 103

Gahereit, brother of Gawain and knight of the Round Table: *Erec*, 22; *Grail*, 437

Galegantin of Wales, knight of the Round Table: *Erec*, 22

Galet the Bald, knight of the Round Table: *Erec*, 22

Galloway [in Scotland]: *Grail*, 419, 440, 443; *William*, 462, 478–79, 491

Galloway, King of: *Erec*, 84–85

Ganedlu, knight of the Round Table: *Erec*, 22

Ganelon, traitor who betrayed Roland: *Cliges*, 100

Garin, Lord: *Grail*, 399–400, 402–404

Garras, King of Cork: *Erec*, 25

Gascony/Gascon [region in France]: *Erec*, 34; *William*, 474

Gassa, Emperor: *Erec*, 30

Gaudin of the Mountain: *Erec*, 28

Gawain, nephew of Arthur and knight of the Round Table, xvi, xix, xxii–xxiii, xxvii; *Erec*, 1, 5, 15–16, 20, 22, 27–29, 50–53, 84–85; *Cliges*, 92–93, 115, 119, 146–50; *Cart*, 173–78, 193, 220, 231–35, 242, 245–46, 249, 252–54; *Lion*, 258, 265, 283–87, 289, 300–301, 303–305, 313, 326–34; *Grail*, 389, 393–414, 418–49

Germany/German: *Erec*, 82; *Cliges*, 119–20, 123, 129–31, 135, 150, 167

Germany, Emperor of, xvii; *Cliges*, 119, 126–28, 135, 138; *Lion*, 322

Ghent [in modern Belgium]: *Cart*, 251

Girflet, knight of the Round Table: *Erec*, 5, 22, 28; *Grail*, 375, 397

Gleolais: *William*, 463–66, 483

Glodoalan, King: *Erec*, 25

Godefroi di Leigni, xx; *Cart*, 256

Godegrains, Count: *Erec*, 25

Gohort. *See* Gornemant of Gohort

Gomeret. *See* Ban of Gomeret

Good Friday: *Grail*, 415, 418

Gornemant of Gohort, knight of the Round Table, xxiv, xxvii; *Erec*, 22; *Grail*, 356–61, 363

Gorre, xx; *Cart*, 213, 244. *See also* Bademagu

Gosselin, Master: *William*, 466–71, 489–91

Governal of Roberdic: *Cart*, 240

Gratienne, wife of William of England: *William*, 450–59, 463–66, 480–83, 487–91

Greece/Greek: xvi–xvii; *Cliges*, 87–88, 90–92, 100–104, 108–113, 116, 119, 122–23, 128–31, 135, 138–40, 168–69; *Grail*, 378

Greoreas: *Grail*, 422–25, 427

Greslemeuf of Finisterre: *Erec*, 25

Gribalo, King: *Erec*, 25

Gringalet, Gawain's horse: *Erec*, 50–51; *Grail*, 414, 425

Guerehet, brother of Gawain: *Grail*, 437

Guinable, Count: *Cart*, 172

Guincel: *Erec*, 28

Guinevere, wife of Arthur, xix–xxi; *Erec*, 2–3, 14–16, 20–23, 30, 50, 54, 85; *Cliges*, 100–101, 103–104, 106, 114–15; *Cart*, 171–73, 177, 183, 187, 209, 214–16, 218–21, 224–31, 235, 238–43, 253; *Lion*, 258–59, 264, 330; *Grail*, 389, 395–96, 437, 449

Guinganbresil: *Grail*, 397–98, 412–14

DAVID STAINES IS PROFESSOR OF ENGLISH AT THE UNIVERSITY OF OTTAWA, AND IS AUTHOR, EDITOR, OR CO-EDITOR OF NUMEROUS ARTICLES AND BOOKS, INCLUDING *TENNYSON'S CAMELOT: THE IDYLLS OF THE KING AND ITS MEDIEVAL SOURCES, STEPHEN LEACOCK: A REAPPRAISAL,* AND *ELEMENTS OF LITERATURE.* HE ALSO SERVES AS EDITOR OF THE *JOURNAL OF CANADIAN POETRY,* AND GENERAL EDITOR OF THE NEW CANADIAN LIBRARY.

EDITOR: JANE SHELLY

BOOK AND JACKET DESIGNER: SHARON L. SKLAR

PRODUCTION COORDINATOR: HARRIET CURRY

TYPEFACE: ASTER

PRINTER: IMPRESSIONS, INC.

BINDER: MALLOY LITHOGRAPHING